ARGENTINA
and the
UNITED STATES
1810-1960

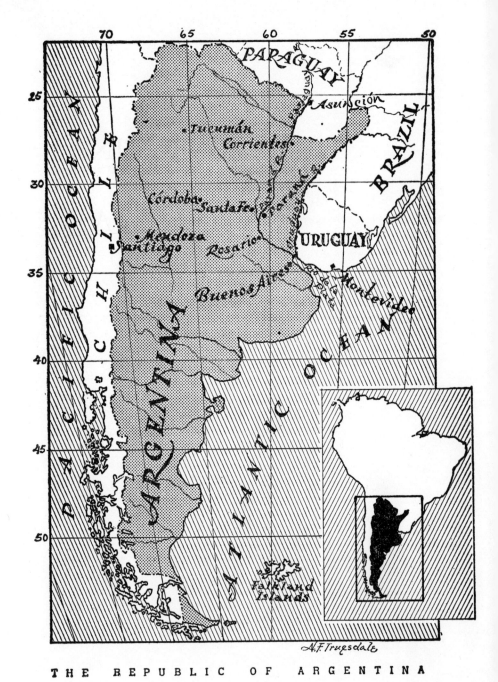

THE   REPUBLIC   OF   ARGENTINA

ARGENTINA
and the
UNITED STATES
1810-1960

by HAROLD F. PETERSON

STATE UNIVERSITY OF NEW YORK • *1964*

ACKNOWLEDGMENTS

Permission to quote copyrighted material from the following books and periodicals is gratefully acknowledged with thanks to the authors and publishers:

THE AMERICAN POLITICAL SCIENCE ASSOCIATION:
Enrique Gil, "The Point of View of Latin-America on the Inter-American Policy of the United States," *The American Political Science Review*. Copyright 1912.

CARNEGIE ENDOWMENT FOR INTERNATIONAL PEACE:
W. R. Manning (ed.), *Diplomatic Correspondence of the United States Concerning the Independence of the Latin-American Nations*. Copyright 1925-1926.
W. R. Manning (ed.), *Diplomatic Correspondence of the United States: Inter-American Affairs, 1831-1860*. Copyright 1932-1939.
The Proceedings of the Hague Peace Conferences. Copyright 1920-1921.

CHICAGO HISTORICAL SOCIETY:
The Diary of James K. Polk. Copyright 1910.

COLUMBIA UNIVERSITY PRESS:
Robert J. Alexander, *The Perón Era*. Copyright 1951.
Charles E. Martin, *The Policy of the United States as Regards Intervention*. Copyright 1921.

CURRENT HISTORY:
J. Lloyd Mecham, "Conflicting Ideals of Pan-Americanism," *Current History*. Copyright December, 1930.

THE FLETCHER SCHOOL OF LAW AND DIPLOMACY, TUFTS UNIVERSITY:
John M. Cabot, *Toward Our Common American Destiny*. Copyright 1955.

vi / *Acknowledgments*

FONDO DE CULTURA ECONOMICA (MEXICO, D.F.):
José L. Romero, *Las ideas políticas en Argentina.* Copyright 1946.

HARVARD UNIVERSITY PRESS:
Robert Bacon and J. B. Scott, *Latin America and the United States. Addresses by Elihu Root.* Copyright 1917.
Thomas F. McGann, *Argentina, the United States, and the Inter-American System, 1880-1914.* Copyright 1957.

THE HISPANIC SOCIETY OF AMERICA:
William B. Parker, *Argentines of To-Day.* Copyright 1920.

HOUGHTON MIFFLIN COMPANY:
William G. McAdoo, *Crowded Years: The Reminiscences of William G. McAdoo.* Copyright 1931.
Charles Seymour (ed.), *The Intimate Papers of Colonel House.* Copyright 1926-1928.

ALFRED A. KNOPF, INC.:
Samuel F. Bemis (ed.), *The American Secretaries of State and Their Diplomacy.* Copyright 1927-1929.

LITTLE, BROWN AND COMPANY:
Charles C. Hyde, *International Law: Chiefly As Interpreted and Applied by the United States.* Copyright 1951.

LONGMANS, GREEN AND COMPANY (COURTESY OF
DAVID MCKAY COMPANY, INC.):
James Bruce, *Those Perplexing Argentines.* Copyright 1953.

THE MACMILLAN COMPANY:
Worthington C. Ford (ed.), *Writings of John Quincy Adams.* Copyright 1913-1917.
Cordell Hull, *The Memoirs of Cordell Hull.* Copyright 1948.
Ysabel F. Rennie, *The Argentine Republic.* Copyright 1945.

THE MANCHESTER GUARDIAN:
The Manchester Guardian. Copyright 1944.

THE NEW REPUBLIC:
The New Republic. Copyright April, 1936.

THE NEW YORK TIMES:
The New York Times. Copyright 1937, 1941, 1942, 1945, 1946, 1947, 1955.

JACOB S. POTOFSKY, GENERAL PRESIDENT,
AMALGAMATED CLOTHING WORKERS OF AMERICA:
Letter in *The New York Times,* June 28, 1945.

FREDERICK A. PRAEGER, INC.:
Arthur P. Whitaker, *Argentine Upheaval: Perón's Fall and the New Regime.* Copyright 1956.

PRINCETON UNIVERSITY PRESS:
William A. Bunkley, *The Life of Sarmiento.* Copyright 1952.

CHARLES SCRIBNER'S SONS:
Frederic J. Stimson, *My United States.* Copyright 1931.

UNIVERSITY OF PENNSYLVANIA PRESS:
Robert Burr and Roland Hussey, *Documents on Inter-American Cooperation.* Copyright 1955.

YALE UNIVERSITY PRESS:
Julius L. Goebel, *The Struggle for the Falkland Islands.* Copyright 1927.

Benjamin Keen, *David Curtis DeForest and the Revolution of Buenos Aires.* Copyright 1947.

PREFACE

During 1959-1960 the Presidents of Argentina and the United States exchanged official visits. In the century and a half of relationships between the southernmost and northernmost of the twenty-one American republics this manifestation of mutual diplomatic courtesies was unique. In Washington and other American cities President Arturo Frondizi received warm and friendly receptions. In Buenos Aires and elsewhere in Argentina President Dwight D. Eisenhower aroused unexpectedly enthusiastic ovations. Whether this newborn glow of cordiality would inaugurate an era of truer friendship between the oft-estranged nations or would prove no more than the hopeful intentions of the two chief executives, their successors in office and the people they govern will have to determine.

Rarely in the long period of Argentine-American intercourse has genuine mutual respect reached to popular levels. To the people of the United States the Argentine Republic has seemed an enigma—always uncooperative, frequently exasperating. For nearly a century after its birth in 1810 geographic separation hampered the growth of intimate relationships with its North American exemplar. When modern inventions reduced the obstacles of time and distance, greater knowledge only bared inbred differences in national goals and ideals. Divergences in internal politics and external policies gradually replaced physical barriers as the basis for disharmony. Although, in many ways, Argentina's historical evolution, economic growth, social development, and manifest destiny paralleled the American pattern, the two republics became rivals more often than partners in international affairs.

To diplomatic officers of the United States as well, Argentina's foreign policies have frequently appeared obstructive, its distinctive brand of ethnocentrism excessive and frustrating. Their well-laid plans for genuine good-neighborliness and inter-American solidarity frequently foundered on the national pretensions of the southern republic. No American approach, cultural or economic, Democratic or Republican, unilateral or multilateral, has served completely to break down apparent Argentine jealousy and suspicion.

For these and other reasons Argentina became and remains a problem

ix

for the American people and their government. When in the late-nineteenth and early-twentieth centuries a remarkable group of Argentine leaders erected the world's greatest surplus food-producing economy, Yankee farmers and businessmen could not ignore the threat of competition. When Britain continuously tightened its grip on Argentina's finances, Yankee bankers could not sit idly by. When Europe's totalitarian ideologies began to infiltrate the Argentine mind, American statesmen could not ignore the challenge to Hemisphere security. When in 1955 an outraged people finally overthrew the repressive dictatorship of Juan Perón, his civilian successors appealed to the United States to rescue their nation from impending insolvency. However small in population, weak in the sinews of war, or remote from the vortex of mid-century strife, the nation behind the Río de la Plata became a force to be reckoned with in Washington's strategic planning. Yet in its reckoning Washington was not always the most understanding of good neighbors.

In its attitude toward the United States, on the contrary, Argentina normally sought only to make its own way and to fulfill its self-assigned mission. Content to be wooed but never won, its leaders from the beginning forged foreign policies that would endure and rarely waver. Through eras of turbulence and stability, of dictatorship and quasi democracy, of immaturity and full-blown nationhood, they have clung to salient guideposts for their nation: political and economic dominance of southern South America; leadership of all the Latin American states; adoption of North Atlantic culture patterns but resistance to foreign intervention; and wariness of multilateral diplomacy, especially security pacts. If Argentines sometimes betrayed irritation or resentment toward the United States, these were attitudes born of abiding belief in their nation's destiny and deep confidence in their ability to achieve it—a belief and a confidence tempered on occasion by a touch of national insecurity.

Historians of both nations have analyzed these discordant relations through study of diverse epochs or episodes. None has attempted to encompass in a single narrative account the entire sweep of diplomatic relations since Argentina's independence. This I have presumed to do in the present volume. Until the Argentine Ministry of Foreign Relations opens its archives for the past century, however, and until scholars of both nations have exploited them to throw light into obscure corners, my delineations and interpretations must necessarily remain tentative.

Though I have sometimes been critical of its leaders or policies, I have not wished to disparage the Argentine nation, for whose people I have considerable affection and great admiration. But the rigidity with which its Foreign Office guards its diplomatic secrets, against both national and alien scholars, has not served to strengthen my powers of synthesis or analysis.

When I went to Buenos Aires in 1940, hoping to complete my research, I placed myself in the willing hands of Dr. Raul Migone, loyal Argentine and sincere friend of the United States, then Chief of the Foreign Ministry's Division of International Conferences and later Minister of Labor in the provisional government of General Pedro Aramburu. His earnest efforts on my behalf with the Under Secretary and the Chief of the Political Division, however, resulted only in frustration. Since no scholar, Argentine or foreign, had used late-nineteenth- and twentieth-century Foreign Office records, a policy had to be made. After weeks of delay, the Ministry created a policy: A foreign researcher might examine unclassified documents; because all documents were filed together, a qualified official must first separate the unclassified from the confidential; but, since many had already been bound, separation was mechanically impossible; therefore, a responsible officer must sit at the researcher's elbow to guard the security of the classified papers; because all available personnel were occupied with wartime problems, none could be spared for weeks of such routine guardianship. Hence, the researcher could examine no records. All this I mention in the hope that future students of Argentine-American relations will have been forewarned and, forewarned, will fare better than I.

Unwilling, evidently, to send a visiting scholar home empty-handed, the Ministry invited me to submit a list of questions on focal issues. These I carefully composed and presented in Spanish. The answers I received, after more weeks of waiting, were not helpful. In spite of Dr. Migone's intercessions at each stage of the negotiations, four months of efforts were barren of results.

Dr. Migone then sought to assist me in the only way left to him. Over luncheon plates and coffee cups he pumped me full of his vast knowledge of the Argentine people and their attitudes toward the United States. Still not content, he urged me to return to Buenos Aires "after the war," when, he ventured, Foreign Office records would surely be available. But after the war, or rather before its close, came Juan Perón and even tighter security measures. And by the end of his dictatorship and the interregnum that followed, I had progressed too far in my composition to consider another research expedition to Argentina. Nevertheless, I must acknowledge my great indebtedness to Dr. Migone, a noble Argentine and a true internationalist.

Elsewhere in Buenos Aires I found only the most gracious response to my requests: from Dr. Héctor Quesada, former Director of the Archivo General de la Nación; from Dr. Emilio Ravignani, former Director of the Instituto de Investigaciones Históricas, Facultad de Filosofía y Letras, University of Buenos Aires; from Dr. Ricardo Levene, former Director of the Museo Mitre; from Abelardo Arenas Fraga, former Chief of the Division of Archives, Ministry of Foreign Relations;

and from the staffs of the Library of the Ministry and the Biblioteca Nacional. I profited greatly from conferences with former President Marcelo T. de Alvear, with Enrique Gil, and with Argentine historians, especially Dr. José Torre Revello and Walter B. L. Bose. Foreign Service officers assigned to the American Embassy in Buenos Aires, Edward P. Maffitt, Second Secretary, and the late Monett B. Davis, Consul General, gave me the benefit of their extended tours of duty in Argentina.

In Asunción, a consul, a diplomat, and an archivist—Edwin Schoenrich of the Department of State, Roque Pérez Stanch of the Ministry of Foreign Relations, and Dr. R. Antonio Ramos of the Archivo Nacional—arranged access to Paraguay's historical manuscripts. In Santiago, the Director of the Archivo Nacional, Dr. Ricardo Donoso Novoa, rendered pleasant my quest for appropriate materials in Chilean archives.

I accomplished a vast portion of my research, of course, in the records of the Department of State, whether housed in its own archives, in the Records Service Center, or the National Archives. Through the sympathetic stewardship of Dr. E. Taylor Parks, Chief, Advisory and Review Branch, and G. Bernard Noble, Chief, Historical Division, I received permission to examine all materials relating to Argentine-American relations through 1941 and selected documents through 1945. During laborious months of note taking in the National Archives, Mrs. Julia Bland Carroll and the late Mrs. Natalia Summers gave me constant stimulation and expert advice. The staff of the Records Service Center, especially Mrs. Mary Ellen Mihar, attended to all my requests. In the use of State Department materials, I have sought to review all pertinent manuscripts, though in my footnote references I have preferred to cite the most available official printed sources, sometimes Argentine, usually American.

In the Department of the Navy I received the most courteous and helpful assistance from Captain Dudley W. Knox, former Chief, Archives Section, Naval Records and Library, and his assistant, Miss E. Craven.

During my Army service with the Joint Chiefs of Staff and the Military Intelligence Division during World War II and in the Officers Reserve Corps after the war, I was fortunate in receiving assignments relating to Latin America, especially the nations of the Río de la Plata. Though regulations, of course, forbade my use of intelligence documents for private research purposes, time has not effaced the opinions I formed or the analyses I made; some of these may have influenced my interpretation of Argentine-American relations.

My thanks must also go to the staffs of many libraries and archives: the Library of Congress, the Columbus Memorial Library of the Pan American Union, the New York Public Library, the Grosvenor and Erie County Public Libraries of Buffalo, the Historical Society of Pennsylvania (Philadelphia), and the libraries of Duke University, the University of

North Carolina, the University of Tennessee, and the State University College at Buffalo.

But my greatest debt is for the inspiration and specific aid I received from four American historians of Latin America or Argentine-American relations: Professor John Tate Lanning, who helped me to understand colonial Argentina and who provided me with letters of introduction to numerous Argentine historians; Professor J. Fred Rippy, who originally suggested the subject and repeatedly urged me to complete it; Professor Arthur P. Whitaker, who over the teacups in a Parisian pension agreed to read critically the entire manuscript and who kept his promise far beyond my expectations; and Professor Watt Stewart, whose extensive writings on the subject pointed my directions and whose constant advice and friendly prodding stimulated my progress. I have paid them the respect of using their writings far more than I cited them.

Finally, I express my appreciation to The Research Foundation of State University of New York, especially the Publications Committee of its Graduate Council, which made possible the publication of this study; to Mr. Francis R. Bellamy, Mrs. Ruth Bellamy, and to the staff of University Publishers, who guided the manuscript through the press with friendly and discerning counsel; to Dr. Samuel Guy Inman and Professor Hubert Herring, who introduced me to many Argentine leaders; to my colleague, Professor Norman F. Truesdale, who designed and executed the maps; to Mrs. Muriel Kam, who carefully typed the completed manuscript; and to my wife, Lucille, who faithfully transcribed thousands of notes and provided inspiration in many discouraging moments.

HAROLD F. PETERSON

State University College at Buffalo
January, 1963

ABBREVIATIONS

AGN, Asun.—Archivo General de la Nación, Asunción
AGN, BA—Archivo General de la Nación, Buenos Aires
Annals of Cong.—Annals of Congress
Cong. Rec.—Congressional Record
Con. Let.—Consular Letters
Cong. Globe–Congressional Globe
Dec. File—Decimal File
Desp. Arg.
Desp. Bra.
Desp. Chile   } Despatches   { Argentina, Brazil, Chile, Paraguay, Paraguay and Uruguay
Desp. Para.   from Ministers
Desp. Para. and Uru.
Dom. Let.—Domestic Letters
F. O.—Foreign Office (London)
For. Rel.—Papers Relating to the Foreign Relations of the United States
HSP—Historical Society of Pennsylvania
H. Doc.—House Documents
H. Ex. Doc.—House Executive Documents
H. Jour.—House Journal
H. Rep.—House Reports
Inst. Arg.
Inst. Bra.
Inst. Min.   } Instructions to Ministers   { Argentina, Brazil, Ministers, Paraguay, Uruguay
Inst. Para.
Inst. Uru.
Inst. to Con.—Instructions to Consuls
LC, MD—Library of Congress, Manuscript Division
Memoria—República Argentina, Ministerio de Relaciones Exteriores y Culto, *Memoria de relaciones exteriores presentada al Congresco Nacional*
MREC, BA—Ministerio de Relaciones Exteriores y Culto, Buenos Aires
Misc. Let.—Miscellaneous Letters
NA, DN
NA, DS   } National Archives   { Department of Navy, Department of State

Notes from Arg. Leg. ⎫   ⎧ Argentine

Notes from Bra. Leg. ⎪   ⎪ Brazilian

Notes from Chil. Leg. ⎬ Notes from Legations ⎨ Chilean

Notes from Uru. Leg. ⎭   ⎩ Uruguayan

Notes to Arg. Leg.—Notes to Argentine Legation

Num. File—Numerical File

RC, AN—República de Chile, Archivo Nacional

Reg. of Deb.—Register of Debates

S1-A2-A4-núm. 8—Sala 1, Armario 2, Anaquél 3, número 8

S. A. Mission—South American Mission

Sen. Doc.—Senate Documents

Sen. Ex. Doc.—Senate Executive Documents

Sen. Jour.—Senate Journal

Sen. Rep.—Senate Reports

Specl. Agts. Ser.—Special Agents Series

Specl. Missions—Special Missions

U.S. Stat. at L.—United States Statutes at Large

CONTENTS

Part One: Introduction

I

TWO AMERICAN PEOPLES IN 1810:
SIMILARITIES

The United States of America and the Argentine Republic are the oldest independent states on the continents of North and South America.[1] In breaking their political ties with England, North Americans set a pattern for the Hemisphere. In severing their allegiance to Spain, Argentines broke ground for all Hispanic Americans.[2] Continuously from the first moments of independence, unlike most of their sister nationalities, Americans and Argentines have maintained sovereign authority under indigenous political institutions.

Both republics came into being as formless clusters of political units—the "united states of America" in 1776 and the "united provinces of the Río de la Plata" in 1810. At the outset, each confederation sheltered seeds of discordant political and economic philosophies as well as essential elements of nationhood. Drawn together by common dangers and common goals, the components of each nascent state slowly conquered intense provincial loyalties and gradually welded themselves into "more perfect union." Only firm leadership and popular resolution, however, exerted through decades of factional strife and seasons of civil violence, would eventually transform nationalities into stable nations.

Geographically, the two pioneer proponents of American independence lay at the extremes of the Hemisphere. This physical separation was symbolic of the broad gulf that would often divide them in their political and cultural orientation toward the rest of the Atlantic world, American and European. Between them, both geographically and politically, lay the rest of the Pan American world-to-be. Just as the examples of the United States and Argentina stimulated other American

---

[1] Among Latin American republics, however, Haiti in the Caribbean gained its independence (1804) earlier than Argentina.

[2] To specify inhabitants of the United States, I have used the term "North Americans" instead of "Americans" only in instances where the meaning might be confused. Regardless of the legal title in any epoch, I have frequently used "Argentina" to refer to the nation now known as "the Argentine Republic" and "Argentines" to designate its residents.

peoples to revolutionary action, so in the distant future would their policies attract the younger states toward the one or the other Hemisphere pole.

The first timid diplomatic steps between the two nations were taken soon after May 25, 1810, day of Argentina's actual separation from Spain. At that time, Buenos Aires and Washington were the newly designated, but not yet the nationally revered, capitals of the independent states. Buenos Aires, an old city, assumed leadership of the new Argentine nation. Washington, newly founded as the capital of the older nation, had national leadership thrust upon it. Youngest of Spain's great viceregal centers in America, Buenos Aires was older by two centuries than Washington, older even than England's first settlement at Jamestown.

By 1810 Buenos Aires had become the chief point of transfer between its vast unexploited hinterland and the principal North Atlantic ports. Released from the restraints of Spain's commercial monopoly, its trade had begun to flow seaward toward Europe and North America rather than landward toward Lima. This escape from the economic isolation with which Spain had smothered its natural expansion opened the gates to the manifold interests which flourish on maritime exchange. Merchandise imported during the first six months of 1810, chiefly cottons and woolens from Britain and flour, lumber, and furniture from the United States, equalled the consumption of the previous six years. Inventories of the shops and warehouses consisted mostly of staple goods but luxury items like skates and warming pans were beginning to dangle from shop fronts. Departing vessels normally loaded with wool, tallow, hides, and skins from the countryside and occasionally with copper and silver from the Andes.[3] Buenos Aires was a port as well as a capital.

Yet these new political and economic advantages did not at once transform the city into a thriving metropolis. It remained in 1810 a drab, unexciting outpost of Spanish civilization with none of the éclat, regal splendor, or architectural elegance of Lima or Mexico. Huddled along the flat shores of the Río de la Plata in rectangular pattern, the city's few dozen streets enveloped three sides of the central plaza, later to become the focal Plaza de Mayo. Flanked by a large fort, the cathedral, the *cabildo,* and other public buildings, the plaza fronted the harbor and the sea beyond.[4]

[3] Reports of Joel Roberts Poinsett, Special Agent to South America, Nov. 4, 1818, and of Caesar A. Rodney, Special Commissioner to South America, Nov. 5, 1818, William R. Manning (ed.), *Diplomatic Correspondence of the United States Concerning Independence of the Latin-American Countries,* I, 454, 504; R. A. Humphreys, *British Consular Reports on the Trade and Politics of Latin America, 1824-1826,* pp. 35, 60-61.

[4] Alexander Gillespie, *Gleanings and Remarks: Collected during Many Months of Residence at Buenos Aires, and within the Upper Country,* pp. 82-83; F. A. Kirkpatrick, *A History of the Argentine Republic,* city plan following p. 54.

The city's 40,000 residents lived in whitewashed single-storied houses of adobe, built closely along dirty, unpaved streets. As many as six hundred shopkeepers, yet only a few tradesmen, served the routine material needs of the population. Religious life was attended by numerous churches, bells freely tolling, six convents, two monasteries, and eleven hundred clerics. Educational opportunities existed only for the children of the governing class; there was no institution of higher learning. A theater and a bull ring provided the only organized public diversion.[5]

Slowly pulling itself out of the muddy, mosquito-ridden marshes of shallow Potomac shores, Washington in the same epoch was an equally unimposing capital. Though the President's house, the unfinished capitol, a few government buildings, and many brick residences had risen on higher ground, there was little evidence yet to suggest the real nature of L'Enfant's plan of radiating avenues or the beauty of the city's future magnificence. From the beginning, Washington was a planned city, lacking the peculiar combination of natural advantages which made Buenos Aires a mart for world trade and world ideas. Since Jefferson's first inauguration, the population of the District of Columbia had grown from 2600 whites and 600 Negroes to a total of 24,000.[6]

In spite of its own weakness and instability, the first provisional government in Buenos Aires boldly struck out to secure the territory it regarded as Argentina's just heritage. It proclaimed the right to control all the provinces which in 1778 Spain had incorporated in the Viceroyalty of La Plata, of which Buenos Aires had been the center. These included the present-day lands of Argentina, Uruguay, Paraguay, and part of Bolivia. Without waiting for governmental stability or formal declaration of national independence, the capital mounted expeditions against Upper Peru (present Bolivia) and Paraguay and contemplated occupation of the Banda Oriental (present Uruguay). But Royalist forces successfully defended Bolivia; the Paraguayans determined to free themselves from Buenos Aires as well as from Madrid; and the Uruguayans prepared to resist the encroachments of both Argentina and Portuguese Brazil.[7] Though the ambitious *porteños* would not succeed in consolidating all their territorial goals, they had effectively asserted Argentina's manifest destiny.

The intentions of the Argentine leaders were not unlike those of the Americans, who spent seventy-five years redeeming what they held to be rightful territorial limits and fulfilling what they proclaimed as America's

[5] Gillespie, *op. cit.*, pp. 69-72, 81-82, 91, 114-122; Juan Probst, "La enseñanza primaria desde sus orígenes hasta 1810," *Historia de la Nación Argentina*, IV, sec. 2, p. 155.

[6] Henry Adams, *History of the United States of America*, I, 30-31; J. A. Krout and D. R. Fox, *The Completion of Independence, 1790-1830*, pp. 185-186.

[7] Ricardo Levene, *A History of Argentina*, pp. 240-254.

manifest destiny. By 1810, when Buenos Aires was just beginning to project its territorial claims, the United States had already doubled its domain by purchasing Louisiana. Yet, even as Argentine expeditions were moving against Upper Peru and Paraguay, American expansionists were edging into Spanish borderlands and clamoring for annexation of Canada.

The lands over which Argentina was eventually able to establish effective control, an area roughly equivalent to the United States east of the Mississippi, made it the seventh largest country in the world. They provided the Argentine people a bountiful countryside to conquer and exploit. From the sun of Buenos Aires, flush against the Atlantic horizon, the lands of Argentina radiate in variegated forms. Beginning at the sun's edge and stretching five hundred miles in a gigantic semicircle, lies the fertile *pampa*, heart of Argentina's pastoral and cereal wealth. Beyond this central plain, north, south, and west, lending diversity to the nation's topography, are other great physiographic regions. Across the Plata is the South American Mesopotamia, grazing lands to the south, tropical forests beyond. To the north, reaching a thousand miles from Buenos Aires to the borders of Bolivia and Paraguay, is the subtropical Chaco, partly scrub-forest, partly grassland, producer of quebracho, cotton, and cattle. To the south, beyond the pampa, pointing sixteen hundred miles to the Strait of Magellan, lie the vast tablelands of Patagonia, source of wool and oil. At the extreme west, fronting Chile more than two thousand miles from Bolivia to Tierra del Fuego, with oases of sugar, vineyards, and natural beauty at its base, stretches the great protective wall of the Andean Cordillera.[8]

The physiographic regions of the United States in 1810 presented no such symmetry as those of Argentina, though in diversity and extent of natural wealth they were superior. Washington, as the capital, was not ordained by man or nature to be the heart of the American body economic. New York would attempt this role, though the American economy would never revolve about a single center to the degree that Argentine business life has concentrated on Buenos Aires. The United States would develop as a confederation of complementary economic regions rather than as an economic unit.

The vast territories which Argentina and the United States sought to encompass were relatively empty of people. At the close of the viceregal period, the population of all the areas claimed by Buenos Aires, excluding Indians, was estimated at 1,080,000. Less than half a million of these —mostly Creoles, a few free Negroes—lived in the provinces that ultimately pledged allegiance to the revolutionary government. Outside the Province of Buenos Aires, the areas of concentrated habitation were Córdoba, Mendoza, and the territories of the northwest, far removed

[8] P. E. James, *Latin America*, pp. 284-285; George Pendle, *Argentina*, pp. 1-9.

from the capital. To the south of Buenos Aires and the pampa, Indians controlled half the country, as devoid of white settlers as the trans-Mississippi United States at the time of Lewis and Clark.[9]

The pattern of settlement in the United States before 1810 was almost the antithesis of that in the United Provinces of La Plata. Where the bulk of Argentina's immigrants had moved overland from Peru to settle in the interior, the great mass of Americans had migrated directly from Europe to find permanent homes close to the seaboard. Streams of pioneers, of course, had long since begun to move westward through the mountain passes and the Mohawk Valley to form islands of population in Kentucky, Tennessee, and Ohio, now counted among the states. Except in Louisiana, which would soon gain statehood, there were few white residents beyond the Mississippi. America's population of 7,240,000 was far greater than Argentina's half-million; yet, because of its diverse national origins, it was also more heterogeneous.

In the consolidation of these sprawling lands and scattered settlements, Washington and Buenos Aires played contrasting roles. As a capital born of political compromise, Washington was the meeting place for the representatives of powerful rival sections, its political institutions the mechanism for the resolution of conflicting sectional interests. The District of Columbia was neutral ground. But from the beginning Buenos Aires was the heart and brain of the Argentine drive for nationhood. Its inspired and aggressive leaders provided not only the initial spark for self-government but also continuing momentum for national unity. Buenos Aires was always a protagonist, never a spectator, in Argentina's political and social evolution.[10]

As the nucleus around which porteño intellectuals after 1810 sought to rally the refractory provinces of the former viceroyalty, Buenos Aires held unique place within the Spanish Empire. For two centuries it had remained a minor star in Spain's firmament of New World cities. Unlike Mexico or Lima, it was a terminus, not the vibrant market of an overland travel route. Unlike Havana or Panama, its harbor was normally closed to the legal trade of both Spain and its rivals. Lacking mineral wealth to assure quick fortunes or fill the King's coffers, its hinterland failed to attract the more greedy conquistadores or the more adventurous noblemen. Without a large, tractable Indian population, its rich agricultural lands did not beckon the highborn who might have established encomiendas. Argentina's settlers, therefore, were of a single class—and that class the lesser nobility.[11]

Poor and isolated, Buenos Aires received from Madrid few favors, little

[9] Report of Theodoric Bland, Special Commissioner to South America, to Secretary of State John Quincy Adams, Nov. 2, 1818, Manning, *op. cit.*, pp. 433, 439; Gillespie, *op. cit.*, p. 334.
[10] José Luis Romero, *Las ideas políticas en Argentina*, pp. 71-84.
[11] Cf. A. W. Bunkley, *The Life of Sarmiento*, pp. 11-12.

surveillance, and less protection. Gradually through the eighteenth century, forced to fend for themselves, the porteños called up unplumbed initiative and self-assurance. When danger threatened, whether from untamed Indians on the pampa, Portuguese frontiersmen to the north, or English and Dutch marauders by sea, they devised their own defensive measures. They learned to deal in contraband with pirates and smugglers. Lacking gold and silver, they discovered the commercial value of hides and began to probe the pampa for herds of stray cattle.

Through policies of isolation and neglect, therefore, Spain drove the porteños to develop cohesion, independence of spirit, and economic self-reliance. The trade in contraband aided the growth of importers and merchants. The demand for hides increased the importance of the Gaucho and gave rise to the rancher class. The exchange of hides for seaborne goods, bringing together land routes and sea lanes, enlarged the port. The potential value of its trade captured the attention of Spain's greatest commercial rivals, the English. With covetous eyes on a new El Dorado, British naval expeditions in 1806-1807 sought to capture and occupy Buenos Aires.[12]

It was Napoleon's subjection of the Spanish government, hard on the heels of porteño resistance to the English, that brought Argentina the opportunity for self-government and independence. Just as the French and Indian War stimulated the Anglo-American colonists to draw together in self-defense, so the English invasions constrained the Argentines to mobilize their own resources. Rid of the immediate danger, like their exemplars they summoned the courage to assert their just rights and prepared to transform their society. In each nation political independence and the social changes that followed were the results of historical evolution, not of a paper declaration or a military campaign.[13]

Penetration of Spain's economic blockade had brought Buenos Aires contraband ideas as well as smuggled goods. Even before 1800 young intellectuals had begun to read Rousseau, Montesquieu, Raynal, and Paine. In absorbing the new philosophies of enlightened politics and economics, they developed revolutionary theories which they deemed compatible with the growing independence of Buenos Aires itself. Once the English were expelled and the Spanish Monarchy proved incapable of defending them, the intellectuals were prepared to inaugurate self-rule according to the new ideas.[14] They moved to take over the cabildo, to create a governing junta, and to open the port. They translated

---

[12] Julio Rinaldini, "Buenos Aires," in Germán Arciniegas (ed.), *The Green Continent,* pp. 384-386.

[13] José Ingenieros, *La evolución de las ideas argentinas,* I, 180-181; Levene, *op. cit.,* pp. 208-209; Bernard Moses, *The Intellectual Background of the Revolution in South America, 1810-1824,* pp. vii, 1-4, 22-24, 64-65.

[14] Romero, *op. cit.,* pp. 50-62; Norberto Piñero, *Escritos de Mariano Moreno,* pp. xli-xlii.

Rousseau's *Social Contract*, founded a public library, and established a newspaper. They sought, by force or persuasion, to win the allegiance of outlying provinces. In sum, they undertook to deal with the twin problems of external independence and internal organization.[15]

Stimulated by French philosophers and American revolutionaries, the untried leaders defied not only the Spanish Monarchy but Spanish intellectual tradition itself. Deeply embedded in the minds of most colonials, especially in the interior provinces Buenos Aires hoped to win, was the concept of loyalty to a king, to a viceroy, to an individual. The substitution of loyalty to ideas or principles for loyalty to a person or even to the symbols of his office was too gigantic a task for a small band of intellectuals, however determined, or even for generations of their successors.[16]

The liberal ideas of the eighteenth century, therefore, as expounded by Mariano Moreno, Bernardino Rivadavia, and Manuel Belgrano, did not take quick root in Argentina. Their decade of experiments led only to a decade of anarchy. Equally determined provincial leaders, wedded to the personalist tradition, balked the liberal experiments at every step. Eventually, loyalty to a national chieftain would overcome loyalty to provincial *caudillos* and even national chieftains would become more rare, but personalism would persist into the twentieth century. In aspiring to self-government for Argentina, the porteño intellectuals accomplished their purpose, but in seeking to consolidate internal organization they introduced the nation to generations of ferment.[17] Whether between city and country, enlightenment and tradition, constitutionalism and personalism, or unitarianism and federalism, bitter conflict endured.

The provisional governments which after 1810 sought to guide the Argentine people from separation to recognized independence were far less stable than the Continental Congress in comparable years, either before or after adoption of the Articles of Confederation. Unlike their North American counterparts, the Argentine patriots who moved with such devotion and enthusiasm to create national institutions operated without benefit of a democratic heritage from the mother country or practical experience in self-government, even at the local level.

In the United States, thanks to their colonial and revolutionary experience and more fortunate legacy from Britain, American patriots produced constitutional unity and national stability much more quickly and with far less civil disobedience. Except for frontier campaigns against the Indians, no intermittent warfare absorbed the energies of

[15] For accounts in English of the Argentine revolution and its background, see Levene, *op. cit.*, pp. 203-239, 255-270, and Kirkpatrick, *op. cit.*, pp. 59-74.

[16] Romero, *op. cit.*, pp. 63-128. See the stimulating discussion of "Hispanic Man" in Bunkley, *op. cit.*, pp. 3-11.

[17] Ingenieros, *op. cit.*, pp. 180ff; Levene, *op. cit.*, pp. 255-270; Bunkley, *op. cit.*, pp. 11-22.

national and sectional leaders. The American people were spared the chaos and the harsh regimes which racked the Argentines. Yet, intellectual and social ferment flourished in the United States as it did in Argentina.[18] For nearly a century after independence, proponents of federal supremacy and partisans of state rights engaged in acrid controversy. The accompanying disagreements over slavery and subsequent social readjustments affected all levels of society. Indeed, the Civil War was physically more destructive than all of Argentina's civil strife. But, by concentrating their violence in a single great conflict, the Americans escaped the enervating turmoil which recurrently sapped the vitality of Argentine life and postponed the attainment of political stability.

Regardless of the speed with which they approached political maturity, the United States and Argentina in 1810 possessed most of the essential elements of nationhood.[19] Both had centralizing institutions, political in the United States, religious in Argentina. Both had, or were developing, military, economic, and colonial traditions. Both peoples revealed love of country and faith in their own destinies. Both eagerly adopted the external symbols of nationalism. In each case, the lack of indigenous cultural tradition and of universal acceptance of political forms was compensated by common historical experience.[20] Each would move energetically, the Argentines handicapped by a late start, to overcome their deficiencies and consolidate their nationality into nationhood. In 1810-1811, as Washington and Buenos Aires contemplated the establishment of mutual diplomatic contacts, the possibility of reinvasion and reoccupation by the mother country presented to each a favorable opportunity for strengthening national loyalties.

These, then, were the Argentine and American people in 1810—their lands, their economies, their traditions, and their aspirations. Both nations needed time to mature and opportunity to develop stability and tranquillity. In the meantime, they would have to confront the world— and each other. In comparable situations, it was natural that their earliest foreign policies should be similar: independence, redemption of national territories, commercial reciprocity, and freedom from entangling international commitments. Divergences would come later—to form the central theme of Argentine-American diplomatic relations in the twentieth century.

---

[18] Merle Curti, *The Growth of American Thought*, pp. 129, 143-156.
[19] Cf. C. J. H. Hayes, *Essays on Nationalism*, pp. 6-26.
[20] Rinaldini, *op. cit.*, pp. 389-391; Curti, *op. cit.*, pp. 143-154, 233-238.

Part Two: The Foundations of a Nation

I I

REVOLUTION IN BUENOS AIRES: ROOTS OF AMERICAN INTEREST, 1810-1816

James Madison must have been somewhat incredulous late in 1807 as he contemplated a communication freshly arrived from Buenos Aires. The writer urged the Secretary of State to send to that city a consul or commercial agent, whose appointment, he asserted, would be highly gratifying to the people and sufficiently favored by the government.[1] Barely six months earlier the Spanish government had decreed that no foreign consuls might reside in its American colonies; it was still more than two and a half years before a revolutionary junta would be created in Buenos Aires.

Rumors of Creole discontent in the Viceroyalty of La Plata may have trickled through Spanish censorship, but Madison could hardly have received trustworthy intelligence that revolution was brewing. At the same time, even on the eve of violent changes in Spain and Portugal, neither the policy of the Jefferson administration nor the sentiment of the American people toward Latin America had crystallized.[2] But whether this recommendation from Buenos Aires met with incredulity or shrugging indifference, certainly it brought within the Secretary's purview the kaleidoscopic changes soon to take place in the Plata area.

Revolution in Buenos Aires

Not until June, 1810, however, after Napoleon's domination of Spain had accelerated developments in Latin America, did Madison, then

[1] David Curtis DeForest to Madison, Oct. 4, 1807, NA, DS, Misc. Let., Jan.-Dec., 1807. DeForest was an adventurous Yankee trader who had first visited the Río de la Plata in 1801. According to his biographer, Benjamin Keen, DeForest had previously sought appointment as consul to Buenos Aires and was to do so again (*David Curtis DeForest and the Revolution of Buenos Aires*, pp. 33, 38, 56). Keen's biography is a most engaging account of DeForest and his contributions to Argentine independence. Also see below, pp. 55-58, 75.

[2] Arthur P. Whitaker, *The United States and the Independence of Latin America, 1800-1830*, pp. 35-38. For interpretation of broad American policy toward Latin America I have relied in many instances on this comprehensive study.

President, respond to the urgings of 1807. Thomas Jefferson's reluctance could become his successor's decision. Madison now appointed Joel Roberts Poinsett, much-travelled South Carolinian, as commercial agent to Buenos Aires.[3] Here on May 25, acting in the name of Ferdinand VII, dissident Creoles had formed the *Junta provisional gubernativa de la provincia del Río de la Plata.* This revolutionary action signalized the beginning of Argentine self-government. A formal declaration of independence was to be delayed for six years, and constitutional stability was not to be attained for nearly half a century; but from May 25, 1810, the Argentine "nation" enjoyed continuous independence from Spain.

Although nominally still loyal to Ferdinand VII, the Junta gubernativa immediately undertook the creation of administrative institutions and the formulation of a national program. It drafted a detailed statement of its prospective foreign policies, though without specifying the attitude to be adopted toward the establishment of relations with the United States. While the Junta was drafting this "Plan de las operaciones," Poinsett prepared to embark for Buenos Aires.[4]

The equanimity with which the Junta began its existence was soon broken by a series of factious quarrels among its members.[5] The chief discord stemmed from the clashing personalities and political views of Cornelio de Saavedra, President of the Junta, and Mariano Moreno, its Secretary. Saavedra, quiet but determined, favored gradual political change with immediate representation of the provinces; Moreno, brilliant but impetuous, preferred revolutionary reform under the sole direction of Buenos Aires. In the six-month struggle between the two patriot leaders, Moreno was forced to resign, twelve provincial deputies were admitted to the Junta, and Saavedra was elevated to temporary leadership of the government.[6] Under his presidency the enlarged Junta grappled with organizational problems until September, 1811, when it instituted government by triumvirate.

[3] See below, pp. 15ff.

[4] For the text of the "Plan de las operaciones que el gobierno provisional de las provincias unidas del Río de la Plata debe poner en práctica para consolidar la grande obra de nuestra libertad e independencia," see Norberto Piñero, *Escritos de Mariano Moreno,* pp. 447-565, and for a detailed analysis see Ricardo Levene, *Ensayo histórico sobre la revolución de Mayo y Mariano Moreno,* II, 203-224. Enrique de Gandía discusses critically the authorship of the plan in his *Las ideas políticas de Mariano Moreno: Autenticidad del plan que le es atribuido.*

[5] Besides Saavedra and Moreno, the Junta was composed of Juan José Castelli, Manuel Belgrano, Juan José Paso, Juan Larrea, business partner of DeForest, and three others (República Argentina, Ministerio de relaciones exteriores y culto, *Digesto de relaciones exteriores, 1810-1913,* p. 294).

[6] On the conflicting ideas of Saavedra and Moreno, see José Ingenieros, *La evolución de las ideas argentinas,* I, 179-194. The feud between them is recounted in Manuel Moreno, *Vida y memorias del Doctor Mariano Moreno,* pp. 250-256, and Levene, *op. cit.,* II, 362-372. See also Harold F. Peterson, "Mariano Moreno: the Making of an Insurgent," *The Hispanic American Historical Review,* XIV (Nov., 1934), 472-475.

In January, 1813, the last of several triumvirates summoned a Constituent Assembly, which promptly avowed its sovereignty, abolished many of the evil remnants of Spanish domination, declared May 25 a national holiday, and adopted nationalistic symbols. Though by its actions it assumed independence to be a reality, the Assembly refused forthrightly to declare it or to enact a constitution. It did, however, in January, 1814, substitute government by "supreme directorate" for that by triumvirate.[7] Although the directors brought the first evidences of political stability, much remained to be done before Argentina would gain recognition by the United States and European powers.

As President Madison despatched Poinsett and his successors, therefore, Buenos Aires was torn by rapid changes in executive power and accompanying military uprisings and economic dislocations. For ten, twenty, and in some phases even fifty years, similar instability persisted.

Despatch of the First American Agents to Buenos Aires

President Madison's decision to send an agent to the turbulent La Plata was an extraordinary event in the evolution of American foreign policy. In the first place, the American government had never previously sent a representative to an unrecognized state.[8] Secondly, Washington had not yet stated its attitude toward the Spanish American rebellions nor even taken specific steps toward the formulation of policy. Already many persons in the United States looked with sympathy upon the revolutionary efforts of the Spanish colonials, and responsible authorities freely admitted their vessels to North American ports. But the belligerency of Buenos Aires had not been officially acknowledged, and independence could hardly be recognized until it was declared.[9] Poinsett was to make his contacts, therefore, not with the legitimist government of the Viceroy but with a revolutionary Junta barely a month old at the time of his commission.

The instructions to Poinsett (June 28, 1810) disclosed the administra-

[7] For a full account of the changing governments, see Ricardo Levene, *Historia de la Nación Argentina desde los orígenes hasta la organización definitiva en 1862,* V, sec. 2, 371-510.

[8] Henry M. Wriston, *Executive Agents in American Foreign Relations,* p. 407.

[9] The general subject of the Spanish American revolutions was not considered by the United States Congress until late 1811. A resolution, introduced in the House of Representatives on December 10 by a special committee, went so far as to refer to the time "when those provinces shall have attained the condition of nations. . . ." (*Annals of Cong.,* 12 Cong., 1 sess., Pt. 1, p. 429). Earlier in the year events in Buenos Aires and Venezuela had roused the interest of American statesmen. See, for example, Secretary of State Monroe to Joel Barlow, Minister to France, Nov. 27, 1811, William R. Manning (ed.), *Diplomatic Correspondence of the United States Concerning Independence of the Latin-American Countries,* I, 12; H. A. Washington (ed.), *Writings of Thomas Jefferson,* V, 580-581, 584, 586-587; Gaillard Hunt (ed.), *Writings of James Madison,* VIII, 171-172.

tion's premonition of the startling changes impending in Spanish America. Because of its geographical position, wrote Secretary of State Robert Smith, the United States must give rare attention to coming events. Poinsett, therefore, was advised

> to proceed without delay to Buenos Ayres, and thence, if convenient, to Lima in Peru or Santiago in Chili or both. You will make it your object whenever it may be proper, to diffuse the impression that the United States cherish the sincerest good will towards the people of Spanish America as neighbors, as having a mutual interest in cultivating friendly intercourse; that this disposition will exist whatever may be their internal system or European relations, with respect to which, no interference of any sort is pretended; and that in the event of a political separation from the parent country and of the establishment of an independent system of National Governments, it will coincide with the sentiments and policy of the United States to promote the most friendly relations and the most liberal intercourse between the inhabitants of this Hemisphere, as having, all a common interest, and as lying under a common obligation to maintain that system of peace, justice and good will, which is the only source of happiness for nations.
>
> Whilst you inculcate these as the principles and disposition of the United States it will be no less proper to ascertain those of the other side, not only towards the United States, but in reference to the great nations of Europe, as also to that of Brazil, and the Spanish branches of the Government there; and to the Commercial and other connections with them respectively, and generally to inquire into the State, the characteristics, and the proportions as to numbers, intelligence and wealth of the several parties, the amount of population, the extent and organization of the military force and the pecuniary resources of the country.[10]

In subsequent instructions, Smith reminded Poinsett of the increase in trade between the United States and La Plata during the preceding decade [11] and of the importance to that trade of the establishment of a consulate. Since the Secretary believed it possible that Poinsett would not be recognized as United States consul, he was commissioned as "agent for seamen and commerce."[12] But, whatever his title, he was directed to attend to all the duties normally performed by a consul.

By his ability to use Spanish, his sympathy for the revolting colonies, his knowledge of men gained from wide travels, and his profound belief in liberal institutions, Poinsett was well prepared for his mission

[10] Manning, *op. cit.*, I, 6-7. Here, as elsewhere, I have followed Manning's slight deviations from the form of the original manuscript. Manuscript sources in the State Department records verify the date of these instructions (NA, DS, Inst. to Con., I, 400-402). J. Fred Rippy, however, believes the date should have been Aug. 27 (*Joel Roberts Poinsett, Versatile American*, p. 58, note 3).

[11] See below, pp. 84-85.

[12] Smith to Poinsett, Aug. 27, 1810, NA, DS, Inst. to Con., I, 399-400.

Moreover, his mind had been conditioned by an unquenchable loyalty to his native land and an unquestioned antipathy for things English.[13] Thus armed, on October 15 the South Carolinian set out on what was to be a stormy, seventy-day voyage to Rio de Janeiro, there to embark for Buenos Aires.

On the very day of his arrival, February 13, Poinsett presented himself to the Junta and received permission to carry out his duties.[14] In accordance with his instructions, he applied himself at once to the task of improving commercial arrangements for American shipping. In interviews with the local authorities he sought to secure lower duties and protested against the preferment of British commerce. He soon reported to Washington that members of the government desired close relations with the United States but that fear and distrust of Great Britain impelled them to court the favor of Spain's ally.[15] He requested more positive instructions to guide him in case independence were declared at an early date. But the policy of the Madison administration toward spreading rebellion in the Spanish colonies had still not been clarified, and Secretary of State Monroe's reply to Poinsett's bald query was noncommittal. He indicated only that the United States would view independent states in South America with stronger friendship than European colonies.[16]

Poinsett experienced some success late in June, when the Junta decreed that commerce of the United States should be given the same privileges as that of Great Britain. At the same time he reported that Britain had appointed a consul to Buenos Aires and urged that the State Department take similar action.[17] His unconcealed opposition to British influence was by now intensifying Anglo-American rivalry, already bitter

[13] On Poinsett's character and ideas, see Herbert E. Putnam, *Joel Roberts Poinsett: a Political Biography*, and J. Fred Rippy, *Joel R. Poinsett, Versatile American.*

[14] Poinsett to the Junta, Feb. 13, 1811, AGN, BA, S1-A2-A4-núm. 8; the Junta to Madison, Feb. 13, 1811, Manning, *op. cit.*, I, 320-321.

[15] Poinsett to Dept. of State, draft, Feb. 16, 1811, HSP, Poinsett Papers, I, 98; Poinsett to the Junta, Feb. 18, 1811, AGN, BA, S1-A2-A4-núm. 8. See also rough notes for letter from Junta to Poinsett, Feb. 18, 1811, *ibid.*; Poinsett to Smith, April 23, 1811, HSP, Poinsett Papers, I, 56; and "Journal to Rio Janeiro, Buenos Ayres and Chile, 1810 & 1811," LC, MD, Poinsett Papers.

[16] Poinsett to Dept. of State, Feb. 16, 1811, draft, HSP, Poinsett Papers, I, 98; Monroe to Poinsett, April 30, 1811, Manning, *op. cit.*, I, 11. The Secretary's reply reached Poinsett seven months after his request for instructions—stark commentary on the painful slowness of diplomatic exchange in precable and presteamship days.

[17] Poinsett to Dept. of State, June 29, July 3, 1811, HSP, Poinsett Papers, I, 86, 90. Poinsett had made the same recommendation on March 9 (*ibid.*, I, 46). On June 29 the agent did not know that Louis Goddefroy, French merchant in Montevideo, had been appointed consul for ports on the Río de la Plata and that he himself had been made consul general to Buenos Aires, Chile, and Peru. Goddefroy's appointment was not confirmed by the Senate (Monroe to Poinsett, April 30, 1811, Manning, *op. cit.*, I, 11; Keen, *op. cit.*, pp. 84-85; W. S. Robertson, "Documents Concerning the Consular Service of the United States in Latin America," *Mississippi Valley Historical Review*, II [March, 1916], 563, 567).

over issues in other spheres.[18] Not daring to provoke the British, yet hoping to win the support of the United States, the authorities continued to steer a middle course.

Toward the end of November, convinced that the time had come for him to move on to Santiago, Poinsett appointed a young American merchant, William Gilchrist Miller, as vice-consul for the port of Buenos Aires.[19] In his residence of nine months the forthright South Carolinian had found Argentine officials generally friendly and the people hospitable. As the citizen of a free government in the Western Hemisphere, he had become an object of great interest and felt overwhelmed "with questions—and caresses." [20] In the fulfillment of his principal mission he had been able to keep the United States before the minds of the leaders and to improve slightly the position of American traders.[21] In frequent reports to Washington he had given his government its first tangible knowledge of the developing situation.[22] Beyond this, if he had not actually taken steps to aid independence, he had at least encouraged progressive action toward it.

The Policy of the United Provinces

Government in Buenos Aires from 1810 to 1816 wavered fitfully as junta gave way to triumvirate and triumvirate to supreme directory. This lack of continuity in administrative form was accompanied by striking consistency in policy toward the United States. Juntas, triumvirates, directories—each in turn manifested great respect for the neighbor to the north and high hopes for friendly and beneficial relations. An obvious motive ran through the tactical wooing of all administrations. Whether arms, trade, or recognition, each sought American aid.

The original Junta gubernativa had no sooner ousted Mariano Moreno and admitted delegates from the outlying provinces than it composed its first note to President Madison, two days before the arrival of Joel Poinsett in February, 1811. The Junta praised the President's magnanimous attitude toward the Province of Caracas (present Venezuela) and dared to hope that "the United States should tighten with the

[18] Poinsett to Dept. of State, Nov. 25, 1811, HSP, Poinsett Papers, I, 110. For the setting of this dispute, see J. Fred Rippy, *Rivalry of the United States and Great Britain over Latin America (1808-1830)*, pp. 9ff.

[19] *Registro oficial de la República Argentina que comprende los documentos espedidos desde 1810 hasta 1873*, I, 127. On December 2 Miller reported that Poinsett had departed three days before (NA, DS, Con. Let., B. A., I, pt. 1).

[20] "Journal to Rio Janeiro, Buenos Ayres and Chile, 1810 & 1811," LC, MD, Poinsett Papers.

[21] Miller to Monroe, Dec. 30, 1811, NA, DS, Con. Let., B. A., I, pt. 1.

[22] A check of the Poinsett Collection in the Manuscript Division, Historical Society of Pennsylvania (Philadelphia), indicates that the Consul wrote about two letters a month to the Department of State during his nine-month residence in Buenos Aires.

Provinces on the Río de la Plata the common chain of nations, by a cordiality more firm and expressive." [23]

This first cautious action of the suitor was followed in June by another, more tangible. Desperately in need of arms, the Junta commissioned two young agents to proceed to the United States on a purchasing expedition. They were Diego de Saavedra, son of its President and a captain of dragoons, and Juan de Aguirre, merchant and Secretary of the Cabildo.[24] Shipping on a cutter owned by William G. Miller, they carried detailed instructions, twenty thousand pesos for expenses, and Poinsett's recommendations.

The instructions defined the volume of purchases, the contractual arrangements, the shipping dispositions, and security regulations. Besides arms and munitions, they were to obtain three or four machines for making flints and to engage technicians, who with their tools and models would go to Buenos Aires to supervise the manufacture of guns and cannon. Shipping instructions were framed to cover such exigencies as North American war with Great Britain and inability to re-enter the Río de la Plata. The secrecy of the mission was to be scrupulously protected. To avoid the risk of compromising the United States with Great Britain, or with any nation, two sets of passports were issued, one bearing the true names of the agents, the other the pseudonyms José Antonio Cabrera and Pedro López.[25] In a personal note soliciting aid and protection for its envoys, the Junta apprised President Madison of these security precautions.[26]

After a journey of nearly four months, including an emergency stop in Rio de Janeiro, the agents arrived in Philadelphia about the middle of October, 1811.[27] Failing readily to find merchants who would agree to do business on the only terms they could offer, they soon moved on to Washington.[28] Secretary James Monroe received them amiably and eagerly solicited information on their homeland, its form of government, the nature of public opinion, the character of the population, and the

[23] Feb. 11, 1811, Manning, *op. cit.*, I, 319-320.

[24] For materials on the Saavedra-Aguirre mission I have gone directly to official manuscript sources in the Archivo General de la Nación, Buenos Aires, but for interpretation I have relied on Samuel Flagg Bemis' *Early Diplomatic Missions from Buenos Aires to the United States, 1811-1824*, pp. 9-16. A shorter account, also based on Argentine archives, is in Daniel Antokoletz, *La diplomatie pendant la révolution*, pp. 202-205.

[25] "Instrucciones que la Junta Provisional Gubernativa . . . comunica á Don Diego de Saavedra y Don Juan Pedro de Aguirre," June 5, 1811, AGN, BA, S1-A2-A4-núm. 9. They were to buy 2,000 pairs of pistols, 4,000 carbines or carbines with bayonets, 8,000 swords or sabers, 10,000 guns with cartridge boxes, and 1,000,000 flints, and were authorized to seek a contract for as many as 30,000 additional shooting arms.

[26] The Junta to Madison, June 6, 1811, Manning, *op. cit.*, I, 321.

[27] Saavedra and Aguirre to the Junta, Oct. 19, 1811, AGN, BA, S1-A2-A4-núm. 9.

[28] Cabrera and López to Monroe, Oct. 25, 1811, NA, DS, Notes from Arg. Leg., I, pt. 1.

state of foreign relations. Through the Secretary, President Madison greeted Saavedra and Aguirre with extreme cordiality. He expressed sympathy with their revolutionary cause, granted them permission to move about the country and export freely the supplies they sought, and offered whatever services the government might render to what must be considered "a province of old Spain." [29]

During the following months, through the firm of Miller and Van Beuren of Philadelphia, Saavedra and Aguirre purchased muskets, bayonets, and flints to the value of $15,713.97, the limit of their funds in hand.[30] Efforts to accomplish the remaining portions of their mission, even in collaboration with Telésforo de Orea, Venezuelan agent in the United States, were unavailing. Early in 1812, after a second trip to Washington and conferences with Secretary Monroe and Attorney General William Pinkney, the agents believed that the government might undertake to sell them arms through the agency of the Philadelphia merchant, Stephen Girard.[31] At this time, however, matters of greater national concern—Cuba, the Spanish borderlands, trade with the Spanish Empire—were boiling over on the presidential doorstep, and President Madison drew back from such a scheme as Silas Deane and Beaumarchais had conceived a generation before. Saavedra and Aguirre, working and waiting in Philadelphia as Cabrera and López, worked and waited in vain. They received no further word from Monroe.

On January 26, much sooner than expected, the envoys received instructions to terminate their mission and return with the supplies purchased.[32] About a month later they sailed in the frigate *Liberty* with their cargo of a thousand each of muskets and bayonets and 363,050 flints.[33] The volume of arms they escorted was small, but the memories of their reception in the United States were pleasant.

In Buenos Aires the return of Saavedra and Aguirre brought forth expressions of enthusiasm for the United States, whose government and people many looked upon as the only true friends of their revolutionary aims. Party feeling soon intervened, however, to prevent adequate explanation of the expedition's reception in the United States. Argentine

[29] Saavedra and Aguirre to the Junta, Nov. 11, 1811, AGN, BA, S1-A2-A4-núm. 9.
[30] "An Account of Sundries purchased by order of Messrs. Don Pedro López and Don Jos. Antonio Cabrera by Miller y Van Beuren," Feb. 3, 1812, AGN, BA, S1-A2-A4-núm. 9.
[31] Saavedra and Aguirre to the Junta, Feb. 16, 1812, *ibid*. On Girard's position in the negotiations, see J. B. McMaster, *Life and Times of Stephen Girard*, II, 168-171.
[32] Saavedra and Aguirre to the Junta, Feb. 16, 1812, AGN, BA, S1-A2-A4-núm. 9.
[33] Saavedra and Aguirre to "Excelentícimo Señor," May 14, 1812, *ibid*. In the Archivo General de la Nación, Buenos Aires, there are about a dozen reports prepared by the envoys, including two itemized statements of expenses, Feb. 3 and May 19, 1812. In both statements the agents treat dollars and pesos as of equal value.

belief in American lukewarmness toward their cause began to grow.[34] The mission from La Plata had visited the United States at a time when the Madison administration was haltingly seeking to resolve a Latin American policy that would synchronize with national interests in Texas, Florida, and Cuba. Under the circumstances, it was significant not that the South Americans secured so few arms but that they gained virtual recognition of their own belligerency and assurance of extremely benevolent American neutrality.[35]

American Offspring Resist Mother Europe

The end of the Saavedra-Aguirre mission coincided roughly with the intensification of serious foreign threats to both nations. In the northern republic, war with Great Britain began on June 18. In the southern state, following the rout of a patriot force at Huaqui in Upper Peru the previous year, the northwestern provinces lay open to advancing Spanish arms. Royalist troops at Montevideo imperiled Buenos Aires itself. During the next four years, consequently, as the two American nations resisted European reconquest, contacts between them were extremely tenuous, though the channels were never closed.

Joel Poinsett's departure for Chile in November, 1811, left Vice-Consul Miller the sole official representative of the United States in the Río de la Plata. If uncertain conditions under the triumvirates rendered his position more difficult, war between the United States and Great Britain made his presence less necessary. North American shipping in the South Atlantic, which by 1811 had shown a lusty rivalry to that of Great Britain, virtually passed from the seas. Nevertheless, Miller sought to convince Monroe that the presence of a frigate in the river would enhance respect for the United States.[36] The position gained by the "dignity" of Poinsett's representation, the Vice-Consul contended, must not be jeopardized.[37]

While commercial relations with Buenos Aires were thus suspended, it became Miller's chief function to recount the political difficulties of the United Provinces. He reported to Washington the instability of the

[34] Miller to Monroe, July 16, 1812, July 26, 1813, NA, DS, Con. Let., B. A., I, pt. 1. The earlier despatch is printed in Manning, *op. cit.*, I, 326.

[35] Whitaker, *op. cit.*, pp. 87-94; Bemis, *op. cit.*, pp. 17-23.

[36] Poinsett's report to Dept. of State, undated, NA, DS, Specl. Agts. Ser., III (1813), J. R. Poinsett; Miller to Monroe, July 16, 1812, Manning, *op. cit.*, I, 329-330. On at least two occasions in 1813-1814, when he accused the British of taking advantage of neutral waters to molest American shipping, Miller regretted the absence of the requested frigate (Miller to Juan Manuel de Luca, Secretary of Supreme Executive of the United Provinces, June 30, 1813, and to Juan Nicolás de Herrera, Minister of Government and Foreign Relations, May 26, 1814, AGN, BA, A1-A2-A4-núm. 8).

[37] Miller to Monroe, Dec. 30, 1811, NA, DS, Con. Let., B. A., I, pt. 1.

triumvirates, the reforms of the Constituent Assembly, the military activities of Manuel Belgrano in Paraguay, and the arrival from Europe of José de San Martín and Carlos M. de Alvear, future liberators of southern South America.[38] Until the close of his official mission in September, 1813, he recurrently evaluated the growth of popular sentiment for independence.[39]

Near the end of Miller's tenure, the United Provinces renewed their courtship of the United States. The Constituent Assembly sent to President Madison a long, carefully phrased solicitation, which deprecated as untimely obstacles to the establishment of direct relations both America's war with Britain and political vacillations in Buenos Aires. Nevertheless, it hoped for the early establishment of a "fraternal alliance, which should unite forever the North and South Americans." [40]

The Supreme Directors courted the United States with equal ardor. Soon after coming to power in January, 1814, Gervasio Antonio de Posadas expressed deep concern to Madison that the United States had failed to support its expressed sympathy for the Spanish American cause. "It is on you," wrote the Director, "we place our present hopes, who have the happiness to govern the only free people in the world, whose philosophic and patriotic sentiments we are ambitious to imitate." [41] The Madison administration, however, still had its hands full elsewhere, and the pleas of Miller, of the Constituent Assembly, and of Posadas were blandly ignored.

Meanwhile, Poinsett had been spending hazardous months in Santiago, where he actively aided José Miguel Carrera and the Chilean moves for independence. Late in 1814 he returned to Buenos Aires. Here he found the British in a more advantageous position than ever; he suspected even that some officials of the government were under English domination.[42]

[38] See his reports to Monroe in NA, DS, Con. Let., B. A., I, pt. 1, some of which are printed in Manning, *op. cit.*, I. For the Argentine background, see Levene, *A History of Argentina*, pp. 249-252, 271-285.

[39] Miller to Monroe, Sept. 13, 1813, NA, DS, Con. Let., B. A., I, pt. 1. Miller continued to live in Buenos Aires for many years. Between 1815 and 1821 he wrote frequently to Poinsett to inform him of conditions in La Plata and to importune his assistance (HSP, Poinsett Papers, I, II).

[40] July 21, 1813, Manning, *op. cit.*, I, 332. On the same day, Manuel Moreno, elder brother of Mariano and many years later minister to England, transmitted to President Madison several public documents, which, he said, would show "the political state in which the Provinces of Río de la Plata are at present, as well as of the noble efforts and sacrifices which the inhabitants have made to obtain their liberty, and that of the American continent" (NA, DS, Notes from Arg. Leg., I, pt. 1).

[41] March 9, 1814, Manning, *op. cit.*, I, 335.

[42] Poinsett to Monroe, Sept. 15, 1814, HSP, Poinsett Papers, I, 151-153. On British interest in the political and commercial affairs of the United Provinces during 1812-1815, see C. K. Webster, *Britain and the Independence of Latin America, 1812-1830*, I, 83-100, and Dorothy Burne Goebel, "British Trade to the Spanish Colonies, 1796-1823," *The American Historical Review*, XLIII (Jan., 1938), 313-315.

Nevertheless, he was able to win new commercial privileges, hollow as they were during the war, which included free entry of specified products from the United States.[43]

Prior to his return to Charleston on May 28, 1815, Poinsett prepared a comprehensive report of his mission to South America. Although primarily concerned with conditions in Chile, he described the parties, characters, and principal events of the revolution in Buenos Aires, as well as the state of society, trade, and military forces. He believed that only contentious struggles prevented Buenos Aires and Chile from laying sound foundations for independence. Then, with astonishing accuracy, he prophesied that

> should these countries struggle through all their difficulties, and finally succeed in establishing their independence, it is to be feared that, harassed at the frequent failure of their political experiments, and finding that all parties, as they alternately fill the seat of government, in order to secure their power, trample on the sacred rights of Liberty, they will despair of obtaining that inestimable blessing, and end them by a military despotism.[44]

Poinsett's return to Charleston marked the end of the first special mission of the United States to South America. By revealing his government's good will the South Carolinian had encouraged revolution and opened the door to more regular intercourse.

Excepting Poinsett's brief residence in late 1814, the United States was not officially represented in the United Provinces during the year and a half after Miller's resignation in September, 1813. Thomas Lloyd Halsey, of Providence, though appointed consul in October, 1812, did not begin his official duties until the early months of 1815.[45] By that time he was a veteran of eight years' experience in Buenos Aires as an importer and exporter; his pioneering enterprise encouraged his appointment as consul. While continuing his private business, he actively sought to improve commercial ties. He introduced breeds of sheep from the United States; he sought lower and reciprocal import duties; he worked for the export of more Argentine commodities to the United States; he urged loans to the revolutionary administration; and he aided the patriots in obtaining war materials.[46] He believed that peace between the United States and

---

[43] Poinsett to Monroe, May 30, 1815, HSP, Poinsett Papers, I, 171. No agreement, however, was effected.

[44] Poinsett's report, undated, NA, DS, Specl. Agts. Ser., III (1813), J. R. Poinsett. The body of the report is divided into eight sections.

[45] Halsey to Monroe, Oct. 21, 1812, Feb. 11, 1815, NA, DS, Con. Let., B. A., I, pt. 1. In the latter note Halsey reported that he had been received by the government. In the Archivo General de la Nación, Buenos Aires, however, there is a letter from Halsey to Nicolás de Herrera, Oct. 27, 1814, in which the merchant refers to himself as Consul (S1-A2-A4-núm. 8).

[46] *Dictionary of American Biography*, VIII, 162-163, and Charles Lyon Chandler, *Inter-American Acquaintances*, pp. 92-93. From the early years of the century until after the wars for independence Halsey intermittently lived in Buenos Aires, where

Great Britain would not only aid commerce but also hasten Argentine independence. Still, he held a very low opinion of the stability of the government and the competence of its leaders.[47] As with many other early agents of the United States in South America, his activities ultimately went under a cloud and he became *persona non grata*. Meanwhile, the United Provinces would send new missions to win North American aid and, ultimately, would declare independence.[48]

Soon after Halsey's recognition, partisan shifts in administration brought to the supreme directorship Ignacio Alvarez Thomas. With the restoration of peace in Europe, peril to the United Provinces began to mount, and the new Director begged the Consul to urge upon "the virtuous sons of Washington" the immediate need of war implements.[49] Not content with this solicitation of the Consul, during the next nine months Alvarez Thomas commissioned no less than three special emissaries to obtain assistance in the United States.

Two of these agents, quite by chance, arrived at Annapolis on January 17, 1816, aboard the same vessel. One was the North American, Thomas Taylor, veteran of naval service for the United Provinces, who came to implement the six privateering patents he carried; the other was the indefatigable Chilean revolutionary, José Miguel Carrera, who came primarily to seek aid for his own homeland.[50] Though neither received official acknowledgment or assistance in Washington, the two men were moderately successful in their missions. Both sailed from the United States in the following December, Taylor in the specially built privateer *Fourth of July* and Carrera in command of three ships bearing thirty recruits and considerable materiel, most of which eventually went to the service of the United Provinces.[51]

---

he amassed a considerable fortune. In the thirties he returned to Providence and became a director of the Providence National Bank. From 1809 to 1839 he was a trustee of Brown University.

[47] Halsey to Monroe, Feb. 11, 1815; to Gregorio Tagle, Secretary of State (Foreign Affairs), July 31, 1815, NA, DS, Con. Let., B. A., I, pt. 1. Part of the first despatch is printed in Manning, *op. cit.*, I, 337. Halsey's correspondence in State Department archives, like that of Miller, is fragmentary. A few of Halsey's letters, mostly unimportant, are in the Archivo General de la Nación, Buenos Aires.

[48] See below, pp. 24-25, 48-58.

[49] May 10, 1815, Manning, *op. cit.*, I, 339.

[50] General Alvarez Thomas advised President Madison of the Carrera mission (May 26, 1815, NA, DS, Notes from Arg. Leg., I, pt. 1). Materials on Taylor and Carrera in the Archivo General de la Nación, Buenos Aires, are almost nonexistent. There is one letter from Taylor to the Supreme Director, Feb. 8, 1816 (S1-A2-A4-núm. 9), and copy of a letter from Carrera to John Skinner, Baltimore postmaster and impresario of privateers, enclosing receipt for a 4,000 peso loan (Correos. División Nacional. 1816. S.v-C.XXIII-A.8-núm. 5).

[51] For brief accounts of the two missions, see Bemis, *op. cit.*, pp. 29-34, and Keen, *op. cit.*, pp. 103-105. Many references to Taylor's privateering activities are found in Lewis Winkler Bealer, *Los corsarios de Buenos Aires*, especially pp. 30-31, 57-59. Carrera's relations with Poinsett are narrated in Rippy, *Joel R. Poinsett*, pp. 61-68.

On the day before Taylor and Carrera landed on American shores, Buenos Aires initiated a far more determined effort to win support. At that time the Supreme Director assured President Madison that the forthcoming congress at Tucumán would declare the independence of the United Provinces. Supported by this assurance, Alvarez Thomas hoped the President would give to a new deputy the same full credit and consideration which would be accorded any ministers he might send to Buenos Aires.[52] The new agent thus introduced was Colonel Martín Thompson, onetime Spanish cadet and veteran of Trafalgar, who, bound by precise instructions, arrived in New York on May 3.[53]

Thompson's instructions went much beyond those of Saavedra and Aguirre five years before. There was a comparable mandate for secrecy and a broad commission to contract for arms, but there the similarities ceased. Thompson was to procure a frigate or two, officers of all grades, who would be properly honored, agreements of mutual interest, and any proposition that would be advantageous. In addition, he was to invite presidential aid in aligning the noncolonial nations of Europe against the colonial powers and to work for the establishment of secret relations with the revolutionaries in Mexico.[54]

Even had the time been more opportune, the assignment might have daunted a statesman. But Thompson was an indiscreet, untested agent, who unfortunately arrived in Washington at a time when the administration had set its eyes on the Holy Alliance and its heart on Florida. The mission of Thompson, therefore, so important to the cause of the United Provinces, was doomed from the outset, even without the blunders he committed and the misfortune he suffered.[55] By executing portions of his instructions without first securing adequate authorization at Washington, he was subjected to early recall.[56] In ill health even upon his arrival in New York, he now became an "unfortunate lunatic agent." [57]

[52] Alvarez Thomas to Madison, Jan. 16, 1816, Manning, *op. cit.*, I, 341-342. Rough notes for this communication are in AGN, BA, S1-A2-A4-núm. 9.

[53] Enrique Udaondo, *Diccionario biográfico argentino*, p. 1041; Thompson to Supreme Director, May 20, 1816, AGN, BA, S1-A2-A4-núm. 9.

[54] A copy of the instructions is filed in *ibid.*

[55] Between May 20 and Nov. 14, 1816, Thompson sent about a dozen reports to his government. They reveal his negotiations for privateers and his contracting with Polish and French officers (AGN, BA, S1-A2-A4-núm. 9). He also communicated with Poinsett (Aug. 8, 1816, HSP, Poinsett Papers, I, 190).

[56] Juan Martín de Pueyrredón, Supreme Director, to Madison, Jan. 1, 1817, Manning, *op. cit.*, I, 346-347.

[57] Jeremy Robinson, who sailed for La Plata in November, 1817, as special agent to Lima, made this allusion to Thompson on Feb. 6, 1818, after paying a visit to the agent's wife (LC, MD, Papers of Jeremy Robinson, Diaries).

Independence of the United Provinces

If the War of 1812 is properly called the "Second War for Independence," then the Treaty of Ghent may be said to have marked the repulse of the English attempt to reconquer its former American possessions. The end of hostilities in Europe, however, gave the Spanish Americans no such assurance. Ferdinand VII's return to the throne of Spain in 1814 was closely followed by the crushing of revolutionary movements in all of Spanish America except the United Provinces. Even there security from reconquest seemed doubtful. The insurrectionary José Artigas was spreading disaffection in the Banda Oriental and in the northeastern districts of the United Provinces. Upper Peru had given way to reinforced Spanish forces. Upon all sides the new state seemed to be in danger.[58] The American Consul in Buenos Aires wrote to his government that

> the situation of this Country is extremely critical, its resources are much diminished, Factions and divisions prevail, & no person of talents & energy appears to take the lead & carry forward the cause of Independance [*sic*], & unless the United States lends some speedy assistance, it will soon be obliged to submit to its old Master.[59]

These were the difficulties which faced the Argentine delegates who assembled at Tucumán in late March, 1816. Their wisdom in selecting Juan Martín de Pueyrredón as Supreme Director inaugurated a three-year period of more stable government. A far more momentous action of the Congress, however, was its declaration on July 9 of the independence of the "United Provinces of South America." [60] Announcement of the declaration was promptly communicated to the American Consul, accompanied by warm tribute to the United States:

> It can not be forgotten that in this hectic revolution the people of the Union have had their eyes fixed in advance upon that great Republic that exists in North America. The United States since their Glorious liberty have been as a luminous constellation pointing the way opened by Providence to the other people of this part of the Globe.[61]

By example and by sympathy, if not by material aid, the government of the United States had aided the cause of independence in the United

[58] Levene, *op. cit.*, pp. 297-299.
[59] Halsey to Monroe, July 3, 1816, Manning, *op. cit.*, I, 343-344.
[60] Complete text of the act is found in *Registro oficial de la República Argentina*, I, 366-367.
[61] Miguel Yrigoyen *et al.* to Halsey, July 24, 1816, Manning, *op. cit.*, I, 345. Rough notes directing this action are contained in AGN, BA, S1-A2-A4-núm. 8.

Provinces. In the ephemeral glow at least, there was a genuine feeling of kinship. The North American press greeted the action with great enthusiasm and helped to pave the way for the administration's next step.[62]

From 1810 to 1816 the policy of the United States was one of observation, delay, and the maintenance of benevolent neutrality.[63] That policy was to continue. The leaders of the United Provinces had been appreciative of such gracious interest, but continuously coveted and actively sought more tangible assistance. That policy, too, would continue.

[62] See many items in *Niles' Register,* including quotations from other journals, as X (Sept. 28, Oct. 26, Nov. 2, 23, 1816), 80, 141, 150, 222. In the first reference, for example, this paragraph appeared: *"Great and good news!*—The united provinces of the *Rio del Plata,* were declared *free and independent by the grand congress at Tucuman, on the 9th of July.* May heaven keep them so!"
[63] Cf. The "Santissima Trinidad," 7 *Wheat.* 283, 5 L. Ed. 454 (1822).

I I I

GROWING PAINS OF A YOUNG NATION:
CHALLENGES TO AMERICAN NEUTRALITY,
1815-1817

Even before the declaration of independence by the United Provinces, the Madison administration had shaped its general policy toward continuing revolution within the Spanish Empire. Looking with cautious eye both eastward at post-Waterloo developments in Europe and southward to the Spanish borderlands and beyond, it was prepared (1) to maintain neutrality, strictly impartial on paper but, in actuality, benevolent toward the rebels; (2) to investigate conditions on the spot—in an area about which the government and its people were singularly uninformed; and (3) to appraise developments on both sides of the Atlantic which might justify more substantial aid.[1] Though modified in one phase or another by domestic and international complications, this was essentially the policy followed by President Madison and his successor, Monroe, until actual recognition in 1822.

By the middle of 1816, however, after Spain had crushed rebellion everywhere except in the Río de la Plata, this policy had become quiescent. To the North American friends of Latin America the United Provinces alone held out hope that revolution might not fail. Self-government had persisted there since 1810. Rebel armies had repeatedly thrust back Spanish attempts at reconquest. Since 1814 General San Martín, Argentine patriot recently returned from military service in Spain, had been patiently preparing his expedition to liberate Chile and areas beyond. His victory at Chacabuco in February, 1817, was soon to give hope that the embers of general revolt might flare up anew. And what was far more immediate, Argentine privateers had begun to enter United States ports and Argentine agents were arriving to contract for additional vessels. All these developments, therefore, focused on the United Prov-

[1] Such a summary has been made by William Spence Robertson in his *Hispanic-American Relations with the United States*, pp. 29-30.

inces the North American interest largely withdrawn from other parts of Spanish America.

In the application of this threefold policy to the United Provinces, the task first of Madison and Monroe, then of Monroe and Adams, was complicated by many circumstances: (1) the temerity of Buenos Aires privateers; (2) the inept conduct of American agents in La Plata; (3) the failure of efforts to secure conclusive intelligence upon which to base an estimate of the situation; (4) repeated requests for recognition by South American envoys in Washington; (5) the political opposition of Henry Clay; and (6) the attitude of the European alliance.[2] All of these considerations hampered the smooth evolution of the policy of the United States toward the United Provinces.

Professed Neutrality

Of all the vexatious problems which challenged the administration's resolution to maintain neutrality, the most pregnant was that presented by the operations of Argentine privateers. As early as July 3, 1815, the Treasury Department had issued an order which legalized the entry into United States ports of vessels flying the new Latin American flags.[3] Protected by this ruling, the privateers began to enter American harbors in 1816 and continued to reappear until 1821.[4] Some of the ships were veterans of the War of 1812; others were specially built in American shipyards. Some vessels represented the personal investment of American merchants or bankers; many were commissioned through Argentine patents purveyed by American adventurers. A majority of the crew members was recruited in American ports; most of the officers were American.[5]

Fitted out with legal or blank commissions, these privateers put out from the ports of the United States and Spanish America in search of Spanish prey. A ship captured or a mission completed, it was simple enough to find excuse to enter or re-enter American harbors. Supplies or ship repairs might be needed. Spoils could be disposed of, or a mutinous crew brought to shore. Whatever the cause, ships of the United Provinces and other Spanish colonies frequented Baltimore and New Orleans or, when more convenient, put in at such ports as Savannah, Charleston,

[2] Points (1) and (2) are discussed in this chapter, point (3) in Chapter IV, and points (4), (5), and (6) in Chapter V.

[3] Secretary of the Treasury A. J. Dallas to the Collector of Customs, New Orleans, July 3, 1815, John Bassett Moore, A *Digest of International Law* . . . , I, 170-171.

[4] Two monographs by American historians, both published in Buenos Aires, describe in great detail the activities of privateers of the United Provinces: Lewis W. Bealer, *Los corsarios de Buenos Aires* . . . , *1815-1821*, and Theodore S. Currier, *Los corsarios del Río de la Plata.* See also *H. Doc.*, No. 48, 15 Cong., 2 sess., pp. 111-121.

[5] Bealer, *op. cit.*, pp. 43-45; Currier, *op. cit.*, pp. iii-xii.

Norfolk, Philadelphia, New York, Providence, and New Bedford.[6] As the legality of their operations—or the fiction of legality—began to wear thin, privateering degenerated into freebooting and slave trading, and American territorial waters, as well as ports, were utilized. Of forty-five to seventy vessels believed to have flown the ensign of Buenos Aires in Atlantic waters alone, perhaps as many as three dozen recurrently visited ports of the United States.[7] The success of these extensive tactics, of course, was facilitated by popular sympathy for the patriot cause and the desire of merchants hungry for increased trade, as well as by liberal interpretation of the Treaty of San Lorenzo and failure to enforce wholeheartedly the neutrality laws.[8]

Against these persistent incursions the Spanish Ministers, Luis de Onís and Francisco Dionisio Vives, protested frequently and vigorously. They denounced the unloading of spoils and the refitting of ships. They decried even their entry into American ports. Almost every ship arrival brought forth an acrid protest. "It is extremely painful to me," wrote Onís on one occasion,

> to interrupt your attention so often, on such unpleasant subjects; but I should be wanting in my duty if I should delay to inform this Government of the manner in which the orders of the President are eluded in Baltimore, in order to heap injury upon injury on a friendly nation, and promote the revolution of its provinces. In vain will it be alleged, in order to cover this proceeding, that the laws are not sufficient to pursue, without a positive evidence, those citizens who commit hostilities against Spain. The treaty which exists between the two nations is a law of the republic; and no tribunal can decline its observance. The proofs of its infraction cannot be more manifest or decisive. . . .[9]

An analysis of the official communications received from the Spanish Ministers in Washington between September 5, 1815, and March 9, 1822, reveals that "the privateering of Buenos Aires required of the Spanish Minister as much attention as all [other] affairs demanded." [10]

[6] Bealer, *op. cit.*, pp. 37-38; Currier, *op. cit.*, pp. 26, 51; Charles C. Griffin, "Privateering from Baltimore during the Spanish-American Wars of Independence," *Maryland Historical Magazine*, XXXV (March, 1940), 1-25.

[7] Bealer, *op. cit.*, p. 42; Currier, *op. cit.*, pp. iii-xii.

[8] For manifestations of popular interest in the privateering enterprises of the United Provinces, see *Niles' Register*, IX (Nov. 11, 1815), 187; XII (March 15, April 5, 1817), 46, 95-96; XIII (Sept. 27, Nov. 15, 1817), 79, 192. For discussions of the neutrality laws and the Treaty of San Lorenzo, see Arthur P. Whitaker, *The United States and the Independence of Latin America, 1800-1830*, pp. 194-199.

[9] To Monroe, Feb. 11, 1817, *American State Papers, Foreign Relations*, IV, 187.

[10] Currier, *op. cit.*, pp. 45-46. For examples of the protests of Onís, see *American State Papers, Foreign Relations*, IV, 184-201, 424, 494, 500, 503. An interesting correspondence on the subject is that between Antonio Argote Villalobos, Spanish Consul at Norfolk, and Charles K. Mallory, Collector at Norfolk and Portsmouth, in April, 1817 (*H. Doc.*, No. 155, 15 Cong., 1 sess., pp. 56-67).

The gist of the Spanish argument was that ships flying the flags of Buenos Aires and the other revolting colonies should be excluded from American harbors. The counter position of the United States, first stated by President Madison in his neutrality proclamation of September 1, 1815, and reaffirmed by Secretary Monroe on January 19, 1816, was followed with reasonable consistency for the next five years. It held that "our ports should remain open to both parties, as they were, before the commencement of the struggle." [11] Nevertheless, Monroe was fully aware —as he demonstrated in his instructions of November 21, 1817, to special commissioners of the United States—that the laxity with which the privateers of Buenos Aires were treated by the United States was not in exact accord with a policy of neutrality.[12] An attempt to clarify the anomaly of the American position was made on March 3, 1817, through the passage of "An Act more effectually to preserve the neutral relations of the United States." [13] But, failure to enforce strictly the provisions of this new act must have demonstrated to Onís that the neutrality of the United States in the war of the United Provinces against Spain was professed, not real.

An Unauthorized Loan

A second consideration which vexed the Department of State in developing its policy toward the United Provinces was the inept or impolitic conduct of its representatives in Buenos Aires. Incapable or overzealous deputies, exceeding their instructions or even acting without authorization, brought frequent embarrassments. In their eagerness to assist the cause of the insurgents, agents impaired their competence as observers and frustrated the administration's efforts to secure reliable intelligence.

In January, 1816, Thomas Lloyd Halsey was still Consul of the United States in Buenos Aires. Nevertheless, learning that an American merchant, John Devereux, was preparing to visit Buenos Aires, Madison invited him to accept appointment as a commercial agent and to obtain information on political developments. He was asked to report especially on military movements, attitude toward the United States, and any changes which might take place in commercial policy toward North American shipping.[14] Devereux, however, apparently dissatisfied at being mere observer and reporter, undertook a more active role. Troubled by the inability of the revolutionary government to secure a foreign loan, he offered to assist the Congress of Tucumán in procuring financial aid in

[11] *American State Papers, Foreign Relations*, IV, 1; Monroe to Onís, William R. Manning (ed.), *Diplomatic Correspondence of the United States Concerning Independence of the Latin-American Countries*, I, 21.

[12] *Ibid.*, p. 49; on the special commissioners, see below, Chapter IV.

[13] *U.S. Stat. at L.*, III, 370-371.

[14] Monroe to Devereux, Jan. 12, 1816, NA, DS, Inst. to Con., I, 371.

the United States.[15] He professed to believe that his government would guarantee such a loan. The suggestion was promptly sanctioned by the Congress and by the Supreme Director. When Halsey reported the proposal to Washington, he manifested no disapproval of the agent's presumption.[16]

Upon the heels of the Consul's report (January, 1817), Pueyrredón informed Madison that he had accepted Devereux's offer as presented by Halsey.[17] The terms of the agreement, signed by the Supreme Director, the Minister of the Treasury, and the Consul, provided for a loan of $2,000,000 at an annual interest of 9 per cent. The principal would not mature until ten years after the close of the war against Spain.[18]

By the time a copy of the contract reached Washington, the Monroe administration had entered office. Acting Secretary of State Richard Rush immediately disavowed Devereux's action, terminated his commission, and ordered that the necessary explanations be made to the government at Buenos Aires.[19] Thereupon, in September, 1817, Pueyrredón was coolly informed that the United States could not "espouse the Cause of the South American Patriots." [20]

An Unauthorized Treaty

About a year after the appointment of Devereux but before receipt of news of his indiscretion, President Madison determined to appoint a special agent for Buenos Aires, Chile, and Peru. For this position, embodying a wider jurisdiction than that of any agent since Poinsett, he selected W. G. D. Worthington. Though a refined man, much given to reading the Bible, the appointee was an egoistic individual, bombastic

[15] Halsey to José Domingo Trillo, Minister of Treasury, Oct. 16, 1816, AGN, BA, S1-A2-A4-núm. 8. In notifying the Congress, June 12, 1817, Pueyrredón said the project was "presented by D. David C. Deforest and by the Consul of the United States D. Thomas Lloyd Halsey in the name of D. Juan Devereux" (Archivo Histórico de la Provincia de Buenos Aires, *Documentos del Congreso de Tucumán*, p. 10).

[16] Halsey to Monroe, Jan. 30, 1817, Manning, *op. cit.*, pp. 347-348.

[17] Jan. 31, 1817, *ibid.*, p. 349. There appeared in Buenos Aires at this time a six-page broadside with the title "Contestación a la Patriota Clara por un Americano del Norte," a series of letters from "Un Ciudadano de los Estados-Unidos" to Padre R. P. Castañeda and to "Pueblo de Buenos-Ayres." It noted that Devereux was supported by "reputable houses" of Baltimore. Its apparent purpose was to encourage the people of Buenos Aires to believe that recognition by the United States was imminent (LC, MD, Broadsides, 310, Argentina).

[18] Terms of the loan contract, dated January 31, appear in *Documentos del Congreso de Tucumán*, pp. 10-11. An English translation is filed in NA, DS, Notes from Arg. Leg., I, pt. 1.

[19] Secretary Rush to Halsey, April 21, 1817; to W. G. D. Worthington, special agent, April 21, 1817, NA, DS, Inst. to Con., II, 7-8, 24-25. On Worthington, see below, pp. 32-34.

[20] Worthington to Secretary Adams, Oct. 1, 1817, Manning, *op. cit.*, I, 354.

in speech and ostentatious in manner. His literary inclinations produced extensive reports and voluminous diaries for the Department of State.[21] Unfortunately, by failing to restrict his actions to his instructions, Worthington revealed his judgment to be no better than Devereux's.

Monroe's instructions indicated the administration's continuing quest for reliable information. The agent was directed to make extensive inquiries regarding population, resources, and revolutionary factions, but, beyond this, he was to explain the mutual advantages of commerce and to promote liberal and stable regulations.[22]

Worthington commenced his mission with discretionary statements and manifestations of his neutral character. He reported the extreme disappointment of the government and the people that he was only an agent and not a minister delegated to make formal acknowledgment of their independence.[23] In anticipation of the information he intended to seek from the United Provinces, he voluntarily prepared for Gregorio Tagle, Pueyrredón's Foreign Minister, a lengthy analysis of the international position of the United States, to which he appended a series of twelve topics upon which he sought data.[24] He seemed to be preparing himself to collect and transmit to Washington the information his superiors so much desired.

But Worthington's overdeveloped pride, self-confidence, and ambition were unsuited to his diplomatic assignment, and his residence in Buenos Aires from September 5, 1817, to January 23, 1818, was climaxed by a startling development. Soon after his arrival he prepared and submitted to the Supreme Director, wholly without authorization by his government, a treaty "Respecting Commerce & Seamen between the United States of America and the Province of Buenos Ayres." In its original draft, the forty-five articles of the treaty included not only provisions for reciprocal tariffs, exchange of consuls, and protection of nationals and their property, but also such principles as freedom of the seas and most-favored-nation treatment.[25] In a series of conferences with the Supreme

[21] Eugenio Pereira Salas, *La misión Worthington en Chile (1818-1819)*, pp. 1-2; Charles Lyon Chandler, *Inter-American Acquaintances*, pp. 92-93; "Mr. Worthington's Diary," NA, DS, Desp. Arg., I, pt. 2. The diary extends to more than three hundred pages; though fluent and witty, Worthington largely ignored critical political and diplomatic problems.

[22] Monroe to Worthington, Jan. 23, 1817 (two despatches), NA, DS, Dom. Let., XVI, 359-360.

[23] Worthington to Adams, Oct. 4, 1817, Manning, *op. cit.*, I, 355-356.

[24] Worthington to Tagle, Oct. 30, 1817, *ibid.*, pp. 358-361. A copy of the enclosure containing the twelve enquiries is filed in NA, DS, Desp. Arg., I, pt. 1.

[25] For a complete draft of the treaty see NA, DS, Desp. Arg., I, pt. 1. It bears the date November 19, 1818, which obviously should be 1817. Although Worthington mentioned the treaty to Tagle as early as October 30, the Spanish draft was not ready until December 17. The agent apparently felt no necessity for "more definite powers" from his government. Although the treaty represented his own ideas, he said, he placed "the two countries on a footing of perfect reciprocity" (Worthington to Tagle, Dec. 17, 1817, NA, DS, Desp. Arg., I, pt. 1).

Director and his deputies, comprehensive revisions were made in the agent's original draft.[26] A copy of the treaty was sent off to Washington and Worthington moved over the Andes to Santiago.[27]

When news of Worthington's action reached him, President Monroe was profoundly irritated. To Adams he said: "Dismiss him instantly. Recall him! Dismiss him! Now to think what recommendations that man had! Dismiss him at once, and send the notice of his dismission by every possible channel. Send it to Halsey, though Halsey himself is recalled." [28] Worthington's proud boast to President Madison that his "intentions will never disappoint their expectations" was thus brusquely deflated.[29]

A Discredited Consul

The indiscretions of Devereux and Worthington were soon followed by those of Halsey. Although since January, 1816, the government at Washington had appointed no less than four special missions to Buenos Aires,[30] Halsey continued to serve as consul, a position to which he had been appointed in 1812. By various acts, including his interposition in the Devereux loan proposal, he had at first ingratiated himself with Pueyrredón; by misconduct, alleged or real, he had by January, 1818, become *persona non grata*. The Supreme Director accused him of spreading seditious and inflammatory literature brought from Baltimore, of meddling in the privateering system, and of conniving with the insurrectionary Artigas in the Banda Oriental.[31]

[26] At these conferences William G. Miller, who was still a resident of Buenos Aires, acted as secretary (see above, pp.18-19). His minutes of the proceedings indicate the tenor of the discussion and the disposition of each article ("Proceedings of the Agency of Mr Worthington's Project of 45 Articles on the Subject of Commerce & Seamen of the 18th Novr. 1817," NA, DS, Desp. Arg., I, pt. 1). See also Worthington to Adams, Jan. 1, 1818, *ibid.*

[27] Worthington to Adams, *ibid.*

[28] Charles Francis Adams (ed.), *Memoirs of John Quincy Adams*, IV, 70. Before the President's commission could be executed, however, Worthington had proceeded to Chile and submitted a similar treaty there. Despatches continued to arrive from him until March 7, 1819, when he composed a long document in Buenos Aires while en route to the United States (NA, DS, Desp. Arg., I, pt. 1). In his *Memoirs* for Nov. 3, 1818, Adams described Worthington as an agent "who has been swelling upon his agency until he has broken out into a self-accredited Plenipotentiary . . ." (IV, 158-159).

[29] Feb. 22, 1817, LC, MD, Madison Papers, LXIV. Upon his return to the United States in 1819, Worthington sought without success to secure approval of his mission from both Monroe and Adams (LC, MD, Toner Collection, Diaries of Worthington, Aug. 19, 1819).

[30] Devereux, Worthington, the South American Mission, and John B. Prevost. The South American Mission did not reach Buenos Aires until February 27, 1818, and Prevost, originally appointed on July 18, 1817, as special agent to Buenos Aires, Chile, and Peru, under changed orders did not arrive in the United Provinces until late in 1819 (see below, pp. 38, 66).

[31] Worthington to Adams, Jan. 10, 1818, Manning, *op. cit.*, I, 368-370. Pueyrredón was greatly irritated at this time by the propaganda activities in Baltimore of a

Halsey's extended consular career in Buenos Aires was finished. On January 7 Pueyrredón ordered him to leave the country within twenty-four hours. Although he subsequently revoked this order, the Director soon requested President Monroe to recall the consul.[32] Meanwhile, Adams had learned of Halsey's alleged participation in privateering enterprises and before receiving Pueyrredón's note had ordered the agent's dismissal.[33] Halsey protested his innocence of aiding privateers and accused David C. DeForest of exciting cabals against him,[34] but the administration stood firm. He, like Devereux and Worthington, felt the ignominy of official rebuff.

In little more than a year, three official agents of the United States to Buenos Aires had failed to accomplish the missions assigned them. All had neglected to appreciate fully the delicate nature of their position within territory claimed by a European power still at peace with their own country. Whether through overzealousness or bad judgment, they had committed acts which Spain could claim violated their status as neutral observers from a neutral nation. In this manner they had complicated administration efforts to maintain the cloak of neutrality while opening American ports to insurgent privateers. Moreover, by involving themselves too actively in affairs of a revolutionary government, they had reduced their own value as seekers of information. In any case, President Monroe had by that time despatched another, more capable mission to Buenos Aires.

---

group of factional opponents whom he had exiled. These included Manuel Moreno, Vicente Pazos, and Pedro José Agrelo. Several pertinent documents are published in *Documentos del Congreso de Tucumán*, pp. 31-32, 59, and the group's activities are described in Whitaker, *op. cit.*, pp. 182-183, and Charles C. Griffin, *The United States and the Disruption of the Spanish Empire, 1810-1822*, pp. 127-128.

[32] Tagle to Halsey, Jan. 7, 8, 1818; Halsey to Adams, Jan. 22, 1818, NA, DS, Con. Let., B. A., I, pt. 2. Pueyrredón's request to Monroe, Jan. 31, 1818, is printed in Manning, *op. cit.*, I, 374-375. Such incidents apparently failed to affect Pueyrredón's attitude toward the United States, for in the midst of the Halsey affair he appealed directly to President Monroe for formal acknowledgment of independence (Jan. 14, 1818, *ibid.*, I, 370-371; AGN, BA, S1-A2-A4-núm. 9).

[33] Adams, *Memoirs*, IV, 44-45; Adams to Halsey, Jan. 22, 1818, NA, DS, Inst. to Con., II, 92. The Department of State was in possession of privateering patents which Halsey had sent to the United States.

[34] Halsey to Adams, Feb. 25, Aug. 21, Sept. 23, 1818, NA, DS, Con. Let., B. A., I, pt. 2; Benjamin Keen, *David Curtis DeForest and the Revolution of Buenos Aires*, pp. 124-125. One American, Jeremy Robinson, defended Halsey's relations with Pueyrredón and DeForest; another, W. G. Miller, criticized his "impudence" in connection with privateering (LC, MD, Papers of Jeremy Robinson, Diaries, Feb. 19-20, 1818; Miller to Poinsett, April 17, 1817, HSP, Poinsett Papers, I, 194). Among the unprinted papers filed in NA, DS, Con. Let., B. A., I, pt. 2, there is an interesting document, dated September 9, 1818, and signed by several notaries, attesting Halsey's innocence of the charge of aiding privateers. On the other hand, evidence of Halsey's participation in the sale of considerable amounts of munitions to the United Provinces is found in Pueyrredón's report to the Congress on the general state of the treasury, July 18, 1817 (*Documentos del Congreso de Tucumán*, pp. 19-24).

I V

THE SOUTH AMERICAN MISSION:
INVESTIGATION AND NONRECOGNITION,
1817-1818

The elevation of James Monroe from the Department of State to the White House in March, 1817, presaged intensified efforts to resolve the problems created by the Spanish American revolts. Early in his administration Monroe's interest was sharpened by developments in Latin America and Europe as well as by heightening attention at home to the revolutionary cause. From the south the President learned not only of San Martín's successes in Chile and of the rekindling of the revolutionary spark in other colonies but also of the spread of factional strife in the United Provinces and Chile. From the east he received intelligence on the inability of the European Concert to unite on a policy of mediation or of intervention.[1] At home, while sympathy for the insurgents persisted, the growing boldness of their agents, propagandists, and privateers led to popular confusion rather than to resoluteness.[2]

The United Provinces were apparently not yet stable enough to justify recognition; the threat of European interposition on behalf of Spain was less imminent; public sentiment in the United States had not yet crystallized. Through these circumstances Monroe was furnished the most valuable resource of diplomacy, time—time to seek fuller information, time to ascertain the true intentions of the European powers, time to postpone the irrevocable decision to recognize independence. But it was not in Monroe's nature to waste time so opportunely granted, and he resolved to act.

[1] See Arthur P. Whitaker, *The United States and the Independence of Latin America, 1800-1830*, pp. 223-229.

[2] Charles C. Griffin capably develops this point (*The United States and the Disruption of the Spanish Empire, 1810-1822*, pp. 121-132).

The South American Mission

Manifold factors motivated the President's determination in late April to despatch a new mission to southern South America.[3] The simple quest for trustworthy information was a motive of great weight.[4] Faulty observation, inadequate reports, and indiscreet conduct had tarnished the careers of American agents in La Plata in 1816 and early 1817.[5] The State Department remained eager, therefore, to learn of the progress of the revolution, the probability of its success, and the capacity and willingness of the people to establish and maintain an independent government. With such evidence at hand, a basis for the future conduct of amicable relations might be established.

The state of popular feeling in the United States produced a second motive. Reports of new revolutionary successes in South America in 1816 reawakened an interest in the independence movement. Though there was no organized pressure for immediate recognition, increased space given to Latin American affairs in newspapers along the Atlantic seaboard and mounting attention in the debates of Congress indicated that popular sentiment had been stirred.[6]

A third reason was the administration's desire to impress the United Provinces with its inherent friendship for their cause. The possibility of multilateral action from Europe was a threat to all republican states in the Western Hemisphere. The American policies of neutrality and nonintervention must be perpetuated, but there was nothing to prevent a display of benevolent diplomacy, or, as Monroe himself later expressed it, the mission might produce "all the advantages of a recognition, without any of its evils."[7] A mission of one or more able and distinguished

[3] My description of the mission leans heavily upon Watt Stewart's "The South American Commission, 1817-1818," *The Hispanic American Historical Review*, IX (Feb., 1929), 31-59.

[4] For expressions of this motive, see Monroe to Poinsett, April 25, 1817, and Rush to Caesar A. Rodney and John Graham, special commissioners, July 18, 1817, William R. Manning (ed.), *Diplomatic Correspondence of the United States Concerning Independence of the Latin-American Countries*, I, 39-40, 42-45; Adams to Albert Gallatin, May 19, 1818, W. C. Ford (ed.), *Writings of John Quincy Adams*, VI, 314-315; Charles Francis Adams (ed.), *Memoirs of John Quincy Adams*, IV, 11; S. M. Hamilton (ed.), *Writings of James Monroe*, VI, 31-32.

[5] See above, pp. 31-35.

[6] In this connection I have surveyed such newspapers as the *Boston Patriot and Morning Advertiser*, *Daily National Intelligencer* (Washington), *Massachusetts Centinel*, *Mercury* (Boston), *Niles' Register*, and *Richmond Enquirer*. See also Griffin, *op. cit.*, pp. 130-132. In his report of Nov. 10, 1818, Commissioner John Graham expressed conviction that the struggle of the United Provinces was "of deep interest to the People and Government of the United States" (NA, DS, S. A. Mission).

[7] "Sketch of Instructions for Agent for South America—Notes for Department of State," March 24, 1819, Monroe, *Writings*, VI, 95.

Americans might help to erase the unsavory effects of inept diplomatic representation.

Other possible motives are discoverable. Perhaps the administration sought to gain time until it worked out a satisfactory recognition policy.[8] Perhaps it felt that the mission would aid the revival of American commerce in the South Atlantic.[9] The war with Great Britain had ceased, but Anglo-American rivalry persisted.

Probably the decisive reason—that is, the reason for its despatch in November, 1817, after a delay of four months—was the desire to apprise the leaders of the United Provinces of the plan to occupy Amelia Island, rendezvous of privateers off the Florida coast.[10] But of all these suggested motives none seems so fundamental as that of the search for information —information which the Monroe administration might use in resolving its Latin American policy.

Commissioners and Their Instructions

It was President Monroe's original intention to send a single agent. Naturally he turned to Joel R. Poinsett, who two years before had returned from a four-year tour of duty in Buenos Aires and Chile. When in April, 1817, Monroe offered the post to him, however, Poinsett had already accepted office in the government of South Carolina.[11]

The refusal of Poinsett to serve as lone commissioner impelled the President to turn to the alternative of a plural commission.[12] Although he made this decision almost at once, seven months passed before final arrangements were completed and the envoys despatched. Two appointments, those of Caesar A. Rodney and John Graham, were promptly made, but the selection of a third member was more difficult. Monroe at first considered the nomination of John B. Prevost, whom he sent instead as special agent to Buenos Aires, Chile, and Peru.[13] Not until November,

---

[8] This suggestion is advanced in Julius Goebel, *The Recognition Policy of the United States*, p. 120, and supported by Stewart as perhaps the most important motive (*op. cit.*, pp. 36-37). Whitaker doubts the accuracy of this interpretation (*op. cit.*, p. 241, note 29).

[9] Upon arrival of the agents, the *Gaceta de Buenos Ayres*, March 7, 1818, listed as one of their objects the intent "to assure a desirable respect for its commerce in every port and of every flag." Instructions to the commissioners did not emphasize this point.

[10] Adams, *Memoirs*, IV, 15. See below, p. 40.

[11] Monroe to Poinsett, April 25, 1817, Manning, *op. cit.*, I, 39-40; Poinsett to Monroe, May 7, 1817, LC, MD, Papers of Monroe, Writings to, XVI, 2017.

[12] Photostatic negative of draft letter, May 19, 1817, LC, MD, Monroe Papers (portfolio of late accessions to the collection, not bound in the original set).

[13] Transportation arrangements on the U.S.S. *Ontario* for Rodney, Graham, Prevost, and Henry M. Brackenridge, secretary, were completed at this time ("B.W.C.," for Secretary of Navy, to Captain James Biddle, July 21, 1817, two orders, NA, DN, Letters to Officers, Ships of War, XIII, 51-52).

when Theodorick Bland accepted appointment, was the personnel of the body complete.[14]

The commissioners were men of wide public experience, most eminent of whom was Caesar A. Rodney, of Delaware. After a term in the House of Representatives, he had been chosen in 1804 to conduct the impeachment trial of Judge Samuel Chase. In January, 1807, President Jefferson appointed him to the post of Attorney General, where he served until his resignation four years later. Rodney was to become the first minister accredited to Buenos Aires, although he died there shortly after his return in 1823.[15] He may be regarded as the leader of the mission.

Because of his knowledge of Spanish, John Graham, of Virginia, was a fortunate choice. Moreover, through long public service, he had become "well acquainted with the routine & etiquet of diplomacy." [16] He had been secretary of legation and Chargé d'Affaires at Madrid (1801-1803), Secretary of the Territory of Orleans, Chief Clerk of the Department of State (1807-1817), and Secretary of State ad interim in the early days of Monroe's administration. President Monroe considered him a man "of very liberal acquirements, an extensive knowledge of our affairs, a sound discriminating mind, and perfect integrity." [17]

Theodorick Bland, least experienced of the three, had been a county judge in Baltimore. Upon learning of the probability of his appointment, Henry M. Brackenridge, secretary of the commission, praised Bland's agreeable manners, his sound judgment and excellent discrimination, his indefatigable inquisitiveness, and the extent of his general information. Subsequent events were to erase, or at least dim, the Secretary's high opinion.[18]

[14] For additional information on the appointments, see Rush to Monroe, June 25, July 20, 1817, LC, MD, Papers of Monroe, Writings to, XVI, 2039, 2051; Rush to Rodney and Graham, July 18, 1817, and Adams to Prevost, Sept. 29, 1817, Manning, *op. cit.*, I, 42-43, 45.

[15] William T. Read, *Biographical Sketch of Caesar Augustus Rodney*, pp. 2-20 *passim;* Henry Adams, *History of the United States of America*, II, 76, 100, 119, 219; III, 444; VI, 429.

[16] LC, MD, Papers of Jeremy Robinson, Diaries, March 7, 1818.

[17] Monroe to Daniel Brent, Chief Clerk, Dept. of State, March 20, 1817, Monroe, *Writings*, VI, 17-18; *Dictionary of American Biography*, VII, 477-478.

[18] Brackenridge to Rush, July 28, 1817, NA, DS, S. A. Mission. During the course of the mission, Bland and Brackenridge developed a feud, which was perpetuated until several years later when the two were rivals for appointment to a federal judgeship in Baltimore. In a conference with Adams in 1820, Brackenridge recited the details of the misunderstanding, which, he said, was the result of Bland's improper conduct as a commissioner. He accused Bland and his son-in-law, J. S. Skinner, of involvement in privateering enterprises and of making loans to the Carrera faction in Chile in return for exclusive commercial privileges for ten years (see above, p. 24). He declared that Bland, Skinner, and their group had used the columns of the *Richmond Enquirer* to agitate for the recognition of Buenos Aires. He charged that a cabal had been responsible for Bland's appointment as a commissioner (Adams, *Memoirs*, IV, 159; V, 56-57). In the Archivo General de la Nación, Buenos Aires, there are several letters related to the Skinner-Carrera trans-

Brackenridge, also of Baltimore, was a former Attorney General for the Territory of Orleans and onetime federal judge. A vigorous advocate of recognition of the South American states, he wrote profusely about those countries, as well as upon other political subjects.[19]

According to the initial instructions, issued at the time of the appointment of Rodney and Graham on July 18, the commissioners were to stop at Rio de Janeiro and Montevideo en route to Buenos Aires. On the return journey they were to touch at São Salvador, Pernambuco, and certain ports of the Spanish Main. In each province they were to observe the strength and leaders of the various factions and their attitude toward the United States, as well as the population, resources, ports and harbors, and commercial problems. Furthermore, the commissioners were to inquire into the form of established government, its probable durability, and "the real prospect . . . of the final and permanent issue." [20]

Although these instructions were detailed to Rodney and Graham in July, a series of circumstances delayed departure of the commission: the President was travelling in the northern states; Acting Secretary of State Rush could not secure the third commissioner; Rodney's son was ill; Monroe's enthusiasm for the mission cooled a bit; John Quincy Adams, finally returned from London to assume the secretaryship, exerted a restraining hand. Not until the important Cabinet meeting of October 30 did the administration make its final decision. Once the Cabinet had agreed to send the Navy to occupy Amelia Island, Monroe and Adams concluded to let the commission depart.[21]

Thereupon, Spain was duly notified, conferences were held between the President and the appointees, final instructions were issued, and the

---

action: Bland, as Skinner's attorney, to Pueyrredón, April 4, 1818, requesting repayment of the $4,000 loan, because, in detaining Carrera's ship in Buenos Aires, the United Provinces had prevented him from repaying; Skinner to the Supreme Director, June 5, 1818, asking reimbursement; Rodney, Graham, and Bland to Pueyrredón, [no date], appealing for release of Carrera (AGN, BA, S1-A2-A4-núm. 8).

[19] After his return from Buenos Aires, Brackenridge was successively judge of the Western District of Florida (1821-1831), congressman from Pittsburgh (1840), and commissioner for the arrangement of the Mexican treaty (*Dictionary of American Biography*, II, 543-544; Carlos A. Aldoa, "American Politics: Argentina and the United States," *Inter-America*, VII, 126-127. This article is a reprint of the author's introduction to a Spanish translation of Brackenridge's work, *Voyage to South America*).

[20] For the complete instructions, see Manning, *op. cit.*, I, 42-45. Some problems connected with preparation of the instructions are discussed in Rush to Monroe, June 25, 28, 1817, LC, MD, Papers of Monroe, Writings to, XVI, 2039, 2042.

[21] On the questions discussed and decisions taken at this meeting, see Monroe, *Writings*, VI, 31-32, and Adams, *Memoirs*, IV, 15. Good analyses of the questions propounded by the President are to be found in Griffin, *op. cit.*, pp. 140-141, and Samuel Flagg Bemis, *Early Diplomatic Missions from Buenos Aires to the United States, 1811-1824*, pp. 52-54.

official commission was prepared.[22] Adams' instructions of November 21 confirmed those of July 18 but added significant new orders. The commissioners were to remonstrate against use of indiscriminate privateering patents and were to explain American action against the freebooters of Amelia Island and Galveston.[23]

Inspection of the United Provinces

The members of the commission, its secretary, and William T. Read, private secretary to Rodney, sailed from Norfolk in the frigate *Congress* about the middle of December.[24] The vessel put in first at Rio de Janeiro, where, in accordance with their instructions, the agents conferred with American Minister Thomas Sumter. Their arrival sharply alarmed both the Portuguese Court and members of the diplomatic corps, as rumors quickly spread that the United States would recognize the independence of the United Provinces. News of the panic aroused in the Spanish Minister at Rio deeply impressed Adams, who concluded that the European Alliance had contemplated settlement of Spanish American affairs without consulting the United States. Now, he wrote to Rush in London, those nations had been shown "that we have some concern with that question, and that they ought . . . not to interfere at all; and most especially not to restore any part of the dominions of Spain." [25] Observing the alarm stirred by a mere mission of investigation, Monroe wondered what sensation a bolder step might create.[26]

Mindful of this cool Portuguese reception, the commissioners moved on to Montevideo and Buenos Aires, where, as anticipated, they received a less restrained welcome. Their arrival quickly reanimated the revolutionary spirit among the porteños, who now saw more tangibly foreshadowed the early establishment of closer relations with the United States.[27]

Following conferences with Thomas Lloyd Halsey, American Consul, and Gregorio Tagle, Secretary of State of the United Provinces, the commissioners secured an interview with the Supreme Director.[28] They

[22] Adams to George W. Erving, Minister to Spain, Nov. 11, 1817, Manning, *op. cit.*, I, 46; Adams, *Memoirs*, IV, 21. For a copy of the commission, see *Annals of Cong.*, 15 Cong., 1 sess., II, 1465.

[23] Adams to Rodney, Graham, and Bland, Nov. 21, 1817, Manning, *op. cit.*, I, 47-49.

[24] *Niles' Register*, XIII (Nov. 29, 1817), 223; Brackenridge, *Voyage to South America*, I, 101.

[25] Adams to Rush, May 29, and to Gallatin, May 19, 1818, Adams, *Writings*, VI, 314-315, 341-342.

[26] Monroe to Madison, April 28, 1818, Monroe, *Writings*, VI, 50-51.

[27] See quotations from the press of Buenos Aires in *Niles' Register*, XIV (July 3, 1818), 326, and Brackenridge, *Voyage to South America*, I, 306-307.

[28] Rodney, Graham, Bland, and Brackenridge to Adams, March 4, 1818, NA, DS, S. A. Mission.

were unanimous in describing the politeness and warmth of Pueyrredón's greeting. He expressed, they said, high regard for the United States, great gratification for the mission, and willingness to satisfy the purpose of their visit.[29] Unlike William Bowles, British naval officer on duty in La Plata, who observed that the Supreme Director wasted "no great cordiality," the commissioners did not question Pueyrredón's sincerity.[30] Perhaps a modicum of wishful thinking clouded the observations of both the Americans and the Englishman.

To assist their collection of data on the United Provinces, the agents obtained the Supreme Director's approval for a series of conferences with his secretary of state. These were held during the next seven weeks, while the men made independent observations. The original instructions had stated that, if it were deemed expedient, one of the envoys might proceed to Chile to inspect the revolutionary government. By April 14, the commissioners decided that Judge Bland should make the trip over the Andes to Santiago and return to Washington later than the others.[31]

Rodney, Graham, and Brackenridge remained in Buenos Aires until April 24 for the final papers Tagle had prepared. They reached Norfolk late in July.[32] Commenting upon their return, Adams wrote to Rush that "their unanimous opinion is that the resubjugation of the Provinces of La Plata, to Spain is impossible. Of their internal condition the aspect is more equivocal."[33]

Reports and Disagreement

For nearly a year after it left, except for an occasional notice in such journals as *Niles' Register* and the *Daily National Intelligencer*, the people of the United States received little information on the progress of the mission.[34] That many people were eager for results of the investiga-

[29] Reports of Bland, No. 2, 1818, and of Rodney, Nov. 5, 1818, born to Adams, Manning, *op. cit.*, I, 384, 514; Brackenridge, *Voyage to South America*, I, 310-311.

[30] Cited in J. Fred Rippy, *Rivalry of the United States and Great Britain over Latin America (1808-1830)*, p. 14. In a letter to Bernardino Rivadavia, Argentine agent in Europe, dated July 31, 1818, Pueyrredón expressed satisfaction with the commission and its activities (*Comisión de Bernardino Rivadavia ante España y otras potencias de Europa, 1814-1820*, I, 194).

[31] Bland had requested this assignment before leaving Baltimore (Bland to Monroe, Nov. 15, 1817, HSP, Gratz Collection, Case 3, Box 25). At the time of his departure for Santiago, Bland wrote to Monroe that the greatest obstacle to the recognition of the United Provinces was the unsettled state of political relations with Chile, Peru, and the Banda Oriental (April 14, 1818, LC, MD, Papers of Monroe, Writings to, XVII, 2140).

[32] Rodney, Graham, and Brackenridge to Adams, May 28, 1818, NA, DS, S. A. Mission; *Niles' Register*, XIV (July 18, 1818), 357. Bland reached Philadelphia from Chile on October 30 (*ibid.*, XV [Nov. 7, 1818], 175).

[33] July 30, 1818, Manning, *op. cit.*, I, 74.

[34] Examples of such items are to be found in *Niles' Register*, XIV (June 13, 20, 1818), 261-263, 288-289; XV (Nov. 18, 21, 1818), 188-190, 202-205.

tion is apparent from the publicity given the reports when, in November and December, 1818, they were finally submitted to the Congress.

Much to President Monroe's consternation, instead of the two reports he had envisioned, four were prepared. Bland's visit to Chile, of course, required preparation of a special document. Rodney and Graham had planned to draft a single report but were unable to agree.[35] Three commissioners presented three divergent estimates, and Poinsett, whom Monroe invited to submit a statement, added a fourth.

Considered in entirety, the reports contained an elaborate picture of conditions in Spanish America and the Viceroyalty of the Río de la Plata during the colonial epoch, as well as detailed accounts of the extent, population, government, resources, and commercial features of the United Provinces and a narrative of the causes, progress, and hopes of the revolution.[36]

Rodney's document consisted of a series of tables, sketches, notes, and outlines, preceded by a brief descriptive statement. Both Monroe and Adams had come to suspect that the former Attorney General's prejudice in favor of the United Provinces would color his observations. His refusal to grant the White House opportunity for preliminary inspection of his report induced presidential fears that the commissioner had come under the influence of Brackenridge, "a mere enthusiast," and of Henry Clay, whose intransigence in Congress was already embarrassing. Moreover, Monroe was alarmed lest Rodney's evaluation give offense to the European Alliance. Though not all of the President's suspicions were well-grounded, the report was clearly "an apologetic eulogium upon the present Government of Buenos Ayres." [37] In an effort to gain a favorable decision for recognition, Rodney sketched the development of the United Provinces in the brightest tones.[38]

Graham's official statement, prepared largely from memory at the last

[35] Adams, *Memoirs*, IV, 155-156.

[36] The original reports of Rodney and Graham, with all their appendices, are filed in NA, DS, S. A. Mission; Poinsett's is in NA, DS, Specl. Agts. Ser., III (1813), J. R. Poinsett; Bland's original was not located in the Archives of the Department of State. The reports, or excerpts from them, were published in many forms, official and unofficial. They are most easily accessible, with small deletions, in *American State Papers, Foreign Relations*, IV, 217-348; and, without appendices, in Manning, *op. cit.*, 382-439, 444-515. Substantial portions appeared in *Niles' Register*, XV (Nov. 28, 1818), 228-240, and in various newspapers. In Great Britain, all the reports were printed in *British Foreign and State Papers*, VI (1818-1819), 558-918, and those of Rodney and Graham were published privately under the title, *The Reports on the Present State of the United Provinces of South America* (London, 1819).

[37] Adams, *Memoirs*, IV, 155-156, 158-159, 388. Clay, however, described Rodney's report as an "independent and impartial exhibition of things as they appeared to you" (to Rodney, Dec. 22, 1818, LC, MD, Rodney Papers).

[38] Adams noted in his *Memoirs* (IV, 119) that Rodney and Brackenridge, through the *Delaware Watchman*, filled the newspapers with articles designed to influence public opinion in favor of recognition.

moment, was brief, devoted chiefly to an analysis of political dissensions within the bounds of the old Viceroyalty. Far more apprehensive than Rodney regarding the guarantees of political liberty, he felt that the revolutionary leaders had done much less than they might have for the protection of popular freedom. In a supplementary report he devoted considerably more space than the other commissioners to the interviews with the Argentine Secretary of State. When Tagle had asked if the United States would not cross "the strict line of neutrality" or at least assist them with loans, Graham had replied only that his government feared the international consequences of such acts.[39]

If appendices are omitted, Bland's report, even excluding the long section on Chile, was the most voluminous. It was by far the most literary and the most scientifically critical. With more fluency than his colleagues he described the conferences with Pueyrredón and Tagle and other engaging features of the trip. He was convinced that the bonds of unity in the United Provinces were only temporary and that not until civil dissensions ceased could the gains of the revolution be consolidated. His whole document betrayed a presentiment for the United Provinces.

Poinsett, because of the years that had intervened since his return from Buenos Aires, was not conversant with current conditions. Moreover, his report was uneven and poorly organized. Still, his extended residence in southern South America, together with his strong memory and skill as an observer, made his judgments of great value to the administration.[40]

Although Brackenridge served only as secretary, he wrote more extensively on conditions in South America than the commissioners themselves. Because much of his work was published for commercial consumption, he reached a wider audience than his colleagues.[41] He embodied his vast material in two volumes with the title *Voyage to South America*.[42] His publication was a forthright appeal for aid to the people of South America, whom he believed "capable of defending themselves, of governing themselves, and of being free."[43] The appearance of

[39] Graham's supplementary report, dated Nov. 10, 1818, is filed in NA, DS, S. A. Mission; it appears not to have been printed. In connection with these interviews, it should be remembered that Graham spoke fluent Spanish.

[40] J. Fred Rippy, *Joel R. Poinsett, Versatile American*, pp. 66-68.

[41] In 1817 he had published a lengthy pamphlet advocating recognition. It was reprinted in 1819 as an appendix to his *Voyage to South America* under the title "A Letter on South American Affairs, by an American, to James Monroe, President of the United States" (II, 313-359). In 1818 it had been printed in Great Britain with the title "North American Pamphlet on South American Affairs" (*The Pamphleteer*, XIII, 36-83). It was also translated into French (Diego Barros Arana, *Historia jeneral de Chile*, XI, 543, note).

[42] Baltimore, 1819. It appeared in London the following year and in Leipzig in 1821.

[43] *Voyage to South America*, I, xiv.

Brackenridge's tract promptly called forth a retaliatory volume, which severely indicted his observations and recommendations.[44]

Effects Upon Recognition

Evaluation of the commission's findings leads to questions regarding its effects. Did the conclusions of the commissioners alter the recognition policy of the United States? How were the international relations of the United States and of the United Provinces affected? Did the mission accomplish its purpose?

In Buenos Aires the arrival of an official mission from the strongest nation in the Western Hemisphere had awakened new zeal. Regardless of its specific purposes, the visit of the distinguished agents was the most unvarnished recognition the United Provinces had received in eight years of independence. To the people, display of hospitality may have been only manifestation of a Latin desire to impress favorably the representatives of the United States; but to the leaders, sympathetic attention must have appeared a prelude to more intimate relations.[45] Certainly the men of government were aware that American acknowledgment of independence would likely lead to recognition by European powers, a much riper plum to pluck.[46]

In Washington the views of the commissioners on stability of government, diverse as they were, clearly did not point the way to the desirability of early recognition. Rodney, of course, strongly approved any step which would lead to that end. Graham, more noncommittal than the others, opposed recognition, at least until greater political stability was attained and the probability of war with Spain reduced. Bland was unequivocally set against acknowledgment of independence until civil dissensions ceased. Poinsett, warm in his sympathy for the South American cause, was, like Bland, strenuously opposed to immediate recognition.[47]

[44] *Strictures on a Voyage to South America* (Baltimore, 1820). It was in the form of letters written by the anonymous author to his "friend." In vitriolic language it described the *Voyage to South America* as "destitute of order, void of perspicuity, wanting in veracity, discolored with gall" (p. iii). Printed as an appendix was a letter written ostensibly by Manuel Moreno, exile from Pueyrredón's government, which accused Brackenridge of unscientific observation. According to the latter's testimony to Adams, the volume was the joint production of Bland, Skinner, Moreno, and Baptis Irvine, journalist and onetime American agent to Venezuela, who claimed to be the sole author (Adams, *Memoirs*, V, 57).

[45] Monroe himself had once written that the United States would do everything but recognize independence (to Rodney, Nov. 20, 1817, LC, MD, Rodney Papers).

[46] As a matter of fact, recognition by the United States did precede that by all European countries except Portugal (see below, p. 73).

[47] Poinsett's reasons are arresting: (1) The European Alliance would become alarmed; (2) the moral effect to be produced upon the colonies had been exaggerated; (3) the government of Buenos Aires had treated the United States as

The effects of the mission's findings upon the process of recognition, therefore, were purely negative. The inability of the commissioners to unite upon conclusions and their consequent submission of widely varying reports convinced the administration that government in the Río de la Plata was not yet stable. Despite the optimism of Rodney, the reports as a whole indicated that nonrecognition would perhaps be a greater spur than recognition to the advancement of the United Provinces. Monroe and Adams had apparently come to agree that recognition must be delayed. When the President addressed Congress on November 16, 1818, he made no recommendations regarding the reports. Failing to vote recognition until 1822, the Congress obviously followed the President's lead.[48]

International Reactions

The sending of a special mission to the Río de la Plata naturally brought distinct responses from other nations. Officials of the Portuguese and Spanish governments had early revealed their apprehensions.[49] The Chileans, whose status and prospects were inspected by Judge Bland, were encouraged by the attention they received.[50] In Great Britain, through publication in newspapers and official journals and under separate cover, wide circulation of the reports of Rodney, Graham, and Brackenridge whetted British interest in Anglo-American rivalry in South America.[51] In France and Germany, publication of translations manifested more than passing interest in developments in southern South America.[52]

The South American mission was disillusioning both to the government that despatched and to the government that received it. President Monroe, from all the information his commissioners had obtained, concluded only that his previous course had been satisfactory and that it

---

a secondary power; (4) the commerce and manufactures of Great Britain had become essential to the people; (5) the government of the United Provinces lacked responsibility and good faith; and (6) the present party in power was dominated by corrupt men (Poinsett to Adams, Nov. 4, 1818, Manning, *op. cit.*, I, 440-442).

[48] The House of Representatives had discussed recognition at great length from March 24 to 30 when Clay introduced as an amendment to an appropriation bill a resolution providing for the sending of a minister to Buenos Aires. The debate originated from House discussion of the clause to provide expenses for the commissioners (*Annals of Cong.*, 15 Cong., 1 sess., II, 1464-1655). For Adams' comments on this debate, see his letter to Gallatin, May 19, 1818, Adams, *Writings*, VI, 314-315.

[49] See above, p. 41.

[50] Barros Arana, *op. cit.*, XI, 542-547.

[51] For writings which appeared in England, see above, notes 36, 41, and 42.

[52] See above, notes 41 and 42.

was proper to adhere to it. Supreme Director Pueyrredón, while pleased with the reports of Rodney and Graham, was greatly disappointed at the failure of the United States to grant immediate recognition.[53] On the other hand, the commission had greatly augmented the knowledge and interest of each people in the status and progress of the other. As a diplomatic episode, it fits precisely into the larger picture of the developing Latin American policy of the United States. It illustrates perfectly the manner in which Monroe's government undertook to maintain neutrality and postpone recognition while investigating conditions and carefully evaluating developments.

[53] When the Supreme Director made this statement to Worthington, he had not seen a copy of Bland's report (Worthington's last despatch from Buenos Aires, to Adams, March 7, 1819, Manning, *op. cit.*, I, 527). Prominent Argentine historians ignore, or at least do not mention, Bland's report (Vicente F. López, *Historia de la República Argentina,* VII, 367; Bartolomé Mitre, *Historia de Belgrano,* III, 72).

V

QUEST FOR DIPLOMATIC RECOGNITION: PERPETUATION OF AMERICAN NEUTRALITY, 1817-1819

Relations between the United States and the United Provinces in 1817 and 1818 did not follow a one-way course. While the United States, through its appointed agents, was scrutinizing conditions in La Plata, the United Provinces with equal persistence were soliciting help in Washington. When one approach failed to accomplish its full purpose, Argentine resourcefulness conceived new techniques—continuing issuance of privateering patents, despatch of agents to purchase arms, executive appeal for recognition, and appointment of an American citizen as consul general. This series of direct approaches kept the cause of independence before the American people, augmented the party opposition of Henry Clay in Congress, focused upon Washington the attention of European chancelleries, and aggravated the task of the administration. But, in the end, Argentine attempts to undermine North American neutrality, like the administration's efforts to investigate the United Provinces, led only to continued nonrecognition.

Pueyrredón Sends an Agent

The government of Alvarez Thomas had commissioned three special agents to the United States—Thomas Taylor, José Miguel Carrera, and Martín Thompson.[1] Taylor and Carrera had dispensed their privateering commissions as best they could and returned to Buenos Aires at the end of 1816. Recall of the unfortunate Martín Thompson in January, 1817, by Alvarez Thomas' successor was only the prelude to a much more ambitious step from Buenos Aires. Pueyrredón's note to President Madison at this time indicated his willingness to appoint "a formal agent . . .

[1] See above, pp. 24-25.

48

upon the first intimation." [2] The intimation came, however, not from Madison but from General San Martín, who had returned to Buenos Aires after his victory over the Spanish at Chacabuco. The Liberator was already planning invasion of Peru by sea and for that venture he needed ships.

In these circumstances, the Supreme Director, as chief of the United Provinces, and the General, acting in behalf of Supreme Director Bernardo O'Higgins, of Chile, collaborated in preparing a new, more pretentious mission to Washington.[3] Jointly and separately, they commissioned Manuel Hermenejildo de Aguirre and Gregorio Gómez to proceed to the United States to "promote whatever conduces to the progress" of the United Provinces and to secure assistance in arming "a squadron destined to the Pacific Ocean." [4] On his part, San Martín furnished Aguirre with 100,000 pesos and the promise of an equal sum in three months for the purchase of two 34-gun frigates and such other warships as could be secured.[5] Pueyrredón, presumably under terms of the Devereux-Halsey loan proposal, provided Aguirre with borrowing power of 2,000,000 pesos.[6] Foreseeing the possibility that the frigates might not be available, the Supreme Director instructed the agents in that case to secure six corvettes of twenty-five to thirty guns each. He specified that the ships must be equipped with good storage facilities, extra sails, and a supply of ship signals and ceremonial bunting. He directed lesser purchases of munitions, extra armament, and side arms. Both agents were promised excellent salaries, attractive bonuses, and travelling expenses. All these arrangements were completed by the end of April.[7]

Supplied with contract and instructions for themselves and with

[2] Jan. 1, 1817, William R. Manning (ed.), *Diplomatic Correspondence of the United States Concerning Independence of the Latin-American Countries*, I, 347.

[3] The most extensive account of this mission, incorporating many of the pertinent documents, is Alberto Palomeque, *Oríjenes de la diplomacia arjentina, misión Aguirre á Norte América*. On Palomeque's use of the sources, however, see Samuel Flagg Bemis, *Early Diplomatic Missions from Buenos Aires to the United States, 1811-1824*, p. 42, note 1. Although I have made independent study of the archival collections in Buenos Aires, I have depended heavily upon Bemis' interpretation (pp. 41-66). Other helpful accounts are Watt Stewart, "Activities of Early Argentine Agents in the United States," *The Southwestern Social Science Quarterly*, XVIII (March, 1938), 3-8; Arthur P. Whitaker, *The United States and the Independence of Latin America, 1800-1830*, pp. 232-235; Carlos Ibarguren, *En la penumbra de la historia argentina*, pp. 61-86.

[4] Commission to Aguirre granted by Pueyrredón, March 28, 1817, and San Martín to Monroe, April 1, 1817, Manning, *op. cit.*, 351-353.

[5] Contract between San Martín and Aguirre, April 17, 1817, Palomeque, *op. cit.*, pp. 123-128.

[6] Aguirre to Supreme Director, Aug. 30, 1817, AGN, BA, S1-A2-A4-núm. 9; Charles Francis Adams (ed.), *Memoirs of John Quincy Adams*, IV, 123-124.

[7] Drafts of instructions to Aguirre and Gómez, April 30, 1817, AGN, BA, S1-A2-A4-núm. 9. The side arms were sabers and pistols to be presented to San Martín, O'Higgins, and other valorous officers.

credentials and letters of introduction to officials in Washington, the agents reached Baltimore in late July, 1817. Aguirre promptly travelled on to the capital, where Acting Secretary of State Richard Rush received him. The envoy presented letters for President Monroe from Pueyrredón, San Martín, and O'Higgins, but retained for later use his credentials from both governments. Pueyrredón's letter introduced him as "Commissary General for War" and "agent" of the government of the United Provinces.[8]

With the President absent from the capital and his own position a temporary one, Rush could do no more than receive Aguirre informally, sympathetically, and helpfully. He reminded his visitor that the government of the United States still adhered to a policy of strict neutrality and that its laws forbade the sale of navy ships—or of any warships—to the citizen of a foreign nation. But Rush also suggested that "as a merchant," which Aguirre professed to be, he might purchase both ships and armament and send them away separately.[9] Fortified by this friendly advice, the two "merchants" moved on to New York to do business.

The business proceeded rapidly: for Chile, the prospects were good; for the United Provinces, poor. By August 17, Aguirre reported to his government that he had contracted for two frigates at a cost of about 100,000 pesos each. These could probably be delivered in Valparaiso by March or April, he wrote, if Chile's second 100,000 pesos were made available as promised. In addition to concluding the contract for the warships, they were able to induce at least three captains to run ships to Chile with cargoes of munitions for San Martín's army. But when it came to floating even a part of the Devereux loan, Aguirre soon found that he could make no headway. Merchants would do business only with cash in hand or with the guarantee of reliable citizens of the United States or England. The government seemed to fear the risk of war with the European nations and to prefer business with great powers to that with new states.[10] The envoy came to feel humiliation at the low reputation of his country in the United States and learned that the 2,000,000 peso loan was a "joke." [11]

---

[8] See Pueyrredón to Monroe, April 28, 1817, Pueyrredón's commission to Aguirre, March 28, 1817, and San Martín to Monroe, April 1, 1817, Manning, *op. cit.*, I, 351-353.

[9] Statement of Richard Rush, Nov. 22, 1817, NA, DS, Notes from Arg. Leg., I, pt. 1; Aguirre to Adams, Nov. 14, 1817, and to Supreme Director, [no date], MREC, BA, Correspondencia del Comisionada Aguirre de Washington. (My references to the Aguirre documents in the Archivo del Ministerio de Relaciones Exteriores y Culto are based on transcripts in possession of the Facultad de Filosofía y Letras, Instituto de Investigaciones Históricas, Buenos Aires, which I used with the kind permission of Dr. Emilio Ravignani).

[10] Aguirre to Supreme Director, Aug. 17, Sept. 12, 1817, and Gómez to Supreme Director, Nov. 13, 1817, AGN, BA, S1-A2-A4-núm. 9.

[11] "*Cosa de broma.*" See Aguirre to Supreme Director, Aug. 30, 1817, *ibid.*

Meanwhile, President Monroe had returned to Washington from his northern swing, and Adams had arrived from London to take over the secretaryship of state. The two men soon grappled with many questions arising from the Spanish American revolutions. Might the executive recognize states conceived in revolution? Should the United Provinces be recognized? Should the piratical establishments on Amelia Island be broken up? Should the South American commission be despatched? These and related questions the President determined to submit to his full Cabinet in the now historic meeting of October 30. The Cabinet's decisions on these questions were of profound importance to Aguirre and his government. Amelia Island would be occupied. The South American commissioners would be sent. But Buenos Aires would not be recognized.[12]

On the day of these decisions, Aguirre was close to the scene of action. He had returned to Washington from New York earlier in October and on the 29th held his first conference with Secretary Adams. At that time he presented his credentials from Pueyrredón and O'Higgins, together with a personal letter to President Monroe explaining briefly the grievances which had led to the declaration of independence of July 9, 1816.[13] For the next three months Aguirre remained in the capital, where he could press the diplomatic ends of his mission; Gómez was busy in New York overseeing the completion of the frigates, seeking to commission privateers, and beseeching his superiors for the second 100,000 pesos.

When Aguirre felt that his D-day had arrived, he adapted his tactics to the progress of debates in the Congress, where Clay and his group were harassing the administration.[14] From the middle of December to the end of January, he besieged the Department of State with one salvo after another. As the attacker followed each conference with a letter of confirmation, the redoubtable Adams countered effectively. When Aguirre formally demanded recognition of independence, Adams questioned his authority. When the agent indicted the inequities of the Neutrality Act of 1817, the Secretary coolly stood behind the law and suggested that a treaty was the proper way to arrange such matters. When the Argentine offered to negotiate a treaty, the American asked about the activities of Artigas and the effective jurisdiction of Pueyrredón's government. When the envoy threatened to bar United Provinces ports to American vessels, the Secretary reminded him that an independent state does not close its harbors to one particular nation without

[12] See above, p. 40, note 21.
[13] Pueyrredón to Monroe, April 28, 1817, and Aguirre to Monroe, Oct. 29, 1817, Manning, *op. cit.,* I, 353, 357-358; Adams, *Memoirs,* IV, 14. See also Bemis, *op. cit.,* p. 51.
[14] *Ibid.,* p. 55.

cause. When Aguirre asked for the return of his commissions, Adams obliged.[15] The Secretary had repulsed a well-mounted attack with a cold, sound, and legalistic counteroffensive, and his adversary retreated to New York to nurse his wounds and regroup his forces.

Clay Crusades for Recognition

Meanwhile, the administration's defenses were being probed from other quarters. By the Cabinet decisions of October 30 and subsequent execution of those decisions Monroe and Adams had avowed their intention to perpetuate the policy of investigation, neutrality, and nonrecognition. [16] But this avowal was not enough to silence the sympathizers of the revolutionary movement. The zeal for Latin American independence which he had manifested several times during Madison's presidency Henry Clay now turned against President Monroe and Secretary Adams.

The Kentuckian opened his crusade for recognition in the congressional session of 1817-1818. By late March administration forces were trying to push through an appropriation bill which contained a $30,000 item for expenses of the South American commissioners. Clay concentrated fire on this clause, just as he had previously opposed the sending of the mission, for to him investigation meant delay and delay obstructed early recognition. As the debate continued, he championed an amendment that would provide $18,000 for a year's salary and outfit for a minister to Buenos Aires. Vigorously he argued that the United Provinces had achieved stability and that Spanish reconquest was inconceivable. His opponents held that recognition of independence would bring no new benefits to either the United States or the United Provinces. As it was, the people and ships of each country were received freely in the other. Trade was not likely to increase. Furthermore, there was always the possibility that recognition might intensify the jealousy of European powers. The proponents of delay were too strong, and Clay won few adherents.[17]

From this vigorous offensive Clay found what consolation he could in the minor changes made in the nation's neutrality laws (Act of 1818), in the embarrassment imposed upon an already burdened administration, and in the popularization of the Spanish American cause through wide

[15] Aguirre to Adams, Dec. 16, 26, 29, 1817, Jan. 6, 16, 1818, Manning, *op. cit.*, I, 361-368, 373; Adams, *Memoirs*, IV, 30, 40-41, 46-47. Dexter Perkins has made a lucid analysis of Adams' position in these negotiations (Bemis [ed.], *The American Secretaries of State and Their Diplomacy*, IV, 39-42).

[16] In a personal letter to Alexander Hill Everett, his former classmate and secretary, Adams revealed something of the caution that guided him at this time (Dec. 29, 1817, W. C. Ford [ed.], *Writings of John Quincy Adams*, VI, 281-282).

[17] *Annals of Cong.*, 15 Cong., 1 sess., II, 1464, 1468, 1481-1482, 1505-1506, 1538-1567, 1655. For the entire debate, see pp. 1464-1655.

distribution of his impassioned speeches.[18] With this defeat Clay's group temporarily dropped its crusade, and the administration turned to the renewed activity of Aguirre and Gómez.

The Agent Crusades for Recognition

When Aguirre returned to New York in February, 1818, he discovered that Gómez had encountered his share of difficulties. He found the two frigates completed, their crews aboard, and all in readiness for sailing—except the payment of the second 100,000 pesos. Believing the time at hand for desperate measures, he sent Gómez off to Buenos Aires to explain their predicament, especially the need for money. In addition, he recommended that San Martín secure his appointment as chargé d'affaires for Chile in order that he might urge the recognition of that state's independence.[19]

Aguirre now turned to other pressing matters, especially a new request for acknowledgment of independence. On March 29, as Clay's campaign for recognition was approaching a climax in Washington, the agent received new instructions. At once he relayed their import to Adams: "I am specially charged by my Government to promote as far as in me lies, the acknowledgment of its Independence by the U. States, . . ." [20] With this he forwarded a well-phrased appeal from Pueyrredón to President Monroe.[21] Thus, Aguirre was placed in the awkward position of having to repeat an assignment he had already fulfilled three and a half months before. His choice of a terse letter in lieu of a personal trip to the capital seemed to indicate his chagrin. A week later, after reading reports of a presidential message to Congress, Aguirre indignantly complained to Adams that Monroe had misinterpreted the envoy's explanation of Artigas' intentions in the Banda Oriental. He asked rectification of this passage, which might do injustice to his fellow citizens. The Secretary curtly refused.[22]

In the following four months, Aguirre waited hopefully in New York for a remittance from Buenos Aires. None came. Meanwhile, alert Spanish agents, whose watchfulness had vexed Gómez from the outset, secured Aguirre's arrest on a charge of violating the neutrality laws. Upon his immediate acquittal and release, he made his last trip to Washington to protest to Adams.[23] The Secretary explained, as both he

[18] Whitaker, *op. cit.*, pp. 245-256; Bemis, *Early Diplomatic Missions from Buenos Aires*, pp. 57-58. For the Act of 1818, see *U.S. Stat. at L.*, III, 447-450.
[19] Aguirre to Supreme Director of Chile, March 18, 1818, MREC, BA, Correspondencia del Comisionada Aguirre de Washington.
[20] March 29, 1818, Manning, *op. cit.*, I, 375.
[21] Pueyrredón to Monroe, Jan. 14, 1818, *ibid.*, pp. 370-371.
[22] Adams to Monroe, March 25, 1818; Aguirre to Adams, April 5, 1818; Adams to Aguirre, April 11, 1818, *ibid.*, 59-61, 376-377.
[23] Aguirre to Adams, Aug. 10, 1818, NA, DS, Notes from Arg. Leg., I, pt. 1.

and Rush had done the previous year, that an agent was not considered a public minister and, therefore, was not exempt from arrest. When Aguirre offered to sell the two ships to the United States, Adams replied that he would consult the President.[24]

While approving his Secretary's handling of the incident and refusing to sanction purchase of the ships, President Monroe was mindful of public reaction in Buenos Aires and the colonies generally, as in the United States. Accordingly, he directed that Adams should temper his formal reply "with all due kindness and courtesy, toward the Colonies." [25] In a warm, almost ingratiating letter, the dutiful Secretary reminded the agent of the President's friendly disposition toward the United Provinces and of the government's extension of free trade and national hospitality.[26] Aguirre, bold from the outset and attempting one finesse after another, had underestimated his opponent and clearly overbid his hand.

By artifice or commercial transaction which the documents do not reveal, San Martín's agent was able to clear the two frigates at New York and deliver them to Buenos Aires in November. The *Curiacio*, later the *Independencia*, saw service in the Pacific, but the captain of the *Horatio*, failing to receive payment, fled Buenos Aires and sold the ship in Rio de Janeiro.[27]

Adams' cool reception of the Aguirre mission had resulted principally from his analysis of Artigas' dissensions in La Plata and the necessity, in view of the undefined intentions of the European Alliance, of maintaining neutrality.[28] The administration had tried to face the situation with prudence, subtly to hold out hope to the United Provinces while awaiting the removal of obstacles to recognition.[29] Moreover, in August Adams was much more favorable to early recognition than he had been six months before. And he had probably revealed his true feelings when he wrote to Monroe: "If Buenos Aires confined its demand of recognition to the provinces of which it is in actual possession, and if it would assert its entire independence by agreeing to place the United States upon the footing of the most favored nation . . . , I should think the time now arrived when its government might be recognized without a breach of neutrality." [30] Punctiliously, however, he had concealed these feelings from Aguirre.

[24] Adams, *Memoirs*, IV, 123-124. The Argentine historian, Palomeque, contends that Aguirre's agency was of a diplomatic character (*op. cit.*, I, 39, note.).

[25] Monroe to Adams, Aug. 17, 27, 1818, LC, MD, Writings of Monroe, V, VI, 72-73; Adams to Monroe, Aug. 23, 1818, LC, MD, Writings to Monroe, XVII; Adams to Monroe, Aug. 24, 1818, Adams, *Writings*, VI, 441-443.

[26] Aug. 27, 1818, Manning, *op. cit.*, I, 76-78.

[27] Bemis, *op. cit.*, p. 65; Ibarguren, *op. cit.*, pp. 75-76.

[28] Cf. Noberto Piñero, *La política internacional argentina*, p. 58.

[29] Two Argentine historians feel that the Aguirre mission was of great worth to the Argentine cause (Ibarguren, *op. cit.*, pp. 75-76; Adrián Beccar Varela, *Juan Martín Pueyrredón*, pp. 159-161).

[30] Aug. 24, 1818, Adams, *Writings*, V, 443.

The United Provinces Send a Consul General

Long before Aguirre's return to Buenos Aires, Supreme Director Pueyrredón had devised bolder tactics to further the quest for recognition. On January 14, 1818, he had appealed directly to President Monroe.[31] Then he resolved to press the issue through citizens of the United States who were sympathetic to the patriot movement. His first appointment was David C. DeForest, the audacious Yankee who years before had been refused appointment as American consul to Buenos Aires [32] and who now, in accordance with the unratified Worthington treaty, was commissioned consul general to Washington.[33]

David DeForest was one of the earliest, if not the first, of the large crop of American adventurers who established firm business roots in La Plata. Having visited one or both shores of the estuary three times between 1801 and 1805, he set up in 1806 the first permanent American business house in Buenos Aires. Although during the next twelve years his star rose and set several times, he ultimately accumulated a considerable fortune—partly from speculation in slaves and privateers—and ingratiated himself with Argentine leaders.[34] A man of undoubted boldness and forthrightness, DeForest was characterized by one fellow American in Buenos Aires as dignified, gentlemanly, and affable, but high-spirited and imperious; by another, as "inflated and impudent in the extreme." [35] But, however he may have impressed his compatriots abroad, his projected retirement to his homeland in 1818 rendered him ideally suited to the purposes of Pueyrredón.

In confidential instructions of February 24, the Supreme Director outlined a mission to challenge the audacity and resourcefulness even of a DeForest. He was empowered to urge recognition of independence as well as to perform the normal functions of a consul. Moreover, he was directed to thwart the anti-Pueyrredón activities of Argentine exiles in the United States, to enlist the services of additional ships as privateers, and to participate in a plan to establish an island base for United Provinces corsairs.[36] DeForest was to carry with him also a letter of appointment, with accompanying credentials, for General William

---

[31] See above, p. 53.

[32] See above, p. 13, note 1.

[33] Pueyrredón to Monroe, May [no day], 1818, Manning, *op. cit.*, I, 377-378.

[34] For most of my data on DeForest's personality and early career in La Plata, I have drawn on Benjamin Keen, *David Curtis DeForest and the Revolution of Buenos Aires* (see above, p. 13). Shorter accounts are J. W. DeForest, *The De Forests of Avesnes (and of New Netherland)* . . . , pp. 113-136, and *Dictionary of American Biography*, V, 196-197.

[35] Henry Hill, *Recollections of an Octogenarian*, pp. 111-114; LC, MD, Papers of Jeremy Robinson, Diaries, Feb. 19, 1818.

[36] Draft of instructions for DeForest, Feb. 24, 1818, AGN, BA, S1-A2-A4-núm. 8.

Winder, of Baltimore, who was invited to become an Argentine *diputado* to the government of the United States.[37]

DeForest arrived in Baltimore late in April and immediately delivered to General Winder the communications from the Supreme Director. The General, who had earned a somewhat tarnished reputation as a commanding officer in the War of 1812, was nevertheless a substantial citizen of the Maryland metropolis and was duly flattered by his appointment.[38] Already friendly to the United Provinces and frankly desirous of serving both countries, he eagerly solicited advice from his friend, James Monroe. Conceding that the United States desired the independence of the United Provinces and that a person enjoying the confidence of both governments could increase mutual understanding, the President declined to advise Winder specifically.[39] In any case, the General refused Pueyrredón's appointment and suggested that he could give greater aid to independence in his normal capacity than as special agent.[40]

Meanwhile, DeForest had gone to Washington, where he soon conferred with the Secretary, visited the President, and arranged a meeting with Henry Clay.[41] In his conference with Adams, the agent was wary, meeting circumspection and aloofness with reserve and cleverness. The Secretary flatly informed him that the Worthington treaty was unauthorized and that, while his communications would be received attentively, DeForest himself could not be recognized, for recognition of a consul meant recognition of a nation, and acknowledgment of the United Provinces was not yet regarded as expedient. The Yankee insisted that he had no wish to embarrass the government and that his principal mission was to prevent the piratical activities carried on by privateers flying the United Provinces flag. Such a gross understatement omitted the major objectives laid down in Pueyrredón's instructions: to solicit recognition, to commission privateers, and to work for the establishment of an insular privateering base. These subjects DeForest completely avoided or touched gingerly. As to recognition, he said that Aguirre had acted without authority and even avowed that the Supreme Director did not wish to press the United States on that subject.[42] Here the agent

---

[37] Supreme Director to Thomas Taylor, Feb. 19, 1818, and draft of note to Winder, Feb. 25, 1818, AGN, BA, S1-A2-A4-núm. 8; Pueyrredón to Monroe, Feb. 25, 1818, NA, DS, Notes from Arg. Leg., I, pt. 1.

[38] Obituary notice in *Niles' Register*, XXVI (May 29, 1824), 202.

[39] Winder to Monroe, May 3, 1818; Monroe to Winder, May 11, 1818, Mary W. Kenway, "Correspondence between General William Winder and President Monroe with reference to proposals made by the United Provinces of South America," *The Hispanic American Historical Review*, XII (Nov., 1932), 457-461.

[40] Winder to Tagle, June 5, 1818, AGN, BA, S1-A2-A4-núm. 8; Winder to Monroe, July 23, 1818, LC, MD, Monroe Papers, Johnson Collection.

[41] DeForest to Tagle, May 17, 1818, AGN, BA, S1-A2-A4-núm. 8.

[42] DeForest to Tagle, *ibid.*; Adams, *Memoirs*, IV, 88-89. Vivid accounts of this interview are presented in Keen, *op. cit.*, pp. 137-140, and Bemis, *op. cit.*, pp. 76-79.

determined to rest his case temporarily. Under the circumstances, it was a skillful performance, but the Secretary, already informed of DeForest's complicity in privateering enterprises, was not deluded.[43]

En route to his native Connecticut, which he had not seen in six years, DeForest stopped in Baltimore to confer with Winder and Manuel Moreno, a leader of the Argentine exiles. Here, too, he sent off his first report to Buenos Aires, where the attitude of the United States caused disappointment and perplexity.[44]

Before the opening of Congress in November DeForest returned to Washington to renew his application. Conditions now, he thought, were distinctly more favorable. Britain had forestalled Franco-Russian plans for intervention in the Spanish American revolution. By clearing central Chile of Spanish armies San Martín had liberated Chile and opened the route to Peru. The South American commissioners had returned in firm agreement that Spain could not reconquer the Viceroyalty of the Río de la Plata. In consultation with Henry Clay, DeForest mapped his strategy. He would arrange that all diplomatic exchanges be confirmed by letter so that, at a propitious time, Clay's group might call for the correspondence.[45]

On the basis of these new developments, DeForest on December 9 reopened his case for recognition as consul general.[46] Five days later, he appeared before Adams, only to receive a second refusal, founded on the same reasoning as that of the previous May.[47] When DeForest requested a written reply, the Secretary obliged in two censorious notes. The one was a rebuke to the Supreme Director for refusing to offer the United States most-favored-nation privileges. The other was a demand for the ending of the piracy which masqueraded as privateering.[48]

In spite of well-intentioned laws and policies, the depredations of Argentine privateers continued to be excessive. In their efforts to chart a course of true neutrality, Monroe and Adams—like so many American

---

[43] Halsey to Adams, Feb. 25, 1818, NA, DS, Con. Let., B. A., I, pt. 2. See also Keen, *op. cit.*, pp. 103-121; *H. Doc.*, No. 48, 15 Cong., 2 sess., pp. 116 ff; and *Annals of Cong.*, 15 Cong., 2 sess., II, 1920-1924.

[44] DeForest to Tagle, May 17, 1818, AGN, BA, S1-A2-A4-núm. 9; *Comisión de Bernardino Rivadavia ante España y otras potencias de Europa, 1814-1820*, I, 304.

[45] Keen, *op. cit.*, p. 143; Bemis, *op. cit.*, p. 79. During his absence from Washington DeForest had sent one report, of a more or less perfunctory nature, to Tagle (Aug. 20, 1818, AGN, BA, S1-A2-A4-núm. 8).

[46] DeForest to Adams, Manning, *op. cit.*, I, 515-516.

[47] Adams, *Memoirs*, IV, 190; DeForest to Tagle, Dec. 16, 1818, AGN, BA, S1-A2-A4-núm. 8. The date of DeForest's report is given as December 18 in Bemis, *op. cit.*, p. 81, note 1, and Keen, *op. cit.*, p. 144, note 39. In any case, it was a full account of his conference with Adams and included a recommendation that the United Provinces should send an "Envoy Extraordinary and Minister Plenipotentiary" to the United States before the next session of Congress. Such a minister, DeForest suggested, should have full powers, a secretary who understands English, and "pecuniary means to live in a style proportioned to his rank."

[48] Dec. 31, 1818, Jan. 1, 1819, Manning, *op. cit.*, I, 82-85, 88-89.

statesmen before and after—were perplexed by the interplay of countless motives. Fixed neutrality acts were but paper laws in contrast to human emotions made pliable by these motives. Adams seemed to be disquieted by the irony of his position: if the United Provinces were denied enjoyment of the rights of a sovereign state, was it just to ask them to abide by the practices of nations? [49] Nevertheless, he wrote DeForest that "the President expects . . . that no instance of this cause of complaint will hereafter be given." [50]

DeForest's reply to Adams' notes of December 31 and January 1, while self-depreciatory, was also overbold and, to Adams, "cunning and deceptive." [51] Moreover, its receipt roughly coincided with a House resolution calling for information on the status of recognition. By this time, Adams was goaded to take conclusive action. In responding to the House request, he forwarded the correspondence with DeForest, carefully explained the refusal to recognize him, and revealed his suspicion of the agent's connivance with party opposition in Congress.[52] When, on January 22, DeForest called on Adams again, the annoyed Secretary confronted him with the bald reality that as a citizen of the United States he was subject to its neutrality laws. Visioning the unhappiness which protracted legal proceedings might bring to his Connecticut retirement, the audacious but vulnerable Yankee yielded to Adams' thrust and hurried to his New Haven sanctuary.[53] Moreover, the signing a month later of the Transcontinental Treaty, by which Florida would become American territory, brought to an end DeForest's undercover efforts to establish a base for privateers in the Gulf of Mexico.[54]

In his long, exciting career in La Plata, David DeForest had contributed in many tangible ways to the origin and the growth of Argentine-American relations. His mission as consul general at Washington, though "a milestone in the establishment of diplomatic relations between the United States and his adopted country," was fruitless in its important objects.[55]

[49] Adams wrote in this vein to Richard Rush, Jan. 1, 1819, *ibid.*, I, 85-88.
[50] Jan. 1, 1819, *ibid.*, I, 88-89.
[51] Jan. 8, 1819, *ibid.*, I, 516-519; Adams, *Memoirs*, IV, 223-224.
[52] This message transmitted information requested by a House Resolution of January 14. See Adams to Monroe, Jan. 28, 1819, Manning, *op. cit.*, I, 89-94, and *Annals of Cong.*, 15 Cong., 2 sess., I, 544; II, 1606-1622.
[53] Adams, *Memoirs*, IV, 224-226; Bemis, *op. cit.*, pp. 83-84; Keen, *op. cit.*, pp. 153-155.
[54] *Ibid.*, pp. 146-152.
[55] *Ibid.*, p. 169. DeForest's commission as consul general was not revoked until 1824 (see below, p. 75).

Proposals of Bilateral Recognition

While the government of the United Provinces was digging deeply into its bag of tricks to win recognition from the United States, Monroe and Adams were becoming increasingly aware that the matter would be determined not alone in Buenos Aires and Washington but more especially in the capitals of Europe. During the latter half of 1818 relations between the two American states shifted distinctly into the center of the world stage. This was a logical consequence of the sending of the South American commission, of the frequent clashes between the United States and Spain over neutrality and the Florida treaty, and of the contemplated mediation of the European Alliance.

Although in his negotiations with South American agents Adams studiedly professed the policy of neutrality and nonrecognition, whenever dealing with the European powers he clearly manifested a desire for early recognition. Repeatedly between April and December, when instructing his ministers in Europe, he stated or implied the probability of early action on behalf of the United Provinces.[56] His hesitation, therefore, must have been induced by uncertainty as to the steps to be taken by the Congress of Aix-la-Chapelle [57] and the necessity of awaiting the reports of the South American commissioners. Later, after the Congress had taken a moderate position, the wide disagreement in the reports of the commissioners increased his wariness of unilateral recognition.[58]

On several occasions after the spring of 1818, however, Adams was prepared to undertake joint recognition of the United Provinces. In May, he wrote to Rush in London that he should "encourage any disposition which may consequently be manifested to a more perfect concert of measures between the United-States and Great-Britain towards that end; the total Independence of the Spanish South-American Provinces." [59] In August, at least according to Adams' own later account, he made a formal proposal to Great Britain, which declined the offer without disapproval. This overture, Adams thought, was responsible for Britain's restraining

---

[56] Adams to George W. Erving, Minister to Spain, April 20, 1818; to Albert Gallatin, Minister to France, May 19, Aug. 20, 1818; to Rush, May 20, Aug. 15, 1818; to George W. Campbell, Minister to Russia, June 28, Aug. 20, 1818, Manning, *op. cit.*, I, 61, 64-66, 69-70, 73, 74, 75.

[57] Like Adams, Bernardino Rivadavia, while on special mission to France, was troubled by the attitude of Russia (to Pueyrredón, April 19, 1818, *Comisión de Bernardino Rivadavia*, I, 260). For a brief discussion of the Congress' deliberations on Latin America, see William Spence Robertson, *France and Latin-American Independence*, pp. 151-158.

[58] See above, pp. 42-45.

[59] May 20, 1818, Manning, *op. cit.*, I, 70. For discussion of this overture in a broader sphere, see Whitaker, *op. cit.*, pp. 254-266.

influence at the Congress of Aix-la-Chapelle.[60] Again in December, even after the South American commissioners had submitted their divergent reports, Adams desired that France and Britain be invited to join with the United States in early recognition of the United Provinces.[61]

By January 1 Adams had framed instructions for Rush. The United States, Adams wrote, had hitherto pursued a course of neutrality, neither acknowledging the independence of the United Provinces nor recognizing their consuls. Now, however, Spain's power had been completely dispelled, and "the President has it in contemplation . . . to recognize the Government of Buenos-Ayres, at no remote period, should no event occur which will justify a further postponement of that intention." The President greatly desired the concurrence of Great Britain in such a plan. When the measure is adopted, Adams concluded, "it will be a mere acknowledgment of the fact of Independence, and without deciding upon the extent of their Territory, or upon their claims to Sovereignty, in any part of the Provinces of La Plata, where it is not established and uncontested." [62]

This proposal for joint recognition was first revealed to the members of President Monroe's Cabinet on January 2. The revelation came as the advisers listened to Adams' reading of the instructions to Rush. In the Secretary's view, the decision to take this step was determined by the convictions, first, that Spain could never restore its control in the Viceroyalty of La Plata, and second, that the privateering irregularities of the United Provinces could be repressed only by granting to them all the rights while holding them to the ordinary duties of sovereign states. After months of investigation, neutrality, and nonrecognition, these were the conclusions Monroe and Adams had reached.[63]

Bilateral recognition of the United Provinces, therefore, despite the unfavorable reports of a majority of the South American commissioners and despite the mediation plans of the European Alliance, seemed a distinct possibility at the beginning of 1819. That recognition did not come—bilaterally or unilaterally—for more than three years was the result of many circumstances.

[60] Adams referred to this instance five years later in an instruction to Richard C. Anderson, Minister to Colombia, May 27, 1823, Manning, *op. cit.*, I, 194-195. The English historian, C. K. Webster, in discussing this letter, concludes that Adams did no more than sound the European powers (*Britain and the Independence of Latin America, 1812-1830*, I, 43-44). See also the appropriate despatches cited above, note 56.
[61] Adams, *Memoirs*, IV, 190, 199. Whitaker discusses fully the possibilities of Anglo-American cooperation at this time (*op. cit.*, pp. 261-266).
[62] Manning, *op. cit.*, I, 85-88.
[63] Adams, *Memoirs*, IV, 203-206.

V I

ANARCHY AND ORDER IN ARGENTINA:
RECOGNITION AT LAST, 1819-1824

The Monroe administration's predilection for Anglo-American collaboration at the beginning of 1819 represented a climax in Argentine-American relations between the War of 1812 and ultimate recognition in 1822. The Department of State had recently released the reports of the South American commissioners, who agreed so emphatically that Spain could not reconquer the Viceroyalty of the Río de la Plata. David DeForest, Pueyrredón's New England-born agent, tactically chose this instant to press for recognition of the United Provinces, which had now maintained self-government for nearly nine years.[1] The recognition of Pueyrredón's government at this point would have been a natural step, and Adams' instructions to Rush seemed to chart the course to be followed.[2] Yet the Argentine people, soon floundering under changing administrations and indecisive leaders, were obliged to wait another three years.

Further Postponement of Recognition

Lord Castlereagh's rejection of Adams' proposal for joint action punctured President Monroe's hopes for cooperation with Great Britain.[3] And the Secretary's crisp handling of DeForest's bold overture scotched the possibility of unilateral action by the United States. Thereupon, active relations between the two American states during 1819 deteriorated more sharply than they had improved during the previous year. After the return of the South American commission, the United States was not again officially represented in Buenos Aires until December, 1819.[4]

[1] See above, pp. 55-58.
[2] See above, p. 60.
[3] Rush to Adams, Feb. 15, 1819, William R. Manning (ed.), *Diplomatic Correspondence of the United States Concerning Independence of the Latin-American Countries*, III, 1451.
[4] See below, pp. 66-67.

Following DeForest's retreat from public affairs, the United Provinces sent no official agent to Washington until two years after the United States extended recognition in February, 1822.[5]

Though the relative influence of each can only be surmised, several circumstances combined to produce this interruption in the fluctuating but obvious trend toward recognition.[6] These circumstances developed simultaneously at all angles of the triangular Atlantic relationship which from the beginning had conditioned development of Argentina's independence movement.

As to the European phase, Castlereagh's decision alone was enough to end American hopes for joint recognition at an early date.[7] Even had France or Russia been receptive, Monroe and Adams could not have afforded to ignore Great Britain. Later, the liberal revolution in Spain seemed for a time to hold out hope that Spanish American grievances might be liquidated. In Buenos Aires, the political anarchy which followed Pueyrredón's resignation in June, 1819, and the disclosure of a plot to create a Bourbon monarchy confirmed the wisdom of Adams' policy of delay.[8] In the United States, wide publication early in 1819 of the divergent reports of the South American commissioners cooled off popular enthusiasm for recognition. During the next two years, acknowledgment of independence would have confronted the Monroe government with the danger of strengthening Henry Clay's already strong position as a political opponent.[9]

A Season of Anarchy in Argentina

For three years after declaring their independence, the United Provinces under the directorate of Pueyrredón had enjoyed relative political stability. Although recognition by foreign powers had not been won, at the beginning of 1819 its early consummation seemed possible. Beneath the surface of this apparent progress, however, seeds of discontent were germinating. The Constituent Assembly, which had been appointed in 1817, hastened the process of disruption by the adoption, in April, 1819, of an unpopular constitution. By means of this instrument the Province of Buenos Aires attempted to impose upon the rest of the

---

[5] See below, pp. 75-79.

[6] Arthur P. Whitaker admirably analyzes several of these circumstances (*The United States and Latin America*, pp. 273-274, 317-343).

[7] Monroe continued to believe in the efficacy of joint recognition ("Sketch of Instructions for Agent for South America—Notes for the Department of State," S. M. Hamilton (ed.), *Writings of James Monroe*, VI, 97; Adams to Smith Thompson, Secretary of the Navy, May 20, 1819, Manning, *op. cit.*, I, 105).

[8] See below, p. 63.

[9] Whitaker, *op. cit.*, pp. 318-320; Charles C. Griffin, *The United States and the Disruption of the Spanish Empire*, pp. 247-252.

United Provinces a government with strong, centralized control.[10] Excessive localism, especially in the riparian provinces, led to two years of discord and anarchy.[11]

Upon Pueyrredón's resignation soon after the promulgation of the new constitution, General José Rondeau became Provisional Director. With the assistance of Manuel Belgrano, leader of many revolutionary campaigns, Rondeau attempted to defeat the armies of Santa Fe and Entre Ríos under the caudillo leaders, Estanislao López and Francisco Ramírez. Rondeau's rout at the battle of Cepeda in February, 1820, led to a succession of governors in Buenos Aires. Although these provincial executives attempted to manage the affairs of the entire country, effective national government was nonexistent. Not until the accession to power of Martín Rodríguez late in 1820 was any form of order restored.[12]

This confusion within the United Provinces during 1819-1920 was augmented by conflict between leaders who were monarchists and those who favored the republican ideal. In 1819 a well-developed plan was under way for calling to the Río de la Plata a French or Spanish Bourbon. Numerous exigencies prevented fulfillment of the project, but its exposure in 1820 improved neither the immediate internal situation nor the country's foreign relations.[13] On the other hand, the denouement of the plot assured the perpetuation of the republican principle in Argentine government.[14]

Clay Renews His Crusade

This succession of events in Buenos Aires—the adoption of the constitution of 1819, the resignation of Pueyrredón, the conflict between Buenos Aires and the provinces, and the project for creation of a monarchy—eventually came to the notice of the American press and of Henry Clay, and was subjected to review by the Department of State. The first reaction of newspapers to the new constitution was one of enthusiasm for its supposedly republican principles and its manifestation

[10] *Registro oficial de la República Argentina*, I, 502-508.

[11] L. S. Rowe, *The Federal System of the Argentine Republic*, pp. 30, 31, 34.

[12] The Argentine historian, Ricardo Levene, has written extensively of the period of anarchy. Most easily available of his accounts are *A History of Argentina*, pp. 336-345, 352-358, and *Historia de la Nación Argentina*, VI, sec. 2, pp. 287-342.

[13] On this project, see Mario Belgrano, *La Francia y la monarchia en el Plata;* W. S. Robertson, *France and Latin-American Independence*, pp. 158-177; and "Memorandum of Baron de Renneval, Minister of Foreign Relations of France to Doctor Don Valentine Gómez, Agent accredited to the said Court by the Government of Buenos Aires," enclosure in Prevost to Adams, March 20, 1820, Manning, *op. cit.*, I, 545-547.

[14] Adolfo Saldías, *La evolución republicana durante la revolución argentina*, pp. 159-214.

of growing political stability.[15] But, in 1820, when news of the internal dissensions and the project for monarchy arrived, the press reflected popular confusion and disillusionment, as well as satisfaction with Adams' policy of delay.[16]

Since March, 1818, Henry Clay's arguments for recognition had been stilled.[17] Now, in April, 1820, undismayed by the undemocratic nature of the new constitution, he again championed the United Provinces and the other insurgent colonies. He introduced a resolution which provided for the sending of a minister to any South American government which was maintaining its independence from Spain. Arguing with his usual zeal, he pushed the resolution through the House on May 10 by a vote of 80 to 75.[18] But Clay's second crusade, attracting little public attention, was no more successful than the first. Consistent with its long-standing policy of nonrecognition, the administration failed to enforce the congressional will.[19]

The United States Renews Investigation

During 1819-1820 Monroe and Adams made no fundamental change in their policy toward the United Provinces. In his annual message of 1819 the President referred to Buenos Aires only in the hollow pronouncement that it "still maintains unshaken the independence which it declared in 1816, and has enjoyed since 1810." [20] Though the negotiations were probably not responsible for postponing recognition, the Secretary was burdened for many months with the task of persuading Spain to approve the treaty transferring Florida to the United States (signed February, 1819).[21] Adams was still determined to await demonstration of political stability by the United Provinces.

The firmness of the administration in withholding recognition did not deter it from pursuing its other policies of investigation and benevolent neutrality. Though the United States had no official observers in Buenos

---

[15] *Daily National Intelligencer*, Aug. 3, 1819; *National Intelligencer* (Triweekly), Oct. 6, 1819; *Niles' Register*, XVI (Aug. 14, 1819), 415-416. Written before news of the new constitution had reached the United States but circulated as propaganda in favor of recognition at this time was the volume of Vicente Pazos, *Letters on the United Provinces of South America, Addressed to Hon. Henry Clay*.

[16] *Boston Patriot*, quoted in *Daily National Intelligencer*, July 17, 1820; *Niles' Register*, XIX (Oct. 28, 1820), 140.

[17] See above, pp. 52-53.

[18] *Annals of Cong.*, 16 Cong., 1 sess., II, 2181-2182, 2225, 2228, 2229-2230.

[19] Griffin, *op. cit.*, pp. 251-252.

[20] J. D. Richardson, *A Compilation of the Messages and Papers of the Presidents*, II, 58-59.

[21] The authorities disagree. See, for example, Griffin, *op. cit.*, pp. 142-143, and Whitaker, *op. cit.*, pp. 273-274.

Aires after May, 1818, this was clearly not the will of the administration.[22] Not only did Monroe and Adams wish to receive a continuous flow of information from Buenos Aires; they were likewise eager that the Argentine leaders should be frequently reminded of American good will toward their cause. Moreover, the persisting abuses of privateering needed adjustment. Perhaps the use of a warship and a naval officer, thought Monroe, could best fulfill these functions.[23] At any rate, in March, 1819, the President turned to the Navy Department.[24]

In collaboration with Secretary of the Navy Smith Thompson, Monroe selected Commodore Oliver H. Perry, hero of the War of 1812, to execute the manifold wishes of the Department of State—in Venezuela first, then in Buenos Aires. The instructions prepared by the Secretary of State were a comprehensive diagnosis of American policies toward the revolution. For both North and South Americans the neutrality policy had been wise, Adams reasoned, for by its tacit recognition of belligerency the United States had effectively neutralized the European Concert and forestalled aid to the Spanish cause. He instructed Perry to assure the Supreme Director that the sympathy of the United States remained "sincere and unabated," but also to press for more careful regulation of privateering.[25]

But these well-laid plans quickly broke down, at least as far as the United Provinces were concerned, for Perry died in August before

[22] The South American commissioners left Buenos Aires in May, 1818; Worthington and Halsey had already been relieved (see above, pp. 34-35). Upon his return to Buenos Aires from Chile in February, 1819, Worthington sent several despatches to the Department of State, including a long report which contained more of human interest than of political or diplomatic import (to Adams, March 7, 1819, Manning, *op. cit.*, I, 519-537). Before his departure, Worthington appointed Nathaniel W. Strong as Acting Consul (Worthington to Tagle, March 4, 1819, AGN, BA, S1-A2-A4-núm. 8; Strong to Adams, April 28, 1819, NA, DS, Con. Let., B. A., I, pt. 2). In December, Strong appointed John C. Zimmerman to act in his stead (Strong to Adams, Dec. 9, 1819, *ibid.*; Strong to Tagle, Nov. 26, 1819, AGN, BA, S1-A2-A4-núm. 8). The Department of State received no despatches of consequence from either Strong or Zimmerman. In the Archivo General de la Nación, Buenos Aires, the last letter from Zimmerman is dated May, 1820.

[23] The matter of privateering and piracy was discussed in the Cabinet meeting of March 16, 1819, when it was proposed to send a public commissioner to Buenos Aires. Poinsett, Rodney, Bland, and Brackenridge were considered for the post, but none was approved (Charles Francis Adams [ed.], *Memoirs of John Quincy Adams*, IV, 298-301). Following this meeting, the President prepared his detailed "Sketch of Instructions for Agent for South America—Notes for Department of State" (Monroe, *Writings*, VI, 99-102).

[24] Smith Thompson, Secretary of the Navy, to Commodore Oliver H. Perry, March 29, 1819, A. S. MacKenzie, *The Life of Commodore Oliver Hazard Perry*, pp. 187-188.

[25] For extracts from Adams' instructions to Perry, see Adams to Thompson, May 20, 1819, Manning, *op. cit.*, I, 101-107. A complete copy is in NA, DS, Dom. Let., XVII. For the several Navy Department orders to Perry, see NA, DN, Private Letters, 1813-1840, pp. 263-292, and Letters to Officers, Ships of War, XIII, 370.

leaving Venezuelan waters.[26] The administration, however, held another trump; a new agent was already on his way to Buenos Aires. He was John B. Prevost, who had been delegated in the summer of 1817 to investigate conditions in Peru and Chile.[27] Prevost, a stepson of Aaron Burr, had served as judge of the Superior Court of the Territory of Orleans by appointment of President Jefferson.[28] For two years he had represented the Department of State on the Pacific coast, but in view of the revocation of the commissions of Halsey and Worthington, Adams now requested that he move over the cordillera to Buenos Aires.[29]

Prevost's instructions were identical with those of Commodore Perry. His reports for the year of his residence (November 13, 1819—October 30, 1820) were illuminating descriptions of the spread of political chaos and the French scheme for creation of monarchy. They furnished rich grist for the Adams mill.[30] Nevertheless, Prevost's overzealousness for the colonial cause eventually brought him under Monroe's suspicion, although he continued in residence until the authorities at Buenos Aires ordered him to leave. By that time, fortunately, his successor, John M. Forbes, had arrived.[31]

John M. Forbes Undertakes a Mission

Forbes's arrival in October, 1820, marked the beginning of a more enduring link between Washington and Buenos Aires than had yet existed. For ten years agents of the United States had moved in and out of the Argentine capital as players in a pageant. Few remained long enough thoroughly to ingratiate themselves with local authorities; nearly all conducted themselves with such imprudence as to be requested to withdraw, either by one government or the other. Forbes, on the contrary, initiated in 1820 a residence which was to last until his untimely death in 1831.

[26] *Niles' Register*, XVII (Oct. 2, 1819), 71-72. Perry's mission was subsequently entrusted to Commodore Charles Morris, who accomplished nothing because his arrival in Buenos Aires coincided with the overthrow of the Directory (Manning, *op. cit.*, I, 131, 540, 541).

[27] Rush to Prevost, July 18, 1817, NA, DS, Inst. to Con., II, 41-42; Adams to Prevost, Sept. 29, 1817, Manning, *op. cit.*, I, 45-46.

[28] Henry Adams, *History of the United States*, II, 220; III, 219, 296. In 1806 Prevost had been suspected of implication in his stepfather's conspiracy (*ibid.*, III, 319).

[29] Adams to Prevost, May 3, 1819, NA, DS, Inst. to Con., II, 162.

[30] Manning, *op. cit.*, I, 537-544, 545-548, 549-557.

[31] Monroe to Adams, June [no day], 1820, LC, MD, Writings of Monroe, V. Three days before Forbes's arrival, Prevost had been summarily ordered to leave Buenos Aires within five days, i.e., by October 25. Government officials resented certain portions of Prevost's despatches which had been published in the United States. The agent remained on an American ship in the harbor until October 30, when he sailed for Chile (Forbes to Adams, Dec. 4, 1820, NA, DS, Con. Let., B. A., I).

As the youngest classmate of John Quincy Adams, Forbes had early come to the Secretary's attention. Between 1802 and 1817 he had been consul and consul general for the north of Europe, living much of the time in Hamburg and Copenhagen. Often troubled with gout, he is said to have chosen for his crest "a gouty foot couchant crossed by two crutches rampant," with the motto "Toujours souffrant, jamais triste." Not the ablest nor the suavest of early diplomats, he nevertheless served his country with vigor and discretion and at least avoided the reprimand of recall.[32]

Adams appointed Forbes agent for commerce and seamen for either Buenos Aires or Chile, his residence to depend upon the location of Prevost.[33] His instructions of July 5 were similar to those given to his recent predecessors. The Secretary advised him to report with "vigilance and discernment, and penetration and fidelity" all political conditions and developments, especially those involving European nations. He was to give particular attention to matters of commercial intercourse and to the repeated violations of American neutrality.[34] By admonishing him that "the performance of these duties will involve also the political relations between those countries and the United States," the administration seems to have attached a special significance to Forbes's appointment.[35]

In supplementary instructions which accentuated contemporary American recognition and commercial policies, Adams directed that Forbes

> take occasion to remark whenever it may be proper that the Government of the U.S. have never intended to secure to themselves any advantage, commercial or otherwise, as an equivalent for acknowledging the Independence of any part of South America. They do not think it a proper subject for equivalent; and they have entire confidence that no exclusive privilege will be granted to any other nation to the prejudice of the U.S. . . .[36]

[32] A. K. Teele, *The History of Milton, Mass., 1840 to 1887*, pp. 566-567; "Diary of John Quincy Adams," in Massachusetts Historical Society, *Proceedings*, 1902, 2d series, XVI, 343-344.

[33] Adams to Forbes, June 17, 1820, NA, DS, Inst. to Con., II, 188. Prevost was to be allowed to choose his post; his misunderstanding with public officials settled the point.

[34] Manning, *op. cit.*, I, 130-132.

[35] H. M. Wriston thinks this portion of Forbes's instructions made his appointment virtually that of chargé d'affaires, although the mission "was so constituted as to avoid recognition" (*Executive Agents in Foreign Relations*, p. 422). There is additional evidence to support this view. In 1821, when Forbes appointed James Robinett as consul, the appointment was officially recognized (Forbes to Juan Manuel de Luca, Secretary of Government and Treasury, May 15, 1821, AGN, BA, S1-A2-A4-núm. 8; De Luca to Forbes, May 16, 1821, *Documentos para la historia argentina*, XIV, 20-21). When Robinett resigned the following December, Forbes advised Rivadavia that he himself would assume consular functions (Dec. 17, 1821, AGN, BA, S1-A2-A4-núm. 8). This circumstance would seem to indicate that Forbes regarded his post as something above that of a consul.

[36] July 12, 1820, Manning, *op. cit.*, I, 140-141.

Even before Forbes's arrival, rumors regarding the purposes of his mission circulated freely. Political malcontents alleged that the United States had authorized recognition and that Forbes had been sent to arrange settlement of claims owed American citizens by former agents of the United Provinces. Except the *Gaceta de Buenos Aires*, newspapers spread the misconceptions.[37] Pressed from the moment of his first appearance in La Plata to participate in factious intrigues, Forbes made every human effort to maintain the inviolability of his position. The agent assured public officials that recognition had no place in his instructions and that he had been sent merely to convey the good wishes of the United States and to communicate upon specified points.[38] Once he had informed the authorities of the true purpose of his mission, Forbes was ready to undertake the specific tasks he had been assigned.

Clay's Final Crusade

Back in Washington, during the winter of 1820-1821, both the President and Congress were again struggling with the problem of Spanish American independence. Reports of renewed activity by the Quadruple Alliance in Europe and the prospect of a threat to independent governments even in the Western Hemisphere added new weight to the arguments for recognition in the United States.

The President, in his annual message to Congress in November, 1820, moved but slightly beyond his position of the previous year. He noted the increased strength with which the colonies resisted Spain and commended the improved order of their internal administration. Unfortunately, he said, factionalism persisted in Buenos Aires. His description of conditions both in Spain and in the colonies revealed his continuing hope for the success of the revolutions.[39]

In Congress, the partisans of South American recognition again granted leadership of their cause to Henry Clay, whose efforts in 1818 and 1820 had been unavailing. Undaunted, he re-entered the lists against the administration in February, 1821. He first attempted to secure repassage of the House resolution which the executive department had ignored the previous May, that a minister should be sent to any government maintaining its independence. This time Clay lost his principal motion but countered on the following day by winning concurrence for a two-part resolution: that the House express its "deep interest" in the South American struggles and that it support the President whenever he

---

[37] Forbes to Adams, Dec. 4, 1820, *ibid.*, I, 557-559; *Gaceta de Buenos Aires*, Nov. 1, 1820.

[38] Forbes to Adams, Dec. 4, 1820, Manning, *op. cit.*, I, 559-561.

[39] Richardson, *op. cit.*, II, 77.

might deem recognition expedient.[40] Again Clay's triumph was empty, for, although House action on both points was conclusive, the administration refused to move. Secretary Adams still resisted.

Forbes's Defense of American Rights

Meanwhile, in Buenos Aires, as Forbes vigilantly observed and faithfully reported the confusion which prevailed, problems involving American rights pressed for his attention—privateering, conscription, and abuses to shipping. Among these he sought first to adjust the vexing issue of privateering, a problem which had plagued his government for five years. Congress in 1817 and 1818 had passed neutrality acts to strengthen the President's hands in dealing with unscrupulous ship captains. The Department of State had instructed its agents to protest vigorously against the excesses committed by ships sailing under the flag and commissions of Buenos Aires. Yet the Argentine government continued to issue blank commissions in quantities. In spite of legislation and official declarations, American citizens persisted in lending aid to Argentine privateers as they sought refuge in ports along the Atlantic seaboard and the Gulf coast. Sympathy for the Spanish American cause and inactivity or corruption on the part of federal officials made difficult the dispensation of justice.[41]

Immediately after the signature of the Transcontinental Treaty in 1819, President Monroe and his Secretary of State had disagreed on administration attitude toward the repeated violations of neutrality. Adams was irritated lest failure to pursue a more vigorous course should postpone or prevent ratification of the treaty.[42] While Monroe was fully aware that a serious situation had developed, he apparently was willing to do no more than send agents to carry official protests to the South American governments.[43] During the next year the missions of Commodore Perry, of his successor, Commodore Morris, and of John Prevost accomplished little.[44] When Forbes arrived in Buenos Aires, therefore, the evil was still rampant.

His despatches to Washington and his strong representations to the government of Buenos Aires throughout the early months of 1821 reveal

[40] *Annals of Cong.*, 16 Cong., 2 sess., pp. 1029-1030, 1071, 1078, 1081-1092. For details on Clay's sponsorship of recognition in Congress, see F. L. Paxson, *The Independence of the South American Republics*, pp. 127-146 *passim*.

[41] Griffin, *op. cit.*, pp. 245-247; Adams, *Memoirs*, IV, 318-319; Theodore S. Currier, *Los corsarios del Río de la Plata*, pp. 58-65.

[42] Adams, *Memoirs*, IV, 298-301. An illuminating analysis of Adams' attitude is that by Dexter Perkins in Samuel Flagg Bemis (ed.), *The American Secretaries of State*, IV, 49-50.

[43] Monroe, *Writings*, VI, 99-102.

[44] See above, pp. 65-66.

the tenacity with which Forbes sought to bring an end to indiscriminate privateering. Frequent changes in public officials frustrated him, especially when he could "ask no official prerogative without involving the recognition of this Government, . . ." [45] Forbes's persistence eventually gained for him an interview with Bernardino Rivadavia, Minister of Foreign Relations of the Province of Buenos Aires.[46] The agent carefully enumerated the evils of privateering and forced the Minister's admission that his government must take immediate action.[47] Further pressure finally brought about the decree of October 6, 1821. In its literal form, it was a complete surrender to the position for which the United States had been contending for five years. It provided for the early revocation of all commissions of privateering issued by the government and for the disarming at the earliest possible moment of all privateers sailing under such commissions.[48] Forbes told Rivadavia that the evils of privateering had done much to curb the enthusiasm of the North American people for the independence of the South Americans, but that the suppression of the abuses would "tend to reanimate their good wishes." [49]

A second problem to which Forbes directed his attentions was the protection of North American seamen. The continuous strife between Buenos Aires and the other provinces led in March, 1821, to an executive order for conscription of foreigners.[50] The disdain with which foreign residents greeted the measure caused the early passage of a similar decree by the Provincial Junta. By this act all foreign shopkeepers, merchants, and other aliens of two years' residence were made liable to the military duties of citizens.[51] Although the terms of the edict fell more heavily upon the British, of whom there were many in Buenos Aires, Forbes felt anxiety for seamen of the United States.[52] His prompt action obtained from the government a resolution which guaranteed exemption

[45] Forbes to Adams, March 10, 1821, Manning, *op. cit.*, I, 572; Forbes to De Luca, April 13, 15, 1821, AGN, BA, S1-A2-A4-núm. 8.

[46] Rivadavia, who had recently returned from an extended mission in Great Britain and France, was named Foreign Minister in July, 1821.

[47] Forbes to Adams, Sept. 2, 1821, and to Rivadavia, Sept. 14, 1821, Manning, *op. cit.*, I, 580-581, 583-584.

[48] Forbes to Rivadavia, Sept. 14, 1821; Rivadavia to Forbes, Sept. 15, Oct. 6, 1821; Minute of a conference between Forbes and Rivadavia, Sept. 17, 1821, Manning, *op. cit.*, I, 583-587, 590-591. Rivadavia transmitted a copy of the decree of October 6 in his note of that date.

[49] Minute of a conference between Forbes and Rivadavia, Sept. 17, 1821, *ibid.*, I, 586.

[50] In LC, MD, Broadsides, 301 (Argentina), there is a printed broadside bearing the notice of Rodríguez' order.

[51] A translation of the decree, dated April 10, was enclosed in Forbes to Adams, April 17, 1821, NA, DS, Con. Let., B. A., I, pt. 2.

[52] Through Captain D. H. O'Brien, commanding British ships off Buenos Aires, British merchants protested severely. Some of the correspondence is printed in *British and Foreign State Papers*, VIII (1820-1821), 1021-1024.

to those American seamen who were properly registered.[53] Forbes exulted that he had gained a point over the British, whose protests were not at first so successful.[54]

Forbes applied himself next to the task of securing an arrangement for the protection of American shipping in La Plata. He had learned of repeated abuses to his country's flag by vessels not authorized to fly it. His protest led to a government order that no vessel professing to be from the United States should be allowed port privileges without the consent of the American agent.[55]

In the meantime, the energetic agent was attending to a variety of lesser matters. He arranged for the performance of consular duties in Buenos Aires.[56] He recounted the demonstrations with which the people received the news of San Martín's capture of Lima.[57] By means of interviews with government officials and the distribution of propaganda he sought to mitigate the prejudice prevailing against the United States.[58] He made suggestions for the improvement of harbor services.[59] And as the months of 1821 wore on, he conferred with the Foreign Minister on the exact status of President Monroe's recognition views [60] and sought to keep his government informed of the growth of stability in the United Provinces.

In this manner did Forbes execute to the letter the instructions of Secretary Adams—vigilant observation, penetrating analysis, faithful reporting, and vigorous representation of American policies and interests. His contributions to the process of recognition were immeasurable.

Recognition a Legal Reality

A series of developments in Buenos Aires and elsewhere in South America during the late months of 1821 convinced President Monroe, if not Secretary Adams, that the time for recognition was approaching. Following the anarchy produced by the overthrow of the "national" government of General Rondeau, order was gradually restored by the

[53] Forbes to Rodríguez, March 22, 1821, AGN, BA, S1-A2-A4-núm. 8. For a copy of the resolution of April 24, see *Documentos para la historia argentina*, XIV, 16-17.

[54] Forbes to Adams, April 24, 1821, NA, DS, Con. Let., B. A., I, pt. 2.

[55] Forbes to Rivadavia, Aug. 24, 1821; Rivadavia to Forbes, Aug. 25, 1821, NA, DS, Con. Let., B. A., II. The order was printed in *Registro oficial de la República Argentina*, I, 584, and in *Niles' Register*, XXI (Dec. 15, 1821), 225.

[56] Forbes to De Luca, May 15, 1821, AGN, BA, S1-A2-A4-núm. 8; De Luca to Forbes, May 16, 1821, *Documentos para la historia argentina*, XIV, 20-21.

[57] To Adams, Sept. 2, 1821, Manning, *op. cit.*, I, 581-582.

[58] Forbes to Adams, Nov. 13, 1821, *ibid.*, pp. 596-597, and Feb. 11, 1822, NA, DS, Con. Let., B. A., II.

[59] To Rivadavia, Jan. 22, Oct. 2, 1822, AGN, BA, S1-A2-A4-núm. 8.

[60] Minute of a conference between Forbes and Rivadavia, Sept. 17, 1821, Manning, *op. cit.*, I, 585-587.

election in September, 1820, of Martín Rodríguez as Governor of the Province of Buenos Aires and his appointment in the following July of the able Bernardino Rivadavia and Manuel J. García as ministers. The manifold reforms which these leaders introduced into the life of the province, it was planned, would eventually be extended to the entire country. Thus would be laid the basis for a revivified nation.[61] Furthermore, the Department of State was gratified to learn from Forbes that the United States had been granted full commercial equality and that privateering had been terminated. To add to this general clarification, Lima had fallen to San Martín in September and Spanish power elsewhere in the Hemisphere was collapsing. These multifarious factors, together with the conclusion of the Florida negotiations, the declining aggressiveness of the Quadruple Alliance, and the growth of Anglo-American trade rivalry in Latin America, contributed to the growing realization that recognition need not be delayed much longer.[62]

A harbinger of the action to be taken appeared in Monroe's annual message, when he said:

It is understood that the colonies in South America have had great success during the present year in the struggle for their independence. . . . At Buenos Aires, where civil dissensions had for some time before prevailed, greater harmony and better order appear to have been established. . . . It has long been manifest that it would be impossible for Spain to reduce these colonies by force, and equally so that no conditions short of their independence would be satisfactory to them. . . . To promote this result by friendly counsel with the Government of Spain will be the object of the Government of the United States.[63]

In Buenos Aires both the press and the government received the President's statement with enthusiastic approval.[64]

In the middle of the succeeding February, the Department of State notified Forbes that the House of Representatives had recently called for the correspondence with the Latin American governments and that some of his despatches would be included in the reply. The despatch also stated that the President would probably be authorized to acknowledge independence.[65] In the message which he submitted to the House on March 8, President Monroe reviewed the struggle for independence in Spanish America, described the attitude of the United States toward it,

[61] Antonio Sagarna, "El gobierno de Martín Rodríguez y las reformas de Rivadavia," in Levene, *Historia de la Nación Argentina*, VI, sec. 2, pp. 343-353; Levene, *A History of Argentina*, pp. 359-369.

[62] Griffin, *op. cit.*, pp. 284-285.

[63] Richardson, *op. cit.*, II, 105.

[64] *El Argos de Buenos Aires*, Jan. 19, 1822; H. Mabragaña, *Los mensajes*, I, 189.

[65] Daniel Brent, Chief Clerk, to Forbes, Feb. 19, 1822, Manning, *op. cit.*, I, 145; *Annals of Cong.*, 17 Cong., 1 sess., I, 825.

and recommended the recognition of independence.[66] Within the next few weeks Congress proceeded with the formalities necessary to implement the recommendations; the bill was signed on May 4.[67] The United States had declared its intention to recognize the government at Buenos Aires; there remained the task of making the new relationship operative.

The government and people of Argentina received the news with genuine rejoicing, for the United States was the first non-Latin nation to grant the long-anticipated recognition.[68] Following years of assiduous effort, it was natural that realization should be heartening. When on May 23 Forbes transmitted copies of the President's message and the accompanying documents, Foreign Minister Rivadavia expressed his great satisfaction.[69] The birthday of the Argentine nation—May 25th—was set apart for a joint celebration of independence and recognition. Forbes was the guest of honor on several occasions, including a dinner at which he heard glowing eulogies of President Monroe, his government, and the American people. Rivadavia spoke for half an hour on the moral influence of the United States in world affairs, an influence exceeded by none.[70]

A Minister Is Sent to Buenos Aires

Following signature of the recognition bill, the administration delayed many months in making it effective for Argentina. Reasons for the delay are obscure, though, of course, during most of the time the Senate was not in session to approve appointments. Even in November, when the Cabinet took up the matter of procedure, there was doubt as to the principles to be established. Should the United States first send its representatives to the new states, or should they be allowed to take the initiative? Adams favored the latter course; the rest of the Cabinet was divided; the President was indecisive. There the matter rested.[71]

Inaction in Washington led to speculation in Buenos Aires, where the news of recognition had been received with such exultation. Forbes, lacking instructions, could only conjecture: the delay might have been

---

[66] Richardson, *op. cit.*, II, 116-118. For the complete report, see *American State Papers, Foreign Relations*, IV, 818-851. Adams' message, together with many of the pertinent documents, was printed in República Argentina, *Tratados, convenciones, protocoles, actos y acuerdos internacionales*, VIII, 135-142.

[67] The record of congressional proceedings is in *Annals of Cong.*, 17 Cong., 1 sess., II, 1314, 1320, 1382-1404.

[68] *Registro oficial de la República Argentina*, pp. 569-570.

[69] Mabragaña, *op. cit.*, I, 193; Rivadavia to Forbes, May 23, 1822, *Documentos para la historia argentina*, XIV, 100-101.

[70] Forbes to Adams, July 10, 1822, Manning, *op. cit.*, I, 604-606; Alexander Caldcleugh, *Travels in South America, during the Years 1819-20-21*, I, 219.

[71] Adams, *Memoirs*, V, 492; VI, 110-111. Earlier, Adams had considered Henry Clay for the post (*ibid.*, V, 495-496).

caused by the recess of the Senate or by the intention to await overtures from Buenos Aires.[72] Not until January, 1823, did President Monroe decide to appoint as minister Caesar A. Rodney, who five years earlier had been a member of the South American commission.[73] He was accredited to the "Government of Buenos Aires," which at that time was conducting foreign relations for the United Provinces.[74] Even yet the process of recognition was incomplete, for another year passed before Rodney was officially presented.

Adams prepared detailed instructions for Rodney.[75] First, he reviewed the general policy of the United States toward independence and described the internal and international status of Argentina. The Secretary then instructed the Minister (1) to promote the adoption of a constitution guaranteeing equal rights to the people, (2) to maintain strenuously the right of the United States to receive most-favored-nation treatment and to negotiate a treaty only on that basis, (3) to remonstrate against certain clauses of the privateering ordinances, should they be renewed, and (4) to explain the efforts of the United States and other maritime nations to suppress the African slave trade.[76] Adams' closing paragraph reminded Rodney that he should

> consider all these instructions rather as advisory than as of positive injunction. Our intercourse with Buenos Ayres, as with all the other new Nations of this Hemisphere, is of recent origin; formed while their own condition has been altogether Revolutionary, and continually changing its aspect. Our information concerning them is imperfect, and among the most important objects of your Mission will be that of adding to its stores; of exploring the untrodden ground, and of collecting and transmitting to us the knowledge by which the friendly relations between the two *Countries* may be extended and harmonized to promote the welfare of both, with due regard to the Peace and good will of the whole family of civilized man. It is highly important that the first foundations of the permanent future intercourse between the two countries should be laid in principles benevolent and liberal in themselves, congenial to the spirit of our Institutions, and consistent with the duties of universal philanthropy.[77]

[72] Forbes to Adams, July 18, Oct. 16, 1822, March 2, 1823, Manning, *op. cit.*, I, 608, 615-616, 618-619.

[73] Adams, *Memoirs*, VI, 121, 122, 127-128.

[74] John Bassett Moore, *A Digest of International Law* . . . , I, 90-91. At the same time, Forbes was designated Secretary of Legation.

[75] May 17, 1823, NA, DS, Inst. Min., IX, 250-265. Extensive portions are printed in Manning, *op. cit.*, I, 186-192.

[76] Manning, *op. cit.*, I, 187-188, 191; NA, DS, Inst. Min., IX, 264.

[77] May 17, 1823, NA, DS, Inst. Min. IX, 264-265. Rodney received unofficial advice for his mission from J. R. Poinsett and Condy Raguet, American Chargé in Rio de Janeiro. Still apprehensive of factious intrigues and of British influence in Buenos Aires, Poinsett warned the Minister to be distrustful (Poinsett to Rodney, April 23, 1823; Raguet to Rodney, Jan. 26, March 20, May 15, 1824, HSP, Gratz Collection, Case 2, Box 20; Case 6, Box 9).

Accompanied by his family, Rodney left the United States in June, but because of stops in Rio de Janeiro and elsewhere did not reach Buenos Aires until the middle of November. His illness then prevented his presentation to the government until December 27.[78] Reporting the unenthusiastic public reception and the perfunctory official greetings, Forbes explained that "Mr. Rivadavia says his prayers, makes all his vows to Europe." [79]

The lingering illness which Rodney contracted en route prevented his full assumption of the responsibilities of office. Scarcely a report from him appears in the official correspondence. In May he was able to participate in a huge banquet commemorating Argentine independence, at which he and Sir Woodbine Parish, British representative, were guests of honor.[80] Two weeks later Rodney died; Rivadavia delivered the funeral oration.[81]

A Minister Is Sent to Washington

The first indication of an Argentine response to the congressional action came not from Buenos Aires but from New Haven. From his retirement there, David C. DeForest, to whom Adams had refused an exequatur as consul general four years before, renewed his application and even asked for reception as chargé d'affaires. Authority for his request, the Connecticut gentleman said, rested upon his former commission. As before, the Secretary denied the claim, this time because the certificate had been issued under an unauthorized treaty by a government which no longer existed. Moreover, the President thought it improper to recognize as chargé a native citizen of the United States living in his homeland.[82]

In Buenos Aires, however, action was less swift. It was not until after the arrival of Rodney that the government selected as its first minister

[78] Forbes to Adams, Nov. 5, 19, 1823, Jan. 3, 1824, NA, DS, Con. Let., B. A., II; *Registro oficial de la República Argentina*, II, 46.

[79] Forbes to Adams, Jan. 3, 1824, Manning, *op. cit.*, I, 631. See also unprinted portion in NA, DS, Con. Let., B. A., II.

[80] Nina Louisa Kay-Shuttleworth, *A Life of Sir Woodbine Parish*, p. 280. Both Rodney and Parish were called upon for toasts, but "Parish won the hearts of all the audience by making his speech in Spanish. . . ."

[81] Antonio Zinny, *La Gaceta Mercantil de Buenos Aires*, I, 12. Details of Rodney's funeral are described in a pamphlet, *Summary of the Public Exercises at the Interment of the Honorable Caesar A. Rodney.*

[82] Adams to DeForest, May 23, 1822, Manning, *op. cit.*, I, 159-160; Adams, *Memoirs*, V, 492. Rivadavia revoked DeForest's commission on March 13, 1823 (*Documentos para la historia argentina*, XIV, 458-460) and instructed Carlos de Alvear to tell DeForest to cease his functions and transmit his records (Alvear to Rivadavia, March 5, 1824, AGN, BA, S1-A2-A4-núm. 10). Among the papers which he returned were 432 commissions and blank patents for "armas veinte goletas, veinte bergantines, seis corbetas y dos fragatas" (Alvear to Rivadavia, Sept. 26, 1824, *ibid.*).

to Washington the veteran military and political leader, Carlos María de Alvear.[83] Like San Martín, Alvear as a youth had received his military education in Spain and with him had returned to Argentina in 1812. He had twice risen to high office, once as Commander in Chief of the Army and once as Supreme Director.[84]

Although Governor Rodríguez officially notified President Monroe of the appointment in January, 1824,[85] credentials and Rivadavia's instructions were not ready until February 26. On his stopover in England en route to the United States, Alvear was to confer with the representatives of foreign governments, especially of the new American states. In Washington, he was to tell the President of the *"distinguida demostración"* with which the announcement of recognition had been greeted. He was especially importuned to encourage the government and people of the United States to formulate the best possible opinion of the political principles of his government and to supply his superiors with precise information regarding influential men, their political affiliation, and their sources of strength. The Minister was directed to secure information on the exact intentions of the United States toward the young American nations and to indicate his government's approval of the principle laid down by Monroe in his message of December 2, 1823 —the noncolonization of American territory by European powers. Most significant of all his assignments, perhaps, was that which bade him enunciate a new principle, namely that no American state should change by force the limits fixed at the time of independence.[86] In national self-interest, Rivadavia was perhaps hoping to halt Brazil's further territorial aggrandizement in the Banda Oriental, but nevertheless he must be given credit for pronouncing a far-seeing principle. His project antedated by a century the essence of the Pact of Paris and the Stimson Doctrine.

In England Alvear spent two busy months. He sent to his government reports on the activities of Iturbide, the Mexican Agustín I in exile, on the possibility of British loans, and on the attitude of European powers toward independence. He held conferences with the representa-

[83] *Registro oficial de la República Argentina,* II, 48. On the appointments, see Rivadavia to Minister of Treasury, Dec. 30, 1823; Alvear to Rivadavia, Jan. 1, 1824; Tomás de Iriarte to Rivadavia, Jan. 2, 1824, AGN, BA, S1-A2-A4-núm. 10. Iriarte, a lieutenant colonel of artillery, was made secretary of legation. In his memoirs, Iriarte has recorded at some length his reactions to the United States, its leaders, and its people (*Memorias: Rivadavia, Monroe y la guerra argentino-brasilena,* III, 140-187).

[84] Levene, *A History of Argentina,* p. 279.

[85] Rodríguez and Rivadavia to Monroe, Jan. 5, 1824, *Documentos para la historia argentina,* XIV, 419-420.

[86] Rivadavia's instructions to Alvear, Feb. 26, 1824, *ibid.,* pp. 453-458. Some of Alvear's instructions may have been transmitted verbally (see Mabragaña, *op. cit.,* I, 201-202).

tives of Brazil, Peru, Colombia, and Mexico, and even with George Canning himself. For the Foreign Secretary he carefully prepared written answers to his many enquiries, including a pointed one on whether the United States had recognized Buenos Aires or all the provinces.[87] About the middle of September, Alvear arrived in New York, just in time to witness the enthusiastic reception given the Marquis de Lafayette, with whom he arranged an interview. While still in New York, he despatched to the Mexican government a proposal to establish Argentine-Mexican diplomatic relations by agreement of their agents in the United States.[88]

Moving on to Philadelphia, where he conferred with the new Colombian Minister,[89] then to Washington, he met Secretary Adams on October 9 and President Monroe two days later. His first interview with the President was brief, marked by the usual formalities. "By the letters which I have the honor to present," said the Minister,

His Excellency the President will be more fully informed of the solicitude and sincere desires which my government feels for intimate union with that of the United States. These arise from the sympathy which naturally exists in all the great American family, produced by a similarity of circumstances and vicissitudes in the glorious course of their emancipation; which, illuminated by the radiant beams spread from the capitol, has established its governments upon the majestic principle of the sovereignty of the people.[90]

Alvear's two-hour conference with Monroe on October 14 provided at the Washington end of the orbit a most auspicious inaugural of formal Argentine-American diplomatic relations. In response to his searching questions, the Minister found the President expansive and completely frank. In a wide-ranging discussion of Hemisphere relations with Europe, Monroe revealed, if the Minister's report is taken at face value, deliberations which he had confided to no other person and of which he has left no other record. Alvear was deeply impressed by the President's frankness, his profound wisdom in the management of public affairs, and his regard for the nascent American states. He wrote Rivadavia that he had experienced "the most agreeable moments" of his life.[91]

The General's confidential report of his satisfying interview is a document of singular significance, both in the evolution of Argentine-American

[87] Alvear to Rivadavia, London, June 15, 29, July 19, 20, 26, 1824, AGN, BA, S1-A2-A4-núm. 10.

[88] Alvear to Rivadavia, New York, Sept. 15, 26, 1824, *ibid.*

[89] Alvear to Rivadavia, Philadelphia, Sept. 30, 1824, *ibid.*

[90] Alvear to Rivadavia, Washington, Oct. 11, 1824, *ibid.*

[91] Alvear to Rivadavia, Washington, Oct. 18, 1824, *ibid.* A skilled analysis of Alvear's conferences with Monroe is found in Thomas B. Davis, Jr., *Carlos de Alvear, Man of Revolution*, pp. 35-50.

relations and in the reanalysis of Monroe's policies toward Latin America.[92] The President asserted that fear of a French expedition to South America had motivated his declaration of 1823 and that before making it he had exacted from the British government a frank statement of its probable course of action should any nation other than Spain undertake reconquest of the new states. Monroe interpreted his proposal to protect the cause of the former colonies as an unequivocal commitment, supported by active rearmament and readiness to use force.[93] As to his long refusal to abandon neutrality, the President declared that active American participation, by precipitating European intervention, might have produced a general war.

To Alvear's inquiry about the attitude of European powers toward independence, Monroe revealed his most recent estimates of Russian, British, and French intentions. Under the Minister's urging, he acknowledged his distrust of monarchies in the New World and his conviction that republican governments must assert themselves. He confessed his desire for republican institutions even in Brazil.

Alvear's report of this conference provided his government with broad intelligence on affairs of the greatest moment to both republics. But great as was his success to this point, the Minister had yet another triumph to record. When, a few days later, he asked Adams if the United States would accept an invitation to mediate in the Argentine-Brazilian dispute over the Banda Oriental, the Secretary "replied favorably, affirming that the Washington government would offer with pleasure to appear as mediator. . . ."[94]

With this happy fulfillment of his important objectives, Alvear was reluctant "to leave so soon a land in which he has received from the most distinguished residents the sincerest demonstration of respect and affection."[95] Returning to New York, the Minister soon received the second modification of his original orders to proceed to Mexico from the United States. First, he had been instructed to return directly to Buenos Aires; now, he was directed to go to Colombia as minister plenipotentiary. This mission, however, did not appeal to Alvear, who

[92] Minute of conference between Alvear and President Monroe, Oct. 14, 1824, AGN, BA, S1-A2-A4-núm. 10. My notes indicate that this statement was sent as an enclosure to Alvear's despatch of October 18, but Whitaker thinks it was transmitted with the report of January 1, 1825 (*The United States and Latin America*, p. 502, note 15). The report is printed in Davis, *op. cit.*, pp. 218-225, and, with some editing, in Carlos Correa Luna, *Alvear y la diplomacia de 1824-1825 en Inglaterra, Estados Unidos y Alto Perú*, pp. 43-56.

[93] The President's statement that American coasts were being fortified and the Navy increased was misleading.

[94] Alvear to Rivadavia, Oct. 19, 1824, enclosure in despatch of Jan. 1, 1825, New York, AGN, BA, S1-A2-A4-núm. 10. Neither as Secretary of State nor as President did Adams seek to implement his promise (see below, p. 91).

[95] Alvear to Rivadavia, Oct. 18, 1824, *ibid.*

found abundant reasons for refusing.[96] Instead, he departed in January, again by way of London, for his homeland, where a new government promptly sent him to confer with Simón Bolívar and José de Sucre in the new Republic of Bolivia.[97]

Thus, after more than a decade of investigation, neutrality, and non-recognition on the part of the United States and repeated requests by the United Provinces for material aid and recognition, the two states formally established diplomatic intercourse. They exchanged civilities and accredited ministers. Unfortunately, the residences of Rodney and Alvear on their respective missions were short, and they were able to make only the barest of official contacts. Neither remained long enough to consolidate the interests of his country with the government of the other. And, what was even more unfortunate, Argentina would have no minister in Washington for fourteen years and the United States would send no diplomatic officer to Buenos Aires until 1844, no minister until 1854.

[96] Rivadavia to Alvear, April 25, 1824, *Documentos para la historia argentina,* XIV, 512-513; García to Alvear, Sept. 22, 1824, and Alvear to Rivadavia, Jan. 1, 1825, New York, AGN, BA, S1-A2-A4-núm. 10.

[97] Alvear to García, April 9, 1825, Buenos Aires, AGN, BA, S1-A2-A4-núm. 10. The appointment papers are numbers 15 and 16, June 10, 1825, AGN, BA, Donación Alvear. Documentos diplomáticos del General Alvear, S1-A1-A1-núm. 5.

VII

PROTECTION OF AMERICAN INTERESTS: VEXATIONS OF A DIPLOMAT, 1823-1831

John M. Forbes, of the gouty foot, the extraordinary memory, and the intense Anglophobia, was the pivot of Argentine-American relations in the twenties. From 1820 to 1831, except for the brief missions of Rodney and Alvear, the New Englander was the sole official contact between Washington and Buenos Aires. First as agent for commerce and seamen, then as secretary of legation, and finally, after Rodney's death, as chargé d'affaires,[1] through his energy and suspicion he placed the stamp of his individuality upon the execution of policy. During the first year of his mission, he obtained a decree abolishing the evils of privateering, secured for North American seamen exemption from enforced military service, and gained safeguards for his country's shipping. In the culminating phase of the process of recognition, he was the intermediary between his government and that at Buenos Aires.[2] After 1824, while the Argentines struggled to consolidate their position as an independent nation, his was the task of harmonizing his country's interests with those of the newly recognized republic.[3]

In spite of recognition and thirteen years of self-government, the Argentine people did not soon attain the national unity for which Monroe and Adams had hoped. From 1820 to 1826 the provincial governors of Buenos Aires assumed direction of both foreign policy and internal administration. Even under the presidency of the respected

---

[1] Forbes was officially recognized as chargé d'affaires on August 26, 1825 (*Registro oficial de la República Argentina*, II, 86). See also Charles Francis Adams (ed.), *Memoirs of John Quincy Adams*, VI, 520. His commission as chargé, Clay to Minister of Foreign Relations, April 14, 1825, together with other Forbes correspondence, is filed in AGN, BA, Estados Unidos, Ministro Plenipotenciario en Buenos Aires D. Juan M. Forbes, 1824 a 1831, S1-A2-A4-núm. 11. Wherever possible, however, I have cited a printed English source.

[2] See above, pp. 69-73.

[3] Watt Stewart has written a sympathetic account of John Forbes in "The Diplomatic Service of John M. Forbes at Buenos Aires," *The Hispanic American Historical Review*, XIV (May, 1934), 202-218.

Bernardino Rivadavia, a new attempt in February, 1826, to unify the nation endured little more than a year. In August, 1827, the interior provinces again defaulted control of national affairs to the Province of Buenos Aires. Through a generation of inter-provincial conflict and harsh dictatorship this political anomaly endured until 1852. War with Brazil from 1825 to 1828 over conflicting claims to the Banda Oriental only sapped national strength and contributed to the perpetuation of internal instability.

Moreover, to add to Forbes's discomfiture, the British by treaty, trade, and pounds sterling were inexorably drawing the Argentines into their orbit. His mounting suspicion of Britain's aims and tactics contributed to the intensification of Anglo-American rivalry. Yet, with all the vicissitudes of carrying on diplomacy in a youthful, turbulent country, Forbes's eleven-year mission was not without its moments of success.

The Monroe Doctrine and the United Provinces

During the brief period of Caesar Rodney's incumbency as minister (December, 1823—May, 1824), John Forbes transacted most legation business. His most important assignment during these months was the transmittal of Monroe's annual message of December, 1823. For the provinces of La Plata, the President framed his principle of nonintervention at a particularly critical time. Confronted by the lack of national government and the growing instability of the Rodríguez administration, the Argentine people, like Forbes, were experiencing intense disquiet over the menace of the Quadruple Alliance.[4] They received Monroe's pronouncement, therefore, with considerable enthusiasm.[5]

As early as February 9, 1824, a porteño newspaper, *La Gaceta Mercantil*, reported the message.[6] It soon reached a wider audience through the columns of *El Avisador Mercantil* and *El Argos de Buenos Aires*, which stressed the import of the noncolonization and nonintervention principles.[7] Rodney mirrored the early reaction of the people, as well

[4] Forbes to Adams, Jan. 24, Feb. 12, 1824, William R. Manning (ed.), *Diplomatic Correspondence of the United States Concerning Independence of the Latin-American Countries*, I, 632, 634. On French policy before and after December, 1823, see William Spence Robertson, *France and Latin-American Independence*, pp. 253-343.

[5] In a personal letter to President Monroe, March 22, 1824, Forbes reported that the message had "produced an electrical effect on the Republican Party, . . . but was received with an unwelcome apathy by the men in power, . . ." (LC, MD, Papers of Monroe). For fuller accounts of Argentine reaction to the Monroe Doctrine, see Watt Stewart, "Argentina and the Monroe Doctrine, 1824-1828," *The Hispanic American Historical Review*, X (Feb., 1930), 26-32, and William Spence Robertson, "South America and the Monroe Doctrine, 1824-1828," *Political Science Quarterly*, XXX (March, 1915), 97-104.

[6] I, 12.

[7] Cited in Norberto Piñero, *La política internacional argentina*, p. 69, and Dexter Perkins, *The Monroe Doctrine, 1823-1826*, p. 159.

as his own enthusiasm, when he reported that "this masterly State Paper, [which] has inspired us here, . . . will have a most extensive influence." [8] He and Forbes promptly arranged for the distribution of Spanish translations in Argentina, Peru, and Chile.[9] Three months later, though his initial enthusiasm had somewhat abated, Rodney thought the message had already produced good effects and would have permanent influence.[10]

Public officials repeatedly emphasized the significance of the message. Foreign Minister Rivadavia sent translations to the governments of Chile, Peru, and Colombia.[11] When preparing the first legation to the United States, he directed Alvear's attention to Monroe's statements and even suggested extension to cover inter-American aggression.[12] Alluding to these instructions before the Legislative Assembly of Buenos Aires on May 3, he reiterated adherence to the principle of nonaggression.[13] When Juan Gregorio de las Heras succeeded Rodríguez as governor of Buenos Aires, he expressed his obligation to the nation which had "constituted itself guardian of the field of battle in order that no foreign power may interfere to give aid to our rival." [14]

Administrative changes in the United States in 1825 and in Buenos Aires in 1826 brought new expressions of adherence. Shortly after Adams' inauguration, Secretary of State Henry Clay instructed Forbes to "urge upon the Government of Buenos Ayres, the utility and expediency of asserting the same principles on all proper occasions." [15] When on the occasion of his presentation as chargé d'affaires Forbes promptly complied, Governor Las Heras reaffirmed his support of Monroe's principles.[16]

Shortly after the reunion of Buenos Aires and the other provinces in 1826 and the subsequent selection of Rivadavia as first President of the "Argentine nation," [17] the possibility of invoking these principles arose. The attempt to form a new national government under a new constitution almost coincided with the opening of the war with Brazil.[18] A conference between President Rivadavia and Forbes on August 17 went to the very core of Argentine-American relations at the time. Apprehensive

[8] To Monroe, Feb. 10, 1824, S. M. Hamilton (ed.), *Writings of James Monroe,* VI, 430.
[9] Forbes to Monroe, March 22, 1824, LC, MD, Papers of Monroe; Rodney to Adams, May 22, 1824, NA, DS, Desp. Arg., II.
[10] Rodney to Adams, *ibid.*
[11] *Documentos para la historia argentina,* XIV, 448.
[12] See above, p. 76.
[13] H. Mabragaña, *Los mensajes,* I, 201-202.
[14] *Ibid.,* I, 211. Cf. Stewart, *op. cit.,* p. 27, and Robertson, *op. cit.,* p. 100.
[15] April 14, 1825, Manning, *op. cit.,* I, 235-236.
[16] Forbes to Clay, Sept. 18, 1825, NA, DS, Desp. Arg., II. The speeches of Forbes and Las Heras were printed in *El Argos de Buenos Aires.*
[17] *Registro oficial de la República Argentina,* II, 111-112, 114.
[18] On the origins of the war, see below, pp. 88-89.

of the close ties existing between Brazil and European powers, the new executive suggested that President Adams might desire to resist European influence in South America.[19] Almost immediately Francisco de la Cruz, Rivadavia's Foreign Minister, questioned Forbes on the scope of Monroe's ideas. Was it applicable, he wished the chargé to enquire of his government, in case a European power assisted the Emperor of Brazil to maintain war against the United Provinces, or in case the Emperor sought aid from the Kingdom of Portugal or any part of its dominions to sustain the war? [20]

The nonappearance of a new Argentine representative in Washington and tardy communication between the two countries delayed Clay's reply nearly two years.[21] Not until July, 1828, was Forbes prepared to transmit the interpretation of the Monroe "doctrine" to José Rondeau, Minister for Foreign Relations ad interim.[22] Clay contended that President Monroe had directed his message expressly at European intervention and that it gave no foreign nation the right to demand its application, a power which Congress alone might exercise. As to the war between Argentina and Brazil, Clay wrote that

the President has seen it with great regret, and would be very glad to hear of its honorable conclusion. But that war cannot be conceived as presenting a state of things bearing the remotest analogy to the case which President Monroe's message deprecates. It is a war strictly American in its origin and its object. It is a war in which the Allies of Europe have taken no part. Even if Portugal and the Brazils had remained united, and the war had been carried on by their joint arms, against the Argentine Republic, that would have been far from presenting the case which the message contemplated. . . .

The general policy of the United States is that of strict and impartial neutrality in reference to all wars of other Powers. It would be only in an extreme case that they would deviate from the policy. Such a case is not presented by the present war.[23]

Although unsuccessful, Argentina's initial effort to invoke application of Monroe's principles disclosed mutually unexpected national points of view. Rivadavia's government revealed not only its approval of the ideas but also its willingness to accept the patronage of the United States for

[19] Forbes's memorandum of conference with Rivadavia, Aug. 17, 1826, and Forbes to Clay, Sept. 5, 1826, NA, DS, Desp. Arg., III.

[20] De la Cruz to Forbes, Aug. 24, 1826, enclosure in Forbes to Clay, Sept. 5, 1826, NA, DS, Desp. Arg., III. On these negotiations, see Perkins, *op. cit.*, pp. 37-39, and Robertson, *op. cit.*, p. 120.

[21] In April, 1826, Manuel Moreno was invited to go to the United States as chargé d'affaires but refused because of ill health (Moreno to De la Cruz, April 20, May 22, 1826, AGN, BA, S1-A2-A4-núm. 9).

[22] July 9, 1828, *ibid.*, núm. 11.

[23] To Forbes, Jan. 3, 1828, Manning, *op. cit.*, I, 293.

the protection of national interests.[24] On the other hand, the Adams administration set the tone for future interpretation of the original statement: it would not pertain to wars among the American states, and it could not be invoked by a Latin American nation.

Anglo-American Commercial Rivalry

During the decade of John Forbes's official residence in Buenos Aires, perhaps no phase of Argentine development perplexed him so much as the growth of British influence.[25] His correspondence from 1820 to 1831 abounds with illustrations of his jealousy, even antipathy, toward the English in the Río de la Plata. Although it was imperative that he observe and report the activities of the British, the impulsive Chargé unwisely revealed his suspicion to Argentine leaders, as well as to English residents,[26] and permitted it to embarrass the objectives of his own country. The Anglo-American rivalry which he heedlessly promoted was particularly obtrusive in commercial relations.

Although since 1800 the trade of the United States with the Río de la Plata had grown appreciably, by the middle twenties it had reached barely a million dollars.[27] The first North American vessels reached Montevideo and Buenos Aires as early as 1798-1799. From that time until 1810 shipping contacts were frequent, though the total volume of trade remained small.[28] After the revolution of May, total United States commerce with Buenos Aires was only one-third that of Great Britain and less even than that of Brazil or Chile.[29] During the first years of Argentine independence, when trade might normally have increased, the War of 1812 virtually shut off North American contacts with southern South America.

The Río de la Plata did not become a regular market for American merchants until after 1815, when the opportunity of selling arms and ammunition opened the way. Soon other commodities from the United States—cotton and woolen goods, hats, boots and shoes, saddlery, furni-

[24] Cf. Robertson, *op. cit.*, p. 105.

[25] For elaboration of this theme, see J. Fred Rippy, *Rivalry of the United States and Great Britain over Latin America, 1808-1830*, pp. 137-149, and Edwin J. Pratt, "Anglo-American Commercial and Political Rivalry on the Plata, 1820-1830," *The Hispanic American Historical Review*, XI (Aug., 1931), 302-335.

[26] Sir Woodbine Parish to Joseph Planta, Feb. 18, 1925, C. K. Webster, *Britain and the Independence of Latin America*, I, 120.

[27] Treasury Department, *American Commerce: Commerce of South America, Central America, Mexico, and West Indies, with Share of the United States and Other Leading Nations Therein, 1821-1898*, p. 3300.

[28] Charles Lyon Chandler has written extensively of these early commercial contacts in *Inter-American Acquaintances*, pp. 23-66 *passim*, and in the several articles listed in my bibliography. Also see Harry Bernstein, *Origins of Inter-American Interest, 1700-1812*, pp. 33-51 *passim*.

[29] LC, MD, South American Pamphlets, B, p. 93.

ture, carriages, naval stores, lumber, flour, fish, and salt provisions—
began to supply markets in the United Provinces and the entire valley
of the Río de la Plata.[30] Nevertheless, this growth was less rapid than
that of the British, whose trade with the River Plate countries, like
that with the rest of South America, had grown steadily since 1800. By
1825 the United States was exporting to Buenos Aires considerably less
than one-fourth the volume of its rival.[31] Moreover, there were far more
British than North American residents, merchants, and shopkeepers
in Buenos Aires.[32]

Throughout the period of Forbes's residence, British trade, British
products, and British prestige were supreme in the Río de la Plata.
Public officials admired England; the people greeted Sir Woodbine
Parish, first British consul to La Plata, with much greater warmth than
Rodney. Awareness of these facts aroused in Forbes both suspicion and
embitterment. He complained to his government that the English
treated him with "deadly hostility and violent opposition" and that
Britain derived from the country all the advantages of colonial dependence. Scarcely a ranking Argentine leader, he wrote, was not
subservient to British influence.[33]

The arrival of Parish as British consul early in 1824 and the departure
of Rivadavia for England in July disturbed Forbes's equanimity.[34] The
grant of a British loan and the increased activity of British merchants
added to his restlessness.[35] But it was rumors of early recognition and
the conclusion of a commercial treaty that caused him greatest uneasiness. By December it was widely known that British recognition—in
the form of a commercial treaty—was imminent.[36]

Forbes chose this moment to protest to Manuel José García, Rivadavia's
successor as Minister of Foreign Relations, and to reaffirm the position
of his government in matters of commercial privilege. The United

[30] "Report on the American Trade in the River Plate by John C. Zimmermann,"
United States Consul, Dec. 31, 1820, NA, DS, Con. Let., B. A., I, pt. 2. During
the years 1818-1820, Zimmermann reported, about two-thirds of American trade with
the Río de la Plata moved through the port of Montevideo, the balance with
Buenos Aires.

[31] Sir Woodbine Parish, *Buenos Ayres and the Provinces of the Río de la Plata*,
p. 361. For a comprehensive analysis of the foreign trade of Buenos Aires in the
twenties, see R. A. Humphreys, *British Consular Reports on the Trade and Politics
of Latin America, 1824-1826*, pp. 28-62.

[32] *A Five Years' Residence in Buenos Ayres during the Years 1820 to 1825*,
pp. 33-35, 37, 49; Rodney to Adams, May 22, 1824, NA, DS, Desp. Arg., II.

[33] See, for example, Forbes to Daniel Brent, July 28, 1822, and to Adams, Jan. 3,
1823, Aug. 13, Nov. 25, 1824, NA, DS, Con. Let., B. A., II; to Monroe, March 22,
1824, LC, MD, Papers of Monroe.

[34] Forbes to Adams, July 5, 1824, Manning, *op. cit.*, I, 638.

[35] Forbes to Adams, Aug. 21, 1822, *ibid.*, I, 610, and Nov. 25, 1824, NA, DS,
Desp. Arg., II.

[36] Forbes to Adams, Dec. 17, 1824, and Rush to Adams, Dec. 30, 1824, Manning,
op. cit., I, 644; III, 1527-1528.

States had originated the liberal system of commercial reciprocity, he said, and consequently should have a fair claim to its advantages. The United States had been open and frank with Argentina on this subject and, while it asked no special concessions, it did expect to be treated as well as the most friendly nation.[37]

Forbes's protests did not impede Parish's negotiations for a treaty of amity and commerce. Signed on February 2, 1825, the pact was soon ratified in Buenos Aires.[38] Forbes's great irritation at British recognition was not shared at home, where Clay and, indeed the nation, saw no cause for alarm.[39]

Argentine ratification of the treaty stimulated Forbes to renew his protests. When García informed the agent that the United Provinces would have concluded a treaty with the United States had it opened negotiations, Forbes explained that his government expected Buenos Aires to initiate them.[40] Later, in a note to the Minister, he became so bold as to

> demand in the name of the United States that every political religious commercial right or privilege conceded to the subjects of His Britannic Majesty by that treaty should simultaneously and ipso facto, be enjoyed by the citizens of the United States of America, with the sole condition that similar reciprocal engagements to those made on the part of His Britannic Majesty shall be agreed and consented to by the United States.[41]

The United Provinces would arrange a treaty with the United States, García replied, on precisely the same basis as that with Great Britain.[42]

Two years before, Secretary Adams had instructed Rodney to conclude a commercial treaty only on the basis of the most favored nation.[43] Clay's instructions to Forbes in April, 1825, veered somewhat from that position. He authorized the Chargé to bring about reciprocal commercial relations either by convention or, preferably, by mutual regulations.[44] In accordance with these instructions, Forbes pressed the Foreign Minister to secure legislation that would bring about perfect reciprocity. To

[37] Forbes to García, Dec. 6, 1824, Manning, *op. cit.,* I, 642-643.

[38] The text of the treaty is published in República Argentina, *Tratados, convenciones, protocolos, actos y acuerdos internacionales,* III, 278-288. On the negotiations, see Emilio Ravignani, *Historia constitucional de la República Argentina,* II, 296-299.

[39] Henry Addington, British Minister to the United States, to George Canning, April 1, 1825, LC, MD, Photostats, F. O. 5, Vol. 197, Folio II.

[40] Forbes to Adams, March 26, 1825, and enclosure, NA, DS, Desp. Arg., II. Cf. below, p. 87, note 47.

[41] Forbes to Adams, March 30, 1825, and enclosures, NA, DS, Desp. Arg., II.

[42] *Ibid.*

[43] See above, p. 74.

[44] Clay to Forbes, April 14, 1825, NA, DS, Inst. Min., X, 260-261. This was the same note in which Clay had instructed Forbes on the Monroe Doctrine (see above, p. 82). Manning omits a portion of the instructions (*op. cit.,* I, p. 235).

prove that the United States had done its part, he enclosed copies of the Laws of March 3, 1815, and January 7, 1824, under which reciprocal trade had been arranged with half a dozen European states.[45] García preferred a treaty; Forbes held out for mutual legislative declarations.[46] At this juncture, there was no clear reason why he should not have concluded a treaty, one which would have placed the United States upon an equal footing with the British. Forbes, however, did not press this alternative,[47] and the United States waited thirty years for its treaty.[48]

The Flour Tariff Controversy

During the very months that the rumors and reality of British recognition most disturbed him, Forbes became involved in a controversy over a decree which forbade the importation of flour. In the export trade of the United States with Buenos Aires, flour had become a leading commodity, its volume reaching 40,000 barrels in six months of 1823-1824.[49] The size and growth of the trade had aroused the national sensibility of the United Provinces, partly owing, or at least so Forbes thought, to British propaganda. The people were led to believe that their agricultural industry would be paralyzed if action were not taken against the importation of North American flour.[50]

This agitation led to the passage in November, 1824, of a law debarring flour. Forbes remonstrated with public officials, sought an explanation for the inability of domestic flour to compete with that from the United States, and suggested a moderate fixed duty rather than an embargo. These efforts were fruitless.[51] His report of the matter brought an early response from Washington, where the Adams administration had taken office. Clay, surprised and regretful at the action, directed Forbes to remonstrate in conciliatory but firm language.[52]

---

[45] *U.S. Stat. at L.*, III, 224; IV, 2-3.

[46] Forbes to García, Sept. 6, 1825, AGN, BA, S1-A2-A4-núm. 11.

[47] However, in a subsequent note to the Department, Forbes insisted that in 1825 he could have negotiated a treaty on even better terms than the English secured, but that he was never "duly instructed and empowered" (March 25, 1829, BA, DS, Desp., Arg., III). See also Watt Stewart, "United States-Argentine Commercial Negotiations of 1825," *The Hispanic American Historical Review*, XIII (Aug., 1933), 367-371.

[48] See below, p. 149.

[49] Rodney to Adams, May 22, 1824, NA, DS, Desp. Arg., II; *A Five Years' Residence in Buenos Ayres*, pp. 49-50.

[50] Forbes to Adams, Nov. 25, 1824, NA, DS, Desp. Arg., II.

[51] *Ibid.*

[52] April 14, 1825, NA, DS, Inst. Min., X, 263. Because the embargo had reduced the number of Yankee ships reaching Buenos Aires, the Chargé had difficulty in communicating with his government at this time (Forbes to Clay, Sept. 18, 1825, NA, DS, Desp. Arg., II).

Through communications and conferences Forbes prodded the Ministry of Foreign Relations. At one time he presented the protests of local merchants; at another he recalled that most Argentine exports were admitted free to the United States. When he proposed mutual national legislation for the settlement of commercial ills, García expressed his preference for a treaty. When the government proposed to levy a duty on imported flour, Forbes thought the duty too high.[53] There seemed to be no common ground for agreement.

Eventually, however, compromise brought settlement. The new customs law for 1826, passed on November 9, 1825, admitted flour, but with a duty of twenty reales per quintal. Forbes saw two advantages in the modified decree. The duty was fixed. Freedom of deposit and transit was secured.[54] On the other hand, feeling that the government had overlooked several pertinent considerations, the Chargé immediately approached García for explanations. Within what period would the authorities permit re-exportation? The Minister replied that flour might remain on deposit in the port for six months; then repayment of duty or re-exportation were the alternatives. How soon would the new law become effective? When informed that eight months must pass, Forbes protested and gained García's promise to place it in operation on January 1, 1826.[55] By this time, however, the United Provinces had become involved in war with Brazil, whose blockade of the Argentine coast soon greatly reduced foreign trade.

The Argentine-Brazilian War

The war between the United Provinces and Brazil was the nineteenth-century continuation of the long struggle between Spain and Portugal for possession of the Banda Oriental, territory which eventually became modern Uruguay. It was not until 1814 that the Uruguayan patriot and former Spanish army officer, José Artigas, had driven out the last Spanish force. Efforts of Argentine leaders to defeat the intractable Artigas and to incorporate the Banda Oriental into the United Provinces of the Río de la Plata gave the Portuguese an opportunity to reinvest the land. This they accomplished in 1820 after a three-year campaign against the arms of Artigas. In 1822, at the time of Brazilian independence, the province was definitely annexed to the Empire, which retained it during the next three years.

[53] On Forbes's correspondence and conferences with García, see Forbes to Adams, March 30, 1825, and to Clay, Sept. 18, Oct. 15, 1825, and their numerous enclosures, NA, DS, Desp. Arg., II. The extensive Forbes-García correspondence is also preserved in AGN, BA, S1-A2-A4-núm. 11.

[54] Forbes to Clay, Nov. 16, 1825, and enclosures, NA, DS, Desp. Arg., II. A copy of the new law is among the enclosures. Twenty reales was about $3.00 U.S.

[55] Forbes to Clay, Nov. 16, 29, 1825, NA, DS, Desp. Arg., II; to García, Nov. 10, 1825, AGN, BA, S1-A2-A4-núm. 11.

Despite this Brazilian success, the Province of Buenos Aires did not forfeit claim to the Banda Oriental. Several attempts—clandestine, diplomatic, military—to win back the lost area originated on the western banks of La Plata after 1822. None, however, was successful until after the incredible exploits of Juan Antonio Lavalleja and his famous *"treinta y tres."* Although the government at Buenos Aires denied complicity with these insurgents, late in 1825 it profited from their achievements by formally reincorporating the Banda Oriental into the United Provinces.[56]

The Brazilian response to this Argentine act was immediate preparation for war. First it made known its intention to blockade the ports of the United Provinces. Declarations of war followed early in December.[57] On the twenty-first, Rodrigo José Ferreira Lobo, commander of the Brazilian squadron, formally declared the blockade of the ports and coasts of the United Provinces, granting the vessels of neutral nations fourteen days to depart.[58] Early in the following year Buenos Aires authorized privateering against the ships and citizens of Brazil.[59]

Since Brazilian initiative prevailed during most of the war, Forbes's representation of American policy was secondary to that of Condy Raguet, the Chargé of the United States in Rio de Janeiro. Nevertheless, the three years' war gave Forbes many opportunities to represent American interests. His activities included: (1) refusal to invoke the Monroe Doctrine, as interpreted by Henry Clay; (2) declarations against the Brazilian blockade; (3) reluctant rejection of the Argentine request for mediation by the United States; and (4) objections to Argentine privateering and defense of the rights and interests of his fellow nationals.[60]

In a despatch to the Brazilian Minister of Foreign Relations on December 13, 1825, Raguet first stated the attitude of American agents toward the blockade. He held strictly to his nation's traditional doctrine that only an effective blockade was legal. Neutral vessels, he contended, might be stopped only before ports where there were adequate blockading forces and only after they had been specifically warned of the

---

[56] Brief treatments of the origins of the war are to be found in Ricardo Levene, *A History of Argentina*, pp. 379-381, and Lawrence F. Hill, *Diplomatic Relations between the United States and Brazil*, pp. 33-36. On the diplomacy attending the war and its origins, see Vicente G. Quesada, *Historia diplomática latino-americana*, II, 95-150.

[57] Viconde de S. Amaro, Brazilian Minister of Foreign Relations, to Condy Raguet, United States Chargé to Brazil, Dec. 6, 1825, *H. Ex. Doc.*, No. 281, 20 Cong., 1 sess., p. 14; *British and Foreign State Papers*, XIII (1825-1826), 775, 783-784; XVI (1828-1829), 1101.

[58] See the manifesto in NA, DS, Desp. Arg., II, printed in *British and Foreign State Papers*, XIII (1825-1826), 783.

[59] *Registro oficial de la República Argentina*, II, 98.

[60] The first of these activities has been discussed earlier in the present chapter (see above, pp. 82-84).

danger of seizure.[61] At Buenos Aires Forbes issued a similar statement. On February 14 he obtained permission from the Argentine Minister of Foreign Relations to send his protest to the commander of the Brazilian blockading force.[62] The position taken by the two diplomats received support from Captain J. D. Elliott, commander of the United States squadron in the South Atlantic. Like Forbes, he communicated directly with Admiral Lobo.[63] Whatever the tenability of these principles, at least the agents were consistent in their position.

In Washington, the prospect of interference with American commerce disturbed the administration. Throughout the late months of 1825 Forbes had repeatedly asked his government for the despatch of ships of war to the South Atlantic.[64] News of the Brazilian blockade had barely reached the United States when merchants specializing in South American commerce began to shower the Navy Department with requests for adequate protection in the waters of Brazil and Argentina.[65] Though the petitions were immediately sent to Congress, Secretary of the Navy Samuel L. Southard reported that there was not a sufficient number of vessels available for the protection requested.[66]

Despite the inadequacy of the Brazilian blockade and the irregularities of its enforcement, American commerce suffered great injury during 1826-1828.[67] British recognition of the blockade did not strengthen the position of the Washington government,[68] nor did Clay find it easy to adapt his instructions to the vexations of agents on the scene. He could only direct Forbes to maintain the position which he had initiated and to exercise, in any case, sound discretion.[69] By the end of 1826 trade of the United States with the Río de la Plata had fallen to a minimum, and, with Raguet active in Rio de Janeiro, there was little Forbes could do in Buenos Aires.[70]

A third matter to which Forbes gave his attention in the Argentine-Brazilian war was that of mediation. His active and vigorous protests

---

[61] Raguet to Brazilian Minister of Foreign Relations, Dec. 13, 1825, *H. Ex. Doc.*, No. 281, pp. 9-14. For a description of Raguet's activities during the war, see Hill, *op. cit.*, pp. 36-52.

[62] Forbes to De la Cruz and to Lobo, Feb. 13, 1826, NA, DS, Desp. Arg., II, printed in *British and Foreign State Papers*, XIII (1825-1826), 821-824.

[63] April 4, 1826, NA, DS, Desp. Arg., III.

[64] Forbes to Clay, June 27, July 6, Dec. 31, 1825, *ibid.*

[65] See copies of numerous letters from agents of merchants in Boston, Philadelphia, Baltimore, and Washington, Feb.-March, 1826, *American State Papers, Naval Affairs*, II, 638-640.

[66] Southard to Speaker, House of Representatives, March 3, 1826, *ibid.*, p. 638.

[67] Joshua Bond, Consul in Montevideo, to Clay, June 30, 1826, NA, DS, Con. Let., Montevideo I; Treasury Department, *American Commerce*, p. 3300.

[68] *British and Foreign State Papers*, XVI (1828-1829), 1111.

[69] Clay to Forbes, Oct. 23, 1826, NA, DS, Inst. Min., XI, 168-169.

[70] Commodore James Biddle to Southard, Jan. 24, 1827, *H. Ex. Doc.*, No. 281, p. 127.

against the Brazilian blockade had already aroused the indignation of the British, whose interests leaned toward the side of Brazil, the more active sea power. Almost from the beginning of the struggle Forbes was apprehensive of British attempts at mediation.[71] Like Raguet, he feared the possibility of British invasion of the Banda Oriental. On frequent occasions during 1826 he wrote to Washington of Great Britain's overweening ambitions in that province, which, he said, would lead to "nothing short of the erection of a neutral and independent Government in the Banda Oriental, *under the guarantee of England.*" [72] If the British government favored the Brazilian cause during the war, the American Chargé was clearly partial to Argentina.

The determination of the Adams administration to follow a policy of nonintervention and neutrality prevented Forbes from substituting American mediation for that proposed by the British. This policy Clay stoutly affirmed when in January, 1828, he side-stepped Rivadavia's request for an application of the Monroe Doctrine.[73] Six months later, when Foreign Minister Rondeau requested that Forbes ask the United States Chargé in Rio de Janeiro to suggest mediation to the government of Brazil, Forbes echoed the language of Clay's communication.[74] Despite his apparent conviction in this reply, Forbes at once wrote to Clay that he believed American mediation would be successful, especially since antipathy for the British had recently grown up in Brazil.[75] British interposition was well under way, however, and aided the settlement of the war before Forbes's suggestion could be considered.[76]

Privateering was a fourth vexatious problem with which Forbes had to grapple. Although the United Provinces had commissioned them at the beginning of the war, Argentine privateers did not immediately interfere with American shipping. Eventually, however, cruising off Santos, Brazil, in September, 1827, the privateer *El Rayo Argentino* seized the American brig *Ruth*.

Forbes objected to the capture on several occasions. He pointed out that the captain of the privateer had announced the blockade of the

---

[71] Rippy has described Forbes's attitude toward the British mediation (*op. cit.*, pp. 143-149).

[72] Forbes to Clay, June 21, 1826, postscript to June 17, Manning, *op. cit.*, I, 654. Forbes's suspicions of the British were also expressed in other notes to Clay, Aug. 3, Sept. 5, Oct. 5, 1826 (*ibid.*, I, 656-659). On the British attitude toward the creation of an independent nation in the Banda Oriental, see Canning to Lord Ponsonby, British mediator, March 18, 1826, and Ponsonby to Canning, Oct. 2, 1826, Webster, *op. cit.*, I, 143-144, 152-156.

[73] See above, pp. 82-84.

[74] Rondeau to Forbes, July 7, 1826, and Forbes to Rondeau, July 9, 1826, NA, DS, Desp. Arg., III. As a matter of fact, Clay's despatch on the Monroe Doctrine and Forbes's reply to Rondeau must have reached the Ministry simultaneously.

[75] July 12, 1826, postscript to July 9, NA, DS, Desp. Arg., III.

[76] For the principal correspondence on Lord Ponsonby's mission of mediation, see Webster, *op. cit.*, I, 149-163.

entire coast of Brazil and declared his intention of seizing every flour-laden vessel of the United States which attempted to run the blockade. On this complaint Foreign Minister Manuel Moreno promised prompt satisfaction.[77] While the *Ruth* was awaiting trial, the government's confidential instructions to captains of privateers became public, whereupon Forbes sent another remonstrance. Moreno immediately replied that these orders were a revival of those used against Spain during the revolutionary wars, but that the government was reforming the objectional clauses.[78] The revision lessened appreciably the scope of the blockade as hitherto decreed.

The modification of the privateering instructions and the subsequent appointment of a commission to consider the claims of neutral nations and their citizens did not at once remove the evil.[79] Even the end of the Argentine-Brazilian war in September, 1828, did not halt the depredations. On March 10, 1829, Forbes urged the recall of all privateering commissions. Within a week the government formally complied.[80] For the second time in his long residence in Buenos Aires, Forbes had been instrumental in securing the abolition of privateering. By greatly diminishing shipping hazards in the South Atlantic, he had opened the way for the early renewal of American trade with La Plata.[81]

The Question of Claims

During the first years of his long residence in Buenos Aires Forbes had dealt with questions of primary international importance—recognition, the Monroe Doctrine, and mediation. In contrast were the issues which occupied him toward the end of his mission, issues of little importance but great irritation. Such, for example, were the diverse claims which he was instructed or requested to assert. All were claims of private citizens of the United States and, as international finance is reckoned, all were comparatively small. Under normal conditions Forbes

[77] Forbes to Moreno, Oct. 13, 1827, and Moreno to Forbes, Oct. 15, 1827, enclosures in Forbes to Clay, Oct. 30, 1827, NA, DS, Desp. Arg., III.

[78] Forbes to Moreno, Oct. 24, 1827, and Moreno to Forbes, Oct. 25, 1827, enclosures in Forbes to Clay, Oct. 30, 1827, *ibid.* At about this time, Commodore James Biddle, U.S. Navy, ordered the *Boston* to Buenos Aires (Biddle to Rodrigo Pinto Guedes, Brazilian Ambassador, Nov. 11, 1827, *British and Foreign State Papers*, XV [1827-1828], 1120).

[79] *Registro oficial de la República Argentina*, II, 231. The commissioners were Mariano Sarratea, Tomás Anchorena, and Manuel H. Aguirre, special agent to the United States in 1817.

[80] Forbes to José Miguel Díaz Velez, Secretary-General of the Provisional Government, March 10, 1829, AGN, BA, S1-A2-A4-núm. 11. Forbes enclosed a copy of the decree of March 19 in his note of March 11 to the Secretary of State (NA, DS, Desp. Arg., III).

[81] Report of the Secretary of the Navy, Dec. 6, 1830, *Sen. Doc.*, No. 1, 21 Cong., 2 sess., p. 38.

might have adjudicated them with comparative ease, but many factors conspired to frustrate his efforts. The patched-up national unity which had prosecuted the war against Brazil gave way to new interprovincial warfare, and within the capital province itself seditious quarrels rendered administration uncertain. Moreover, the public treasury was depleted and public credit worthless. The refusal of the Adams administration to apply Monroe's principles or to undertake mediation had decreased American prestige. And, finally, the severance of commercial relations during the war had nullified Argentine dependence upon the United States.

Many of the claims which Forbes presented grew out of capture of North American vessels by Argentine privateers during the Brazilian war. The procedure followed in connection with the *Ruth* claim was typical of the evasion which confronted Forbes.[82] The vessel had been captured in September, 1827, and by December the cargo had been condemned by a prize court and turned over to the owners of the privateer. On the ground that the brig and the cargo belonged to the same person and could not justifiably be separated in a court decree, Forbes protested the injustice of the decision. His report of the case to Washington brought from the Secretary of State instructions for firm action. "The capture of that vessel and her cargo," wrote Clay,

is an outrage which requires immediate and full indemnity. It cannot be excused, or justified upon the ground of the pretended secret blockade of the coast of Brazil. It would be a mockery gravely to discuss such a spurious and illegal blockade. The sense of the Buenos Ayrean Government, in regard to it, was manifested by the prompt revocation of it upon your representation. On what pretext a discrimination was made between the cargo and the vessel, we are at a loss to conjecture. The american [*sic*] character of both was incontestible, and does not appear to have been contested. . . . I am charged by the President to instruct you to make an immediate and urgent demand of full satisfaction and indemnity in behalf of the owner of the Ruth and her cargo, for the injury which they have sustained by the capture and detention of the cargo; and to express his expectation that there will be no delay in a compliance with this demand.[83]

In the meantime, after a second court in Buenos Aires had ordered the *Ruth* and its cargo restored to the original owners, the captors had

[82] The story of the *Ruth* claim may be pieced together from Forbes's despatches to the Department of State (to Clay, Dec. 27, 1827, Jan. 16, May 2, Sept. 17, Nov. 5, 1828; to Martin Van Buren, Oct. 15, Nov. 12, 1829, April 9, 1830, NA, DS, Desp. Arg., III, IV) and from his notes to the Ministry of Foreign Relations in Buenos Aires (to Ramón Balcarce, April 2, 1828; to Rondeau, Sept. 3, 1828; to Tomás Guido, Oct. 27, 1828; to Tomás de Anchorena, March 22, 1830, AGN, BA, S1-A2-A4-núm. 11).

[83] March 13, 1828, NA, DS, Inst. Min., XII, 69-70.

appealed the case to the highest tribunal. Pressing for a final decision, Forbes obtained an order in September, 1828, for the liberation of the cargo and the payment of probable damages. The Chargé prepared a detailed statement of damages and expenses, amounting to about $57,000 in Argentine currency. At this juncture the government appointed a commission of three Argentines to liquidate claims against owners of privateers. A year passed, however, without settlement, when a new commission, composed of three natives and two Englishmen, undertook to establish the amounts of the claims. To this body Forbes again presented the claims of the owners of the *Ruth*. By April, 1830, because the two Englishmen refused to consider any but British claims, the commission was obliged to suspend its functions.[84] By such procedure, although Forbes protested at every step of the way, was the payment of damages avoided.

Most of the other claims which Forbes presented antedated the Argentine declaration of independence.[85] Because of the persistent instability of the struggling government, these claims had never received vigorous attention. Now, with the insistence upon the collection of the claims against privateers, the others were revived. In this class were such claims as those of Thomas Lloyd Halsey, William P. White, Captain Silas Atkins, and the owners of the brig *Hope*.[86] Most of these grew, directly or indirectly, out of activities of the revolutionary governments. Most were comparatively small. None of the accounts was settled as a result of the diplomatic pressure of Forbes; several were obliged to wait thirty years for final adjudication; and most were never liquidated.[87]

Forbes and Internal Politics

His continuous residence in Buenos Aires during the vexatious twenties naturally made Forbes a close observer of internal affairs. Constant

[84] Andrew [?] Jamieson and Thomas Duguid, British members of the commission, to Minister of Foreign Relations, March 26, 1830, and Tomás Manuel de Anchorena to president of the commission, March 29, 1830, AGN, BA, S1-A2-A4-núm. 11.

[85] Information upon these claims is most readily available in NA, DS, Claims Division, where the correspondence and affidavits are filed and indexed. They are referred to as Buenos Ayres Claims, Miscellaneous, Folders 1-20. A fairly complete list, together with a very brief description of the nature of each claim, is printed in *Sen. Ex. Doc.*, No. 18, 35 Cong., 2 sess., pp. 119-120.

[86] The *Hope* case grew out of the British boarding of the ship in the neutral waters of the port of Buenos Aires during the war of 1812 (William Miller to Nicolás de Herrera, Secretary of Government and Foreign Relations, May 26, 1814, AGN, BA, S1-A2-A4-núm. 8).

[87] A survey of the correspondence of American agents in Buenos Aires after 1831 reveals that these claims were pressed on many occasions, but with little success. By 1865 only three had been liquidated: the Halsey claim (William A. Harris, United States Minister to Argentina, to Secretary of State Daniel Webster, Oct. 14, 1851, NA, DS, Desp. Arg., VIII); and the Atkins and White claims (*Registro oficial de la República Argentina*, V, 41-42, 84-85).

shifting of executives, rivalries of factions, jealousies of Buenos Aires on the part of the other provinces, and international complications—all these rendered the decade one fraught with interest and frustration for the representative of a foreign nation. Through the many contacts which he made with public leaders, Forbes was enabled to share in internal politics. Although never projecting his interest to the point of indiscretion, he did upon occasions become influential in local affairs.

One of the problems toward which Forbes helped to shape policy was the limitation of the African slave trade. In his original instructions to Caesar A. Rodney in May, 1823, Secretary Adams had urged the Minister to seek Argentine support, either by law or by treaty, for the abolition of the slave traffic.[88] In September, 1824, Forbes sent to the Foreign Minister a formal statement which intimated the possibility of a convention. García was amenable. Out of these negotiations came the Argentine law of November 15, 1824, which declared traffic in African Negroes an act of piracy and provided punishment for citizens who participated in the trade.[89]

Upon the occasion of Bolívar's invitations to the Panama Congress of 1826, Forbes pressed his influence with President Rivadavia. In a conference with the executive in March, the Chargé reported that the United States would send an agent but not a minister to the conference. Professedly delighted at this decision of President Adams, Rivadavia announced that he likewise would not send a minister. Moreover, he said that he was "determined not to deviate, in the slightest degree, from the march of the United States, who, from the wisdom and experience of their Cabinet, as well as their great national Character and strength, ought to take the lead in American policy." [90] If the man whom Forbes had once accused of making all his vows to Europe spoke from conviction, it was unfortunate for American interests that his conversion had been so long delayed and that his presidency was so short.

During the civil commotions which racked Argentina in the late twenties, Forbes found opportunities for dabbling in internal politics. At the conclusion of the Argentine-Brazilian war, Manuel Dorrego, Governor of Buenos Aires, able politician and statesman, and once an exile in the United States, found himself opposed by a mutinous army division

[88] Adams to Rodney, May 17, 1823, NA, DS, Inst. Min., IX, 264.

[89] Forbes to García, Sept. 17, 1824; García to Forbes, Sept. 20, 1824; Forbes to Adams, Oct. 6, Nov. 25, 1824, NA, DS, Desp. Arg., II. Adams approved Forbes's action, but directed that he cease negotiations for a convention. The Senate had just refused to ratify a similar arrangement with Colombia, and the Secretary feared the same fate for a treaty with Buenos Aires (Adams to Forbes, April 14, 1825, NA, DS, Inst. Min., X, 258-259).

[90] Forbes to Clay, March 20, 1826, NA, DS, Desp. Arg., II. In August, 1825, the executive had been authorized to appoint one or more ministers plenipotentiary (Facultad de Derecho y Ciencias Sociales de la Universidad de Buenos Aires, *La política exterior de la República Argentina*, pp. 37-39).

commanded by General Juan Lavalle. Conflict between the two men eventually led to the assassination of the Governor at the hands of the rebel leader.[91] Forbes intervened too late to save the life of Dorrego, although Lavalle subsequently informed the agent that under no circumstances could his wishes have been granted.[92]

Dorrego's murder late in 1828 set off the violent civil wars which lasted with little respite for the next year. This new descent into political barbarism greatly disturbed John Forbes, who wrote to Martin Van Buren that

> my long residence in this Country has brought me through the greatest vicissitudes of its political fortunes. Arriving in the year 1820, a state of things too much resembling those of the present moment I witnessed the morning twilight of their regeneration, I had the felicity to partake with them of the brilliant, but short lived, meridian of their national prosperity, and have now the distressing spectacle of their falling through the evening twilight of despondency into the darkness of an almost hopeless anarchy.[93]

Out of the gloom Forbes revealed came Juan Manuel de Rosas, the strong, ruthless caudillo of the southern plains. By conceding this dashing Gaucho leader the powers of a dictator, the nation gained for itself a period of stability in government but postponed for a generation reasoned progress toward an organic society.

The phase of the civil wars which most nearly complicated Argentine-American relations was the peremptory decree requiring military service of all foreigners not exempted by treaty. Objecting to the decree on the ground that American citizens were guaranteed the same rights as the English, Forbes advised his countrymen not to comply. When he proposed to the English Chargé and the French Consul General that foreigners be allowed to participate in an "Urbane Guard," Sir Woodbine Parish demurred. The militant attitude of the Englishman was effective; the government soon withdrew the decree.[94] Although it revived compulsory service in 1830, citizens of the United States were not affected.[95]

By the close of 1830 the irritations and vicissitudes of his long career in convulsive Buenos Aires had undermined Forbes's health. As a matter of fact, as early as the time of Rodney's arrival in 1824 the agent had begged Monroe to relieve him of his post. Then, as later, he complained of his "protracted and unwilling residence" in Buenos Aires and of the

---

[91] Levene, *op. cit.*, pp. 385-390.
[92] Forbes to Clay, Dec. 8, 23, 1828, and enclosures, NA, DS, Desp. Arg., III.
[93] July 1, 1829, NA, DS, Desp. Arg., III.
[94] Forbes to Secretary of State, March 25, April 13, 1828; to Van Buren, May 25, 1829, *ibid.*
[95] Forbes to Van Buren, Nov. 29, 1830, and enclosures, *ibid.*, IV.

heavy drain upon his personal finances. He longed for surcease from his "cheerless exile." [96] Again in 1827 he requested leave, only to be told that the exigencies of the Brazilian War demanded his continuous presence. Finally, in February, 1831, failing health forced him to prepare for withdrawal. Death prevented his departure.[97]

John M. Forbes rendered a decade of significant service both to the United States and to the United Provinces. Though his influence on Argentine-American relations was rarely decisive, his long residence in Buenos Aires and his forthright representation of American rights and interests gave the Department of State a tangible medium of contact with the newly recognized government. His friendliness for the United Provinces and his personal acquaintance with many Argentine leaders helped the young nation through its difficult formative years. If his record was not that of a skillful diplomat, at least it was satisfactory to his government and respected by that at Buenos Aires.

[96] Forbes to Monroe, March 22, 1824, LC, MD, Papers of Monroe. Forbes's interesting "Account Book of House Expenses, June 25, 1825 to July 6, 1830" is preserved in LC, MD, J. M. Forbes.

[97] Forbes to Van Buren, Feb. 14, 1831; George W. Slacum, United States Consul since 1824, to Van Buren, June 14, 1831, NA, DS, Desp. Arg., IV. In the Archivo General de la Nación, Buenos Aires, there are at least seven letters, dated from 1827 to 1831, in which Forbes announced his absence from duties or public functions because of ill health (S1-A2-A4-núm. 11).

Part Three:

Argentina, Pawn of Power Politics

V I I I

THE FALKLAND ISLANDS:
A DIPLOMATIC INCIDENT AND
THE AFTERMATH, 1831-1960

The death of John M. Forbes in June, 1831, left the United States without diplomatic representation in Buenos Aires on the eve of discordant relations between the two countries. The diplomatic incident of 1832—the only serious blemish in the first century and a third of intercourse—grew out of a controversy over sovereignty in the Falkland Islands, bleak, barren sentinels of the South Atlantic. Although they lay strategically only two hundred miles east of the Strait of Magellan, these forbidding islands long had discouraged exploration; before 1750 only whalers, sealers, and intrepid navigators had touched their shores. After the middle of the eighteenth century, the need for protected trade routes lifted the islands from their obscurity. Once brought into the stream of world affairs, the Falklands have remained a point of controversy.

Argentina Inherits the Falklands

Resolute French settlers planted the first colony in the Falkland Islands in 1764.[1] Defying this action, the British took formal possession of

---

[1] The brief summary of early Falklands history which follows is based largely upon Julius Goebel, Jr., *The Struggle for the Falkland Islands: A Study in Legal and Diplomatic History*, pp. 1-433, *passim*. This superb treatise also contains an analysis of the Argentine-American controversy of 1831-1833 (pp. 438-455), upon which I have relied heavily for this chapter. The best study from the Argentine point of view is Adolfo Saldías, *Historia de la Confederación Argentina*, II, ch. XIX. A comprehensive popular description and history of the islands was published in the United States in 1842 (Robert Greenhow, "The Falkland Islands: A Memoir; Descriptive, and Political," in *The Merchants' Magazine and Commercial Review*, VI [Feb., 1842], 105-151). This article was reprinted with the title "Memoria sobre las Islas Malvinas" in *La Revista de Buenos Aires*, XII, 142-154, 299-309, 448-454; XIII, 170-186, 352-360, 500-526.

the islands in January, 1765, and in the next year established a settlement at Port Egmont. When under authority of the Treaty of Utrecht Spain took over the French and English colonies in 1767 and 1770, it further complicated the question of sovereignty. After lengthy negotiations Great Britain formally abandoned its settlement on May 20, 1774. The withdrawal of the British left Spain free to exercise full control over the islands and their contiguous waters. The Spanish then ordered the absolute exclusion of all alien fishing and whaling vessels.

The much disputed islands were in Spanish hands, therefore, at the beginning of the revolutionary struggles in La Plata. On March 16, 1811, Xavier Elío, Viceroy of the Río de la Plata, notified the Spanish King that the rebel government had ordered the withdrawal of the colonists on the Falklands.[2] The vicissitudes of the United Provinces during the next decade, however, precluded attempts at recolonization, and, fortunately for Argentine national interests, no other nation sought to acquire them. In 1820, as the provincial government of Buenos Aires determined to unite all the territory in the old viceroyalty, it sent Colonel Daniel Jewett in the frigate *Heroína* to assume formal possession of the Falklands. The government maintained its control during the ensuing years, and in 1823 appointed Pablo Areguati as Governor. At about the same time, it granted the right of settlement and exclusive use of fisheries and cattle to several individuals, including Lewis Vernet, cosmopolitan adventurer of French origin but long a resident of Germany and the United States. Though his colony did not maintain itself continuously, in January, 1828, Vernet secured wide privileges to the island of Soledad, or East Falkland.[3]

During the subsequent months the colony grew vigorously. By June, 1829, the Governor of Buenos Aires, General Juan Lavalle, resolved to claim for Argentina all the possessions of Spain in its former Viceroyalty of Río de la Plata. To insure permanent possession of the Falkland Islands and Tierra del Fuego, Lavalle placed them under a political and military governor. This officer would enforce all Argentine laws in the islands, especially those protecting the seal fisheries. To the scheming Vernet went this appointment. With official support he could now execute his ideas regarding the fisheries. Bluntly he warned masters of fishing vessels that he would tolerate no infringement of his monopoly.[4]

---

[2] Pedro Torres Lanzas, *Independencia de América: Fuentes para su estudio*, 1st series, II, p. 485, no. 2932.

[3] *British and Foreign State Papers*, XX (1832-1833), 420-421.

[4] *Registro oficial de la República Argentina*, II, 238; Antonio Zinny, *La Gaceta Mercantil de Buenos Aires* (June 13, 1829), I, 213. On February 10, 1831, the Department of State directed Forbes to remonstrate against these measures, but his death prevented compliance (Secretary Van Buren to Forbes, William R. Manning [ed.], *Diplomatic Correspondence of the United States: Inter-American Affairs, 1831-1860*, I, 3-4).

Seizure of American Ships

If by such an order Vernet hoped to protect the seal fisheries from foreign depredations, he soon saw the futility of his desire. Alien ships, including several vessels of the United States, continued to transgress the rights of his concession. Vernet vainly appealed to Buenos Aires for a warship.[5] Concluding that the situation demanded a more drastic course, in August, 1831, he seized three of these ships, the *Harriet*, the *Superior*, and the *Breakwater*.[6] The *Breakwater*, promptly escaping, returned to the United States.[7] After several weeks of negotiations, the captains of the other vessels accepted a contract with the Governor stipulating disposition of their ships.[8] By this agreement the *Superior* was to continue fishing operations on the west coast of South America, while the *Harriet* sailed to Buenos Aires for trial. Vernet cunningly arranged, therefore, that one of the ships visit the sealing grounds while its trial was in progress, although he planned to institute condemnation proceedings against both vessels. Should they be condemned, the Governor would share in the proceeds of the voyage. This understanding concluded, the *Harriet*, with Vernet on board, proceeded to Buenos Aires.[9]

For both Argentina and the United States the *Harriet* reached La Plata at an acutely unpropitious moment. Throughout the Province of

[5] Tomás Manuel de Anchorena, Minister of Foreign Affairs, to Vernet, July 12, 1831, AGN, BA, Archivo de Vernet, Sl-A4-A5-núm. 2. In the Archivo General de la Nación, Buenos Aires, there is an extensive collection of Vernet manuscripts. Most of this material, however, relates not to the strictly diplomatic aspects of the incident but to colonization projects, contractual relations with the captains of captured ships, and claims for damages subsequently suffered at the hands of the American warship *Lexington* (see below, pp. 105-106).

[6] In his "Memoirs on the Falkland Islands," Vernet says that the *Superior* had been warned in 1829 and 1830, the other two ships in 1830, but that all returned (AGN, BA, Archivo de Vernet, S1-A4-A5-núm. 10f).

[7] *Ibid.*, núm. 3. Suit against insurance underwriters for recovery of losses was brought by the owners of the *Breakwater* and the *Harriet* in the United States Circuit Court, Boston.

[8] The original contract is filed in AGN, BA, Archivo de Vernet, S1-A4-A5-núm. 5. For a copy, see Manning, *op. cit.*, I, 68-69.

[9] George W. Slacum, U.S. Consul, to Anchorena, Nov. 21, 1831, *ibid.*, I, 65. This note, together with most of those dealing with the diplomatic controversy of 1831-1832, is printed in many places. The Argentine government issued the correspondence in 1832 in two publications, one Spanish and one English, with some slight differences in the documents included (*Colección de documentos oficiales con que el gobierno instruyo al cuerpo legislativa de la provincia del origen y estado de las cuestiones pendientes con la República de los E. U. de Norte América, sobre las Islas Malvinas; Papers Relative to the Origin and Present State of the Questions Pending with the United States of America, on the Subject of the Malvinas*). In 1836 they were printed in *British and Foreign State Papers*, XX (1832-1833), 311-441. They are also available in Manning, *op. cit.*, I. In cases where the documents have been printed, I have cited the most readily available source, usually Manning.

Buenos Aires and the back country turbulence prevailed. Assumption by the capital province of the management of national affairs had aroused political factionalism and widespread dissatisfaction. Moreover, its attempt to conscript aliens for military service involved the government in acrid disputes.[10] Neither Argentina nor Brazil had yet completely acquiesced in the British settlement of the Uruguayan problem.[11]

As to the United States, the death of Forbes in June left only a consul, George W. Slacum, as its official representative in Buenos Aires.[12] Forbes's ability and experience, together with his acceptability to the Argentine government, might have enabled the nations to pass through the crisis without tension. But Slacum, a tactless diplomatic novice, was particularly suited to inflame Argentine officials.[13] His arbitrary and militant attitude, supported in Washington by a suspicious and impolitic administration, quickly sharpened a vexing issue.

Slacum swung into action immediately following the *Harriet's* arrival. His correspondence breathed indignation. In his first despatch to Tomás Manuel de Anchorena, Minister of Foreign Affairs, he wrote he could not understand the grounds for the capture. He inquired if the government intended to avow the seizure. He was dissatisfied when Anchorena explained that the Ministry of War and Marine was investigating and that the Governor would soon act.[14] Although he held no rank but that of consul and had no specific instructions from Washington,[15] Slacum promptly lodged a formal protest against the acts of Vernet. Denying that Argentine officials had the right of seizure or the right to restrain American citizens from use of the fisheries, he said he regarded Anchorena's note as an avowal of Vernet's captures. He protested against the decree of June 10, 1829. Anchorena, considering the Consul unauthorized to act, refused to regard Slacum's position as the official attitude of his government. He hoped for an amicable settlement. Nevertheless,

---

[10] See above, pp. 95-96.

[11] See above, pp. 90-91.

[12] Slacum had served as consul since April, 1824 (Manning, *op. cit.*, I, 65, note 1).

[13] As an illustration of his tactlessness, see correspondence on a feud which grew up among Slacum, Commander Silas Duncan, and Dr. Joshua Bond, American Consul in Montevideo. Plans were made for a duel to settle the dispute (Bond to Captain Edgar S. Hawkins, U.S. Army, Oct. 8, 1832, enclosure in Hawkins to Secretary of State Edward Livingston, Dec. 15, 1832; Slacum to Bond, Aug. 9, 1832, NA, DS, Con. Let., B. A., IV; Duncan to President Jackson, March 6, 1832, NA, DS, Misc. Let., Jan.-March, 1833). See also Vernet to Lewis Krumbhaar, correspondent of Vernet in Philadelphia, May 29, 1832, AGN, BA, Archivo de Vernet, S1-A4-A5-núm. 3.

[14] Slacum to Anchorena, Nov. 21, 1831; to Livingston, Nov. 23; Anchorena to Slacum, Nov. 25, Manning, *op. cit.*, I, 65-70.

[15] Slacum may have taken authorization from Van Buren's instructions to Forbes on February 10, 1831 (cf. Slacum to Livingston, Nov. 23, 1831, Manning, *op. cit.*, I, 70).

he took the opportunity to assert that the United States possessed no rights to the islands or to the fisheries.[16]

The "Lexington" Retaliates

This exchange of notes, revealing Slacum's open hostility and Anchorena's subtle intimations, made good tinder for a heated diplomatic controversy. At this critical moment the U.S.S. *Lexington* sailed into the harbor of Buenos Aires. It was commanded by a fiery, high-spirited young officer, Commander Silas Duncan. The arrival of the warship in the hands of the aggressive Duncan was hardly the restraining influence with which to temper a tense situation.[17] Upon learning the facts of the seizures, the officer decided his duty lay in the protection of American citizens and commerce in the Falklands. When on December 6 Slacum reported Duncan's decision to Anchorena, he laid down a virtual ultimatum. Within three days, he said, unless the government of Buenos Aires promptly suspended the right of capture and promised immediate restoration of the *Harriet* and other captured property, the *Lexington* would proceed to the Falklands. To buttress this position Commander Duncan also communicated with the Foreign Minister. He accused Vernet of piracy and robbery and demanded his immediate trial in the courts of either the United States or Buenos Aires.[18]

The firmness of the British position at this time may have stimulated Slacum's "bold front and truculent behavior."[19] At the very beginning of the controversy, Woodbine Parish had reminded the Argentines that Great Britain had not surrendered its claim to the Falklands by withdrawal in 1774 and that the United Provinces had no legitimate basis for their possession.[20] Whatever his inspiration, Slacum recommended to Livingston that "it is indeed time Sir that *'this Government should be made sensible of their obligations* to respect our rights and to *render justice to our Citizens.'* "[21]

When Anchorena failed to comply with Slacum's intemperate demands within the three-day limit, Commander Duncan and the *Lexington* sailed for the islands.[22] The Foreign Minister's belated reply was far from an

---

[16] Slacum to Anchorena, Nov. 26, 1831; Anchorena to Slacum, Dec. 3, 1831, *ibid.*, I, 71-73.

[17] V. F. Boyson, *The Falkland Islands*, pp. 94-95.

[18] Slacum to Livingston, Dec. 9, 1831, and enclosures; Slacum to Anchorena, Dec. 6, 1831, Manning, *op. cit.*, I, 73-78 and notes; Duncan to Anchorena, Dec. 7, 1831, *British and Foreign State Papers*, XX (1832-1833), 319-320.

[19] Goebel makes this suggestion (*The Struggle for the Falkland Islands*, pp. 442-443).

[20] Parish clearly stated the British position in a note to the Argentine Foreign Office on Nov. 19, 1829 (Manning, *op. cit.*, I, 109, note 2).

[21] Slacum to Livingston, Dec. 9, 1831, *ibid.*, pp. 77-78.

[22] Slacum to Livingston, Dec. 20, 1831, *ibid.*, p. 85.

acquiescence. His government viewed the whole controversy as a private litigious affair. Moreover,

> if the Señor Commandant of the Lexington or any other person belonging to the said Government shall commit any act, or use any measure which may tend to a denial of the right which this Republic has to the *Malvinas* . . . and to impede the seal fishery which it may wish to exercise in them, and especially in the first, the Government of this Province will address a formal complaint to that of the United States, under the firm confidence that it will cause to make valid and respected its rights, by all the means it may esteem convenient. . . .[23]

Finally, the Foreign Minister coldly informed Slacum that his government refused to treat with a consul who usurped diplomatic powers. The Consul retaliated with a blanket denial of virtually all of the Minister's contentions. He announced that he was referring the whole affair to Washington.[24]

During this epistolary bout in Buenos Aires, Commander Duncan and the *Lexington* had reached the Falklands, where late in December the vessel entered Berkeley Sound allegedly flying the French flag.[25] Duncan proceeded to disarm the island, loot the settlements, and arrest some of the inhabitants. He declared the island government at an end and carried away as prisoners Matthew Brisbane, one of Vernet's aides, and six other persons.[26] When on February 3 the *Lexington* returned to Montevideo (rather than an Argentine port), Duncan advised Slacum that he would hold the prisoners until the government of Buenos Aires made arrangements for their disposition.[27]

Reaction in Buenos Aires and in Washington

News of the *Lexington's* raid aroused sharp reactions in Buenos Aires. Popular resentment flared. *La Gaceta Mercantil* and *El Lucero* reprinted a letter of Vernet's exposing the details of Duncan's acts and defending his own former position in the Falklands.[28] Less denunciatory, *The*

[23] Anchorena to Slacum, Dec. 9, 1831, *ibid.*, pp. 79-80.

[24] Slacum to Anchorena, Dec. 15, 1831, *ibid.*, pp. 81-85.

[25] Boyson, *op. cit.*, p. 95.

[26] The entire incident was reviewed when Carlos María de Alvear, Argentine Minister to the United States, presented the Argentine case to Secretary of State John Forsyth, March 31, 1839, Manning, *op. cit.*, I, 210-226 and notes.

[27] Duncan to Slacum, Feb. 2, 1832, *ibid.*, pp. 93-98, note 5; Duncan to Levi Woodbury, Secretary of Navy, Feb. 3, 1832, NA, DN, Letters from Masters Commandant, Jan.-June, 1832; *La Gaceta Mercantil* (Feb. 8, 1832), II, 13. The Argentine government accepted responsibility for the prisoners (*Registro oficial de República Argentina*, II, 287).

[28] *La Gaceta Mercantil* (Feb. 9, 15, 20, 1832), II, 14, 15, 29; *El Lucero*, Feb. 10, 21, 1832. Both journals published editorials, articles, and documents on the controversy.

British Packet and Argentine News published a letter which assumed that the government of the United States would acquit itself honorably.[29] The Argentine government did nothing to quell the agitation. Rather, it issued a public proclamation denouncing the *Lexington's* violent attack. Popular indignation was fully justified, the government said, as it promised satisfaction of its rights.[30] Moreover, it notified Slacum that it would no longer recognize him as the official representative of the United States. Because of the prejudices aroused by his irregular ideas and by Duncan's unwarranted proceedings, the government felt obliged

> to remove with the greatest care all that directly or indirectly might aggravate the feelings or change the moderation and temperance with which negotiations between civilized and friendly Governments should be conducted, . . .[31]

Slacum's immediate response was unyielding. He declined to appoint a successor, he said, because his government had not dismissed him nor authorized him to select a substitute.[32]

In communicating these developments to Washington, Slacum reported that the government had resorted to every device to inflame the minds of the people. He was unable to determine the causes of the Argentine attitude toward him, but he was certain that "if this signal outrage is passed over without *immediate* and *ample* satisfaction, we may bid adieu to all security for our Citizens and commerce." [33]

Meanwhile, the Jackson administration had determined upon an aggressive Falklands policy. Although he received no official report until long after,[34] the President had alluded to the *Harriet's* capture in his annual message of December 6, 1831. He announced that the right of fishing in the Falklands, never before denied to citizens of the United States, had been transgressed "by a band acting, as they pretend, under the authority of the Government of Buenos Ayres." He had already despatched an armed vessel, he said, to protect trade in the South At-

[29] See issue of February 11.
[30] *Papers Relative to . . . the Malvinas*, p. 23, no. XIV; *Registro oficial de la República Argentina*, II, 288.
[31] Manuel J. García, Foreign Minister, to Slacum, Feb. 14, 1832, Manning, *op. cit.*, I, 88-89.
[32] Slacum to García, Feb. 16, 1832, *ibid.*, pp. 89-90.
[33] To Livingston, Feb. 20, 1832, *ibid.*, p. 91. Slacum had kept the Department advised of each new development in the crisis (Nov. 23, Dec. 9, 20, *ibid.*, pp. 66-70, 75-78, 85-88).
[34] Slacum's first report, dated November 23, did not reach Washington until long after December 6. It seems certain that the President's only source of information was the crew of the escaped *Breakwater*. News of its return was printed in the *Columbian Centinel* (Boston) and reprinted in *La Gaceta Mercantil* (Jan. 2, 1832), II, 5.

lantic and would send a minister to examine Argentina's claim to the islands.[35]

Secretary of the Navy Levi Woodbury officially approved Commander Duncan's decision to proceed with the *Lexington* to the Falklands.[36] But neither his position nor Jackson's was precisely consistent with that of Edward Livingston, Secretary of State, who ordered the United States Minister in Spain to inquire into the legal sovereignty of the Falklands.[37] Nor was Jackson's policy congruous with the attitude of Commodore George W. Rodgers, commanding American forces in the South Atlantic, who hoped no event in the Falklands would render necessary the presence there of a war vessel.[38] However, in the face of Slacum's boldness and the brusqueness of Jackson, the efforts of Livingston and Rodgers to meet the crisis judiciously were fruitless.

The militancy of the White House was reflected but dimly among the people of the nation. Newspapers of Washington and the larger cities noted the actions of Vernet and Duncan with interest but not with indignation. In Buenos Aires, too, popular resentment abated after its first fury, and by May Rosas resolved to await the arrival of a minister from the United States.[39]

Jacksonian Diplomacy on Paper

The chargé d'affaires selected by President Jackson to undertake settlement of the controversy was Francis Baylies, Massachusetts lawyer, politician, journalist, and author.[40] A political henchman of the President without diplomatic experience, he impressed John Quincy Adams as "one of the most talented and worthless men in New England." [41] Be-

[35] J. D. Richardson, *A Compilation of the Messages and Papers of the Presidents*, II, 553.

[36] Woodbury to Duncan, Feb. 15, 1832, NA, DN, Letters to Officers of Ships of War, XX (Aug. 5, 1831-May 7, 1834).

[37] To C. P. Van Ness, Jan. 11, 1832, NA, DS, Inst. Min., XIII, 269-270.

[38] Rodgers to Vicente López, Argentine Foreign Minister, April 24, 1832, enclosure Woodbury to Livingston, July 25, 1832, NA, DS, Misc. Let., July-Dec., 1832.

[39] Message to the Legislature, May 7, 1832, H. Mabragaña, *Los mensajes*, I, 260.

[40] Manning, *op. cit.*, I, 4; Paul Groussac, *Les Iles Malouines: nouvel exposé d'un vieux litige*, p. 27, note.

[41] Adams confided to his *Memoirs* the following rancorous characterization of Baylies:

> . . . Baylies, in 1825, had, as a member of Congress, voted for Jackson as President, libelled me in the newpapers, and lost his election in consequence. He thought Jackson undervalued him, by the offer of the Collectorship of New Bedford, and Jackson, to appease him, gave him as a second sop the office of Chargé d'Affaires at Buenos Ayres. He went there; stayed there not three months—just long enough to embroil his country in a senseless and wicked quarrel with the Government; and, without waiting for orders from his Government, demanded his passports and came home. Nothing but the imbecility of that South American abortion of a state saved him from indelible disgrace and this country from humiliation in that concern. . . . (Charles Francis Adams, [ed.], *Memoirs of John Quincy Adams*, IX, 446-447).

cause of his inexperience and high-strung temperament, Baylies was clearly unqualified to fulfill the task to which Jackson assigned him.[42]

Even before he learned of Duncan's acts, Livingston drafted instructions for Baylies. They were lengthy, detailed, often inaccurate, and typical of Jacksonian aggressiveness.[43] In depicting Vernet's "lawless and piratical" actions, the Secretary wrote that the President questioned the authenticity of the decree which authorized them. If by its decree of June 10 the government of Buenos Aires sought to delegate authority, it ought to have informed Forbes, either by special notification or by special interpretation. Seizure of a vessel without previous warning was a hostile act,[44] committed in this case while the United States was on friendly terms with the government of Buenos Aires. Citizens of the United States had enjoyed shelter and fishing in the Falklands for more than fifty years. Assuming, therefore, that Vernet had acted without authorization, the President had ordered all available warships to the area to protect American interests.

Baylies' primary duties, then, were to justify the protective measures taken by President Jackson and to insist upon the right of Americans to share in the fisheries of the islands. The Secretary upheld the traditional rights of all nations to the enjoyment of ocean fishery and the use of shores adjacent to the fishing grounds. For precedent he pointed to the Anglo-American treaty of 1782 and the Anglo-Spanish treaty of 1790.

This approach brought him to the point of questioning the right of Buenos Aires to inherit Spanish sovereignty in the islands. He instructed Baylies, therefore, to negotiate for the settlement of the following points:

1. The perfect right of the United States to the free use of the fishery—on the ocean, in every part of it, and on the bays, arms of the sea, gulfs, and other inlets, which are incapable of being fortified.

2. To the same perfect right on the ocean within a marine league of the shore, when the approach cannot be injurious to the sovereign of the country, as it cannot be on the shores which are possessed by savage tribes, or are totally deserted, as they are to the south of the Rio Negro.

3. To the same use of the shores when in the situation above described.

4. That even where a settlement is made, and other circumstances would deprive us of the right, that a constant and uninterrupted use will give it to us.[45]

---

[42] See the comment by the Argentine historian, Enrique Vera y González, *Historia de la República Argentina*, I, 211-213.

[43] January 26, 1832, Manning, *op. cit.*, I, 4-12.

[44] Warnings had been given on several occasions (see above, p. 103, note 6).

[45] Manning, *op. cit.*, I, 11.

Livingston authorized Baylies to sign a treaty which acknowledged these rights, and, if occasion arose, to conclude a treaty of amity and commerce. Finally, he should demand restitution of the vessels captured, indemnity for property destroyed, and disavowal of Vernet's acts. Livingston's blunt, unrelenting instructions were characteristic of Jackson's South American policy.[46]

Jacksonian Diplomacy in Action

Baylies arrived in Buenos Aires in early June and received immediate recognition.[47] A few days later, in a lengthy narrative of his government's attitude, he initiated negotiations. He reviewed Vernet's offenses against American citizens and commerce: the capture of the fishing vessels; the extortion of a mercantile contract; the exposure of seven men on one of the islands; the seduction of North American seamen; and the seizure of property. He complained particularly because the United States had been singled out as the victim of these crimes. Furthermore, Baylies' accusations continued,

> the Governor chose a time for the exercise of his power in acts of despotism, when no high diplomatic functionary [of the United States] was here to advocate and protect the interests and the rights of his countrymen—and remained unchecked and uncontrolled, until an American naval commander was found of sufficient energy and patriotism, to defend and protect those rights on his own responsibility.[48]

Baylies' note complied fully with Livingston's instructions. But not content to rest his case there, he announced that he saw no justification for Slacum's suspension and suggested his reinstatement.[49]

Such indecorum on the part of an agent whose mission Buenos Aires had thought to be that of conciliation must have been disconcerting. Nevertheless, Manuel Vicente de Maza, the Acting Minister of Foreign Affairs, promptly replied with dignity (June 25). The serious nature of Baylies' declarations, he said, required that they be referred to Governor Rosas. The government would question Vernet and the others indicted at once and would reach a verdict without attempt to impair the rights of American citizens or to sacrifice those of the Argentine Republic. Baylies' response on the following day revealed much less reserve. He said that the questioning was unnecessary, since Vernet had admitted

---

[46] On the basis of an unofficial report of Duncan's departure for the Falklands, Livingston later instructed Baylies to justify the action to the Argentine government. When news of Duncan's acts at the Falklands arrived, the Secretary ordered that these, too, be justified (Feb. 14, April 3, 1832, Manning, *op. cit.*, I, 12-13, 14-15).

[47] *Registro oficial de la República Argentina*, II, 291.

[48] Baylies to Manuel Vicente de Maza, Acting Foreign Minister, June 20, 1832, Manning, *op. cit.*, I, 99-105.

[49] *Ibid.*, p. 105.

his guilt; the pertinent problem was to determine the measure of guilt. The United States did not pretend to doubt Argentine rights but did wish to establish its own.[50]

From De Maza's note of June 25 Baylies concluded that the Minister was trying to evade the main issue, to involve him as an accuser of Vernet, and to replace the question between the United States and Buenos Aires with one between the United States and Vernet.[51] No further communication reached the Chargé until July 10, when De Maza wrote that the gravity of the controversy demanded the most thorough investigation.[52] In the meantime, Baylies had prepared a comprehensive historical diagnosis of "the original rights of Spain and the derivative rights of the Argentine Republic" to the Falklands, in which he sought to show the weakness of the Argentine claim. He contended for American rights to free fishery.[53]

When nearly a month passed without reply, the impatient Baylies determined to insist upon an answer to his demands of June 20. Because of the Chargé's alleged prejudice and his insistence upon Slacum's reinstatement, however, De Maza preferred to negotiate directly with the Department of State. His letter, written as a defense of Slacum's suspension, presented an adroit explanation of the Argentine position. His government had omitted no effort, he said, to keep the question within its lawful limits.[54]

Within a week De Maza informed Baylies of the only basis upon which Governor Rosas would permit negotiations to continue. Viewing Duncan's conduct of the *Lexington's* raid as barbarous and palpably outrageous, the government had resolved to insist upon "prompt and complete satisfaction for said outrages, and reparation and indemnification, not only to the Argentine Republic, but to Comandante Vernet, and the Colonists . . . , for all the damages and injuries. . . ."[55] Duncan's actions were made the core of the whole controversy. Until the United States satisfied Argentine demands for reparation, negotiations could not proceed.

Baylies' exaggerated sense of national loyalty apparently could not tolerate this decision. Four days later (August 18), he returned unread the copy of Vernet's detailed report which De Maza had transmitted and, at the same time, demanded his passports.[56] The Chargé returned

---

[50] *Ibid.*, pp. 106-108.

[51] Baylies to Livingston, June 30, July 24, 1832, *ibid.*, pp. 108, 127-128.

[52] *Ibid.*, pp. 110-111.

[53] July 10, 1832, *ibid.*, pp. 111-126.

[54] Baylies to De Maza, Aug. 6, 1832; De Maza to Livingston, Aug. 8, 1832, *ibid.*, pp. 138-139, 141-145. For a brief description of the Argentine position, see J. B. Alberdi, *Escritos póstumos*, XVI, 376-377.

[55] De Maza to Baylies, Aug. 14, 1832, Manning, *op. cit.*, I, 151.

[56] Baylies to De Maza, *ibid.*, p. 152.

the report because he felt that consideration of it might make the United States a litigant against Vernet in Argentine courts.[57] Although he thought Buenos Aires might be desirous of war, he betrayed no resolution to prevent it when he wrote to Livingston, "We have attempted to soothe, and conciliate and coax these wayward & petulant fools long enough." [58]

Failure to reach an agreement by written communication induced De Maza to invite Baylies to a conference on August 27 for the consideration of certain controversial points. To the Minister's request for an explanation of the return of Vernet's report, the Chargé recited his desire to keep the United States from private litigation. The Minister had demanded satisfaction and reparation for Duncan's raid as a prerequisite to negotiation on other matters; therefore, since he was not authorized to deal with that topic, Baylies must insist upon his passports. But De Maza, believing the Chargé to have been given full authorization, could not comprehend this overt act. The Argentine suggested that Baylies might request new instructions or that they might invite the arbitration of a neutral. He saw no reason for severance of amicable relations. When the Minister insisted that they must settle the *cuestión de hecho* concerning Duncan's depredations before the *cuestión de derecho* regarding the fisheries, Baylies persisted in his uncompromising attitude.[59] Since he apparently felt that he had exhausted all possibilities of a settlement, further conferences were impossible. Receiving his passports on September 3, the impetuous Chargé soon departed for the United States.[60]

In Buenos Aires the departure of Baylies occasioned widespread comment. *La Gaceta Mercantil* characterized the Chargé as lacking "in the possession of all those qualities which are indispensable in a political agent of his rank," and charged the aggravated situation to his "unskilfulness and imprudence" as well as to his lack of instructions.[61] De Maza stooped to no such criticism but declared that Baylies had prevented an accommodation by his insistence upon justifying Captain Duncan.[62]

---

[57] Extensive documentary evidence assembled by Vernet to substantiate his claim against the United States is preserved in AGN, BA, Archivo de Vernet, S1-A4-A5-núm. 10a and 10e. A brief of the claim is filed in *ibid.*, núm. 3.

[58] Aug. 19, 1832, Manning, *op. cit.*, I, 153-154.

[59] This account is based upon three "minutes" of the conference by De Maza, J. D. Mendenhall, an American citizen, who served as interpreter, and Francis B. Stockton, purser from the United States Navy, who knew Spanish. De Maza's minute is printed in *British and Foreign State Papers*, XX (1832-1833), 437-440; those of Mendenhall and Stockton are in NA, DS, Desp. Arg., IV, the former printed in Manning, *op. cit.*, I, 155-157.

[60] De Maza to Baylies, *ibid.*, p. 158.

[61] (Sept. 22, 1832), II, 65.

[62] De Maza to Livingston, Oct. 13, 1832, Manning, *op. cit.*, I, 166.

Although the leaders of both countries exhibited an unmistakable coolness both before and after the withdrawal of Baylies, there seems little doubt that each was earnestly desirous of an early renewal of diplomatic intercourse. When on September 18 De Maza transmitted the correspondence to the Legislature, he expressed confidence that the United States would make adequate redress at an early date.[63] Within a month his government determined to send a minister to Washington, and within three months selected General Carlos María de Alvear, only previous Argentine Minister to the United States.[64] In Washington, where the House of Representatives requested pertinent correspondence on the Falklands affair, President Jackson refused on grounds that it might be inconsistent with the public interest. "Negotiations . . . are not considered broken off," said he, "but are suspended only until the arrival of a minister, . . ." [65]

Great Britain Fills a Vacuum

Relations between Washington and Buenos Aires had reached this turn when British reoccupation of the Falklands startlingly transformed the situation. Reasserting rights which they had ostensibly relinquished in 1774, the British late in 1832 moved in before the Argentines could re-establish their colony. By this sudden coup the British settled in fact, if not in debate, the question of sovereignty.[66] Whether or not Captain Duncan's destruction of the Argentine colony inspired the British action is a matter of speculation.[67] Certainly, British agents in Washington and Buenos Aires knew that relations between the two countries were strained. They doubtless assumed that the United States would not prevent a British occupation or lend support to Argentina.[68]

This *fait accompli* by Great Britain gave Argentina its second opportunity in less than a decade to invite an application of Monroe's principles. In this case, unlike that of the Brazilian War in 1826, it did not immediately make such a request. Nor did the government at Wash-

---

[63] These documents were published as mentioned above, p. 103, note 9.

[64] De Maza to Livingston, Oct. 13, Dec. 20, 1832, Manning, *op. cit.*, I, 166, 167; *Registro oficial de la República Argentina*, II, 302.

[65] *Reg. of Deb.*, 22 Cong., 2 sess., IX, pt. 1, 900-901; Richardson, *op. cit.*, II, 608-609. Meanwhile, the government was maintaining in the South Atlantic an adequate protecting force for American commerce and fisheries (Woodbury to Livingston, Dec. 24, 1832, NA, DS, Misc. Let., July-Dec., 1832).

[66] The Falklands have remained a British possession in spite of Argentine "irredentism."

[67] See Baylies' view in his note to Livingston, April 23, 1833, Manning, *op. cit.*, I, 179-180.

[68] Charles Bankhead, British Minister to the United States, to Viscount Palmerston, LC, MD, Photostats, F. O. 5, Vol. 273, Folio III; Goebel, *op. cit.*, pp. 454-455.

ington undertake to protest to Great Britain. The national interest in 1833 clearly did not dictate a decisive stand against the British move.[69] Moreover, once Great Britain had reaffirmed its claim by actual reoccupation, it was obvious that Jackson would be unwilling to deny British sovereignty as he had previously that of Argentina.

The Sequel—A Decade Later

The abrupt departure of Chargé Baylies in September, 1832, precipitated a *de facto* suspension of diplomatic relations, which endured for more than a decade. Although each government repeatedly made friendly overtures to the other, they did not renew formal diplomatic intercourse until 1844. Argentine intentions to send a minister to Washington soon after Baylies' withdrawal were suspended by the British *démarche* in the Falklands [70] and further delayed by a series of domestic and international complications.

The delay of 1832 grew into months, then years, and no Argentine minister reached Washington until 1838.[71] Each year the Argentine Legislature was apprised of the failure to renew negotiations. Periodically the Congress of the United States was informed that a minister would soon arrive.[72] When in July, 1834, Secretary of State John Forsyth appointed a new consul for Buenos Aires, he addressed the Minister of Foreign Relations in the friendliest of terms. The postponement of a minister's arrival, he said, was disappointing to the President, who was ready to entertain propositions which would lead to an accommodation.[73]

Of the manifold factors which postponed Argentine action, the lack of continuity in the nation's administration was most disturbing. General Rosas resigned in December, 1832. Before his return to the governorship in April, 1835, three executives struggled to quell dissensions within the province. Rosas' campaign against the Indians in the southern wilderness (1833) added to his personal popularity and prompted a demand for his return to office. Civil war between the provinces of Salta and Tucumán (1834), opposition to Rosas after his return to power (1835), war against the Republic of Bolivia (1837), and a break in relations with

[69] Dexter Perkins, *The Monroe Doctrine, 1826-1867*, pp. 8-9; S. F. Bemis (ed.), *The American Secretaries of State and Their Diplomacy*, IV, 253-254.

[70] Eben R. Dorr, Consul at Buenos Aires, to Forsyth, Jan. 1, 1835, Manning, *op. cit.*, I, 187-188.

[71] For correspondence on this delay, see *ibid.*, pp. 184-185, 186-191, 193-195, 186-197.

[72] Mabragaña, *op. cit.*, I, 281, 290, 309; Richardson, *op. cit.*, III, 27, 151.

[73] July 29, 1834, Manning, *op. cit.*, I, 15-16; Forsyth to Dorr, July 29, 1834, NA, DS, Inst. to Con., VI, 32-33. Until the arrival of Dorr, the United States had had no official representative in Buenos Aires since the departure of Baylies and Slacum in September, 1832.

France (1837-1838)—all these developments, together with depletion of public funds, pushed relations with the United States into the background.[74]

General Alvear, appointed Minister to the United States in December, 1832, did not depart for his post. Manuel Moreno, ordered in September, 1835, to transfer to Washington from London, could not comply because of illness, physical or diplomatic.[75] Three more years elapsed before General Alvear, then reappointed, reached Washington.[76] In the meantime, the United States maintained only a consulate in Buenos Aires and made no move to send a minister.

Alvear's instructions, prepared by Rosas' Foreign Minister, Felipe Arana, included a flat mandate to secure satisfaction from the United States for Duncan's depredations and Slacum's effrontery. They did not mention British reoccupation or the Monroe Doctrine. Alvear was ordered (1) to promote the most satisfactory reparation for the insults inflicted upon Argentine sovereignty by Duncan's destruction of Vernet's colony, by his capture of innocent persons and their removal to foreign lands, and by Slacum's lack of respect for Argentine authority; (2) to promote reparation to the Argentine Republic, Vernet, and the colonists for all damages caused by Duncan's aggression; and (3) to clarify and defend Argentine rights to the Falklands and to fisheries along their coasts. If Alvear failed to secure suitable satisfaction on the first point, he was not to take up the others and was to terminate his mission.[77]

The Minister laid his case before the Department of State in a conference with Secretary Forsyth on January 14, 1839. Alvear learned for the first time that the American government had long since approved Commander Duncan's conduct. In support of the naval officer's actions, the Secretary sought to argue from allegory; in rebuttal, the Minister erected his proof upon established laws and upon human and neutral rights. If there were a choice between Great Britain and Argentina as possessors of the Falklands, said Forsyth, the United States would of course prefer the American state, but it could not set itself up as judge of rightful ownership. Nevertheless, Forsyth declared to Alvear, the

[74] Ricardo Levene, *A History of Argentina*, pp. 404-409; Manning, *op. cit.*, I, 196-202.

[75] Arana to Forsyth, Sept. 13, 1836, *ibid.*, pp. 193-195; Arana to Moreno, Sept. 19, 1835, AGN, BA, S1-A2-A4-núm. 9.

[76] *Registro oficial de República Argentina*, II, 388; Alvear to Arana, July 4, 1837, May 25, 1838, AGN, BA, S1-A2-A4-núm. 13.

[77] "Instrucciones que deberán regir al Ministro Plenipotenciario Extraordinario cerca del Gobierno de los Estados Unidos de la América del Norte," May 22, 1838, AGN, BA, S1-A1-A1-núm. 5. Vernet also provided Alvear with "Breves observaciones sobre los daños y perjuicios ocasionados por la destrucción de la colonia en las Islas Malvinas por el Comandante de la Corveta de los Estados Unidos Lexington, en 31 de Diciembre de 1831" (*ibid.*).

United States "will never permit that any European nation take pos-session of one inch of land in any point of all America," a promise which Alvear found of "great use and mutual interest for all the American continent." The Secretary closed the conference by assuring the General that he would lay the whole matter before the President and by remind-ing him that the United States also had claims against Argentina.[78]

Alvear's documentary presentation of the case two months later, couched in far gentler language than his own instructions, made little if any impression upon President Martin Van Buren or his Secretary of State.[79] At any rate, willfully or otherwise, they forced a distinguished hero of Argentine independence to set something of a record for cooling diplomatic heels. They permitted the two remaining years of their administration to run out without reply to the Argentine demands. Nine more months passed before Secretary of State Daniel Webster finally stated the American position. Webster asserted simply that the United States must suspend final judgment upon Alvear's request until Argentina and Great Britain adjusted their dispute. If the Argentine government was willing to acquiesce in this postponement, then the United States would agree to a reopening of diplomatic relations.[80] Lacking instructions to deal with such a proposal, Alvear avoided a direct reply. Since Rosas seemed unwilling—or unable—to make up his mind to accept Webster's proposal, the Minister received no guidance from Buenos Aires.[81] The Tyler administration, therefore, proceeded on the basis of the Secretary's stated position.[82] Diplomatic wheels have rarely ground so slowly.

The Sequel—A Half-Century Later

Although full diplomatic relations were restored in 1844, the Argentine claim lay dormant another forty years.[83] Except for the writings of an occasional journalist, politician, or political theorist, the controversy over

[78] This account is based upon Alvear's minute of the conference, AGN, BA, S1-A1-A1-núm. 5. Thomas B. Davis, Jr. has written extensively of Alvear's fruitless negotiations with the Department of State (*Carlos de Alvear: Man of Revolution*, pp. 112-121).

[79] Alvear to Forsyth, March 21, 1839, and enclosures, Manning, *op. cit.*, I, 210-226.

[80] Webster to Alvear, Dec. 4, 1841, *ibid.*, pp. 18-19.

[81] Davis, *op. cit.*, pp. 119-120.

[82] J. C. Calhoun, Secretary of State, to William Brent, Jr., appointed Chargé d'Affaires at Buenos Aires, July 15, 1844, Manning, *op. cit.*, I, 22-23. In every annual message to the Legislature from 1840 to 1844, Rosas or his ministers expressed hopes for a settlement (Mabragaña, *op. cit.*, I, 4, 23, 39-40, 55, 72).

[83] In 1866 Vernet solicited aid from Domingo F. Sarmiento, Argentine Minister to the United States. Sarmiento wrote the Foreign Minister from New York that he had been given no instructions on the subject (April 6, 1866, *Obras de D. F. Sarmiento*, XXXIV, 209-215). Vernet died in 1871.

the Falklands remained a dead issue in Argentine-American relations.[84] Finally in 1884, near the close of Chester A. Arthur's administration, the claim was resurrected by Luis L. Domínguez, Argentine Minister to the United States. Twice, through formal notes to Secretary F. T. Freling-huysen, he presented the Argentine claim for indemnity and damages.[85] He received no reply. Twice more, during the first four months of the first Cleveland administration, the Minister addressed formal statements to Secretary Thomas F. Bayard.[86] The last of these four communications finally brought the persistent Argentine a reply which reverted to the reasoning of Daniel Webster. The case must remain in abeyance until Argentina settled its differences with Great Britain.[87] To this argument Domínguez responded that Argentina was willing to arbitrate, even with the Chief Justice of the United States Supreme Court as arbiter. There was no rejoinder.[88]

In his annual message of 1885 President Grover Cleveland handled this revival of the old claim with unfortunate bluntness:

> The Argentine Government has revived the long dormant question of the Falkland Islands by claiming from the United States indemnity for their loss, attributed to the action of the commander of the sloop of war *Lexington* in breaking up a piratical colony on those islands in 1831, and their subsequent occupation by Great Britain. In view of the ample justification for the act of the *Lexington* and the derelict condition of the islands before and after their alleged occupation by Argentine colonials this Government considers the claim as wholly groundless.[89]

Dr. Vicente G. Quesada, just beginning a seven-year mission to the United States, waited less than twenty-four hours to score Cleveland's errors in fact. He described as unjust the President's references to the *"piratical colony"* and the *"derelict condition of the islands."* The claim could not fairly be called *"wholly groundless,"* he contended, until it had been adjudicated.[90] Bayard's reaction echoed Frelinghuysen and re-echoed Webster. Admission of the claim for reparation would be tacit recognition of Argentina's sovereignty over the islands; and sovereignty

[84] In the Archivo General de la Nación, Buenos Aires, there is an extensive file of newspaper clippings illustrating press revival of the issue. Few of these, however, antedate 1884 (Archivo de Vernet, S1-A4-A5-núm. 8).

[85] Sept. 24, 1884, Jan. 23, 1885, NA, DS, Notes from Arg. Leg., III. Much of the correspondence on the revival of the claim has been printed in *Memoria, 1885*, pp. 126-143; *1886*, pp. 48-64; *1887*, pp. 193-278.

[86] May 4, June 27, 1885, NA, DS, Notes from Arg. Leg., III.

[87] July 20, 1885, NA, DS, Notes to Arg. Leg., VI, 240-242.

[88] July 27, 1885, NA, DS, Notes from Arg. Leg., III.

[89] Richardson, *op. cit.*, VIII, 325.

[90] To Bayard, Dec. 9, 1885, NA, DS, Notes from Arg. Leg., III. Quesada has written of his activity on behalf of the Falklands claim in *Recuerdos de mi vida diplomática: misión en Estados Unidos (1885-1892)*, pp. 155-205.

was a question for Great Britain and Argentina to resolve. Even if Argentine sovereignty should be established, there was still justification for Captain Duncan's actions of 1832. Moreover, this was not a case in point for an application of the Monroe Doctrine, because that principle pretended no retroactive features.[91] Quesada's reply was a cogent exposition of the Argentine position, but it failed to persuade Cleveland and Bayard.[92]

This prolonged correspondence brought to an end active agitation for settlement of the Argentine-American debate over sovereignty in the Falkland Islands.[93] During the long controversy, the United States had adhered to four rules of action: (1) nonapplication of the Monroe principle where the dispute antedated 1823; (2) nonapplication of the doctrine in a retroactive sense; (3) the denial of the right of a foreign government to demand an enforcement of the principle of reparation for injuries resulting from its nonapplication; (4) the right of the United States "to abate a nuisance involving lawless aggressions upon the persons and property of its citizens, without regard to the question of territorial jurisdiction."[94] Argentina had based its case upon the legality of Spain's claim to sovereignty, the inheritance of that claim by Argentina in 1810, and continuous exercise of Argentine jurisdiction until 1832.

The Sequel—A Century Later

The disappearance of the Falklands question from direct Argentine-American negotiations did not signify Argentina's dropping of its claim to the islands nor end its agitation for return of the "unredeemed" territory. Persistently it maintained the legitimacy of its position and especially during and after World War II acted more aggressively to sustain its rights. Turning their resentment toward Great Britain during these later years, Argentine leaders, nevertheless, utilized the machinery of the Inter-American System to project and support their contention. As the issue reappeared on the agenda of successive conferences, American statesmen from Cordell Hull and Sumner Welles to John Foster

[91] March 18, 1886, NA, DS, Notes to Arg. Leg., VI, 256-267, printed in *Memoria, 1886*, pp. 49-56.

[92] May 4, 1887, NA, DS, Notes from Arg. Leg., III, printed in *Memoria, 1887*, pp. 201-273.

[93] In 1897, when the Bureau of the American Republics officially listed the Falkland Islands as a British possession, the Argentine Minister in Washington, Martín García Mérou, protested to the Department of State (García Mérou to William R. Day, Assistant Secretary of State, Nov. 23, 1897, NA, DS, Notes from Arg. Leg., IV; Day to García Mérou, Dec. 1, 1897, NA, DS, Notes to Arg. Leg., VII, 15). The Bureau, of course, was not an agency of the United States government.

[94] These principles are well stated by Charles E. Martin, *The Policy of the United States as Regards Intervention*, p. 126. See also Perkins, *The Monroe Doctrine, 1867-1907*, pp. 62-64.

Dulles found themselves caught between a Hemisphere neighbor and a European friend.

At the very outset of World War II British efforts to fortify the Falklands against possible German occupation, such as Admiral von Spee had attempted in 1914, placed a heavy strain on Anglo-Argentine friendship. Porteño leaders looked upon the recruitment of young Britons within Argentine territory for service in the islands as a violation of their neutrality and sovereignty.[95] When, at Panama in October, 1939, the First Consultative Meeting of Foreign Ministers resolved to create a broad security zone around the Hemisphere, the Argentines flatly reserved their legitimate rights to the possession they had lost in 1832.[96]

Seven months later, after Nazi armies had occupied Holland and France, the Argentines took further steps to re-establish their claims to the islands. When the United States proposed that the American republics recognize no transfer of Hemisphere territory from one non-American power to another, the Argentines countered with the proposition that no European colony should exist within the Americas. They ratified the Convention of Havana, tailored by the Second Consultative Meeting of Foreign Ministers along the lines of the American proposal, but only with the reservation that it did not apply to the Falklands, "since they are a part of Argentine territory and are included within its dominion and sovereignty." [97]

During the post-World War II decade the chauvinism engendered by Juan Perón created appropriate atmosphere for the reassertion of Argentina's claims. Its threats to lay the Falklands case before the United Nations inspired Prime Minister Clement Atlee's assurance to the House of Commons that Britain would not be "cheeked or chivvied" out of its territories anywhere in the world. Periodically, by issuing stamps showing the islands as the "Islas Malvinas" or as a British crown colony, the one or the other nation renewed the "battle of the postage stamps." [98] Even as late as 1958 the famed old wheel horse of the Socialist Party, Alfredo L. Palacios, could publish the third edition of his nationalist volume, *Las Islas Malvinas, archipiélago argentino*. The issue may have been one essentially of "honor" between two long-time friends, yet it sometimes provoked the strategic movement of warships.[99]

At successive inter-American gatherings after the war—Rio (1947), Bogotá (1948), and Caracas (1954)—Perón's representatives renewed their familiar cry. While re-emphasizing Argentine rights to the Falklands

[95] *The New York Times*, Oct. 23, 1939.
[96] See below, p. 402, note 12.
[97] See below, pp. 404-405.
[98] *The New York Times*, June 4, Oct. 6, 1946, Feb. 24, 1948. For a summary of Argentine agitation against Great Britain, see C. A. Silva, *La política internacional de la Nación Argentina*, pp. 641-646.
[99] *The New York Times*, Feb. 16, 1948.

and other territories in the South Atlantic and Antarctica, they sought and won Latin American approval for their opposition to all colonialism in the Western Hemisphere. In loyalty to their European allies, American delegates to the regular Inter-American Conferences at Bogotá and Caracas felt compelled to withhold support from anticolonial resolutions.[100]

For more than a century and a quarter the Argentines have mourned the loss of the strategic Falklands. During the first part of that time, by insisting upon reparations, they clearly held the United States responsible for violation of their sovereignty. Failing to win the indemnification they sought, more recently they have switched their animus, with equal lack of success, toward Great Britain. These repeated failures help to account for Argentina's current hostility toward colonialism within the Americas and its unaccustomed resort to multilateral diplomacy to achieve national aims.

[100] See below, pp. 467, 469, 488.

I X

VORTEX OF INTERNATIONAL POLITICS: FOREIGN INTERVENTION, 1838-1850

For more than a decade after the Falklands dispute, the United States chose to ignore the Argentine Republic. After the withdrawal of Francis Baylies in 1832, the Jackson administration waited two years even to replace George W. Slacum, the refugee consul. Three successors, appointed to Buenos Aires in 1834, 1836, and 1837, received identical admonitions not to exercise "any functions of diplomatic character." [1] When the first of these asked that he be made chargé d'affaires, Secretary of State Forsyth ignored his request.[2] When he offered formal explanation to the Argentine government for criticism of its leaders in the American press, the Secretary speedily censured and recalled him.[3]

Neither the arrival of General Alvear in 1838 nor his continued residence in the United States prompted the Van Buren administration to resume diplomatic relations. Even the shift from Democrats to Whigs in 1841 brought no immediate change in policy. Not until 1844 did Washington resolve to send a diplomatic agent to Buenos Aires. Through its lack of representation, therefore, the United States was impotent in the late thirties and early forties, when France and Great Britain directed their aggressive diplomacy toward the complicated politics of the River Plate region.

[1] John Forsyth, Secretary of State, to Eben R. Dorr, July 29, 1834; to Thomas Lumpkin, Sept. 17, 1836; to Alfred M. Slade, Sept. 22, 1837, NA, DS, Inst. to Con., VI, 32-33; IX, 143, 230-231.

[2] Dorr to Forsyth, Dec. 28, 1835, NA, DS, Con. Let., B. A., IV.

[3] The newspaper article, which quoted a letter purporting to have been written by an officer of the U.S.S. *Natchez*, was reprinted in the New York *Commercial Advertiser* (May 28, 1835) from the *Alexandria Gazette*. See Dorr to Forsyth, Jan. 16, Oct. 15, 1836, Jan. 12, April 20, 1837, NA, DS, Con. Let., B. A., V; Forsyth to Dorr, May 10, 1836, Jan. 11, 1837, NA, DS, Inst. to Con., IX, 119, 178-179. Much of the correspondence was published in Antonio Zinny, *La Gaceta Mercantil de Buenos Aires* (Dec. 12, 1835), II, 268.

Geography and Politics in the Plata Valley

Geography and politics—the geography of the mighty La Plata river system and the politics of the Spanish viceroyalty which grew up along its shores and in its hinterland—combined to produce the domestic turmoil and the foreign intervention which engulfed Argentina from 1838 to 1850.

The broad estuary of the Río de la Plata is formed by water from the Rivers Paraguay, Uruguay, and Paraná, whose tributaries stretch from the Andes of Bolivia to the coffee lands of Brazil. This web of rivers drains all of Paraguay, most of Uruguay and northeastern Argentina, a fourth of Bolivia, and much of southeastern Brazil. Though not geographically a part of the Plata system, the great Argentine pampa, with its millions of acres of farm and pasture lands, is a natural economic complement of the port cities. Before the coming of the railroad and the highway, and even after, this tremendous system of waterways provided the principal commercial arteries for over a million square miles of rich agricultural soil, tilled by the population of five rising nations. The capitals of three nations—Buenos Aires, Montevideo, Asunción— grew up along the river shores.

Before the movements for independence, these three nations had been provinces of the last viceroyalty created in Spain's American Empire. In Buenos Aires, seat of the viceregal government, where after 1810 Spanish leaders never restored their authority, divergent political beliefs and overweening imperialist ambitions split wide the Creole leadership in the Plata valley, prevented unification of the Viceroyalty, and postponed for decades the attainment of political stability.

In the creation of an independent government, fledgling political philosophers and ambitious local caudillos clashed over administrative forms best suited to secure national unity and popular support. In the capital city, where young Creoles had absorbed French eighteenth-century philosophy, strong leadership advocated a unitary system like that of France. In the outlying regions, where untamed Gauchos cherished their independence, equally zealous forces sought a federal state with adequate local autonomy.[4] Until 1880, Unitarians and Federalists waged intermittent political and military warfare to win or keep power. Only during the rigid dictatorship of Juan Manuel de Rosas (1835-1852) did the Argentine people enjoy relative freedom from civil strife. In matters of foreign policy Rosas gave little voice to provincial leaders. Vigorous opposition came from the river provinces—Corrientes, Entre Ríos, and Santa Fe—where local chieftains sometimes refused to submit to porteño control.

[4] José Luis Romero, *Las ideas políticas en Argentina*, pp. 65-128.

Whether unitarian or federalist, the leaders at Buenos Aires almost unanimously dreamed of subjecting all parts of the old viceroyalty to their authority. Paraguay, its homogeneous Guaraní population isolated a thousand miles up the rivers, resented the nascent imperialism of Buenos Aires. Until 1840, under the inscrutable Dr. Francia, and later, under Carlos Antonio and Francisco Solano López, Paraguay resisted outside penetration and frustrated absorption into a larger state.

Across the Río de la Plata, on the eastern shore, the Spanish Americans of the Banda Oriental were equally reluctant to accept domination from Buenos Aires. Not only from the west but also from Portuguese Brazil on the north the Uruguayans were exposed to aggression. Here was the inevitable meeting ground for the competing expansionism of Argentina and Brazil, nineteenth-century sequel to the Spanish-Portuguese rivalry which had persisted from the sixteenth. Brazilians, with arms of the Plata system reaching into their lands, could not concede Argentine occupation of both sides of the estuary; nor could Argentines complacently submit to Brazilian control of the eastern shore and its Spanish inhabitants. The logical compromise, at the close of a three-year war (1828), was the creation of Uruguay as a buffer state in the European tradition—a pawn which both nations could seek to control.

Moreover, after independence, domestic conflict in Uruguay invited outside interference. Its first President, Fructuoso Rivera, granted asylum to Unitarian émigrés from Buenos Aires, who used Montevideo as a sanctuary from which to plot against the entrenched Argentine Federalists. Rivera's successor, Manuel Oribe, electing to play the Rosas game, in 1835 agreed to curb the political activities of the Argentine exiles. Later, when Rivera initiated active rebellion against President Oribe, Rosas' enemies joined up with the revolting leader.[5]

Borrowing from Rosas his reliance upon party symbols, Oribe decreed use of a white emblem bearing the motto "Defensores de leyes." To compete with the symbolism of Oribe's *Blancos*, the Gaucho adherents of Rivera, adopting a red standard, formed the *Colorados*. Turbulent Uruguay, therefore, long the victim of Argentine-Brazilian rivalry, was now drawn more deeply into the bitter maelstrom of Argentine factional politics. Not until 1850 would Uruguay escape the shadow of the Gaucho dictator and the international complications he brought to the whole Plata valley.

Interference of the French, 1838-1840

The determination of Jackson and his successors to avoid involvement in the tumultuous politics of the Plata region coincided with aggressive actions by Great Britain and France. Anglo-American rivalry, which

[5] Ricardo Levene, *A History of Argentina*, p. 426.

had risen to a high pitch in the twenties, gradually gave way in the thirties and forties to Anglo-French competition. Despite Argentine resentment at seizure of the Falklands, Britain continued to dominate the Río de la Plata, both in prestige and in foreign trade. France between 1831 and 1841 increased its exports to the area,[6] and in 1837 the Molé government sought to placate factional opposition at home by intensifying its pressure against Argentina.

Concurrently with naval action in Mexico, France injected itself into the heart of River Plate affairs by reviving an old quarrel with the Argentine government. In 1828-1830, like the English and Americans, the French had been irritated by the attempt of General Lavalle to conscript resident aliens for military service.[7] During 1836-1837, a vice-consul, Aimé Roger, demanded for French nationals the same privileges enjoyed by British residents under the treaty of 1825. Failing to establish his contention, the Consul, in November, 1837, combined this demand with some specific claims of French citizens and insisted upon early satisfaction. Burdened with the cares of foreign war and local disaffection, Rosas punctiliously refused to treat with a consul upon diplomatic affairs. Roger obtained the consent of his government to use coercion, and on March 24 Admiral Leblanc appeared before Buenos Aires with a French squadron. The officer immediately presented three peremptory demands and enjoined a reply within forty-eight hours. When Rosas refused to negotiate under threat of force, Leblanc declared the port and the coast under blockade.[8]

The Van Buren administration received prompt notification of the blockade from its agents in southern South America: Eben Ritchie Dorr, Consul in Buenos Aires, William Hunter, Minister in Rio de Janeiro, and Commodore J. B. Nicolson, commanding officer of United States ships in the South Atlantic. Dorr and Nicolson, on the spot, believed that Leblanc could enforce the blockade.[9] Hunter, a thousand miles away, contended that, without a declaration of war or despatch of an adequate naval force, the French blockade was illegal.[10]

The failure of President Van Buren and Secretary Forsyth to main-

[6] *The Merchants' Magazine and Commercial Review*, VIII, 445-447.

[7] See above, p. 96.

[8] This summary is based upon "Memorandum of a Conference at the Department of State with De Alvear," Oct. 27, 1838, William R. Manning (ed.), *Diplomatic Correspondence of the United States: Inter-American Affairs, 1831-1860*, I, 208-209; William Hunter, U.S. Minister to Brazil, to Forsyth, April 16, 1838, *ibid.*, II, 223-224; *British and Foreign State Papers*, XXVI (1837-1838), 920-1024; and John F. Cady, *Foreign Intervention in the Río de la Plata, 1838-1850*, pp. 22, 31. Cady's work is a comprehensive survey. Although devoted especially to Anglo-French policies during the intervention, it deals at length with those of the United States. I have used it freely in the preparation of this chapter.

[9] Dorr to Forsyth, April 7, 1838, Manning, *op. cit.*, I, 201; Nicolson to Mahlon Dickerson, Secretary of Navy, April 1, 1838, NA, DN, Captain's Letters, April, 1838.

[10] Hunter to Forsyth, May 4, 1838, Manning, *op. cit.*, II, 225-226.

tain diplomatic representation in Buenos Aires during the French intervention militated against the conduct of effective diplomacy. Successive consuls, instructed to avoid diplomatic activity, failed even to submit adequate intelligence reports.[11] Nevertheless, had the administration chosen to reassure Rosas in his stand against French violation of Hemisphere waters, it could have communicated with him through Carlos de Alvear, who in August arrived in the United States on his second mission.[12]

Although Alvear's primary mission in Washington was adjustment of the Falklands dispute,[13] his instructions reveal Rosas' desire for American good will during the intervention. He directed his emissary to assure the Secretary of State that the Argentine Confederation had determined to resist at whatever cost the French challenge to its national independence and dignity. To enlighten the American people and to win their favor for the Argentine cause, Alvear was to utilize, widely but prudently, the American press. Moreover, he should explain the Argentine case to diplomatic representatives, even to the French envoy.[14]

When in October General Alvear received his first appointment with the Secretary of State, he carried out his instructions to the letter. He described the provocative actions of the French agents; he explained the legal position and the conciliatory reaction of the Rosas government. While affirming Argentine determination to retaliate, at no time, either during this interview or later, did Alvear ask or receive assurance that the United States would take a firm stand against the French blockade.[15]

While the French, in the meantime, were making no headway against the resoluteness of Rosas, the blockade was stifling American commerce and threatening the neutral position of American naval forces. Lacking specific instructions from Washington and handicapped by his admitted incompetence in international law, Commodore Nicolson followed a generally commendable course. While carefully reporting the progress of Franco-Argentine negotiations, he strove to protect American shipping without deviating from strict neutrality.[16]

[11] Forsyth to Slade, Jan. 1, 1839, Jan. 1, 1841, NA, DS, Inst. to Con., IX, 347, 490.
[12] Alvear to Arana, Aug. 4, Sept. 13, 1838, AGN, BA, S1-A2-A4-núm. 13. Alvear's second mission to the United States lasted until his death in 1852. Thomas B. Davis recounts at length the Minister's frustrating efforts to secure American aid for Rosas during both the French and the Anglo-French interventions (*Carlos de Alvear, Man of Revolution*, pp. 122ff).
[13] See above, p. 115.
[14] Instructions to Alvear, [May 22, 1838], AGN, BA, S1-A1-A1-núm. 5.
[15] "Memorandum of a Conference at the Department of State with De Alvear," Oct. 27, 1838, Manning, *op. cit.*, I, 208-209.
[16] Nicolson to Dickerson, April 1, May 31, 1838; to James K. Paulding, Secretary of Navy, Oct. 1, Nov. 5, 10, Dec. 3, 1838, March 18, 1839, NA, DN, Captain's Letters, April, May, Oct., Nov., Dec., 1838, March, 1839; Paulding to Nicolson, June 17, 1839, NA, DN, Letters to Officers of Ships of War, XXVII (May 24, 1838—Sept. 30, 1839).

After action of the French blockading force had twice threatened to provoke hostilities with his command, the naval officer, without the authorization of his government, determined in April, 1839, to attempt a mediation between Rosas and the French. Having studied carefully the correspondence on the origin of the blockade,[17] Nicolson secured the authority of the French agents to present terms of negotiations to Rosas.[18] But his earnest efforts to facilitate an accommodation failed either to move refractory adversaries or to please his superiors. French terms proved unacceptable to the stubborn Rosas; the dictator's counterproposals were inadmissible to the obstinate French.[19] Though the officer speedily terminated his project, the Secretary of the Navy warned him that such moves, unless expressly authorized, might not conform to government policy.[20]

Nicolson's activities and the entire sequence of events connected with the French intervention gained little attention in the United States. The press carried news of the French blockade and the mediation, but there was little editorial criticism of Van Buren's failure to protest European aggression.[21] The apathy of the public was but a reflection of that of the administration. When in May, 1838, Hunter in Rio de Janeiro offered to visit Buenos Aires for a conference with Rosas, his suggestion was disregarded.[22] The Argentine Foreign Minister's direct appeal for the "sympathetic sentiments" of the United States availed him nothing.[23] Even General Alvear's personal explanation of the blockade, Commodore Nicolson's well-intentioned project of mediation, and Hunter's warning

---

[17] The relevant documents were published in Buenos Aires in 1838 in a pamphlet of sixty-eight pages, under the title *Oficio del consul encargado interinamente del consulado general de Francia en Buenos-Aires, al Sr. ministro de relaciones exteriores de la Confederación argentina, . . .* A supplementary publication was issued later in the year.

[18] Rosas to Nicolson, April 4, 7, 1839; Nicolson to Rosas, April 9, 1839, NA, DN, Captain's Letters, April, 1839. The Rosas-Nicolson correspondence, including the latter's original letters, is preserved in the Archivo General de la Nación, Buenos Aires, S1-A2-A4-núm. 9. It was also published in English in Buenos Aires with the title *Correspondence Sustained between the Government of Buenos Aires, . . . and Captain John B. Nicolson, . . .*

[19] Rosas to Nicolson, April 12, 17, 1839; Nicolson to Arana, April 22, 1839, NA, DN, Captain's Letters, April, 1839. Because of Rosas' position in this negotiation, J. B. Alberdi described the French intervention as an affair between Rosas and the French, not between Argentina and the French (*Obras selectas*, VI, 275).

[20] Paulding to Nicolson, July 8, 1839, NA, DN, Letters to Officers of Ships of War, XXVII.

[21] News accounts of the events, but little more, appeared in such journals as the *Daily National Intelligencer*, *Globe* (Washington), *Richmond Enquirer*, and *Niles' Register*. Alvear supplied some information to newspapers (see Davis, *op. cit.*, pp. 128-129).

[22] Hunter to Forsyth, May 15, 1838, NA, DS, Desp. Bra., XI.

[23] Arana to Forsyth, Nov. 13, 1838, Manning, *op. cit.*, I, 210.

of French intrigues failed to animate the State Department.[24] The Congress paid little attention to the whole affair, although, in considering the French blockade of the Mexican coast, Senator Caleb Cushing, of Massachusetts, called upon the President for correspondence relating to the blockade of La Plata.[25] Neither the threat of French occupation of South American soil nor the striking decrease in American commerce with Argentina shook the indifference of the Van Buren administration.[26]

The French intervention persisted until October 29, 1840, when the Mackau Convention brought about its termination.[27] The reopening of La Plata to foreign vessels after more than two years and a half stimulated a sharp revival in the trade of North American vessels with the South Atlantic, in spite of the commotions which rocked Argentina's internal peace and for a time threatened the tenure of Rosas.[28] Although the government of the United States had played an inconspicuous role in Argentine affairs during the period of French interference, Rosas and his aides manifested no unfriendliness toward the northern republic.[29]

Beginnings of Anglo-French Interposition

The lifting of the French blockade enabled Rosas to war more vigorously against Uruguay. Upon Fructuosa Rivera's accession to the presidency in March, 1839, Rosas had allied himself with ex-President Oribe's Blancos. The entente between the Argentine and Blanco chiefs, greatly strengthened by the French intervention, became a central factor in the confused politics of the Río de la Plata during the forties. Recurrently throughout the decade the dictator found himself opposed not only by President Rivera and his Colorados, but by Britain, France, Brazil, Paraguay, and even some of the fluvial provinces of Argentina itself, notably Entre Ríos and Corrientes. About this struggle between Oribe and Rivera for control of Uruguay revolved the chaos which embroiled the Río de la Plata until the expulsion of Rosas.[30]

By their desire to protect commerce with Buenos Aires and Monte-

---

[24] "Memorandum of a Conference at the Department of State with De Alvear," Oct. 27, 1838; Hunter to Forsyth, Dec. 29, 1839, Manning, *op. cit.*, I, 208-209; II, 240-241.

[25] *H. Jour.*, 25 Cong., 3 sess., p. 159; *H. Ex. Doc.*, No. 211, 25 Cong., 3 sess., p. 33.

[26] Treasury Department, *American Commerce: Commerce of South America, Central America, Mexico, and West Indies, with Share of the United States and Other Leading Nations Therein, 1821-1898*, p. 3300.

[27] *British and Foreign State Papers*, XXIX (1840-1841), 1089-1091.

[28] Amory Edwards, Acting U.S. Consul at Buenos Aires, to Forsyth, Dec. 28, 1840, Manning, *op. cit.*, I, 227.

[29] Commodore Charles G. Ridgely, commanding U.S. Naval Forces on the coast of Brazil, to Secretary of State, Dec. 25, 1840, NA, DS, Con. Let., B. A., VI.

[30] Levene, *op. cit.*, pp. 426-427.

video, Britain, France, and the United States were drawn into the imbroglio. After January, 1841, Rosas blockaded Uruguayan ports with exasperating frequency and with deplorable injury to foreign commerce. From August, 1842, to 1850, British and French mediators repeatedly sought to resolve the anarchy. Actual Anglo-French intervention did not occur until September, 1845, but by that time Rosas' foreign affairs were deeply involved.[31]

Renewal of Diplomatic Relations

Into this chaos, in September, 1843, the Washington government determined to send a diplomatic representative. The Tyler administration, seeking to rehabilitate American shipping to the South Atlantic, was concerned over commercial preferences granted to Great Britain. It felt urged to ascertain the objects of Anglo-French policies toward the nations of La Plata. It needed authentic information on the internal affairs of a nation where no United States diplomat had been assigned for more than a decade. Claims of American citizens awaited diplomatic pressure. To accomplish these purposes President Tyler appointed as special agent a Tennessean, Harvey M. Watterson, first in a long line of Southerners to represent the nation in Buenos Aires.[32]

Watterson's arrival in Buenos Aires in January, 1844, coincided with mounting hatred of Britain, France, and Brazil for their activities against the Argentine blockade of Uruguayan ports. In these circumstances, Rosas displayed complete willingness to exchange diplomatic missions with the United States. Opposed in his policies by neighboring nations and by European powers, Rosas was naturally eager to receive an agent from the United States.[33] To his affability and flattery the American quickly succumbed.[34] He continued to write of "the friendly feeling of the government of Buenos Ayres towards that of the United States and of its citizens." [35]

The Tennessean was given little opportunity to test Rosas' sincerity, for in June the Senate refused to ratify his appointment as chargé d'affaires.[36] To replace him, John C. Calhoun, Secretary of State, appointed a Virginian, William Brent, Jr., Democrat, Anglophobe, and neophyte in diplomacy. Except that he was specifically authorized to work for a commercial treaty, Brent's instructions were similar to those

---

[31] See Cady, op. cit., pp. 92-159.
[32] Abel P. Upshur, Secretary of State, to Watterson, Sept. 26, 1843, NA, DS, Inst. Arg., XV, 1-5, extract printed in Manning, op. cit., I, 20-22.
[33] Edwards to Upshur, Jan. 23, 1844, ibid., pp. 230-233.
[34] Watterson to Dept., April 27, 1844, NA, DS, Desp. Arg., V.
[35] Watterson to Calhoun, Sept. 8, 1844, Manning, op. cit., I, 233.
[36] St. George L. Sioussat, "John Caldwell Calhoun," in S. F. Bemis (ed.), The American Secretaries of State and Their Diplomacy, V, 216.

of his predecessor.[37] Departing from New York in August, Brent was recognized as chargé d'affaires on November 15.[38]

The Voorhees Affair

Prior to the departure of Watterson and the arrival of Brent a flurry blew up to disturb the newborn calm in Argentine-American relations. The disturbance centered around Captain P. F. Voorhees, who in March, 1844, had been sent to Montevideo with the frigate *Congress* for the protection of commerce. His superior, Commodore Daniel Turner, had ordered him to be

> extremely particular in all your *Official & Private* intercourse with the MonteVidean and Buenos Ayrean Governments, bearing always in mind that it is not only, the Policy of our Government, but their earnest desire, to maintain a strict and unqualified neutrality in all things relating to the Belligerents, and to those countries generally.[39]

Voorhees arrived in the Río de la Plata to find Montevideo blockaded at sea by an Argentine squadron and besieged on land by the forces of General Oribe, claimant to the Uruguayan presidency. Although the pretender occupied most of Uruguay outside the capital itself, Britain and France recognized his opponent, Rivera, as the legal ruler. Moreover, though formal war did not exist, the European powers generally admitted belligerent rights to the contestants.[40]

On September 29, Oribe's armed schooner *Sancalá*, in pursuit of a Montevidean fishing boat attempting to run the blockade, fired carelessly into the American ship *Rosalba*. Captain Voorhees promptly seized the *Sancalá* and its crew as well as the officers and ships of the Argentine squadron, with whose commander the offending vessel had communicated. The officer also liberated several fishing boats held by the blockading force and released some Montevidean prisoners and American seamen. Though he soon dismissed the Argentine ships, Voorhees detained the *Sancalá* and its crew under charge of displaying a false flag.[41]

---

[37] Calhoun to Brent, July 15, 1844, NA, DS, Inst. Arg., XV, 8, extract printed in Manning, *op. cit.*, I, 22-23.

[38] *Niles' Register*, LXVI (Aug. 17, 1844), p. 397; *Registro oficial de la República Argentina*, II, 432.

[39] March 14, 1844, NA, DN, Brazilian Squadron, Commodore Daniel Turner, April 19, 1844-April 28, 1845. (Hereafter cited as Brazilian Squadron, Turner.) Much of the correspondence on the Voorhees episode is transcribed in a separate volume in Department of State Archives, called "Correspondence of Captain Voorhees."

[40] John Bassett Moore, *A Digest of International Law* . . . , I, 178-179.

[41] Watterson to Calhoun, Oct. 11, 1844, and enclosures, Manning, *op. cit.*, I, 242-245.

Voorhees' precipitate actions offended both Rosas and Oribe. Tension quickly mounted. Through their respective Foreign Ministers, Felipe Arana and Carlos G. Villademoros, the dictator and his Uruguayan ally sought explanations and retribution,[42] demands with which the American agent in Buenos Aires and the Consul in Montevideo found it difficult fully to comply. Watterson, with the utmost tact, deplored the incident, expressed his regrets, and sought to curb Argentine indignation.[43] On the eastern shore of the Plata, however, where the Consul, R. M. Hamilton, was advised and animated by Voorhees, calm was not so quickly restored. The determined officer, who regarded Oribe's men as "a set of sanguinary barbarians," refused to recede from his position.[44] To the commander of the Argentine squadron he complained of discrimination against American ships by the blockading force and announced that he would no longer grant the right of search.[45] Only the arrival of Commodore Turner from Rio de Janeiro late in October clarified the charged air. Refusing to support the aggressive position of his junior officer, Turner notified the Argentine commander that the United States would respect the blockade.[46]

For the time being this decision apparently satisfied the Argentine government, for Brent experienced no difficulty in securing recognition.[47] In describing the Voorhees incident to the legislature late in December, Rosas announced that both the Chargé and the commander of the United States squadron had disapproved the officer's temerity. He had instructed the Argentine Minister in Washington, he said, to claim reparation and complete satisfaction. He hoped that friendly relations would continue.[48]

The authorities in Washington soon revealed their concern. Secretary Calhoun, after conferring with the Secretary of the Navy, advised Brent to extend the "deep regret" of the United States and to assure the authorities that Voorhees would receive proper punishment.[49] This much was done at once. Repeated requests and reminders by Carlos de

[42] Villademoros to R. M. Hamilton, Consul in Montevideo, Sept. 30, Oct. 1, 1844; Arana to Watterson, Oct. 6, 1844, and enclosures, Manning, *op. cit.*, I, 235, 236, 237-240.

[43] Watterson to Arana, Oct. 11, 1844, *ibid.*, pp. 241-242.

[44] Voorhees to Hamilton, Oct. 2, 1844; Hamilton to Oribe, Oct. 3, 12, 1844; Villademoros to Hamilton, Oct. 10, 1844, NA, DN, Brazilian Squadron, Turner; Voorhees to Henry A. Wise, U.S. Minister to Brazil, Nov. 1, 1844, NA, DS, Correspondence of Captain Voorhees.

[45] Voorhees to Admiral Antonio Toll, Oct. 22, 1844, NA, DN, Brazilian Squadron, Turner.

[46] Turner to Toll, Nov. 3, 1844, *ibid.*

[47] Brent to Secretary of State, Dec. 11, 1844, NA, DS, Desp. Arg., V.

[48] H. Mabragaña, *Los mensajes*, II, 72-73.

[49] John Y. Mason, Secretary of Navy, to Calhoun, Dec. 13, 1844, and enclosure, NA, DS, Misc. Let., Nov.-Dec., 1844; Calhoun to Brent, Dec. 28, 1844, Manning, *op. cit.*, I, 23-24.

Alvear, however, failed to accelerate the labored process of interdepartmental conferences, court-martial, Cabinet meeting, and Presidential action.[50] Ultimately, in October, 1845, Secretary Buchanan notified Alvear that the Navy had suspended Voorhees for three years.[51] Rosas could now convey to his legislature appreciation for "this testimony of the good policy and fine friendship of the illustrious government of the United States."[52] On the eve of intensified Anglo-French intervention, the Voorhees incident had tested but not impaired the newly established friendship between the two American nations.

American Agents Protest the Blockades

Even the presence in Buenos Aires of William Brent, a fully accredited diplomatic officer, failed to restore complete harmony in the policy of the United States. On two occasions in 1845, Brent disputed appropriate courses of action with Captain G. J. Pendergrast, commanding the U.S.S. *Boston*. The first instance was the Argentine blockade of Montevideo and Maldonado; the second was the Anglo-French blockade of Uruguayan coasts controlled by Oribe. In each case, Brent's stand favored Rosas and Oribe, while Pendergrast's position followed more closely that taken by the British and French naval officers.

The first of the incidents arose from the strict blockade which Rosas decreed on January 11, 1845.[53] Brent assumed that his government would recognize its validity.[54] Pendergrast, on the other hand, observing that Rear Admiral Lainé, Commander in Chief of French Naval Forces in La Plata, had refused to acknowledge the blockade, informed the Argentine admiral that he would expect equal immunities and advantages for American ships. Arguing that such action was a violation of neutrality and an invasion of Argentine sovereignty, the Chargé sought to move Pendergrast from his position.[55] Although the commander of the Buenos Airean squadron off Montevideo, Admiral William Brown, supported this view, the American captain stubbornly refused to "admit the right or

---

[50] Alvear to Calhoun, Feb. 7, 1845; Alvear to Buchanan, March 27, April 13, May 17, 1845, Manning, *op. cit.*, I, 260-268; Calhoun to Alvear, Feb. 20, March 3, 1845; Buchanan to Alvear, May 29, 1845, *ibid.*, pp. 24-26. On the actions taken by the United States Government, see Mason to Calhoun, March 3, 1845, and enclosures, NA, DS, Misc. Letters, Jan.-March, 1845; Secretary of Navy to Secretary of State, May 27, 1845, and enclosure, Manning, *op. cit.*, I, 26-27; and *The Diary of James K. Polk during his Presidency*, I, 41-43.

[51] Buchanan to Alvear, Oct. 25, 1845, and enclosures, Manning, *op. cit.*, I, 27-29.

[52] Mabragaña, *op. cit.*, II, 94.

[53] Arana to Admiral William Brown, Commander in Chief of the Argentine Squadron, Jan. 11, 1845, Manning, *op. cit.*, I, 252, note 2.

[54] Brent to Pendergrast, Feb. 11, 1845, *H. Ex. Doc.*, No. 212, 29 Cong., 1 sess., p. 11.

[55] Pendergrast to Brown, Jan. 30, 1845; Brent to Pendergrast, Feb. 11, 1845, *ibid.*, pp. 5, 12-13.

propriety of any foreign officer or government to dictate to him a particular course of conduct." [56]

Though neither Brent nor Brown was able to sway Pendergrast, the officer was forced to bow to the interpretation of the secretaries of the State and Navy Departments. Supported by President Polk, they held that Pendergrast was

> wrong in his position that a blockading squadron must have the force and power to resist effectually all opposition, and that the failure on the part of the Argentine republic to maintain her belligerant [*sic*] rights against the opposition of the French naval force justified him refusing to conform to the strict blockade. [57]

In his first brush with the naval officer, the diplomat had scored the more heavily.

Brent's second disagreement with Pendergrast resulted from the Anglo-French blockade of Montevideo. Toward the end of July, the British and French mediators, W. G. Ouseley and Baron Deffaudis, began to differ with Rosas over terms of an armistice with Uruguay. Failing to secure Rosas' agreement to retire his troops from Uruguay, on August 1 the negotiators withdrew from Buenos Aires, satisfied temporarily to establish a blockade over the Uruguayan ports held by Oribe. [58]

Having already urged his government to adopt a more forthright position in Platine affairs, Brent now sought to enlist Pendergrast's aid in opposing the European intervention. In a long letter filled with allusions to international law, Brent asked the captain to confer with the European commanders. While informing them that the declaration of a blockade by a neutral state was illegal, he should seek for American shipping the same concessions they had previously wrung from Rosas in his blockade of Montevideo. [59]

In the preceding May, when Buchanan instructed Brent to ensure that Argentina conduct the blockade "on the established principles of public law," [60] he could hardly have expected that the agent would undertake a lengthy academic discussion of the subject for the edification of a naval officer. At any rate, Brent's approach was not one to convert Pendergrast. Moreover, the officer had not the pro-Rosas bias of the chargé. Except to demand some special privileges for American

[56] Brown to Pendergrast, Feb. 19, 1845; Pendergrast to Brown, Feb. 22, 1845, *ibid.*, pp. 9, 10.

[57] George Bancroft, Secretary of Navy, to Turner, May 27, 1845, *ibid.*, p. 39; Buchanan to Brent, May 26, 1845, Manning, *op. cit.*, I, 26.

[58] Brent to Buchanan, Aug. 2, Nov. 14, 1845, Manning, *op. cit.*, I, 291, 305-306.

[59] Brent to Pendergrast, Aug. 30, 1845, *ibid.*, pp. 295-298.

[60] Buchanan to Brent, May 26, 1845, *ibid.*, p. 26.

vessels, Pendergrast paid little heed to Brent's requests.[61] In his second encounter with the naval officer, the diplomat achieved no triumph, nor was his opposition to the intervention diminished in the slightest.

When on September 22 he learned that the British and French proposed to extend their restrictions to Buenos Aires within forty-eight hours, Brent hotly protested the "so-called and misnamed blockade," declared its invalidity, and threatened to demand indemnification for losses suffered by American citizens.[62] On this occasion, Pendergrast, too, raised objections, calling the blockade "unjust and unnecessary . . . hasty and inconsiderate." [63]

Throughout his mission in Buenos Aires, William Brent displayed obvious prejudice for the Argentine cause and equally apparent dread of English predominance in the Río de la Plata. Even while offering to serve as mediator, his despatches to Washington manifested abhorrence of British imperialism and fear of the limits it might reach in southern South America.[64]

Abortive Attempts to Mediate

Brent paralleled his protests against the blockades with efforts to intercede in the successive crises. On three occasions in 1845-1846 he initiated or abetted plans for mediation between Argentina and her foes. Partly because of his ambition and prejudice but mainly because of his government's refusal to support him, the Chargé failed in each attempt.

In the conflict between Argentina and Montevideo, Brent first offered his services to Rosas on April 11, 1845, shortly before the arrival of the European mediators, Ouseley and Deffaudis.[65] The dictator, promptly responding to the American's initiative, insisted upon Brent's inclusion as an active participant in the Anglo-French mediation.[66] Although Brent agreed to cooperate with them, the Europeans complained that they lacked instructions for such a plan.[67] Even Brent's proposal to allow Argentina to suspend or resume his services at will failed to relieve the tenseness. The European mediation, like the American, was abortive.[68]

[61] Pendergrast to Rear Admiral S. H. Inglefield, Commander in Chief of British Naval Forces in Río de la Plata, and to Admiral Lainé, Sept. 5, 1845, *H. Ex. Doc.*, No. 212, pp. 19-23.

[62] I. du Mareuil, French Chargé d'Affaires, to Brent, Sept. 22, 1845; Brent to Ouseley, Sept. 23, 1845, Manning, *op. cit.*, I, 292, 293-294.

[63] Pendergrast to Inglefield, Oct. 14, 1845, *H. Ex. Doc.*, No. 212, p. 28.

[64] Brent to Buchanan, Nov. 14, 1845, Feb. 2, 1846, Manning, *op. cit.*, I, 312, 323-325.

[65] Brent to Arana, April 11, 1845, NA, DS, Desp. Arg., V.

[66] Brent to Buchanan, Aug. 2, 1845, Manning, *op. cit.*, I, 290-291.

[67] Brent to Arana, June 12, 1845; Brent to Buchanan, Aug. 2, 1845, *ibid.*, pp. 269, 290.

[68] Brent to Arana, July 26, 1845, *ibid.*, p. 275.

Meanwhile, in Rio de Janeiro, the United States Minister, Henry A. Wise, was conceiving other plans for halting hostilities and frustrating Anglo-French intentions in La Plata. As early as November, 1844, the Brazilian Minister of Foreign Affairs, Ernesto F. França, had asked him what the United States would do to prevent European intervention in American affairs. Would it not be willing, he asked, to "unite with Brazil in putting an end to that war by force, if necessary, rather than permit England or France to interpose and acquire a dominant influence in the Platte [Plata] country?" Wise reported the proposal to Calhoun and enthusiastically suggested the possibility of such a mediation under his agency or that of Brent.[69] Receiving no encouragement—or discouragement—from Washington during the next six months, the Minister sought, without success, to urge the Brazilian government to action.[70] Without instructions, he was unable to go further. Apparently at the end of his resources, a fortuitous occurrence gave him new opportunity.

Wise's newborn hopes emerged from the arrival in Rio de Janeiro late in July, 1845, of Edward A. Hopkins, specially appointed by President Polk to investigate conditions in Paraguay. Young, vigorous, ambitious, Hopkins had the unlimited energy required for an inspection tour of the isolated land, though his overzealousness and indiscretion were to lead him into a stormy career in Paraguay and the Río de la Plata.[71] Thrice tried between 1842 and 1845 for misconduct and insubordination, the United States Navy had finally dismissed him.[72] The record of his activities in Paraguay and Argentina during the next half century reads like fiction.[73] He became an enterprising pioneer in frontier lands, but never a diplomat. Nevertheless, his unexpected appearance, en route to Asunción, with specific instructions to consult Wise, brought the Minister an exciting windfall.

In Wise's extravagant dreams, the United States, without departing from its established policies of nonintervention and avoidance of entangling alliances, would become the great protector and benefactor of American nations. It would vastly extend its commerce. Rio de Janeiro would become the center of operations in South America. But, to accomplish all this, hostilities in the Río de la Plata must be stopped, and

[69] Nov. 1, 1844, Manning, *op. cit.*, II, 269-271.

[70] Wise to Calhoun, Feb. 25, 1845; to Buchanan, March 28, May 2, 19, July 2, 31, 1845, *ibid.*, pp. 275-282 *passim*, 286-294.

[71] Henry M. Wriston, *Executive Agents in American Foreign Relations*, pp. 440-443.

[72] The complete story of Hopkins' career in the Navy, including his court-martial, is to be found in the Navy Department Manuscripts in the National Archives. See Harold F. Peterson, "Edward A. Hopkins: A Pioneer Promoter in Paraguay," *The Hispanic American Historical Review*, XXII (May, 1942), 246-247, notes 5-8.

[73] On Hopkins' colorful career, see Peterson, *op. cit.*; Victor L. Johnson, "Edward A. Hopkins and the Development of Argentine Transportation and Communication," *The Hispanic American Historical Review*, XXVI (Feb., 1946), 19-37; and Hopkins, *Historico-Politico Memorial upon the Regions of the Río de la Plata. . . .*

the English and French must not be the ones to halt them. First of all, however, Paraguay must not go to war with Argentina. With these ideas Wise sought to imbue Hopkins, a thoroughly receptive pupil.[74]

Hopkins represented the Polk administration's desire for more intimate relations with Paraguay. In clear, unmistakable terms, stressing the need for tact, Secretary Buchanan directed the youth to determine the fitness of Paraguay and its government for recognition, After evaluating Argentine intentions toward the nation, he should assure President Carlos Antonio López that the United States would seek to induce Rosas to keep the Río de la Plata open to the trade of all nations. He should inform López of American sympathies for his country and suggest that he follow the American policy of avoiding entangling alliances.[75]

Stimulated by the zeal of his mentor in Rio de Janeiro, Hopkins moved on by boat, foot, and wild horse to Asunción.[76] His fire and zest won the immediate favor of President López, an advantage which the agent turned to quick profit. In his first interview he committed his government to recognition and tendered its good offices for mediation between Paraguay and Rosas.[77] The stimulant of Wise's plans, intensified by his own enthusiasm, was exerting its effect. Unless Paraguay were invaded, López responded, his armies would remain inactive for four months or until Rosas clarified his position. Negotiation of permanent terms must await Argentine recognition of Paraguayan independence and guarantee of territorial integrity.[78] After gaining some commercial privileges for himself, Hopkins left Asunción in late December.[79]

Before Hopkins' return to Rio de Janeiro, Wise informed Brent of the agent's successes, especially of López' promise to suspend hostilities against Rosas pending the mediatorial efforts of the United States.[80] Though Brent had already offered his services to Argentina, he now urged immediate action. On February 26 Arana pronounced acceptance of the offer. A day later Rosas ordered General Urquiza not to invade Paraguay.[81]

Meanwhile, Hopkins had returned to Rio de Janeiro, where Wise, still without authorization, sent him on to Buenos Aires to exert his influence with Rosas.[82] The agent reached the capital on the 27th, in

[74] Wise to Buchanan, July 31, 1845, Manning, *op. cit.*, II, 284, 294-295.
[75] Buchanan to Hopkins, June 10, 1845, Manning, *op. cit.*, X, 29-32.
[76] Hopkins to Buchanan, Aug. 26, Sept. 16, 19, Nov. 1, 1845, *ibid.*, 57-63.
[77] Hopkins to Buchanan, Nov. 31 [*sic*], 1845, *ibid.*, pp. 64, 65, 74.
[78] Wise to Brent, Jan. 12, 1846, Manning, *op. cit.*, I, 319-320, note 1; *Mensajes de Carlos Antonio López . . .* , p. 45.
[79] Brent to Buchanan, March 31, 1845, and enclosure, Manning, *op. cit.*, I, 349, note 5.
[80] Wise to Brent, Jan. 12, 1846, *ibid.*, pp. 319-320, note 1.
[81] Brent to Arana, Jan. 31, 1846; to Buchanan, Feb. 2, 1846; Arana to Brent, Feb. 26, 1846, and enclosures, *ibid.*, 319-321, 325-329.
[82] Wise to Buchanan, Feb. 18, 1846, Manning, *op. cit.*, II, 318-321.

time to receive news of Brent's successes. Here, however, Hopkins' mounting enthusiasm received a quick chilling, when Rosas brusquely refused to confer with an agent who bore no credentials directed to the Argentine Republic.[83] It was the first rebuff his great plans had suffered. He became sulky and vindictive.

By announcing the terms he would grant to Paraguay, Rosas stimulated Hopkins' next step. The dictator was willing to concede territorial integrity, home rule, and use of the rivers on an equal basis with other members of the Argentine Confederation, but not independence.[84] Two days later Hopkins withdrew from the country. His parting thrust at Rosas' tyranny was a long, bitter letter, flaming with indecorum and impudence. With insolent and provoking phrases the diplomat described Argentina's chaos and offered possible remedies. He advised recognition of Paraguayan independence, immediate declaration of war against Britain and France, confiscation of English and French property, purification of the press, and conclusion of a treaty with Brazil. To the head of an independent state, in glowing rhetoric, he sketched the alternatives for Argentina's future:

> The power by actions unmistakable and not to be construed to your discredit, to make for yourself a far greater, a far nobler, a far more lofty name in the history of the world than otherwise will ever be yours, is with you. But to do this you must entirely change your policy and government—Which do you prefer? The Character of a Francia or a Santa Anna, or that of a Washington or a Bolivar? Would it be more agreeable to your last moments, when the rapid review of your life passes before you, to be able to say, I have desolated my Country; impoverished it; ruined it, and gloated over the blood of my enemies; than to feel as the death chill creeps upon your spirit, that you die calm and contented, for your Country is happy and at peace, and you alone had caused it? Would it be more agreeable to your soul as it wings its flight to other regions, to hear the frantic joy occasioned by your death, or the sorrow moans of a weeping people, that they had lost their father? [85]

Such an outburst demanded immediate apologies. While suggesting that the Argentine government handle the case through its minister in Washington, Brent revealed his own indignation at the "unprovoked insult." [86] Even before news of Hopkins' greatest indiscretion reached Washington, the State Department had recalled him. It now extended

[83] Arana to Brent, March 12, 1846, and enclosure, Manning, *op. cit.*, I, 333-337.
[84] Arana to Brent, March 16, 1846, Manning, *op. cit.*, II, 327-328.
[85] Hopkins to Rosas, March 19, 1846, Manning, *op. cit.*, I, 343-346. The original of this letter was forwarded to Alvear on March 23 (AGN, BA, S1-A2-A4-núm. 13) and delivered to Buchanan with the Minister's note of July 20 (Manning, *op. cit.*, I, 383-385). In the National Archives, it is bound in Notes from the Argentine Republic, I.
[86] Brent to Arana, March 25, 1846, Manning, *op. cit.*, I, 346-347.

profuse apologies to General Alvear. [87] Rosas expressed his satisfaction with these arrangements.[88] Hopkins returned to the United States to continue his fight for Paraguay—and for Hopkins—by extensive writing and speaking.[89]

Brent's role in the Wise-Hopkins fiasco was essential though inconspicuous. He did not share in conception of the plan and at no time did he undertake seriously to direct its course. Having received no criticism from Washington on his first offer of mediation and without instructions after May, 1845, the chargé was left to his own resources.

The withdrawal of Hopkins, therefore, simply meant to Brent that he alone should continue the Wise project. At once he submitted his good offices to López, as he had previously to Rosas, and in June dispatched his son, George Lee Brent, and the United States Consul in Buenos Aires, Joseph L. Graham, to Asunción.[90] The elder Brent knew that López would never consent to Rosas' terms but evidently believed that a commission might arrive at some sort of a compromise. The commissioners, however, found the Paraguayan President greatly embittered at the United States for its repudiation of Hopkins' golden promises and for its apparent friendliness toward Rosas. Except for current information on Paraguay, the agents returned to Buenos Aires in December with empty portfolios.[91]

By this time, the State Department had long since recalled William Brent. President Polk was greatly disturbed that his agent should have shown "so little discretion and judgment" as to proffer American good offices to Rosas.[92] Though the administration did not publicly disavow Brent's mediation, it expressly commanded his successor not to renew the offer.[93] When news of the overture to López reached Washington, Buchanan announced that the United States would not be responsible.[94] Brent's three unauthorized offers of American aid to resolve the Argentine chaos of the mid-forties had brought him only dismissal from his post.

[87] Buchanan to Hopkins, March 30, 1846, Manning, *op. cit.*, X, 32-34; Buchanan to Alvear, Aug. 14, 1846, Manning, *op. cit.*, I, 35-36.

[88] Mabragaña, *op. cit.*, II, 118-119.

[89] See Peterson, *op. cit.*, pp. 251-252.

[90] Brent to López, April 29, June 8, 1846, Manning, *op. cit.*, I, 365, 368.

[91] William A. Harris, Brent's successor, to Arana, Dec. 14, 1846, and enclosures, *ibid.*, pp. 401-411. The report of the commissioners was among the enclosures. George Lee Brent also submitted a report directly to Arana on January 18, 1847. (Copies of this and other papers relating to the mediation are preserved in the collections of the Instituto de Investigaciones Históricas, Facultad de Filosofía y Letras, Universidad de Buenos Aires, filed in a *legajo* called "Intervención Anglo-Francesa Mediación de los Agentes de EE. UU., 1845-1846." They have been copied from manuscripts in the Archivo del Ministerio de Relaciones Exteriores y Culto.)

[92] *The Diary of James K. Polk*, Sept. 25, 1846, II, 155.

[93] Buchanan to Harris, March 30, 1846, Manning, *op. cit.*, I, 31.

[94] Buchanan to Harris, Nov. 12, 1846, *ibid.*, pp. 36-38.

Reactions in the United States

The Polk administration pursued a policy of complete noninvolvement in Argentina's difficulties. It refused to use its good offices for purposes of mediation. It failed to support its agents when they initiated mediation without authorization. Though in his annual message of December 2, 1845, the President asserted that the people of the United States could not be indifferent to European attempts to interfere with the sovereign rights of American states, he was willing to apply Monroe's principles only to North America.[95] Even the invasion of Argentine waters by an Anglo-French naval expedition failed to budge him.[96]

To this passive policy American shipping interests,[97] a portion of the press,[98] and a small group of Congressmen reacted vigorously. They urged the President to challenge British leadership in South America and to strike out boldly against European interference anywhere in the Hemisphere. These forces, however, inadequately mobilized, were unable to persuade the administration to broaden its affirmed position. In his eagerness to avoid war with Britain over Oregon and to forestall Anglo-French opposition to his dreams of expansion in the southwest, Polk had no intention of forcing a showdown over the faraway La Plata.[99]

The dictator Rosas, confronted by a formidable international coalition and desperately in need of foreign friends and foreign aid, could turn only to the United States. Yet where Brent had failed to arouse support for the Argentine cause, Minister Alvear realized that he had little chance to succeed. His one hope, both he and Rosas knew, lay in an aroused public sentiment. Throughout 1845-1846, therefore, the Minister used available funds and staff to reach the American public.[100] On behalf of the Argentine Republic, he planned and executed a propaganda campaign unequalled by a Latin American republic in mid-nineteenth-

[95] J. D. Richardson, *A Compilation of the Messages and Papers of the Presidents,* IV, 398-399.

[96] Brent to Buchanan, Nov. 14, 1845, Manning, *op. cit.,* I, 311. Arana protested to Brent the participation of the American ship *Creole* in the expedition (Oct. 29, 1845; Brent to Arana, Nov. 27, 1845, *ibid.,* pp. 299-300, 312-314).

[97] *Sen. Jour.,* 29 Cong., 1 sess., p. 254; *Niles' Register,* LXX (March 21, 1846), 36.

[98] See, for example, *The Union* (Washington), Feb. 18, 1846; *The Daily Union* (Washington), Feb. 17, 18, 1846; *Richmond Enquirer,* Jan. 31, 1846. Alvear forwarded to his government copies of these and many other newspapers (AGN, BA, S1-A1-A1-núm. 5). See also Caleb Cushing, "English and French Intervention in the Rio de la Plata," *The United States Magazine and Democratic Review,* XVIII (March, 1846), 163-184.

[99] Cady, *op. cit.,* pp. 185-192.

[100] Alvear to Arana, Feb. 7, 1846; Arana to Alvear, Aug. 10, 1843, AGN, BA, S1-A1-A1-núm. 5.

century America. He employed Americans to prepare material in the American idiom. He submitted articles to city newspapers. He appointed Americans as Argentine consuls. He stimulated petitions to the government.[101] Through friends he sought to arouse congressmen to the dangers of European intervention in the New World.[102] When opportunity presented, he appealed directly to the Secretary of State. He urged

> the Government of the United States to employ in the present crisis all the moral influence in its power, as a consequence of the acceptation of the principle of non-intervention, which has been proclaimed on various occasions by the Presidents of the United States.[103]

Patiently but persistently Alvear sought to pierce the indifference of the Polk administration.

But all the activities of Brent in Buenos Aires and Alvear in the United States were fruitless. Though several Democratic senators introduced a resolution calling upon the President to declare American intention to enforce Monroe's principle of nonintervention, it never reached the floor.[104] The House of Representatives twice requested the President to communicate information on the foreign intervention in La Plata.[105] Beyond that, neither the Congress nor the President would go. The Polk administration was facing west, not south.

Reactions in Argentina

When Brent's successor, William Harris, reached his post in June, 1846, he found a growing hostility toward the United States. This loss in popularity the Chargé attributed to the "blunders, mistakes, and follies" of American agents and to the failure to send a minister instead of a chargé.[106] Moreover, the Argentine government was particularly incensed when several North American vessels accompanied the Anglo-French expedition up the Paraná.[107] And the feelings of the people

[101] Many of Alvear's reports on his propaganda activities are preserved in the Archivo General de la Nación, Buenos Aires, and filed as "Donación Alvear" (S1-A1-A1-núm. 4, 5, and 6). Other materials on this phase of Alvear's mission are to be found in S1-A1-A4-núm. 9 and 13. All of this material has been well synthesized in Davis, *op. cit.*, pp. 140-161.

[102] Joshua A. Dodge, Alvear's propaganda assistant, to Alvear, Dec. 17, 1845, March 8, 1846, AGN, BA, S1-A1-A1-núm. 4; Davis, *op. cit.*, p. 153.

[103] Alvear to Buchanan, Nov. 1, 1845, Manning, *op. cit.*, I, 300-302.

[104] *Cong. Globe*, 29 Cong., 1 sess., XV, 197-198, 239-248.

[105] Feb. 18, May 4, 1846, *H. Jour.*, 29 Cong., 1 sess., pp. 411, 746.

[106] Harris to Buchanan, July 14, 1846, and enclosure, Manning, *op. cit.*, I, 372-378.

[107] Arana to Brent, Oct. 29, 1845, *ibid.*, pp. 299-300; Nov. 26, 1845, AGN, BA, S1-A2-A4-núm. 12; Buchanan to Messrs. Kirkland and Chase, Baltimore, Aug. 19, 1846, John Bassett Moore, *The Works of James Buchanan*, VII, 67.

were offended when they learned that the United States had declared war against Mexico, a war they regarded as one of conquest.[108]

To allay this new wave of anti-Yankee sentiment Harris distributed five hundred copies, printed in Spanish, of President Polk's message to Congress on the origins of the Mexican War. He requested Rosas to permit publication in his official organs of pro-American articles and documents.[109] Through the next three years, as the hated Anglo-French intervention persisted, as the United States continued to pronounce against it, and as Rosas turned to praise of the American attitude, popular enmity gradually abated. In his annual messages of 1847-1849 the dictator specifically lauded American policy.[110]

Last Phases of the Intervention

Until 1849-1850 Great Britain and France strove almost ceaselessly to liquidate their differences with Rosas.[111] In accordance with his instructions, Harris contented himself largely with routine functions— reporting the progress of the European mediation, improving the Argentine attitude toward the United States, and insisting upon the rights of his fellow citizens.[112] He remained as chargé until 1851.

Harris' efforts to influence Argentine opinion paralleled closely successive Anglo-French mediation efforts. The unsuccessful mission of the British Consul at Montevideo, T. S. Hood, was followed by a new commission, consisting of Lord Howden and Count Walewski. Upon their arrival in May, 1847, Harris informed them that he would be glad to cooperate in any way possible, but that if the negotiations broke down, he would certainly protest continuance of the blockade.[113]

True to his word, on July 1 the Chargé sent identical notes of protest to the two commissioners. He said the United States would never condone the policy of intervention and could not continue indefinitely to abide by the blockade. The United States could not sanction the establishment of permanent political influence by European nations in the River Plate area.[114] When Harris reported to his government, he explained that

[108] Harris to Buchanan, Sept. 15, 1846, and enclosure, Manning, *op. cit.*, I, pp. 396-398. In the United States, Alvear grew fearful of "the spirit of conquest which has possessed a large part of the American people" (to Arana, April 23, 1849, AGN, BA, S1-A2-A4-núm. 13). See also Davis, *op. cit.*, pp. 161-180.

[109] Harris to Buchanan, June 16, 1847, Manning, *op. cit.*, I, 423-424; Zinny, *La Gaceta Mercantil* (June 6, 23, 1845), II, 152, 155; *Archivo Americano y Espíritu de la Prensa del Mundo*, series 2 (May 15, 1849), pp. 21-26.

[110] Mabragaña, *op. cit.*, II, 155, 203-204, 301.

[111] See Cady, *op. cit.*, pp. 193-298.

[112] Buchanan to Harris, March 30, 1846, Manning, *op. cit.*, I, 29-32.

[113] Harris to Buchanan, May 25, July 15, 1847, *ibid.*, pp. 419, 423.

[114] Harris to Howden and to Walewski, July 1, 1847, *ibid.*, pp. 424-427.

the course which I have thought proper to pursue, in regard to these matters, was not precisely embraced by my instructions, yet from the peculiar state of affairs here; the nature of public opinion; the positions and purposes of the parties to the intervention; the injury which was inflicted upon our neutral and lawful commerce, in my judgment pointed out my duty as clearly, as if I had been specially instructed to perform it.[115]

Harris' attempts to stiffen American policy, like those of Brent before him, failed to interest Polk and his Cabinet. When the Chargé recommended that Washington despatch a war vessel to La Plata and make official inquiry in London and Paris of Anglo-French intentions, Buchanan did not respond.[116] Soon after the failure of the Howden-Walewski mission, British forces temporarily withdrew from Argentine waters. The French were left alone to enforce the blockade. Their procedure now was to require all vessels entering and leaving Buenos Aires to stop at Montevideo to pay duties and transship in small craft. When the Chargé reported this "piracy" to Washington, the authorities took no action to protect American shipping.[117]

In November, 1849, Great Britain finally was able to conclude a convention for the re-establishment of friendly relations; France was obliged to wait until the following August.[118] During the last months of the French negotiations Rosas was sometimes indifferent, sometimes refractory. With war actually threatening, Harris tried to convince him and various members of the Congress that they should not rely on the United States for active assistance. When Rosas insisted that "he was sustaining American doctrine against foreign intervention, and that the United States government was morally bound to support him," Harris claimed that Washington had already fulfilled its moral obligation.[119]

The policies of the United States, economic and political, toward the Anglo-French intervention were passive but consistent. To the Polk administration commerce with the Río de la Plata was important but not essential. In its view, the economic interests of the nation lay in Texas, the far Southwest, and the Northwest, where Mexico and Britain were the foes. The government had its hands full in those quarters without taking on a quarrel in distant Argentina. Agents in South America might evaluate the threat differently, might desire to prohibit European interposition, and might let their zeal lead them into un-

---

[115] Harris to Buchanan, July 15, 1847, *ibid.*, p. 431.
[116] *Ibid.*, pp. 437-438.
[117] Harris to Buchanan, Oct. 17, 1847, *ibid.*, p. 450.
[118] República Argentina, *Tratados, convenciones, protocolos, actos y acuerdos internacionales*, VIII, 229-233, 319-326.
[119] Harris to John M. Clayton, Secretary of State, May 14, 1850, Manning, *op. cit.*, I, p. 499.

authorized steps. But the administration need not follow where agents led. If Polk and Buchanan believed the intervention to be a violation of Monroe's principles, they failed to support their views by words or action. Nor did the Congress or the people ever vigorously demand that the intervention be halted.[120] Although Argentine opinion of the United States shifted frequently during the forties, it is doubtful if by 1850 its policy of noninterference had appreciably advanced or retarded the prestige of the northern republic in the southern.

---

[120] Some of these ideas are well summarized in Cady, *op. cit.*, pp. 270-271.

X

THE BEGINNINGS OF COMMERCE:
TRADE AND NAVIGATION UNDER HANDICAPS,
1824-1870

In January, 1852, a new American chargé d'affaires in Buenos Aires sent a perceptive intelligence report to Washington. Because of revolutionary political changes about to occur, John S. Pendleton predicted to Secretary of State Webster, conditions in Argentina would soon be auspicious for the improvement of economic relations. According to his estimate of the situation, rebellious forces under Justo José de Urquiza would presently overthrow the entrenched dictatorship of Rosas. This accomplished, the powerful caudillo of Entre Ríos Province would seek to form a government more representative of the entire nation. During this formative stage, advised Pendleton, the United States should initiate negotiations for the treaty it had long coveted.[1]

During the thirty years since recognition, a succession of international crises—the war with Brazil, the Falkland Islands episode, Rosas' interference in Uruguayan difficulties, the French blockade, and the Anglo-French intervention—had frequently impeded the movement of American ships in Argentine ports. The Department of State had instructed each diplomatic agent since Rodney to seek a commercial treaty that would protect American commerce. Yet the very foreign complications which provoked the blockades, followed usually by intervals of domestic uncertainty, had frustrated successful negotiations. This combination of recurring blockades and lack of treaty protection produced inevitable fluctuations in the volume of Argentine-American trade.

Fluctuations in Trade

At no time during Rosas' long regime did the dollar value of American exports to Argentina reach more than a negligible figure. The annual

[1] Pendleton to Webster, Jan. 4, 1852, William R. Manning (ed.), *Diplomatic Correspondence of the United States: Inter-American Affairs, 1831-1860*, I, 521.

average of fewer than a half-million dollars placed American exporters far behind those of England and France.[2]

A variety of circumstances operated to keep American products virtually unknown to the people of the Río de la Plata. During recurrent periods totaling more than eight years blockades and domestic turmoil wholly or partially closed Platine ports to Yankee ships. At times increasing production of breadstuffs in Argentina or capricious imposition of discriminatory port charges reduced American imports; at others, depression in the United States or concentration on more dependable markets decreased interest in the turbulent land of Rosas. But, always, American exporters of manufactures, lumber, tobacco, and other goods felt the need of the treaty protection enjoyed by the British.[3]

Argentine sales to the United States, on the other hand, consistently prospered, as exporters of wool, hides, skins, horse hair, and soap stuffs found ready buyers. Exports which annually averaged a little more than a half-million dollars between 1826 and 1830 grew to nearly a million in the thirties, more than a million and a third in the forties, and nearly three millions in the fifties. Excepting the two years of the French blockade (1839-1840), Argentina maintained a balance of trade in its favor, often two, sometimes three, to one.

TABLE 1

VALUE OF ARGENTINE TRADE WITH THE UNITED STATES
(ANNUAL AVERAGE BY DECADES): 1826-1880

Years	Argentine Exports	Argentine Imports	Argentine Excess of Exports (+); of Imports (−)
1826-30	$ 574,884.40	$ 388,142.10	+
1831-40	996,643.80	558,405.90	+
1841-50	1,383,950.10	389,582.10	+
1851-60	2,805,717.10	898,563.90	+
1861-70	4,815,032.80	1,840,842.10	+
1871-80	5,590,352.00	1,903,462.00	+

SOURCE: The figures are adapted from *American Commerce*, pp. 3300-3301.

After 1849, however, trade in both directions began to rise sharply. In Argentina, as blockades ceased, commerce moved more normally.[4] In the United States, with the discovery of California gold, construction

[2] Treasury Department, *American Commerce: Commerce of South America, Central America, Mexico, and West Indies, with Share of the United States and Other Leading Nations Therein, 1821-1898*, p. 3300. Unless otherwise stated, the commercial statistics in this chapter are based upon this source.

[3] As samples of consular reports stressing these causes, see Eben Ritchie Dorr to John Forsyth, Secretary of State, Jan. 16, 1836; Amory Edwards to Forsyth, Dec. 28, 1840; to Secretary of State, Jan. 2, April 12, 1842, Jan. 2, 1845; to Webster, July 12, 1842, NA, DS, Con. Let., B. A., V, VI, VII.

[4] William A. Harris, Chargé d'Affaires at Buenos Aires, to James Buchanan, Secretary of State, Aug. 1, 1846, NA, DS, Desp. Arg., VI; to John M. Clayton, Secretary of State, Oct. 10, 1849, Manning, *op. cit.*, I, 489-490.

of railroads, settlement of the Mississippi Valley, and extension of the agricultural domain, the time was ripe for expansion of foreign trade.[5] Journals began to urge the advantages of markets in southern South America.[6] The upward trend was clear by 1851, when in Argentina rebellion flared against the long-established dictatorship. Few citizens of either nation would regret Rosas' departure, for out of the temporary chaos there would soon come new leaders, a new government (two, in fact), a new constitution—and the first treaties with the United States.

A New Government and New Treaties

John S. Pendleton, who reached Buenos Aires on the eve of these dramatic developments, was a man of experience in public life.[7] Like his three predecessors and five successors, he was a Southerner. As a sixth-generation Virginian, he had represented his district in the Assembly and the Congress. But, more valuable for his new post, he had served three years in Santiago at a time when Domingo F. Sarmiento and other fugitives from Rosas were agitating against him from their Chilean sanctuary.[8] The Chargé was well prepared, therefore, to forecast impending changes and to evaluate probable trends.

Since 1846 strife had been brewing between Rosas and General Urquiza, Governor of Entre Ríos. Primarily, the feud was personal. It had deeper roots, however, in the enduring conflict between proponents of centralized and of federalized forms of government. Politically, centralization had become the goal of the conservative landed aristocrats of Buenos Aires who would control the nation, federalization the objective of the largely unrepresented masses of the provinces. But the rivalry carried economic and social as well as political overtones.[9] It had been the fundamental cause of Argentine instability since 1810.

By accepting or usurping responsibility for the conduct of Argentine foreign relations the provincial government of Buenos Aires had maintained a semblance of national unity. Though avowedly a federalist, Rosas had governed and directed foreign policy without genuine representation of the provinces. This, obviously, was an expediency which

[5] Emory R. Johnson, *History of Domestic and Foreign Commerce of the United States*, II, 46-48, 50.

[6] See, for example, Edward A. Hopkins, "Navigation of the Confluents of the Rio de la Plata," *The Merchants' Magazine*, XXI (July, 1849), 80-87. See also the issue for Nov., 1849, p. 558.

[7] *Registro oficial de la República Argentina*, II, 474; Webster to Minister of Foreign Affairs, April 28, 1861, Adolfo Saldías, *Papeles de Rozas*, II, 133.

[8] *Dictionary of American Biography*, XIV, 422; Louise Pecquet de Bellet, *Some Prominent Virginia Families*, IV, 264.

[9] Although it emphasizes economics, a trenchant study on federalism is Miron Burgin's *The Economic Aspects of Argentine Federalism, 1820-1852*. Also useful are Francisco Ramos-Mejía, *El federalismo argentino*, and L. F. Rowe, *The Federal System of the Argentine Republic*, especially pp. 19-22, 29-31.

could not endure. The root problem must be settled. When, therefore, the vigor of Rosas' power began to wane and when, in May, 1851, Urquiza withdrew the authority delegated to him by Entre Ríos, he paved the way for revolutionary change on a grand scale.[10]

Urquiza began his "march to Rome" in the succeeding October, when he invaded Uruguay, defeated Rosas' ally, Oribe, and raised the long siege of Montevideo. Crossing the Paraná into Santa Fe Province, he led augmented forces toward Buenos Aires. Suddenly the movement ignited the powder magazine upon which Rosas had built his dictatorship, wrecked the hollow superstructure, and in February, 1852, sent its architect fleeing to England from the battlefield of Caseros. Urquiza soon entered Buenos Aires and installed himself as the leader of an ostensibly united nation.[11]

These were the momentous events that Pendleton had foreseen in the first months of his residence, when he advised Webster that the time was at hand to push for the commercial treaty. Skillfully now he sought

> to maintain the most friendly relations with the Gov^t *de facto*, carefully avoiding every thing that might possibly disturb the friendly relations that exist between this Gov^t and that of the U. States.[12]

His suggestion received support from Robert C. Schenck, who while on leave from his legation in Rio de Janeiro witnessed Rosas' defeat at Caseros. He thought the time favorable, too, for securing the opening of the Río de la Plata to the free navigation of all nations.[13]

After years of open disdain toward their agents' recommendations, the Department of State in this instance acted promptly to follow their advice. Webster directed Schenck to return to Buenos Aires and to cooperate with Pendleton in arranging treaties for the protection of American commerce and for the opening of the Plata river system.[14]

[10] The contest between the Province of Buenos Aires and the Argentine Confederation, as recounted in this chapter, is founded primarily upon Ricardo Levene, *A History of Argentina*, pp. 434-442; F. A. Kirkpatrick, *A History of the Argentine Republic*, pp. 157-170; and Rowe, *op. cit.*, pp. 37-54.

[11] On this occasion forty marines landed to protect the Legation and Consulate of the United States and the mercantile establishments of its citizens. Headed by Pendleton, a deputation visited Urquiza to urge his moderation in dealing with the residents of Buenos Aires (Pendleton to Webster, Feb. 8, 1852, Manning, *op. cit.*, I, 525; Charles S. Stewart, *Brazil and La Plata: The Personal Record of a Cruise*, pp. 307-313).

[12] Nov. 1, 1851, Manning, *op. cit.*, I, 516; Courtney Letts de Espil, "John Pendleton and His Friendship with Urquiza," *The Hispanic American Historical Review*, XXXIII (Feb., 1953), 152-167.

[13] To Webster, Feb. 14, 1852, NA, DS, Desp. Bra., XIX.

[14] They were instructed to negotiate treaties with Uruguay and Paraguay as well as with the Confederation (Webster to Pendleton, April 28, 1852, and to Schenck, April 29, 1852, Manning, *op. cit.*, I, 41-42; II, 166-167).

While these instructions were en route, Urquiza was proceeding with the establishment of his government. In April, he called an assembly of all provincial governors to meet at San Nicolás, two hundred miles north of Buenos Aires. Here, on May 31, the delegates promulgated the *Acuerdo de San Nicolás*, which enjoined the early assembly of a constituent congress and gave Urquiza extensive powers as provisional director of the new confederation.[15]

Pendleton personally accompanied Urquiza to this meeting, the only foreign representative so favored. He received the only advance copy of the proceedings given to a foreign agent.[16] He could report, therefore, that the Director was "exceedingly anxious to cultivate the most friendly relations with the U States, and as much as possible, to assimmilate [sic] the institutions of his Govt, to those of the U. States—." [17]

The leaders of Buenos Aires Province received announcement of the Acuerdo with impetuous opposition. Not until he closed its legislature and appointed himself provisional governor was Urquiza able to restore temporary peace. Pendleton grew skeptical now about the possibility of successful treaty negotiations.[18] Upon Schenck's arrival, nevertheless, the two promptly interviewed Urquiza and his minister of foreign affairs, Luis José de la Peña. The Minister was willing to negotiate a commercial treaty but proposed that a pact for free navigation of the Plata river system should await agreement among the powers and concerting of policy by the provinces. Though satisfied that they had won the Director's good will, the agents realized the futility of pushing treaty negotiations until greater domestic tranquillity prevailed.[19]

Urquiza's departure for Santa Fé, where the constituent assembly was to be organized, was the signal for overt action by the capital province. Buenos Aires now withdrew from the Confederation and prepared to assume all the functions of an independent state. This revolutionary change of November 11 initiated a seven-year period during which the Province and the Confederation existed side by side as separate entities.

The provincial governor, Valentín Alsina, authorized consuls to continue in performance of their duties until they received instructions from their governments.[20] Confederation leaders notified diplomatic agents

---

[15] *Registro oficial de la República Argentina*, II, 279.
[16] Thomas J. Page, *La Plata, the Argentine Confederation, and Paraguay*, p. 564.
[17] To Webster, April 28, 1852, Manning, *op. cit.*, I, 528.
[18] Pendleton to Secretary of State, July 7, 1852, NA, DS, Desp. Arg., VIII.
[19] Pendleton to Webster, July 29, 1852, Manning, *op. cit.*, I, 529-531; *Memoria, 1852*, pp. x-xi. Shortly after this meeting, Pendleton and Schenck succeeded in negotiating a treaty with Uruguay (Schenck to Secretary of State, Sept. 4, 1852, NA, DS, Desp. Bra., XIX). On March 4, 1853, Pendleton concluded a treaty of commerce and navigation with Paraguay (Pendleton to Secretary of State, March 4, 1853, Manning, *op. cit.*, X, 104-105).
[20] Joseph Graham, U.S. Consul, to Alsina, Sept. 30, 1852, NA, DS, Con. Let., B. A., VIII.

that Paraná would henceforth be the center of the Argentine government and that they should move their residences at the earliest practical moment. Pendleton prepared to comply.[21]

When the Constituent Congress assembled in Santa Fé on November 20, 1852, Buenos Aires refused to send delegates. Without it, the other thirteen provinces could muster only one-third of the population and barely one-fourth of the country's wealth. Moreover, since the metropolis was the only port of entry, a new government would be compelled to function without customs dues as a source of revenue. In the face of these realities, nevertheless, the convention began its work and by May 1, 1853, completed the new charter. Twenty-four days later, General Urquiza proclaimed it the supreme law of the land.[22] "The land" did not include Buenos Aires, however, for the provincial legislature refused to approve either the constitution or the law.

In guiding principles and structural form, the new constitution closely resembled that of the United States. Like its model, it provided a strongly federalized government with separation of powers and a system of checks and balances.[23] But, unlike the model, it embodied several centralizing features—notably, the rights to proclaim "state of siege" and to intervene in provincial governments—which were to negate on many occasions the advantages of federalization.[24] Without fundamental change, however, it was to endure until 1949, when the Perón dictatorship forced a considerable overhauling.

During these months of transition, disorder and apprehension pervaded Buenos Aires and surrounding territory. "Now," wrote a foreign observer,

> in place of peace, there is war; in place of quietude and order, anarchy and confusion; in place of safety, danger; and of seeming prosperity, apprehended ruin! All business, foreign and domestic, is suspended; the mole is like a place of the dead, the shops and houses are all closed, the streets deserted; every male inhabitant, between the years of sixteen and sixty, under arms and on daily duty, and the city begirt, within a dozen squares

[21] Pendleton to Webster, Oct. 10, 1852, and enclosure; to Edward Everett, Secretary of State, Dec. 5, 1852, Manning, *op. cit.*, I, 535, 537.

[22] *Registro oficial de la República Argentina*, III, 65-73. In forwarding a copy of the constitution to his government, Pendleton wrote, "You will find it to be almost an exact copy of the Constitution of the United States" (To William L. Marcy, Secretary of State, June 1, 1853, NA, DS, Desp. Arg., VIII).

[23] The lineal relationship between the constitutions of the United States and Argentina has not yet been adequately traced. Much material for such a study exists in the works of J. B. Alberdi and other constitutional theorists. See, among others, Alberdi, *Obras selectas*, X; Alberto Padilla, *La constitución de Estados Unidos como precedente argentino;* José Nicolás Matienzo, *El gobierno representativo federal en la República Argentina* (Vol. XIV in "Biblioteca de ciencias políticas y sociales"); and Rowe, *op. cit.*

[24] Austin F. Macdonald, *Government of the Argentine Republic*, pp. 143-144, 169-188.

of its centre, by hostile troops composed of its own people. By these, all intercourse between the city and the country is prevented, and all supplies of provision cut off; . . .[25]

United States Marines were held in constant readiness to protect property of American citizens.[26] On one occasion, a Confederation official specifically invited Pendleton to utilize the "means by which you think it possible to save that city." [27]

Realizing the barriers to early *rapprochement* between Province and Confederation, the representatives of foreign states, including Pendleton and Schenck, moved to conclude treaties with Urquiza for the free navigation of the Paraná and the Uruguay. Both governments had already paved the way for protection of their foreign trade by decreeing that the rivers should be open to all ships.[28] Representatives of the United States, England, and France were now able to secure Urquiza's guarantee of this privilege, during wartime as well as peacetime, in identical treaties.[29]

On paper at least, the treaties precluded repetition of the blockades and counterblockades of the thirties and forties. American diplomacy had successfully promoted its long-standing principle that international rivers should be legally navigable by ships of all nations, not merely by those of riparian states. Argentine commentators have come to regard these treaties as the herald of a new day in the international relations of the nation.[30]

This treaty concluded, Pendleton and Schenck had less difficulty in arranging a pact of friendship, commerce, and navigation. They were now able to consummate the diplomatic and commercial arrangements the United States had sought for thirty years. The signatories agreed not only to guarantee mutual freedom of commerce but also to apply the most-favored-nation principle to diplomatic and consular services as well as to commerce and navigation.[31] The two pacts were ultimately proclaimed on April 9, 1855.

[25] Stewart, *op. cit.*, pp. 418-419.

[26] Graham to Webster, Jan. 31, 1853, NA, DS, Con. Let., B. A., VIII. In July, Urquiza was forced to flee Buenos Aires. The American steamer *Water Witch* gave him asylum and passage to his home in San José de Flores.

[27] Angel Elías, secretary to Urquiza, to Pendleton, April 13, 1853, Manning, *op. cit.*, I, 545.

[28] *Registro oficial de la República Argentina*, III, 243; Pendleton to Secretary of State, Oct. 26, 1852, NA, DS, Desp. Arg., VIII.

[29] For complete texts of the United States-Argentine treaty, see William M. Malloy, *Treaties, Conventions, International Acts, Protocols, and Agreements between the United States and Other Powers, 1776-1909*, I, 18-20, and República Argentina, *Tratados, convenciones, protocolos, actos y acuerdos internacionales*, VIII, 143-150.

[30] For example, see Mariano A. Pelliza, *Historia argentina desde su origen hasta la organización nacional*, II, 620-621.

[31] Malloy, *Treaties*, I, 20-24; República Argentina, *Tratados*, VIII, 151-158.

Dual Governments in Argentina

While foreign representatives were negotiating treaties with Urquiza, deepening domestic strife decreased the probability of their immediate enforcement. As the leaders of both the Argentine Confederation and the Province of Buenos Aires proceeded with the organization of their governments, they rendered more incisive the breach which prevented reunion. Under its new constitution of May 1, 1853, the Confederation raised Urquiza to the presidency and removed its seat of government to Paraná, a small river port in the Province of Entre Ríos. By April, 1854, the Province adopted a constitution and selected Pastor Obligado its first constitutional governor.

The hostility between the rival governments was nowhere more bitter than in the opposition of the Province to the Confederation's treaties on the navigation of the rivers. Signatures on the documents were barely dry when the provincial leaders formally protested to the agents of Great Britain, France, and the United States. They argued that the signatories had no power to deprive the Province of the right of blockade, that Urquiza had no authority to negotiate on its behalf, and that he was deliberately seeking to avenge himself upon the Province.[32] Buenos Aires naturally resisted the loss of the monopoly of foreign commerce and customs it had enjoyed so long. Clearly, the laxity or rigidity with which the treaties of 1853 were enforced would determine the future independence of each government.

This political cleavage complicated the position of the United States. Since 1810 it had transacted its business with or through the Province of Buenos Aires; now, it must still adjudicate its claims and conduct the bulk of its commerce with that agency. And yet it had established treaty relations with the Confederation, with which its commercial connections were negligible. How should a diplomat function? The conclusion of new treaties of navigation and commerce with the Province would operate against the validity of those already signed with the Confederation. Such a step would offend Urquiza's government by the recognition of a state over which it claimed constitutional sovereignty. This contingency also prevented the United States from inviting Buenos Aires to adhere to the treaties already concluded.[33] Pendleton found

[32] The formal statement of protest was included in a despatch from Lorenzo Torres, Minister of Foreign Affairs of Buenos Aires, to Marcy, Sept. 30, 1853, Manning, *op. cit.*, I, 559-564.

[33] The vagaries of the political situation which prevailed in Argentina were effectively presented, probably by Alberdi, in a Paraná newspaper, *Nacional Argentino*, Feb. 16, 1856 (Peden to Secretary of State, April 23, 1856, and enclosure, NA, DS, Desp. Arg., X).

himself in the anomalous position of being accredited to one government and having to do business with another.[34]

The Department of State was even deeper in a quandary as to how to proceed. Only after conferences with an agent of the British government, a visit from Urquiza's representative, and several years of vacillation was it able to evolve its policy. As early as January, 1854, the English government instructed its minister in Washington to determine what policy the administration contemplated toward the appointment of consuls to Buenos Aires and the reception of its consuls in the United States. He learned that while the Department of State had already issued exequaturs to certain consuls, it had acted only for convenience and had no intention of recognizing the Province as a separate government.[35] Yet, within less than five months, by commissioning a minister resident to the government of Buenos Aires, the Department reversed itself. The appointee was James A. Peden, of Florida, the first minister sent to the Río de la Plata since Rodney in 1823.[36] But Secretary William L. Marcy elected to play two angles. He also gave Peden a letter of credence to the Confederation and instructed him,

in determining the priority of the presentation of these respective letters, . . . [to] be governed by the relative position of the two powers at the time of your arrival in that quarter, for this Department is not so fully advised in respect to the present political condition of the Argentine Confederation and the province of Buenos Aires, as to prescribe the course which under all circumstances will be the most judicious.[37]

Marcy authorized the Floridian not only to exchange ratifications of treaties with the Confederation and with Uruguay but also to enter into treaty relations with the government of Buenos Aires.

Peden's problems beset him almost upon arrival. He barely received recognition in Buenos Aires when the government of the Confederation invited him to remove his establishment to Paraná.[38] He discovered that there were not only two governments to be dealt with but factions in each.[39] Moreover, at intervals the provincial authorities confronted him with formal protests against certain clauses of the treaties of 1853.[40]

Meanwhile, the State Department's policy was slowly crystallizing. In

---

[34] Pendleton to Marcy, Dec. 2, 1853, Manning, *op. cit.*, I, 564.

[35] John F. T. Crompton to the Earl of Clarendon, Jan. 13, 1854, LC, MD, Photostats, F. O. 5, Vol. 593, Folio II.

[36] Marcy to Peden, July 12, 1854, NA, DS, Inst. Arg., XV, 75.

[37] Marcy to Peden, June 29, 1854, Manning, *op. cit.*, I, 44-46.

[38] Juan María Gutiérrez, Minister of Foreign Affairs, to Peden, Jan. 30, 1855, circular, *ibid.*, 570-572.

[39] Peden to Marcy, Oct. 27, 1854, *ibid.*, 565-566.

[40] Peden to Secretary of State, June 18, Aug. 14, 1855, NA, DS, Desp. Arg., IX.

June, 1855, en route to London, Urquiza's representative, Juan B. Alberdi, visited Washington for consultations with President Franklin Pierce, Secretary Marcy, and Attorney General Caleb Cushing.[41] The Argentine diplomat, who had contributed extensively to the writing of the constitution of 1853, described at length the situation in his country. As to the protests of Buenos Aires against the treaties of 1853, he convinced Marcy that "her object must be to deprive these Powers of the benefits of their respective treaties, and to withhold from the Argentine Republic the advantages it might derive from them."[42]

After weighing the statements of Alberdi, the President changed course again. He now determined to "make a new appointment of a minister to the Argentine Republic" without accrediting him or any other diplomatic agent to the government of Buenos Aires. He would support the position of the Confederation on the opening of La Plata. He directed James Buchanan in London and John Y. Mason in Paris to seek British and French concurrence in this arrangement.[43]

In accordance with this policy, Marcy commissioned James A. Peden, fifth in the line of Southern diplomats to Buenos Aires, as minister resident to the Confederation. Not until July 18, 1856, however, was he informed that his

> Government considers it to be its duty to transfer you to the Argentine Confederation. You are therefore instructed to take your leave of the Government of Buenos Ayres. On doing this you will explain the views of your Government as herein presented in the manner which may be most acceptable to it, and assure the authorities of Buenos Ayres that this course is not taken in any unfriendly spirit toward that State, or with the intention to interfere in the controversies which may exist between it and the Argentine Confederation. . . .[44]

In Washington, the Department had required two years to determine that it should recognize only the Confederation. In Buenos Aires, where the decision arrived in October, Peden had already negotiated a treaty of friendship, commerce, and navigation with the provincial government.[45] Moreover, after two years of observation, he was convinced that

[41] Alberdi to [his government], June 13, 1855, Alberdi, *Escritos póstumos*, XVI, 420.

[42] Marcy to Buchanan, June 16, 1855, Manning, *op. cit.*, VII, 116. Some months after Alberdi's visit to the United States, there appeared in Hartford a 37-page pamphlet entitled *A Memorial on the National and Territorial Unity of the Argentine Republic.* . . . It was obviously propaganda for the cause of the Argentine Confederation and may have been written by Alberdi.

[43] Buchanan to Marcy, Sept. 4, 1855, Feb. 29, 1856, and enclosures, Manning, *op. cit.*, VII, 610-611, 637-638.

[44] Department to Peden, July 18, 1856, *ibid.*, I, 48-50.

[45] Peden to Marcy, Sept. 29, Oct. 4, 1856, *ibid.*, pp. 608-610. He enclosed a copy of the treaty.

the Province exerted preponderant influence in La Plata and would sustain its independence. He elected, therefore, to remain indefinitely in Buenos Aires.[46] Not until the following May did he move, reluctantly, to Paraná. Thanks to a seven months' delay in mails, his arrival preceded that of the stinging rebuke he received for basing his decision on personal discretion instead of departmental directive.[47]

When Peden interviewed the Foreign Minister of the Confederation, he candidly explained his late arrival by saying "more than once during the conversation, that my course was predicated on my own knowledge of the country, and views of its relations with the United States." He complained that without his knowledge Alberdi had been authorized to make certain representations in Washington while he remained the official American representative in Argentina.[48] The Buchanan administration evidently felt that Peden's partisanship rendered him unfit for further service in Argentina, for it soon appointed his successor. It selected a former president of Texas, Mirabeau Buonaparte Lamar, to convey explanations to Urquiza's government.[49] Before his departure, however, the Department of State transferred him to Nicaragua. A year and a half passed before another appointee, Benjamin C. Yancey, of Georgia, reached Paraná.[50]

The Yancey Mediation

By the time of Yancey's arrival tension between Buenos Aires and the Confederation had greatly mounted. All efforts of the two governments to coexist, as well as outside attempts to assist them, had proved futile. Free navigation of the rivers and the derivative rights to regulate foreign commerce and control customs dues remained the key issues. Rivalry over these questions continued to involve the rights of the United States and other signatories of the treaties of 1853. Yancey's greatest interest during his brief service in Argentina was the reconciliation of the estranged parties, though neither his enthusiasm nor the timeliness of his proposals was sufficient to effect a solution. He did, however, vigorously assert the treaty rights of the United States.

[46] Peden to Marcy, Oct. 13, 1856, *ibid.*, p. 612.
[47] Marcy to Peden, Feb. 10, 1857; Peden to Lewis Cass, Secretary of State, April 26, 1857, *ibid.*, pp. 52-53, 640.
[48] Memorandum of conference with Bernabé López, Minister of Foreign Affairs, May 19, 1857, *ibid.*, pp. 641-642.
[49] Cass to Lamar, July 23, 1857, C. A. Gulick, Jr. and Winnie Allen, *The Papers of Mirabeau Buonaparte Lamar*, IV, pt. II, 42; Cass to Lamar, Oct. 23, 1857, Manning, *op. cit.*, I, 53-58. Late in August the British Minister had reminded Cass of the policy upon which Britain and the United States had agreed during the previous administration (Lord Francis Napier to the Earl of Clarendon, Aug. 29, 1857, LC, MD, Photostats, F. O. 5, Vol. 673, Folio IV).
[50] Yancey to Cass, Dec. 2, 1858, NA, DS, Desp. Arg., XIII.

Yancey's best opportunity to insist upon strict enforcement of the treaties grew out of a Confederation decree of May 20, 1859. By this order the executive closed the Confederation's ports to all intercourse with the Province of Buenos Aires and denied admission to foreign vessels which stopped at provincial ports.[51] In a long, reasoned despatch, the Minister vigorously contended that the decree was an outright violation of the Confederation's treaties and by enjoining absolute non-intercourse virtually invalidated them. The decree, he urged, was devoid of all legal and constitutional requisites. Had it been the intention of the Confederation to suspend intercourse with the Province in case of war or rebellion, such a clause should have been inserted in the treaty. Moreover, he regarded Buenos Aires as a *de facto* government and conceded to it all the rights of a belligerent, even retaliation against Urquiza's blockade.[52] The Department of State upheld Yancey's views. In September the Confederation rescinded the objectionable decree.[53]

However persuasive Yancey's legalistic interpretation of treaty rights, it could hardly lessen the certainty with which the two governments were drifting toward a renewal of civil war. Motivated by his own deep desire to forestall new hostilities as well as by a memorial from American merchants in Buenos Aires, the Georgian offered to both governments his services as mediator.[54]

General Urquiza accepted Yancey's good offices without reservation, giving him carte blanche; the provincial authorities were reluctant, questioning the General's good faith.[55] The Minister shuttled between Buenos Aires and Paraná to assure that hostilities would remain suspended during the mediation. Governor Alsina, ultimately consenting to proceed, demanded the right to counter Yancey's bases for negotiation with suggestions of his own. Though the proposals agreed on essential components for reunion of all provinces by 1863, they differed in two significant particulars. First, the Province demanded Urquiza's complete retirement from public life, not mere ineligibility for re-election. Secondly, it insisted that the United States guarantee com-

---

[51] A copy of the decree was forwarded to Yancey by Elías Bedoya, Acting Minister of Foreign Affairs, May 23, 1859, Manning, *op. cit.*, I, 697-698.

[52] Yancey to Bedoya, May 27, 1859; Yancey to Cass, June 23, 1859, *ibid.*, pp. 702-721.

[53] Cass to John F. Cushman, Minister to Argentina, Sept. 12, 1859, *ibid.*, pp. 59-60; Yancey to Cass, Sept. 10, 1859, NA, DS, Desp. Arg., XIII.

[54] Yancey described his mediation in detail in communications to Cass, July 20, 1859, and to Buchanan, Aug. 22, 1859, Manning, *op. cit.*, I, 721-731.

[55] The correspondence with Urquiza and Governor Alsina was printed in an official publication of the Argentine Confederation, *Documentos oficiales. Mediación del encargado de negocios de los Estados Unidos de América D. Benjamin Yancey . . .* , pp. 16-17, 18, 25. (Hereafter cited as *Mediación de Yancey*.)

mercial privileges and freedom as defined in the treaties of 1854-1855 between Buenos Aires and the Confederation.[56]

Negotiations revolved around these differences. As to the second, Yancey asserted that American policy was strict neutrality in the wars and internal dissensions of foreign nations. As to the first, he sought to persuade the provincial authorities not to make the person of General Urquiza an insuperable obstacle to national reunion. His logic and persuasion, however, were futile, for on August 10 the provincial leaders refused to continue the parleys except on the basis of Urquiza's immediate retirement. This *sine qua non* abruptly terminated Yancey's mediation. Nevertheless, Urquiza and the Confederation Congress were profuse in their praise of the Minister's efforts.[57] His successor to Paraná, John F. Cushman, of Mississippi, believed that the subsequent mediation by General López of Paraguay sprang from Yancey's preliminaries.[58]

When Benjamin C. Yancey left his post in the following September, Argentine-American relations were as salutary as they had ever been. "I shall leave the Legation," he wrote, "without leaving a single question between our Govts. and I am gratified to be enabled to say that I shall leave the country entertaining the most cordial friendship, among it's people and in it's Gov't, towards our Gov't." [59] When he stopped in London on his return voyage, the Confederation Minister, Juan B. Alberdi, presented him to Lord John Russell as a competent analyst of affairs in La Plata.[60]

The Growth of Trade and Related Interests

In the growth of Argentine-American commercial relations during the nineteenth century, the year 1853 marked a turning point. In the first place, under the bilateral treaties of commerce and navigation negotiated in that year American shipping could operate on an equal footing with the British and French. American diplomats could now argue treaty rights in defending American interests. In fact, diplomatic relations for the next decade revolved largely around interpretations of the treaties and defense of treaty rights.

Secondly, from 1853 the total dollar value of American exports grew steadily. It reached a million dollars for the first time in 1856, and two

[56] On the bases of negotiation, see *Mediación de Yancey*, pp. 28-30, and Manning, *op. cit.*, I, 728-730.

[57] Baldemero García, Acting Minister of Foreign Affairs, to Yancey, Sept. 3, 1859, NA, DS, Desp. Arg., XIII; República Argentina, *Diario de las sesiones de la Cámara de Diputados, 1859-1860*, p. 314.

[58] Cushman to Cass, May 22, 1860, Manning, *op. cit.*, I, 756-757.

[59] Yancey to Cass, Sept. 10, 1859, NA, DS, Desp. Arg., XIII.

[60] Alberdi to De la Peña, Nov. 8, Dec. 5-7, 1859, Alberdi, *Escritos póstumos*, XIV, 334-335, 339.

million in 1867. The annual average for the fifties almost doubled in the sixties, then levelled off in the depression seventies. In spite of growth, the totals remained strikingly small. Flour, lumber, furniture, and machinery continued to be the chief items of commerce.

Thirdly, only in 1862, at the depth of the Civil War, would annual Argentine exports to the United States fall below the total of 1852. The value of merchandise reaching the United States in the fifties annually averaged close to three million dollars; in the sixties, nearly five million; and in the next decade, about five and a half million. Raw wool, hides, and skins were still the most desired products.

Finally, as these figures demonstrate, the treaties of 1853 opened the way to steady increase in total Argentine-American trade. With slight fluctuations, this upward trend continued—through the panic of 1857 and the Civil War in the United States and through internal discord and the Paraguayan War in Argentina—until the depression years 1874-1877. Continuously the balance of trade remained in Argentina's favor, usually by a wide margin.[61] But, more important, the total trade of the United States with Argentina still ran a poor third to that of Great Britain and of France, which had also signed bilateral treaties in 1853.[62] It would require more than equal treaty rights to narrow that gap.

To this problem both the American government and its citizens began to give attention. In 1858 the Department of State appointed a commercial agent for Rosario, chief port of entry of the Confederation after the withdrawal of Buenos Aires.[63] In the early sixties, it instructed its agents to encourage diverse enterprises which would bring Argentina, Uruguay, and Paraguay into closer contact with the commercial world. These included a project for an international postal convention, the establishment of international telegraphic communication,[64] and limited cooperation with an English group in the contemplated opening of the Salado River, a tributary of the Paraná.[65] The two countries concluded the postal convention in 1872, but direct telegraph lines and other projects awaited future entrepreneurs and more aggressive administrations.[66]

Next to the construction of an intercontinental telegraph, a direct shipping service was the greatest need of American commerce. Since

[61] See above, p. 144, Table 1.

[62] *Statistical Abstract for the United Kingdom, 1853-1867*, pp. 16-17, and *1859-1873*, pp. 22-23; *Annuaire statistique de la France, 1882*, pp. 348-349.

[63] Peden to Secretary of State, July 15, 1857, NA, DS, Desp. Arg., XI; Benjamin Upton, first commercial agent to Rosario, to Cass, May 14, Nov. 13, 1858, NA, DS, Con. Let., Rosario, I.

[64] Official correspondence on these projects was printed in *Memoria, 1863*, pp. 130-141, and *1866*, pp. 121-127.

[65] F. W. Seward, Assistant Secretary of State, to Hinton R. Helper, United States Consul, April 3, 1863, NA, DS, Inst. to Con., XXXIII, 104-105.

[66] *Memoria, 1872*, pp. 1-24, and *1873*, pp. 627-637; República Argentina, *Tratados*, VIII, 163-169, 171.

1810 this lack had handicapped both merchants and diplomats. Great Britain and France, connected with Buenos Aires for years by direct ship lines, were at least fifteen travelling days closer than east coast ports of the United States. Aware of this handicap, two Americans in Argentina—Hinton R. Helper, author of *The Impending Crisis,* and Edward A. Hopkins, pioneer Yankee promoter seeking new ventures —agitated for governmental subsidies to steamship lines.[67]

Buenos Aires made an immediate proposal; Washington took no action. In 1865 the Argentine Congress authorized an annual subvention of $20,000 for not more than eight years to promote a direct line of steamers making monthly calls.[68] The Argentine Minister in Washington, Domingo F. Sarmiento, urged American cooperation. Subsequently, in a petition to the United States Congress six hundred influential Argentine citizens and aliens endorsed the project.[69] The Johnson administration failed to respond to these pressures, however, leaving American exporters to meet European competition with the handicaps imposed by inferior communication and transportation facilities.

Meanwhile, private citizens were contributing essential talents to the improvement of relations between the two peoples. Specialists in diverse areas were helping Argentina to conquer its frontier and to strengthen its science, technology, transportation, and education.[70] Thomas Jefferson Page, a Virginian in the employ of both governments, spent thirty years after 1853 exploring the tributaries of the Río de la Plata and plumbing the economic potentialities of their hinterland.[71] William Wheelwright, of Massachusetts, veteran steamship promoter and railroad builder on the Pacific coast of South America, built the first extensive railroad line in Argentina, from Rosario to Córdoba, and for his labors merited a commemorative biography by Juan B. Alberdi.[72] Edward A. Hopkins, of Vermont, whose aggressive energy brought exile from Paraguay, gave forty years of pioneering zeal to Argentina,

---

[67] Helper to Seward, March 13, 1863, Dec. 27, 1864, Aug. 21, 1866, NA, DS, Con. Let., B. A., X, XI; Robert C. Kirk, Minister to Argentina, to Seward, July 26, 1865, NA, DS, Desp. Arg., XV.

[68] Kirk to Seward, Aug. 21, 1865, NA, DS, Desp. Arg., XV; *Diario de sesiones de la Cámara de Senadores, 1865,* p. 269.

[69] Sarmiento to Seward, Nov. 11, 1865, Jan. 17, 1868, NA, DS, Notes from Arg. Leg., II; Alexander Asboth, Minister to Argentina, to Seward, June 20, 1867, NA, DS, Desp. Arg., XVII.

[70] J. Fred Rippy, *Latin America and the Industrial Age,* pp. 105-114.

[71] On Page's explorations for the Navy Department, see his *Report . . . to the Secretary of the Navy, 1856,* and *La Plata, the Argentine Confederation, and Paraguay,* as well as John P. Harrison, "Science and Politics: Origins and Objectives of Mid-Nineteenth Century Government Expeditions to Latin America," *The Hispanic American Historical Review,* XXXV (May, 1955), 192-200. Also see below, pp. 168-170.

[72] *The Life and Industrial Labors of William Wheelwright in South America,* Boston, 1877.

consummating few projects, but pinpointing and spotlighting numerous needs.[73] Domingo Sarmiento, as Minister to the United States, enlisted the services of Benjamin A. Gould, of Massachusetts and the United States coastal survey, to found and direct an astronomical observatory. As President after 1868 he recruited dozens of Yankee schoolteachers to found Argentina's system of normal schools.[74] Where these pioneered, other technicians followed.

In Washington, however, where after Appomattox new winds were beginning to blow, the atmosphere was less salubrious for Argentine economic health. Until 1867, trade between the two countries had moved without significant restrictions from domestic tariff laws. Then, with American protectionists firmly in the saddle, a strong combination of woolgrowers and manufacturers secured a prohibitive duty upon raw wool, long a leading Argentine export. The new rates virtually excluded the commodity from American markets at a time when England, France, and Italy admitted it free.[75]

The Argentine government sought in various ways to win modification of the restrictive legislation. First, its minister in Washington promoted a propaganda campaign. Through interviews with influential persons, articles in newspapers, and wide distribution of an eighteen-page pamphlet, Manuel R. García attempted to show that the interests of manufacturers, merchants, and consumers required a reduction of the rates.[76] Next, he proposed a new treaty, which would provide fixed rates on leading items of trade, such as lumber, breadstuffs, farm implements, wool, hides, and canned goods. Secretary of State Hamilton Fish ruled such a treaty inadvisable because of the most-favored-nation clause in many bilateral treaties.[77] Finally, in its tariff for 1870, the Argentine Legislature sought to woo the United States by placing some items on the free list and by giving the executive discretionary power to exempt others.[78] When, a short time later, the United States Senate

---

[73] On Hopkins' multifarious activities, diplomatic and economic, official and private, in Paraguay and Argentina, see Harold F. Peterson, "Edward A. Hopkins: A Pioneer Promoter in Paraguay," *The Hispanic American Historical Review*, XXII (May, 1942), 245-261, and Victor L. Johnson, "Edward A. Hopkins and the Development of Argentine Transportation and Communication," *ibid.*, XXVI (Feb., 1946), 19-37. Also see above, pp. 134-137, and below, pp. 165-168.

[74] Rippy, *op. cit.*, pp. 108-110; *Dictionary of American Biography*, VII, 448.

[75] *Sen. Ex. Doc.*, No. 7, 45 Cong., 3 sess., pp. 5-7.

[76] García to Mariano Varela, Minister of Foreign Affairs, May 5, Dec. 31, 1869, *Memoria, 1869*, pp. 167-169, and *1870*, p. 106. The pamphlet, published in Washington, was entitled *Remarks Concerning the Means to Re-establish the Declining State of Commerce between the United States and the Argentine Republic by the Proper Reduction of the Present Tariffs*.

[77] García to William Seward, Secretary of State, May 10, 1869, NA, DS, Notes from Arg. Leg., II; Hamilton Fish, Secretary of State, to García, May 14, 1869, NA, DS, Notes to Arg. Leg., VI, 71-73, both printed in *Memoria, 1869*, pp. 171-173.

[78] García to Fish, Nov. 22, 1869, NA, DS, Notes from Arg. Leg., II.

asked Secretary Fish to explain the unsatisfactory state of trade with the Spanish American nations, he failed to emphasize tariff policy.[79]

With Republican majorities in Congress now committed to protectionism, all Argentine attempts to increase the flow of trade were abortive. Though their reactions at the time were tactful and correct, on more than one occasion in the future Argentine statesmen would refer to the Wool and Woolens Act of 1867 as a misguided step in the promotion of Argentine-American harmony.

During the years after Rosas' fall, the United States gradually developed a more positive commercial policy toward Argentina. In the thirties and forties international complications had restricted reciprocal trade. After 1850 the domestic cleavages that rocked each nation still hampered commercial expansion. In Argentina, as in the United States, depressions, civil turmoil, expanding economy, and growing population were overriding problems. The drive in each to unify a divided people while conquering a sprawling land was a consuming interest. In spite of handicaps at each pole, however, American statesmen sought to liberalize the economic policies of Argentina and its neighbors and to win equal rights for American shipping in their river ports. To these ends they concluded the nation's first commercial treaties with Argentina, Uruguay, and Paraguay and secured recognition of the principle that international rivers should be open to ships of all nations. As economic barriers to commerce diminished after 1852, diplomatic relations between the two states improved, though on several occasions events in Paraguay were to complicate them anew.

[79] *Sen. Ex. Doc.,* No. 112, 41 Cong., 2 sess., pp. 10-11.

Part Four: Paraguay, Focus of
Argentine-American Diplomacy

X I

IMBROGLIO IN PARAGUAY:
IMPRUDENCE OF AMERICAN AGENTS,
1853-1860

Even before conclusion of the 1853 treaties, both Argentina and the United States had zealously advocated free navigation of international rivers in South America. In August, 1852, General Urquiza had incorporated the principle in a treaty recognizing Paraguayan independence and in October had decreed the Paraná and the Uruguay open to the merchant vessels of all nations.[1] As early as September, 1851, Robert Schenck in Rio had recommended the principle to Washington [2] and, along with John Pendleton in Buenos Aires, received prompt authorization to secure the adherence of Paraguay and Uruguay as well as of Argentina.

With laudable despatch the envoys negotiated treaties with the three nations, though before consummation of that with Paraguay tactless agents had incensed its irritable, sometimes impulsive dictator, Carlos Antonio López. Their indiscretions produced not only ruptured relations with Paraguay but an apparent threat to the security of Argentina.

Discordant incidents were pressing to a climax in Asunción when in his first annual message President Buchanan requested authority to use force to support his demand for redress. American grievances, he said, were Paraguay's (1) refusal to ratify the projected treaty, (2) confiscation of a business enterprise and insults to its managers, and (3) attack upon an exploring vessel, the *Water Witch*.[3]

The difficulties continued until 1859, when by effective use of his good offices Urquiza minimized Buchanan's threat of coercion and salvaged the principle of free navigation. The Republic of Paraguay, long

[1] See above, p. 149.
[2] To Webster, Sept. 25, William R. Manning (ed.), *Diplomatic Correspondence of the United States: Inter-American Affairs, 1831-1860*, II, 414-415.
[3] J. D. Richardson, *A Compilation of the Messages and Papers of the Presidents*, V, 449.

isolated by geography and by policy, thus became the focus of Argentine-American relations,[4] a status it was to retain throughout the sixties.

An Unratified Treaty

The Fillmore administration in 1852 laid careful plans for opening up the Río de la Plata and its tributaries. In April Secretary of State Webster directed Minister Schenck to proceed from Rio to Buenos Aires, there to associate himself with Pendleton in negotiating treaties with the three Platine nations. In the case of Paraguay, he specifically ordered Schenck not to transfer to Asunción but, if possible, to treat with López' agent in Rio or in Buenos Aires.[5]

Schenck reached Buenos Aires in mid-July to find Argentina deeply enmeshed in problems of national reorganization. Since Rosas had never recognized Paraguayan independence, no diplomatic representative of President López resided in the Argentine capital. In the face of these circumstances, Schenck felt obliged to return to his post and to leave affairs in the hands of Pendleton.[6] December came before the chargé could proceed.

Meanwhile, in Washington the administration grew impatient. Failing perhaps to appreciate the deep turmoil which handicapped agents in the field, President Fillmore determined to utilize the Navy to achieve the treaty with Paraguay. On February 1, 1853, he authorized Lieutenant Thomas J. Page, then preparing to lead a scientific expedition to the Río de la Plata, to assist Pendleton and Schenck or, if necessary, to proceed alone.[7] Though its terms would expire within a month, the Whig administration resolved that the United States should open up Paraguay as it was preparing to open up Japan.

Long before the Page expedition reached La Plata, however, Pendleton decided to act. Urged by the veteran British Minister, Sir Charles Hotham, he moved to Asunción, where the two joined the French and Sardinian ministers in negotiating treaties wtih President López.[8] In accord with administration plans, Pendleton's treaty provided free navigation of the Paraguay River and the Paraguayan section of the

---

[4] The most complete study of the treaty negotiations and other antecedents of the American expedition against Paraguay in 1859 is the first volume of Pablo Max Ynsfran's *La expedición norteamericana contra el Paraguay, 1858-1859*. For a short article, see Harold F. Peterson, "Urquiza y el enredo paraguayo-norteamericano," Academia Nacional de la Historia, *Segundo congreso internacional de historia de América, reunido en Buenos Aires en los días 5 a 14 de julio de 1937*, IV, 320-330.

[5] Webster to Schenck, April 29, 1852, Manning, *op. cit.*, II, 166-168, and to Pendleton, April 28, 1852, *ibid.*, I, 41-42.

[6] Schenck to Webster, Oct. 14, 1852, *ibid.*, II, 419-421.

[7] Edward Everett, Secretary of State, to Page, Feb. 1, 1853, *ibid.*, X, 35.

[8] Pendleton to Everett, Dec. 5, 1852, *ibid.*, I, 537-538.

Paraná. However reluctant he had been to surrender any part of his absolute control over national waterways, López immediately proclaimed ratification of the pact.[9]

With American ratification of this treaty, therefore, and of similar ones soon to be completed with Uruguay and the Argentine Confederation, Washington would have attained its ambitions for the unimpeded navigation of the Río de la Plata and its confluents. But, so far as Paraguay was concerned, its hopes were to be delayed more than six years.

Though the Senate promptly approved the treaty, it did so only after editing Pendleton's inept use of such terms as "United States of North America" and "North American Union." Ultimate proclamation of the amended document, therefore, required resubmission to López and reratification by him.[10] Efforts of the naval officer Page in 1854 and a special commissioner, Richard Fitzpatrick, in 1856 to secure the second ratification were unavailing. Meanwhile, as unfortunate events intervened to embitter relations between the two governments, López again grew apprehensive of the treaty.

The Imprudence of a Consul

The first of these incidents stemmed from the provocative activities of Edward A. Hopkins, who returned to Asunción at this juncture in the dual roles of American consul and ambitious entrepreneur. Soon after his arrival he bluntly stated that the United States would never ratify the treaty.[11] This strange declaration of a government agent about to assume an official post while launching a private business venture was consistent with Hopkins' long record of indecorum.

Less than a decade earlier the Yankee adventurer had gambled with the fortunes of two dictators, Rosas and López—and lost. But the loss of one hand only whetted his dazzling hopes for Paraguay and swelled ambitions for himself.[12] Abruptly he shifted his career from amateur diplomat to that of propagandist. Half of the next five years he spent

[9] Correspondence on the negotiations has been printed in Manning, *op. cit.*, X, 95-111, and *Historia documentada de las cuestiones entre el gobierno del Paraguay y él de los Estados Unidos*, pp. 21-25. The latter volume was published by the Paraguayan government in 1858 while the American fleet was en route. Though a tract, it contains copies of many documents no longer available in Paraguayan archives.

[10] Lewis Cass, Secretary of State, to James B. Bowlin, United States Commissioner to Paraguay in 1858-1859, Oct. 6, 1858, Manning, *op. cit.*, X, 40; Ynsfran, *op. cit.*, I, 155-156.

[11] Page to W. L. Marcy, Secretary of State, Oct. 23, 1853, NA, DS, Desp. Arg., VIII.

[12] Much of the material in this section has been published in Peterson, "Edward A. Hopkins: A Pioneer Promoter in Paraguay," *The Hispanic American Historical Review*, XXII (May, 1942), 250-256.

in Paraguay and adjoining lands. He came to know the leading citizens and familiarized himself with all sections of the country.[13] Back in his homeland between South American journeys, Hopkins sought to focus the interest of commercial groups on the vast new regions which awaited their enterprise. Of all the new nations in the valley of the Río de la Plata, he contended, Paraguay was most deserving of American attention.[14] His shrill trumpetings of the nineteenth-century Potosí echoed through diverse American journals.[15]

But Hopkins' glowing reports were much more than empty bleatings. He was the harbinger of several fundamental policies the Department of State was to pursue during the next generation. As early as 1846 he urged the United States to become the champion of the principle of free navigation of international rivers.[16] In defending the Monroe Doctrine, he complained because President Polk failed "to carry it out as it was originally intended." [17] He pleaded for the appointment of diplomatic representatives to Latin America on some more rational basis than "the reward of sycophancy, relationship, and oftentimes unscrupulous party services, without one single reference to competency for the office." [18] He advocated the despatch of a governmental hydrographic survey long before Lieutenant Page entered the Paraná with the *Water Witch*.[19]

Moreover, during these years of travel and writing, Hopkins was laying the groundwork for his own promotional ventures. He proposed a steamship company which would operate boats on Paraguayan rivers. If he were guaranteed a monopoly on the machines and inventions he would introduce, he offered to organize a manufacturing company.[20]

Meanwhile, Hopkins sought reappointment to the post from which Secretary Buchanan had once summarily dismissed him. Though the

[13] Edward A. Hopkins, *Historico-politico Memorial upon the Regions of the Río de la Plata and Coterminous Countries, to President Buchanan,* pp. 6-7. A manuscript copy of this memorial was sent to Cass on Jan. 25, 1858, NA, DS, Misc. Let., Jan., 1858.

[14] Hopkins, "The La Plata and the Parana-Paraguay," *DeBow's Review,* XIV (March, 1853), 250.

[15] His writings appeared in *DeBow's Review, The Merchants' Magazine, The American Review, Weekly National Intelligencer,* and the *Bulletin of the American Geographical and Statistical Society.*

[16] Hopkins to Henry A. Wise, Minister to Brazil, March 27, 1846, NA, DS, Desp. Bra., XV; Hopkins, "The Republic of Paraguay; Since the Death of the Dictator Francia," *The American Review,* VI (July, 1847), 245-260.

[17] *Ibid.,* p. 259.

[18] *Weekly National Intelligencer* (Washington), May 12, 1849, p. 7.

[19] Hopkins to Webster, June 30, 1851, NA, DS, Misc. Let., June, 1851; *Bulletin of the American Geographical and Statistical Society,* I, 66-69.

[20] *El Seminario de Avisos y Conocimientos* (Asunción), Aug. 26, 1854, p. 6; Juan A. Gelly, Paraguayan Chargé in Rio de Janeiro, to Hopkins, Dec. 15, 1848, *Commission under the Convention between the United States & Paraguay,* pp. 143, 145. *El Seminario* was the official newspaper of López.

sin of his petulant letter to Rosas continued to militate against him until 1852, the State Department finally granted him the appointment.[21]

Now at last, Hopkins was ready for his greatest adventure. Armed with his commission as United States consul, he would have official position from which to direct his commercial undertakings. Home from his third trip to Paraguay, he set about the organization of a company to underwrite his enterprises. He induced a group of Rhode Island capitalists to charter a corporation, with an initial capitalization of $100,000. The chief purpose of The United States and Paraguayan Navigation Company was to build and navigate vessels on the seas and rivers of South America, though it was also authorized to transact any "other lawful business." [22]

The company soon despatched its first expedition, a river steamer loaded with the latest American industrial equipment. It also carried several scores of American and Cuban workmen, principally machinists, cigar makers, and common laborers.[23] Upon the ship's arrival in Paraguay, Hopkins immediately acquired land and buildings at Asunción and San Antonio, ten miles below the capital, where water power could be developed. President López aided the company in diverse ways, including patent rights and exemption from import duties on the machinery and manufacturing processes introduced.[24] Hopkins immediately launched various enterprises. By the early months of 1854 business seemed to be thriving.

Nevertheless, Hopkins' great hopes for Paraguay—and for himself and his company—were never to be realized. The domain of López, which the Consul had so zealously advertised for ten years, was no longer the hospitable paradise he had envisaged. By diverse indiscretions, including an angry exchange over an alleged insult to his brother, Hopkins provoked the dictator to drastic action. López accused him of smuggling, contempt for officials, disregard of port regulations, and other excesses. Alleging infractions of Paraguayan laws, in August, 1854, he first paralyzed, then closed Hopkins' enterprises and withdrew his exequatur as consul.[25] Clearly, the American's arrogant and tyrannical deportment intensified his controversy with the stubborn López.

[21] See above, p. 136. Many letters written by him and for him are filed in NA, DS, Appointment Records, Hopkins, in various volumes of Misc. Let., and in LC, MD, Webster Papers, XII.

[22] *Charter and By-Laws of the United States and Paraguay Navigation Company*, pp. 3-4.

[23] *Commission under the Convention between the United States & Paraguay*, pp. 105, 123 ff.

[24] Ynsfran, *op. cit.*, I, 135.

[25] AGN, Asun., Vol. IX, no. 23, Decretos circulares de gobierno sobre prohibición de comprar de esclavos. . . .

To him, Hopkins' entire demeanor had become anathema. He put an abrupt end to the Consul's promotional career in Paraguay.[26]

In January, 1855, The United States and Paraguayan Navigation Company requested government intervention to redress its grievances.[27] President Pierce termed the acts of the Paraguayan government "violent and arbitrary" and proposed to hold it accountable. On two occasions—April, 1856, and October, 1858—the State Department despatched special agents to Asunción to demand satisfaction for the company's losses. Eventually, with the aid of the American Navy, the Buchanan administration forced a settlement. Long before, however, Washington had initiated other steps to secure Paraguayan approval of the controversial treaty.

The Affair of the "Water Witch"

Hopkins' unrestrained conduct in Asunción frustrated the mission of Lieutenant Page and eventually rendered his position untenable. In the officer's original instructions of 1853 Secretary of the Navy John P. Kennedy ordered him to take the steam vessel *Water Witch* "to the La Plata for the purpose of exploration and survey of the upper streams above their falls." His objectives, in order of priority, were promotion of commerce and navigation and extension of the bounds of science.[28] The decision to employ Page to negotiate the treaty with Paraguay was an afterthought of President Fillmore.[29]

Reaching Argentina in May, Page promptly secured Urquiza's authority to navigate the waters of the Confederation for scientific purposes.[30] In Asunción, where he arrived ten days before Hopkins, he wrung from López limited navigation privileges on Paraguayan rivers.[31] During his wait for the dictator's reluctant approval, he met Hopkins and spontaneously formed a low opinion of him. He wasted no time in

[26] In flaming language, Hopkins stated his case again and again. See, for example, his reports to Marcy, Manning, *op. cit.*, X, 120-141, and his tirade published in Buenos Aires in 1856, *La tiranía del Paraguay, a la faz de sus contemporáneos*. A long statement of the Paraguayan case, sometimes mendacious and vituperative, was presented in *Historia documentada*, esp. pp. 31-76. For an historian's account, see Ynsfran, *op. cit.*, I, 175-191.

[27] W. M. Bailey, treasurer of the company, to Marcy, Sept. 28, 1855, and enclosure, NA, DS, Misc. Let., Sept., 1855. During the next four years agents of the company continued to send memorials to the Department of State.

[28] NA, DN, Record of Confidential Letters, No. 2 (March 1, 1849-Feb. 28, 1853), pp. 422-423; Page, *La Plata, the Argentine Confederation, and Paraguay*, p. 567.

[29] Everett to Page, Feb. 1, 1853, Manning, *op. cit.*, X, 35.

[30] Page to Secretary of Navy, May 28, 1853, NA, DN, Letters from Page.

[31] Page's Report to the Secretary of the Navy, August 4, 1856, *Sen. Rep.*, No. 60, 35 Cong., 1 sess., pp. 11, 12.

recommending that the State Department rebuke the Consul for his "idle bombast" against the treaty Pendleton had negotiated with López.[32]

While Hopkins was setting up his enterprises in the capital, Page was exploring the Paraguay and Upper Paraná Rivers. He was in the Argentine port of Corrientes in August, 1854, when Hopkins appealed to him to bring the *Water Witch* to Asunción to restrain the government from "its blind vengeance." [33] The naval officer had no intention of involving his command in a vindication of the Consul's actions or absolving him from blame for the predicament into which his own folly and want of discretion had led him. Yet, feeling a duty to protect American citizens and their property, he gave Hopkins refuge.[34] Three days after the Consul's flight, López ordered all Paraguayan rivers closed to foreign warships.[35]

The officer's assistance to Hopkins' exit, however reluctant, placed him in an awkward position two weeks later when he received Secretary Marcy's order to attempt an exchange of treaty ratifications with López.[36] Because Parguayan waters were now closed to his vessel, he was forced to ask permission to proceed. When he framed the request in English, unaccompanied by a translation, López denied approval.[37] Page and the treaty paid the price of Hopkins' wounded honor.

But Page's Paraguayan career, like that of the *Water Witch*, had not yet chronicled its most unfortunate experience. The activities of his ship were now legally restricted to the rivers of the Argentine Confederation. Nevertheless, Page sent Lieutenant William N. Jeffers to explore the Paraná where it formed the boundary between Paraguay and the Province of Corrientes. When Paraguayan authorities attempted to halt the vessel for violating national waters, the young commander contemptuously refused to comply. As it passed under the fort of Itapirú, Paraguayan guns opened fire and killed the pilot.[38] Page at once withdrew his expedition and, except for reports to his superiors and a brief journalistic feud with President López, did not again figure prominently in United States-Paraguayan relations. Without intention perhaps, Page

[32] Page to Marcy, Oct. 23, 1853, NA, DS, Desp. Arg., VIII.
[33] Hopkins to Page, Aug. 13, 1854, NA, DN, Letters from Page.
[34] Page to James C. Dobbins, Secretary of the Navy, Sept. 1, 1854, *ibid.*
[35] *Historia documentada,* pp. 79-80; Manning, *op. cit.,* X, 142, note 1.
[36] Marcy to Page, June 2, 1854, *ibid.,* p. 36.
[37] Page to José Falcón, Acting Minister of Foreign Affairs, Oct. 16, 1854; Falcón to Page, Oct. 21, 1854, *ibid.,* 142-143, 144.
[38] Page to Dobbin, Feb. 5, 1855, and enclosures, NA, DN, Letters from Page; Peden to Marcy, Feb. 10, 1855, and enclosures; Falcón to Marcy, Feb. 4, 1855, and enclosure, Manning, *op. cit.,* X, 150-153. By reference to maps, geodetic data, and sovereign rights, Ynsfran presents a convincing justification of Paraguay's position (*op. cit.,* I, 205-228).

and his vessel had twice sharpened the acrid dispute which Hopkins had provoked.

James A. Peden, on the other hand, reading the officer's reports in Buenos Aires, left no doubt about his intentions. With great indignation he advised the State Department of the attack upon the American flag. Several times he recommended that sufficient naval armament be sent to demand satisfaction for American grievances. These he listed as the expulsion of Hopkins' company, the refusal to ratify the treaty, and the firing upon the *Water Witch*.[39]

Pierce Conciliates; Buchanan Threatens

The Pierce administration was not yet willing to adopt Peden's jingoistic recommendations. Though two of its agents, in attempting to improve commercial and diplomatic relations, had served only to embroil them, it resolved to try another conciliatory gesture. On August 5, 1856, nearly two years after Page's debacle, it delegated Richard Fitzpatrick, secretary of the Legation at Buenos Aires, as special commissioner to López.[40]

Fitzpatrick lacked the experience and resourcefulness to accomplish the assignment. To him, the exchange of treaty ratifications was the fundamental duty and a prerequisite to negotiations upon other problems. Nicolás Vásquez, Paraguayan Minister of Foreign Affairs, on the contrary, sought to postpone conversations upon the treaty until other matters had been adjusted.[41] The diplomats had reached a stalemate and soon broke off negotiations. Fitzpatrick's failure left relations in this strained position as the new administration entered office.

President Buchanan analyzed the situation promptly and determined to act. By imposing harsh restrictions on intercourse with foreigners, the President reasoned, López had defied the United States; only a threat of force could now bring him to book.[42] As soon as Congress convened he urged liquidation of the nation's grievances against Paraguay. "A demand for these purposes will be made in a firm but conciliatory spirit," he declared. "This will the more probably be granted if the Executive shall have authority to use other means in the event of a refusal." [43] Six months later, the Congress conceded him powers "to adopt such measures and use such force as, in his judgment, may be necessary and advisable, in the event of a refusal of just satisfaction

---

[39] Peden to Marcy, Feb. 10, April 6, 20, 1855, Manning, *op. cit.*, X, 154-162.

[40] Marcy to Fitzpatrick, Aug. 5, 1856, NA, DS, Inst. Arg., XV, 99-101. A portion of this instruction is printed in Manning, *op. cit.*, X, 37-38.

[41] *Ibid.*, pp. 171-179; *Historia documentada*, pp. 102-108.

[42] John Bassett Moore, *The Works of James Buchanan*, XII, 243.

[43] Richardson, *op. cit.*, V, 449.

by the government of Paraguay." As if an afterthought, it later appropriated funds for a special commissioner to negotiate with López.[44]

Buchanan's choice of a commissioner left no room for criticism. He appointed James B. Bowlin, a St. Louis attorney with long experience as a judge and representative in Congress, who had recently served as minister to Colombia.[45] Secretary Cass's instructions to Judge Bowlin were as specific as those to Page and Fitzpatrick had been vague, his powers as broad as theirs had been limited.

The Secretary directed the commissioner to demand (1) an apology for the attack upon the *Water Witch* and the rude treatment of the overtures of Page and Fitzpatrick, (2) indemnification to representatives of the seaman killed, (3) reparations for the losses and damages to Hopkins' company, and (4) ratification of the 1853 treaty or a new one. Having presented these demands, he should fix a time for their acceptance; refusal would provoke the use of force. Should hostilities ensue, they were to be maintained only until the Paraguayan government indicated a willingness to resume negotiations on the proposed bases.[46]

Long before the State Department had drafted these instructions, however, the Navy had begun preparations of an expeditionary force. As early as July it ordered ship captains to rendezvous at Montevideo.[47] The fleet assembled by December consisted of nineteen vessels, armed with two hundred guns and manned by twenty-five hundred sailors and marines. It was placed under the command of Commodore W. B. Shubrick,[48] whose orders left no doubt of the administration's intentions. Should Bowlin's negotiations break down, the naval officer would establish an effective blockade of Paraguay, destroy fortifications that might endanger safe passage, and use force, if necessary, to take possession of the capital.[49]

Buchanan's position was clear-cut. He empowered Judge Bowlin to deliver an ultimatum, with time limit. President López would acquiesce or face bombardment from Shubrick's guns. Since the days of Polk the Latin American policy of Democratic presidents had turned a cycle. The nation which would not raise a word against European interven-

[44] *U.S. Stat. at L.*, XI, 319, 370. For the debates in Congress, see *Cong. Globe*, XXXVI, pt. 1, 624; pt. 2, 1704-1705, 1727-1728, 1782-1786, 1929, 1961, 1963; pt. 3, 2547.

[45] J. H. Brown (ed.), *Lamb's Biographical Dictionary of the United States*, I, 367.

[46] Oct. 6, 1858, Manning, *op. cit.*, X, 38-46.

[47] NA, DN, Confidential Letters, Oct. 20, 1857—Sept. 6, 1861.

[48] NA, DN, *Annual Report*, 1859, pp. 1137; Isaac Toucey, Secretary of Navy, to Flag Officer French Forrest, Commander Brazilian Squadron, Aug. 30, 1858, NA, DN, Confidential Letters, No. 4.

[49] Toucey to Shubrick, Oct. 9, 1858, *ibid.*, No. 4, pp. 103-104.

tions in the forties was now itself intervening—with firepower. And not in North America but in the remote interior of South America.

The sending of this formidable squadron by the largest and most powerful nation in the Hemisphere to threaten one of the smallest and most obscure quickly kindled widespread alarm among the peoples and governments of Paraguay and its neighbors.[50] The chauvinistic press swung into action.

In Paraguay, López' official papers, *El Seminario* and *La Reforma Pacífica,* heaped vilification upon President Buchanan and demanded restitution for the crimes of Hopkins and Page.[51] In the Confederation, the semiofficial *El Nacional Argentina,* though less abusive, published extensive tirades from *El Seminario* and López' "blue book," *Historia documentada.*[52]

Foremost organs of the American press showed remarkable restraint, revealing no enthusiasm for the administration's policy. The *Daily National Intelligencer* (Washington) criticized the President for originating a policy which emphasized defiance instead of forbearance.[53] *The New York Times* thought belligerence hardly necessary against a nation as small as Paraguay.[54] The *Daily Union* (Washington), while defending Buchanan, hoped for a peaceful settlement.[55]

Urquiza and the Settlement

General Urquiza, President of the Argentine Confederation, was the dominant figure in the Platine states at the time of the Paraguayan controversy. For nearly twenty years he had led his fierce Gauchos, cloaked in red ponchos, up and down the valleys of the Paraná and the Uruguay. Ambitious, though responsive to national needs, ruthless, yet attentive to social welfare, he was said to have made himself "feared and obeyed, but not detested." [56] Supreme power in his own province and the Confederation, master of Uruguayan policies, and avowed friend of López, he enjoyed wide prestige. He was also skillful in exploiting a situation for his own advantage. In the conflict which impended between a neighbor and a foreign power, he saw that media-

---

[50] In reality, however, though well equipped for an engagement in open waters, the fleet was ill suited to its mission. Its ships were unmaneuverable in the treacherous rivers and its manpower was too small for land operations. The expedition "was not a model of tactical foresight or strategic wisdom" (Ynsfran, *op. cit.,* II, pp. 157-158).

[51] For examples, see *El Seminario,* April 24, Oct. 3, 9, 22, Nov. 13, Dec. 4, 1858, and *La Reforma Pacífica,* Dec. 3, 4, 5, 1858.

[52] Nov. 7, 8, 9, Dec. 14, 15, 1858. On the *Historia documentada,* see above, p. 165, note 9.

[53] Oct. 1, 1858. Also see issues of Sept. 2, Oct. 4, 8, 26, 1858.

[54] Oct. 12, 1858.

[55] Oct. 2, 3, 1858.

[56] W. H. Koebel, *The Romance of the River Plate,* II, 487.

tion might relieve the neighbor and cement friendship between the Confederation and the power. The threat stimulated him to action.

To prepare the ground and arrange the details of his intervention, Urquiza delegated his trusted minister, General Tomás Guido, veteran of half a century in Argentine politics. As a youth, Guido had fought to bring independence to several South American nations. Under successive Argentine administrations, he had held more than seventy offices, civil, diplomatic, and military. Seven times he served as minister of state, twenty times as plenipotentiary to Latin nations.[57] In 1846, while Minister to Brazil, he had conferred with Henry A. Wise on the Wise-Hopkins-Brent proposal for mediation between Rosas and López.[58] To Guido fell the assignments first of converting López to Argentine mediation and eventually of consummating the agreements that would restore United States-Paraguayan harmony.

Long before Bowlin, Shubrick, and the fleet sailed for La Plata, the Argentine leaders made preliminary overtures to López. Beginning in March, Guido regularly informed him of belligerent developments in the United States—of Buchanan's request for congressional authority, of fleet preparations, and of probable demands. Even before Congress passed its joint resolution in June, Guido advised López that he should "expect the worst." Gradually, he prepared the Paraguayan chief for the probability of friendly intervention—first, Argentine good offices; then, personal mediation by Urquiza; and, finally, joint interposition by Argentina, Brazil, and Uruguay. The seasoned diplomat reminded the proud executive that, however just he believed his cause, he should remember a lesson of history, that justice is impotent against brute force.[59]

By September López agreed to consider bases for the proposed joint mediation, though he rejected in advance any alternative that would sacrifice Paraguay to its neighbors' security and resolved to stand alone, if necessary, against the American colossus. He proposed and Urquiza approved a December meeting at an intermediate site for the discussion of mutual interests.[60]

---

[57] Estanislao S. Zeballos (ed.), "Diario del Brigadier General Tomás Guido durante su misión al Paraguay (1858-1859)," *Revista de Derecho, Historia y Letras,* VI (June, 1900), 485-486. The complete text of the diary is printed in *ibid.*, VI, 485-510; VII (July, Aug., 1900), 34-52, 195-208. The original manuscript is deposited in AGN, BA, Archivo del General Tomás Guido, 1858. The printed version is hereafter cited as "Diario del General Guido."

[58] Wise to Hopkins, Feb. 11, 1846, Manning, *op. cit.*, I, 331.

[59] Guido to López, March 30, May 22, June 28, Aug. 25, Sept. 14, 24, 1858, drafts, AGN, BA, Archivo del General Guido, 1858.

[60] López to Urquiza, Sept. 20, Nov. 22, 1858; to Guido, Oct. 9, 1858, *ibid.* An Argentine account of Urquiza's mediation, including many pertinent documents, is contained in C. A. Silva, *La política internacional de la Nación Argentina,* pp. 308-319.

The early arrival of American warships in the Río de la Plata prevented this meeting and forced Urquiza to turn to the second stage of his program.[61] As Bowlin's ship neared Montevideo, the General prepared to win the American's approval of his mediation. First, he alerted his close friend José de Buschenthal, German-born adventurer who, after varied careers in Spain and Brazil, had established himself in Uruguay as a rich banker and citizen of parts. Urquiza invited the banker to approach the commissioner with offers of his cooperation and mediation and requests for suggested bases of settlement.[62] Upon Bowlin's arrival, Buschenthal complied.[63]

Not content with a single approach to the American commissioner, Urquiza invited Minister Yancey to confer with Vice-President Salvador María del Carril. Apprised of the alarm generated by the approaching fleet, Yancey quoted Buchanan's latest despatch to demonstrate his peaceful intentions. But if the commissioner failed, inquired the Vice-President, would the United States accept the mediation of the Confederation, Brazil, and Uruguay? Yancey replied that Bowlin would have to answer, but he himself was certain that his superiors would not discuss with other governments the question of national honor or the principle of liability for damages to alien property.[64]

Later, as vessels of the fleet moved up the Paraná to Rosario, Del Carril invited Yancey to communicate two requests to Bowlin. Would he be willing to discuss pending problems with President Urquiza at Paraná? Would he deem it expedient to order the squadron to remain within the waters of the Confederation until the conclusion of negotiations in Asunción? [65]

The projected interview took place on January 10. It was a high-level conference involving the President, Vice-President, and Guido, now Acting Minister of Foreign Affairs, as well as Bowlin, Yancey, and Samuel Ward, secretary and interpreter to the commission.[66] When Urquiza promptly offered the mediation of the three nations, Bowlin as promptly refused. When the President volunteered to go to Asunción,

---

[61] Urquiza's report to his government, Feb. 5, 1859, Julio Victorica, "Los Estados Unidos, el Paraguay and la mediación Argentina de 1859," Revista de Derecho, Historia y Letras, VII (Sept., 1900), 369.

[62] Urquiza to Buschenthal, Dec. 13, 1858, Manning, op. cit., X, 188-189; Enrique Udaondo, Diccionario biográfico argentino, p. 190. Urquiza also authorized Buschenthal to solicit American aid, or at least sympathies, for the Confederation's efforts to unify the nation.

[63] Bowlin to Cass, Dec. 29, 1858, Manning, op. cit., X, 188.

[64] Yancey to Cass, Dec. 15, 1858, ibid., I, 664-666.

[65] Yancey to Cass, Jan. 6, 1859, ibid., pp. 675-676.

[66] Samuel Ward's "Memorandum of a conference," Manning, op. cit., X, 196-198, note 3. For an engaging narrative of Ward's subsequent relations with President López, see Pablo Max Ynsfran, "Sam Ward's Bargain with President López of Paraguay," The Hispanic American Historical Review, XXXIV (Aug., 1954), 313-331.

ostensibly to visit his Paraguayan friend, in reality to promote a settlement for his American friends, Bowlin hastened to accept his good offices.[67]

Urquiza and Bowlin, with their suites, then moved separately to Asunción. The Argentine arrived eight days before the American; the steamer *Fulton*, escorted by the *Water Witch*, found too many sand bars.[68] Meanwhile, in a succession of conferences, the General sought to convince López that American intentions had been much exaggerated and that a peaceful settlement could be effected.[69] Now, he undertook to orient Bowlin. He arranged his appointments, gave him friendly tips on how to approach López, and begged him to let no hitch interfere with negotiations. The discerning commissioner was receptive to these suggestions.[70]

The Argentine President did not function as the official mediator he hoped to be, but, aided by the resourceful Guido, he was the catalyst producing the settlement. During sixteen days in Asunción, he repeatedly consulted with López. Upon Guido, however, who conferred almost daily with the principals, fell the essential but less honored tasks of ironing out details and, after Urquiza's departure on February 1, of clinching the agreements.[71] Loyal to his chief, Guido believed that the President's prestige and impartiality had saved Paraguay from a calamity. Yet only the Minister's experience and acumen had successfully bridged numerous treacherous spots.[72]

With preliminaries so thoroughly planned and conferences so dexterously arranged, Bowlin's contribution was little more than perfunctory. Within a week after his arrival, he could report substantial agreement on all issues that had plagued United States-Paraguayan relations since 1853. The omnibus settlement included (1) a new treaty, at last opening Paraguayan ports to American ships, (2) a special convention providing

[67] Manning, *op. cit.*, X, 198. Urquiza said he owed this service to the United States, whose agents had saved his liberty and perhaps his life at a crucial moment (see above, p. 149, note 26).

[68] Shubrick to Toucey, Jan. 25, 1859, NA, DN, Paraguay Expedition and Brazil Squadron, Flag Officer Wm. B. Shubrick, Sept., 1858—May, 1859. Besides the manuscripts in this collection, useful sources on the naval expedition are "Report of the Secretary of the Navy, Dec., 1859," *Sen. Ex. Doc.*, III, 36 Cong., 1 sess., pp. 1135-1184, and Amos L. Mason (ed.), *Memoir and Correspondence of Charles Steedman, Rear Admiral, United States Navy*, pp. 155-265.

[69] "Diario del General Guido," Jan. 16-21, 1859.

[70] *Ibid.*, Jan. 24-30, 1859; Bowlin to Cass, Jan. 25, 1859, Manning, *op. cit.*, X, 200-203.

[71] "Diario del General Guido," Jan. 16-Feb. 21, 1859; Urquiza to Guido, Jan. 31, 1859, AGN, BA, Archivo del General Guido, 1859. In his diary Guido enumerates nineteen conferences with López, as well as many sessions with Bowlin, his secretary, and other diplomats. Also see Ynsfran, *op. cit.*, II, 106-153.

[72] "Diario del General Guido," Jan. 30, 1859.

arbitration of the company claims in Washington within twelve months,[73] (3) a letter of explanation and apology for the attack upon the *Water Witch*, (4) a sight draft for $10,000 for the representative of the slain seaman, and (5) a special letter authorizing admission to the Paraguay and the Paraná of an American exploring vessel. By February 6th the participants had completed all documents. Five days later Paraguay ratified the treaty and proclaimed the convention.[74]

Satisfaction with the Settlement

During the following weeks, exchanges of appreciation and congratulations circulated freely among the executives and their agents.[75] Surely no international settlement ever stimulated such an abundant flow of deferential rhetoric.

President Urquiza extended his personal congratulations to President Buchanan for Bowlin's achievement. "Not only has peace been restored," he said,

between the great and powerful nation over which your Excellency presides and that young and wealthy Republic, so as to promote all the elements of progress, of commerce, and of industry; but you have also, through the example of a policy, high, just and friendly, drawn to you the respect and the affection of these young Republics of the South towards their powerful Sister of the North, whom they claim as their great pattern.[76]

[73] On the work of the arbitration commission, see *Commission under the Convention between the United States & Paraguay*, and J. B. Moore, *History and Digest of the International Arbitrations to Which the United States Has Been a Party*, II, 1485-1549. Though the award was in favor of Paraguay, President Buchanan sought to revive the claim in a special message to Congress in 1861 (Richardson, *op. cit.*, V, 664-668). Later administrations, in response to pressure from Hopkins and other representatives of the company, continued to press the claim against Paraguay until 1888 (NA, DS, Inst. Para., I, 42-50, 154-158; Inst. Uru., I, 192-193, 244; and Desp. Para. and Uru., V).

[74] Bowlin to Cass, Feb. 17, 1859, Manning, *op. cit.*, X, 208-210; Guido's "Resumen de la conferencia que terminó las diferencias entre el Paraguay y E.E.U.U.," Feb. 1, 1859, AGN, BA, Archivo del General Guido, 1859. For the treaty and convention, see William M. Malloy, *Treaties, Conventions, International Acts, Protocols, and Agreements between the United States and Other Powers, 1776-1909*, II, 1364-1369, and also Manning, *Arbitration Treaties among the American Nations*, 45-48.

[75] On the way home from Asunción Commodore Shubrick took the *Fulton* and the *Water Witch* up the Uruguay River, so that he, Bowlin, and their staffs might accept Urquiza's invitation to visit him at his country home at San José de Flores. On this occasion, the General presented to the naval officer the sword he had worn while signing the first official act of the Confederation (Shubrick to Toucey, March 10, April 12, 1859, and enclosures, NA, DN, Paraguay Expedition and Brazil Squadron).

[76] March 1, 1859, Manning, *op. cit.*, I, 679.

Buchanan acknowledged his "grateful recognition of the noble and successful efforts of your Excellency in aiding Mr. Bowlin in the holy work of restoring peace and friendship." [77]

But among all these congratulatory messages probably none was composed with deeper sincerity than that of Bowlin to the venerable Guido:

> The labours of my mission over, it remains to me to execute one pleasing task; which is to offer my sincere thanks for the zealous co-operation of your friendly offices, which have on several occasions, removed thorns from my arduous path, and materially accelerated the progress of my negotiations.[78]

In Buenos Aires, the Argentines greeted final settlement of the Paraguayan question with general satisfaction. Though they squandered no love on Paraguay, they felt relief at withdrawal of the American threat.[79] From Paris, Minister Juan B. Alberdi reported the honor Urquiza's success had brought to the Argentine government and, what was more practical, the increased movement to La Plata of capital and industrial enterprises.[80] Clearly, Urquiza's intervention had not been inspired solely by idealism.

In Washington, President Buchanan expressed great satisfaction with the achievements of the naval expedition. He was convinced that

> the appearance of so large a force, fitted out in such a prompt manner, in the far-distant waters of the La Plata, and the admirable conduct of the officers and men employed in it, have had a happy effect in favor of our country throughout all that remote portion of the world.[81]

With the help both of General Urquiza and of the American Navy, Buchanan had resolved the crisis with Paraguay. But however proud he may have been of the success of his policy, future generations in the United States as well as in remote portions of the world would question the wisdom of using gunboat diplomacy to produce "a happy effect" among other peoples.

By the end of the fifties the United States had established treaty relations with all three nations of the Plata region. It had won recognition of the principle of free navigation of international rivers and in the competition for markets placed itself on an equal footing with

[77] August 10, 1859, *ibid.*, pp. 58-59.
[78] Feb. 11, 1859, AGN, BA, Archivo del General Guido, 1859.
[79] John F. Cushman, Minister to Argentina, to Cass, Nov. 20, 1860, Manning, *op. cit.*, I, 768-769.
[80] To Urquiza, April 7, May 6, 1859, Alberdi, *Escritos póstumos*, XIV, 761, 774.
[81] Richardson, *op. cit.*, V, 560.

European powers. In Uruguay and the Argentine Confederation, American diplomats had fulfilled their missions and raised the prestige of their country in the eyes of local leaders. In Paraguay, however, tactless or inexperienced agents, handicapped by vague or limited instructions, had served only to antagonize the government. Peculiarly, the display of force against López had brought about closer relations with President Urquiza. This favored position was to be short-lived, however, for in Buenos Aires new and younger leaders would soon unseat the Confederation chief and accelerate the process of unifying the nation. In any case, for the next decade all-absorbing wars—civil in the United States, international in La Plata—would check the normal evolution of North-South relations.

XII

THE PARAGUAYAN WAR:
DEFENSE OF DIPLOMATIC RIGHTS, 1865-1870

During the five-year interval 1859-1864 no storm winds blew up to disturb the even course of Argentine-American relations. Reciprocal demonstrations of good will in 1859—Yancey's well-received mediation between Buenos Aires and the Confederation and Urquiza's effective conciliation between the United States and Paraguay—ushered in a season of calm. The few despatches which ministers sent to the Department of State reported little more than the status of internal affairs. Instructions from the Department to its agents were rare. Argentina sent no representative to Washington. Intercourse between the two nations settled down to commercial routine.

Internal conditions, however, did not reflect the calm in their mutual relations. In both nations domestic turmoil absorbed the energies of administrations and total populations. In the United States, the bitter controversy between sections and the rebellion which followed turned the nation's energies inward.

In Argentina, the smoldering struggle between the Confederation and the Province flamed into open warfare. At the ravine of Cepeda (October 23, 1859), Urquiza won the first victory and soon set in motion machinery which would reunite province and nation.[1] New differences, however, rendered peace short-lived. The Confederation triumph at Cepeda was reversed at Pavón (September 17, 1861), battlefield which Argentines have come to regard as the symbol of reunion. New compromises made Buenos Aires again the capital of the nation (1862), and new elections made the dynamic Bartolomé Mitre the first constitutional President of an undivided republic.

Unfortunately these settlements did not wholly still the bitter rivalry. The national government must stamp out guerrilla uprisings in the frontier provinces. The government of long-independent Buenos Aires Province must learn to coexist in the same city with the government

[1] *Registro oficial de la República Argentina*, IV, 250-251, 334-343.

of the nation or must move. But problems of greater urgency—conquest of the southern frontier, expansion of agriculture, construction of railroads, war with Paraguay—claimed priority.

From its involvement in the internal commotions of Uruguay in 1863 Argentina gradually slipped into the Paraguayan War. From 1865 to 1870 Argentines joined Uruguayans and Brazilians in the subjugation of their neighbor. Upon several occasions the ramifications of the war ran athwart American interests and involved official relations with the Argentine Republic.[2]

Origins of the Paraguayan War

The Paraguayan War was the disastrous climax of accumulating international tensions. The principal source of these tensions was the establishment and growth of the two greatest South American nations. Argentina's ever-increasing nationalism and Brazil's expanding economy periodically threatened to engulf Paraguay and Uruguay, sandwiched between the rising giants.[3] The two powers clashed repeatedly with the smaller states over boundaries, navigation of rivers, control of commerce, and even domestic politics. Three major problems, all involving Paraguay, arose from this situation: (1) the question of boundaries with Brazil; (2) the question of boundaries with Argentina; and (3) the issue of Argentine-Brazilian intervention in the internal affairs of Uruguay.

Paraguay owed its early attainment of national unity and stability to the absolutism of José Gaspar Rodríguez Francia, dictator from 1816 to 1840. To his successor, Carlos Antonio López, Francia bequeathed a nation made potentially strong by its intense nationalism, but rendered vulnerable because of its disregard for the rights of others. During the regime of the two dictators hostility developed with Brazil over boundaries unfixed since the days of Spanish-Portuguese colonial rivalry. Moreover, Brazil persistently demanded certain fluvial rights in the Río Paraguay.[4]

With Argentina, Paraguay's disputes involved vast sections of intervening land. Both nations, together with Bolivia, claimed the unknown Gran Chaco, a wilderness lying west of the Paraguay and between the Vermejo and Bahía Negra. Both hoped to establish jurisdiction over the territory of Misiones, stretching from the Argentine Province of Corrientes to the borders of Brazil and filling the bottleneck formed by the converging courses of the Paraná and the Uruguay.[5]

[2] The name "the Argentine Republic" (*La Republica Argentina*) was officially adopted on October 8, 1860 (*ibid.*, IV, 346).
[3] Pelham Horton Box, *The Origins of the Paraguayan War*, I, 9. I have based my summary of the war largely upon Box's convincing analysis.
[4] *Ibid.*, I, 20-53.
[5] *Ibid.*, I, 54-69. See map, p. 206.

When he succeeded his father in 1862, Francisco Solano López inherited not only the malignant national traditions developed by Francia but also the bitter boundary questions. Here was the powder keg and the tinder. It was necessary only to inject the spark. Steeped in the glory of the Napoleonic tradition through two years of study in Paris, the younger López created in the heart of the tropics one of the strongest armies in South America. He was prepared to touch off the explosion.

Argentine-Brazilian intervention in Uruguayan politics in 1864 gave López the opportunity he needed. When General Venancio Flores, leader of the Blanco element, revolted against the government in Montevideo, both powers came to his assistance, Argentina under the cloak of neutrality, Brazil by the use of troops. When the Empire rebuffed both his offer of mediation and his stern protest, López prepared for retaliation.[6]

The Paraguayan moved first against Brazil, then challenged Argentina. Without a declaration of war, he seized a Brazilian steamer on the Paraguay and sent his troops into its Province of Mato Grosso. Then, planning to invade Río Grande do Sul, he sought permission to cross the Province of Corrientes. When the Argentine government refused, López seized two Argentine ships and assaulted the city of Corrientes.[7]

President Bartolomé Mitre promptly took the initiative in building a cordon around Paraguay to check López' powerful armies. On May 1, 1865, he signed with Brazil and the friendly Colorado government of Flores in Uruguay the Treaty of the Triple Alliance. The terms of the secret pact, soon made public, revealed the latent imperialistic designs of Argentina and Brazil. Each was promised its territorial claims in full: Argentina to receive all the Gran Chaco and all of Misiones to the Brazilian boundary; Brazil to gain all land to a line connecting the sources of the Ríos Apa and Igurey. In case of defeat, López was to be unseated and Paraguay was to bear the entire burden of the war's cost.[8] That the Allies were aiming at far more than their own security and national honor is evident from the treaty clauses; that Paraguay did not lose all of the disputed territory was partly owing to the arbitration of President Rutherford B. Hayes.[9]

The five-year war which resulted from these origins was a grim

[6] *Ibid.*, I, 70-178. The efforts of the Blancos to obtain the assistance of López is revealed in the story of Juan José de Herrera, Uruguayan Foreign Minister, written by his son, Luis Alberto (*La diplomacia oriental en el Paraguay*). On the American attitude at this time, see below, pp. 194-195.

[7] Box, *op. cit.*, I, 211-219, 239-269. On both the causes of the war and López' preparations for it, Professor Harris G. Warren, author of *Paraguay, An Informal History*, suggests the need for revisionist interpretation (paper read at the annual meeting of the American Historical Association, Washington, D. C., Dec. 29, 1961).

[8] *Registro oficial de la República Argentina*, V, 209-211.

[9] See below, pp. 204-207.

struggle. It numbed and stifled the very life of Paraguay. It brought forth many of the inglorious phases of twentieth-century warfare—violations of international law and the rights of neutrals, infringement of treaty rights of both combatants and noncombatants, mutual charges and denials of atrocities, and use of the press to influence public opinion at home and abroad. Until his death on March 1, 1870, López drove his dogged people. War's end found the country desolate and prostrate and its people all but annihilated.[10]

The sequence of events in this worst of Latin American wars challenged the interests and prestige of the United States. These developments involved significant principles and procedures of international law and custom: notably, (1) rights of a minister en route to his post, such as free and unimpeded transit; (2) rights of a minister in residence, including asylum, unobstructed intercourse with his government, exemption from judicial process, and immunity of persons other than heads of missions; (3) attempted mediation between the combatants; and (4) arbitration of a boundary dispute.[11]

Minister vs. Admiral

Charles A. Washburn, whose years of service in Paraguay before and during the war furnished him material for a two-volume history, was a colorful and tenacious, if controversial and choleric, figure.[12] He was one of five brothers who attained prominence in American public life. Three, Israel, Elihu, and Cadwallader, were members of Congress from different states, Maine, Illinois, and Wisconsin. The fourth, William Drew, was editor of the Minneapolis *Tribune*. Israel was one of the founders of the Republican Party and Elihu a leading advocate of the impeachment of President Johnson. The diplomat came from vigorous stock.[13]

In January, 1865, after three years' residence, Washburn left Asunción for a deserved leave.[14] During his absence López' war against Brazil had involved Argentina and Uruguay and the three allies had erected an undeclared blockade around Paraguay. In returning to his post the diplomat encountered exasperating obstacles.

Learning of the blockade upon his return to Rio de Janeiro in early October, Washburn turned to the United States Navy for transportation. The commander of the South Atlantic Squadron, Acting Rear Admiral

[10] Estimates of Paraguayan casualties vary widely. For examples see John L. Stevens, American Minister to Uruguay, to Hamilton Fish, Secretary of State, Aug. 8, 1872, *For. Rel., 1872*, pp. 466-467; W. H. Koebel, *Paraguay*, pp. 198-199; Charles E. Akers, *A History of South America, 1854-1904*, p. 187.

[11] Points (3) and (4) are discussed in Chapter XIII.

[12] *The History of Paraguay* was published in Boston in 1871. Because of his bias against López, Washburn's work must be used with caution.

[13] *Dictionary of American Biography*, XIX, 495-496, 502-506.

[14] Washburn, *op. cit.*, I, 438; II, 10-11, 114-115.

S. W. Godon, was chary of challenging the blockade. Ship repairs, he said, would prevent immediate detail of a vessel to accommodate the Minister. Moreover, he quickly formed a low opinion of Washburn's diplomatic capabilities. While the Minister was moving to Buenos Aires by means of English transportation, the Admiral was conceiving additional excuses for frustrating him.

In Buenos Aires after November 4, Washburn awaited Admiral Godon or a ship of his command. Both arrived in December. As a naval commander, Godon resourcefully found reasons to postpone assignment of the ship. He lacked instructions from Washington. The trip to Asunción would be too expensive. American interests in Paraguay were insignificant. The weather was too warm, the mosquitoes numerous, the season unhealthy.

As a diplomatic officer, Washburn could see advantages in the use of a naval vessel. It would assist the execution of the President's orders. It would be in harmony with Navy tradition. A diplomat's presence in Asunción might facilitate the exchange of war prisoners. A neutral ship standing by might hasten the war's end by providing a means of escape to López.

Unable to break down the Admiral's obstinacy, Washburn resolved to get to Corrientes by merchant vessel and to Asunción by any means available. He reached Corrientes on January 30 only to find new impediments barring his path.[15] For the time being his dispute with Godon passed into the background.[16]

Combatants, Neutrals, and International Law

Military policy and divergent interpretations of diplomatic rights now replaced interdepartmental feuding as obstructions to the Minister's passage to Asunción. Had Godon acted promptly or had Washburn not insisted on a warship, he might have reached Paraguay without hindrance. By January, 1866, however, the military situation had changed and field commanders were eager to prevent the Minister's transit through military lines. They believed that the American's return at this critical juncture would brighten the horizons for López and his harassed people

[15] Washburn to William H. Seward, Secretary of State, Nov. 9, Dec. 15, 1865, Jan. 16, Feb. 1, 1866, *For. Rel., 1866*, II, 548-551, 554-559; Godon to Gideon Welles, Secretary of Navy, Jan. 23, 1866, NA, DN, South Atlantic Squadron, Brazil, Rear Admiral S. W. Godon; Welles to Godon, March 12, April 26, 1866, NA, DN, Letters to Flag Officers, No. 5, pp. 402, 433-435. Some of the Navy correspondence was published in *H. Ex. Doc.*, No. 79, 40 Cong., 3 sess., pp. 1-31.

[16] In 1869, when a House committee undertook a comprehensive investigation of Paraguayan affairs, both officials were called to testify. A minority resolution dissented from the majority decision to censure Godon; the House took no action (*H. Rep.*, No. 65, 41 Cong., 2 sess., xxix-xxx; *Cong. Globe*, 41 Cong., 2 sess., IV, 3261).

and might increase the tenacity of their resistance. They feared that the presence of an American warship might permit López to escape capture.[17]

Immediately after his arrival at Corrientes, Washburn went to the field headquarters of President Mitre, now generalissimo of the allied armies, from whom the Minister requested safe conduct to Asunción. As analyzed later by an American authority on international law, "The United States asserts that according to the law of nations a diplomatic officer is entitled to a right of transit to his post, by sea, or through the national domain, whether land or water, of a State other than that to which he is accredited." [18] By the injection of this principle, Washburn brought his government into direct clash with Argentina and Brazil.

Although he admitted the Minister's right to proceed, General Mitre said that he must withhold permission until he had consulted his advisers in Buenos Aires and his fellow commanders in the field.[19] Washburn, returning to Buenos Aires for his family, secured the Foreign Minister's concurrence with the President's views.[20]

Soon back in Corrientes, satisfied that Argentine approval was assured, Washburn was confronted with Brazilian intransigence. To maintain an united front Mitre must have yielded to the views of Admiral Tamandaré, commander of the allied blockading fleet.[21] The Admiral's refusal apparently represented the official attitude of his government as soon stated by the Foreign Minister:

> The Government of His Majesty the Emperor is obliged, unavoidably, to differ from the United States as to the manner of application to this case of the International Laws. *It* holds that from the right to make war upon its enemy, and to effectively blockade his waters, arises the right to impede the transit even of the Diplomatic Agent of a Neutral power. . . .[22]

Throughout May, June, and July, in Corrientes and in Buenos Aires, in person and by letter, Washburn plied Mitre for reconsideration of his

---

[17] Washburn to Seward, Feb. 8, 1866, *For. Rel., 1866,* II, 562; Washburn, *op. cit.,* II, 117.

[18] Charles C. Hyde, *International Law: Chiefly As Interpreted and Applied by the United States* (Boston: Little, Brown & Co., 1951), II, 1261. (Footnotes in original text are omitted.)

[19] Washburn to Seward, Feb. 8, 1866, *For. Rel., 1866,* II, 562. Much of the correspondence between Mitre and Washburn and between Mitre and other Argentine officials is reproduced in *Archivo del general Mitre,* II, 260, 280; III, 153-154, 304-306; IV, 210-225; V, 103-119, 139-140. I have preferred, however, to cite the more readily available volumes in the series *Foreign Relations* and *Memoria de relaciones exteriores.*

[20] Washburn to Seward, March 16, 1866, *For. Rel., 1866,* II, 564.

[21] Washburn to Seward, April 27, 1866, *ibid.,* p. 569.

[22] José Antonio Saraiva, Brazilian Minister of Foreign Affairs, to William V. Lidgerwood, Chargé d'Affaires, July 17, 1866, *ibid.,* pp. 314-315.

position. At each stage the General seemed willing to endorse the right but reluctant or unable to invoke it for Washburn's benefit. Though professing Argentine friendship for the United States, Mitre still refused and in mid-July advised the Minister to deal directly with the government in Buenos Aires, not with field commanders.[23]

Stiffening Policy of the United States

During these protracted exchanges Washburn received no specific guidance from Washington or effective assistance from his colleagues in Buenos Aires and Rio de Janeiro. Slow communications, of course, hampered the State Department's efforts to keep in intimate touch with its ministers. Moreover, at the height of the difficulties, Minister Robert C. Kirk retired from Buenos Aires and Minister James Watson Webb took leave from Rio.

Secretary William H. Seward's earliest statement on Washburn's predicament (April 21) supported the Minister's position. "We sincerely hope to learn," he wrote to Kirk,

> that the President of the Argentine Republic has neither ordered, nor approved of this hindrance to the passage of our diplomatic representative of the United States, so disrespectful in itself, and so entirely inconsistent with the laws of nations.[24]

He directed legation chiefs both in Buenos Aires and in Rio to request explanations.

Learning of no change in allied policy by June 27, Seward became concerned about the affront to "the sovereignty and honor of the United States." Resolved now to take peremptory action, he ordered his agents to demand explanations from Argentine and Brazilian leaders and, failing to receive them within eight days, to ask for passports. At the same time he instructed Washburn to demand safe passage from Mitre; if Mitre still refused, Admiral Godon would provide convoy for a public vessel.[25]

Without advising Mitre of Seward's instructions, Washburn returned to Buenos Aires. With some reason he felt that he had exhausted all possibilities of securing the Argentine's approval, that even a demand would be fruitless. Moreover, surely now Admiral Godon would obey

---

[23] Washburn to Seward, May 28, July 26, Aug. 10, 1866, *ibid.*, pp. 580-581, 589-590, 593; Washburn to Mitre, July 21, and to Rufino de Elizalde, Minister of Foreign Affairs, Aug. 13, 1866, *Memoria, 1867*, pp. 128-133, 137-138; Washburn, *op. cit.*, II, 117-119.

[24] *For. Rel., 1866*, II, 280-281.

[25] To Alexander Asboth, Kirk's successor, to Webb, and to Washburn, June 27, 1866, *ibid.*, pp. 284, 307, 585.

Department orders to get him to his post.[26] But the Admiral was on cruise to Rio. It would take six weeks to exchange despatches.

In Buenos Aires, meanwhile, Washburn discovered that Seward's orders were common knowledge. Americans rejoiced in his condemnation of allied policy and his decision to use a naval force to escort the Minister to his destination.[27] At least one porteño newspaper criticized the "great blunder" of the government in unnecessarily bringing the "great Colossus of the North" into the controversy with López.[28] But the Argentine government still refused to act. Foreign Minister Rufino de Elizalde stated that it had neither refused nor granted the Minister permission to proceed to Asunción. And once again it neither refused nor granted it. Washburn was convinced that Argentina and Brazil were "passing the buck," each placing blame for refusal on the other.[29]

The allied policy, however, was no more frustrating to Washburn than Admiral Godon's position. When in late September the officer replied to his August 8th request for transportation, he said he would do nothing until the Minister had fulfilled the letter of his June instructions by making one more application for safe conduct to General Mitre.[30]

Notwithstanding Brazil's earlier adamant objection, the first break in the log jam against Washburn came from Rio. In late August American representatives succeeded in getting Brazil to withdraw all obstructions. This news Minister Webb at once communicated to Washburn.[31] It is not precisely clear why he did not seize upon this breach in the united front. Perhaps it was Godon's insistence that he would not comply with his instructions until the Minister had faithfully carried out the letter of his. Or perhaps, as Godon alleged, it was Washburn's insistence that he be transported on a warship.[32]

At any rate, in the midst of this stalemate, a new minister resident arrived in Buenos Aires. He bore firm orders from Seward to declare that "the President of the United States cannot consent to hold relations of peace and friendship with even friendly Nations, when they make their own interests the rule of exposition, instead of the law of nations." [33] Two days after he was accredited as Kirk's successor (October 22),

[26] Washburn to Seward, Aug. 10, 1866, *ibid.*, p. 593; to Godon, Aug. 8, 1866, NA, DN, South Atlantic Squadron, Brazil, Godon.
[27] Washburn to Seward, Aug. 10, 1866, *For. Rel., 1866*, p. 593.
[28] *The Standard* (Buenos Aires), Aug. 11, Sept. 11, 1866.
[29] Helper to Seward, Aug. 13, 1866, and enclosures, NA, DS, Con. Let., B. A., XI; Washburn to Asboth, Oct. 22, 1866, *For. Rel., 1866*, II, 295-296.
[30] Sept. 16, 1866, NA, DN, South Atlantic Squadron, Brazil, Godon.
[31] Webb to Godon, Sept. 16, 1866, *ibid.*; to Seward, Sept. 19, 1866, *For. Rel., 1866*, II, 523. See also Lawrence F. Hill, *Diplomatic Relations between the United States and Brazil*, pp. 191-194.
[32] Godon to Washburn, Sept. 16, and to Welles, Oct. 24, 1868, NA, DN, South Atlantic Squadron, Brazil, Godon.
[33] Seward to Asboth, Sept. 24, 1866, *For. Rel., 1866*, II, 285.

Alexander Asboth invited Elizalde's attention to the Brazilian action of the previous August. Within twenty-four hours Washburn received Argentine consent to proceed to Paraguay.[34]

At precisely the same time Seward was framing further instructions to Washburn. Though they were now useless, they revealed the Secretary's ultimate understanding of the true situation. "If this despatch find you outside of the Republic of Paraguay," Seward wrote,

> the President expects you to overlook all points of ceremony, and of past offense real or imaginary on the part of the allied governments, or any of them, and of past neglect, real or imaginary on the part of Admiral Godon, and adopt whatever course in your discretion may seem best to reach Asuncion.[35]

For nearly a year the Argentine Republic had violated the free navigation clause of its 1853 treaty with the United States. In defiance of the widely accepted principle of freedom of transit, it joined Brazil to keep an American diplomat cooling his heels.[36] Throughout, Minister Washburn had been forced to rely almost wholly upon his own resourcefulness. He had received few effective instructions from the Department —and these sometimes too late. At critical junctures of the negotiations, regularly accredited ministers were absent from Buenos Aires and Rio de Janeiro. The responsible naval officer had chosen not to cooperate.[37] In view of Washburn's subsequent conduct in Asunción, Godon's evaluation of his diplomatic incapacity was probably correct. But, in defense of the Minister, it must be said that through months of travail he stolidly defended an American policy.

In Washington, the Argentine Minister, Domingo Sarmiento, had taken no actions except to transmit official explanations of Argentine policy and to influence public opinion through propaganda.[38]

[34] *Registro oficial de la República Argentina*, V, 298; Asboth to Elizalde, Oct. 22, and Elizalde to Asboth, Oct. 23, 1866, *For. Rel., 1866*, II, 289-290, 293.

[35] Oct. 23, 1866, *ibid.*, p. 613.

[36] Washburn's patience eventually wore thin. On October 13, he wrote Seward that he was returning home on the next steamer (*ibid.*, p. 610).

[37] Godon's actions were approved on at least four occasions by Secretary Welles and, according to Welles, by Secretary Seward, Welles to Godon, March 12, Dec. 22, 1866, Feb. 1, May 25, 1867, NA, DN, Letters to Flag Officers, No. 5, pp. 402, 578, 590; No. 6, p. 65.

[38] Sarmiento to Minister of Foreign Relations, Nov. 22, 1866, *Obras de D. F. Sarmiento*, XXXIV, 228-236; Sarmiento to Seward, Dec. 17, and Seward to Sarmiento, Dec. 20, 1866, *For. Rel., 1867-1868*, II, 241-242; Allison W. Bunkley, *The Life of Sarmiento*, pp. 426-427.

The Minister Reaches His Post

Washburn wasted no time in taking advantage of Argentina's acquiescence. On October 24 he sailed for Paraguay on the United States sloop *Shamokin*. With his family he reached Asunción fifteen days later, more than fourteen months after departure from New York and almost a year after he planned.[39]

As the allied leaders had anticipated, the Paraguayan people hailed the return of the American Minister. The government's official newspaper, *El Seminario*, joined in welcoming him.[40] José Berges, Foreign Minister, wrote to Washburn that

> my government welcomes your return to this country to continue the good relations with the friendly government of the United States; it commends your heroic conduct in overcoming the difficulties so unjustly placed in your way by the allied forces; and I am pleased to rejoice with you that the flag of the great American republic has forced the outrageous blockade of the triple alliance, commanded that respect and justice it deserves, saluted the national banner of the republic, waving in triumph over the battlements of Curupaiti, in support of the cause of liberty that has just finally triumphed in the United States of America.[41]

Despite the warmth and felicity of its welcome, the country to which Washburn and his family returned was no longer the delightful region of their former residence. The war had spread and intensified. Industry was paralyzed. Human and financial costs were mounting. Liberties were suppressed. López' rule grew more tyrannical. Through the senseless war López was pushing the Paraguayan people toward a cultural and economic degradation they would endure for decades.

Resignation and Exit

Resuming his official functions in Asunción, Washburn could not have been aware of the trials he would still endure. Provoking as were the hindrances which had delayed his re-entrance into Paraguay, even greater difficulties would molest the fulfillment of his mission. And when his usefulness came to an end, his exit would bring a threat to personal safety and reputation.

When allied forces began to envelop Paraguay and to menace Asunción itself, the Minister committed a series of acts which ruptured his

[39] Washburn to Seward, Nov. 6, 1866, *For. Rel., 1866,* II, 613.
[40] Washburn to Seward, Dec. 25, 1866, *ibid.,* p. 706; Washburn, *op. cit.,* II, 141-142.
[41] Nov. 30, 1866, *For. Rel., 1866,* II, p. 709.

steadily deteriorating relations with López. On February 23, 1868, under the approach of allied gunboats, López ordered the complete evacuation of the capital. Washburn determined to remain in Asunción and, as the only minister in residence, to give what protection he could to foreign nationals and their property. Some fifty aliens sought refuge for themselves and security for their valuables in the spacious legation.[42] By granting asylum to foreigners, after Paraguayans had fled, Washburn defied the dictator and jeopardized the safety of all. During the next six months the legation remained under close guard, the occupants virtual prisoners.

When López requested release of the Portuguese consul, Washburn surrendered only to pressure. When he demanded Porter C. Bliss, an American, and George R. Masterman, an Englishman, the Minister claimed they were members of his staff.[43] When López alleged that Washburn was using the legation as headquarters of a conspiracy against him, he placed the American in a dire situation.[44]

As early as the previous January, Washburn had realized the hopelessness of his predicament. He first requested, then demanded, his immediate recall.[45] Even before the charge of conspiracy, he had applied to López for passports for himself, family, and suite. Ultimately on September 2, after a second request, López consented to the departure of the Minister and his family but of no others.[46]

Now that he had wrung permission to leave, a new hazard arose. In three years few persons had entered or left the country without the aid of warships.[47] Even departure was not a pleasant prospect for one who had so recently endured a year's struggle to secure passage through military lines. Naval officers of the South Atlantic Squadron, however, as well as superiors in Washington, had foreseen the emergency and sought clearances. The Argentine authorities in this instance offered no objection to the passage of the U.S.S. *Wasp*. Only Brazil, which now

[42] Washburn to Seward, April 7, 1868, *ibid.*, pp. 645-655.
[43] On the cases of Bliss and Masterman, see *For. Rel., 1868*, II, 657-658, 670-723, 741-829; *H. Ex. Doc.*, Nos. 69, 79, 40 Cong., 3 sess.; *H. Rep.*, No. 65, 41 Cong., 2 sess.; John Bassett Moore, *A Digest of International Law . . .* , II, 824-831. Each of the men published a book on his experiences: Bliss, *Historia secreta de la misión del ciudadano norte-americano Charles A. Washburn cerca del gobierno de la República del Paraguay* (Asunción, 1868) and Masterman, *Seven Eventful Years in Paraguay* (London, 1869). Bliss later maintained that his violent attack on Washburn was written under duress from López.
[44] There seems to have been some evidence of plotting against López. See *For. Rel., 1868*, II, 751-752, 760-815, 825-829; *Une question du droit des gens. M. Washburn, ex-ministre des Etats-Unis a l'Assumption et la conspiration paraguayenne;* and A. Rebaudi, *Guerra del Paraguay; la conspiración contra S. E. el Presidente de la República, Mariscal Don Francisco Solano López.*
[45] Washburn to Seward, Jan. 13, April 17, 1868, and Seward to Washburn, June 2, 1868, *For. Rel., 1868*, II, 650-652, 667.
[46] *H. Rep.*, No. 65, 41 Cong., 2 sess., pp. xiv-xvii.
[47] Washburn to Seward, April 17, 1868, *For. Rel., 1868*, II, 667.

had assumed principal responsibility for the prosecution of the war, proved obdurate. In Rio Minister Webb had used his hardfisted tactics since May to persuade Brazilian authorities to recede from the same steadfast position they had taken in 1866.[48]

On September 10, thanks to the toughness of Webb in Rio and the firmness of the *Wasp's* commander with López, Washburn and his family escaped Paraguay. His two aides, Bliss and Masterman, were seized as they left the legation.[49] When the harried minister reached Buenos Aires, he found the Argentine press as jubilant about his arrival as had been the Paraguayan two years before.[50]

A New Minister and His Recall

Had Secretary Seward been able to foresee the circumstances of Washburn's withdrawal, he would certainly not have drafted a successor's instructions in the spirit he did—or perhaps not have appointed the successor at all. But writing during the very week of Washburn's flight, he was still unaware of the depth to which American prestige had fallen. He wrote, therefore, in the normal diplomatic vein of a neutral seeking to convey its friendliness toward a war-torn belligerent.[51]

The appointee who bore this gesture of good will was a retired major general, Martin T. McMahon, native of Quebec and onetime aide-de-camp to General George B. McClellan. Though in Rio Minister Webb apprised the General of the changed situation, advised him to demand the release of Bliss and Masterman, and sought to dissuade him from presenting his credentials, he managed only to antagonize him.[52] McMahon moved on to Buenos Aires, where without delay the allied governments authorized his passage. Escorted by Rear Admiral C. H. Davis, now commanding the *Wasp*, he reached Paraguay in early December.

Preceding McMahon to army headquarters, Admiral Davis followed Webb's counsel to the extent of persuading López to free Washburn's protégés, Bliss and Masterman. He agreed, however, only after exacting the inglorious promise that the men would be evacuated as prisoners and tried in Washington for their alleged crimes.[53] McMahon then pre-

[48] Webb to Seward, July 7, Aug. 7, and Seward to Webb, Aug. 17, Sept. 15, 1868, *ibid.*, pp. 273-275, 294-299; Rear Admiral C. H. Davis, commander of South Atlantic Squadron, to Welles, May 20, June 8, 25, July 23, 1868, and enclosures, NA, DN, South Atlantic Squadron, Davis, I; *Memoria, 1869*, pp. 162-164.

[49] Washburn to Seward, Sept. 26, 1868, *For. Rel., 1868*, II, 670-673; Commander Kirkland to Davis, Sept. 22, and Davis to Welles, Oct. 10, 12, 1868, NA, DN, South Atlantic Squadron, Davis, II.

[50] *The Standard*, Sept. 30, Oct. 11, 1868.

[51] *For. Rel., 1868*, II, 669-670.

[52] Hill, *op. cit.*, pp. 204-205.

[53] Davis to Welles, Dec. 12, 1868, NA, DN, South Atlantic Squadron, Davis, II.

sented his credentials and established his residence near López' headquarters.

Factional politics in Washington rendered McMahon's mission short-lived. As a reward for his services in the election of 1868, Elihu Washburne [54] became President Grant's first Secretary of State. The new administration could ill afford to perpetuate in Paraguay an agent whose good relations with López might be regarded as a rebuke to the Secretary's brother. Though Elihu served only twelve days (March 5-16), until his replacement by Hamilton Fish, that was long enough to effect McMahon's recall.[55]

During his first five months in Paraguay McMahon remained isolated from the outside world. Apprehensive when no communication from him reached Buenos Aires, Minister Henry G. Worthington in March sent the *Wasp* to carry official mail to him. When both the ship and the despatches failed to get through, Worthington complained to Argentine authorities. Foreign Minister Mariano Varela offered the now familiar explanation, military necessity: because the Allies were mounting an attack, they must tighten the blockade.[56] Worthington's report came to the attention of Hamilton Fish. In the manner of Seward three years before, Fish became indignant and ordered Worthington to protest the Argentine refusal to pass diplomatic despatches.[57] Again, however, as in 1866, instructions arrived after conditions had changed. McMahon had long since received his recall and departed Paraguay.[58]

In Buenos Aires the Argentines slandered and vilified McMahon for his failure to take an anti-López position.[59] Rumors had leaked through to President Sarmiento that the American Minister was giving encouragement to López and advising him on military strategy.[60] Certainly McMahon did believe that Washburn and allied propagandists had given the world a one-sided picture. Without defending alleged Paraguayan atrocities, he accused allied armies of equally inhuman practices.

[54] Elihu had added an "e" to the family name.

[55] S. F. Bemis (ed.), *The American Secretaries of State and Their Diplomacy*, VII, 120-121.

[56] Worthington to Secretary of State, March 11, April 12, 1869, and Varela to Worthington, April 16, 1869, NA, DS, Desp. Arg., XVII; Davis to Secretary of Navy, March 13, 16, April 12, 13, May 14, 1869, NA, DN, South Atlantic Squadron, Davis, II.

[57] Fish to Kirk, June 17, 1869, NA, DS, Inst. Arg., XV, 317-318.

[58] McMahon to Fish, July 13, 1869, NA, DS, Desp. Para., III; Davis to Secretary of Navy, June 19, 1869, NA, DN, South Atlantic Squadron, Davis, II.

[59] McMahon to Fish, July 13, 1869, NA, DS, Desp. Para., III.

[60] Sarmiento to García, Feb. 12, 1869, Manuel R. García-Mansilla, *Cartas confidenciales de Sarmiento a M. R. García*, pp. 41-42, 50; Sarmiento to Mary Mann, Dec. 30, 1869, Alice Houston Luiggi, "Some Letters of Sarmiento and Mary Mann, 1865-1876, Part II," *The Hispanic American Historical Review*, XXXII (Aug., 1952), 352-353. In an *aide memoire* to the Department of State García protested McMahon's alleged partisanship for Paraguay (NA, DS, Notes from Arg. Leg., II).

A Propaganda Battle

McMahon's return to the United States in October sharpened the rancorous public discussion which Washburn's arrival had set off. Public opinion, which earlier in the war had favored the underdog, now seemed anti-López. In speeches, articles, and testimony before a congressional committee, McMahon sought to temper this attitude. Argentine spokesmen, as well as Washburn and Bliss, whose personal reputations were at stake, entered the fray.[61]

From the very beginning of the war Argentine authorities had been sensitive about American hostility toward the Triple Alliance and attraction for López and the Paraguayan cause. After his arrival as minister in May, 1865, Sarmiento had sought to counteract American prejudice for the underdog. He published articles in American newspapers and founded his own journal, *Ambas Américas*.[62]

In February, 1869, after assuming the presidency, he had alerted his successor in Washington, Manuel R. García, to the rumors of McMahon's pro-López activities in Paraguay. Because of Mrs. Horace Mann's influence on certain American publications, he advised the Minister to consult with her. Aware of Washburn's political connections with President-elect Grant, he urged García to stimulate the former envoy's sympathies in Argentina's favor.[63]

After McMahon's return to Washington, the Argentine Legation quickened its activities. In signed atricles to newspapers the secretary of the legation, Bartolomé Mitre y Vedía, protested McMahon's calumnies against the army commanded by his father.[64] Later the Minister himself published a forty-page pamphlet and distributed copies to members of Congress and other influential persons.[65] Even Secretary Fish's lecture on diplomatic manners did not at once end the Argentine propaganda.[66]

Meanwhile, as Congress continued its exhaustive probe into Paraguayan relations, the Allies pushed their campaign against López to its inevitable conclusion. After his death on March 1, 1870, successors soon accepted peace terms. House resolutions on the conduct of American officials were reported out of committee in May.[67] In Argentina the anti-American feeling engendered by the propaganda war died slowly.

[61] Bliss was reputedly the author of a book criticizing McMahon's views, *General McMahon's Opinions in Regard to the Paraguayan War*.

[62] Bunkley, *op. cit.*, p. 426.

[63] García-Mansilla, *op. cit.*, pp. 41-42.

[64] García to Fish, Nov. 11, 1869, NA, DS, Notes from Arg. Leg., II. The statements were published in *The New York Times* and other newspapers.

[65] *Paraguay and the Alliance against the Tyrant Francisco Solano López* (New York, 1869); García to Varela, Dec. 31, 1869, *Memoria, 1870*, pp. 105, 106.

[66] Fish to García, Nov. 5, 1869, NA, DS, Notes to Arg. Leg., VI, 78-79.

[67] *H. Rep.*, No. 65, 41 Cong., 2 sess., pp. xxix-xxx.

Of the several diplomatic rights challenged by one or more of the belligerents in the Paraguayan War, only two involved American relations with Argentina: the right of a diplomatic officer to pass to his post through the territory of a third state and the right to exchange official communications with his government through military lines. The Department of State contended that by violating these rights Argentina had broken the "law of nations" as well as the free navigation clause of the Treaty of 1853. Argentine authorities did not deny the correctness of the American position; they simply delayed action and at times appeared to follow Brazilian leadership. In seeking to enforce American rights, the Secretary of State directed ministers first to request explanations, then to demand them, and finally to withdraw within fixed time limits. The threats were not carried out. Ministers and naval officers were repeatedly handicapped by the irresoluteness of their superiors, who sometimes failed to enforce cooperation between the services or to draft adequate instructions. At many stages of the war the Department was embarrassed by the imprudence or tactlessness of agents in the field. This was especially true during the attempts to end hostilities through mediation.

X I I I

THE PARAGUAYAN WAR:
MEDIATION AND ARBITRATION, 1864-1878

Insistence upon the rights of its diplomats was not the only basis for American involvement in the Paraguayan War. On two occasions, one during the war, the other after, administration officials extended American good offices on behalf of peace. In 1866-1868 President Johnson and Secretary Seward attempted to end the war through mediation.[1] In 1877-1878 President Hayes arbitrated a boundary dispute between Argentina and Paraguay. The first failed completely; the second succeeded eminently.

The First Proposals of Mediation

Earnest attempts by several countries in 1866 to mediate in the Paraguayan War were a logical sequel to a decade of warfare in the western world. In Europe, Sebastopol, Solferino, and Schleswig-Holstein were symbols of recent conflict. In North America, Gettysburg and Vicksburg were still bitter memories. Elsewhere in the Western Hemisphere, Spain was waging war against the independent Spanish-American nations on the Pacific coast. Whether motivated by remorse, by sympathy for small states, or by genuine good will, interested nations—the United States, England, France, Chile, Bolivia, Peru, and Ecuador—proposed mediation in the Paraguayan struggle.

In the earliest stages of the Argentine-Brazilian intervention in Uruguay, President Lincoln had expressed concern for republican institutions in the Hemisphere and had authorized the use of his influence to avert hostilities. On January 2, 1864, Secretary Seward instructed repre-

[1] The portion of this chapter dealing with American mediation proposals is reproduced, with considerable change, from Peterson, "Attempts of the United States to Mediate in the Paraguayan War," *The Hispanic American Historical Review*, XII (Feb., 1932), 2-17.

sentatives in Argentina and Paraguay to determine what outside efforts national leaders would accept in the interests of preserving harmony.[2] Though both urged acceptance of American good offices, Robert C. Kirk in Buenos Aires conceded leadership to James Watson Webb in Rio.[3] In view of the information he received, Seward decided not to offer the "umpirage" of the United States but merely to continue the tender of good offices.[4] In late 1864, however, the guns immobilized the pens.

After two years of war the Johnson administration revived the policy. In October, 1866, Seward directed his ministers to express American concern for peace and to encourage requests for good offices. In his note to Washburn in Asunción he also emphasized the importance of trade with the area and the unfortunate interference with the commercial and navigation treaties of the fifties. In all the instructions Seward underscored American reluctance to interfere in foreign controversies.[5]

The inspiration for Seward's action at this time apparently came from General Webb, long an intimate friend. In early August, a variety of motives impelled the Minister to ask authority to offer United States mediation. He suspected the early intervention of England and France, a development which the United States sought to discourage, especially in view of recent success against the French in Mexico. To convince the Latin Americans that it is "their interest and their duty, to look to the United States for protection and advice," the nation should assume "her *right* to interpose in all international conflicts on this continent."[6] Webb was projecting clear-cut arguments for the "moral protection" principle of the Monroe Doctrine soon to be whispered by Grant and Fish and later shouted by Cleveland and Olney.

Before receiving Seward's instructions both Alexander Asboth[7] and Charles Washburn had urged the need for American interposition. In reporting Argentina's refusal of mediation offers from Chile, Bolivia, Peru, and Ecuador, the General reiterated Webb's rumors of Anglo-French intervention. Soon after his return to Paraguay in November, Washburn recommended mediation, if not intervention.[8]

[2] Seward to Kirk and to Washburn, Jan. 2, 1864, NA, DS, Inst. Arg., XV, 187-188, and Inst. Para., I, 59-60.

[3] Kirk to Webb, Aug. 27, 1864, and to Seward, Sept. 12, 1864, NA, DS, Desp. Bra., XXX, and Desp. Arg., XV.

[4] Seward to Kirk and to Webb, Nov. 15, 1864, NA, DS, Inst. Arg., XV, 203-204, and Inst. Bra., XVI, 88-90.

[5] Seward to Asboth, Oct. 10, 1866; to Webb, Oct. 15, 1866; to Washburn, Oct. 17, 1866, *For. Rel., 1866*, II, 286, 326, 611.

[6] Webb to Seward, Aug. 7, 1866, *ibid.*, p. 320; L. F. Hill, *Diplomatic Relations between the United States and Brazil*, p. 195.

[7] Kirk's successor.

[8] Asboth to Seward, Dec. 15, 1866; Washburn to Seward, Dec. 25, 1866, *For. Rel., 1867-1868*, II, 113, 706-707. On the mediation offers of the Latin American nations, see *Memoria, 1867*, pp. 30-32, 42-45, 52-54, 59-74; *1869*, pp. 25-32.

Before he received these reports congressional action forced Seward's hand. In December the House of Representatives passed a resolution recommending executive action to extend friendly offices.[9] The Secretary immediately notified ministers of the resolution and through a circular letter despatched specific proposals to each of the combatants. According to his plan, an armistice would be arranged as soon as all belligerents had accepted the propositions. Plenipotentiaries would convene in Washington, one from Paraguay and one or three from the allied nations, authorized to treat of all matters of difference and to consider terms of permanent peace. Each side would have a single vote; in case of disagreement, the president would designate an umpire. He would also appoint the presiding officer, who might give information and advice but not vote.[10]

In Buenos Aires the government had not yet replied to Seward's October enquiry when his December proposals arrived. General Asboth immediately set to work. First he sent Seward's plan to Foreign Minister Elizalde.[11] Then he asked Admiral Godon to convey the proposals to Montevideo, where there was no American minister.[12] Finally, in order to assure Washburn's receipt of the proposition, he also requested the Admiral to transport him to Paraguay.[13] Earlier, Webb had communicated both messages to the Brazilian Foreign Office.[14]

When Domingo Sarmiento learned of the congressional action, he confided his inner feelings to Minister Kirk, just returned from Buenos Aires. While the United States had the moral influence to accomplish mediation, he suggested, neither Asboth nor Washburn possessed the knowledge or influence to conduct it. A month later, however, when Seward showed him a copy of the official proposals, Sarmiento took the official line that the war must be pushed to its conclusion.[15]

From Buenos Aires General Asboth reported that all Argentines except those profiting from the war favored immediate peace and early escape from growing Brazilian domination of River Plate affairs. Even suppres-

---

[9] *Cong. Globe,* 39 Cong., 2 sess., XXXVII, pt. 1, p. 152. The House resolution proposed also that American offices be used to halt the war between Spain and the South American states on the Pacific coast, because both wars were "destructive of commerce and injurious and prejudicial to republican institutions."

[10] Seward to Asboth, Dec. 20, 1866, *For. Rel., 1867-1868,* II, 114-115.

[11] Asboth to Elizalde, Jan. 1, 26, Feb. 6, 1867, *ibid.,* pp. 116, 122, 132-133; *Memoria, 1867,* pp. 176-177, 178, 182-185.

[12] Asboth to Godon, Feb. 7, 1867, NA, DN, South Atlantic Squadron, Godon.

[13] Feb. 16, 1867, *For. Rel., 1867-1868,* II, 136; Godon to Welles, March 9, 1867, NA, DN, South Atlantic Squadron, Godon.

[14] Webb to Seward, Jan. 24, 1867, and to Antonio Coelho de Sa'e Albuquerque, Jan. 21, 1867, *For. Rel., 1867-1868,* II, 245, 247.

[15] Sarmiento to Kirk, Dec. 20, 1866, and to Argentine Minister of Foreign Relations, Jan. 21, 1867, *Obras de D. F. Sarmiento,* XXXIV, 236-242.

sion of newspapers and arrests of private citizens throughout the country, he said, did not intimidate those who advocated acceptance of mediation.[16]

Procrastination and Refusal

The three ministers worked throughout January, February, and March, 1867, to push the belligerents to a decision. Brazil, which resisted the mediation most firmly, believed that it would soon strike the fatal blow at Paraguayan resistance. Aware that Brazil was now the backbone of allied strength, Argentina was in no position to act alone.[17]

In Asunción, on the other hand, his relations with Lopez still friendly, Washburn had no difficulty in winning Paraguayan approval.[18] But the zealous Washburn visualized a greater conquest. By presenting the proposition to the Marquis de Caxias, now Commander in Chief of the allied armies, he would gain Brazilian acceptance as well. Though not accredited to Brazil, he was not reluctant to approach its military leader on a purely diplomatic mission; the General was equally willing to assume diplomatic functions.

Caxias' reply to Washburn was instantaneous and categoric. The Allies would consider no terms for ending hostilities which did not prescribe the resignation of López and his immediate retirement from Paraguay. Though balm for Paraguayan leaders, the Minister's subsequent denunciation of a *sine qua non* which denied Paraguay's rights of self-government was ignored by the Brazilian commander.[19]

Meanwhile in Buenos Aires and Rio de Janeiro, Asboth and Webb were exerting all the pressure they could muster. They met evasion after evasion, however, until it was apparent even to British diplomats in the South Atlantic that the Allies would reject the offer. They thought the entire plan ill-conceived. Washington was too distant a place for convening; the necessity of communicating with home governments would protract negotiations; the delay would be advantageous to López, who might augment his depleted resources. Moreover, the English ministers reported to London, allied leaders maintained that they had

---

[16] Asboth to Seward, Jan. 22, Feb. 2, 1867, *For. Rel., 1867-1868*, II, pp. 119, 129-131. Clippings from various Argentine newspapers are filed in NA, DS, Desp. Arg., XVI.

[17] Asboth to Seward, Feb. 2, 25, Mar. 25, 1867, *For. Rel., 1867-1868*, II, 129-131, 137, 150; Elizalde to Asboth, Feb. 18, 1867, *Memoria, 1867*, pp. 185-186.

[18] Berges to Washburn, March 4, 1867, *For. Rel., 1867-1868*, II, 713.

[19] Washburn to Caxias, March 11, 19, 1867; Caxias to Washburn, March 12, 1867; Washburn to Seward, March 26, 1867; Berges to Washburn, March 24, 1867, *ibid.*, pp. 718-722; Washburn, *The History of Paraguay*, II, 184-185.

undertaken the war to expiate a point of honor and that they themselves must determine the terms of its satisfaction.[20]

The Foreign Ministers of Argentina, Uruguay, and Brazil eventually sent notes of refusal, the first on March 30, the second on March 31, and the third on April 26. Each contended that the Allies were resisting the unbounded ambition of a tyrant, whose extinction their armies must guarantee.[21]

American Insistence and Latin Resentment

Sarmiento's skepticism of Minister Asboth's ability to guide negotiations for mediation proved well founded. The General was unwilling to accept Elizalde's refusal at face value. First he convinced himself that Argentina's decision to continue the war was inconsistent with domestic welfare. Then he undertook to convert the Argentines to his view. Undismayed by his brief opportunity for observation, he drafted for the Foreign Minister's benefit a critical analysis of Argentina's afflictions. The Civil War general sketched the war-weariness induced by loss of life, waste of money, paralysis of trade, and ruin of agriculture. As proof of the popular desire for peace, he chronicled instances of rebellion, anarchy, disaffection, and frontier disorders.[22]

Argentine authorities resented Asboth's gloomy diagnosis of the state of their nation and his affront to the wisdom of their policies. Both in Buenos Aires and Washington they protested. Elizalde was curt and satirical when he replied to Asboth that "the Argentine government must refrain from entering into an appreciation of your excellency's remarks, . . . although it recognizes the noble sentiments which inspire them." [23]

Chargé Mitre y Vedía's protest to Seward, though tactful, was frank and demanding. He reviewed the causes of the war, the purposes of the Triple Alliance, and the history of mediation attempts. Pulling no punches, he indicted Asboth's departure from diplomatic practices as well as Washburn's prejudice and ill-considered approach to a general.[24]

Seward assured Mitre y Vedía that he would take the matter up with

[20] W. G. Lettsom, British agent in Uruguay, to Lord Stanley, March 29, 1867; G. Buckley Mathew, English Minister to Argentina, to Stanley, April 6, 1867; Edward Thornton, English Minister to Brazil, to Stanley, April 8, 1867, *British and Foreign State Papers*, LXVI (1874-1875), pp. 1289-1293.

[21] Elizalde to Asboth, March 30, 1867; Albuquerque to Webb, April 26, 1867, *For. Rel., 1867-1868*, II, 158-160, 253; Alberto Flangini, Uruguayan Minister of Foreign Affairs, March 31, 1867, NA, DS, Notes from Uru. Leg., I.

[22] Asboth to Elizalde, April 10, 1867, *For. Rel., 1867-1868*, II, 161, and *Memoria, 1867*, pp. 192-193.

[23] Elizalde to Asboth, April 22, 1867, *For. Rel., 1867-1868*, II, 188, and *Memoria, 1867*, p. 194.

[24] Mitre y Vedía to Seward, July 9, 1867, *For. Rel., 1867-1868*, II, 242-243, and *Memoria, 1867*, pp. 276-279.

the two ministers.[25] As a matter of fact, he had already approved As-both's note to Elizalde and congratulated him on his discreet expression of the Department's views. Only after this endorsement had the Secretary added the caution, as if an afterthought, that the Minister should not let his zeal for peace lead him to an invasion of Argentina's sovereignty or dignity.[26] Asboth eventually closed the incident by sending an explanation to Elizalde's successor, Marcelino Ugarte.[27]

After these developments little was heard of the American mediation from July, 1867, until the following January. Ardor of the ministers doubtless cooled, for they permitted initiative in matters of mediation to pass to English representatives.[28]

Final Failure

In his annual message to Congress in 1867 President Andrew Johnson could report only that the South American belligerents had been receptive to the State Department's mediation efforts. If future opportunity presented itself, he said, he would renew conciliatory offers.[29]

When Seward revived the project a few weeks later, he entrusted the conduct of negotiations to his friend General Webb.[30] In view of Brazil's increased responsibility for prosecution of the war, this seemed an appropriate move. Mindful of the effects of General Asboth's earlier overzealousness,[31] he assured the belligerents that the United States was not wedded to its own views and that the right to choose the terms of peace belonged to them.[32] But to ask Webb to be completely circumspect was to expect too much. In his note to the Brazilian Foreign Minister he said he fully absolved Brazil from all responsibility for starting the war. This imprudence called for another of Seward's slaps on the wrist. He reminded Webb of the risks of pronouncing on the

[25] Seward to Mitre y Vedía, July 11, 1867, *For. Rel., 1867-1868*, II, 243-244, and *Memoria, 1867*, pp. 279-280.
[26] Seward to Asboth, May 27, 1867, *For. Rel., 1867-1868*, II, 178.
[27] *Ibid.*, pp. 228-230, and *Memoria, 1868*, pp. 281-284.
[28] For details on the mediation efforts of G. Z. Gould, secretary of the British Legation in Buenos Aires, see *For. Rel., 1867-1868*, II, 206, 234-235, 730-733; *Archivo del Mitre*, II, 260-262, 284-287; George C. E. Thompson, *The War in Paraguay*, pp. 217-220. According to Washburn, both sides agreed to all terms except the allied condition that López must leave Paraguay (to Seward, Sept. 27, 1867, *For. Rel., 1867-1868*, II, 730).
[29] J. D. Richardson, *A Compilation of the Messages and Papers of the Presidents*, VI, 578.
[30] Seward to Webb, Nov. 26, 1867, *For. Rel., 1867-1868*, II, 255-256.
[31] Seward to Webb, June 17, 1867, *ibid.*, p. 254.
[32] Webb to João Lustoza da Cunha Paranaguá, Brazilian Minister of Foreign Affairs, Jan. 27, 1868, and to President of the Argentine Republic, Feb. 1, 1868, *ibid.*, pp. 262, 264.

merits of the controversy, but only after commending his renewal of the mediation offer.[33]

In this case Webb's indiscretion was of little importance. The allied nations soon reiterated their refusals of the previous year. Each said simply that the reasons were those they had given before.[34]

In December, 1868, the President reported to Congress that the state of the Union's relations with the belligerent nations remained unchanged.[35] However inept their methods, American ministers had probably not precipitated rejection of mediation, but, on the other hand, they had lacked the finesse to convert the demurring Latin Americans to acceptance. The war ended early in 1870 but the mediation of the United States played no part in its termination.[36] Webb had failed in his efforts to establish American "right to interpose in all international conflicts on this continent." No South American government acknowledged his contention that they should look to the United States for protection and advice. Washburn had not succeeded in opening Paraguayan rivers to American commercial interests. Asboth died in Buenos Aires before the renewal of mediation proposals in 1868. As they left office, therefore, President Johnson and Secretary Seward could report no victory for American diplomacy, nor even improved conditions for American commerce.

The Question of Boundaries

The irritations produced during the war by State Department policies and by imprudent representatives did not grow into postwar barriers to friendly intercourse. The Grant administration repeatedly revealed to the nations its continuing interest in the progress of peace negotiations and the settlement of their contentious problems. This interest encouraged Argentina and Paraguay to select the American president as the arbiter of their protracted boundary dispute. But a succession of crises postponed this peaceful conclusion until 1878.

The issues which generated recurring threats to Paraguayan security throughout the seventies were the ancient ones of unresolved boundaries and Argentine-Brazilian rivalry.[37] Crushed by allied arms, its people and economy prostrate, Paraguay feared extinction of its nationality.

---

[33] Seward to Webb, March 23, 1868, *ibid.*, p. 270.

[34] Webb to Seward, April 25, 1868, and enclosures, *ibid.*, pp. 271-273.

[35] Richardson, *op. cit.*, VI, 685.

[36] In February, 1869, without authorization Minister McMahon offered his services as mediator to President López, who refused because of his conviction that the Allies would not negotiate with him upon his own invitation (Luis Caminos, López' secretary, to McMahon, Feb. 7, 1869; McMahon to Fish, May 12, 1869, NA, DS, Desp. Para. and Uru., III).

[37] See above, pp. 180-181.

If the victors remained faithful to their war aims, they would absorb much of Paraguay's territory and saddle its people with reparations of $400,000,000. Sorely in need of friends, early in 1871 the Paraguayan executive sought President Grant's friendly offices to moderate the demands of Argentina and Brazil. There was little Grant could do but tactfully urge restraint upon the victorious powers.[38]

Brazil was the first nation to collect its pound of flesh. In the preliminary peace of June 20, 1870, the Empire had joined Argentina and Uruguay to impose upon Paraguay the terms of their alliance, though conceding its leaders the privilege of suggesting modifications of boundary clauses.[39] In the negotiations for a definitive treaty, the Argentine delegate, Manuel Quintana, cut a sharp rift in the united front. When he demanded all of the Gran Chaco, the Brazilian envoy supported Paraguay's refusal. Quintana's withdrawal from the conference at this point opened the door to a separate Brazilian peace.[40] The Paraguayans promptly signed four treaties, which covered such matters as peace, friendship, boundaries, extradition, commerce, navigation, and consular privileges.[41]

By this settlement Brazil moved a long way toward establishing hegemony over Paraguay and overreaching Argentina in the contest for domination of the inland waterways. By exacting Paraguayan agreement to a huge indemnity, broad territorial concessions, and support of an army of occupation, as well as to Brazilian guarantee of its government, the Empire converted the vanquished nation into a virtual protectorate.[42]

Reports of this Brazilian expansionism aroused the fears of Secretary Fish that Paraguay might lose its independence or at least its territorial integrity and chances for prosperous recovery. He directed the American representative in Brazil to express American interest in Paraguayan welfare and concern for its independence.[43]

Argentine-Paraguayan Differences, 1872-1876

The conclusion of the Brazilian treaties drastically altered the face of diplomatic relations among the ex-belligerents. Until recently the backbone of the Triple Alliance, Brazil was now at peace with Para-

---

[38] John L. Stevens, American Minister to Uruguay, to Fish, Aug. 8, 1872 [1?]; Fish to Stevens, Oct. 5, 1871, *For. Rel., 1872*, pp. 467-468.

[39] *British and Foreign State Papers*, LXIII (1872-1873), pp. 322-325.

[40] Dexter E. Clapp, Chargé d'Affaires ad interim to Argentina, to W. Hunter, Assistant Secretary of State, Feb. 13, 1872, *For. Rel., 1872*, pp. 29-30.

[41] W. R. Manning (ed.), *Arbitration Treaties among the American Nations to the Close of the Year 1910*, pp. 91-92; *British and Foreign State Papers*, LXII (1871-1872), pp. 277-290.

[42] Clapp to Hunter, June 12, 1872, *For. Rel., 1872*, p. 36.

[43] Fish to James R. Partridge, United States Minister to Brazil, April 20, 1872, *ibid.*, p. 97.

guay and in a favorable position to dominate its policies. Argentina, although responsive to Brazilian leadership throughout the war, now found its ally barring the way to settlement of national claims against their former foe. Paraguay, once the cause of allied unity, had become the bone of contention between its conquerors. Uruguay, whose factional politics had touched off the five-year war, took little part in postwar rivalries.

The burning issue between Argentina and Paraguay was the territory of the Gran Chaco. Since the wars for independence both nations, together with Bolivia, had laid claim to this wild land west of the Río Paraguay. Brazil's support of Paraguayan claims stemmed from the desire to protect its own monopoly of tropical products on the upper rivers. By aiding Paraguay it hoped to prevent the construction of a railroad long planned by Argentina and Bolivia to traverse the Chaco from the highlands to the Paraguay.[44]

Soon after Quintana's withdrawal from the 1871-1872 peace conference, President Sarmiento formalized Argentina's claim to the Gran Chaco by declaring it an Argentine province. He designated Villa Occidental as the capital. Paraguayan authorities contended that the region had always been a part of their territory and that submission to Argentina's actions would threaten its national sovereignty.[45] Secretary Fish, now as concerned about Argentine pretensions as he was about Brazilian, repeated his urgings of American interest in a strong, republican Paraguay.[46]

Argentine apprehension toward Brazil's growing influence over Paraguayan policies intensified the antagonism produced by the Empire's conclusion of separate treaties. By mid-1872 from his seat in the Senate ex-President Mitre led the fight to stiffen President Sarmiento's too-pacific policies. As war fever mounted in both countries, the President selected his predecessor and opposition leader to undertake the settlement of all matters of disagreement with Brazil.[47] During this period of tension, only a chargé represented the United States in Buenos Aires, a reality of which the Argentine Minister reminded Fish. It was an opportune time, said Manuel García, for a skillful American diplomat to exert great moral influence in his country.[48]

After five months of delicate negotiations, General Mitre was able to effect a settlement of all questions pending with Brazil. The protocol of November 19 proclaimed the treaty of the Triple Alliance still in

[44] Clapp to Hunter, June 12, 1872, *ibid.*, pp. 36-37.
[45] Clapp to Hunter, Feb. 13, June 12, 1872, *ibid.*, pp. 30, 37.
[46] Fish to Clapp, April 19, 1872, *ibid.*, p. 35.
[47] W. H. Jeffrey, *Mitre and Argentina*, pp. 227-228.
[48] June 26, 1872, NA, DS, Notes from Arg. Leg., II.

effect. The three nations agreed to share in reparations and jointly to guarantee Paraguayan independence. Allied armies would evacuate Paraguay within three months. Separately or jointly Argentina and Uruguay would be free to make peace with Paraguay.[49]

General Mitre's diplomatic success in Rio prompted his immediate appointment to conclude the definitive treaty with Paraguay. He might have succeeded equally in this mission had not his superiors decided to increase their demands after the start of negotiations. Having won Paraguayan agreement to cede the Chaco up to the Pilcomayo River as well as the territory of Misiones, he now received instructions to demand Villa Occidental as well. This village, the only populated center in the Chaco, was strategically located on the Paraguay only a few miles from Asunción. When Paraguay refused to yield it, Mitre returned empty-handed.[50] The Argentine-Paraguayan boundary in the Gran Chaco remained unsettled.

At the height of Argentine-Brazilian tension, Sarmiento had replaced his Foreign Minister, Varela, by Carlos Tejedor, proponent of a more aggressive policy toward Paraguay. In a "Memorandum on the Question of Limits with Paraguay," dated October 14, 1873, he announced that his government was prepared to accept either of two solutions of the boundary question: (1) arbitration of all territory between the Pilcomayo River and Bahía Negra, including Villa Occidental; or (2) a definitive settlement on the line of the Pilcomayo, with Villa Occidental reserved for Argentina. Paraguay was not interested.[51]

Little was heard of the Tejedor proposals for a year and a half as the Argentine people lived through another season of war scares, an election campaign, and Mitre's unsuccessful revolt to prevent the inauguration of President-elect Nicolás Avellaneda.[52] Finally, in April, 1875, Tejedor went to Rio de Janeiro to present to Brazilian and Paraguayan representatives the proposals of his memorandum.[53] Villa Occidental remained the apple of Argentine desire. When the envoy offered to cancel Argentina's war indemnity in return for Paraguayan agreement to cede the strategic region, Paraguayan leaders wondered

[49] *British and Foreign State Papers*, LXVIII (1876-1877), 83-86; *Annual Register*, 1872, CXIV, 303.

[50] Clapp to Hunter, April 15, 1872, *For. Rel., 1873*, p. 38; J. B. Moore, *History and Digest of the International Arbitrations to Which the United States Has Been a Party*, II, 1935; Jeffrey, *op. cit.*, pp. 230-231.

[51] A copy of the memorandum was forwarded to Secretary Fish by Thomas O. Osborn, United States Minister to Argentina, April 12, 1875, *For. Rel., 1875*, I, 26-28.

[52] Ricardo Levene, *A History of Argentina*, pp. 482-483; F. A. Kirkpatrick, *A History of the Argentine Republic*, pp. 183-186.

[53] Osborn to Fish, Sept. 12, 1874. March 15, June 24, 1875, *For. Rel., 1875*, pp. 3-4, 24-25, 37-41; *British and Foreign State Papers*, LXVI (1874-1875), 1077-1078.

how their concession to a compromise could consist of territory which Argentines claimed had never been Paraguay's.[54] Though both Brazil and Paraguay refused Tejedor's offer, the conference paved the way for the eventual arbitration by President Hayes.

The Arbitration of President Hayes

After six years of tense rivalry, checkered by conferences, special missions, press campaigns, mutual charges of overweening ambitions, and war scares, Argentina and Paraguay ultimately resolved their differences. On February 3, 1876, they signed treaties of peace; of friendship, commerce, and navigation; and of limits. The third pact provided settlement of all boundaries, including those of the Gran Chaco.[55]

Without contention Paraguay now ceded the island of Cerrito, strategically situated at the confluence of the Paraná and the Paraguay, and yielded her interest in the territory of Misiones, long occupied by Argentina. The disputants divided the Gran Chaco into three parts, with east-west boundaries to follow the courses of the rivers Verde and Pilcomayo. Paraguay retained the northern section, that between Bahía Negra and the Verde. Argentina received the southern portion, bounded by the Vermejo and the Pilcomayo. The question of ownership of the central area, lying between the Verde and the Pilcomayo, they agreed to submit to the arbitration of the president of the United States. Within a year the two governments were to present essential statements, plans, and documents.[56]

President Avellaneda's formal invitation of January 25, 1877, addressed to the "President of the United States," acknowledged "the friendly interest which you have ever taken in everything connected with the peace and cordiality of the American States." In truth, through the despatches of Secretary Fish, President Grant had many times expressed his hopes for peaceful settlement of South American disputes. For him it was unfortunate, therefore, that the invitation reached Washington in March, after the inauguration of his successor.[57] A year later, Manuel R. García and Benjamín Aceval, Argentine and Paraguayan representatives in the United States, submitted to President Hayes the

[54] Moore, *op. cit.*, II, 1935.

[55] *British and Foreign State Papers*, LXVIII (1876-1877), 86-100.

[56] Moore, *op. cit.*, II, 1923; V, 4783-4785; Manning, *op. cit.*, pp. 105-109.

[57] García forwarded the invitation to Secretary of State Evarts on March 19, 1877, NA, DS, Notes from Arg. Leg., II. Two years earlier Osborn had recommended arbitration by the Supreme Court, but Fish advised that arbitration was the constitutional prerogative of the executive. In any case, the United States would not interpose its good offices except upon formal invitation (Osborn to Fish, Sept. 11, 1875, NA, DS, Desp. Arg., XX; Fish to Osborn, Oct. 28, 1875, NA, DS, Inst. Arg., XVI, 93).

memoranda and documentary evidence from their governments.[58] In each brief the litigant built up pertinent legal and historical backgrounds for its claims to the contested lands.[59]

To an American historian of arbitrations it appeared that Argentina based its claim on inheritance after independence of all territory in the Spanish Viceroyalty of the Río de la Plata and on its subsequent attempts to prevent Paraguayan secession. Paraguay founded its case on various expeditions and settlements in the Chaco and its successful repulse of Argentine attempts to absorb the homeland itself. The evidence seemed to indicate that neither the Argentine historical claims of rightful legacy nor the Paraguayan claims of prior exploration and settlement bore effectively on the question of legal title. The decision seemed to swing on the fact that until 1865 Paraguay had exercised some jurisdiction over the disputed area while Argentina had exercised none.[60]

Whatever the reasoning of the principals, President Hayes's review of the evidence apparently convinced him of the justice of the Paraguayan case. On November 12, 1878, he awarded to the Republic of Paraguay the whole of the area not definitely settled by the treaty of 1876.[61] Consistent with its oft-proclaimed doctrine that "victory gives no rights," Argentina accepted the President's judgment without dissent.

In his annual message to the Congress three weeks later President Hayes reported that

> a boundary question between the Argentine Republic and Paraguay has been submitted by those Governments for arbitration to the President of the United States, and I have, after careful examination, given a decision upon it.[62]

Soon the Paraguayan government changed the name of Villa Occidental to Villa Hayes.[63] In this form the strategic site so much prized for a time by both nations appears on maps of South America—a symbol of inter-American harmony and of an arbitration that succeeded.

Each American administration from Lincoln to Hayes expressed its neighborly interest in the welfare of Argentina and the other nations

[58] García to Evarts, March 25, 1878; Aceval to Evarts, March 27, 1878, *For. Rel., 1878*, pp. 17-18, 709-710. See also República del Paraguay, Ministerio de Relaciones Exteriores, *Chaco paraguayo: memoria presentada al arbitro por Benjamin Aceval*, and *Appendix and Documents Annexed to the Memoria Filed by the Minister of Paraguay, on the Question Submitted to Arbitration*.

[59] Moore, *op. cit.*, II, 1928-1940. A summary of the arbitration from the Argentine point of view is contained in Ernesto Quesada, *La política argentino-paraguaya*, pp. 170-211.

[60] Moore, *op. cit.*, II, 1941.

[61] Evarts to García, Nov. 13, 1878, and to Aceval, Nov. 13, 1878, *For. Rel., 1878*, pp. 18, 710-711.

[62] Richardson, *op. cit.*, VII, 497.

[63] Moore, *op. cit.*, II, 1944.

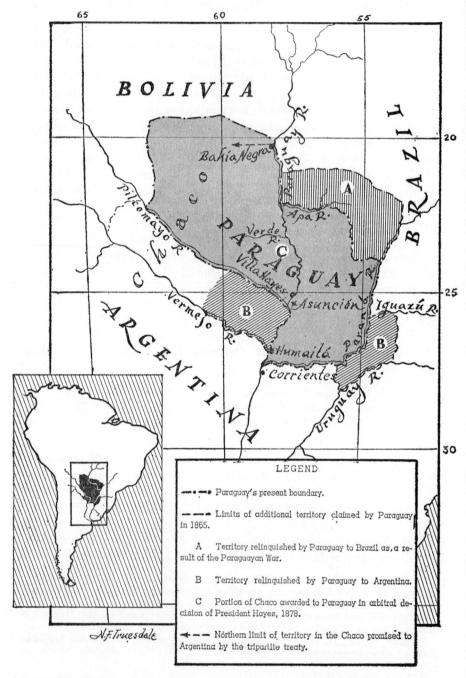

LEGEND

–•–•► Paraguay's present boundary.

– – –► Limits of additional territory claimed by Paraguay in 1865.

A   Territory relinquished by Paraguay to Brazil as, a result of the Paraguayan War.

B   Territory relinquished by Paraguay to Argentina.

C   Portion of Chaco awarded to Paraguay in arbitral decision of President Hayes, 1878.

◄– – Northern limit of territory in the Chaco promised to Argentina by the tripartite treaty.

N.F.Truesdale

ARGENTINE-PARAGUAYAN BOUNDARY SETTLEMENT, 1878

Adapted from map, p. 368, HISTORY OF THE LATIN-AMERICAN NATIONS, by William Spence Robertson. 2nd ed., rev. and enl., copyright, 1932, D. Appleton and Co. By permission of Appleton-Century-Crofts, Inc.

involved in the Paraguayan War. The eagerness to offer mediation during hostilities and the willingness to arbitrate a postwar dispute were the principal manifestations of good will. But on many other occasions Secretaries Seward and Fish conveyed American hopes for an early return of stability and prosperity. With Argentina minor irritants occasionally molested harmonious relations, but these were assuaged without damage to normal intercourse. In these instances Domingo Sarmiento and Manuel García gave Argentina forthright but judicious representation in Washington. Only the latent questions of Falklands reparations and American tariff policy remained as barriers to completely friendly relations as each nation surged from a period of postwar reconstruction into an era of national expansion.

Part Five:

The Expansion of National Interests

XIV

NATIONS IN MIDSTREAM:
FERMENT AND UNITY IN TWO REPUBLICS,
1860-1880

The eighteen-sixties and seventies were epochal years for the United States and the Argentine Republic. In the domestic growth of each, as well as in their mutual relations, the period formed a historical watershed. What went before was prelude; what came after was plot unfolding. In each nation for half a decade bitter war absorbed the energies of government and people. Through another decade war-damaged economy and impaired morale required painful rebuilding. But out of war and reconstruction each people found a newborn national unity which would stimulate material and cultural expansion. As each progressed toward political maturity at home and economic and cultural leadership among its neighbors, new influences developed to replace those which had long conditioned relations between them.

Influences on Policy Trends: The Past

The United States and Argentina were born of revolution against European colonial powers. After independence each nation sought to make what it could of its heritage and environment without interference from external forces. Except the singular inspiration set Argentine patriots by American revolutionaries, neither exerted conspicuous influence on the development of the other. Though the very similarity of location and experience served at some points to draw them together, deeper circumstances prevented the growth of intimacy. In any case, during the years of prelude to dramatic mid-century events, contradictory influences molded their relationship.

The first of these was distance. The relationship between the United States and Argentina until after mid-century was little more than a flirtation of two youthful nations seeking to develop a friendship over the barriers of geographic separation and mutual skepticism of too close association. Without rapid communication and transportation, the seven thousand miles which separated Washington and Buenos Aires were a prohibitive obstacle to growth of community of interests. Exchanges of correspondence which took three, often six months, in moments of tension deprived ministries of fresh information and agents of timely instructions. Similarly, the lack of regular, direct transportation between ports invalidated efforts of American merchants to compete with Europeans for the markets of the Río de la Plata. Argentina's remoteness helped to account, too, for its relative isolation from the political and cultural streams of the North Atlantic.

Secondly, there was little natural affinity between the American and Argentine peoples. Argentines, like all Spanish Americans, looked to the mother country and Western Europe for their commerce and their political and cultural inspiration. An occasional political theorist might read Thomas Jefferson or Joseph Story with interest or another might borrow features from the American constitution, but until Domingo Sarmiento no Argentine statesman or publicist advocated extensive adoption of the American pattern. Few, if any, American politicians or diplomats looked to Argentina even with respect, much less with hope that it could make a contribution to American life.

The attitude of European powers, especially Great Britain and France, was a third influence in Argentine-American relations. Through the vagaries of internal politics European governments frequently sought foreign adventures, and when their attention focused upon the Río de la Plata, Washington officials felt the need of wariness if not of countermeasures. American reaction in these instances ranged from apprehension of British predominance and desire to prevent European interposition to apathy, disregard of Argentine interests, and even approval of European policy.

A fourth influence was the topography of the Plata valley. The Río de la Plata and its tributaries—the Paraná, the Paraguay, and the Uruguay—provided an avenue to a vast hinterland, rich in raw materials, foodstuffs, and potential markets. Control of the estuary was perhaps the richest prize to be won by the growing nations of the South Atlantic. Before conceding self-alleged natural rights to the Banda Oriental, Argentina and Brazil contested long and bitterly. If Paraguay and the southern provinces of Brazil were to enjoy intercourse with the outside world, free, unimpeded passage of the rivers was essential. Any blockade of these strategic waterways affected not only the littoral nations but also foreign shipping interests. On many occasions—1826-1828, 1838-1840, 1843-1850, 1853-1859, 1865-1870—this feature of Argentina's topography involved the diplomacy of the United States.

Arising from the configuration of the Plata valley was a fifth influence, the rivalries of bordering states, which often pushed athwart the interests of the United States. The competition of Argentina and Brazil for supremacy in the Banda Oriental, Argentina's reluctance to recognize the independence of Paraguay and Uruguay, and the factional struggles between Blancos and Colorados in Uruguay and between Unitarians and Federalists in Argentina were sparks which at any time might burst into flame. The commerce, diplomatic rights, and the property of the United States and its citizens were frequently affected.

Sixthly, the similarity of environmental conditions perpetually retarded the growth of commerce. Though the seasons were reversed, both countries were endowed with temperate climates and rich agricultural potential. Until after the mid-century wars, each government attempted to attain economic and political stability by dependence upon an agricultural empire. American flour shipped to La Plata was obliged to meet the competition of the local product; Argentine wool was rarely able to enter the United States without the handicap of a protective tariff. Irritating episodes as well as low trade volume, especially for American commercial interests, were the results.

In the seventh place, American exporters devoted much less attention to the development of Argentine markets than to those of Cuba, Mexico, and Brazil. Commercial contacts were constant but never great. Until after 1880 the balance of trade was perpetually in Argentina's favor. Though admitted violations of Monroe's pronouncements, English occupation of the Falkland Islands and Anglo-French interventions in Platine politics left the United States indifferent. In its relations with Argentina, as elsewhere in Latin America, Washington normally pressed political principles only when the economic interests of its nationals were involved.

Eighth, more often than not the United States was represented in Argentina by incapable or overzealous agents. From 1810 to 1880 no more than three representatives left deep impressions upon the minds of Argentine leaders or people. Of the remainder, most committed indiscretions of one sort or another. The State Department's failure to send more able men to Buenos Aires may have emanated from the comparative lack of interest in the region. But whatever the reason, the situation led to a vicious circle in the representation of American interests —faulty observation, imperfect reports to Washington, State Department failure to understand conditions, inadequate instructions, and faulty observation again. Though distance and slow communication handicapped the agents and foreign ministers of both countries, Argentine representatives in Washington, when they were sent, were usually able diplomats.

The final influence was the continuity throughout the period of foreign policies, Argentine and American. From the revolution of May,

1810, Argentina steadfastly maintained four cornerstones of policy. It aspired to spread its control, military and political at first, then economic and cultural, to the limits of the former viceroyalty. It resisted intervention in its affairs from whatever source, Latin American, American, or European. By reasons of both propinquity and common origins, it asserted its special ties with the other states of Latin America. It refused to participate in multilateral arrangements for the protection of its own security. Adherence to these cornerstones of policy transcended all changes in executive leadership, whether peaceful or violent, from junta through dictatorship to constitutional president.[1] By their very nature all four traditions excluded intimacy with the United States.

During its early relations with the Western Hemisphere, the United States also adopted policies that became traditional if somewhat less fixed than cornerstones: the Monroe Doctrine, expansion of commerce, Manifest Destiny, and promotion of peaceful settlement. But, for the most part, Argentina lay outside the scope of these policies. Neither by its own volition nor by Argentine invitation did the United States invoke the Monroe Doctrine in its behalf. Though in several instances, notably the 1853 treaty on navigation of rivers, the United States revealed concern for the free movement of trade, its citizens displayed little economic interest in Argentina. Although Argentine spokesmen attacked it, American territorial expansion did not threaten their national interests. In the promotion of peaceful settlement, including the by-product of nonintervention by one state in the affairs of another, American and Argentine views ran parallel. Both preached it and both violated their preachings.

Ferment and National Unity

The ferment in the Argentine Republic from 1860 to 1880 followed closely the pattern of mid-century revolution in the United States. In the northern republic, the nation turned the full cycle from unity, however tenuous, through secession, war, military occupation, and reconstruction, back to unity, at last firm and unyielding. Without plan or intention, within a few years Argentina duplicated each phase of the American cycle.

The American people endured four years of civil war to stamp out secession and restore the Southern states to the Union. The Argentines, too, used force to attain effective control over all the nation's territory. Their leaders sometimes regarded the Paraguayan conflict as a war against secession or as a campaign to restore lands that were a rightful

---

[1] This summary of Argentine policies follows Arthur P. Whitaker's interpretation in his *The United States and Argentina*, pp. 85-88.

part of the Argentine heritage from Spain.[2] At war's end, Paraguay remained independent but not without conceding "repatriation" of a considerable portion of the Argentine claims.

After the war, as before, Argentina was confronted with another, more immediate kind of secession, the control exercised over regions of the nation by rebellious caudillos. By 1876 the worst of these were liquidated and the disease of *caudillismo* largely eliminated.[3]

In the perpetually incipient rebelliousness of the Province of Buenos Aires, Argentina faced still a third kind of secessionism. Since 1862, representing the unitarist point of view against the federalism of the other provinces, Buenos Aires had been held in the nation by a precarious truce that made its capital also the capital of the republic. During the election of 1880, the question broke out anew with provincial refusal to cede its public domain to the central government. In a brief civil war, national forces frustrated the threat of secession, separated the city from the province, and federalized it as the permanent national capital.[4] The republic could be effectively governed only from Buenos Aires and now, for the first time, it became the legal capital of an undivided nation.

The Civil War in the United States was followed by a decade or more of physical, financial, political, and moral reconstruction that reached every fiber of the nation's being. After the Paraguayan War, Argentines were equally beset by problems of postwar reconstruction —war debts, rising import-export deficits, unbalanced budgets, internal disorders, financial panic, international boundary disputes—not to mention epidemics of cholera and yellow fever.

The withdrawal of the last federal troops from the South in 1877 symbolized the reduction of states' rights as an explosive issue and the acceptance of federal supremacy in the nation. The American republic at last was permanently unified. In Argentina, the recall of troops from Paraguay and the defeat of the last of the caudillos in 1876, followed by federalization of Buenos Aires in 1880, symbolized the end of secessionism and the assurance of national unity.

The ridgepole of war and reconstruction, therefore, defined a line of far-reaching shifts in the United States and Argentina. In both republics it marked the settlement of divisive constitutional issues and the acknowledgment of supremacy of the federal principle. In both it indicated submergence of old issues of secession and emergence of new problems of overcentralization. In both it signalized defeat of deep-rooted sectional cleavages and victory of truer national unity.

[2] *Obras de D. F. Sarmiento,* XXXIV, 240; J. B. Moore, *History and Digest of the International Arbitrations to Which the United States Has Been a Party,* II, 1941.
[3] A. W. Bunkley, *The Life of Sarmiento,* pp. 449-456, 470-483.
[4] *Ibid.,* pp. 479-482; W. H. Jeffrey, *Mitre and Argentina,* pp. 231-234.

Sarmiento, Link Between Republics

Ties between the two republics during these years of turmoil were unsubstantial. Diplomatic and commercial relations were still rudimentary. Argentine tracing of the American pattern was wholly fortuitous. And yet, through the personality of one gigantic figure, there was a link. The link was Domingo F. Sarmiento, one of the titans of Argentine mid-century change. Through him future Argentine adherence to the American model would become purposeful.

As Argentine Minister to Washington from 1865 to 1868 and as President from 1868 to 1874, Sarmiento served his nation, indeed both nations, at the height of ferment in each. He arrived in New York just three weeks after the assassination of Lincoln and four days after the start of the Paraguayan War. He came in time to sense the impact on the American people of a terrible war just concluded and to feel the pulsations of throbbing war industry, awaiting conversion to peacetime boom. He would see a dynamic people, released from the despair of war, turn their energies to planning the future.

Sarmiento was brilliantly suited to accomplish the mission he bore. As a youth in remote San Juan, he read widely, learned French, adopted Benjamin Franklin as his model. As a young man, he fought against the local caudillo, fled to Chile, taught school, studied English, Italian, and Portuguese, translated Sir Walter Scott, and founded a newspaper. His opposition to tyrannical government drove his pen to sharp attacks on Argentine dictators and brought him three more seasons of exile in Chile. Not until 1855, at the age of forty-four, did he settle down in Buenos Aires to edit a newspaper, serve as provincial senator, and direct the provincial school system. Later, after three years as senator from San Juan, President Mitre appointed him minister to the United States.[5]

From his manifold instructions Sarmiento selected two for emphasis. He wished to represent Argentina to Americans in a favorable light and to learn from American institutions whatever might assist him in guiding his own nation's moral and material progress.[6] These purposes he could accomplish best, he believed, not by diplomatic formalities in Washington but by living in New York and travelling throughout the country. In this manner he carried out his mission.

Sarmiento first undertook to know people. He renewed acquaintance with the widow of Horace Mann, who during his previous visit had

[5] Bunkley, *op. cit., passim.*
[6] *Obras de D. F. Sarmiento,* XXXIV, 184; Sarmiento to President of the United States, Nov. 9, 1865, NA, DS, Notes from Arg., II.

excited his enthusiasm for public education. He learned English, read books, collected a library, founded another newspaper, and wrote a life of Lincoln. He inspected schools and colleges, attended professional meetings, and addressed distinguished groups.[7] He came to respect the American people and to appreciate American life. "It is the province of the United States," he once told an American audience, "the highest mission intrusted by Providence to a great people, that of conducting others through the new paths opened by mankind to advance firmly to their great destinies." [8]

So by 1868, returning to Argentina as President-elect, Sarmiento was prepared to assume office as protagonist of "Northamericanization" and American regionalism and as opponent of continued Europeanization and Hispanicism. Though critical, like all Argentines, of some American policies toward Latin America, he clearly hoped to convey to his nation something of the spirit he admired in the American people and in their society, education, economy, and government.[9]

Argentine Consolidation and Expansion

From his position as President from 1868 to 1874 Sarmiento became the dynamo for the reorientation and transformation of Argentine life. His predecessor, Bartolomé Mitre, even in the midst of war, had set distant beacons. His unimpressive but shrewd successor, Nicolás Avellaneda, would follow where the two had led. But it was Sarmiento's energy and imagination that placed Argentina on the road to economic and cultural leadership in Latin America. The administrations of the three, unmarred by successful revolutions against them, spanned the two decades of mid-century watershed. Except for statistics, the chronicle of their achievements reads like the history of post-bellum United States.

It took no Mitre or Sarmiento to realize that Argentina's paramount need was people. Its first census, taken in 1869, revealed what every leader knew, that three centuries of immigration had brought few people to the country, only 1,800,000, about two for each square mile of land. Now, by colonization schemes and other inducements, the annual flow of five thousand in 1857 and 34,000 in 1868 was increased to 76,000 in 1873. It would reach 219,000 in 1889. Moreover, if the political orientation of the nation were to be changed, it needed non-Hispanic

[7] Bunkley, *op. cit.*, pp. 420-442.
[8] Quoted in *ibid.*, pp. 433-434.
[9] Bunkley (ed.), *A Sarmiento Anthology*, pp. 17, 22, 33, 35-38, 309-311, 327-332; Whitaker, *op. cit.*, pp. 94-95.

people. Spaniards continued to come, but most were Italians and many were French, English, Germans, or Swiss.[10]

Settlers on the land, no matter how industrious, could get bulky crops to market only with adequate transportation. The rich pampa was almost roadless and riverless. Sarmiento's extensive travels through the American countryside had taught him the indispensability of a rail network to a rural hinterland. His efforts by 1874 doubled the 1870 mileage of 454. His successors doubled the mileage again by 1880, quadrupled that figure by 1890, and quadrupled it again to 20,805 by the end of 1913. The increase in monthly ship arrivals at Buenos Aires from four to nineteen between 1868 and 1874 vastly augmented the movement of Argentine products into the channels of world commerce.[11]

But a revolution in ranching and farming would not be made by men and rails and ships alone. Better livestock, more advanced methods, more nutritious grasses, and modern inventions must come. In 1866 a small but visionary group of cattle raisers founded the Sociedad Rural, soon to become the strongest force for revolutionizing the cattle industry and eventually a powerful pressure group influencing Argentine foreign policy. Through propaganda and livestock shows, beginning in 1875, they preached the advantages of thoroughbred stock and sought to replace the Argentine longhorn with the English Shorthorn and the local Merino with the imported Lincoln. They introduced alien clover and alfalfa to supplant native grasses. Refrigeration came in 1877 when the first refrigerator ship carried congealed meat from Argentina. Within a decade fifty-seven ships were transporting beef and mutton to whet English appetites. With the building of the first packing plant by 1883, the Argentines had assembled all the ingredients for a pastoral revolution.[12]

An agricultural revolution followed the pastoral. The introduction and widening use on the treeless pampa of barbed-wire fencing, steel windmills, reapers, and threshers enabled the growing population to increase at dizzy rates production of cereals. The per capita acreage in cultivation rose from less than half an acre in 1869 to three in 1895. Agricultural products which totaled only 2 per cent of Argentine exports in 1880 grew to 65 per cent by 1908. Wheat, corn, sugar, wine, and linseed were the commodities most widely produced. Through its mounting production of meat and cereals Argentina was moving

[10] For the statistics in this and subsequent paragraphs I have not gone to the sources. See J. Fred Rippy in A. Curtis Wilgus (ed.), *Argentina, Brazil, and Chile Since Independence*, p. 113; Hubert Herring, *A History of Latin America*, pp. 619, 623; Whitaker, *op. cit.*, pp. 41-42; Bunkley, *The Life of Sarmiento*, p. 469.

[11] *Ibid.*, p. 469; Rippy, *op. cit.*, p. 117.

[12] Ysabel F. Rennie, *The Argentine Republic*, pp. 143-150; Whitaker, *op. cit.*, pp. 32-33.

toward its twentieth-century reputation of world's largest exporter of surplus food products.[13]

The frontierward march of barbed-wire fencing during Avellaneda's administration (1874-1880) incited anew the few fierce Indians remaining to impede the white man's invasion. It was General Julio A. Roca, the astute, vigorous minister of war, who in 1879 wiped out the threat to pioneer settlement and as "the Conqueror of the Desert" won for himself a reputation that would elevate him to the presidency (1880-1886). The way was now open to the southernmost pampa and beyond to Patagonia.

But cheap land and labor, new breeds and seeds, imported methods and inventions, and improved transportation were not enough to complete the economic revolution Mitre and Sarmiento had started. If Argentines wanted their new economy of scientific stock raising and commercialized agriculture to supply meat and bread for the expanding labor force of industrial England and Europe, they must have capital. The road and rail net must be expanded, port facilities built, cities modernized, *frigoríficos* constructed, and technological improvements imported from Europe and the United States. And capital in volume was forthcoming, as since 1825 it had been available in small amounts, primarily from British investors.[14]

Argentina's economic revolution, of course, ran far beyond the visions of Mitre and Sarmiento. But it was they, together with their predecessor, Urquiza, and their successor, Avellaneda, who created the favorable atmosphere and set in motion the forces which made the revolution possible. Meanwhile, during his presidency, Sarmiento gave attention to goals that were much closer to his heart and mind and to his plans for Northamericanization. His highest hopes were to introduce government by law and by the people, and through education to prepare the people for their participation in government. While material progress moved inexorably forward, he undertook to accomplish these less certain but more rewarding tasks according to the American, English, and French patterns he had observed. In no area of his broad program was he more successful than in the founding of an elementary school system that would become the best in Latin America.[15]

[13] *Ibid.*, pp. 32-33; Rippy, *op. cit.*, pp. 115-116, 119.

[14] *Ibid.*, pp. 117-118; J. H. Williams, *Argentine International Trade under Inconvertible Paper Money, 1880-1900*, p. 13.

[15] Bunkley, *A Sarmiento Anthology*, pp. 23-25, and *The Life of Sarmiento*, pp. 467-469; Watt Stewart and W. M. French, "The Influence of Horace Mann on the Educational Ideas of Domingo Faustino Sarmiento," *The Hispanic American Historical Review*, XX (Feb., 1940), 12-31.

Influences on Policy Trends: The Future

As a link between the northern and southern republics, Domingo Sarmiento contributed far more than any Argentine—or American—toward building closer relations. Much of his program of North-americanization could never be undone. Yet his most cherished aims remained, and would remain, unfulfilled. He failed to eliminate personalism from Argentine politics. He could not transform the Gaucho of the pampa. The Creoles did not recede from their devotion to Hispanic culture. The new immigrants, largely illiterate, collected in the cities in unassimilable masses, still loyal to their homelands.

Out of the years of ferment and transformation, two well-defined socio-economic classes emerged. Since the 1880's they have contended for control of Argentine politics. One was the conservative oligarchy of great landowners and the merchants and bankers who throve on the commerce provided by their huge *estancias*. The other was the great, amorphous mass of Creoles and immigrants which slowly and painfully became a political force to be reckoned with. It would be unfair to hold Sarmiento responsible for the rise of these groups, yet his policies contributed to their evolution.

The oligarchs, who grew fat on the land they pre-empted before and during the days of boom expansion, dominated the nation's economy and with it the nation's politics and foreign policies. They built vast country estates and magnificent town houses. They travelled and lived in Europe. They were homogeneous and aristocratic and regarded themselves as socially superior.

For decades the oligarchy provided distinguished cultural and political leadership to Argentina. Their success brought national strength and prosperity. They created Argentina's renowned free press and proclaimed respect for liberal principles. But, paradoxically, they believed that they could represent the interests of the nation better than the Creole-immigrant mass. Therefore they framed their political methods to implement their beliefs. They increased the power of the state while keeping in their own hands the instruments of government. Their liberal principles became principles for themselves.

The great flood of late-nineteenth-century immigrants contributed to the formation of the second group. Their temper was determined by the motive which drove them to emigrate—the economic. They planned to return to their homelands and preferred to regard themselves as foreigners. Nevertheless, their economic fortunes in the urban centers tended to coincide with those of the Creoles. A rapid, extensive Tower-of-Babel intermingling resulted. By 1890, beginning to feel class consciousness, they organized the Unión Cívica Radical and eventually, in

1916, elevated their champion, Hipólito Irigoyen, to the presidency. They retained control of the executive until 1930 only to see the Army intervene to restore the oligarchy to power.

The Unión Radical developed a political line contrary to that of the oligarchy—popular democracy. Because it was antioligarchic, however, it became antiliberal. Gradually along the way the Creole-immigrant group developed increasing trust in the preponderance of the state in industrial activities and personalist leadership in government. Though they contributed from their numbers to the growth of a new middle class, they also revealed sympathy for principles of totalitarian demagogy or at least a willingness to return to nineteenth-century authoritarianism. Rosas, not Sarmiento, became their beau ideal.[16]

On this side of the mid-nineteenth-century watershed, therefore, the two principal Argentine groups have entrusted more and more of their welfare to state control. This development coincided, even antedated, similar trends in Europe. Though many other forces, internal and international, were at work, this enigmatic but inexorable trend in Argentine politics was to become a powerful influence on relations with the United States in the twentieth century. Perhaps it was the decisive one.

[16] On the growth of socioeconomic groups, I have relied upon José Luis Romero, *Las ideas políticas en Argentina*, especially pp. 167-226. See also Whitaker, *op. cit.*, pp. 39-42, 55-62, 77-79, and T. F. McGann, *Argentina, the United States, and the Inter-American System, 1880-1914*, pp. 9-65.

X V

THE EXPANSION OF COMMERCE: NEW DIRECTIONS AND OLD BARRIERS, 1871-1914

Commerce between the United States and Argentina in the quarter-century after the Paraguayan War did not respond to the quickened pace that stirred their domestic economies. Diverse factors, many of which had operated throughout the century, continued until the late nineties to keep commercial interchange at low figures. Spasmodic efforts to stimulate trade were not immediately effective. At the turn of the century, however, trade volume began to grow steadily, then like a jet plane approaching and breaking the sound barrier soared in a sharp upward spiral that culminated in the inflated figures of World War I.

Sluggish Growth to the Mid-Nineties

The dollar value of Argentine-American trade between 1871 and 1895 increased at no more than the torpid rate that had prevailed for half a century. The annual average by half-decades grew from a little under seven millions (1871-1875) to about nine and a half millions (1891-1895). In only one year (1889) did the figure approach fifteen millions.[1] At the same time, Argentine business with England exceeded $81,000,000, that with France, $55,000,000, with Germany, $42,000,000 and with Belgium, $27,000,000.[2] Total American trade with Argentina ran far behind that with Brazil, sometimes as much as one to eight.[3]

Argentine sales to the United States in each five-year period deviated

[1] Figures adapted from Treasury Department, *American Commerce: Commerce of South America, Central America, Mexico, and West Indies, with Share of the United States and Other Leading Nations Therein, 1821-1898*, pp. 3300-3301.

[2] W. E. Curtis, *Trade and Transportation between the United States and Spanish America*, pp. 65-66.

[3] *American Commerce*, pp. 3301-3303.

little from an annual average of five million dollars. Actually, exporters sold less in the American market between 1891 and 1895 than between 1871 and 1875. The best buyers for Argentine pastoral and agricultural products were still the English and French, with Belgians and Germans

TABLE 2

VALUE OF ARGENTINE TRADE WITH THE UNITED STATES
(ANNUAL AVERAGE BY HALF-DECADES): 1871-1915

Years	Argentine Exports	Argentine Imports	Argentine Excess of Exports (+); of Imports (−)
1871-75	$ 6,834,156	$ 2,012,143	+
1876-80	4,346,548	1,794,781	+
1881-85	5,106,963	3,737,281	+
1886-90	5,176,202	7,183,015	−
1891-95	5,546,347	4,009,226	+
1896-00	7,845,751	7,982,969	−
1901-05	10,761,276	14,648,623	−
1906-10	20,362,386	34,220,459	−
(1910-14	32,877,726	47,169,111)	−
1911-15	47,804,570	47,252,035	+

SOURCE: The figures are adapted from *American Commerce*, pp. 3300-3301, and appropriate volumes of *Statistical Abstract of the United States.*

now better customers than the Americans.[4] The astronomical increases in the production of grains, meats, hides, and wool found outlet among the growing populations of Western Europe but not in the United States.

If American producers yearned to plumb the Argentine market, dollar sales did not reflect their deep interest. The annual value did not reach five million dollars until 1883 and exceeded that figure only five times before 1895. The annual average for the quarter-century after 1871 was less than four millions. England and France consistently outsold the United States by a wide margin; even German and Belgian exports were often larger than the American. Though the American share of bilateral trade lacked the steadiness of the Argentine, beginning in the eighties it did reveal a tendency toward sharper increase.[5] The products of the developing American industry, especially farm implements, rolling stock, and wood and steel products, began to reach Argentine markets.

As it had without break since the French blockade of 1840, the balance of trade remained in Argentina's favor until 1884. For the next decade and a half, as domestic circumstances affected buying power, the favorable balance shifted between the two nations.[6] But after 1898,

[4] *American Commerce*, pp. 3300-3301; Curtis, *op. cit.*
[5] *Ibid.*; *American Commerce*, pp. 3300-3301.
[6] *Ibid.*

except during the abnormal conditions of World Wars I and II, Argentina rarely regained the black side of the ledger.[7]

Real Barriers and Ineffective Countermeasures: Tariffs

Foremost among many barriers to increased Argentine-American commerce was the similarity of their rich pastoral and agricultural lands and the noncomplementary nature of their economies. Republican protectionists after the Civil War determined to foster the products of American farm and factory. Unless Democratic opposition or Argentine diplomacy could modify this policy, importers would lack the exchange to purchase American manufactured goods in volume. At the heart of the impasse was the tariff on wool.

Exportation of wool was indispensable to Argentine prosperity. In spite of the conversion of the pampa to the production of beef and grain, the sheep population increased in geometric proportions. The number rose from 14,000,000 in 1860 to 41,000,000 in 1870, 61,000,000 in 1880, and 91,000,000 in 1895. In the forty years after 1860 the wool volume increased 1500 per cent.[8] The wool clip constantly found ready markets in Western Europe and, until 1867, in the United States.

The tariff levied on wools in 1867 by the post-bellum Republican Congress set the tone of Argentine-American economic diplomacy for a generation, perhaps longer. Wool became the perennial Argentine whipping boy. A succession of able diplomats—Sarmiento and García-Mansilla in the sixties and seventies, Domínguez and Quesada in the eighties, and Zeballos and García Merou in the nineties—reasoned, petitioned, pleaded, and even propagandized for modification of American policy. Like reform groups and Democratic oppositionists, they failed to overcome the barrier erected by American vested interests.

Tinkerings with the tariff in 1872 and 1875 produced no helpful reduction of the duties on wool. In 1883 the Tariff Commission, headed by the secretary of the American Wool Manufacturers Association, John L. Hayes, proposed new schedules which provided no relief for Argentine wool. In protest, Argentine Minister Luis L. Domínguez drafted for Secretary F. T. Frelinghuysen a comprehensive analysis of his nation's commercial relations with the United States.

The tariff of 1867, he said, within a year reduced importations of Argentine wool from 37,000,000 pounds to 12,500,000. By 1882 the figure had plummeted to 2,000,000, less than 1 per cent of Argentine total wool exports and a fraction of American total imports of 64,000,000 pounds. Beyond this, the Minister reminded Frelinghuysen, in the same

[7] See below, pp. 233, 320-321, 341-342, 358-359, 412.
[8] *American Commerce*, p. 3169.

year the United States purchased less than 5 per cent of Argentina's total exports. Whereas his government admitted American timber, railroad rolling stock, and agricultural implements free of duty or at low rates, the United States virtually excluded the commodity which represented more than half of Argentina's exports. "It is futile to search for ways of increasing the commerce between the two countries," he submitted, "if the obstacles which the government imposes by means of the duty are not removed." [9]

Throughout the eighties leaders and representatives of both nations ineffectively sought ways to relieve the stalemate. From Buenos Aires Ministers Thomas O. Osborn and Bayless W. Hanna and Consul Edward L. Baker, all energetic officials, zealously relayed Argentine bids for reciprocity, especially through annulment of export duties on wool, hides, and linseed.[10] In Washington, Domínguez reminded Secretary Thomas F. Bayard that elimination of the duty on wool would bring better shipping facilities, and better shipping would enlarge commerce in general.[11] Near the end of its tenure, the Arthur administration despatched a commission to the Central and South American states to ascertain "the best modes of securing more intimate international and commercial relations." In Argentina it learned firsthand that wool was the key to any agreement on mutual trade. None of its well-intentioned recommendations of 1885 was implemented.[12] Similarly, Cleveland's oft-cited tariff message of 1887 resulted only in the abortive Mills bill.

Every effort, in Washington as in Buenos Aires, failed to change American policy. And at the end of the decade, the duty on wool was one of the rocks upon which Secretary James G. Blaine's hopes for an American customs union foundered. Because of his own party's intransigence, the Commercial Bureau of the American Republics very nearly suffered a stillbirth.[13]

Blaine's determination to correct the unfavorable trade balance with Latin America by developing markets for manufactured goods received a boon in the reciprocity clause of the McKinley Tariff Act of 1890. This section placed sugar, molasses, tea, coffee, and hides on the free list, but empowered the president to reimpose duties against any nation

[9] Domínguez to Frelinghuysen, Sept. 29, 1883, and to Bayard, Aug. 15, 1885, NA, DS, Notes from Arg. Leg., II, III, printed in *Memoria, 1897,* pp. 277-280; Martín García Merou, *Estudios americanos,* pp. 401-405.

[10] As examples, see Osborn to Frelinghuysen, July 30, 1884; Hanna to Bayard, Nov. 19, 1887, NA, DS, Desp. Arg., XXV, XXVI; República Argentina, *Diario de sesiones de la Cámara de Diputados, 1884,* II, 816-818; *1887,* II, 1163-1164.

[11] See above, note 9.

[12] *H. Ex. Doc.,* No. 50, 49 Cong., 1 sess., pp. 5, 396. See also Inst. to Spec. Com. to C. and S. A. States, Aug. 27, 1884, NA, DS, Specl. Missions, III, 352-359; Domínguez to Minister of Foreign Relations, Aug. 27, 1885, República Argentina, Ministerio de Relaciones Exteriores, *Boletín mensual,* Oct. 1885, pp. 707-708; *Memoria, 1885,* pp. xv-xx.

[13] See below, pp. 283-284.

which treated American goods unequally or unreasonably. On January 3, Blaine invited the Argentine Minister, Vicente G. Quesada, to negotiate a reciprocal agreement. When the Secretary offered free admission of hides in exchange for free entry of tanned leather, shoes, and soles, the Argentine claimed lack of instructions. When the Minister raised the question of woolens, Blaine postponed further discussion until the arrival of the instructions.[14] Upon Quesada's subsequent absence from the country, negotiations shifted to Buenos Aires, where under a new president the authorities were trying to lead the nation out of deep political and economic distress.

Faced with the responsibility of enforcing the McKinley Act, the Department of State on August 3 directed Minister John R. G. Pitkin to press Argentina for action.[15] For nearly a year Pitkin carried on a verbal and written duel with Foreign Minister Estanislao S. Zeballos, soon to become minister to the United States and later jurist on the Hague Court of Arbitration. Neither had broad compass for action. Pitkin was bound by the terms of the McKinley Act, which permitted no concessions on wool. His nation always dependent upon custom-house duties as the chief source of revenue and his government now virtually bankrupt, Zeballos was in no position to concede free entry of imports in volume. Moreover, in Pitkin's belief, Argentina could adopt no policy which might offend English, French, German, and Italian commercial or banking interests.

The Argentine Foreign Minister professed apprehension that a reciprocal arrangement with the United States would violate the spirit of most-favored-nation treaties, provoke retaliation by France and other leading customers, and by international compromise endanger Argentina's domestic financing. Though Argentine tariffs had always been extremely liberal, the United States, at least since 1867, had been disdainful of Argentine markets; the commission of 1884 had spent only a few hours in Buenos Aires. Instead of seeking new concessions at this time, Zeballos ventured that a more just approach would have been to ask equal treatment for American pine and Argentine wool. In any case, he suspected that the American policy of reciprocity was transitory, resting solely upon executive decree, and would disappear with a change in internal politics. The Argentine constitutional system, he said, required that changes in tariffs be consummated by legislative action. To penetrate the American shield of prohibitive duties on wool without risking the danger of retaliatory rates upon hides, the Argentine jabbed and feinted. In what must have been an unguarded moment, Zeballos

---

[14] NA, DS, Notes to Arg. Leg., VI, 314-315; Quesada to Eduardo Costa, Minister of Foreign Relations, Feb. 12, 1891, *Memoria, 1891,* pp. 210-211.

[15] NA, DS, Inst. Arg., XVI, 583-585.

admitted that he was actuated by "the spirit in which a girl coyly repels her sweetheart to invite greater fervors and a closer approach." [16]

Pitkin parried the Argentine arguments with finesse, with erudition, or, when necessary, with boldness. He pointed out that Argentina had no special commercial agreements with any European nation except Portugal. He argued that in the most-favored-nation clause international law recognized "no surrender of the right to make reciprocal concessions based upon adequate consideration." As evidences of sincere American interest in Argentine markets, he offered its initiation of the 1889-1890 Conference and its eagerness to secure regular shipping service.[17]

In the end, the tariff situation was little changed. Hides and skins would be admitted free of duty into the United States; farm machinery and unworked pine and spruce would be untaxed in Argentina.[18] But the incident would have broader repercussions. Continued American refusal to concede the slightest reduction of wool tariffs thickened the accumulating veneer of resentment which had long overlaid relations with Argentina. In microcosm, the year of debate brought forth the basic differences which had prevented and would continue to prevent the growth of completely harmonious relations.

Two years later, in the Wilson-Gorman Tariff Act, the Cleveland administration lifted the barrier against Argentine wools. As a result, Argentine total exports to the United States in 1895 reached the highest value in history. The 1896 figure trebled that for 1894 and the 1897 rose still higher.[19] Unfortunately, by taking its action in a diplomatic vacuum the Democratic Congress failed to capitalize on its revolutionary action.

As the bill moved through Congress, Zeballos, now in Washington as Minister, followed closely the course of committee hearings and congressional actions. In January, 1894, he advised the Secretary of State that the Argentine Congress had added crude petroleum to its free list out of consideration for the Ways and Means Committee recommendation for free wool. The Secretary forwarded this information to the Committee.[20] In late July, while the bill was still before the

[16] On Zeballos' exposition of Argentine views, see especially his long despatch to Pitkin, Dec. 24, 1891, *Memoria, 1891-1892*, pp. 391-404. Many other documents, including exchanges among Argentine cabinet members, are printed in *ibid., 1891,* pp. 210-219, and *1891-1892*, pp. 366-438.

[17] For Pitkin's instructions and reports, see NA, DS, Inst. Arg., XVII, 10-13, and Desp. Arg., XXIX, XXX, especially his despatches of Oct. 7, 1891, Jan. 9, 20, Feb. 20, 26, May 30, 1892, with their enclosures.

[18] Pitkin to John W. Foster, Secretary of State, July 11, 1892, and enclosures, NA, DS, Desp. Arg., XXX.

[19] *American Commerce*, p. 3301.

[20] Zeballos to Gresham, Jan. 30, 1894, *For. Rel., 1894*, pp. 3-4; *H. Rep.*, No. 2263, 54 Cong., 1 sess., p. 79. This report gives a detailed account of Argentine offers of reciprocity (pp. 77-104).

Senate, the Argentine Foreign Minister cabled his determination to "respond with all possible exemptions." The Secretary advised the Finance Committee.[21] Without even congressional acknowledgment of the Argentine overtures, the tariff bill moved on to legislative approval. When, subsequently, Secretary W. Q. Gresham directed William I. Buchanan in Buenos Aires to seek concessions, the Minister met the stone wall of Argentine pride. The Argentine Congress felt under no obligations to reciprocate. It understood fully that the American action was motivated solely by internal politics, not by intention to benefit Argentina. Buchanan was able to report only minor concessions in the Argentine tariff law of 1895.[22] As a result, the United States Treasury lost in revenues ten times the amount gained in American exports to Argentina.[23]

In the long run, therefore, neither Republican nor Democratic tariff policy toward Argentine wool improved the atmosphere of diplomacy. In 1891-1892, the Republicans, adamant against placing wool on the free list, fruitlessly invited Argentina to negotiate a reciprocity agreement. But, in 1894, the Democrats, willing to remove all duties from wool, consummated their purpose without inviting Argentina to grant reciprocal advantages or even acknowledging its offers to do so. In the Argentine view, the Harrison administration lacked foresight, the Cleveland, tact. In neither instance did American policy satisfy the sensitive Argentines. Nor was the 1897 Dingley Act of the McKinley administration to improve their attitude.

Though issues and negotiations under the new Republican measure differed in some respects from those of 1891, the results were the same. Argentine sugar, coming into commercial production in Tucumán Province, was now added to wool as a bone of contention.[24] Receding from their former demand for free wool, the Argentines now indicated willingness to settle for a nominal reduction in rates.

Argentina was represented in the United States at this time by Martín García Merou. During eight years of residence between 1896 and 1905 he became a close student of American life and public policy, upon which he published a five-hundred-page volume called *Estudios americanos*.[25] In an extended chapter he analyzed American tariff policy and commercial relations with Argentina. In friendly but critical fashion, he concluded that "if the United States wishes to gain our commerce,

[21] *Ibid.*, p. 80; Zeballos to Gresham, July 30, 1894, *For. Rel.*, *1894*, pp. 5-6.
[22] Gresham to Buchanan, Aug. 7, 1894, and Buchanan's subsequent reports, *For. Rel.*, *1894*, pp. 6-17; *1895*, pp. 3-4; J. D. Richardson, *A Compilation of the Messages and Papers of the Presidents*, IX, 626.
[23] *H. Rep.*, No. 2263, p. 82.
[24] *Memoria*, *1898*, pp. 47-56; NA, DS, Notes from Arg. Leg., IV, and Notes to Arg. Leg., VII, 11-13, 15-16, 20-21.
[25] Buenos Aires, 1900.

they must make some efforts to secure it."[26] He borrowed a considerable portion of the chapter from the extensive report he had sent to his government in October, 1896, after observing Republican efforts under Cleveland to restore the tariff on wool.[27] Within two months after the inauguration of President William McKinley, in a long note to Secretary John Sherman, he summarized the Argentine views on the proposed duties on wool.[28] The Dingley Act signalized the failure of García Merou's efforts.

The McKinley administration was represented in Buenos Aires by a Cleveland appointee, William I. Buchanan, an extremely able business-man-diplomat.[29] After the passage of the Dingley Act, Buchanan used his prestige to convince the Argentines that the measure was "not to be considered in the slightest degree designed to prejudice the commercial interests of the Argentine Republic." He worked to forestall retaliatory measures against American products.[30] Ultimately authorized in December, 1898, to negotiate a reciprocal agreement under the bargaining clause, he signed a convention in which Argentina granted reduced rates on pine lumber, furniture, canned goods, and oils in exchange for 20 per cent reduction on sugar, hides, and wool.[31] Though the Argentine government twice granted the United States extension of time for exchange of ratifications, American woolgrowers persistently obstructed Senate approval.[32] After three years had passed without favorable action, an Argentine newspaper forecast that it would be "a long time before the Argentine Government will enter into negotiations for another treaty of reciprocity with the United States."[33]

[26] Pp. 381-432. The quotation is from page 432.

[27] To Amancio Alcorta, Minister of Foreign Affairs, Oct. 10, 1896, *Memoria, 1897,* pp. 251-330.

[28] May 1, 1897, NA, DS, Notes from Arg. Leg., IV.

[29] A. W. P. Buchanan, *The Buchanan Book,* pp. 472-474.

[30] Sherman to Buchanan, Nov. 8, 1897, Jan. 6, 11, 1898, and to François S. Jones, Chargé d'Affaires, April 5, 1898, NA, DS, Inst. Arg., XVII, 285-287, 303-313, 332-333; Buchanan to Sherman, Sept. 15, Dec. 22, 1897, Jan. 6, 8, 1898, NA, DS, Desp. Arg., XXXV; S. F. Bemis (ed.), *The American Secretaries of State and their Diplomacy,* IX, 14-15.

[31] John Hay, Secretary of State, to Buchanan, Dec. 9, 1898, NA, DS, Inst. Arg., XVII, 409; Buchanan to Hay, July 10, 1899, NA, DS, Desp. Arg., XXXVIII; República Argentina, *Tratados, convenciones, protocolos, actos y acuerdos internacionales,* VIII, 199-204.

[32] William P. Lord, Minister to Argentina, May 9, 1900, May 7, 1901, NA, DS, Desp. Arg., XXXIX, XL.

[33] As quoted from *The Buenos Aires Herald* in Lord to Hay, May 3, 1902, NA, DS, Desp. Arg., XL. In concluding an Extradition Convention, ratified by both governments in 1900, Buchanan was more successful in his treaty negotiations (W. M. Malloy, *Treaties, Conventions, International Acts, Protocols, and Agreements between the United States and Other Powers, 1776-1909,* I, 25-28).

Other Barriers and Countermeasures

This succession of tariff controversies was by no means the only impediment to improved commerce. Other obstacles, only slightly less thorny, barred the way to a more favorable climate. Upon its return in 1885, President Chester A. Arthur's Central and South American Commission suggested several of these barriers when it recommended to Congress (1) regular and direct steamship communications, (2) increase and improvement of consular service, (3) establishment of branch mercantile houses, (4) more intimate knowledge of the needs of the people, (5) a system of banking connections, and (6) more liberal credits by exporting merchants.[34]

Slow, irregular, and indirect communication with Argentina had constituted a problem since the days of Joel Roberts Poinsett. After the decline of the clipper ship, the American flag became a rare sight in Argentine harbors. In 1873 not a single American steam vessel arrived in Buenos Aires. In 1887, British sailing ships outnumbered American by 662 to 74 and steamships, 363 to 7. From 1893 to the end of 1906, an American consul reported, no American steam vessel stopped in Buenos Aires.[35]

The most persistent American attacks upon the problem came in the eighties and early nineties. Under repeated hammerings by American agents, Presidents Arthur, Cleveland, and Harrison used their annual messages to urge congressional aid for direct American shipping lines to South American ports.[36]

In Argentina, every president from Mitre in the sixties to Roca in the nineties advocated government support for a direct line to New York. In 1865, the Congress had authorized a standing offer of $20,000 a year to any company that would promise monthly voyages.[37] Several later congresses renewed and increased the original amount.[38] Entrepreneurs like the American, Colonel W. P. Tisdel, agent of the United States and Brazil Mail Steamship Line, and the Englishman, Robert P. Houston, negotiated for Argentine aid in the eighties.[39]

---

[34] "Report from the Central and South American Commissioners," *H. Ex. Doc.*, No. 226, 48 Cong., 2 sess., p. 4.

[35] George S. Brady, "American Shipping in Argentina," *The American Weekly of Buenos Aires*, I (April 12, 1924), p. 6; Curtis, *op. cit.*, pp. 74-75; Snyder to Asst. Sec. of State, Dec. 18, 1906, NA, DS, Numerical File, Vol. 183, case 1700/30-37.

[36] Richardson, *op. cit.*, VIII, 251, 516-517; IX, 12, 57, 125, 199.

[37] See above, p. 157.

[38] Osborn to Evarts, Sept. 22, 1880, *For. Rel.*, *1880*, pp. 33-34; Hanna to Bayard, Nov. 20, 1887, *ibid.*, *1888*, II, 2-4; *Diario de sesiones de la Cámara de Diputados, 1887*, II, 1176-1178.

[39] Blaine to Osborn, Oct. 5, 1881, NA, DS, Inst., Arg., XVI, 224-225; Hanna to Bayard, Nov. 20, 1887, and enclosures, *For. Rel.*, *1888*, I, 2-4.

But none of these recommendations, negotiations, or standing offers was attractive enough to tempt private capital. Until long after 1900 American and Argentine exporters faced a dilemma: either accept the long, two-way crossing of the Atlantic via Europe on regular routes or submit to the irregular sailings and noncompetitive rates of direct communication.

Commerce, of course, followed the mails, and orders could move no faster than the ships that carried them. Even with the best of connections mail orders could rarely be filled in less than ninety days. Combined with dependence upon alien shipping and lower prices on competitive goods, these delays drove potential American business into the arms of English and continental merchants.[40]

Business by cable, except in real emergency, offered no alternative. British firms, first in the field, had secured monopolistic cable-landing rights in Brazil, Uruguay, and Argentina. Not only were they able to impose discriminatory charges on messages to and from American exporters, but, more important, they were in a strategic position to intercept valuable business information.[41] Beginning in 1868, James A. Scrymser, founder of the Central and South American Telegraph Company, drove aggressively to lay a direct cable to Brazil and Argentina. Seward and each succeeding secretary of state supported his persistent efforts.[42] Surprisingly, Argentine business and government leaders were eager to break the British monopoly.[43] But even the winning in 1885 of landing rights in Argentina remained a paper gain until the expiration of exclusive British rights in Brazil and Uruguay.[44] Though some relief was afforded in 1892, when the American company secured direct access to Buenos Aires through Valparaiso, Chile, the first direct Atlantic cable from New York to Argentina was not opened until 1919.[45]

Other hindrances to increased commerce were neither so persistently aggravating nor so difficult to overcome as those of high tariffs, poor ship connections, slow mails, or expensive cables, but they were, nonetheless, influential. Niggardly treatment of its consular service by the

[40] Ministers and consuls in Buenos Aires reported frequently on the handicaps of slow mail service to both business and diplomacy.

[41] Frelinghuysen to Osborn, Dec. 12, 1883, Dec. 29, 1884, NA, DS, Inst. Arg., XVI, 302-304, 344; *For. Rel., 1885*, p. 1.

[42] For summaries of the long struggle to break the English monopoly, see L. F. Hill, *Diplomatic Relations between the United States and Brazil*, pp. 303-305, and John L. Merrill, President of the company, to Secretary of State, Feb. 11, 1919, NA, DS, Decimal File, 1910-1929, 835.73/89. (In subsequent references to the Decimal File only the decimal numbers are cited.)

[43] Osborn to Frelinghuysen, March 8, 1884, NA, DS, Desp. Arg., XXIV.

[44] Osborn to Bayard, July 16, 1885, *For. Rel., 1885*, p. 5.

[45] Robert Lansing, Secretary of State, to Ministers of Foreign Affairs of Uruguay and Argentina, Dec. 19, 1919, NA, DS, 835.73/34a, 109. By this time, the Central and South American Telegraph Company had been merged with All America Cables, Inc.

United States Congress left offices inadequately staffed to supply essential data on local needs to American merchants and manufacturers. No agent knew this better than Consul Baker, devoted public officer who served in Buenos Aires from 1874 until his death in the saddle twenty-three years later. In 1883, when recommending the elevation of his office to the level of the Argentine Consulate General in New York, he reported the need of clerical assistance he could not afford on his $3,000 salary. Fourteen years later, he was still asking for more assistance than his one clerk could supply.[46]

Moreover, American commercial houses too often solicited business solely by letters to the legation or consulate. Unlike the British, they failed to set up branch houses or even send personal representatives. Unlike the Germans, they failed to study the needs of the people and revealed little interest in catering to local tastes. Unlike most European merchants, they refused to give liberal credit terms. To lend prestige to the national interests of the United States, as late as 1887 there were fewer than six hundred Americans living in Buenos Aires.[47] Until after 1900 neither Argentine bonds nor Argentine industries attracted much American capital. And until 1914 United States law forbade the establishment of branch banks abroad.

On the other hand, financial conditions and government policies in Argentina during these years, however auspicious for the English and Europeans, were not always conducive to good business for Americans. The eighties were a time of great boom, checkered by suspension of specie payments, large issues of paper money, heavy foreign loans, and great speculation. The early nineties brought panic, collapse of the national banking structure, and bankruptcy of federal and provincial governments. Only in the late nineties did the nation find the way to slow recovery, revived foreign trade, and stabilized currency.[48]

To Argentine economic life in these tumultuous years, as in much of the twentieth century, contact with the North Atlantic nations was indispensable. If the United States, enmeshed in its own expansion, was not a suitor for Argentine attractions, then the nation must court the swains of Western Europe. They had the capital it needed for the development of agricultural resources; they had the mouths to feed.

The basic similarity of the geography and the economies of the two

[46] Baker to Hunter, June 2, 1883, and to W. W. Rockhill, Asst. Sec. of State, Dec. 8, 1896, NA, DS, Con. Let., B. A., XIX, XXIII.

[47] Henry L. Vilas, sec. of legation in Argentina, to Blaine, July 25, 1889, NA, DS, Desp. Arg., XXVII. As early as 1887 the Argentine Government established an official information agency in New York (Quesada to Bayard, March 11, 1887, NA, DS, Notes from Arg. Leg., III).

[48] This summary is based upon J. H. Williams, *Argentine International Trade under Inconvertible Paper Money, 1880-1900*, and H. E. Peters, *The Foreign Debt of the Argentine Republic*.

nations and the basic differences between their social orientations probably outweighed all other barriers to speedier increase of commerce and greater harmony in economic diplomacy. Continued expansion of American industry, however, and accelerated exploitation of Argentina's soil would soon reduce the noncomplementary nature of their nineteenth-century economies.

Rocketing Growth to World War I

During the years prior to World War I Argentine-American commerce experienced the first boom period in its history. Trade movements in both directions enjoyed flush times. The 1891-1895 annual average of about nine and a half million dollars in goods soared by 1910-1914 to more than eighty millions.[49] By 1914, though it still trailed Germany and Britain in bilateral trade, the United States had passed Belgium and France.[50]

Argentina's average annual exports to the United States for 1910-1914 were six times those for 1891-1895, about thirty-three million against five and a half.[51] In spite of this striking growth, however, the American share of Argentina's total exports remained relatively constant. As late as 1913, England, Germany, France, and Belgium still were better customers.[52]

American exports to Argentina underwent even more spectacular growth. As the two nations emerged from financial stress in the early nineties, Argentine purchases from the United States began to mount. By 1910-1914 the annual average had jumped twelvefold, from four million dollars to forty-seven million. The American portion of Argentina's total business now surpassed those of France and Belgium and approximated that of Germany. Britain, as usual, took the lion's share.[53]

The salient change in the pattern of trade was Argentina's loss of the favorable balance. Only five times between 1895 and 1914—three of these, 1895-1897, the years of free wool—did Argentina retain the advantage it had so long enjoyed.

This was also the period in which Argentina became the world's leading exporter of surplus beef. In the United States between 1901 and 1914 population growth far outran the increase in beef supply; in

[49] Rising prices, of course, accounted for a portion of the growth. (Trade statistics in this section for the years through 1898 are adapted from *American Commerce*, p. 3301, and those for 1899 and after from appropriate volumes of *The Statistical Abstract of the United States*. All figures are based upon fiscal years ending June 30; the period 1910-1914 has been used in order to avoid the abnormalities caused by World War I.)

[50] *The Argentine Year Book, 1915-1916*, p. 209; Julius Klein, *Frontiers of Trade*, p. 307.

[51] See above, p. 223, Table 2.

[52] *The Argentine Year Book, 1915-1916*, p. 209.

[53] *Ibid.*

Argentina the reverse was true. American beef exports of nearly 352,000,-000 pounds in 1901 dropped to barely 6,000,000 pounds in 1914. Argentina was prepared to fill the vacuum. As the American people came to require all the fresh beef their ranches could produce, Argentine chilled beef replaced American exports on English and European tables. It was "not that meat production in the Argentine has had an effect upon the industry in the United States, but that the decline in the surplus production of beef in the United States has had a most profound effect on the industry in Argentina." [54]

New Directions and Old Barriers

These increases in trade came about in spite of perpetuation into the twentieth century of old barriers. Business, financial, agricultural, and government leaders had already set new directions for national economies which would eventually reduce their noncomplementary nature and free the waters of stagnant reciprocal trade.

In Argentina, the same economic forces which had transformed sprawling provinces into an united nation now elevated the nation to leadership in Latin America. The snowball of pastoral and agricultural expansion became an avalanche. From 1890 to 1912 the production of wheat grew sixfold. Between 1901 and 1913 the corn crop advanced from 96,000,000 bushels to 263,000,000. The linseed yield, which totalled a thousand tons in 1880, touched a million by 1913. The ninety-million-dollar meat shipments of 1914 exceeded by eight times the value of those of 1894. In the same two decades, population doubled, national wealth quadrupled, and per capita acreage in cultivation increased from three to eight.[55] By World War I Argentina had fulfilled its promise of the eighties. It had become the world's greatest exporter of surplus food products and industrial raw materials.

Meanwhile, by following a divergent course the United States was realizing its nineteenth-century promise. Without reducing its pastoral and agricultural production, it turned toward economic diversification. Its investment capital, with accretions from European bankers, flowed into manufacturing, transportation, and the extractive industries. Except cotton, products of the new commercialized agriculture were largely reserved for domestic consumption. Thus, by 1900 the United States had matured to the point where its industries needed Argentina's wool, hides, skins, linseed, and quebracho, and its industrial population could

[54] A. D. Melvin and G. M. Rommel, "Meat Production in the Argentine and Its Effects upon the Industry in the United States," *Yearbook of the United States Department of Agriculture, 1914*, pp. 386-387.

[55] J. F. Rippy in A. C. Wilgus (ed.), *Argentina, Brazil and Chile Since Independence*, pp. 119-120.

absorb some of the pampa's vast food surpluses. But, more significant, before 1914 the United States moved into a position where it could surpass France, vie with Germany, and challenge England in Argentine markets.

Other factors, too, contributed to the sharp increases in commercial exchange. Diverse private and public agencies—the National Association of Manufacturers, independent companies, the Department of State, and the newly created Department of Commerce and Labor—began to study more systematically and extensively Argentine needs and resources.[56] As early as 1899, moving to more spacious quarters, the American Consulate was reported to be the busiest in Buenos Aires, with three to four hundred enquiries each month.[57] Shipping and banking services improved, though American and Argentine shippers were still at the mercy of alien proprietors. With the advent of American packing houses in 1907, Yankee capital made its first important intrusion into the Argentine economy; by 1914 five American companies were exporting 63.3 per cent of Argentina's beef.[58]

At the same time, most of the influences which before 1895 had militated against improved trade relations continued to operate. Unt:' 1913 tariff policies of the two nations remained essentially unchanged, though there occurred no series of diplomatic controversies like those of the eighties and nineties. An occasional Argentine voice was raised against wool and sugar duties, but in the main leaders seemed to have accepted the inevitable—though without forgiveness.

Several developments which halted or threatened to halt the flow of trade involved diplomatic negotiations, but they were settled without leaving permanent scars. For the first time, the hoof-and-mouth disease appeared as an obstacle to commerce. Embargoes against Argentine livestock or fodder were declared in 1907 and 1910 and against the American in 1908 and 1915. In none of the instances, however, was the ban of long duration, nor did either nation threaten permanent exclusion of the other's livestock or meat products.[59]

The diplomatic flurry which blew up in 1911 over Argentine-American competition for Brazilian flour trade was promptly calmed. American exporters had long enjoyed a 20 per cent differential in Brazilian flour duty. When the United States secured an increase to 30 per cent, the

[56] *For. Rel., 1896*, pp. 1-2; *Memoria, 1897*, pp. 70-84; Francis B. Loomis, Act. Sec. of State, to Daniel Mayer, Consul at Buenos Aires, Aug. 5, 1903, NA, DS, Inst. to Con., B. A., Vol. 188, pp. 211-212; Secretary of State to Richard Bartleman, Consul General, Aug. 28, 1913, NA, DS, 635.11/2a.

[57] *The Buenos Aires Herald*, April 5, 1899.

[58] U.S. Federal Trade Commission, *Food Investigation: Report of the Federal Trade Commission on the Meat-Packing Industry*, I, 164-165, 174-175.

[59] Alban G. Snyder, Consul General, to Asst. Sec. of State, March 18, 1907, NA, DS, Minor File, 1906-10, X; various despatches in Num. File, Vol. 966, case 16563, and Dec. File, 600.1156 and 611.3556.

Argentine government threatened to raise duties on American petroleum, lumber, and other staples. This threat brought from the State Department the formal declaration that it had no thought of seeking further concessions and would give Argentina six months' notice of any future negotiations.[60]

Until World War I, inadequate shipping facilities continued to molest the movement of mails and cargoes. The American flag remained singularly absent from Argentine harbors. In 1908 only four American sailing vessels, with a total tonnage of 4,074, arrived at Buenos Aires.[61] Of 28,303 arrivals in the three years before the outbreak of war, only two steamers and thirty sailers were American.[62] Ship subsidy bills were passed by the Argentine Congress in 1905 and introduced into the American Congress in 1905 and 1914, but with no more success than the first Argentine offer of 1865.[63] Supported at every step by the Department of State, the Central and South American Telegraph Company worked to complete the coveted all-American Atlantic cable to Argentina or even to improve its sea-land connection through Valparaiso. All its efforts to improve communications were fruitless.[64]

Some Argentine leaders, including President Victorino de la Plaza, advised Americans that they could expect to strengthen reciprocal interests with Argentina only by investing capital, as the British had done for a century.[65] If this were true, the American case at the moment was not hopeful. By 1913, its financiers had invested only $40,000,000, principally in meat packing, to compete with the British $1,860,700,000. As to government securities, only one Argentine issue had been floated in New York, that a mere one-fifth of the £10,000,000 internal loan of 1909.[66]

The complete lack of American banking facilities until 1914 continued to force American business to operate through English and German bankers and to pay the tribute exacted. This situation, however, was finally remedied on November 10, 1914, when under the Federal

[60] Unsigned *aide-mémoire*, June 13, 1911, NA, DS, 611.3231/210. See also *For. Rel., 1911*, pp. 30-34, and *Memoria, 1910-1911*, pp. xxi-xxii.

[61] Snyder to Asst. Sec. of State, Jan. 14, 1909, NA, DS, Num. File, Vol. 183, case 1700/83-96.

[62] Brady, *op. cit.*

[63] *Diario de sesiones de la Cámara de Diputados, 1905*, II, 121-127; *Cong. Rec.*, 59 Cong., 1 sess., XL, pt. 1, p. 526, and 63 Cong., 2 sess., LI, pt. 13, pp. 13134-13141, 13276. In his annual messages of 1907 and 1908, President Roosevelt called attention to the problem (Richardson, *op. cit.* [Washington, 1913], X, 7487, 7611).

[64] The voluminous correspondence on this subject after 1910 is found in NA, DS, 832.73.

[65] Roger Babson, *The Future of South America*, p. 42; Pan American Union, *Proceedings of the Pan American Commercial Conference, February 13-17, 1911*, p. 42.

[66] Max Winkler, *Investments of United States Capital in Latin America*, pp. 284-285; Peters, *op. cit.*, p. 76.

Reserve Act the National City Bank of New York established the first American branch bank in Buenos Aires.[67]

All the former criticisms of American business methods—short term credits, disregard of local desires, nonfulfillment of contract terms, failure to send personal agents—continued to be heard. "It cannot be denied," wrote an American chargé,

> that an American firm which writes a letter in English from its home office and accompanies it with a catalogue printed in the same language, quoting prices in dollars and cents, weights in avoirdupois and measurements in feet and inches, labors at a disadvantage in competing with a firm which has an agent on the ground to explain and demonstrate his wares.[68]

These, of course, were the complaints of American diplomats in all parts of the world.

Throughout the nineteenth century the two maturing republics sought without success to find a common basis for commercial exchange. Despite the growth of population, domestic stability, and national incomes, their economies remained essentially competitive, their reciprocal trade unproductive. But toward the end of the century leaders in the two countries envisioned divergent national horizons. Pursuit of these horizons led inexorably in the early twentieth century to the emergence of economies which were more nearly complementary. The greatest obstacle to trade expansion was similarity of environments. The greatest stimulant was the evolution of national disparities in manufacturing skills, entrepreneurial ambitions, and stages of industrial development. The economic demands of World War I and the booming twenties would put the new relationship to severer test.

---

[67] W. S. Robertson, *Hispanic-American Relations with the United States*, p. 272. The First National Bank of Boston followed in July, 1917 (*Bulletin of the Pan American Union*, XLVI, p. 97).

[68] Robert W. Bliss, Chargé d'Affaires ad interim, to Secretary of State, Jan. 23, 1911, NA, DS, 635.29/no document number. For the friendly criticism of the Argentine Ambassador on this subject, see Rómulo S. Naón, "Trade Expansion with Argentina," in *The Pan-American Magazine*, XX (March, 1915), 10-16.

X V I

PARTNERSHIP IN PEACEFUL SETTLEMENT: ARGENTINE BOUNDARIES, 1878-1899

In seeking a common basis for the promotion of mutual trade, Argentina and the United States frequently contended over vital national interests. In its initiation and extension of the Pan American idea, the United States recurrently encountered Argentine skepticism of its intentions and obstructionism to its projects.[1] In these areas, the two nations were at best healthy competitors, at worst stubborn rivals. In spite of disagreements over these basic national policies, however, their record of collaboration in another direction—the maintenance of Western Hemisphere peace—was extensive and salutary. In the first century of their relations, they were often partners in the promotion of peaceful settlement.

Both nations were signatories to pacts creating peace machinery in the Americas. The two collaborated, with each other and with others, in extending good offices to third parties among the American states. Each nation accepted the mediation of the other in international disputes and, in the case of Argentina, in a domestic problem. Each, in good grace, accepted the other as arbiter of vital national interests.

Diplomatic controversies over the rights of nationals or over the sovereign rights of nations were rare. A few small financial claims involving damages to property of American citizens were settled, though sometimes very slowly, through routine negotiation. Only in the case of the Paraguayan War did the United States vigorously protest violation of its diplomatic rights. Only as a result of the Falkland Islands incident did Argentina claim damages to the property of its nationals or violation of its sovereign rights. Indeed, the Falklands affair was the only serious exception to a century of cooperation in the encouragement of peace in the Hemisphere.

[1] See below, Chapter XVIII.

The Record of Peaceful Collaboration

On at least fifteen occasions before World War I the two nations, or their representatives, collaborated to promote the spirit of peaceful settlement. American agents recurrently used the prestige or the good offices of the United States to assist Argentine resolution of troublesome questions: Commodore Nicolson during the French intervention (1839); Brent and Wise during the Anglo-French blockade (1845-1846); Yancey during the strife between the Argentine Confederation and the Province of Buenos Aires (1859); Seward and his agents in the early months of the Paraguayan War (1865-1866); and the Taft administration at the time of the Argentine-Bolivian break in 1909-1910.[2] In several other instances the United States indicated its availability to serve as mediator.

Argentine leaders twice served as mediators of disputes involving the United States: General Urquiza during the 1859 negotiations with Paraguay and Romulo S. Naón, in conjunction with Brazilian and Chilean representatives, in the 1914 controversy with Mexico. In 1909 the United States approved Argentine jurists as members of commissions to arbitrate pecuniary claims of its citizens against Venezuela and national counterclaims against the British position on North Atlantic fisheries.[3]

On two occasions, both in 1910, the two nations joined in extending their good offices to aid in the adjustment of perennial boundary disputes: between Ecuador and Peru and between Peru and Chile.[4] That most of these efforts, Argentine and American, resulted in failure or only partial success did not negate the tradition of peaceful settlement engendered.

By far the most important of the conciliatory services, certainly the most successful, were the American contributions to the settlement of Argentina's boundaries.[5] Between 1878 and 1899, through its chief executives or its diplomatic agents, the United States participated in the adjudication of the greater portion of Argentina's long-unfixed territorial claims against neighboring states. In 1878 and 1895 Presidents Hayes and Cleveland were the arbiters of Argentine claims to territories contested by Paraguay and Brazil.[6] In 1881 Thomas O. Osborn and Thomas A. Osborn, Ministers in Buenos Aires and Santiago, were indispensable links in the negotiation of an Argentine boundary treaty with

[2] See above, pp. 126-127, 133-135, 153-155, 194-200, and below, pp. 266-267.
[3] See above, pp. 172-176, and below, pp. 271-274.
[4] See below, pp. 267-271.
[5] Paul D. Dickens, "Argentine Arbitrations and Mediations with Reference to United States Participation Therein," *The Hispanic American Historical Review*, XI (Nov., 1931), 464-484.
[6] See above, pp. 204-207, and below, 246-250.

Chile. Finally, at the end of the century, the same governments invited an American, William I. Buchanan, to sit on a three-man commission to iron out wrinkles in the Andean boundary line.

The Ministers Osborn and the Chilean Boundary

None of Argentina's boundaries was as difficult to adjust as that with Chile. None was as productive of diplomatic controversy and threat of conflict. At two critical stages—the 1881 negotiations over the Andean border, Patagonia, Tierra del Fuego, and the Strait of Magellan and the 1899 conferences on the northernmost three hundred miles of frontier—American ministers were key figures in the settlements.

Under Spanish dominion, Argentina had been the heart of the Viceroyalty of the Río de la Plata, Chile the southern extension of the Viceroyalty of Peru. After 1810 the boundary between the colonial provinces, vaguely fixed, was accepted as the border between the independent states. These limits crowded the Chilean population into the narrow corridor between the mountain wall and the Pacific, comprising desert to the north and fog-bound islands to the south. Along the tumbled Andean Cordillera and along the strategic Strait of Magellan ownership of numerous focal points remained to be determined.

Chile moved first to affirm its claims in the southernmost regions. In 1843 it established a settlement on Brunswick Peninsula. Claiming the entire peninsula, Argentina in 1847 protested the action but took no overt countermeasures. Two years later Chilean settlers began to move into the area of Punta Arenas, midway along the strait. When the two nations signed a general pact of friendship in 1855, they recognized the boundaries of 1810 and agreed to eventual arbitration of any questions that could not be settled peaceably as they arose.[7]

Soon, however, in search of guano and coal Chileans began to probe the area north of the strait, while the Araucanian Indians spilled over the mountains into Southern Patagonia. Meanwhile, their southward advance blocked until Roca's defeat of the Indian menace, the Argentines grew increasingly concerned over Chilean incursions. A series of conferences and proposals in the late seventies ended in stalemate.[8] By 1879, as Argentina appeared to be preparing for conflict, hostilities threatened.[9] Before it could act, however, internal political strife inter-

---

[7] For Argentine interpretations of the background, see [Bernardo de Irigoyen], *La cuestión de límites entre la República Argentina y Chile,* and Luis V. Varela, *Histoire de la démarcation de leurs frontières despuis 1843 jusqu'a 1899.* For the Chilean side, see Diego Barros Arana, *Exposición de los derechos de Chile en el litijio de límites sometido al fallo arbitral de S. U. B.*

[8] Estanislao S. Zeballos, *Demarcación de límites entre la República Argentina y Chile,* pp. 5-6; T. H. Holdich, *The Countries of the King's Award,* p. 1.

[9] T. O. Osborn to W. M. Evarts, Secretary of State, June 12, July 31, 1879, NA, DS, Desp. Arg., XXII.

vened to weaken national unity, while impending war with Peru impelled Chile to make concessions to its eastern neighbor. Neither had diplomatic representation in the capital of the other. Sensing this propitious atmosphere, the American Ministers in Buenos Aires and Santiago moved promptly to facilitate a settlement. They made themselves as indispensable to "The Wire Treaty" as the telegraph lines between the two capitals.[10]

The Ministers Osborn were diplomats of long residence in the nations to which they were accredited. Thomas O. had served in Buenos Aires since 1873, Thomas A. in Santiago since 1877. Thomas O., a Chicagoan, had served through the Civil War as an infantry commander, ultimately brevetted major general for bravery in action. After some years in the Illinois Senate, he accepted diplomatic assignment under Grant.[11] Thomas A. was a Pennsylvanian who in 1857 migrated to Kansas. Within fifteen years he became state senator, organizer and director of the Northern Kansas Railroad Company, and, at thirty-six, governor. His extended travels, wide associations, and calm manner made him well-suited for a diplomatic post. In October, 1880, aboard the U.S.S. *Lackawanna*, he presided over the abortive American attempt to end the War of the Pacific.[12]

Soon after return from this mission, Thomas A. Osborn interviewed President Aníbal Pinto about the Argentine boundary problems. The President revealed Chilean eagerness for peaceful settlement and willingness to arbitrate all questions. The arbitrable questions, he felt, might be those stated in the Treaty of 1855 or those formulated by the president of the United States or by the arbitrator. On November 15, 1880, Thomas A. despatched these views to Thomas O. in Buenos Aires.[13] After consulting President Roca and his cabinet, Foreign Minister Bernardo de Irigoyen agreed to the proposal for arbitration, but with the reservation that boundary questions only and not the whole of Patagonia be included. Thomas O. forwarded these reactions to his colleague in Santiago.[14]

For nearly four months Chile failed to respond to these overtures.

[10] Osborn used this expression in a despatch to Secretary James G. Blaine, Oct. 27, 1881, *ibid.*, XXIV.

[11] *The Washington Post*, March 28, 1904; *The Inter-Ocean* (Chicago), March 28, 1904. Remaining in Argentina after the end of his duty in 1886, Osborn secured a concession to build a link in the railway from Argentina through Bolivia to Peru.

[12] C. S. Gleed, "Thomas A. Osborn," in *Transactions of the Kansas State Historical Society, 1897-1900*, VI, 284-287; D. W. Wilder, *The Annals of Kansas*, pp. 955, 1055.

[13] Both ministers were extremely dilatory in reporting these and subsequent developments to Washington. See T. O. Osborn to Evarts, April 4, 1881, and to Blaine, July 1, 1881, NA, DS, Desp. Arg., XXIII; T. A. Osborn to Secretary of State, July 22, 1881, Desp. Chile, XXXI. Each of these despatches contained many enclosures; only the covering letters are printed in *For. Rel., 1881*, pp. 6-8, 134.

[14] Jan. 4, 1881, NA, DS, Desp. Arg., XXIII.

Meanwhile, as the Roca administration in Buenos Aires stepped up its war preparations, the Chilean Consul reported Argentine conviction that it should await further initiative from Santiago.[15] This was the moment General Osborn chose for action. Conceding his lack of authority from Washington, on April 5 he recommended to his counterpart that they tender their good offices, establish "lines" acceptable to each government, and after appraising national differences seek to prevent hostilities.[16] Thomas A. presented the proposition to Foreign Minister Melquíades Valderrama, who took three weeks to give assent.[17] Patiently awaiting Chilean action, Irigoyen promptly agreed, then offered the ministers free use of national telegraph lines. The General volunteered to send no wire without Irigoyen's prior approval.[18] Preparations were now complete for the negotiation of "The Telegraph Treaty." On almost a daily basis from May 9 to June 26 the ministers consulted the foreign secretaries in the two capitals and almost as frequently exchanged telegrams with each other.[19]

On May 9, in submitting the first definite proposals, Chile revealed its disposition to settle the entire boundary with Argentina. Valderrama proposed (1) that the Andean border from Bolivia south to 52° latitude should follow the *divortia aquarum* (watershed) of the Andes, (2) that the southern border across Patagonia should follow the fifty-second parallel to 70° longitude, then a deviating line to Cape Vírgenes on the Atlantic, (3) that all land west and south of the line except Staten Island should be Chilean, (4) that the Strait of Magellan should be neutralized, and (5) that the entire settlement should be definitive unless one party demanded arbitration.[20]

Within forty-eight hours, Irigoyen accepted points (1) and (4). Thus, the disputants were already in agreement on the long Andean boundary. As to the other points, Irigoyen proposed to substitute for Cape Vírgenes a point slightly to the south, Point Dungeness, and to submit all territory south of the Patagonian line to the arbitration of the president of the United States.[21] During the next three weeks, discussion focused on two questions, the location of the Patagonian line and the choice between

[15] Francisco de B. Echeverría to Minister of Foreign Relations, Jan. 22, Feb. 8, 1881, República de Chile, Archivo Nacional, Cónsules de Chile en el extranjero, 1881, XLVI.

[16] NA, DS, Desp. Arg., XXIII.

[17] T. A. O. to T. O. O., April 28, 1881, *ibid*.

[18] T. O. O. to Blaine, July 1, 1881, *ibid*.

[19] Copies of most of the telegrams were forwarded to the Department of State in T. O. Osborn's despatch of July 1. Many were printed in the annual volumes of the Ministries of Foreign Relations of Argentina (*Memoria, 1882*, pp. 3-37) and Chile (*Memoria, 1881*, pp. 132-168). In many cases where the dates do not agree I have used those of the manuscript copies in the Department of State archives.

[20] T. A. O. to T. O. O., May 9, 1881, NA, DS, Desp. Arg., XXIII.

[21] T. O. O. to T. A. O., May 11, 1881, *ibid*.

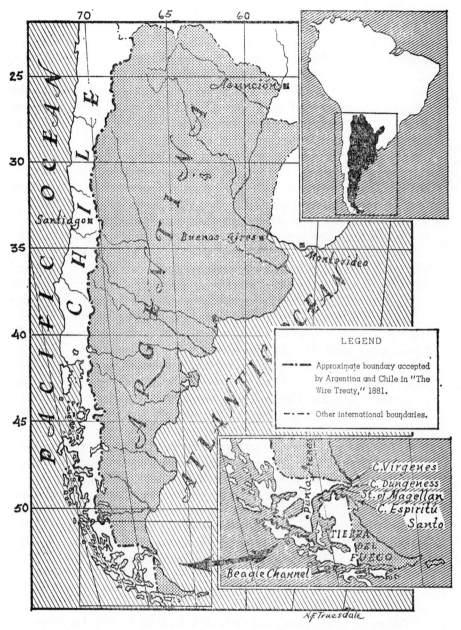

ARGENTINE-CHILEAN BOUNDARY SETTLEMENT, 1881.

arbitration and direct settlement. By the end of May, the nations compromised on the Patagonian boundary (as it exists today) and agreed to direct settlement.[22] President Pinto, addressing the Chilean Congress at this juncture, commented that Argentina had not unjustly pressed the boundary issue during Chile's war. The Chilean Consul in Buenos Aires believed that Argentina was willing to renew diplomatic contacts.[23] The Osborns were making progress.

Valderrama then prepared six formal bases which on June 3 he asked Thomas A. Osborn to forward to Buenos Aires. These bases, slightly amended upon Argentine insistence, became the basic text of the treaty soon to be signed: (Base 1) The mountain boundary from north to south shall follow the highest peaks of the cordillera "which divide the waters"; any question on the "water-parting" shall be resolved by two experts, one from each country, or in case of disagreement by a neutral expert. (Base 2) From the intersection of the mountain line and 52° latitude, the boundary shall be that already agreed upon. (Base 3) The island of Tierra del Fuego shall be divided by a line running from Cape Espíritu Santo south to the Beagle Channel, Chile to retain the western portion, Argentina the eastern; Chile shall also receive all islands south of the Beagle Channel to Cape Horn and west of Tierra del Fuego, and Argentina, Staten Island and adjacent islets. (Base 4) The same experts designated under Base 1 shall settle problems arising under Bases 2 and 3. (Base 5) The Strait of Magellan shall be neutralized and open to the ships of all nations. (Base 6) Any question subsequently arising shall be submitted to a friendly power.[24]

Within twenty-four hours Irigoyen announced that he would accept Valderrama's proposals if the Osborns could secure two minor amendments. He wished to have incorporated in Base 1 the clarifying expression "and shall pass between the slopes which descend one side and the other" and in Base 5 a more unequivocal prohibition of fortifications.[25] Valderrama accepted the first but was reluctant to agree to the second.[26] Aware of the deference which Irigoyen had shown repeatedly, General Osborn urged his namesake in Santiago to persuade the Chilean

[22] T. A. O. to T. O. O., May 18, 21, 28, 1881; T. O. O. to T. A. O., May 20, 23, 31, 1881, *ibid.*

[23] *Discurso de su excelencia el presidente de la República [de Chile] en la apertura del Congreso Nacional de 1881,* p. 4; Echeverría to Minister of Foreign Relations, May 16, June 1, 1881, RC, AN, Cónsules de Chile en el extranjero, 1881, XLVI.

[24] Valderrama to T. A. O., NA, DS, June 3, 1881, Desp. Arg., XXIII. See map and text, Gordon Ireland, *Boundaries, Possessions, and Conflicts in South America,* pp. 20-23.

[25] Irigoyen to T. O. O., June 4, and T. O. O. to T. A. O., June 6, 1881, NA, DS, Desp. Arg., XXIII.

[26] Valderrama to T. A. O., June 10, and T. A. O. to T. O. O., June 11, 1881, *ibid.*

Foreign Minister.[27] By June 26 a compromise statement was concluded [28] and on July 23 the treaty was signed.[29]

Meanwhile, in Washington Secretary Blaine had received Thomas O. Osborn's April 4th report of the situation and on June 13 advised both Osborns that the United States did not seek but would not refuse the position of arbitrator.[30] Even before the instruction was framed, however, the recipients had all but completed their self-assigned mission.

In Buenos Aires, Santiago, and Washington, Thomas O. Osborn, Thomas A. Osborn, and James G. Blaine received the most enthusiastic expressions of gratitude from Argentine and Chilean officials. In the Argentine view, by smoothing away difficulties and keeping negotiations under the influence of moderation and kindly feeling General Osborn had kept hopes for settlement alive.[31] But none of these sentiments is so rare in diplomatic annals as the special protocol, suggested by the Argentine Irigoyen, which was attached to the treaty and printed in official publications. In this protocol, the two signatories agreed that they

should express in this act and in the name of their respective governments the deep appreciation in which they hold the benevolent assistance which the Most Excellent Ministers of the United States accredited to the Republic of Argentina and to that of Chile, Major General Thomas O. Osborn and Mr. Thomas A. Osborn, contributed to the negotiations which brought about the definitive agreement which they have just signed.[32]

Following the signature of the treaty on July 23, the two nations engaged in a three-month debate over which should ratify first.[33] Whether the point at issue was simply a misunderstanding or a matter of protocol is not clear. In any case, General Osborn urged both Irigoyen and the American Minister in Santiago, now General Judson Kilpatrick, to press

[27] Irigoyen to T. O. O., and T. O. O. to T. A. O., both June 14, 1881, *ibid.*

[28] T. O. O. to T. A. O., June 27, 1881, *ibid.*

[29] Osborn to Blaine, July 23, 1881, *For. Rel., 1881*, p. 9. The text of the treaty is found in República Argentina, *Tratados, convenciones, protocolos, actos y acuerdos internacionales*, VII, 118-121.

[30] *For. Rel., 1881*, pp. 6, 130-131.

[31] *Ibid.*, pp. 10-11, 15-17; República Argentina, *Memoria, 1882*, pp. 44-45, 125-127; NA, DS, Notes from Chil. Leg., IV; H. Mabragaña, *Los mensajes*, IV, 47; J. D. Richardson, *A Compilation of the Messages and Papers of the Presidents*, VIII, 42.

[32] República Argentina, *Tratados*, VIII, 121.

[33] Echeverría to Minister of Foreign Relations, Aug. 9, 12, 22, 26, Sept. 9, 12, 17, 22, 29, Oct. 4, 8, 11, 12, 17, 1881, RC, AN, Cónsules de Chile en el extranjero, 1881, XLVI; Valderrama to Echeverría, Aug. 20, Sept. 6, 10, 21, 1881, and José Manuel Balmaceda, Minister of Foreign Relations, to Echeverría, Sept. 21, 24, 1881, RC, AN, Correspondencias a los cónsules chilenos, 1879-1882, pp. 185-186, 188-192, 196-197.

for exchange of ratifications.[34] The exchange was consummated on October 22.

Argentina's controversy over its long frontier with Chile would again become acute in 1898, when another American minister would provide the leaven for settlement. In the meantime, its statesmen were free to attend to the shorter boundary with Brazil.

President Cleveland and the Brazilian Boundary

The Argentine Territory of Misiones lies like a scimitar along the flanks of Brazil's rich southern provinces. Thrusting upward between the Rivers Uruguay and Upper Paraná, its point aims at the Province of Paraná and its cutting edge brushes against Santa Catarina and Rio Grande do Sul. In 1895 President Grover Cleveland held in his hands the power to permit Argentina to force the weapon more deeply into the side of its neighbor. Instead, by awarding Brazil an area as large as Belgium, he prevented Argentina from dismembering Santa Catarina and crowding it into a two hundred-mile corridor along the Atlantic between the pastoral states of Paraná to the north and Rio Grande to the south.

Since the Papal Bull of 1493 and the Treaty of Tordesillas of 1494, the Misiones area had occupied a conspicuous place in the diplomacy of Hispanic Europe and Hispanic America. For three centuries it was a kind of American Alsace-Lorraine, a buffer between the westward march of Portuguese Paulistas and the eastward expansion of Spanish colonizers. Until the expulsion of the Jesuits in 1767 it was the scene of impressive mission activities among the Guaraní Indians. After independence, as Argentina and Brazil inherited the imperialistic pretensions of the Spanish and Portuguese, aggressive leaders sought to establish hegemony over the area. At the end of the century President Cleveland became the arbiter of the last unsettled boundary heritage of the four-hundred-year-old rivalry.

Beginning in 1750 the diplomats first of Spain and Portugal, then of Argentina and Brazil, negotiated treaty after treaty to settle their frontier line through Misiones. In the demarcation which followed the Treaty of Madrid (1750), the Iberian nations agreed that the boundary between the Uruguay and the Upper Paraná should be the Rivers Pepirí-Guazú, the San Antonio, and the Iguazú. This treaty annulled in 1761, the line was reaffirmed by the mother countries in the Treaty of San Ildefonso (1777) and by the daughter countries in the

---

[34] Osborn to Blaine, Oct. 8, 1881, and enclosures, NA, DS, Desp. Arg., XXIV; Balmaceda to Kilpatrick, Sept. 29, Oct. 12, 17, RC, AN, Diplomáticos extranjeros, 1880-1883, pp. 148-149, 158-161.

Treaty of Paraná (1857). In ratifying the Treaty of Paraná, the Argentines claimed that the Pepirí-Guazú and San Antonio were in reality two rivers two hundred miles east of those claimed by Brazil. In refusing to ratify, Brazil contended that these were the Chapecó and the Chopim. Argentina had introduced a Schoodiac-Magaguadavic (St. Croix) confusion involving four rivers instead of two. The nations were now in agreement that their boundary should follow the courses of the rivers Pepirí-Guazú and San Antonio and the highlands between their sources. Their only problem was to determine which pair of rivers legitimately bore those names.[35]

Between 1859 and 1885 both nations took steps to exercise control over the disputed area. In 1885 they created a mixed commission to explore and map all four rivers and the land between them.[36] Before the commission completed its work in 1891, however, two significant events occurred. In September, 1889, the nations signed a treaty which provided arbitration of the region by the president of the United States if friendly settlement did not follow within ninety days after announcement of the commission's report.[37] Four months later, following the collapse of the Brazilian monarchy, Argentine Foreign Minister Zeballos nearly effected a diplomatic coup which would have negated the arbitration agreement. He signed with the Brazilian Foreign Minister a treaty which divided the territory on a completely new basis, the watershed between the Uruguay and the Iguazú. This would have guaranteed Argentina roughly half the contested area. When the Brazilian Congress refused to approve, settlement reverted to the 1889 agreement on arbitration by the American president.[38]

The treaty of 1889 gave the arbiter an extremely clear-cut assignment. He had only to decide, according to the evidence submitted by the contestants, which rivers were the Pepirí-Guazú and San Antonio. But upon this simple decision rested the disposition of 12,000 square miles of territory considered of great strategic value by two highly competitive nations. It was the area bounded by the Uruguay to the south, the Pepirí-Guazú and San Antonio to the west, the Iguazú to the north, and the Chapecó and Jangada [39] to the east. A decision for

[35] This summary of the diplomatic background is based upon J. B. Moore, *History and Digest of the International Arbitrations to Which the United States Has Been a Party*, II, 1970-2020; Ireland, *op. cit.*, pp. 10-14; W. S. Robertson, *Hispanic-American Relations with the United States*, pp. 157-158.

[36] Repúblic Argentina, *Tratados*, II, 541-550.

[37] *Ibid.*, pp. 637-642.

[38] Ireland, *op. cit.*, p. 15.

[39] In 1888 Argentina had switched its claim from the Chopim to the Jangada, farther to the east (*Statement Submitted by the United States of Brazil to the President of the United States of America as Arbitrator . . .*, p. 2. Hereafter cited as *Statement Submitted by Brazil*).

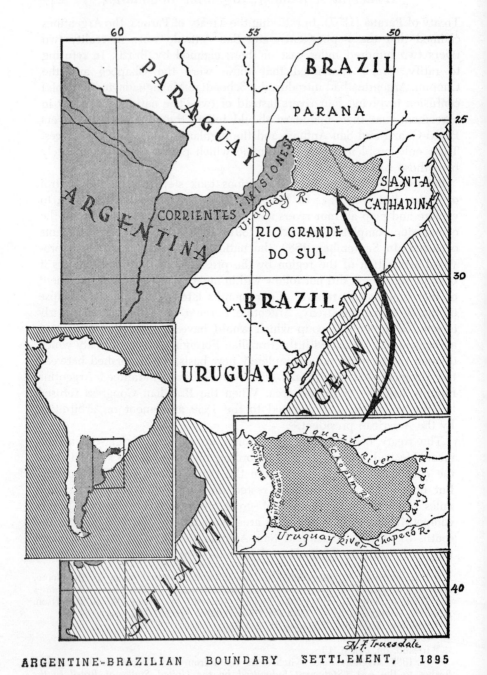

ARGENTINE-BRAZILIAN BOUNDARY SETTLEMENT, 1895

LEGEND ▨▨▨▨ Territory awarded to Brazil in arbitral decision of President Cleveland, 1895.

Map adapted from data in BOUNDARIES, POSSESSIONS, AND CON-, FLICTS IN SOUTH AMERICA, by Gordon Ireland. Copyright, 1938. By permission of The President and Fellows of Harvard College.

the Argentine line would deprive Brazil of virtually half the Province of Santa Catarina (as constituted today), permit Argentina to drive a formidable wedge between the two largest states of South Brazil, and move its rival to within two hundred miles of the Atlantic in the center of Brazil's pastoral heartland. A decision for the Brazilian contention would be less damaging, strategically, to Argentina, though wounding to its national pride and territorial ambitions. These were the alternatives placed before the president of the United States.

Contrasting with the initiative of the Osborns in the 1881 dispute over the Chilean boundary, the American opportunity to serve the cause of Hemisphere peace in this instance came wholly without solicitation. Argentine and Brazilian invitations to serve as arbitrator arrived from Presidents Carlos Pellegrini and Floriano Peixoto in April, 1892. President Harrison accepted at once.[40] Since the litigants had twelve months following receipt of the acceptance in which to file their cases, the decision became the responsibility of President Cleveland.

On February 10, 1894, the disputants presented their arguments, accompanied by voluminous documents and maps. Chief of the Brazilian delegation to Washington was the Baron Rio Branco, son of an illustrious Empire statesman. His case was a brilliant exposition.[41] Chairman of the Argentine commission was Estanislao Zeballos, exponent of Argentine opposition to McKinley reciprocity in 1891. As Foreign Minister, Zeballos had negotiated the 1889 arbitration treaty with the Empire. Now, as newly appointed Minister to Washington, he presented the Argentine case under the treaty he had initialed.[42] In addition to his official brief, Zeballos published in New York and Buenos Aires a volume designed to rebut the Brazilian case and to influence public opinion throughout the Hemisphere.[43]

As directed in the 1889 treaty, President Cleveland announced his award on February 5, 1895, a year after the presentation of the briefs. His decision was in favor of the westerly system of rivers, those claimed by Brazil.[44] The American President, therefore, denied to Argentina possession of the entire area in dispute. The Brazilian authorities and

[40] *For. Rel., 1892*, pp. 1-4, 17-19.

[41] *Statement Submitted by Brazil;* Moore, *op. cit.,* II, 1989-2020.

[42] *Argument for the Argentine Republic upon the Question with Brazil in regard to the Territory of Misiones, Submitted to the Arbitration of the President of the United States, in Accordance with the Treaty of September 7, 1889;* Moore, *op. cit.,* II, 1970-1989. See also Zeballos, *Cuestiones de límites entre las Repúblicas Argentina, el Brazil y Chile.*

[43] *Arbitration of Misiones. Statement Made by the Late Minister of Foreign Affairs of the Argentine Republic to Refute Mistakes of Brazilian Origin and to Enlighten Public Opinion in South and North America.*

[44] Moore, *op. cit.,* pp. 2020-2023; República Argentina, Ministerio de relaciones exteriores y culto, *La frontera argentino brasileña,* II, 129-133; Richardson, *op. cit.,* IX, 626.

people, of course, received the award with great rejoicing.[45] Argentina acknowledged the President's services with formal thanks but with none of the enthusiasm which had hailed the work of the Osborns in 1881.[46] Several of the more sensational porteño newspapers severely criticized Zeballos for incapacity and Cleveland for favoritism toward the important Brazilian market. They argued against future arbitration of pending boundary disputes.[47] The more conservative papers, however, like *La Prensa* and *La Nación,* assumed that the President had acted upon the evidence.[48]

Minister Buchanan and the Puna de Atacama

The 1881 settlement, so enthusiastically hailed in Buenos Aires, Santiago, and Washington, did not bring an end to Argentine-Chilean boundary disputes nor to American participation in their resolution. Demarcation experts became impaled on divergent interpretations of the treaty phrase "the most lofty peaks of the Cordillera which divide the waters." [49] Argentina persisted for the chain of highest peaks; Chile claimed the line of the watershed. The implementing conventions of 1888 and 1895 and a clarifying protocol in 1893 failed to allay popular animosities or the recurrent threat of war.[50]

In a new convention signed on April 17, 1896, the nations sought to narrow the area of their disagreement. Any differences which arose over the mountain frontier south of latitude 26° 52' 45" were to be submitted to the British government for arbitration. North of that point to the 23° parallel, a distance of about three hundred miles, the boundary was to be worked out in conjunction with Bolivia.[51] The region between 23° and 26° 52' 45" was the bleak, largely uninhabited plateau, the Puna de Atacama.

The Puna is a South American Tibet, a vast, forbidding wasteland lying at the northwest angle of Argentina's frontiers with Chile and Bolivia. Scanty in water, sparse of vegetation, poor in resources, it

[45] President Prudente J. de Moraes Barros to President of the United States, Feb. 14, 1895, NA, DS, Notes from Bra. Leg., VII; T. L. Thompson, Minister to Brazil, to W. Q. Gresham, Secretary of State, Feb. 15, 1895, Desp. Bra., LVIII.

[46] Amancio Alcorta, Minister of Foreign Affairs, to Zeballos, April 3, 1895, NA, DS, Notes from Arg. Leg., IV; Mabragaña, *op. cit.,* V, 214.

[47] Buchanan to Gresham, Feb. 11, 1895, NA, DS, Desp., Arg., XXXI; *The Southern Cross,* Feb. 8; *Tribuna, El Tiempo,* and *The Standard,* all Feb. 7.

[48] Feb. 7 and Feb. 8, 1895.

[49] See above, p. 244.

[50] República Argentina, *Tratados,* VII, 144-150, 151-156, 182-183. These and subsequent agreements are helpfully summarized in Ireland, *op. cit.,* pp. 19-27.

[51] *Ibid.,* pp. 184-186.

offers no attractions to man or beast. In 1898 fewer than a thousand primitive Indians braved alternate frigid blasts and scorching sun to eke out a wretched existence.

The twelve-thousand-foot floor of the Puna is dissected by a maze of lofty ridges and pierced by snow-capped peaks reaching more than sixteen thousand feet. Surrounded by the two great spinal columns of the Andean Cordillera, the Puna's drainage system is independent of the continental divide. Since its waters drain into neither the Atlantic nor the Pacific, the 1881 principle of the *divortia aquarum* offered no solution to the boundary question.[52]

Argentina, Bolivia, and Chile had laid claim to the Puna de Atacama since the expulsion of Spain. After decades of negotiation, Bolivia in 1889 ceded its rights to Argentina. But Chile, whose troops had occupied the area during the War of the Pacific, was not a party to that treaty and refused to recognize the validity of Argentina's title.[53] Thus, its disposition unresolved by the 1881 treaty, the Puna became the symbol of Argentine-Chilean national fervors and the subject of separate diplomatic settlement.

The controversy reached its most ominous phase between June and November, 1898. The Chilean Foreign Minister, J. J. Latorre, reporting to Congress in June, produced the impression that Argentina was responsible for the delay in boundary demarcation. When the Argentine Minister took umbrage, several exchanges of sharp notes followed.[54] Only prompt and effective diplomatic action in Santiago, Washington, London, and Buenos Aires prevented resort to arms. To calm the troubled atmosphere the Foreign Minister decided to solicit the assistance of the United States. On July 25, he directed Minister Eliodoro Infante to suggest discreetly that the United States might find it opportune to repeat its 1881 tender of good offices. But he must assure that any American offer appear spontaneous and not the result of Chilean solicitation.[55]

In a series of conferences lasting until August 6, Infante learned that the State Department was reluctant to trespass upon Great Britain's position as arbitrator. Moreover, it did not wish to intervene in any controversy unless the situation were extremely grave nor to join

---

[52] Holdich, *op. cit.*, pp. 22-24; *Chilo-Argentine Boundary. The Puna de Atacama. Memorandum Presented by the Government of Chile to the Government of the United States of America*, pp. 1-3. (Hereafter cited *Chilo-Argentine Boundary*.)
[53] *Ibid.*, pp. 3-4, 23-24; Ireland, *op. cit.*, pp. 3-6.
[54] Norberto Piñero, Argentine Minister to Chile, to Latorre, June 20, July 11, 1898; Latorre to Piñero, June 21, July 12, RC, AN, Gobierno y legación de la República Argentina en Chile, 1898 a 1899.
[55] Infante to Minister of Foreign Relations, Aug. 9, 1898, RC, AN, Legación de Chile en los Estados Unidos de Norte América, 1898, II.

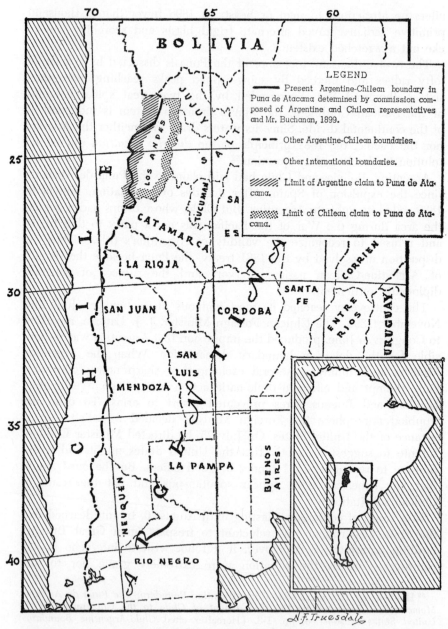

ARGENTINE-CHILEAN BOUNDARY SETTLEMENT, 1899.

Map adapted from data in BOUNDARIES, POSSESSIONS, AND CONFLICTS IN
SOUTH AMERICA, by Gordon Ireland. Copyright, 1938. By permission of The
President and Fellows of Harvard College.

Germany or any other power in seeking to settle problems of third parties.[56] On July 29, nevertheless, as he directed Ministers in Buenos Aires and Santiago to urge speedy arbitration, Secretary William R. Day confidentially advised them of American willingness to respond to an invitation for assistance.[57]

In relaying Day's hopes for settlement by arbitration, Ministers William I. Buchanan and Henry L. Wilson found both governments eager to avoid hostilities. They observed, however, that passions continued to rise and relations to deteriorate. Wilson in Santiago suspected Argentine intransigence. Buchanan in Buenos Aires believed that Chile was seeking to bring about arbitration of the entire frontier rather than of specific differences.[58] During late August and most of September, he was in daily touch with Foreign Minister Amancio Alcorta. He held conferences with the Chilean Minister.[59] Meanwhile, the State Department ascertained that Britain had no objections to American interposition.[60]

In September the center of diplomatic jockeying returned to Santiago, where the limits commissioners labored day by day to find the key that would halt troop movements and naval preparations. A ray of hope flickered on September 15, when the Chilean Foreign Minister tentatively acceded to Argentine insistence upon separate treatment of the Puna de Atacama.[61] But the nations endured another six weeks of tension before the diplomats succeeded in framing a specific plan.[62] By agreement of November 2 an international conference of ten delegates, five from each nation, was to meet in Buenos Aires to trace the Atacama line. If not successful after ten days of study, its task should be turned

---

[56] *Ibid.*

[57] *For. Rel.*, 1898, p. 1.

[58] Wilson to Latorre, Aug. 1, 6, 1898, RC, AN, Gobierno y legación de los Estados Unidos de Chile, 1898; Buchanan to Day, Aug. 5, 1898, NA, DS, Desp. Arg., XXXVI; Wilson to Day, Aug. 8, 1898, Desp. Chile, XLVI.

[59] Buchanan to Day, Sept. 22, 1898, NA, DS, Desp. Arg., XXXVII; Chilean Minister of Foreign Relations to Joaquín Walker M., Minister to Argentina, Aug. 29, 1898, RC, AN, Copiador oficios diplomáticos chilenos, 1898, I.

[60] J. B. Moore, *A Digest of International Law . . .* , VI, 435-436; Carlos Morla Vicuña, Chilean Minister to the United States, to the Minister of Foreign Relations, Sept. 22, 1898, RC, AN, Legación de Chile en los Estados Unidos de Norte América, 1898, II. At this stage the State Department was concerned over a rumor that Germany was exerting its influence in the South American dispute.

[61] *Memoria presentada al tribunal nombrada por el gobierno de Su Majestad Británica . . .* , I, viii; II, 1121 (hereafter cited *Memoria presentada por Argentina*); *Esposición que por parte de Chile i en respuesta a la esposición arjentina se somete al tribunal . . .* , V, 37. These memorials were also published in English (see Bibliography).

[62] Buchanan to Day, Sept. 22, 1898, NA, DS, Desp. Arg., XXXVII; Wilson to Day, Sept. 16, Oct. 31, 1898, Desp. Chile, XLVI.

over to a demarcation commission with definitive powers. The commission was to be composed of one Argentine, one Chilean, and the Minister of the United States to Argentina, William I. Buchanan.[63]

By naming Minister Buchanan as the third arbitrator the rival nations recognized the American contribution to the settlement of 1881. They also paid tribute to Buchanan's long and respected service in Argentina. President Cleveland had first appointed him to the post while he was still serving as director of the Departments of Agriculture, Live Stock, and Forestry of the World's Columbian Exposition in Chicago. Until his retirement in 1899, he was retained by President McKinley.[64]

This was but the first in his long series of diplomatic missions. He became "a sort of diplomatic free lance, always at the call of the State Department in Latin-American affairs."[65] After an interim as director-general of the Pan American Exposition in Buffalo, he became successively delegate to the Second Pan American Conference, first Minister to Panama, chairman of the delegation to the Third Pan American Conference, delegate to the Second Hague Conference, delegate to the Central American Peace Conference of 1907, and special commissioner to settle United States claims against Venezuela.[66] Alvey A. Adee, long-time career officer in the Department of State, believed Buchanan to possess more of the "instinct of diplomacy" than any man he knew.[67] Even before the agreement of November 2, the Chilean Minister in Washington had expressed his government's eagerness to secure Buchanan's services.[68] Later, the Argentine Minister requested permission to appoint Buchanan because he "enjoys the greatest esteem of the Argentine government for his high intellectual endowments and the precision and uniform tact of his official and private actions."[69]

The joint conference authorized in the November 2 agreement met in Buenos Aires in early March, 1899. When each proposal for tracing the line from 23° to 26° 52′ 45″ resulted in a vote of five to five, the demarcation commission of three was convened, affording Buchanan

[63] República Argentina, *Tratados*, VII, 212-218; *For. Rel., 1898*, pp. 179-181.
[64] A. W. P. Buchanan, *The Buchanan Book*, p. 472.
[65] This characterization of Buchanan was written by Huntington Wilson, Assistant Secretary of State (*The Chicago Daily Tribune*, Oct. 18, 1909).
[66] Buchanan, *op. cit.*, pp. 472-474.
[67] *The Evening Star* (Washington), Oct. 18, 1909.
[68] Memorandum of conversation between Chilean Minister and the Assistant Secretary of State, Oct. 31, 1898, NA, DS, Notes from Chil. Leg., VI; John Hay, Secretary of State, to Buchanan, Inst. Arg., XVII, 403.
[69] Martín García Merou to Hay, Dec. 15, 1898, *For. Rel., 1898*, pp. 2-3; Richardson, *op. cit.*, X, 176. Buchanan was not formally invited to accept the post of arbitrator until February 17, 1899 (Buchanan to Hay, Feb. 25, 1899, and enclosures, NA, DS, Desp. Arg., XXXVII; Hay to Buchanan, Feb. 23, 1899, Inst. Arg., XVII, 438-439; *Tratados*, VII, 229-231).

opportunity to play his decisive role.[70] He freely admitted his lack of scientific knowledge about the principles of *"divortia aquarum"* and the "mountain chain." But, once appointed to the commission, he read and reread, he said, "every book, pamphlet, report, study, and prominent newspaper or magazine article written on the subject." [71]

The commission held four sessions, on March 21, 22, 23, and 24. The Argentine and Chilean delegates, José E. Uriburu, former President, and Enrique MacIver, presented proposals for marking the Atacama boundary. Both plans were rejected, with Buchanan casting each deciding vote. The Minister then submitted his proposal—a division of the line into seven sections, with a separate vote on each. Four times Buchanan voted with the Argentine representative, twice with the Chilean. On one section, with the terminal points fixed, the vote was unanimous.[72] In this simple and expeditious fashion the respected American Minister resolved the troublesome question of the relatively worthless Puna de Atacama.

Popular approval of the commission's decision was by no means unanimous, either in Argentina or Chile, but again, as in 1881, the American Minister in Buenos Aires was officially acclaimed for removing grounds of misunderstanding between two American peoples.[73] Four months later, when he retired from his post, *La Prensa* remarked, "Mr. Buchanan embarked yesterday for the United States. The noble Minister was bid affectionate farewell by his many friends and acquaintances, and many of them accompanied him to the steamer." [74] Buchanan had helped to clear the atmosphere for acceptance of the King's Award of 1902 and for the erection of the "Christ of the Andes."

During the twenty years from 1878 to 1899 Argentina repeatedly called upon the United States to assist in adjustment of its frontiers. American

[70] *Memoria presentada por Argentina,* II, 1131-1134; *Tratados,* VII, 240-242; Buchanan to Hay, April 7, 1899, and enclosure, NA, DS, Desp. Arg., XXXIX.

[71] Soon after the completion of the commission's work, Buchanan prepared a forty-three-page report, in which he described the proceedings and his share in them (to Hay, April 7, 1899, NA, DS, Desp. Arg., XXXIX).

[72] The original minutes are filed in RC, AN, Legación de Chile en la Argentina, 1893-1907. Together with other official documents of the episode, Mr. Buchanan's original pencilled memorandum on the voting is bound in a letter book now filed in the collections of the Grosvenor Library, Buffalo, N. Y. ("Chilian-Argentine Boundary Arbitration: Private Papers, W. I. Buchanan, Deciding Member of the Commission, 1899"). See also *Tratados,* VII, 245-256; República de Chile, *Memoria, 1899,* I, 50-59; and *British and Foreign State Papers,* Vol. 96 (1902-1903), 379-383.

[73] Buchanan to Hay, and newspaper enclosures, NA, DS, Desp. Arg., XXXIX; Wilson to Hay, April 11, 1899, Desp. Chile, XLVI; García Merou to Hay, April 19, 1899, *For Rel., 1899,* p. 3; Mabragaña, *op. cit.,* V, 344.

[74] July 12, as quoted in François S. Jones, Chargé d'Affaires, to Hay, July 25, 1899, NA, DS, Desp. Arg., XXXVIII.

diplomacy contributed to the tracing of every mile of Argentina's borders except those with Uruguay and Bolivia. The United States had been both mediator and arbitrator. Though a few spokesmen alleged American partisanship toward Argentina's neighbors—and would continue to do so—the assistance of the United States, in the main, was accepted gracefully. Not every decision was definitive; still other arbitrations and adjustments would be necessary. But, during this epoch of their relations at least, the two nations often collaborated to promote the concept of inter-American peace.

X V I 1

PARTNERSHIP IN PEACEFUL SETTLEMENT: CONFLICTING DOCTRINES AND COOPERATIVE ACTIONS, 1900-1914

The record of Argentine-American collaboration in the promotion of peaceful settlement after 1900 is by no means as dramatic or significant as that of preceding decades. Early in the century a statesman of each nation conceived a new doctrine designed to protect small American states from belligerent intervention by European powers. Later, both nations participated in bilateral and multilateral attempts to create more effective peace machinery in the world. In the years preceding World War I each nation utilized its good offices to rescue the other from a vexatious controversy with a neighbor, and jointly they cooperated with Brazil to prevent hostilities among other American states. In none of these attempts to fortify the Hemisphere against strife, however, did Argentina or the United States enjoy spectacular success. The growth of each to a more dominant position in its own region, as well as allegiance to more urgent national policies, tended to chasten the enthusiasm of their cooperation.

Peace Doctrines and Peace Machinery

Since the mid-nineteenth century, joint efforts to maintain peace had been stimulated only by threats from within the Hemisphere. Moreover, in every instance of mediation or arbitration, one of the nations, usually Argentina, had been a party to the dispute. In enforcing the principles of Monroe, the United States did not invite Argentine assistance nor did Argentina ever formally volunteer its support. At the First Pan American Conference in 1889, the two states approved the principle of

257

arbitration for the Americas but could agree only on a mild, ineffective project.[1] Argentina there began to assert its leadership—to become so vigorous in the twentieth century—of Latin American opposition to any policy or project which might lead to foreign intervention and loss of national sovereignty.

To safeguard national control of their colonial economies and revolution-ridden governments against invasion of European capital, the Latin American states developed reliance upon the doctrine of sovereign immunity from external intervention. The combination of Argentina's own economic imbalance, political turbulence, and national aspirations to Latin American leadership contributed to its championship of the concept of equality of American states. As early as 1868, the Argentine jurist Carlos Calvo had projected the doctrine that alien investors had no recourse beyond the courts of the nation to which their capital migrated. It was wholly consonant, therefore, with national traditions and policies that another Argentine jurist, Luis M. Drago, should inject an extension of the Calvo Doctrine into the Venezuelan debt controversy of 1902.

The Anglo-German blockade of Venezuelan coasts, designed to force collection of debts owed European nationals, posed a challenge both to the American policy of the Monroe Doctrine and to the Latin American position on nonintervention. Conceivably, Venezuela could become a beachhead directed both against American supremacy in the Caribbean and against Argentine leadership in South America. As President Roosevelt acted for the United States, so Foreign Minister Drago spoke for Argentina and Latin America.

Drago first projected his concept of a nonintervention policy in a long despatch to Minister García Merou in Washington on December 29, 1902, for transmission to the Department of State. Acutely aware of the attractions of South American riches to the covetous eyes of European expansionists, he revealed his apprehension that official intervention to collect public debts from unstable American governments might conceal serious efforts to acquire territory. "The collection of loans by military means," he alleged,

> implies territorial occupation to make them effective, and territorial occupation signifies the suppression or subordination of the governments of the countries on which it is imposed. Such a situation seems obviously at variance with the principles many times proclaimed by the nations of America, and particularly with the Monroe Doctrine, sustained and defended with so much zeal on all occasions by the United States, a doctrine to which the Argentine Republic has heretofore solemnly adhered.

[1] See below, pp. 282-283.

Coming to the heart of his proposal, the Foreign Minister declared that

> the only principle which the Argentine Republic maintains and which it would, with great satisfaction, see adopted, in view of the events in Venezuela, by a nation that enjoys such great authority and prestige as does the United States, is the principle, already accepted, that there can be no territorial expansion in America on the part of Europe, nor any oppression of the peoples of this continent, because an unfortunate financial situation may compel some one of them to postpone the fulfillment of its promises. In a word, the principle which she would like to see recognized is: that the public debt can not occasion armed intervention nor even the actual occupation of the territory of American nations by a European power.[2]

This unsolicited and unanticipated support for the Monroe Doctrine, initiated by the nation most consistently opposed to inter-American action, focused Washington's attention upon its author. Only recently appointed to the post of foreign minister, Luis María Drago was virtually unknown outside his native land, though, as the grandson of former President Bartolomé Mitre, he came from eminent Argentine administrative lineage. He had served the bulk of his twenty-year public career as a judge of civil and criminal courts in the capital province. Deeply concerned with the life habits and thought patterns of the criminal classes, he had given little indication of the juridical abilities that would eventually win the respect of the United States and gain him a place among the world's leading international jurists. Impressed by his conduct at the Second Hague Peace Conference, the United States in 1909 would nominate him to arbitrate the pecuniary claims of its citizens against Venezuela and would later designate him one of the arbiters of the North Atlantic fisheries dispute with Great Britain.[3] To honor Dr. Drago's distinguished services in the cause of peace, Columbia University in 1912 would confer upon him an honorary doctorate of laws, and the Carnegie Endowment for International Peace would recognize him as "the highest exponent of the intellectual culture of South America."[4]

But in 1902 these expressions of American confidence in Drago's integrity remained for the future to unfold. In the midst of the Anglo-German threat to Venezuela, State Department officials missed the full import of the Argentine's memorandum. Concentrating upon envisioned European reaction against the projected policy, they apparently failed

---

[2] The entire note is printed in *For. Rel., 1903*, pp. 1-5. Also see W. P. Lord, Minister to Argentina, to John Hay, Secretary of State, Dec. 29, 1902, NA, DS, Desp. Arg., XLI.

[3] W. B. Parker, *Argentines of To-day*, I, 11-14. Drago resigned from the first appointment in order to serve on the fisheries case.

[4] *Ibid.*, p. 14. In 1920 Dr. Drago represented Argentina at the League of Nations.

to see it as the economic corollary to the Monroe Doctrine intended by Dr. Drago.[5] Mindful of possible future American need to intervene in the unstable Caribbean republics, they were unwilling to concede any modification of Monroe's unilateral policy.[6] In the depth of these concerns about possible European resentment and the protection of private American interests, they failed to assess Drago's overture for what it really was—a singular innovation in Argentine foreign policy. By proposing for the Western Hemisphere a policy of multilateral resistance to any European intervention to collect public debts, Luis Drago moved his nation closer to the concept of American regionalism than any of his predecessors or successors.[7]

In his memorandum, however, the Argentine foreign minister made no demand upon the United States for endorsement of his views. Nor did Secretary John Hay reply until late February when the Venezuelan problem was well on the way to settlement. In the meantime, the despatch was put through the mill of State Department analysis. "If the United States Government should definitely abandon all right of forcible intervention," advised Solicitor W. L. Penfield, "there are some communities, subject to the licentious sway of ephemeral rulers, in which Americans might henceforth be repeatedly and completely despoiled with impunity to the wrongdoers." Assistant Secretary Alvey A. Adee, urging emphasis upon American confidence in arbitration, recommended mere acknowledgment of the note without comment on the kernel of Drago's proposition.[8]

In his reply to the Argentine foreign minister, Secretary Hay followed Adee's recommendations. He quoted the state-of-the-union message of 1901, in which President Roosevelt had assured the Latin American states against loss of territory but not against other forms of punishment for their "misconduct." He repeated the President's guarantee of December 2, 1902, that "no independent nation in America need have the slightest fear of aggression from the United States." But the Secretary carefully side-stepped either approval or disapproval of Drago's overture.[9]

American public opinion, on the other hand, already aroused by the European threat against Venezuela, expressed enthusiastic concurrence

---

[5] Carlos A. Silva, *La política internacional de la nación Argentina*, p. 507.

[6] See below, pp. 261-262.

[7] For fuller development of this interpretation, see A. P. Whitaker, *The Western Hemisphere Idea*, pp. 87-88. Drago had even solicited Brazilian and Chilean support for his proposal (see Drago to José A. Terry, Argentine Minister to Chile, Jan. 20, 1903, Drago, *Discursos y escritos*, II, 68-69, and Silva, *op. cit.*, p. 506).

[8] Memoranda dated Feb. 5 and 6, 1903, NA, DS, Notes from Arg. Leg., V.

[9] *For. Rel., 1903*, pp. 5-6; J. D. Richardson, *A Compilation of the Messages and Papers of the Presidents* (Washington, 1913), IX, 6663, 6758.

in Drago's tentative proposals. Almost without dissent, leading newspapers from Boston to Los Angeles and from Minneapolis to Atlanta applauded them.[10] A writer in *The North American Review* optimistically asserted that "Our State Department must refrain, hereafter, from assisting our native creditors in the collection of ordinary debts from the Governments of Latin-American Commonwealths."[11] Because Argentina had never officially adopted the Monroe Doctrine, said *Harper's Weekly*, Drago's note marked "the beginning of an epoch."[12]

In Buenos Aires the American reaction was received with reciprocal enthusiasm. In his annual message of 1903, President Julio A. Roca expressed satisfaction that the Argentine note had not fallen into a vacuum, even though the United States had not committed itself to a policy on compulsory collection of public debts.[13] Foreign Minister Drago promptly published a book in which he reproduced the American press clippings with which García Merou showered him.[14] *La Nación* was convinced that popular support in the United States would "eventually lead the American Government to declare itself definitely in favor of our doctrine."[15]

The Drago Doctrine, of course, contributed nothing to settlement of the Venezuelan question. A distinguished American historian, who believes Argentine self-interest may have inspired the proposal, has characterized it as not particularly novel nor inevitably corollary to the Monroe Doctrine.[16] Nevertheless, at an opportune moment an Argentine foreign minister had outlined a clear-cut position from which the American states might resist European interventions. The forecast of *La Nación* was accurate. Ultimately the United States would endorse the principle, in substance at the Hague Conference of 1907 and without qualification in the Buenos Aires Declaration of Solidarity in 1936.[17]

But not yet prepared to surrender the right of intervention, the United States chose to shape its own policy on forceful collection of public debts. Secretary Hay's noncommittal note of February, 1903, left the door open for President Roosevelt to formulate a strictly American doctrine. This was the "Roosevelt Corollary of the Monroe Doctrine." The European powers could not intervene if they had no excuse for

---

[10] See quotations from numerous American newspapers in Drago, *La República Argentina y el caso de Venezuela*, pp. 246-294; García Merou to Drago, May 23, 1903, *Memoria, 1902-1903*, pp. 186-187; Edward W. Ames, Chargé d'Affaires ad interim to Argentina, to Hay, May 5, 1903, *For. Rel., 1903*, p. 6.
[11] Vol. 176 (March, 1903), 321-335.
[12] Vol. XLVII (March 28, 1903), 521.
[13] H. Mabragaña, *Los mensajes*, VI, 47-49.
[14] Drago, *op. cit.*
[15] May 3, 1903.
[16] Dexter Perkins, *The Monroe Doctrine, 1867-1907*, pp. 352-353.
[17] See below, pp. 263, 392.

intervening. By policing the Caribbean and strengthening impotent governments, the United States would prevent the financial defaults that might invoke the use of force. Roosevelt's agreements with the Dominican Republic, point of departure for subsequent interventions in the Caribbean, left no room for Argentine or inter-American cooperation.[18]

The immediate reaction to President Roosevelt's justifications of his policy did not portend the bitter indignation that was to flow in later years from the pens of Argentine publicists and from the mouths of Argentine statesmen. Though a sector of the press, led by *La Prensa*, was extremely critical, *La Nación* and other influential journals were extremely laudatory.[19] President Manuel Quintana expressed no misapprehension.[20] In a speech that prompted Secretary Elihu Root's personal thanks, Foreign Minister Carlos Rodríguez Larreta assured the Chamber of Deputies that he understood the Monroe Doctrine as a "doctrine of friendship" among the American republics.[21] Luis M. Drago, now an Argentine deputy, refused appointment as a delegate to the Third Pan American Conference because, among other reasons, he anticipated attacks upon Monroe's principles at the Rio assembly.[22] When, in his message to the Congress in 1906, President Roosevelt quoted Dr. Drago's views, the former Foreign Minister called in person at the American Legation to ask that his thanks be transmitted to the President.[23]

Roosevelt's reference to Drago was but one in a series of steps antecedent to partial recognition of the Argentine doctrine. At the Rio Conference the previous August, the United States had supported a resolution inviting the Second Hague Peace Conference to examine the question of forcible collection of public debts.[24] Secretary Root had won the favor of the Latin Americans when he declared that the United States deemed "the independence and equal rights of the smallest and weakest member of the family of nations entitled to as much respect

---

[18] S. F. Bemis, *The Latin American Policy of the United States*, pp. 156-159; Perkins, *op. cit.*, pp. 407-411.

[19] Issues of Dec. 8, 11, 1904; A. M. Beaupré, Minister to Argentina, to Hay, Dec. 12, 1904, and many newspapers enclosed, NA, DS, Desp. Arg., XLIV. Dexter Perkins has provided an interesting analysis of Argentine press reaction (*op. cit.*, pp. 451-454).

[20] Beaupré to Elihu Root, Secretary of State, Jan. 22, 1905, NA, DS, Desp. Arg., XLVI.

[21] Beaupré to Root, Oct. 24, 1905, *For. Rel., 1905*, pp. 48-49; Dec. 30, 1905, and enclosure, NA, DS, Desp. Arg., XLVI.

[22] Drago, *op. cit.*, pp. 80-85.

[23] Richardson, *op. cit.*, X, 7440; Beaupré to Root, Dec. 31, 1906, NA, DS, Minor File, 1906-1910, III.

[24] J. B. Scott, *The International Conferences of American States, 1889-1928*, pp. 135-136.

as those of the greatest empire." [25] Finally, the United States had exerted its influence to secure representation of the Latin American states at the Hague Conference. Luis Drago and Roque Saenz Peña were among the Argentine delegates.

But the Roosevelt administration had no intention of urging the Conference to endorse the Drago Doctrine in the spirit its author had conceived it. Already, by a succession of actions, it had made clear its unwillingness to approve the Argentine project in its pristine form, especially its absolute proscription on intervention and its proposal for multilateral enforcement. Secretary Hay's reply to Drago's note in 1902 had left the United States uncommitted. But two years later President Roosevelt's own corollary, while broadening the meaning of intervention, had reserved the right for exclusive use by the United States. Acting under Secretary Root's instructions at the Rio de Janeiro Conference in 1906, United States delegates successfully removed the Doctrine from Hemisphere jurisdiction. Moreover, the Argentine Foreign Office itself had retreated from the advanced position Dr. Drago had sought to establish. In instructions to its Rio delegation it viewed the Doctrine as properly a matter for global, not Hemisphere, application—an additional reason for Drago's refusal to serve.[26]

When, therefore, at the Hague Conference the United States delegation proposed a thinned-out version of the Argentine doctrine, Dr. Drago faced the necessity of defending his principles with less than wholehearted support from his own government. As introduced by General Horace Porter and eventually approved in Resolution II, the American proposal forbade the use of force to collect public debts—but only until arbitration or an arbitral award had been refused by the debtor state. To this perversion of his original project, Drago was not a silent witness. "At a memorable time," he declared in one of many speeches at The Hague,

the Argentine Republic proclaimed the doctrine which excludes from the American continent military operations and the occupation of territory having Government loans as their causes.

Although based on very serious and fundamental considerations, the principle here involved is one of policy and of militant policy which cannot be and which we shall not see discussed or voted on in this assembly.

I announce it, nevertheless, in order to reserve it expressly and to declare,

[25] Robert Bacon and J. B. Scott, *Latin America and the United States, Addresses by Elihu Root*, p. 10. Though not an official delegate to the Rio Conference, Root addressed the opening session. Some months later, in April, 1907, the American Society of International Law, with Root in the chair, adopted a resolution condemning the use of armed force to collect public debts (*La Prensa*, April 23, 1907).

[26] Mabragaña, *op. cit.*, VI, 167-168; White to Root, May 30, June 15, 1906, NA, DS, Desp. Arg., XLVIII.

in the name of the Argentine delegation, that the latter intends to maintain it as the political doctrine of its country with all the energy manifested in the dispatch sent on December 29, 1902, by our Government to its representative at Washington on the occasion of the Venezuelan episodes.

It is with this reservation which will be duly recorded and which relates to the public or national debt arising from Government loans, that the Argentine delegation will accept arbitration, thus doing fresh homage to a principle which its country has often endorsed.[27]

Though the Argentine delegation eventually approved Resolution II, it expressly attached the reservation that

public loans, secured by bond issues and constituting the national debt, shall in no case give rise to military aggression or the material occupation of the soil of *American* nations.[28]

By restricting application of his policy to American nations Dr. Drago achieved a passing victory over his fellow delegate, Dr. Roque Saenz Peña, veteran diplomat and frequent critic of the United States. To him

the doctrine and the note of 1902 should be, not a guarantee on behalf of South America against Europe, but a universal protection of all weak states against all strong states which might abuse their power in order to debase a sovereignty and which might declare war for a coupon.[29]

In further wrestling with the American resolution, Dr. Drago sought by amendment to salvage one other bit of consolation for himself and Argentina, the proviso that arbitration should be utilized only after recourse to the courts of the debtor country. Failing to secure passage of his amendment, he made this, too, a reservation to Argentine approval of the American proposition.[30] But, however hedged about, a convention admitting any right to resort to coercive measures was unpalatable to most Latin American leaders. Neither Argentina nor any other South American state ratified it.

Throughout its consideration of Dr. Drago's project, from 1902 to 1907, the Roosevelt administration had treated the foreign minister with circumspection. At each turn, it betrayed its determination to cling to the self-assigned right of intervention. In the end, by refusing to support the well-intentioned suggestions of an imaginative Argentine statesman, it frustrated a gesture that might have led to truer Argentine-

[27] Carnegie Endowment for International Peace, *The Proceedings of the Hague Peace Conference. The Conference of 1907*, II, 251.

[28] *Ibid.*, I, 549. Italics are mine.

[29] Argentine Republic, Delegación a la Segunda Conferencia de la Paz, *La República Argentina en la Segunda Conferencia Internacional de la Paz*, pp. 28-29. Dr. Saenz Peña did not use the accent mark on his paternal name.

[30] *Proceedings of the Hague Peace Conference*, I, 549.

American friendship and prompter Latin American acceptance of Western Hemisphere regionalism.[31]

Convention II embodied another clause which was to involve Argentine-American efforts to promote Hemisphere peace. This was the provision which created a procedure for arbitration, by a tribunal of five jurists, under the Permanent Court of Arbitration. As its members of the Court, Argentina named its perennial Minister of Foreign Affairs, Estanislao S. Zeballos, and three other veterans of diplomacy, all ex-foreign ministers, Saenz Peña, Rodríguez Larreta, and Drago.[32] Twice during 1909 the United States enthusiastically agreed to invite Dr. Drago to sit as the fifth jurist on troublesome disputes submitted to the Hague Court.[33]

Though both Argentina and the United States were signatories of the Hague Convention of 1907, they were not successful in consummating a bilateral treaty which would require them to submit their disputes to the peace machinery created under it. Late in 1908, the administration of President José Figueroa Alcorta willingly signed an arbitration convention. Like the twenty-four others negotiated by Secretary Root, it excluded from arbitration certain questions, particularly those affecting "the vital interests, the independence, or the honor" of the two nations. The succeeding administration, that of Saenz Peña, sought to substitute for the key phrase a new formula: "with the exception of those which might affect constitutional principles." This formula, argued the Argentines, was more precise, more judicial, and more acceptable to Argentine needs. Neither nation would recede from its established position.[34] Five years later, Secretary Bryan signed a conciliation or "cooling-off" treaty with Argentina, but it suffered a similar fate.[35] Both conventions were approved by the United States Senate, but ratifications were never exchanged.[36]

[31] Cf. Whitaker, *op. cit.*, pp. 96-97.

[32] Beaupré to Root, Aug. 9, 1907, and Sherrill to Knox, Aug. 29, 1909, and enclosures, NA, DS, Num. File, Vol. 216, Case 2098/58, 201-205, 228.

[33] See above, p. 259.

[34] Bemis, *The American Secretaries of State and Their Diplomacy*, IX, 225; NA, DS, Num. File, Vol. 955, Case 16210. A congressional leader of the opposition to the Root principle was Carlos Saavedra Lamas, son-in-law of President Saenz Peña and twenty-five years later Minister of Foreign Affairs (Robert W. Bliss, Chargé d'Affaires ad interim to Argentina, to Secretary of State, June 20, 1911, NA, DS, Dec. File, 711.3512/1).

[35] Bryan to Rómulo S. Naón, Argentine Minister to the United States, Jan. 23, April 18, 1914; George Lorillard, Chargé d'Affaires to Argentina, to Secretary of State, Sept. 19, 1914, NA, DS, 711.0012/249c, 512, 655a.

[36] Department of State, *List of Treaties Submitted to the Senate, 1789-1931*, pp. 12, 13.

The United States Assists Argentina

Just as presidents of the United States were called upon to arbitrate Argentina's boundaries, so was an Argentine executive invited to settle a limits question between Bolivia and Peru. In July, 1904, the two states invited President Roca to arbitrate their boundary northward from Lake Titicaca to the Brazilian Territory of Acre. The exact frontier had remained undetermined since colonial days. The end of Roca's term and the death of his successor, Manuel Quintana, left responsibility for the decision in the hands of José Figueroa Alcorta.[37]

President Figueroa's award of July 9, 1909, gave three-fifths of the disputed area to Peru. Discovering in advance the nature of the conclusions, Bolivia ordered its minister not to attend the formal promulgation of the decision. By drawing a new line instead of accepting the claim of one or the other disputant, alleged the Bolivian authorities, the Argentine President had exceeded his authority. In La Paz, inflammatory speeches incited mob action against the Argentine Legation and minister. On July 21, after ordering the Bolivian minister to leave within twenty-four hours, Argentina broke off all diplomatic relations. Bolivia retaliated with similar action.[38]

On the same day, without solicitation, American ministers in La Paz and Buenos Aires were invited by the Argentine and Bolivian governments to take charge of their respective legations. Cables from the two men, reaching Washington at almost the same moment, convinced Secretary Knox of the confidence of the two countries in the United States. He directed Charles H. Sherrill in Buenos Aires and James F. Stutesman in La Paz to accept the invitations but to restrict their activities to good offices on behalf of nationals and to avoid diplomatic representation of governments.[39] Fulfilling these instructions until the renewal of relations on January 9, 1911, the American ministers often became intermediaries between the estranged administrations.

The Republics of Chile and Peru, perpetual rivals for the good will of neighboring nations, separately sought authority to negotiate for a renewal of Argentine-Bolivian relations.[40] Bolivian leaders made it clear from the beginning, however, that they preferred the friendly offices of the United States. On at least five occasions between December, 1909,

[37] Gordon Ireland, *Boundaries, Possessions, and Conflicts in South America*, pp. 104-105.

[38] James F. Stutesman, Minister to Bolivia, to Secretary of State, Nov. 26, 1909, NA, DS, Num. File, Vol. 71, Case 534/143.

[39] *For. Rel.*, *1909*, pp. 10-11.

[40] Sherrill to Secretary of State, Dec. 2, 1909, NA, DS, Num. File, Vol. 1127, Case 22224/5.

and December, 1910, they invited, or revealed a willingness to accept, American intervention.[41] In each instance the Department of State indicated its desire to serve, but only on the formal request of each government.[42] Argentina, the offended nation, was in no hurry to act. It rebuffed successive Bolivian overtures, each transmitted through the American ministers.

Argentine authorities capitalized on every opportunity to postpone an adjustment. After awaiting publication of the Bolivian "Red Book" on the rupture, they challenged Bolivia's good faith. They refused to invite Bolivia to send delegates to the Fourth Pan American Conference to convene in Buenos Aires in July; through the American ministers they merely sent formal notice that the assembly would be held, then expressed resentment that Bolivia was not represented. The Argentine Senate deliberately rejected a protocol which would have adjusted a disputed boundary. President Figueroa felt that his administration could not overlook the insult which his own action had provoked. His successor, Saenz Peña, would make no advances.[43]

Eventually, toward the end of 1910, a former Bolivian president, José Manuel Pando, initiated direct negotiations with the Argentine Minister of Foreign Affairs to restore friendly relations.[44] It was still several months, however, before ministers were exchanged and the United States formally relieved of its Argentine responsibilities in La Paz. Though American agents took no part in the final settlement, Secretary P. C. Knox received effusive Argentine thanks for "great and friendly services" throughout the diplomatic break.[45]

The United States and Argentina Assist Others

In few seasons during a century and a half were Argentine-American relations more genuinely amicable than in the year 1910. While American representatives were assisting Argentina to adjust its disagreement with Bolivia, the two nations were working hand in glove to resolve two of the most enduring boundary disputes in the history of the Americas.

[41] Stutesman to Secretary of State, Dec. 30, 1909, Feb. 1, March 2, 1910, *ibid.*, no. 4, and Dec. File, 724.35/10, 11; Alexander Benson, Chargé d'Affaires to Bolivia, to Secretary of State, Oct. 25, Dec. 3, 1910, *ibid.*, nos. 24, 32.

[42] Knox to American Legation in La Paz, Jan. 4, 1910, and Knox to Sherrill, Feb. 14, 1910, NA, DS, Num. File, Vol. 1127, Case 22224/3, 9; Knox to Bliss, Nov. 14, 1910, Dec. File, 724.35/26.

[43] Sherrill to Secretary of State, Jan. 6, March 22, April 6, Aug. 13, 23, 1910, NA, DS, Num. File, Vol. 1127, Case 22224/6; Dec. File, 724.35/19, 20, and 724.3515/4, 5. See also Mabragaña, *op. cit.*, VI, 412-414.

[44] Bliss to Secretary of State, Nov. 8, Dec. 13, 1910, Jan. 10, 1911, NA, DS, 724.35/34, 36, 41.

[45] Naón to Knox, May 11, 1911, NA, DS, 701.3524/2.

These were Peru's controversies with Ecuador over their eastern limits and with Chile over Tacna-Arica. Both conflicts at times threatened South American peace.

Like almost every international boundary in South America, the Andean-Amazonian frontier between Ecuador and Peru had remained unfixed since independence. Finally, in 1904, the nations had submitted the area to the arbitration of the King of Spain. When reports reached Quito early in 1910 that the award would be unfavorable to Ecuador, a heedless press stimulated popular violence against Peru's Legation, consulates, and nationals. Typically, Peruvians in Lima and Callao attempted reprisals and the government ordered mobilization.[46]

With tension rising, both nations requested American assistance. On March 24 Secretary Knox instructed representatives in Lima and Quito, as well as in Buenos Aires, Petropolis, and Santiago, to confer with the various foreign ministers. He suggested that the United States or another disinterested nation bring together delegates of the disputants to discuss suspension of the King's Award and settlement by direct negotiations.[47]

From Buenos Aires Minister Sherrill reported the most enthusiastic spirit of cooperation. Its foreign commerce rapidly increasing, Argentina was eager to exert greater influence in international affairs. Already at loggerheads with Bolivia and Brazil, Argentine leaders were seeking friends. Foreign Minister Victorino de la Plaza, soon to be inaugurated vice-president, fell in completely with Knox's proposal. Not only did he approve the Secretary's policy, but, uniquely, he revealed his determination to follow American guidance "in all matters touching South American affairs." [48] De la Plaza's subsequent actions proved the sincerity of his words. On no fewer than fifteen occasions during the next ten months, he endorsed Knox's initiative and executed his requests. Throughout the mediation soon to be undertaken, it was Brazil, not Argentina, that obstructed progress.[49]

When reports of troop movements continued to reach Washington, Secretary Knox determined to move with despatch. On May 12, he cabled Department agents in Argentina and Brazil to propose a tripartite mediation with the United States. He suggested that the three nations present identical communications to the foreign ministers of Ecuador and Peru. If the two governments would agree to withdraw their armies from the frontier, suspend mobilization and other military preparations, and await developments, the three nations would seek a solution through mediation. The King's Award must not be repudiated in

[46] Ireland, op. cit., pp. 226-227.
[47] For. Rel., 1910, pp. 440-441.
[48] Sherrill to Knox, March 28, 1910, NA, DS, 711.35/14.
[49] The essential documents were published in For. Rel., 1910, pp. 461-507, and 1911, pp. 177-186, but many others are filed in NA, DS, Dec. File, Case 17554 and 722.2315.

advance. Mutual expressions of regret for acts of violence would be exchanged.[50] Within forty-eight hours both Argentina and Brazil accepted the invitation as well as the proposed text of the communication.[51]

Representatives of the mediating nations delivered the joint notes on May 22. Because the proposal implied settlement by arbitration, Peru accepted with enthusiasm; Ecuador, hoping for adjustment by direct negotiation, agreed more reluctantly.[52] Events then moved swiftly. Mindful of world opinion, Knox had already urged immediate publication of the notes. On May 28 he suggested that demobilization begin within a week. Four days later he recommended preparation of expressions of mutual regret.[53] With all of these proposals De la Plaza complied without the slightest compunction.[54] Moreover, through the Spanish minister, he undertook to persuade the King to resign his post as arbiter.[55]

In late June Secretary Knox presented to the other mediators the draft of a protocol for the signature of the contesting nations. The draft incorporated details of the mediation plan, together with statements of regret and readiness to arrange damages.[56] When in mid-July the three representatives submitted the protocol, Peru agreed to sign without reservation. Willing to express regrets but hostile to indefinite postponement of the boundary solution, Ecuador refused. Meanwhile, as Ecuador made no move to withdraw its frontier troops, Knox urged his fellow mediators to bring all possible pressure, Argentina through Chile, and Brazil through Bolivia and Colombia.[57]

Subsequent overtures by the mediators were equally abortive. Though Argentina secured the withdrawal of the King of Spain as arbiter, Ecuador remained intractable.[58] When in December, through Knox's initiative, the mediators proposed submission of the dispute to the Hague Court, Ecuador's blunt refusal cancelled Peru's acceptance.[59] Several

[50] *For. Rel., 1910*, pp. 449-450.

[51] Sherrill to Knox, and Irving B. Dudley, Ambassador to Brazil, to Knox, both May 14, 1910, *ibid.*, pp. 451-452.

[52] Leslie Combs, Minister to Peru, to Knox, May 23, 1910; *Aide-mémoire* to Ecuadoran Legation, June 1, 1910, *ibid.*, pp. 456, 463-464; Combs to Knox, May 23, 1910, NA, DS, Dec. File, Case 17554/168.

[53] Knox to Sherrill, May 15, 28, June 1, 1910, *For. Rel., 1910*, pp. 452, 460-461, 463.

[54] Sherrill to Knox, May 16, 29, June 3, 1910, *ibid.*, pp. 453, 461, 466.

[55] Sherrill to Knox, June 5, 23, 1910, NA, DS, Dec. File, Case 17554/221, 269.

[56] Huntington Wilson, Asst. Sec. of State, to Sherrill, June 23, 1910, and enclosure, *For. Rel., 1910*, pp. 475-476, 479-480.

[57] Wilson to Combs, July 14, 1910, and to Argentine Chargé d'Affaires, July 21, 1910, *ibid.*, pp. 485, 489-490; Wilson to Sherrill, Aug. 31, 1910, NA, DS, 722.2315/418A.

[58] William C. Fox, Minister to Ecuador, to Knox, Nov. 25, 1910, *ibid.*, no. 475.

[59] Knox to Bliss, Dec. 19, 1910, *For. Rel., 1910*, p. 504; Combs to Knox, Jan. 4, 1911, and Fox to Knox, Jan. 17, 1911, NA, DS, 722.2315/512, 519.

times during 1911 and again in 1913, foreign ministers of the three nations revived negotiations on the joint project. Slowly, however, without formal conclusion, the mediation faded out. The frontier would remain unsettled until 1942. Nevertheless, in the views of the presidents both of Argentina and the United States, the intervention of 1910 had prevented outbreak of hostilities that might have involved neighbor nations.[60]

In yet another instance in 1910 Argentina maintained its policy of intimate cooperation with the United States. This was the perennial conflict between Peru and Chile over Tacna-Arica, which flared up anew just as Peru became embroiled with Ecuador. Because of the three-nation mediation in the one conflict, it was natural that their intervention should be considered in the other. In the Peruvian view at least, Chile's support of Ecuador made the two problems logically inseparable.[61]

Since the War of the Pacific (1879-1883) the status of the parched coastal territory of Tacna-Arica had produced discord between Peru and Chile. Because the two nations could not agree on conditions of the plebiscite authorized in the Treaty of Ancón, Chile continued its occupation long after the ten years stipulated. Peru, however, never forfeited its claim and in 1910 severed diplomatic relations.

Finding themselves in diplomatic deadlock with neighbors north and south, the Peruvian leaders appealed to Brazil for assistance. Foreign Minister Rio Branco eagerly grasped the opportunity. Without first clearing his scheme with other nations concerned, he proposed that Chile join Peru in submitting the controversy to Argentina, Brazil, and the United States for decision.[62] When news of this overture leaked to Buenos Aires, De la Plaza was incensed that the Brazilian had offered the participation of Argentina without its express consent. It required several conferences in Buenos Aires and Washington, as well as a flurry of cables, to convince the Argentines that the Brazilian gesture was purely exploratory and that no action would be taken without Argentine acquiescence.[63]

The attitude of Argentina toward the Brazilian project conformed to the general policy it had followed since 1908—close cooperation with the United States.[64] As in the mediation of Peru's dispute with Ecuador,

[60] *For. Rel., 1911*, p. 4; Richardson, *op. cit.*, X, 8151-8152.

[61] William P. Cresson, Chargé d'Affaires to Peru, to Knox, March 19, 1910, and M. de Freyre, Peruvian Minister to the United States, to Act. Sec. of State, Oct. 26, 1911, NA, DS, 723.2515/111, 241.

[62] Dudley to Knox, March 17, 1910, *ibid.*, no. 110.

[63] Record of conversation between Act. Sec. of State and Argentine Minister, [no date]; Knox to Sherrill, April 1, 1910; Sherrill to Knox, April 1, May 2, 1910, *ibid.*, nos. 119, 129, 146, 161.

[64] On four occasions during 1908-1909, Argentine representatives had indicated their eagerness to proceed with the United States on the Tacna-Arica problem (NA, DS, Num. File, Vol. 131, Case 944/17, 44; Sherrill to Knox, Nov. 4, 1909, *ibid.*, Vol. 1137, Case 22715).

it would adhere to American leadership at every step, with or without Brazil. With Brazil alone, it would not participate.[65]

But the seeds Rio Branco sowed in Santiago fell on soil as barren as that of Tacna and Arica. Chile was not ready to join Peru in requesting mediation from Brazil or any combination of nations. The United States remained true to its policy of refusal to intervene in any controversy unless invited by all parties. Later, in 1911, 1914, and 1918, as tension over Tacna-Arica boiled up again and again, the possibilities of joint mediation were discussed, always with the same frustrating outcome.[66]

All efforts of the United States, working closely with the two most powerful South American states, to resolve two treacherous disputes were fruitless. Yet, significantly for Argentine-American harmony, the joint mediation and the projected intervention had demonstrated the ability of the two nations to cooperate closely in reinforcing Hemisphere peace.

Argentina Assists the United States

In their long series of mutual efforts to promote Hemisphere peace, Argentina had usually followed where the United States led. With the exception of General Urquiza in 1859,[67] no Argentine executive had tendered his nation's good offices to settle an American dispute, internal or international. Early in President Wilson's administration, however, the shoe was moved to the other foot. It was Argentina's friendly minister, Rómulo S. Naón, who in 1914 initiated Latin American aid to rescue the United States from its embroilment with Mexico.

At the moment of Wilson's severest tempest with General Victoriano Huerta, Minister Naón was nearing the middle of his eight-year mission in the United States. He had arrived in Washington in December, 1910; he was to remain throughout the difficult years of World War I. After the reciprocal elevation of legations in late 1914, he would become his country's first Ambassador to the United States. A former Superintendent of Public Instruction in his homeland, he would receive honorary degrees from both Harvard and Yale during the midst of the mediation negotiations he inspired. An expert in international law, he was motivated now to save the peace for two sister republics in North America. An Argentine who in 1913 alleged that Pan Americanism existed only in Washington took steps a year later to spread the ideal to South America.[68]

[65] Sherrill to Knox, March 28, April 1, 9, 12, 1910, NA, DS, 711.35/4; 723.2512/132, 135, 146.

[66] Correspondence on these instances is filed in *ibid.*, 723.2515. Also see *For. Rel.*, *1919*, I, 128ff.

[67] See above, pp. 172-177.

[68] Parker, *op. cit.*, I, 546-549; Frank H. Severance, "The Peace Conference at Niagara Falls in 1914," in Buffalo Historical Society, *Peace Episodes on the Niagara*, pp. 12, 52; George H. Blakeslee, *The Recent Foreign Policy of the United States*, pp. 134-135.

Woodrow Wilson's determination to stimulate the regeneration of Mexican politics through "moral diplomacy" enmeshed him in a chain of difficulties he did not foresee and with which he could not cope. The seizure of American sailors at Tampico in early April, followed by demand for a salute to the American flag, ultimatum to Huerta, decision to use force, and occupation of Vera Cruz, pushed Wilson and the nation to the edge of a war they had no will to wage.[69] Naón's initiative and the ABC mediation offered an alternative.[70]

Accompanied by his colleagues the Brazilian ambassador and the Chilean minister, the Argentine appeared before Secretary Bryan on April 25. In the interests of Hemisphere peace, they offered their joint services to settle the conflict with Mexico.[71] The idea apparently was the minister's own, for until the eve of the invitation Argentine authorities had repeatedly asserted their decision that the nation remain an impartial spectator. Receiving Naón's proposal earlier that day, the Argentine Foreign Office had hastily consulted Santiago and Rio de Janeiro before authorizing the action.[72] In Washington, before the day was over, Bryan conferred with the President, then accepted the good offices.[73] By the 29th, President Huerta and the leader of the Constitutionalist insurgents, Venustiano Carranza, had also accepted.[74]

Convening usually in the Argentine Legation, the mediators proceeded to prepare arrangements. They secured Huerta's agreement, though not Carranza's, to an armistice during negotiations. Over strong opposition within the State Department they determined to meet on neutral ground, in Niagara Falls, Ontario. The Conference formally opened on May 20.[75]

As American commissioners President Wilson appointed Joseph R. Lamar, an Associate Justice of the Supreme Court, and Frederick W. Lehman, Solicitor General in Taft's administration. But Wilson held all cards close to his vest. Huerta must go. Carranza, committed to internal reforms, must come in. Only Mexico's salvation, not Huerta's failure

[69] Howard F. Cline, The United States and Mexico, pp. 155-162.

[70] Throughout the Conference Naón acted without instructions from his government (Lorillard to Secretary of State, May 13, 26, 1914, NA, DS, 812.00/12166, 12332). See also Memoria, 1913-1914, pp. 9-38.

[71] For. Rel., 1914, pp. 488-489; Clarinda Pendleton Lamar, The Life of Joseph Rucker Lamar (1857-1916), pp. 245-246.

[72] Lorillard to Secretary of State, March 12, April 22, 29, 1914, NA, DS, 812.00/11492, 11630, 12096. For fuller account of the official position, see C. A. Silva, La política internacional de la Nación Argentina, pp. 343-351.

[73] Ray Stannard Baker, Woodrow Wilson, Life and Letters, IV, 334-335; For. Rel., 1914, p. 489.

[74] Severance, op. cit., p. 8. This account, written almost contemporaneously, is replete with interesting sidelights on the Niagara Falls Conference.

[75] Ibid., pp. 8-9; Memorandum on Place of Conferences of Mediators and Representatives to attend on behalf of the United States, May 1, 1914, NA, DS, 812.00/11800-1/2.

to salute the flag, must constitute the conference agenda. All these conditions the President made clear to mediators and American delegates alike. Even on these questions he would make the American decisions. Carranza was equally adamant. He would not let other nations decide the fate of Mexico's internal politics or economic directions.[76]

Hedged about by Wilson's ideas of diplomatic finesse and by Carranza's refusal to accept an armistice and failure to send delegates, the mediators were left little room for effective action. From May 20 to June 30, threatened often by complete breakdown, they entertained statements by representatives of Wilson and Huerta and offered their own proposals for a solution. Rarely, except in four plenary sessions, did the contending delegates face each other.[77]

By securing agreement to fragmentary protocols Naón and his associates ultimately pieced together a final memorandum. It made no reference to the break in diplomatic relations or the sequence of events which had produced it. It dealt only with the status of Mexico. The Mexicans would create a provisional government committed to free elections, general amnesty, and settlement of claims of foreigners. The United States, promising to claim no indemnity, would join the ABC states in prompt recognition.[78] Without assuring the signature of the Americans or inviting the approval of the Constitutionalists, the mediators voted an indefinite recess. Two weeks later Huerta resigned and fled, opening the gates of Mexico City and the presidential palace to Carranza and the Constitutionalists. On November 23, President Wilson ordered the evacuation of American troops.[79]

It is easy, in retrospect, to stress the failures and scout the successes of the Niagara Falls Conference. The fall of Huerta was predetermined. The settlement did nothing to satisfy American honor or redeem Wilsonian diplomacy. It was not accepted by the strongest force in Mexico. It did not permanently pacify the troubled republic. And yet, whether in spite or because of the mediation, war did not come. To Wilson and other American leaders the Latin Americans demonstrated the intensity of their faith in the sovereign equality of all states. For a time at least, the South American republics were reassured as to the direction of American intentions. Wilson demanded no indemnity, no oil concessions, no territory.[80] The mediators may not have continentalized the

[76] Baker, *op. cit.*, pp. 337-338, 340; Severance, *op. cit.*, pp. 9-10.

[77] An extensive selection of documents on the Conference was published in *For. Rel., 1914*, pp. 488-563. Additional materials are in NA, DS, 812.00/12631-1/2.

[78] *For. Rel., 1914*, pp. 548-553.

[79] E. E. Robinson and V. J. West, *The Foreign Policy of Woodrow Wilson, 1913-1917*, p. 38.

[80] Paul D. Dickens, "Argentine Arbitrations and Mediations with Reference to United States Participation Therein," *The Hispanic American Historical Review*, XI (Nov. 1931), 483-484; Bemis, *The Latin American Policy of the United States*, p. 180; Lamar, *op. cit.*, pp. 256, 263-264; Baker, *op. cit.*, pp. 349-350.

Monroe Doctrine or inaugurated the millennium in Pan American relations.[81] But, in the words of Walter Hines Page, on the eve of World War I, for the first time South Americans were admitted to the North American game.[82]

Perhaps the most tangible result of the mediation did not appear until a year later. Unceasing warfare between Carranza and his colorful but uncompromising lieutenants drove Mexico more deeply into chaos. By June, 1915, Wilson again felt compelled to act. But this time, upon Robert Lansing's counsel, he resorted not to unilateral force but to "Pan American" consultation. In July, the Acting Secretary sought the advice of the six ranking Latin American diplomats in Washington, the ambassadors of the ABC nations and the ministers of Bolivia, Guatemala, and Uruguay.[83] In all the negotiations which ensued Naón was not only an eager participant but several times Lansing's counsellor.[84] As a result of this consultation, though not without difficulties, all the nations on October 19 recognized the *de facto* government of General Carranza. The Mexican problem receded from the forefront of Argentine-American relations, thanks in part to the tactful political science lessons given the professor-President by the educator-Ambassador.

But whatever the balance shows, Argentina made the most of the role Naón had played, especially in the 1914 mediation. Its press and its public officials basked in the thanks and congratulations received from Bryan, Huerta, and leaders of other governments.[85] In annual reports to the Congress a year later, and again two years later, President De la Plaza praised what his Foreign Minister described as "an event of distinguished results in the history of Pan-American politics." [86]

The ABC mediation brought to a close three quarters of a century of frequent partnership—always friendly, sometimes intimate—in the encouragement of peaceful settlement. During and after World War I both nations would continue to promote Hemisphere peace and security but usually under the aegis of the Pan American movement, in which they were more often rivals than partners.

[81] Charles H. Sherrill, "Practical Mediation and International Peace," *The North American Review*, Vol. 200 (Dec., 1914), 887, 892; Cline, *op. cit.*, 161.

[82] Page to the President, July 5, 1914, B. J. Hendrick, *The Life and Letters of Walter H. Page*, III, 119-120.

[83] Department of State, *The Lansing Papers, 1914-1920*, II, 541; Cline, *op. cit.*, pp. 172-174; Baker, *op. cit.*, pp. 359-360; Sen. Doc., No. 324, 64 Cong., 1 sess., pp. 9-10.

[84] *The Lansing Papers*, II, 542-554; Naón to Lansing, Aug. 27, 1915, and Lansing to Naón, Oct. 5, 1915, NA, DS, 812.00/21337.

[85] *For. Rel., 1914*, p. 559; *Memoria, 1913-1914*, p. 21; *La Prensa*, June 27, 1914; Lorillard to Secretary of State, July 7, 1914, NA, DS, 812.00/12712.

[86] *Memoria, 1913-1914*, pp. v-vi; *For. Rel., 1915*, p. 28, and *1916*, pp. 16-18.

X V I I I

RIVALRY IN INTER-AMERICAN AFFAIRS:
PAN AMERICANISM IN PEACETIME, 1889-1910

The aura of harmony which surrounded their joint efforts to promote peace within the Western Hemisphere did not grace Argentina and the United States as they searched for effective policies to secure the Americas against the world. In settling their own disputes or those of their neighbors, the maturing republics repeatedly demonstrated their ability to cooperate intimately. But in their attempts to organize the continent or gird it against Europe, friction was the rule. At the heart of the friction were essential disagreements over the concept of the Western Hemisphere and the desirability of creating regional instruments to protect it. In short, leaders of the two nations never saw eye to eye on the feasibility of a Hemisphere ideology, whether Pan American, Latin American, or Spanish American. Without mutual understanding of the idea, they could rarely agree on the policies or international machinery to promote it. By 1889, therefore, when Secretary Blaine proposed an organization of the American states, the seeds of Argentine-American rivalry were already sown.

Argentine-American Roots of Pan Americanism [1]

In the evolution of the Pan American movement and the Western Hemisphere idea upon which it rests, the voices of Argentine leaders, some constructive, many obstructionist, were often heard. Influential,

---

[1] For the inspiration and basic organization of this section, I acknowledge great indebtedness to two American historians of Pan Americanism, Joseph B. Lockey (*Pan-Americanism: Its Beginnings,* New York, 1920) and Arthur P. Whitaker (*The Western Hemisphere Idea,* Ithaca, 1954). On the subject of Argentine-American relations within the Pan American movement and the diverse inter-American organizations, see Thomas F. McGann, *Argentina, the United States, and the Inter-American System, 1880-1914,* Cambridge, 1957, and R. N. Burr and Roland Hussey, *Documents on Inter-American Cooperation, 1881-1948,* Philadelphia, 1955.

too, were the views and actions of Americans specifically responsible for the framing or execution of policies toward the South American republic. From the moment of Argentina's independence these voices began to speak on the shores of both the Río de la Plata and the Potomac. Dissonant though they were at both poles of the Hemisphere, they nevertheless contributed to the character and form of inter-American machinery.

It was Mariano Moreno, brilliant secretary of Argentina's first governing junta, who raised the beacon light that has since guided his successors around the shoals of foreign entanglements. In aspiring to unify the diverging parts of the former viceroyalty and to assert his nation's leadership in South America, he is given credit for formulating two traditional Argentine policies. In opposing plans for federating Spain's former colonies, he is said to have initiated Argentina's consistent opposition to any form of continental union.[2] But, like George Washington's oft-cited counsel on foreign entanglements, Moreno's views may have become warped with the years, for his writings make transparent his awareness of the concept of "America" and his beliefs in mutual support, even close alliance, among the new Latin American governments.[3]

Three years later, in addressing an appeal for protection to President Madison, Moreno's successors went much further in visualizing the idea of inter-American cooperation. "The dispositions arising from an analogy of political principles," they wrote,

> and the indubitable characters of a National sympathy, ought to open the road to a fraternal alliance, which should unite forever the North and South Americans, by adopting in the Congress of the United States and the Constituted Assembly of the United Provinces of Rio de la Plata, the basis of social beneficence in all its extent, in order to demonstrate by its effects, that between the Governments of the two Americas, there does not exist those fatal distinctions which separate political morality, nor those artificial manoeuvres which deform the Cabinets of the Old World.[4]

On the American side, the Hemisphere concept was envisioned with equal clarity. In his instructions to Joel Roberts Poinsett, first envoy to

[2] Ricardo Levene, *A History of Argentina*, pp. 260-261; Lockey, *op. cit.*, pp. 283-285, 434-435.

[3] See above, p. 14, note 4, and Moreno's "Sobre las miras del congreso que acaba de convocarse, y constitución del estado," Ricardo Rojas, *Doctrina democrática de Mariano Moreno*, especially pp. 249, 271, 274-275. See also Whitaker, *op. cit.*, p. 24.

[4] The Constituted Assembly of the United Provinces of the Río de la Plata to President Madison, July 21, 1813, W. R. Manning (ed.), *Diplomatic Correspondence of the United States Concerning Independence of the Latin-American Countries*, I, 332-333.

the government Moreno was seeking to guide, Secretary Robert Smith wrote,

It will coincide with the sentiments and policy of the United States to promote the most friendly relations, and the most liberal intercourse, between the inhabitants of this hemisphere, as having all a common interest, and as lying under a common obligation to maintain that system of peace, justice, and good will, which is the only source of happiness for nations.[5]

From the writings of Henry M. Brackenridge, secretary to President Monroe's South American mission, Henry Clay received strong support for his "American System." "The United States will be the natural head of the New World," Brackenridge predicted.[6] Upon recognition of Argentine independence in 1822, Monroe's secretary of state, John Quincy Adams, was much more cautious. "To any confederation of Spanish American provinces for that end [independence from Europe]," he instructed Caesar A. Rodney, first Minister, "the United States would yield their approbation, and cordial good wishes."[7]

Throughout the wars for independence, the United Provinces joined their fellow colonies in waging a common struggle against the mother country. But no pressure developed in Buenos Aires, not even on the wings of San Martín's armies, for any form of political union with the other provinces. Of all the Argentine revolutionary patriots, only Bernardo Monteagudo—and he after exile from the land he helped to free —became a spokesman for Spanish American federation.[8]

When President Monroe determined to base an American policy upon a regional concept of the Hemisphere, he broadened considerably the foundations upon which Latin American federationists were already working. While Argentine leaders greeted his message with polite warmth, they failed at the time to endorse its nonintervention declaration. Three years later, however, deeply enmeshed in war with Portuguese Brazil, the Argentines sought to invoke the new doctrine, only to discover that their understanding disagreed with the American interpretation. Secretary Clay himself composed the rebuff.[9]

No event in Latin America's formative years better symbolizes discordant Argentine-American thought on the Pan American idea than the Panama Congress of 1826. Neither nation was represented, Argentina by choice, the United States by default. The leaders at Buenos Aires, as before, had little interest in a continental union, least of all one under

---

[5] June 28, 1810, *ibid.*, p. 7.
[6] See above, p. 44 and note 41. The quotation is from *The Pamphleteer*, XIII, 67.
[7] May 17, 1823, Manning, *op. cit.*, I, 189. Also see above, pp. 74-75.
[8] Lockey, *op. cit.*, pp. 308-311; R. N. Burr and R. D. Hussey, *op. cit.*, I, 42-47.
[9] See above, pp. 81-84, 91, and Whitaker, *op. cit.*, pp. 34-40.

the leadership of Simón Bolívar and Colombia. Neither President Adams nor Secretary Clay approved an organization which might limit the nation's freedom of action or usurp its leadership.[10] By their very absence, two strongly nationalistic peoples, one at each end of the Hemisphere, snubbed the overtures of intervening states for some form of confederated whole.

During the next forty years, while leadership of Spanish American internationalism shifted from Colombia to Mexico and Peru, Argentina and the United States expanded their respective brands of isolationism. The southern republic, soon dominated by Rosas and then rent by factional strife, continued to exclude itself from all organized plans for continental security. In 1862 its foreign minister, Rufino de Elizalde, tersely defined the Argentine belief—that "independent America is a political entity which neither exists nor is possible to constitute by diplomatic combinations."[11] Involved in North American expansion, the slavery controversy, and the Civil War, the United States gradually pared down the Hemisphere-wide scope of Monroe's original pronouncement.

Successive Democratic presidents, withdrawing from the advanced positions occupied by Clay and Monroe, turned aside every Argentine gesture that might have drawn the two nations into the Hemisphere stream. Jackson and his successors, both Democratic and Whig, refused Argentina's pleas for help against Britain in the Falklands case. Van Buren did not support a naval officer who sought to whittle down the threat of French intervention.[12] Polk regarded with only superficial concern the Anglo-French interference that endured throughout his tenure. Through his secretary of state, James Buchanan, he turned a deaf ear to Rosas' repeated appeals for assistance based on the principle of American solidarity against Europe.[13]

Furthermore, Buchanan received without recorded comment what was probably the most comprehensive statement of twentieth-century Pan American aims made in the nineteenth. This was the proposal of Edward A. Hopkins—chimerical, to be sure—that "now is the proper time to revive Gen¹. Bolívar's plan of the *General Congress.*"[14] In 1846, Hopkins was a diplomatic fledgling of twenty-four; he may not have known that twenty years before his superior had strongly resisted American participation in the very plan he was now proposing to revive.

The imaginative but imprudent Hopkins had already visited Paraguay and written his inflammatory letter to Rosas.[15] Now, on March 27, 1846,

---

[10] Lockey, *op. cit.,* pp. 393ff, 426-427, 448ff; Burr and Hussey, *op. cit.,* I, 47-49.
[11] *Ibid.,* I, 151.
[12] See above, pp. 114-116, 125-127.
[13] See above, pp. 133-139.
[14] Hopkins to Henry A. Wise, Minister to Brazil, March 27, 1846, enclosure in Wise to Buchanan, April 29, 1846, NA, DS, Desp. Bra., XV.
[15] See above, pp. 134-137.

from his sanctuary in Montevideo, he envisioned a Pan Americanism that belonged to the nineteen-thirties, one which

> will give to Europe a lesson which she will never forget, and which will put a stop to all future attempts like the present on any quarter of our continent, in showing her that we can & will take care of our own affairs, whether of the Northern or Southern continent, & will not tolerate any foreign interference whether *guaranteed* or not.

He would convoke a congress to settle boundaries, regulate the navigation of rivers and "spread throughout America ideas of fraternity & community in interests hitherto unknown." [16]

An impractical youth about to be recalled and rebuked for his stumbling tactics along the Río de la Plata was obviously in no position to influence the policy of his superiors on the Potomac. Nevertheless, for twentieth-century Americans, the breadth of the gulf between Hopkins' vision and Buchanan's realism dramatizes the distance that would have to be travelled before the broad Pan Americanism of Franklin Roosevelt could replace the limited continental views of James Polk. It was the same Buchanan, of course, who thirteen years later aroused the fears of Argentina by sending a strong naval expedition coursing through its inland rivers to satisfy American claims against Paraguay. [17]

During the sixties and seventies, Argentina continued to spurn invitations to Spanish American conferences. Bartolomé Mitre, president during the Paraguayan War, successfully averted all American attempts to mediate. In writing his epochal history of General San Martín, he belittled the significance of the Panama Congress. [18] Juan B. Alberdi, writing on "The Crime of War" in the twilight of his career, saw regional organizations as an essential step to world government, but he no longer exerted decisive influence on Argentine policy. [19]

Of the great nineteenth-century Argentine leaders, only Domingo Sarmiento contributed distinctively to the evolution of the Pan American idea. And even he, strongly opposed to an "American Congress" in 1844, came only gradually to support the concept of inter-American cooperation. By 1865 and after, however, his firsthand knowledge of Latin peoples, his opposition to European influence, his devotion to the North American pattern, and his qualified endorsement of Monroe's principles became essential ingredients of his dictum, "Let us be America, as the

[16] Hopkins to Wise, *loc. cit.*; Pablo Max Ynsfran, *La expedición norteamericana contra El Paraguay, 1858-1859,* I, 85-94.

[17] See above, pp. 169-172.

[18] Lockey, *op. cit.*, p. 317 note; Whitaker, *op. cit.*, p. 57.

[19] *Ibid.*, pp. 54, 55, 65-66; W. R. Crawford, *A Century of Latin-American Thought,* p. 31.

sea is the ocean." [20] Though his continental views were helpful in the shaping of a doctrine for the Hemisphere, they failed to steer his own nation from its traditional policies. In the flood tide of the economic expansionism he promoted there was little room for the American solidarity in which he believed. Barely a year after his death in 1888, a younger generation of Argentine leaders resisted uncompromisingly James G. Blaine's hopes for Pan American union.

The Washington Conference and Its Sequel

As Secretary of State under Presidents Garfield and Harrison, Blaine was in a position to undertake the initiation of inter-American cooperation that Sarmiento had coveted for the South American states. In 1881, Blaine invited the nations to a Pan American conference which never met and, curiously, in 1889 presided over one he did not originate.[21] For both opportunities he was deeply in debt to Hinton Rowan Helper, President Lincoln's consular appointee to Buenos Aires. From his five years of service in Argentina the Consul returned brimming with fervor over the potentialities of Latin America. The zeal with which he had once pushed the antislavery crusade he now turned to a pro-Pan American one.

By means of personal letters, pressure on influential citizens, and memorials to Congress, the enthusiastic publicist sought support for his vision of a Pan American railroad running from Hudson Bay to the Strait of Magellan.[22] After several unsuccessful attempts, in 1886 he secured passage of a law which authorized the convening of a conference to consider closer commercial relations in the Americas. To Helper, stimulated by his residence in Argentina, must be given considerable credit not only for the calling of the First Pan American Conference but also for the diversity of its agenda.[23]

The Washington Conference provided the first arena where spokesmen of Argentine and American foreign policies met face to face in the presence of all their continental colleagues. The two nations which had most persistently shunned involvement in inter-American conventions at last agreed to send their representatives into the lists. National policies which each had projected and defended during three-quarters of a

---

[20] On Sarmiento's evolving views, see Burr and Hussey, *op. cit.*, pp. 79-83, 94-97, 161-163; Whitaker, *op. cit.*, pp. 67-74; and Crawford, *op. cit.*, p. 51. See also above, pp. 216-217.

[21] Lockey, "James Gillespie Blaine," in S. F. Bemis, *The American Secretaries of State and Their Diplomacy,* VIII, 164ff.

[22] *Dictionary of American Biography,* VIII, 517.

[23] A. Curtis Wilgus, "James G. Blaine and the Pan American Movement," *The Hispanic American Historical Review,* V (Nov., 1922), 670 note, 687; Whitaker, *op. cit.*, pp. 77-81.

century could now be debated in open forum. From the opening session to the final vote, thanks to American initiative and Argentine aggressiveness, conference proceedings revolved around the duel between the two determined antagonists.

In personnel of national delegations the Argentine Republic was much the better equipped. The American group was larger but the Argentine superior in quality. Its members were Vicente G. Quesada, Manuel Quintana, and Roque Saenz Peña. Quesada, who had been minister in Washington since 1885, decided he could more effectively fulfill the duties of his regular post if he avoided participation in the Conference.[24] But Quintana and Saenz Peña were more than equal to their assignments. They were veterans of Argentine politics and diplomacy; they were able speakers and skilled parliamentarians. Both would later achieve the presidency.[25]

The American delegation was composed largely of men whose training had not prepared them for the kind of thrust-and-parry debate that was to ensue. John B. Henderson had been a senator and William H. Trescott was a veteran diplomat, but the other eight, including Andrew Carnegie and Clement Studebaker, were wealthy merchants or industrialists. Blaine, who became chairman of the Conference, was not a member of the delegation.[26]

To a reader of the proceedings it might appear that the Argentine delegates came to Washington with the avowed intention of scuttling the Conference. This would be too harsh a judgment. Rather it seems likely that they came with a determination to project Argentina's bid for leadership in the Hemisphere, at least in Latin America, a policy for which the nation had stood since Moreno. Perhaps, too, by "boring from within" they hoped to forestall any decision that might limit in any degree their own freedom of action or involve the Hemisphere in multilateral security measures for which they had no stomach.

Whatever the purposes of the Argentine strategy, many of their tactics were sheer tedium and picayune. Serving only to increase tension before the principal agenda items were introduced, Quintana and Saenz Peña repeatedly challenged decisions on routine organization and procedure. Because they believed that only a regular delegation member should serve as chairman, they opposed the selection of Blaine, then, to avoid

[24] República Argentina, Ministerio de Relaciones Exteriores y Culto, *Boletín mensual*, Feb., 1889, p. 547; Vicente G. Quesada, *Recuerdos de mi vida diplomática; misión en Estados Unidos (1885-1892)*, p. 119. A provocative, though adulatory, account of Saenz Peña's role in the conference is that by his biographer, Felipe Barreda Laos, *Roque Saenz Peña*, pp. 112-142.

[25] T. F. McGann, *op. cit.*, pp. 75-76, 101-102. For my interpretation of Argentine-American relationships at the Conference, I have relied heavily on this excellent volume.

[26] *Ibid.*, pp. 130-131.

the necessity of voting against him, boycotted the opening session. They refused to participate in their host's six-thousand-mile railroad tour of the eastern states. They maintained that all delegates should certify minutes and that Blaine, not a committee on committees, should select all committee members.

On other organizational and procedural matters, the Argentine actions were more justifiable. They insisted not only upon equality of languages but upon official secretaries who could speak both Spanish and English. Against the rulings of Blaine or over the opposition of American delegates, they secured restriction of the agenda to topics of the convening act, recognition of speakers in the order they requested the floor, and exclusion of private secretaries from official sessions.[27] By the time preliminaries were cleared away, Quintana and Saenz Peña had served notice on Blaine, Henderson, and their colleagues that they were equipped to battle for every inch of ground on the important propositions to be considered.

The line of cleavage between Argentina and the United States was most sharply drawn on the issues of arbitration and a customs union, the two essentials in Blaine's hopes for the Conference. The Argentines led the fight on each proposal, outgeneraled the Americans at every stage, and secured the approximate objectives they sought.

Quintana and Henderson were members of the committee directed to draft a plan of arbitration. Both were eager to exert leadership in devising a workable formula for the Hemisphere. The Argentine favored a mild form of arbitration, one which would respect the equality of all states, safeguard their independence, and reject every type of intervention. The American favored compulsory arbitration on a broad basis. Quintana's case was clearly the more appealing to the small Latin American states, whose support Argentina was seeking. The Americans were forced to a losing choice. They could propose a weaker plan, which they did not want, or a stronger plan, for which they could not win support, or they could accept the Argentine proposition. The victory was Argentina's.[28]

The same committee proposed a closely related recommendation on "Claims and Diplomatic Intervention," to be adopted by the nations as a principle of American international law. It declared that "a nation has not, nor recognizes in favor of foreigners, any other obligations or responsibilities than those which in favor of the natives are established, in like cases, by the constitution and the laws." The United States alone

---

[27] *Ibid.*, pp. 133-135, 137-140.

[28] *Ibid.*, pp. 145-148; *Minutes of the International American Conference*, pp. 107-108, 689-690, 695-697; *International American Conference: Reports of Committees and Discussions Thereon*, II, 1078-1083. (These two works are hereafter cited as *Minutes* and *Reports*.)

opposed it and thus laid bare its position on a problem that was to plague Pan Americanism until the nineteen-thirties.[29]

The climax of Argentine-American disagreement was reached in the rancorous debate touched off by Blaine's proposal for a Pan American customs union. Henderson and Saenz Peña were the protagonists. With the American concurring, the committee quickly dismissed the customs union as utopian and impractical. There, however, agreement ended. Going beyond the agenda, Henderson and the majority recommended that bilateral and multilateral reciprocity treaties be utilized to develop a free trade area. Saenz Peña, supported by his Chilean colleague, contended that the Conference was empowered only to approve or reject the customs union; their minority report proposed rejection, nothing more.[30]

Had either report been voted on at once, eliminating the angry clashes which followed, the prospects for inter-American solidarity as well as for Argentine-American harmony might have been brighter. But Blaine had set his sights on some measure to increase Hemisphere trade, and the Argentines, intent on protecting their European markets, determined to slug it out, even at the risk of sabotaging the Conference. Saenz Peña alone made sixteen speeches on the reciprocity resolution.[31]

The Argentine delegate praised his nation's trade position and the intimacy of its relations with Europe. He attacked the commercial policies of the United States, especially its protective tariff and disregard of South American markets. He accused Blaine of seeking to make economic tributaries of sovereign Latin states.[32] In a dramatic exhortation he struck out for leadership of Latin America. "Let us respect the sovereignty of all these states," he said, "and let us found upon them and for their benefit a single society with a common destiny, with a view to the defense of this part of America from dangers common to all." [33] His Latin oratory reached its brilliant zenith in a passage that was to echo through Pan American corridors for decades:

> Let the century of America, as the 20th century is already called, behold our trade with all of the nations of the earth free, witnessing the noble duel of untrammeled labor in which it has been truly said God measures the ground, equalizes the weapons, and apportions the light. *Let America be for humanity.*[34]

[29] *Reports*, II, 937. For the reports of the Argentine delegates to their government, see *Memoria, 1891*, especially pp. 17-19, 24.

[30] *Minutes*, pp. 293-297.

[31] McGann, *op. cit.*, pp. 154-155.

[32] *Ibid.*, pp. 155-163; *Minutes*, pp. 297-324, 600-616; *Cong. Rec.*, 51 Cong., 1 sess., XXI, pt. 7, 6257-6258.

[33] Saenz Peña, *Escritos y discursos*, I, 162, quoted in Bemis, *op. cit.*, VIII, 175.

[34] *Minutes*, p. 324.

The rebuttals of Henderson and his colleagues were adequate to carry the recommendation for reciprocity, but only after acrimonious debate had incited personal clashes and national animosities. The Argentine motion to reject a customs union already rejected did not come to a vote.[35]

In spite of Argentina's unblushing representation of its own national interests, Blaine, Helper, and their fellow spirits had inaugurated the Pan American "movement." Its course would be tortuous, its growth slow. And growth could come, usually, without Argentine support or, at best, with its grudging cooperation. At Washington, Quintana and Saenz Peña charted the course for Argentina's twentieth-century aversion to Pan Americanism. By proclaiming the championship of "humanity," they protected the nation's traditional ties to Europe without relaxing its bonds to America. They kept it free from any involving pledge to Hemisphere unity. They demonstrated its will to lead, not follow, other American states. By sternly confronting American statesmen on American ground, they revealed a hard confidence in Argentina's own policies and challenged the soundness of its rival's.[36] For the indefinite future they had fixed the tone of Pan Americanism.

During much of the decade after the Washington Conference Argentina maintained its attitude of aloofness toward the Pan American idea and the principles for which Blaine had sought Hemisphere approval. After 1891, the administration of Luis Saenz Peña and José E. Uriburu, allegedly for reasons of economy, refused even to pay Argentina's annual share of $700 for the maintenance of the Commercial Bureau of the American Republics. Their foreign ministers regarded the Bureau as an international depository and publisher of official national documents and objected to its assumption of greater powers.[37] What truly restrained Argentina's participation, however, was its belief that the Bureau was to all intents and purposes no more than "an adjunct of the State Department." [38]

When, under the McKinley Tariff Act, Blaine undertook to reduce Hemisphere tariff barriers through bilateral reciprocity treaties, the Argentines held fast to their position that without free wool in American markets there could be no reciprocity. Under the Wilson-Gorman Tariff Act, the Cleveland administration failed to barter for the reciprocity it might have gained. When President McKinley and the Republicans re-

[35] *Ibid.*, pp. 653-654, 859-874.
[36] Cf. McGann, *op. cit.*, pp. 163-164; and Whitaker, *op. cit.*, pp. 84-85.
[37] For example, see Amancio Alcorta, Minister of Foreign Relations, to W. I. Buchanan, Minister to Argentina, Aug. 29, 1896, Jan. 21, 1898, NA, DS, Desp. Arg., XXXIII, XXXV. See also many instructions to the American ministers, NA, DS, Inst. Arg., XVI, 534-535; XVII, 24, 166-169, 401-402, 428-430.
[38] Buchanan to Hay, Dec. 19, 1898, NA, DS, Desp. Arg., XXXVII.

newed overtures for reciprocity without free entry of wool, the Argentines returned to their adamant position of 1891.[39]

Involvement of the United States with other areas of Latin America during the nineties stimulated only official neutrality on the part of successive Argentine administrations but left a residue of anti-American feeling among influential sectors of the population. In the case of American estrangement from Chile over the *Itata* and *Baltimore* incidents in 1891, Argentina officially sympathized with the United States, but its attitude was based more upon anti-Chilean than pro-American sentiment.[40]

President Cleveland's invocation of the Monroe Doctrine during the Anglo-Venezuelan boundary dispute of 1895 aroused anew Argentine fear and mistrust of American ascendancy. Supported by the strong pro-British press, ex-President Carlos Pellegrini led the attack upon Cleveland's use of the Doctrine allegedly to renew Blaine's policy of commercial aggressiveness. He reindicted American policies toward the Falkland Islands in the thirties and toward Mexico in the forties. Though Cleveland's position won support from Acting President Roca and ex-President Mitre, Pellegrini's views were the most popular.[41]

McKinley's intervention in Cuban affairs two years later brought a similar outcry against American policy. Through mass meetings and vitriolic press articles, the powerful Spanish and Italian minorities attacked American expansionism. Most native Argentines approved Cuban independence, but faced with the need for national unity against Chile the authorities maintained a studied neutrality.[42] Needing settlers to exploit vacant acres, they could ill afford to alienate the principal fountains of immigrants.

The Mexico City Conference—and After

At the end of a decade of troublesome episodes tending to produce tension and mutual distrust, official relations between the two republics for a time became more propitious for the growth of the Pan American idea. The change became apparent shortly after the inauguration in October, 1898, of Julio A. Roca, "the wily fox," who in the interests of South American peace was soon to exchange official visits with the

[39] See above, pp. 225-229.

[40] John R. G. Pitkin, Minister to Argentina, to Blaine, Jan. 30, March 28, 1892, NA, DS, Desp. Arg., XXIX.

[41] Buchanan to Richard Olney, Secretary of State, Dec. 19, 26, 1895, and enclosures, *ibid.*, XXXII; Dexter Perkins, *The Monroe Doctrine, 1867-1907*, pp. 212-213.

[42] Daniel Mayer, Consul to Buenos Aires, March 11, 1898, NA, DS, Con. Let., BA, XXIII; François S. Jones, Chargé d'Affaires to Argentina, to John Sherman, Secretary of State, April 12, 1898; Buchanan to Sherman, July 14, 1898, Desp. Arg., XXXVI.

Brazilian president and to conclude peaceable settlement of the boundary dispute with Chile.[43]

It was the friendly and understanding attitudes of resident envoys in the two capitals, however, that served most to reduce, at least temporarily, the rivalry between their nations. Martín García Merou, while recognizing that "not all is luminous in the picture of this nation," came to believe, nevertheless, long before the end of his eight years of duty in Washington, that

> the imitation of its methods of work, of the energy of its enterprises, of its spirit of order and justice, will strengthen our good natural endowment and will improve our political and social customs.[44]

He developed the greatest respect for William I. Buchanan and believed his continuance as minister in Buenos Aires by two administrations was evidence of American desire for cordial relations.[45] In spite of his own government's attitude, he accepted the Secretary of State's invitation to sit on the executive committee of the Bureau of American Republics. Aware that even Chile had entered the Bureau, soon after the inauguration of President Roca he urged that Argentina resume its support.[46]

In Buenos Aires, Buchanan repeatedly prodded the Uriburu administration to fulfill its fiscal obligations and re-enter the union of American states. Not until the advent of Roca, however, did Foreign Minister Amancio Alcorta shift his position from criticism of American domination of the Bureau to acquiescence in Argentine reaffiliation.[47]

In view of the respect and understanding which each minister had gained for the homeland of the other, it was fortunate that both were named delegates to the next Pan American conference, held at Mexico City in 1901-1902. García Merou was chief of his nation's mission; Buchanan was the key figure in the Yankee delegation. Tempered somewhat by their moderation, the Argentine and American representatives minimized the verbal fireworks which had exploded in the halls of the Washington Conference.

Four months before receipt of Mexico's formal notification of August 15, 1900, President Roca announced to the Argentine Congress that he had accepted the invitation of the United States to attend the conference, wherever it might be held. He had already suggested to Secretary Hay that Buenos Aires would be happy to entertain a congress which "can

---

[43] Jones to Hay, Aug. 3, 1899; Wm. P. Lord, Minister to Argentina, to Hay, Nov. 3, 1900, ibid., XXXVIII, XXXIX.

[44] Estudios americanos, pp. 220-221.

[45] Ibid., p. 301.

[46] Hay to Buchanan, Nov. 7, Dec. 17, 1898, NA, DS, Inst. Arg., XVII, 401-402, 413.

[47] Buchanan to Hay, Dec. 19, 1898, NA, DS, Desp. Arg., XXXVII. The decision was made just after the Argentine government had agreed to the appointment of Buchanan as the neutral member of the commission to settle the Atacama boundary with Chile (see above, p. 254).

be fruitful to the relations of the American States living far apart, notwithstanding that common interests and aspirations demand closer
ties." [48] A strong sector of the Argentine press, recalling American territorial gains from Spain and "scheming" against Cuba, was less hopeful
of improved inter-American relations.[49]

But the feelings of friendship exemplified by García Merou and
Buchanan were incapable of bridging the deep cleavages which separated the two republics on matters of basic national policy. On the
central issues of arbitration, rights of aliens, pecuniary claims, and commercial reciprocity, they perpetuated at Mexico City their rivalry for
Hemisphere leadership.

As at the Washington Conference, all the nations were prepared to
agree to a treaty recognizing the principles of arbitration. The Argentine
and American delegations, however, found their positions of 1890 precisely reversed. The Argentines now proposed obligatory arbitration, even
of pending disputes. Buchanan and the Americans supported the Mexican
proposal, which was essentially an endorsement of the voluntary arbitration principles of the Hague Convention. Chile, concerned about disputes
pending with each of its neighbors, favored obligatory arbitration but
only of future disputes.[50]

Arguing for a broad plan of compulsory arbitration, García Merou's
colleagues appealed for concrete steps to promote a practical Pan
Americanism. Opposing the coercion of any nation, they proposed that
each group of states contract among themselves for the plan they
endorsed.[51] In this deadlock, García Merou appealed directly to Secretary Hay to save the Conference by throwing American influence behind
obligatory arbitration. Hay replied that American pressure might produce the very failure the Argentine Minister feared.[52] In the end, the
Argentines gained the approval of nine states for the plan they proposed.
By securing adherence of all nations to the Hague Convention, the
Americans preserved some measure of Conference unanimity.[53]

[48] H. Mabragaña, *Los mensajes*, V, 361; Lord to Hay, March 26, April 24, 1900,
and enclosures, NA, DS, Desp. Arg., XXXIX.
[49] Mayer to Department, May 28, 1901, and enclosures, NA, DS, Con. Let.,
B. A., XXIV.
[50] For the day-to-day actions of the American delegates on arbitration and other
issues, see NA, DS, Records of the United States Delegation to the Second International Conference of American States, 1901-2.
[51] *Second International American Conference, Mexico: 1901-1902*, pp. 316-328,
357-360.
[52] García Merou to Argentine Legation in Washington, Nov. 22, 1901, NA, DS,
Notes from Arg. Leg., V; Hay to Argentine Legation, Nov. 23, 1901, Notes to
Arg. Leg., VII, 92-93.
[53] W. I. Buchanan, "Latin America and the Mexican Conference," *Annals of the
American Academy of Political and Social Science*, XXII (July, 1903), 53-54; J. B.
Scott, *The International Conferences of the American States, 1889-1928*, pp. 61-62,
100-104.

As to the rights of aliens to the diplomatic protection of their government, an issue upon which the United States had suffered a 15-to-1 defeat in 1890, the Argentines again led the Latin attack against diplomatic interventions. This time Buchanan and his associates abstained from discussion and voting. A kindred convention providing compulsory arbitration of pecuniary claims provoked still another clash between the rivals, though, without achieving all its objectives, the United States eventually signed and ratified it.[54]

Though they secured the adoption of no treaty or resolution on reciprocal trade, the Argentine delegates managed to renew their attacks upon American tariff policy. In an extensive report to the Conference, paying unexpected tribute to the inspiration of James G. Blaine, they berated continued American duties on hides and wool.[55]

Without resort to the histrionics of their predecessors at the Washington Conference, the Argentines had maintained their independence of views and reasserted their claims to leadership of the Spanish states. At the same time, Buchanan, in optimistic retrospect, could properly praise the Conference's "spirit of cordial confidence and good-will," for at least his nation's hopes for Pan Americanism had been kept alive.[56] He and his colleagues had effectively fulfilled President Roosevelt's instructions to refrain from assuming leadership of the Conference.

The reversal of Argentine and American views on arbitration at the Mexico City Conference was soon followed by a far more significant shift of their positions on the Pan American idea itself. Argentina, traditionally wary of international commitments, now became the exponent of multilateral inter-American diplomacy, while the United States, emerging from its nineteenth-century isolationism, turned to a "lone-wolf" internationalism.

Luis Drago's proposal (December, 1902) of a Pan American fiat against European armed intervention to collect public debts was far more than a recommendation for the creation of stronger machinery to guarantee the security of the Hemisphere.[57] It was an extension not only of Monroe's principles but of the highest hopes of Blaine and Sarmiento for inter-American cooperation. It was an overture for a multilateral policy based upon the regional concept of the Western Hemisphere. It was a harbinger of the dynamic Pan Americanism the United States was eagerly to propose and Argentina reluctantly to accept thirty years

---

[54] *Ibid.*, pp. 90-91, 104-105; McGann, *op. cit.*, pp. 213-215.

[55] *Report Which the Delegation of the Argentine Republic Submits to the Second Pan-American Conference*, pp. 64-66.

[56] Buchanan, *op. cit.*, p. 55. For a detailed review of Argentine-American rivalry at the Conference, see McGann, *op. cit.*, pp. 203-217.

[57] Cf. above, pp. 257ff.

later. It was a complete turnabout to Argentina's policy of a century's tradition.[58] Thanks to the American reaction, it proved but an aberration.

Unfortunately for the improvement of Argentine-American relations within the inter-American framework, Drago's suggestions reached the desk of the wrong American president at an inopportune time. Under the leadership of Theodore Roosevelt, the United States was irretrievably committed to its new Manifest Destiny, encompassing an expanding economy, a quest for new markets and investment opportunities, and reliance upon sea power. Strengthened in its position by fresh understanding with Great Britain, the nation felt emboldened to undertake its own brand of internationalism.[59] As it had during the disputes over the Venezuelan boundary and Cuban independence, so now in the cases of Venezuelan debts, Panamanian independence,[60] and Dominican insolvency, Washington chose to move without consulting the Latin American states.

Roosevelt's reply to an Argentine proposition that might have led to genuine Pan Americanization of the Monroe Doctrine was his own unilateral corollary. Drago was not openly rebuffed, but Argentina's singular offer to play the Pan American game was brusquely frustrated and would soon be withdrawn. Whichever side of the coin they called, the Argentines seemed fated to confront North American rivalry.

The Rio de Janeiro Conference

William I. Buchanan, who had followed his mission to the Mexico City Conference by a brief term as first Minister to the new Republic of Panama, was named chairman of the American delegation to the Third Pan American Conference at Rio de Janeiro in 1906. Of the Argentine leaders who for a season at the turn of the century had manifested unexpected interest in Pan Americanism—President Roca, Foreign Minister Drago, Minister García Merou—none was now closely associated with the shaping of foreign policy.

President Figueroa first proposed to appoint as delegates Roque Saenz Peña, whose oratorical barbs in 1890 had pierced Blaine's Pan American balloons, and Luis Drago, still friendly to the United States. But Saenz Peña went instead to Spain to attend the wedding of Alfonso XIII and Drago refused to be bound by instructions that precluded

---

[58] See Whitaker's excellent discussion of "Drago's Economic Corollary to the Monroe Doctrine," in *The Western Hemisphere Idea*, pp. 88-107.

[59] *Ibid.*, pp. 89-95.

[60] A forerunner of later inter-American policy on multilateral recognition was Argentina's decision to recognize the independence of Panama in concert with Bolivia, Brazil, Chile, Paraguay, and Uruguay (John Barrett, Minister to Argentina, to Secretary of State, Dec. 24, 1903, NA, DS, Desp. Arg., XLII).

acceptance of Monroe's doctrine and perverted the Pan American implications of his own.[61] Figueroa then appointed four delegates, including García Merou's successor in Washington, Epifanio Portela.[62] Except Portela, they were men of little experience outside Argentina and, in the view of the American chargé in Buenos Aires, represented "the conservatism of the old regime rather than the developing openmindedness toward which the country is tending." [63] Clearly, the Argentine government was prepared perfunctorily to meet its Pan American obligations but not to generate real enthusiasm for the movement.

At the same time, Argentine newspapers did little to modify the lukewarm attitude of the government except to chill it further. Once it was announced that the Third Conference would meet in Rio rather than Buenos Aires, the porteño press initiated a drumfire of criticism. It attacked the selection of the site and the hollowness of the agenda as well as the Monroe Doctrine and Roosevelt's Latin American policy.[64] The *Buenos Aires Herald* predicted "a general discussion of second rate themes, a flood of platitudes, a vast expenditure of parabole and hyperbole, and as a residue the *status quo*." [65] Only *La Nación*, seeking to guide public opinion along broad, fair-minded paths, maintained a reasonably moderate tone.[66]

The Rio Conference brought out none of the bitter cross fire that had checkered the first meeting or even the forthright clashes that had marked the second. Secretary Root's appearance at the opening ceremonies, his support of Latin American representation at the Hague Conference, and his soothing reassurances helped to allay incipient mistrust. The showdown debate which might have developed over the Drago Doctrine was thwarted by preliminary actions of the two governments. In his instructions to delegates, the Argentine foreign minister took the position that prohibition of force to collect public debts was properly a matter for jurisdiction of world law, not regional policy.[67] Secretary Root directed American representatives to seek transfer of the subject to the Hague Conference.

To the proponents of Hemisphere solidarity the decision to transpose

[61] Charles D. White, Chargé d'Affaires to Argentina, to Root, May 30, June 15, 1906, *ibid.*, XLVII.

[62] *Boletín oficial de la República Argentina*, No. 3786, June 16, 1906.

[63] White to Root, June 15, 1906, NA, DS, Desp. Arg., XLVII.

[64] A. M. Beaupré, Minister to Argentina, to Root, Dec. 4, 1905, *ibid.*, XLVI.

[65] April 7, 1906.

[66] March 28, May 30, 1906. See also White to Root, May 30, 1906, NA, DS, Desp. Arg., XLVII.

[67] White to Root, June 15, 1906, *ibid.*; Whitaker, *op. cit.*, p. 102. Argentina's position on arbitration, pecuniary claims, and American tariff policy had not changed (República Argentina, Delegación a la Tercera Conferencia Internacional Americana, *Memoria de la delegación de la República Argentina presentada a la Tercera Conferencia Internacional Americana reunida en Rio de Janeiro*, pp. 28-30, 147-153).

Drago's proposal to The Hague was the most far-reaching action taken at Rio. Roosevelt's representatives and Drago's Argentine opponents had agreed—agreed to scotch Drago's bid for a practical Pan Americanism. What happened at The Hague was merely postlude.[68]

Secretary Root's good-will visit to Buenos Aires while the Rio Conference was still in session was an unqualified success. By officials and public alike he was received with genuine warmth.[69] His public statements, especially those against forcible collection of public debts, effectively stilled press criticism. Impressed by the popular reaction to Root's frankness, the American minister concluded that "the Argentine people and those of the United States [were] made friends on the surest of certain foundations—that of mutual acquaintance, understanding, and confidence." [70]

"Battleship Diplomacy"

The newborn glow of cordiality did not endure. Argentine-American harmony, like the Pan American unity to which it was indispensable, was soon befogged by the rise of power politics and a naval armaments race among the South American states.

The struggle for place between Argentina and Brazil reached its pre-World War I zenith in the years between the Third and Fourth Pan American Conferences. On the very day the Rio meeting convened the Brazilian government signed contracts with British shipyards for the construction of three modern battleships. Apprized of this startling intelligence three weeks after the Conference adjourned, the American ambassador at Rio forecast the grave situation that promptly developed. After some months of agitation, Argentina determined to respond with an expensive armaments program of its own.[71]

At the time the Brazilian action burst upon the Argentine horizon, no important unsettled diplomatic questions divided the two nations. But this challenge to Argentina's confidence in its own naval superiority over other South American states created tensions and inflamed passions that threatened to spread beyond its borders. Fortune dictated that the foreign ministries at this moment should be occupied by the two men who had matched their diplomatic talents before President Cleveland in the Misiones boundary dispute. Whatever hope existed that national

[68] See above, pp. 258-265.
[69] Mabragaña, *op. cit.*, VI, 214; República Argentina, *Diario de sesiones de la Cámara de Diputados,* July 4, 1906, pp. 188-189; *For. Rel.,* 1906, I, xlvi-xlix, 21ff. For the complete report on Root's visit, see Beaupré to Secretary of State, Aug. 14-21, 1906, NA, DS, Num. File, Vol. XXX, Case 194/99-139.
[70] *For. Rel.,* 1906, I, 24-25, 29.
[71] Lloyd C. Griscom, Ambassador to Brazil, to Root, Sept. 17, 20, 1906, NA, DS, Num. File, Vol. 139, Case 1070/1-3.

pride might be quickly soothed was sacrificed by the continuance in their portfolios of Baron do Rio Branco and Estanislao Zeballos, who had been estranged for more than a decade.[72]

Under these circumstances it was inevitable that century-old suspicions should be revived. Brazilians were apprehensive that Argentina was seeking to re-establish sovereignty over former viceregal territories. Argentines suspected that Brazil was supporting Uruguay's firm stand on the question of territorial jurisdiction over the waters of the Plata.[73]

Contributing to Argentina's uneasiness were the frequent public demonstrations of close friendship between the United States and Brazil. The Brazilian banquet tendered American delegates to the Hague Conference and the effusive welcome accorded a Brazilian admiral and his staff at the White House, turned to account by the Brazilian press, were assumed to lend plausibility to rumors of a military alliance and American encouragement of Brazilian rearming. Argentines could never understand why the United States maintained an ambassador in Rio but only a minister in Buenos Aires.[74]

No calculated tactics of Rooseveltian diplomacy could have more direly offended the sensitive Argentines in this period of tension than the blunders committed in sending the United States fleet around South America in late 1907. On August 28 the Navy Department advised the Secretary of State that the President had ordered the cruise of sixteen naval vessels through the Strait of Magellan to San Francisco. The fleet would coal at Trinidad, Rio de Janeiro, Punta Arenas, Callao, and Magdalena Bay.[75] The State Department interposed no policy objections to the omission of Buenos Aires and Valparaiso.

On January 15, while the fleet was in the harbor at Rio, Roosevelt sent the Brazilian president a warm message in which he referred to the warships as "messengers of friendship and good will commissioned to celebrate with you the long continued . . . amity . . . of the two great Republics." [76] News of Roosevelt's greetings struck Foreign Minister Zeballos like a bomb blast. In violent reaction, he called the fleet's bypassing of Argentina "an act of hostility," caustically upbraided his minister in Washington for inactivity, and ordered him, even at that late hour, to obtain visits of some ships to Buenos Aires or Bahía Blanca. Helpless, but without losing his sense of humor, the Argentine envoy

[72] Irving B. Dudley, Ambassador to Brazil, to Root, May 5, 1908, *ibid.*, Vol. 490, Case 6047/9; Charles L. Wilson, Chargé d'Affaires ad interim to Argentina, to Root, June 25, 1908, *ibid.*, Vol. 397, Case 4519/37-38.

[73] Dudley to Root, May 21, 1908, *ibid.*, nos. 10-11; Wilson to Root, Nov. 7, 1907, *ibid.*, Vol. 494, Case 6084/8-9.

[74] Beaupré to Root, Aug. 19, 24, 1907; Wilson to Root, July 23, 1908, *ibid.*, Vol. 490, Case 6047/1-5, 12-14.

[75] Asst. Sec. of Navy to Secretary of State, *ibid.*, Vol. 597, Case 8258/no number.

[76] *Ibid.*, nos. 70-71.

converted himself into a *"boue emissaire"* and begged Root to tell him what to reply.[77] Arrangements were hastily made to send a flotilla of destroyers to Buenos Aires.[78]

Five days after Roosevelt's cable to Brazil, Secretary Root undertook to pacify Zeballos. The cruise, he said, was strictly for training purposes, "determined upon and announced by the Navy Department without there having been any communication on the subject to or through the State Department." [79] But this explanation, tardily delivered and inaccurate in detail, was not the end of the matter. When the President and Secretary of State acknowledged telegrams from their Argentine opposites only by a directive to the American chargé, the Foreign Minister expressed surprise and regret. On the same day, Figueroa and Zeballos received directly the personal messages they felt obliged to solicit.[80] Roosevelt and Root had wasted away much of the official good will they had so carefully built up eighteen months before.

As these offenses to Argentine pride piled up, both governments were able to exploit the situation for the satisfaction of national ends. Jingoistic groups in Argentina inflated the incidents to whip up popular support for a naval-building program to match Brazil's.[81] Ultimately convinced by despatches from Buenos Aires that the United States must take some action, Assistant Secretary Adee laid the matter before his chief. "The Argentines have a strong impression," he wrote in an office memorandum, "that the United States shows a preferential friendship for Brazil. Is there any way of convincing them that we love them just as much as the Brazilians?" [82] Thus, the potential Argentine market for warships provided an outlet for the growing American urge to build them.[83]

Argentine legislators and strong press interests responded reluctantly to the pressure of the naval expansionists. Annually from 1906 to 1908 administration requests for vast naval appropriations touched off Cabinet crises and bitter congressional debates.[84] Not until December, 1908, thirty months after Brazil signed its battleship contracts, did President Figueroa

---

[77] Zeballos to Portela and Portela to Root, Jan. 16, 1908, *ibid.*, nos. 83-84.

[78] Root to Portela, Jan. 21, 1908, *ibid.*

[79] Root to Beaupré, Jan. 20, 1908, *ibid.*, no. 64.

[80] For the exchange of telegrams, dated Jan. 29, 1908, see *ibid.*, nos. 89, 90, 92, 93.

[81] Wilson to Secretary of State, Aug. 11, 1908, and Henry D. Janes, Chargé d'Affaires ad interim to Brazil, to Root, Oct. 4, 1908, *ibid.*, Vol. 490, Case 6047/15-16, 20-25.

[82] See Adee's longhand notations on Spencer F. Eddy, Minister to Argentina, to Secretary of State, Sept. 16, 1908, *ibid.*, Vol. 938, Case 15865/1.

[83] On the relationship of Argentina-American negotiations to the entire American policy on naval armament in South America, see Seward W. Livermore, "Battleship Diplomacy in South America," *The Journal of Modern History*, XVI (March, 1944), 31-48.

[84] Beaupré to Root, Oct. 11, 1906, and Wilson to Root, Sept. 9, 1907, NA, DS, Num. File, Vol. 139, Case 1070/4, 14; Eddy to Root, Sept. 16, 1908, *ibid.*, Vol. 938, Case 15865/1.

succeed in forcing his program through Congress. The law authorized approximately $55,000,000 for two battleships and eighteen destroyers, with an escalator clause providing for a third battleship and seven additional destroyers, if deemed necessary.[85]

American arms manufacturers were not caught napping. Three months before the bill became law, a representative of the Bethlehem Steel Corporation, personally endorsed by Charles M. Schwab, approached the American minister in Buenos Aires for official assistance.[86] After the Argentine government announced that its Legation in London would receive all bids, agents of arms producers from seven countries descended on the British capital. These included Schwab for Bethlehem, Admiral Francis T. Bowles, president of the Fore River Ship Building Company of Quincy, Massachusetts, and representatives of other American companies.[87] To aid the American firms, the State Department would go no further than to authorize Minister Spencer F. Eddy in Buenos Aires and Ambassador Whitelaw Reid in London to secure for them "equality of treatment" with other bidders.[88] To the close of the Roosevelt administration, initiative to gain an American share in the arms traffic was taken exclusively by the manufacturers themselves.

Taft and Knox, however, had bolder ideas. They committed themselves at once to a policy of "battleship diplomacy," complementary to "dollar diplomacy" in other economic spheres. They waited only three days to solicit from Argentina the "most favorable opportunity" for American competitors. They reminded the Argentines of the $10,000,000 loan, first in history, recently floated in the United States. At a critical point in the negotiations, they lifted the duties on Argentine hides. The pressure was polite but persistent. Moreover, their early reorganization of the State Department brought into existence the Division of Latin American Affairs, soon to be of special use both to the administration and to the shipbuilders.[89]

The most self-evident manifestation of Taft's policy was his appointment to the legation post in Buenos Aires of a close friend, to whom he gave the specific mission of securing at least one of the battleship contracts. Charles H. Sherrill, long a corporation lawyer in New York City and an active supporter of Taft's election, was peculiarly suited to this special assignment. His ebullient personality, developed from

---

[85] Eddy to Root, Nov. 25, Dec. 17, 1908, *ibid.*, Vol. 139, Case 1070/26, 36-37.
[86] Eddy to Root, Oct, 22, 1908, *ibid.*, no. 23.
[87] Eddy to Secretary of State, Dec. 18, 1908; Bowles to John C. O'Laughlin, Asst. Sec. of State, Feb. 10, 1909; S. C. Dumaine to George von L. Meyer, Secretary of Navy, Feb. 26, 1909, *ibid.*, nos. 25, 38-39, 43.
[88] Adee to American Legation, Sept. 18, 1908; Department to Reid, Feb. 11, 1909, *ibid.*, nos. 16, 38-39.
[89] Memorandum of Huntington Wilson, March 7, 1909; Memorandum of Adee, Sept. 24, 1909, *ibid.*, nos. 42a, 91; Knox to the President, March 30, 1911, NA, DS, 835.34/270.

wide travels and twenty years of campaigning for the Republican Party, placed him at home with both businessmen and statesmen. He delighted in bringing them together. He was the author of several books and would write many more. As a Yale undergraduate, he had been the American 100-yard-dash champion and had invented the crouch start for runners. His were the energetic hands to which Taft entrusted the execution of a policy.[90]

Sherrill wasted no time in softening up his clients for the wares he undertook to sell. En route to Buenos Aires, he conferred with the Argentine ministers in London and Paris, from whom he received introductions to porteño social circles.[91] Within sixty days after presenting his credentials (June 30), he had discussed battleships and inter-American diplomacy with all officials concerned, twice with President Figueroa and five times with Foreign Minister De la Plaza. Both, he believed, were favorable to American shipbuilders and steel manufacturers. He exerted special persuasion upon Roque Saenz Peña, who as Minister to Rome inclined to Italian firms and who as probable President-elect wielded influence. He conferred repeatedly with the editors of *La Prensa*, spearhead of the press campaign for naval expansion and champion of the American cause. Moreover, as agents of interested American firms shuttled in and out of Buenos Aires, he entertained them and established their contacts.[92]

Meanwhile, following closely reports of intense activity by rival bidders, the administration pushed its policy relentlessly. Under constant pressure from the heads of American companies,[93] the Secretary exhorted State Department personnel to "bend every effort," to "redouble your efforts," and to "force this battleship question to a successful issue." [94] Frequently he enlisted the services of the Navy Department. He reminded the Argentine minister of free hides and American loans, as well as of the favorable effects to be gained for ship subsidies, better banking facilities, and improved national feeling toward Argentina.[95]

[90] Sherrill, *The Sherrill Genealogy*, pp. 172-174; Taft to President of Argentina, April 7, 1909, NA, DS, Num. File, Vol. 1039, Case 18551/2; Sherrill to Knox, July 8, 1909, Vol. 139, Case 1070/72.

[91] Sherrill to Knox, June 24, 1909, *ibid.*, Vol. 325, Case 3501/38.

[92] The Minister's despatches on his conference were frequent. See, for example, those of July 29, Aug. 21, 27, Sept. 4, 9, Dec. 23, 1909, *ibid.*, Vols. 139-140, Case 1070/75, 77-79, 89, 102, 168.

[93] In addition to the Fore River Ship Building Company and the Bethlehem Steel Company, three other firms were active in the bidding: New York Ship Building Company, Newport News Shipbuilding and Dry Dock Company, and the Cramps Ship Building Company, of Philadelphia.

[94] Knox to American Legation, Dec. 7, 1909; Memorandum to Division of Latin American Affairs, Jan. 7, 1910; Adee to American Legation, Jan. 15, 1910, NA, DS, Num. File, Vol. 140, Case 1070/125, 154, 160.

[95] Memorandum of Huntington Wilson to Adee, Sept. 24, 1909, *ibid.*, Vol. 139, Case 1070/91.

Through the late months of 1909, Sherrill was confronted by one obstacle after another. When in July Argentina severed diplomatic relations with Bolivia, he feared his assigned role of intermediary would handicap the battleship negotiations. Diverse British maneuvers to secure reclassification of bidders' priorities, reopening of bids, and lowering of estimates gave repeated setbacks to Sherrill's progress with Argentine officials. When at a crucial juncture Secretary Knox demanded that Chile settle the Alsop claims case, Argentines resented his imperious tone.[96] To strengthen Sherrill's hand, the new Division of Latin American Affairs hastily conceived a prospectus of six special concessions to Argentine desires.[97]

After seven months of "constant, aggressive, and prompt action," the administration's efforts bore fruit.[98] On January 21, 1910, the Argentine naval commission awarded contracts for two battleships larger than any afloat to the Fore River Ship Building Company. The Bethlehem Steel Corporation received contracts to manufacture artillery for the torpedo boats to be built in European yards.[99] In competition with thirty or more bidders from England and five other nations, the new alliance of American diplomacy and private enterprise had gained a lion's share.[100]

American officials from Taft to Sherrill were singularly proud of their success in initiating the nation's first venture into the world's shipbuilding and ordnance-making competition. When a year later the United States Senate resolved to investigate the suspected release of naval secrets, Secretary Knox seized the opportunity to emphasize the vast prestige and efficiency the battleship contracts had brought to American labor, industry, and commerce.[101]

Little attention was paid at any level, public or private, to the possible effects of battleship diplomacy upon Hemisphere solidarity. By contributing to Argentine naval parity the United States helped to stabilize the power struggle in South America. By awarding naval contracts to American builders Argentina negated whatever intentions it might once have had of allying with Brazil and Chile to neutralize American influence on the continent. The negotiations required by building, servicing, and repairing the battleships placed Argentine and American naval interests in a favorable intimacy that was to endure. On the other hand, Pan American solidarity could hardly be expected to flower in the

---

[96] Sherrill to Secretary of State, July 22, Dec. 23, 1909, *ibid.*, Vol. 71, Case 534/20, and Vol. 140, Case 1070/168. Also see Livermore, *op. cit.*, pp. 37-39.

[97] Jan. 7, 1910, NA, DS, Num. File, Vol. 140, Case 1070/161.

[98] Memorandum of the Division of Latin American Affairs to the Secretary, Jan. 22, 1910, *ibid.*, no. 175.

[99] Sherrill to Secretary of State, Jan. 21, 1910, two cablegrams, *ibid.*, nos. 169, 170.

[100] *Sen. Doc.*, No. 3, 62 Cong., 1 sess., p. 3.

[101] The two battleships, named the *Moreno* and the *Rivadavia*, were launched in 1911 and turned over to Argentina in 1915.

shadow of a naval armaments race encouraged by the United States. Fortunately, as the Fourth Pan American Conference approached, other, more salutary influences were at work.

The Buenos Aires Conference

Two months after the awarding of the battleship contracts, Foreign Minister De la Plaza, soon to become vice-president, assured Minister Sherrill of his complete satisfaction with Taft-Knox policies in South America and his determination to follow where the Secretary led. During the following year the two nations cooperated more intimately than at any time in the history of their relationship. Upon Knox's initiative they joined Brazil in seeking to mediate Peru's dispute with Ecuador. Upon De la Plaza's insistence they resisted Brazil's proposal to intervene in the Tacna-Arica crisis. The United States represented Argentine interests in Bolivia and stood ready to assist restoration of relations.[102] None of these projects, of course, diminished Argentina's influence in South America nor did they in any degree commit the nation to the larger Pan American diplomacy.

The fourth general meeting of the American republics gave the Taft administration an opportunity to emphasize the importance of expanding trade with Latin America, an interest projected in the Republican platform, the President's inaugural address, and Secretary Knox's instructions to Minister Sherrill. Sherrill was as equal to this assignment as to that of battleship contracts. Even before his appointment was confirmed, in letters to Business Men's Republican Associations he himself had organized, he urged that each send a small delegation to Buenos Aires at the time of the Conference, still more than a year away. To leading members of the New York Chamber of Commerce he stressed the need for branch banks in Argentina.[103] Five days after arrival in Buenos Aires, he requested Knox to appoint as secretary of legation "a young unmarried man of means and companionable nature," qualified to take charge of entertaining delegates to the Conference.[104] Without the slightest hint from the Department, he secured Argentina's consent to change the opening date from May 25 to July 9, in order that more foreign guests might come and the United States might send a stronger delegation.[105]

Now that Argentina was at last to entertain the conference it had desired in 1901 and in 1906, it was even more foresighted than the

---

[102] See above, pp. 266-271. In May the United States had contributed to the success of Argentina's centennial celebration by sending Major General Leonard Wood as "Special Ambassador" and a Special Service Squadron of four battleships (*For. Rel., 1910*, pp. 4-7).

[103] Sherrill to Knox, April 5, 1909, NA, DS, Num. File, Vol. 766, Case 11302/20-21.

[104] Sherrill to Knox, June 24, 1909, *ibid.*, Vol. 325, Case 3501/38.

[105] *Ibid.*, Vol. 766, Case 11302/29, 30, 34.

zealous Minister. Two years in advance it appointed its committee on arrangements and its delegates nearly a year.[106] The Argentine press, with an enthusiasm for Pan Americanism it had never before shown, steadily prepared public opinion for the occasion. After personal interviews with President Taft, Secretary Knox, and ex-Secretary Root, a special representative of *La Prensa* wrote, "The public relations of Argentina with the United States, then, cannot be on a better footing. . . . The cause of panamericanism . . . has triumphed." [107] Moreover, the convening of the Conference in Buenos Aires would become the culminating event in Argentina's grand and enthusiastic celebration of its century of independence.

President Figueroa's nine appointees represented a total experience in foreign affairs unequalled by an Argentine delegation to any international conference before or since. Six had been ministers of foreign relations, five were veterans of previous Pan American conferences, four were members of the Permanent Court of Arbitration, and two had been ministers to Washington. In diplomatic experience the American delegation could not match the Argentine, although it included such distinguished Americans as Henry White, chairman, General Enoch H. Crowder, David Kinley, John Bassett Moore, Bernard Moses, and Paul S. Reinsch.[108]

The combination of Argentine hospitality, De la Plaza's endorsement of Knox's policies, and recent instances of cooperative diplomacy placed Argentine-American relations, and therefore the atmosphere of the Conference, on a plane of cordiality unique in inter-American affairs. When the Brazilian delegation sought to introduce a move to endorse the Monroe Doctrine, De la Plaza discussed with both White and Sherrill the advisability of the action; no resolution came to the floor. On other occasions, the Foreign Minister repressed the incipient turbulence of his own delegates.[109] White found excessive the deference of the Latin Americans, especially as the Argentines, Brazilians, and Chileans fell in line with American views.[110] Unfortunately, however, except for the item on pecuniary claims, the agenda did not deal with problems of deep significance.

President-elect Roque Saenz Peña, who had stunned the first conference with his "America for humanity" speech, returned to Buenos Aires from Italy in time to attend the closing sessions. It was in his

[106] Beaupré to Root, March 24, 1908; Sherrill to Knox, Aug. 25, 1909, *ibid.*, nos. 4, 48.

[107] Wilson to Secretary of State, May 3, 1909, *ibid.*, Vol. 928, Case 15504/7-8.

[108] Sherrill to Knox, Aug. 25, 1909, *ibid.*, Vol. 766, Case 11302/48; *Cuarta Conferencia Internacional Americana, 1910*, I, xxvii-xxviii.

[109] Sherrill to Secretary of State, July 27, Aug. 29, 1910, NA, DS, 710.D/270, 275.

[110] White to Knox, Sept. 5, 1910, *ibid.*, no. 329; Allan Nevins, *Henry White; Thirty Years of American Diplomacy*, pp. 308-311.

presence, therefore, that the new foreign minister, Carlos Rodríguez Larreta, uttered the closing panegyric:

> Gentlemen, in this year the majority of our republics complete a century of independent life. We can now say, as in Washington, "America for humanity," because we are sovereign nations and the place we occupy in the world we owe to strength of our own arm and to our blood heroically shed. But let my last words be to send from here a message of acknowledgment to the great nation which initiated these conferences, which preceded us in the struggle for independence, which afforded us the examples of a fruitful people organized as a republican nation, which on a day memorable in history said: "America for the Americans," and covered as it were with a shield the independence we had won.[111]

The Foreign Minister's encomium was undoubtedly an appropriate finale to the most tranquil of all general conferences of the American republics, but it was neither indicative of Argentina's past record nor prophetic of its future performance. Of the thirteen conventions it had signed at previous Conferences, Argentina had ratified only two. It would ratify none of the four signed at Buenos Aires. Nor, indeed, was the Minister's tribute a portent of continuing harmony in Argentine-American relations. The Buenos Aires Conference was but a mild season in stormy years of rivalry under the Pan American aegis.

---

[111] "Fourth International Conference of American States," *Sen. Doc.*, No. 744, 61 Cong., 3 sess., p. 54.

Part Six: World and Inter-American Affairs

XIX

WORLD WAR I:
NEUTRALITY AND BELLIGERENCY, 1914-1918

The outbreak of world war in 1914 staggered the unsuspecting governments and populations of Argentina and the United States. Encumbered as they were by problems of domestic evolution, Argentines in the agony of financial depression and Americans in the ferment of progressive reforms, both peoples were shocked by the war's suddenness. Neither psychologically nor economically were they prepared to adjust quickly to the rapid spread of the conflict. As potential sources of the sinews of war, agricultural and industrial, neither state could expect to avoid some degree of involvement, whatever the wishes of its people or the intentions of its government.

Devoted from birth to their characteristic varieties of isolationism, both nations recurrently found historic interests and policies defied by the belligerents. Both suffered the challenges to national honor and self-respect implicit in Germany's submarine aggressions and in Britain's more subtle economic warfare. From within and without, both received assaults of propaganda from nations with which they had traditional ties. Like other American states with which they could commiserate but not join in effective unity, they endured the European flouting of the Hemisphere security they had vainly tried to establish.

At the height of their attempts to maintain the neutrality they coveted, the two nations concurrently passed through the stress of presidential election campaigns. Subsequent contests between executives and electorates over the issue of war served to edge the northern republic more surely into the path of total involvement and to anchor the southern more securely to nonintervention.

Legations Become Embassies: Naón and Stimson

The importance of their relations in wartime was symbolized at the outset by the reciprocal elevation of missions from legations to embassies.[1] The first ambassadorial appointees were Rómulo S. Naón and Frederic Jesup Stimson. With a continuity rare in their century of intercourse, Argentina and the United States maintained these chiefs of mission throughout the war. Actually, Naón served eight years in Washington, Stimson six and a half in Buenos Aires.

Rómulo Naón, scholar and youthful veteran of provincial and national policies, was first appointed Minister to the United States by President Saenz Peña in December, 1910. Until his resignation at the close of the war, he served continuously as minister and ambassador under presidents of two parties. In a variety of ways he labored to harmonize Argentina's relations with the United States, to induce its full participation in the war, and to promote inter-American solidarity.[2]

Frederic Stimson, professor of comparative legislation at Harvard University, was a neophyte in diplomacy but a veteran member of several Massachusetts public commissions and of Democratic national conventions. He had written novels as well as legal textbooks and would publish his memoirs and translate José Enrique Rodó's *Ariel*. Nearly sixty when Wilson appointed him, he retained his interest in golf, managing during leave in 1916 to sandwich in at least one diplomacy-flavored match with his friend, Naón.[3] He was a man of charm and puckish humor. In Buenos Aires, where the porteños have a penchant for nicknames, his erect carriage, grey hair, and pointed beard won him the title of "Jesus in a dress-suit." [4]

The United States and Argentina Test Neutrality

Left dazed and unprepared by the coming of war, the peoples of the United States and Argentina raised no protests against the prompt neutrality declarations (August 4 and 5) of Presidents Wilson and De la Plaza. At first flush, to the overwhelming majority in each nation the war was Europe's, unfortunate and deplorable but remote and unthreatening to the Americas.

More compellingly than the masses of other American republics, however, they soon found their loyalties drawn toward the participants, especially the Allied Powers. Argentines were bound to Britain by a

---

[1] *Memoria, 1913-1914*, pp. 183-205; William J. Bryan, Secretary of State, to American Legation, May 16, 1914, NA, DS, 124.35/10b. The formalities were not concluded until December (*ibid.*, 701.3511/109).

[2] Robert W. Bliss, Chargé d'Affaires ad interim to Argentina, to Secretary of State, Nov. 19, 1910, *ibid.*, no. 23; W. B. Parker, *Argentines of To-Day*, I, 546-549.

[3] Robert Lansing, Acting Secretary of State, to George Lorillard, Chargé d'Affaires to Argentina, Sept. 21, 1914, NA, DS, 123.St5/a; *Buenos Aires Herald*, April 20, 1921; Stimson, *My United States, passim*.

[4] Hugh Wilson, *The Education of a Diplomat*, p. 119. Wilson was Stimson's secretary.

century of economic reciprocity, Americans by ties of race, language, and political principles. Argentines felt a deep cultural affinity for France, Americans a genuine sentimental attachment. Both populations were in the process of absorbing millions of Italian immigrants, their affections still close to the homeland. Argentina had no such sizable German minority as the United States, yet it could ill afford to sacrifice the huge commerce it had built up with the strongest of the Central Powers.[5]

For many reasons, whether they chose or not, Argentina and the United States were indispensable to the salvation of each belligerent. They were the storehouses of the agricultural resources and raw materials whose possession—or denial to the enemy—might decide the conflict. The United States was the only Western power not committed to the war. To most European governments Argentina was the acknowledged leader of Latin America. Both nations, therefore, became fair prey for twentieth-century techniques of propaganda and economic warfare.

At the outset the derangement of merchant shipping and the dislocation of foreign markets acutely affected the economies of both republics. German cargo carriers were soon sealed in port. Allied vessels were sometimes diverted to more strategic purposes. The lack of regular direct ship connections between east coast ports and Buenos Aires, scored for a century, was now temporarily disastrous. Argentine purchases of luxury goods, even of necessities, sharply declined. Imports of fresh capital ceased. For Argentina, long reliant upon the English market, no economic effect was so grave as the destruction of its developing trade with Germany. In 1913, Germany had been more than four times as good a customer as the United States. As a supplier of goods, it exceeded the United States and approached Great Britain.[6]

As the war settled down to its enduring pattern, however, and the needs of the combatants expanded, American and Argentine economies were bound to prosper. By the end of 1915 both countries were geared to supply Allied demands. At the same time, United States-Argentine trade mounted in astronomical proportions. American exports, which dropped to $27,000,000 in 1914, jumped to $53,000,000 in 1915, $77,000,-000 in 1916, and $107,000,000 in 1917. Argentine dollar sales to the United States in 1918 ($228,000,000) were double those of 1916, which in turn had doubled those of 1914. For the first time since 1902, the United States surrendered the favorable balance of trade.[7]

Defense of the neutral rights often involved in this vast movement of

[5] Percy Alvin Martin, *Latin America and the War*, pp. 173-186.

[6] Department of State memorandum, signed by Harry G. Seltzer, July 21, 1917, NA, DS, 611.35/2.

[7] *Statistical Abstract of the United States, 1920*, p. 411.

commerce was a far more difficult task for both nations than the mere observance of neutrality. Considering its reputation as an uncooperative, even pro-German, neighbor during World War I, Argentina from 1914 to 1917 revealed a surprising eagerness to act jointly with the United States and the other American republics. At numerous crucial points Argentine leaders sought American guidance, suggested joint action, or promoted Pan American consideration of common problems.

During the first month of war Ambassador Naón requested Secretary Bryan to advise his government on neutral rights not covered by the Hague Convention. Specifically, he requested direction on treatment of armed merchantmen and wireless apparatus on belligerent vessels.[8] Six weeks later, concerned about British interpretation of conditional contraband and rules of search and seizure, he suggested "the gratification with which the Argentine Government would see the establishment of a close understanding between our governments upon the doctrine which would best protect the common interests." Bryan was willing to agree with Argentina to keep each other informed but not to adopt a policy of joint representation to the British government.[9]

As early as August and twice more before the end of November, Naón or his superiors urged the advisability of Pan American agreement on rules and procedures for neutrality.[10] Unable to get a conclusive answer from Bryan, the Ambassador presented the problem at a meeting of the Governing Board of the Pan American Union on December 8. The Board authorized the creation of a special commission of nine members, with the Secretary of State as chairman, to study and report on problems presented by the war. With White House approval, neither Secretary Bryan nor his successor, Lansing, pushed the commission or its subcommittee on neutrality to decisive action.[11]

Failing to press for the Pan American unanimity he might have secured, President Wilson nevertheless became the champion of neutral rights for the American states. Each time he protested the rival retaliations of the belligerents, Ambassador Stimson was able to report from Buenos Aires that the De la Plaza administration or the Argentine press strongly approved the action. *La Nación* was the strongest supporter of Wilson's policies, as it praised the "triumph of American diplomacy and spirit," the "service which humanity has received at the hands of

[8] Naón to Bryan, Aug. 20; Naón to Lansing, Aug. 28; Lansing to Naón, Aug. 21, 29, 1914, NA, DS, 763.72111/223, 224.

[9] Naón to Bryan, Nov. 9, and Bryan to Naón, Nov. 13, 1914, *For. Rel., 1914,* Supplement, pp. 433-435.

[10] See note 8 above, and Lorillard to Secretary of State, Nov. 18, 1914, *ibid.,* pp. 437-438.

[11] Minutes of the Governing Board of the Pan American Union, Dec. 8, 1914, Nov. 1, 1916, *For. Rel., 1914,* Sup., p. 444, and NA, DS, 710.001/121,165; R. S. Baker, *Woodrow Wilson, Life and Letters,* V, 298.

the United States," and "the deepest fellow-feeling" with which the American republics received Wilson's policy.[12]

The President's leadership of the neutrals might have been even more eagerly accepted had he chosen to consult more closely with their leaders or if suspicion had not lingered that the United States might itself one day enter the war and abandon them to their own resources. Even in enthusiasm for his Pan American Peace Pact, Wilson failed to press home the fullest advantages of his position.[13] In the early months Bryan was lukewarm toward the idea of Hemisphere solidarity. And by the time Lansing took over, the very diplomatic crises which stimulated the need for Pan American unity drew the President's energies toward Europe. When by July, 1916, President De la Plaza volunteered Argentine willingness to act with the United States in common leadership of the American states, it was too late.[14]

American Belligerency and Argentine Neutrality

Transition of the United States from leadership of the neutral nations to association with the Allied Powers marked the parting of the way with Argentina. The breaking of diplomatic relations with Germany in February, 1917, followed by four months the inauguration of Hipólito Irigoyen and by three the re-election of President Wilson. The coincidence of Germany's resumption of maritime aggression and presidential elections in the two nations determined the character of their relations for the duration of the war.

In electing Irigoyen in 1916, the Argentine people ousted the caste which had ruled for a generation and placed in the presidency for the first time a candidate of the Radical Party. The new election law of 1912, providing secret, compulsory voting, gave the Argentine citizenry an unrestricted presidential choice it had never enjoyed. It was Roque Saenz Peña, Blaine's adversary of 1890, who sponsored the law. Curiously, therefore, a foremost representative of the Conservative Party opened the Casa Rosada to a political opponent who would assert Argentina's will to independence of action as vigorously as had he at the First Pan American Conference.

When Ambassador Stimson received news of Wilson's decision to break with Germany, he sought audience at once with the President and the Acting Foreign Minister. Though he had been in office since October, Irigoyen had not yet appointed a chief of the Ministry but saddled its duties upon his minister of agriculture, Honorio Pueyrre-

---

[12] Stimson to Secretary of State, Feb. 18, Sept. 2, 1915, April 21, 1916, NA, DS, 763.72/1474, 2177, 2604, 2705; *La Nación*, Sept. 2, 1915, April 21, 1916.

[13] See below, pp. 326-328.

[14] Stimson to Secretary of State, July 15, 17, 1916, NA, DS, 711.35/23, 24.

dón.[15] The Ambassador had been instructed not only to announce the diplomatic break but also to convey Lansing's circular invitation that all neutrals follow the American course.[16] But the former professor was not one to apply Big-Power pressure. Recalling the important interview at a later date, he sympathetically recorded Irigoyen as saying:

> You have come to the end of a way—when my country is only at its beginning. You have seen Germany sink scores of your ships—destroy hundreds of American lives—Argentina, not one. It is nearly two years since the *Lusitania,* one year since the *Sussex.* Your patience is at last extinguished. But we of Argentina have not suffered. It is a terrible thing for me to involve my people in the Great War. *I cannot do it for sympathetic reasons alone.* I must have a concrete injury, a *casus belli.* Germany has broken no promise to us. We have only the same note from them that you have—and we shall answer it.[17]

The Argentine reply to Lansing's formal announcement was a simple note of acknowledgment, without the expression of sympathy or word of "Pan-American confraternity" Stimson had suggested. In reply to Germany's notification of renewed submarine warfare, however, true to Irigoyen's commitment to the Ambassador, Pueyrredón wrote that "the Argentine Government deplores that His Imperial Majesty should have seen fit to adopt such extreme measures." [18]

Two months later, when the United States declared war, the official Argentine reaction followed the same pattern. As in the case of every declaration of war by an American nation against Germany, Irigoyen scrupulously avoided formal pronouncement of neutrality. To him, neutrality was the normal state of nations; there was no need to declare it.[19] On the other hand, since the United States was defending principles of international law in which Argentina believed, Pueyrredón's response to Stimson's note expressly recognized the justice of the American cause.[20] To Secretary Lansing, this reply was disappointing; to the German Minister, Count Karl von Luxburg, it embodied unneutral language; to Irigoyen, it left the door open for future Argentine actions.[21]

The mass of the Argentine people reacted with mixed feelings. A large group of intellectuals and former officials, headed by Luis Drago,

[15] Stimson to Secretary of State, Feb. 6, 1917, NA, DS, 763.72/3235.

[16] *For. Rel., 1917,* Sup. 1, p. 108.

[17] Stimson, *op. cit.,* p. 368.

[18] *For. Rel., 1917,* Sup. 1, pp. 225-228; República Argentina, Ministerio de Relaciones Exteriores y Culto, *Documentos y actos de gobierno relativos a la guerra en Europa,* pp. 45-46 (hereinafter cited as "Blue Book").

[19] Lucio M. Moreno Quintana, *La diplomacia de Yrigoyen,* pp. 445-446; Ricardo Ryan, *La política internacional y la presidencia Yrigoyen,* p. 22n.

[20] "Blue Book," pp. 49-50; Stimson to Secretary of State, April 10, 16, 1917, *For. Rel., 1917,* Sup. 1, pp. 249-250, and NA, DS, 763.72/4764.

[21] Stimson, *op. cit.,* pp. 368-372.

sent President Wilson a message of tribute and sympathy, delivered in person to Ambassador Stimson.[22] Pro-Allies speeches, processions, and mass meetings, usually sponsored by opponents of the administration, were common. But approval of Irigoyen's course, proclaimed by huge meetings in Córdoba, Mendoza, and Buenos Aires, was also widespread. The Socialist Party, defying the views of its leaders, voted against intervention.[23]

To many statesmen and journalists on both sides of the Atlantic, Hipólito Irigoyen was pro-German and anti-American. Probably he was neither of these. Certainly he was pro-Argentine, extremely so. As an idol of the masses he had led for twenty-five years, he undoubtedly believed that he could best serve their interests by avoiding intervention in a war they were totally unprepared to fight. Severance of diplomatic relations or declaration of war by the United States, or by Brazil and other Latin states, might be the soundest courses of action for them, but only for them. Since these were his beliefs, he would let no force, Argentine or alien, weaken his will to abide by them. Though many of Irigoyen's actions are open to conjecture, his decisions on Argentine neutrality were usually unhesitating and consistent.[24]

In Stimson's view, Irigoyen's neutrality was not based on pro-German sympathies. It may have been founded in part on his dislike of the English and his hatred of the long-standing alliance between British financiers and Argentine oligarchs. By 1914 the German community in Argentina had grown large, rich, and powerful. During half a century its influence had penetrated Argentine education, business, journalism, and society. Since 1912 a German military mission had trained the politically important Army. Until Britain closed the seas to its merchant ships, Germany had been for Argentine exporters a rich market. Should it bring about the prostration of Germany, therefore, Allied victory might restore and perpetuate the British commercial and financial monopoly.[25]

[22] The original message is filed in NA, DS, 763.72/4765. See also J. B. Scott, "Argentina and Germany: Dr. Drago's Views," *The American Journal of International Law*, XII (Jan., 1918), 140-142.

[23] Stimson to Secretary of State, April 10, 13, 14, 22, May 1, 1914, NA, DS, 763.72/3761, 3824, 3839, 4001, 4213, 4760.

[24] Cf. Stimson, *op. cit.*, pp. 368-371; Moreno Quintana, *op. cit.*, pp. 445-446; Martin, *op. cit.*, pp. 251-253; A. P. Whitaker, *The United States and Argentina*, pp. 98-100; Hugo Wast, "President Irigoyen of Argentina," *Current History*, XXX (Aug., 1929), p. 872.

[25] Stimson, *op. cit.*, pp. 369-372; Stimson to Secretary of State, Sept. 16, 24, 1917, NA, DS, 763.72/4764, 6983; unsigned Department memorandum, attached to Stabler to Harrison, June 23, 1917, 862.20235/16.

Neutral Argentina Salutes the American Fleet

However strait-laced President Irigoyen sought to be in his policy toward America's quarrel with Germany, he repeatedly revealed basic pro-American leanings. On several occasions he made use of the door he told Ambassador Stimson he would hold open for future freedom of action. When the United States broke relations, Argentina deplored Germany's resumption of submarine warfare. When the United States declared war, Argentina endorsed the action—and Count Luxburg officially enquired if he should ask for his passports. Most unneutral of all was Argentina's welcome to an American fleet, again prompting the German to ask if he was expected to leave. Lacking the *casus belli* he said he must have to justify intervention, Irigoyen refused to sign on Lansing's dotted line, but his pro-German vote was obviously not in Luxburg's pocket.[26]

The reasons, diplomatic or strategic, for the fleet's visit to Buenos Aires in July, 1917, are none too clear. After entering the war, the American Navy took over patrol of the South Atlantic from the British. Arguing that it needed the same privileges in Argentine waters it had already been granted in Brazilian and Uruguayan,[27] the Navy reasoned that a four- or five-day visit by American warships would force Argentina to revoke its neutrality.[28] Whether or not President Wilson agreed with the Navy's views, the State Department directed Stimson to secure Argentine approval for a visit by Admiral Caperton's fleet.[29]

The Ambassador performed his mission promptly. On June 30 the Argentine Senate in secret session unanimously agreed that the American fleet should be received if its commanders decided to call at Buenos Aires. Four days later, July 4th, at a mass meeting staged by Irigoyen's opponents to force his hand on the invitation, Stimson delivered the opening address. On the 14th the formal invitation was tendered and accepted.[30]

But these actions were largely window dressing, perhaps for public

[26] Stimson, *op. cit.*, pp. 368, 372, 388.

[27] On June 18, while still neutral, Uruguay decreed that "no American state, which, in defense of its rights, finds itself in a state of war with nations of other continents, will be treated as a belligerent" (Juan Carlos Welker, *Baltasar Brum: verbo y acción*, pp. 175-176; Stimson, *op. cit.*, p. 385). The Uruguayan action was a forerunner of a similar resolution passed by all of the American states at the third meeting of Ministers of Foreign Affairs at Rio de Janeiro in January, 1942.

[28] Memorandum from Division of Latin American Affairs to Frank L. Polk, Acting Secretary of State, July 13, 1917, NA, DS, 811.3335/20. The memorandum was prepared after a conference with the Department of Navy.

[29] Stimson, *op. cit.*, p. 386.

[30] *Ibid.*, pp. 386-388. The Senate resolution is printed in *Memoria, 1917-1918*, pp. 269-270.

consumption. On the day before the Senate session, briefed by the Foreign Minister himself, Pueyrredón had advised Stimson that his government hoped the fleet would come and that an Argentine squadron would meet it at the mouth of the Plata. The Ambassador cleared his Fourth of July speech with the Minister. The two diplomats worked out in conference the phraseology of the notes to be exchanged. When the State Department insisted that the fleet visit must be unconditional, that ships must be permitted to enter ports for any purpose, President Irigoyen ruled that no conditions would be attached to the invitation if assurance was given that it would be accepted. No attempt was made to restrict the stay to the twenty-four hours authorized by the Hague Convention.[31]

The appearance of Admiral Caperton's vessels in the harbor of Buenos Aires gave pro-Allies Argentines an opportunity to air their pent-up sympathies. The recent German sinking of two ships flying Argentine flags increased the intensity of their feelings. As Stimson put it, Buenos Aires "threw her house out of the window." Perhaps 200,000 porteños greeted the arrival of the warships and the parade of their sailors and marines. Under arms, they marched through the capital's avenues to permit their commander to lay wreaths at the statues of San Martín and Washington. President Irigoyen and other officials warmly received and entertained the Admiral and his staff. Upon their departure, Irigoyen asked Stimson to advise President Wilson that the welcome came from the hearts of the people and invited Admiral Caperton to stay longer if he desired.[32] Nothing like it had happened in Buenos Aires before.

German Submarines, Argentine Ships, and Luxburg

At the moment when Buenos Aires was lavishing its hospitality on the American fleet the Argentine government was in the midst of diplomatic controversy with Germany over the sinking of the *Toro*. This was the second of three German affronts to Argentine sovereignty between April and September, each threatening for a time to end the nation's neutrality. The first was the torpedoing of the *Monte Protegido;* the third was the revelation of Count Luxburg's insolence and cynicism.[33]

---

[31] Stimson, *op. cit.,* pp. 387-388. The correspondence is printed in *For. Rel., 1917,* pp. 5-8, and "Blue Book," pp. 105-106. Placing a different interpretation upon the use of "unconditional," Moreno Quintana says that Stimson announced that the fleet "would enter unconditionally" (*op. cit.,* pp. 153-156). See also Estanislao Zeballos, "Gobierno radical: la visita de la escuadra americana," *Revista de Derecho, Historia y Letras,* LVII (Aug., 1917), 526ff.

[32] *For. Rel., 1917,* pp. 7-8; Stimson, *op. cit.,* pp. 391-396.

[33] A comprehensive discussion of the effects of these events on Argentina's attitude toward the war is contained in Martin, *op. cit.,* pp. 199-254. Many of the documents on these three events are reproduced in C. A. Silva, *La política internacional de la Nación Argentina,* pp. 525-544.

Argentina first felt directly the sting of German submarine warfare in the destruction on April 4 and June 22 of its merchant ships *Monte Protegido* and *Toro*. In neither sinking was there loss of Argentine lives. In the first case, Argentina accepted prompt German settlement in the form of regrets, reparation in full, and a salute to the Argentine flag. Diplomatic negotiations over the *Toro* were more complicated, but Pueyrredón's near ultimatum eventually brought about apparent capitulation. On August 28 Germany not only granted the concessions made in the earlier sinking but also agreed to recognize the freedom of the seas upon which Argentina insisted.[34]

Though each incident aroused the hopes of the interventionists (*rupturistas*), neither led to strong popular demand for the end of neutrality. On the basis of the diplomatic exchanges the Irigoyen administration could claim a complete diplomatic victory over the German Empire.[35] That Germany could ill afford to antagonize one of the last important uncommitted American neutrals or to jeopardize the status of its rich economic interests was not at the moment a significant factor in Argentine consideration. Nor was it known until later that President Irigoyen had made a secret commitment to Luxburg that Argentine ships would not enter the war zone.[36]

Eleven days after settlement of the *Toro* incident, the third and by far the most sinister violation of Argentine sovereignty—and sensitivity—was revealed. On September 8 the American government released for publication three Luxburg cablegrams intercepted by the British and transmitted to the State Department for tactical use. Two of these included the Minister's oft-quoted recommendation that Argentine ships be "sunk without a trace"; the third characterized Pueyrredón as a "notorious ass and anglophile."[37] Although Secretary Lansing disclosed the intercepts to Ambassador Naón on September 7 and advised him of his determination to publish them, he had neither sought prior approval of the Argentine government nor given it advance notification.[38] Unfortunately, Naón's report failed to reach Buenos Aires until many hours after the porteño press carried the sensational news.[39]

Reaction in Argentina to Luxburg's callous recommendations was instantaneous. Demand for severance of relations with Germany was loud and general, yet by no means unanimous. The administration acted with prompt severity—against Luxburg but not against his government.

[34] "Blue Book," pp. 85-90, 93-102.
[35] Stimson to Secretary of State, April 15, May 5, June 26, 1917, *For. Rel., 1917,* Sup. 1, pp. 255, 275-276, 303.
[36] Martin, *op. cit.,* pp. 211-212, 222-224.
[37] Lansing to Stimson, *For. Rel., 1917,* Sup. 1, pp. 322-323.
[38] Secretary Lansing recounts his handling of the entire incident in *War Memoirs of Robert Lansing,* pp. 326-329. See also David J. Hill, "The Luxburg Secret Correspondence," in *The American Journal of International Law,* XII (Jan., 1918), pp. 135-140.
[39] Sept. 10, 1917, *Memoria, 1917-1918,* pp. 58-59.

Without giving Berlin the chance to recall him, Pueyrredón on September 12 handed the minister his passports. On the same day, while notifying the German government of Luxburg's dismissal, the Foreign Minister thanked it for "the magnanimous and dignified manner" in which it had settled the *Toro* incident.[40] Irigoyen evidently reasoned that the envoy and not his government had committed the affront.

The President's unwillingness to use Luxburg's conduct as a cause for breaking relations did not satisfy large sectors of the Argentine press, population, and Congress. *La Epoca*, long an administration supporter, and *La Nación* wasted no time in demanding rupture. [41] The people of Buenos Aires, as they usually do when aroused, organized vast demonstrations and mass meetings. Their chief spokesman was again Dr. Luis M. Drago, who declared that the German government, as well as its agent, was guilty of contemptuous and reprehensible actions. Other intellectuals and anti-Irigoyenists supported his views.[42] Even after listening to briefings by the Foreign Minister, the Senate and the Chamber of Deputies voted overwhelmingly (September 19 and 25) that the President should suspend diplomatic relations.[43]

When on September 21 Irigoyen received the German government's regrets and complete disavowal of Luxburg's ideas, he was ready to regard the incident as closed.[44] As the initial shock and pain of wounded pride diminished, the *neutralistas* moved into the open. They formed a neutrality committee headed by the well-known writer Ernesto Quesada. Various groups, especially in the provinces, flooded administration newspapers with petitions supporting neutrality. Estanislao Zeballos, ex-foreign minister and special envoy to the United States, publicly supported Irigoyen's attitude toward both Luxburg and Germany. Pro-German elements sought to foment discord between Argentina and Brazil and censured the United States for publishing the Luxburg telegrams without Argentine approval.[45]

Lansing's calculated risk that revelation of Luxburg's insolence would bring Argentina into the war missed its mark. Convinced that the Department had overplayed its hand, Stimson was unable to discern the trend in Argentine policy the Secretary had hoped to promote.

---

[40] Pueyrredón to Luxburg, and to Luis B. Molina, Argentine Minister to Germany, *ibid.*, pp. 64-65.

[41] Stimson to Secretary of State, Sept. 10, 1917, NA, DS, 862.20235/34.

[42] Scott, *op. cit.*, p. 141.

[43] *Diario de sesiones de la Cámara de Senadores*, p. 567; *Diario de sesiones de la Cámara de Diputados*, p. 2662; *For. Rel.*, 1917, Sup. 1, pp. 328, 330.

[44] Molina to Pueyrredón, Sept. 22, 1917, *Memoria, 1917-1918*, pp. 95-96; Stimson to Secretary of State, Oct. 17, 1917, NA, DS, 862.20235/149.

[45] Stimson to Secretary of State, Oct. 3, 10, 13, *ibid.*, no. 131, and 763.72/7096, 7270; Zeballos, "Gobierno radical: incidente del Conde Luxburg," *Revista de Derecho, Historia y Letras*, LVIII (Oct., 1917), 254-255. On American efforts to counteract German propaganda, see J. R. Mock, "The Creel Committee in Latin America," *The Hispanic American Historical Review*, XXII (May, 1942), 263ff.

Though the Ambassador cabled fifty-six messages in forty-eight days, Lansing thrice chided him for inadequate intelligence coverage.[46]

In his memoirs and official despatches Stimson has left his record of the Argentine attitude toward involvement in the war. His analyses shed light on the enigma of Irigoyen's stubborn neutrality. By yielding to every Argentine demand on the *Monte Protegido* and *Toro* sinkings, the German Foreign Office left no cause for a diplomatic break. In five months Irigoyen had wrung from Germany greater concessions than Wilson had secured in two years. When the German minister violated the simplest rules of humanity and diplomacy, Argentina immediately dismissed him. His phrases were evil and offensive, but he had taken no Argentine lives. For two years after 128 Americans were lost on the *Lusitania* the United States had tolerated Count von Bernstorff.

In Irigoyen's view, Congress did not represent the will of the people. He looked upon its actions as political maneuvers to "put him in a hole." Moreover, resolutions were only statements of congressional views, not bills demanding executive action.

But behind Irigoyen's rationalization of contemporary decisions, thought Stimson, were basic goals: to even the balance between belligerents, to keep alive the threat of German competition against English interests, and to promote Argentine leadership of the neutrals Wilson had abandoned. In pursuing his aims, he may have been strongly influenced by pro-German and pro-Spanish advisers, but the aims themselves were pro-Argentine.

At the root of popular and congressional failure to force Irigoyen's hand, reasoned Stimson, was deep resentment, veiled but widespread, against the United States for releasing Luxburg's despatches without Argentine consent or knowledge. The German's contemptuousness was offensive enough without its airing by a friendly power. Lansing's policy may have frustrated the very Argentine decision it was designed to promote.[47]

At any rate, the Secretary did not make the same mistake a second time. When Argentina asked the State Department to decode copies of some four hundred captured Luxburg despatches, Lansing suggested to Ambassador Naón simultaneous publication of the translations. On December 21, forty of the messages were published in both countries.[48]

---

[46] Lansing to Embassy, Sept. 18, Oct. 24; Polk to Embassy, Sept. 28; Stimson to Secretary of State, Oct. 25, 1917, NA, DS, 862.20235/44, 107a, 159a, 160.

[47] Stimson to Secretary of State, Oct. 4, 15, Dec. 6, 10, 1917, NA, DS, 763.72/7645, 7774, 8002 (confidential file), 8468; Stimson, *op. cit.*, pp. 406-411.

[48] *War Memoirs of Robert Lansing*, p. 328; Lansing to Embassy, Dec. 14; Stimson to Secretary of State, Oct. 31, Dec. 15, 20, 21, 1917, NA, DS, 862.20235/175, 196, 201, 206; *For. Rel., 1917*, Sup. 1, pp. 392-393. In the United States, many of the intercepted despatches were published in Committee on Public Information, *The Official Bulletin*, Oct. 31, Dec. 21, 1917.

Although their appearance at this time was something of an anticlimax, exciting little reaction in Buenos Aires,[49] editorial treatment of their contents by the *Washington Post* created a passing tempest. "Is the Argentine Government independent," asked the Post, "or is it directed by Germans?" After half a dozen questions in the same vein, it continued, "If it is argued that some of these questions pertain solely to Argentina and do not concern the United States, it ought to be answered that the United States cannot remain indifferent to the attitude of any American nation in its relations with Germany." Officials quickly patched up the offense, but only after the Argentine press had whipped up considerable ill-feeling over the editorial strictures by what *La Epoca* called an official organ of the American government.[50]

For Ambassador Naón and his relations with both governments, the *Post's* slurs on Argentine integrity came at an unfortunate moment. After seven years of residence in the United States, he had become a strong supporter both of American policy and of Pan American solidarity. He earnestly believed that Argentina's faith in right and justice demanded a more active role in the war and closer cooperation with the other American republics. In language that presaged the Rio Pact he once told Irigoyen he regarded an attack upon the United States as an attack upon Argentina.[51] Throughout 1917 he had urged his government to place Argentina at the side of its sister states. With Lansing, he had hoped the revelation of the Luxburg telegrams would tip the balance. Now, in the middle of controversy, he penned these ideas in his resignation and soon sailed for Buenos Aires.[52]

Argentine Economic Aid to the Allies

Before the end of 1917, the Irigoyen government had molded a satisfactory pattern of conduct toward the two groups of belligerents. In acknowledging Wilson's proclamation of war, it had endorsed American defense of international principles in which Argentina believed. By securing full indemnification for the sinking of its vessels, it had salvaged national honor without resorting to a diplomatic break. By welcoming the American fleet in violation of the rules of neutrality, it had revealed Argentine sympathy for the American cause. By dismissing Luxburg but absolving his government of responsibility for his offenses, it had

---

[49] Stimson to Secretary of State, Dec. 22, 1917, *For. Rel., 1917*, Sup. 1, pp. 393-394.

[50] *Washington Post*, Dec. 22, 1917; República Argentina, Ministerio de Relaciones Exteriores y Culto, *Circular informativa mensual*, No. 7 (Dec., 1917), pp. 13ff; Lansing to Embassy, Dec. 24, and Stimson to Secretary of State, Dec. 26, 1917, Jan. 4, 17, 18, 1918, NA, DS, 862.20235/210, 215, 221, 259, 260.

[51] Department of State memorandum, July 16, 1918, NA, DS, 611.3531/61.

[52] A copy of Naón's resignation, dated Dec. [no day], 1917, is filed with Stimson to Secretary of State, Nov. 29, 1918, NA, DS, 701.3511/695.

evened the balance of its unneutral favoritism toward the warring sides. By inviting the Latin nations to a conference of neutrals, it had reasserted Argentine claims to leadership of Latin America.[53] Now, its determination to neutrality established, it could devote greater attention to the nation's economic welfare in the face of war.

The paramount instance of wartime cooperation with the Allies was the Wheat Convention of January 14, 1918.[54] Largely through the interposition of the United States and Ambassador Stimson, Argentina assured markets for its surpluses by contracting to sell two and one-half million tons of wheat to Great Britain and France.[55] Although actual negotiation of the Convention required only two months, preliminary preparations began in Washington as early as July, 1917.

While the administration was still preparing to institute domestic wheat controls, the State Department warned Stimson that "every large wheat-growing country and the nations friendly to the Allied cause are expected to make similar sacrifices or readjustments in their export distribution." It directed him discreetly to present this point of view to the Argentine government.[56] Between July and November, representatives of the Treasury Department, Food Administration, and the British Embassy discussed with Secretary Lansing the relationship of Argentina to wheat shortages and the alternatives for financing purchases. The Latin American Division recommended that any proposals on wheat should be closely related to negotiations for Argentine wool and interned German ships.[57]

Lansing's instructions to Stimson on November 14 grew out of a decision reached in London by the Assistant Secretary of the Treasury, the Chancellor of the Exchequer, and the French Minister of Finance. The European governments would buy cereals and provide the shipping if Argentina would agree to work out some plan of financing. The Secretary expected the Ambassador to facilitate the transaction in every possible way.[58]

Though admonished not to commit the United States to any agreement, Stimson became the agent of the successful negotiations. Providing credit up to forty million pounds sterling, a draft convention was prepared within a week. It then required two months to complete the jockeying for most advantageous terms.[59] Argentina's acute coal shortage,

[53] See below, pp. 332-336.
[54] "Blue Book," pp. 115-116.
[55] Stimson summarized the negotiations in *My United States*, pp. 415-418, and in his despatch to Secretary of State, Jan. 15, 1918, NA, DS, 835.6131/59.
[56] Polk to Stimson, July 6, 1917, *For. Rel., 1917*, Sup. 1, p. 306.
[57] Herbert Hoover to Lansing, Aug. 27, 1917, NA, DS, 635.119/Orig.; Memorandum of Division of Latin American Affairs, Nov. 2, 1917, NA, DS, 835.6131/11.
[58] *For. Rel., 1917*, Sup. 1, pp. 366-367.
[59] Stimson to Secretary of State, Nov. 22, 1917, and many other despatches, NA, DS, 835.6131/14ff.

rather than its reluctance to grant so large a credit or Allied haggling over terms, was the major hurdle. In the end, Stimson provided the key to settlement. He secured Department approval for his written promise to Pueyrredón that the United States would assist "by permitting so far as possible . . . the exportation in the ships coming from the United States for said wheat, of coal for the actual requirements of the Argentine people." When President Irigoyen submitted the convention for congressional approval, he lauded the United States for its generosity in releasing coal from its own wartime stocks.[60]

Ambassador Naón, who did not share in the wheat negotiations, sailed for Buenos Aires on January 17, not to return until July. Long out of touch with his government and people and deeply convinced that Argentina should have openly declared its loyalty, he had resigned his post but could not secure administration acceptance. Assigned meanwhile to the Foreign Office, his position was anomalous.[61] Still unwilling to accept his nation's complete isolation from the war, he sought to develop some plan which would firmly align Argentina's economy with the Allies, if not bring about a rupture with Germany.

Naón conceived a kind of economic alliance between Argentina and the United States, Great Britain, France, and Italy. He prepared a draft treaty providing what he termed mutual economic and financial services. Neither Lansing nor the foreign secretaries of the other powers were able to see the advantages of such a pact. When the Ambassador spoke vaguely of commercial interchange, stabilization of exchange, financing of Argentine industries, and conversion of interned German ships, Lansing directed Stimson "to make no personal comment."[62] Whether Naón was seeking to involve Argentina in the war in spite of Irigoyen's resolution, to ensure his return to the United States with a specific mission, or to accomplish some other purpose is not clear from available documents.

Undaunted by lack of Allied enthusiasm for his proposals, the Argentine succeeded in getting himself appointed as Special Ambassador to Washington, with the additional title of "High Financial Commissioner."[63] Promptly upon return, he reassured State Department officials of his continued friendship for the United States and his desire to have Argentina in the war. Late in July he presented his project for a treaty on the conduct of commercial relations in wartime.[64] The Department

[60] Stimson to Pueyrredón, Jan. 14, 15, 1918, *ibid.*, nos. 51, 59, and "Blue Book," pp. 115-116.

[61] Stimson to Secretary of State, Feb. 23, 27, April 2, 1918, NA, DS, 701.3511/131-133.

[62] Stimson to Secretary of State, Feb. 26, March 2, 26; Secretary to Stimson, March 1, 1918, *For. Rel., 1918*, Sup. 1, Vol. I, 671-673, 678-680.

[63] *Memoria, 1917-1918*, pp. 177-178.

[64] *Note verbale* from Argentine Ambassador, July 29, 1918, NA, DS, 611.3531/59.

submitted the draft to a high-level conference which included Bernard Baruch, Edward N. Hurley, Vance McCormick, and representatives of other wartime boards. The conferees dismissed Naón's treaty but suggested that the Secretary answer him "somewhat vaguely" and request him to submit specific plans on unlimited credit, wool purchases, and use of German ships.[65] On October 4 Lansing advised the Ambassador that the United States could not negotiate the proposed treaty but that the War Trade Board or other agencies might consider some of the proposals.[66] Thirty-eight days later the war ended and Naón resigned his ambassadorship.

Two other Argentine actions designed to improve the American economic position during the war were more successful. In October, 1917, Argentina decided to admit armed merchantmen to its ports with only minor restrictions.[67] During late 1917 and several times in 1918, to bolster the sagging dollar and stabilize exchange, Argentina granted gold credits up to $100,000,000. Under the American gold embargo and the Gold Agreement of January, 1918, no gold was to be shipped to Buenos Aires until the signing of the peace.[68]

Complications of Economic Warfare

As the most important Latin American neutral and as a reservoir of essential foodstuffs, Argentina felt keenly the backlash of economic and political warfare. The welfare of its people was closely bound to British and American policies on trading with the enemy, licensing of imports, restricting of exports, allocating of ship space, and use of interned German ships. Failure of the two powers to concert their policies often caused conflict of interests and damage to Allied prestige. As commercial restrictions impinged upon the Argentine economy, pro-German propagandists effectively exploited Anglo-American tactlessness.

After passage of the Enemy Trading Act in December, 1917, the State Department and War Trade Board sought to cooperate with the British in enforcement of the black lists. Believing the policy of black-listing to be oppressive, un-American, and incapable of just enforcement, Consul General W. Henry Robertson was convinced that in Argentina it played directly into the hands of British commercial interests. Even before passage of the act, as well as after, he hammered away at British exploitation of their black list to damage American trade. The British, he reported, supplied goods to the very companies

[65] Department of State memorandum, Sept. 5, 1918, *ibid.*, no. 60.

[66] *For. Rel., 1918*, Sup. 1, Vol. I, 730-733.

[67] Stimson to Secretary of State, Oct. 11, 1917, NA, DS, 763.72111/5654.

[68] William G. McAdoo, Secretary of Treasury, to Lansing, Dec. 28, 1917, and L. S. Rowe, Acting Secretary of Treasury, to Secretary of State, May 6, 1918, NA, DS, 635.119/77, 430; *Memoria, 1917-1918*, pp. 167-168.

they proscribed to the Americans. They utilized the manifests of American ships for the advantage of British merchants. He cited other offenses.[69] Even Embassy officials believed the British showed more zeal in securing the local market for their nationals than in destroying German trade. They reported the unpopularity of the policy among Argentines.[70] Washington eventually took note of Robertson's protests but believed the remedy lay in closer cooperation with the British, not in official representations.[71]

The operation of the black lists, together with lack of adequate shipping, rising freight rates, and Allied export controls, produced acute shortages in Argentina. Especially in late 1917 and in 1918, the Argentine economy felt the pinch in such items as coal, newsprint, agricultural implements, and transport equipment. The knottiest problem was treatment of the powerful Compañía Alemana Transatlántica de Electricidad, which supplied power for the Anglo-Argentine Tramways Company and lighting for Buenos Aires and controlled subsidiaries in other cities of Argentina and neighboring countries. It secured not only coal but copper, lubricants, and electrical equipment from the United States. Pueyrredón asked specifically that its coal supplies be maintained. When in late 1917 Lansing proposed to cut off shipments unless the Argentine government sequestrated the property, Stimson advised that it would be better to let coal exports dwindle than to threaten Irigoyen.[72] Able to get little coal from any source, even at five times the 1914 prices, the company was forced to use oil, wood, and bran.

Restricted production of newsprint in the United States and Canada and establishment of priorities on exports by the spring of 1918 reduced to narrow margins the reserve supplies of Argentine newspapers. Appreciating the indispensability of supporting the pro-Allies press, Lansing struggled to meet the current requirements of *La Nación* and other "approved" publications.[73]

As the movement of American troops and supplies to Europe in 1918 made shipping space increasingly tight, the Argentine authorities contemplated the purchase of interned German ships, especially the 15,000-ton *Bahía Blanca*. Providing it carried no enemy personnel and followed satisfactory routes, Lansing was inclined to grant approval of the

[69] Robertson to Secretary of State, June 15, 1917, Feb. 18, May 28, 1918, NA, DS, 600.001/123; 763.72112/7914, 9342.

[70] Stimson to Secretary of State, Jan. 10, 1918, NA, DS, 600.001/194; Warren D. Robbins, Chargé d'Affaires ad interim to Argentina, to Secretary of State, Aug. 21, 1918, 635.4115/8.

[71] Polk to Embassy, Nov. 22, 1918, *ibid.*

[72] Stimson to Secretary of State, June 7, Dec. 4, 1917, and Lansing to Embassy, Nov. 30, 1917, NA, DS, 600.119/106; 635.119/48b, 51.

[73] Stimson to Secretary of State, May 6, 1918, and Lansing to Embassy, May 25, 1918, *ibid.*, no. 427.

ship's transfer. Feeling assured of American consent, the Argentines moved ahead with repair and reconditioning of the vessel, when unexpectedly just before the war's end the British interposed objections. On the eve of postwar readjustments, therefore, Lansing's support of Britain, appearing to Pueyyredón to be an about-face, provoked Argentine resentment against both nations.[74]

At several critical moments during and just after the war—September and December, 1917, and January, 1919—widespread strikes engulfed Buenos Aires and other ports. Work stoppage and violence on the railroads, at the docks, and in the meat packing establishments seriously interfered with the unloading of ships and the movement of foodstuffs. Stimson believed that German, as well as Bolshevist, influences were responsible. But there was little he could do except ask police protection for the American *frigoríficos* and their employees and underscore the inestimable losses to both Argentina and the Allied nations.[75]

Benevolent Neutrality Pays

Argentine economy, like its diplomacy, during the last year of the war became more and more polarized toward the United States and the Allies. In spite of frequent irritations caused by economic warfare, it became increasingly clear to most Argentines, whatever their sympathies, that the nation must revolve within the Allied orbit.

However provoking the shortages of both necessities and luxuries, Argentina was prosperous. As its farmers and ranchers increased the acreage of wheat, corn, and linseed and multipled the production of livestock, they brought the nation the highest per capita wealth in the world. [76] In the year ending May 31, 1918, bank deposits in Buenos Aires increased fifty per cent, from $751,827,600 to $1,050,173,900.[77] In lending $250,000,000 to Allied nations between 1917 and 1920, Argentina played for the first time the part of a creditor nation.[78] Total foreign trade in 1918 reached the unprecedented figure of $1,263,007,000, almost twice that of 1914.[79] As total bilateral commerce in 1918 surpassed

[74] The correspondence is printed in *For. Rel., 1918*, Sup. 1, Vol. II, 1746-1754. See also Thomas A. Bailey, *The Policy of the United States toward Neutrals, 1917-1918*, pp. 333-334.

[75] Stimson to Secretary of State, Sept. 25, Oct. 16, Dec. 1, 1917, Jan. 28, Feb. 8, 1919, NA, DS, 835.5045/7, 21, 32, 69, 76.

[76] Frederic M. Halsey, *Investments in Latin America and the British West Indies*, pp. 23, 25.

[77] Memorandum from the Commercial Attaché to the Ambassador, June 25, 1918, NA, DS, 701.3511/149.

[78] H. E. Peters, *The Foreign Debt of the Argentine Republic*, p. 95.

[79] Fourth Pan American Commercial Conference, *Foreign Trade of Latin America, 1910-1929*, p. 27.

$333,000,000, the United States became the best market for Argentine goods as well as the leading supplier of its needs.[80]

Under these circumstances, the Irigoyen government could afford to take no steps which would seriously impair its relations with the Allies or modify its less-than-neutral policies. The President and the majority of his Cabinet and party remained avowedly neutral, but Foreign Minister Pueyrredón, Marine Minister Alvarez de Toledo, most leading Conservative politicians, and many prominent intellectual leaders were as openly pro-Allies.[81]

Cordiality toward the United States, even admiration and sympathy for its stand in the conflict, appeared to increase as the climax of the war approached. Irigoyen expressed his respect for President Wilson and his approval of the lofty American objectives. With the exception of the pro-German *La Unión*, the press grew increasingly friendly. Expressions of homage to the United States and its representatives became more frequent and uninhibited.[82]

In Washington, Ambassador Naón fretted his way to the end of the war, unable to influence his own government or to sell his economic pact to the United States. Abruptly and irrevocably, on November 11 he penned his resignation, a revelation of his frustration and complete dissent from Argentine international policy during the war. In a long statement announcing acceptance of the resignation, President Irigoyen defended the rectitude of his policy at every step of the war. The Ambassador's critical despatch and the President's self-righteous decree climaxed the internal conflict which had gripped Argentina throughout 1917 and 1918.[83]

By the end of 1918 Argentine-American relations revealed the effects of twenty-five years of failure to unite the Hemisphere. America's entry into World War I, while Argentina remained aloof, brought the ultimate separation of national courses which had run remarkably parallel. This parting of the ways in wartime, symbolized by the divergent appeals to continental solidarity of Presidents Wilson and Irigoyen, marked the beginning of a more permanent clash of interests and cleavage of policies.

[80] *Statistical Abstract of the United States,* 1920, p. 411.
[81] Robbins to Secretary of State, Aug. 26, 1918, NA, DS, 835.00/155.
[82] *Ibid.;* Stimson to Secretary of State, April 13, 1918, NA, DS, 763.72/9540; Naón to Pueyrredón, July 12, 1918, and enclosure, *Circular informativa mensual,* No. 16 (Sept., 1918), p. 1; Zeballos, "Gobierno radical: política internacional," *Revista de Derecho, Historia y Letras,* CX (May, 1918), 118-120.
[83] Copies of resignation and decree are bound in NA, DS, 701.3511/164.

X X

RIVALRY IN INTER-AMERICAN AFFAIRS: PAN AMERICANISM IN WARTIME, 1910-1918

The years of World War I were an arid season in the evolution of the inter-American organization. Instead of stimulating collective action among the twenty-one republics, the threat to Hemisphere security served rather to devitalize a promising trend toward solidarity. No individual nation or statesman arose to arrest the play of exclusively national interests or resolutely lead the way to effective continental diplomacy. The failure of the nations to draw together even in the face of stark challenge to their neutral rights revealed the weakness of the structure they had erected, the absence of real confidence in its potentialities, and the conflict of divergent regional concepts.

Long competitors for leadership of the other republics, Argentina and the United States continued their rivalry in wartime. Several Argentine attempts in the first weeks of the war to bring about united action received no encouragement in Washington. Without success, executives of both nations later initiated Hemisphere projects consonant with their own national aims. From late 1914 to early 1917 President Wilson promoted a Pan American peace pact which he never consummated. After American entry into the conflict, President Irigoyen issued invitations first to a conference of neutrals, then to a congress of Latin American states, neither of which convened. Wilson's increasing involvement in European affairs militated against fulfillment of his own plan; his opposition to a conference which excluded the United States was a factor in blocking Irigoyen's intentions. Beneath these surface moves lay a deepening ideological conflict between the Pan Americanism of the United States and the Latin Americanism of Argentina.

Pan Americanism vs. Latin Americanism

Accelerated by Hemisphere developments during World War I, the decade from the Buenos Aires Conference through the Versailles Conference brought into focus the conflict between Argentina and the United States for leadership of the Latin American republics. Two events, one in each nation, precipitated a cleavage in international policy that had been incipient for a generation. First, the election of Hipólito Irigoyen in 1916 gave political voice to the aspiring masses of Creoles and immigrants. Long unenfranchised, these groups now expressed deeper interest in social reforms and defense of the national economy than in the professed liberalism and international affiliations of the oligarchy. Of the new leaders and their aspirations Washington had little knowledge.

The second event was Wilson's decision to abandon neutrality and isolation for defense of what he believed to be Hemisphere ideals. His action could win the approval of intellectuals and Conservative leaders but not the active support of Irigoyen and his heterogeneous supporters, who had given little thought to international affairs.

It was the entrenched leaders of the Conservative Party who in 1910 had sponsored the Fourth Pan American Conference and encouraged for a time greater cordiality toward the United States. Without conceding basic national principles, they had participated in a series of multilateral mediations.[1] Concerned by Brazil's growing power and naval arming, they had favored American companies in the awarding of battleship contracts and secured consent to train Argentine naval officers on American warships.[2] When he felt obliged to refuse Secretary Knox's invitation to visit Washington, President-elect Saenz Peña paid eloquent tribute to American secretaries of state who had promoted the Pan American movement.[3] Twice during the first two years of his presidency, he sought to send Vice-President De la Plaza to acknowledge the invitation he had been unable to accept.[4] Argentine efforts to offset American influence in South America by drawing closer to Chile or Brazil, or both, were dropped in the early years of President Saenz Peña's term.[5]

While official Argentina in 1910-1913 moved slightly toward a more pro-American and pro-Pan American orientation, a new force was spawning to hold the nation to its more traditional course. Even before the Buenos Aires Conference, the first cries of what was to become

[1] See above, pp. 266-274.

[2] See above, pp. 291-297. Also see C. H. Sherrill, Minister to Argentina, to Secretary of State, April 9, 1910, and enclosure, and Secretary of Navy to Secretary of State, May 16, 1910, NA, DS, 811.32735/5, 8.

[3] Knox to American Embassy in Paris, June 27, 1910; Henry C. Ide, Minister to Spain, to Secretary of State, July 8, 1910; Everit S. Swenson, Minister to Switzerland, to Secretary of State, July 15, 1910, NA, DS, 835.00/78A, 88, 89.

[4] Robert W. Bliss, Chargé d'Affaires ad interim to Argentina, to Secretary of State, Oct. 21, 1910, and George Lorillard, Chargé d'Affaires to Argentina, to Secretary of State, Dec. 18, 1912, NA, DS, 701.3511/17, 63.

[5] Department memorandum, Jan. 28, 1912, NA, DS, 725.3211/33.

a strident Yankeephobia issued from the articulate pen of the Argentine propagandist, Manuel Ugarte. Writing in Paris, he condemned Pan Americanism as favoring only the United States. To him inter-American gatherings were "useless and deceitful" and represented no more than congresses of "mice presided over by a cat." He urged the republics of Latin culture to "unite among themselves to cultivate and fortify their own nationalities." [6] In his "Open letter to the President of the United States" in 1913, he decried American financial intervention, denied Argentina's need for the Monroe Doctrine, asserted his nation's consideration for the other Latin republics, and inflated the solidarity of Latin America.[7]

In Buenos Aires other, less shrill voices took up the pro-Argentine and pro-Latin American arguments. José Ingenieros, scientist turned sociologist, touted Argentina as the only nation qualified to exert leadership in South America. From economic and philosophical points of view, Alejandro E. Bunge and Manuel Gálvez rose to the defense of the Argentine land and spirit.[8]

Even less nationalistic Argentines joined in criticism, more constructive, to be sure, of American policies. Enrque Gl, lawyer, professor, and friend of the United States, though condemning Ugarte's extremism and blindness, challenged the "tutelage" of the Monroe Doctrine and the unilateral character of Pan Americanism. Addressing the American Political Science Association in 1911, he besought the United States to disclaim the vague concept of Latin America and to substitute "wise management towards each of the Republics individually." Argentina also has a "manifest destiny," he contended.[9] Even Minister Naón, who was to become the staunchest advocate of Hemisphere solidarity, believed in 1913 that "there is no Pan-Americanism in South America; it exists only in Washington."[10]

President Wilson's heralded statements of a new Latin American policy, made after a Cabinet meeting on March 11, 1913, and at Mobile on October 27, received a cold reception in Buenos Aires. His chief critic was ex-Foreign Minister Zeballos, no longer an Argentine official but now a widely read editorial writer for *La Prensa*. He sharply criticized Wilson's apparent intention to set the United States up as

[6] Ugarte's article," Le prochain congrés Pan-Américain," first appeared in *La Revue* (Paris) in March, 1910, and was widely reprinted in Latin America. For example, see *El Tiempo*, Caracas, June 15, 17, 1910.

[7] Reprinted in *La patria grande* (Madrid, 1924), pp. 11-21.

[8] J. F. Normano, *The Struggle for South America*, pp. 122-123, 138-140, 148-150; Rex Crawford, *A Century of Latin-American Thought*, pp. 124-126, 152-153.

[9] "The Point of View of Latin-America on the Inter-American Policy of the United States," *The American Political Science Review*, VI (Feb., 1912, supplement), 164-182.

[10] J. Lloyd Mecham, "Conflicting Ideals of Pan-Americanism," *Current History*, XXXIII (Dec., 1930), 402.

judge of the constitutionality of political regimes in Latin America.[11] Shortly after the Mobile speech, in conferring an honorary degree upon Theodore Roosevelt, Zeballos thanked the United States for its past protection but protested that the Monroe Doctrine "is no longer necessary now that our civilization has been attained." [12]

Proud, sensitive Argentines of whatever party loyalty resented their inclusion on the same political plane with Nicaragua and the Dominican Republic. The best intentions of Wilson's "missionary diplomacy," [13] therefore, played into the hands of publicists and propagandists who would pluck the strings of Argentina's national greatness and its destiny to lead the Latin republics.

Meanwhile, staunch proponents of Pan Americanism were urging closer ties among the American states. Charles H. Sherrill, former Minister to Argentina, was writing and speaking widely on "The South American Point of View" and "A Pan-American Triangle for Peace." [14] The newly founded Carnegie Endowment for International Peace was organizing national societies for conciliation. Its representative, Robert Bacon, former Ambassador to France, received special greetings in Buenos Aires from Dr. Zeballos and Dr. Luis Drago.[15] Secretary Bryan was seeking to negotiate his "cooling-off" treaties, including one with Argentina. Minister Naón's initiative in the ABC mediation between Wilson and Huerta revealed at least passing Argentine interest in promoting inter-American diplomacy.

In the midst, therefore, of attack and counterattack upon the rival regional concepts, the American republics completely lacked the solidarity necessary to facilitate a united front in the face of European war. There was little sentiment even for convening a congress to promote unity. Chile, scheduled to entertain the Fifth Conference in November, 1914, could not afford it. Secretary Bryan was unable to leave Washington to attend. Argentine Foreign Minister José Luis Murature was convinced that past conferences had been futile and that another would be impractical. The Santiago Conference did not meet until 1923.[16]

In spite of Murature's opposition to a conference, he urged Ambassador Naón to support a Peruvian proposal for Hemisphere agreement on uniform neutrality procedures. Secretary Bryan gave the Ambassador no encouragement. After waiting nearly four months, Naón presented on

[11] Lorillard to Secretary of State, March 17, 1913, NA, DS, 710.11/124.

[12] "Theodore Roosevelt y la política internacional americana," *Revista de Derecho, Historia y Letras*, XLVI (Dec., 1913), 561, 565-568.

[13] Cf. Arthur S. Link, *Woodrow Wilson and the Progressive Era, 1910-1917*, p. 82, and A. P. Whitaker, *The Western Hemisphere Idea*, pp. 120ff.

[14] Sherrill, *Modernizing the Monroe Doctrine*, pp. 111-114. See also his pamphlet, "The South American Point of View," *International Conciliation*.

[15] Robert Bacon, *For Better Relations with Our Latin American Neighbors*, pp. 11-12, 92, 95.

[16] Lorillard to Secretary of State, Sept. 23, 29, 1914, NA, DS, 710.E/29, 37.

December 8 a concrete plan to the Governing Board of the Pan American Union. The Board referred the problem to a special commission headed by the Secretary of State.[17] Thus, with President Wilson's subsequent approval, Bryan and Lansing effectively frustrated Naón and side-stepped the Latin American overtures for Pan American unanimity on rules of neutrality.

Argentina and Wilson's Pan American Pact

By reducing Latin American pressure for uniform rules on neutrality, the State Department in effect opened the door for President Wilson to regain the initiative in Pan American affairs.[18] The President lost no time, therefore, in responding to Colonel Edward M. House's urging to formulate some plan of Western Hemisphere union. Eight days after the meeting of the Governing Board, he pencilled a rough draft of his "Pan-American Peace Pact." [19] The idea was not new, for twice within the previous year the project of a nonaggression treaty had been suggested to him, once by an American congressman, again by a Latin American diplomat.[20]

Wilson's first draft of a convention comprised two brief articles:

1st. Mutual guaranties of political independence under republican form of government and mutual guaranties of territorial integrity.

2nd. Mutual agreement that the Government of each of the contracting parties acquire complete control within its jurisdiction of the manufacture and sale of munitions of war.[21]

The President directed House to initiate informal discussions with the ambassadors of Argentina, Brazil, and Chile, each of whom had participated in the recent Mexican mediation.

Colonel House approached the South American envoys at once, on December 19th. Through the intercession of Justice Lamar, American delegate to the Niagara Falls Conference, he met first with Rómulo Naón. Deeply impressed, especially with the first article, Naón was confident of Argentine approval. He asked to be allowed to keep Wilson's personally typed memorandum, "an historical document of much value" he wished to preserve. Three days later, the Ambassador reported that his government had received "with sympathy the proposition with the

[17] See above, p. 306.
[18] R. S. Baker, *Woodrow Wilson, Life and Letters*, V, 297-298.
[19] Charles Seymour, *The Intimate Papers of Colonel House*, I, 207-210.
[20] On the genesis of the idea, see S. F. Bemis, *The Latin American Policy of the United States*, pp. 194-197, and M. W. Graham, *American Diplomacy in the International Community*, pp. 162-173.
[21] Seymour, *op. cit.*, pp. 209-210.

understanding that [it] tends to transform the one-sided character of the Monroe Doctrine into a common policy of all the American countries." This, of course, was precisely the advantage Wilson and House had hoped the Latin American leaders would visualize. Naón himself, now a veteran of four years' service in Washington, was less restrained than his superiors. "It will be such a great accomplishment that there will be nothing he [Wilson] can ever do afterward that can approach it in importance," he told House. President Wilson accepted the Argentine's recommendations on tactics—that the four nations should first agree on the terms and that the ABC countries should present the proposal to the other republics.[22]

From the moment of House's first approach until the fading of the project two years later, Naón's support never wavered nor did his government reverse its willingness to sign. Through various extensions and editings of the original abbreviated draft, Naón either endorsed the terms without dissent or, after submitting revisions, approved the compromise statements. Accepting the first formal proposal without modification (February 1, 1915), he urged immediate action for the purpose of impressing the European belligerents.[23]

But House's drive and Naón's zeal were not able to speed negotiations. Unenthusiastic, perhaps because of the Colonel's interposition, Bryan did not move with despatch. The President, in House's view, did not press the project with vigor.[24] The principal cause of delay, however, was the reluctance of Chile. Deeply involved in the Tacna-Arica dispute, the Pacific republic raised multiple objections, mainly to the guarantees of territorial integrity.[25] Eventually, hoping to persuade Chile, it was Naón who secured elimination of a time limit for the settlement of boundary disputes. The Argentine accepted without reservation Lansing's final draft of November, 1915.[26]

Just before sailing for Europe in December, House convinced the President that the time had come to go ahead. In addressing the Pan American Scientific Conference on January 6, Wilson made the first public announcement of his proposals.[27] But Chile still hung back, and soon border troubles with Mexico produced an atmosphere unfavorable to the conclusion of a nonaggression treaty. On June 27, with tension

[22] *Ibid.*, pp. 211-217.
[23] Bryan to Naón, Feb. 1, 1915, and Bryan to Wilson, March 8, 1915, Department of State, *Papers Relating to the Foreign Relations of the United States. The Lansing Papers, 1914-1920*, II, 473-474.
[24] Seymour, *op. cit.*, II, 18-19.
[25] Bryan to Wilson, April 21, 1915, *The Lansing Papers*, II, 476-479; Department confidential memorandum, undated, NA, DS, 710.11/200-1/2a.
[26] Lansing's draft of October 20 and Naón's counterdraft of the following day are filed in *ibid.*, no. 211-1/2. See also *The Lansing Papers*, II, 488-492, and Seymour, *op. cit.*, pp. 226, 233-234.
[27] *Ibid.*, pp. 227-228.

running high over the Mexican crisis, Naón for the first time indicated his government's hesitation to proceed. By August, however, on a Massachusetts golf course, he told Stimson that he was again authorized to sign.[28]

Hastening to Washington from his diplomatic triumph at golf, Stimson informed Lansing that he "had Argentina's signature in [his] pocket." The Secretary quickly chilled this enthusiasm. The Brazilian ambassador was at sea and action must await his return. When Stimson proposed that the nations sign separately, Lansing saw no need for haste. Nor would he permit the diplomat to take the matter to the White House. Naón was never again approached about the treaty.[29]

In any case, with or without Argentina's signature, Wilson's pact was doomed. The President was soon absorbed with the election campaign and the chain of events that led to war. Moreover, Chile had shown no sign of relenting. Brazil's ardor had cooled.[30] And in Argentina, on October 12, Irigoyen had been inaugurated.

Argentina's compliant attitude throughout the negotiations perplexed the State Department. The suspicion existed that Naón had gone beyond his government or that Argentina was simply letting Chile or Brazil bear the onus of killing the treaty.[31] In view of his repeated demonstrations of candor and his enthusiasm for the United States and Pan American solidarity, however, it seems unlikely that Naón would have played the double game. As to Argentina, such duplicity would have been remarkably inconsistent with its long record of forthrightness in American relations. Stimson was inclined to blame the State Department itself for the treaty's fate.[32] Until Argentina's archives are available, therefore, explanations of its unique amenability must be inconclusive.

Argentina and the International High Commission

President Wilson's policies toward Latin America, however well-intentioned for Hemisphere peace and security, provided few rallying points for proponents of Pan Americanism. In the face of growing criticism from exponents of Latin Americanism, a series of contradictions in Wilson's actions militated against promotion of the Pan American

[28] Department memorandum, H. P. Fletcher, in charge of the treaty negotiations, to Lansing, *The Lansing Papers*, II, 496-497; Frederic J. Stimson, *My United States*, p. 349.

[29] *Ibid.*, pp. 349-350; Seymour, *op. cit.*, 232-233.

[30] *Ibid.*; Department memorandum, signed by H. P. F. [Fletcher], Aug. 9, 1916, *The Lansing Papers*, II, 496-497.

[31] Unsigned Department memorandum, strictly confidential, Jan. 21, 1916, NA, DS, 710.11/230.

[32] Stimson, *op. cit.*, p. 350.

spirit by its enthusiasts.[33] Ambassador Naón and the Argentine Republic were involved in each of these situations.

In his dispute with Huerta, Wilson accepted the mediation of Naón and his Brazilian and Chilean colleagues, but narrowly circumscribed their powers. At a moment when Hemisphere problems cried out for common action, he concurred with Argentina and Chile in postponement of the Fifth Pan American Conference. When Naón and other Latin Americans urged uniform Hemisphere policies on rules and procedures for neutrals, the President approved the State Department's interment of their enthusiasm in a subcommittee of the Pan American Union. He failed to exploit their eagerness for the benefit of American leadership.

In the midst of negotiations for his nonaggression pact, Wilson sent a military force across the Rio Grande, occupied Haiti, and perpetuated interventions in other Caribbean republics. He permitted his secretaries of state to move at such a slow pace that war developments overtook the natural evolution of the treaty. Moreover, for more than a year his representatives conducted the negotiations in secret, exclusively with the ABC nations, and when he decided to make public announcement of the pact, it was at an unpropitious moment and without benefit of fanfare.

Exceptions, however, to this unwitting frustration of the Pan Americanists were the First Pan American Financial Conference and the International High Commission it created. The convening of the Conference in Washington and the subsequent assembling of the High Commission in Buenos Aires provided platforms for Pan American spokesmen as well as committee rooms for consideration of economic problems.

As the coming of the war brought dislocations in exchange, banking structure, and movement of goods and capital, financiers and businessmen of all American nations were suddenly struck with the threat to their material welfare and the need for common action.[34] For Americans, the blockade of German exports and the drying up of the springs of British capital opened new opportunities in Argentina. For Argentines, the same circumstances, together with the loss of German markets, forced reconsideration of traditional economic patterns. In whatever degree, all the American states felt the economic impact of war.

Bankers, industrialists, and finance ministers responded eagerly, therefore, to the American invitation to discuss "closer and more satisfactory financial relations between their countries and the United States."[35]

[33] Cf. Julius W. Pratt, *A History of United States Foreign Policy*, pp. 431-432, and Bemis, *op. cit.*, pp. 198-199.

[34] Normano, *op. cit.*, pp. 101-104; H. E. Peters, *The Foreign Debt of the Argentine Republic*, p. 77.

[35] *Proceedings of the First Pan-American Financial Conference*, p. 7.

Leaders who had not previously concerned themselves with matters of continental ideology awakened to the meaning of Pan Americanism. Appropriately, as the Financial Conference convened in Washington in May, 1915, Wilson's son-in-law and Secretary of the Treasury, William G. McAdoo, became the keynoter. He struck a common chord when he announced that

> it is not from selfish motive or sordid desire for material gain that this conference draws its inspiration. It has a deeper and a finer meaning. We meet for the purpose of considering how and in what manner the great Republics of the Western Hemisphere, representing as they do common ideals of liberty, justice, and self-government, and dedicated as they are to the highest and best interest of humanity, may, through common action and interest, not only conserve their material welfare, but become a more homogeneous and powerful moral force for the preservation of peace and the good of humanity.[36]

For Argentine-American relations in wartime, the most significant action of the Conference was its creation of an International High Commission to consider uniform legislation on bills of exchange, customs regulations, and other aspects of burgeoning Hemisphere trade. To prosecute the work in its country, each government was to appoint a High Commission of nine men, with its finance minister as chairman. Buenos Aires was selected as the site of the first gathering.[37] Originally scheduled for the succeeding November, the meeting was postponed to April 3, 1916.

Besides McAdoo, who served as chairman, Andrew J. Peters, Assistant Secretary of the Treasury, and Duncan U. Fletcher, senator from Florida, Wilson appointed to the American section a member of the Federal Reserve Board, the governor of the Federal Reserve Bank of San Francisco, and the head of the United States Chamber of Commerce. With their staff of secretaries, interpreters, translators, and stenographers, all attended the first meeting.[38]

Buenos Aires greeted its distinguished guests with another of the effusive welcomes the porteños can prepare so well. McAdoo was impressed by Argentine friendliness and hospitality. Yet, to accomplish his mission within ten days, he refused most of the social invitations he received.[39]

[36] *Ibid.*, p. 114.
[37] Lansing to diplomatic officers in Latin America, July 10, 1915, *For. Rel., 1915*, pp. 20-21.
[38] McAdoo to Secretary of State, March 4, 1916, NA, DS, 810.51/553; Stimson, *op. cit.*, p. 332.
[39] *Crowded Years: The Reminiscences of William G. McAdoo*, p. 357.

The Secretary was pleased, too, at first flush, with the success of the meeting. At least he could claim all the organizational victories for the Americans. The Conference agreed to hold a financial conference every two years, with the 1917 meeting to be held in Washington. It made permanent the International High Commission and selected Washington as the first headquarters. It created a Central Executive Committee, with McAdoo as President, John Bassett Moore as Vice-President, and Leo S. Rowe as Secretary-General.[40]

The delegates considered a broad agenda of thirteen items, ranging from trademarks to transportation. Most practical of the projects, thought McAdoo, were organization of steamship lines, extension of banking services, enlarged radio developments, increased cable facilities and decreased cable rates, and completion of the railway from the United States to Buenos Aires.[41]

Evaluating the Conference rather from the human side, Ambassador Stimson was less sanguine of American success with the Argentine people. In his distinctively puckish interpretation of what is proper, he recited in his memoirs the delegation's offenses against Argentine good taste. In a day when women had small place in the Spanish political mind, American delegates brought their wives, including the President's daughter, thus lending the impression that social entertainment was at least as important as uniform legislation.

Accompanied only by a Conservative Party leader, during the most revolutionary presidential election Argentina has had, Secretary McAdoo visited a polling booth. Unaccompanied by the Argentine foreign minister, he paid a personal call upon President De la Plaza. Yet he proposed to ignore an *agasajo* at which the President was to be an honored guest. To the finance minister, who would soon become a "lame duck," he presented a $6,000 silver service.[42]

When he received President Wilson's confidential cable that the United States was close to war, McAdoo determined to return to Washington at once, ignoring the host government's invitation to a week's grand tour to southern estancias, the Córdoba hills, and the Andes.[43] So, in Stimson's words, McAdoo and his colleagues took "French leave" from Argentina, but not before committing what the Ambassador considered the paramount blunder. In his farewell speech, while praising the delegates for their labors for peace, McAdoo an-

[40] *Ibid.*, p. 358.
[41] *Ibid.*, pp. 359-360; Lansing to American Embassy in Chile, Dec. 13, 1915, *For. Rel., 1915*, pp. 23-24; Stimson to Secretary of State, Feb. 19 [?], 1916, and McAdoo to Lansing, May 6, 1916, NA, DS, 810.51/505, 657.
[42] Stimson, *op. cit.*, pp. 329, 334-337.
[43] Stimson does not suggest that McAdoo might have been exacting recompense for failure of the Argentine delegates to accompany Blaine's grand tour in 1889.

nounced that "when the United States *was* forced to draw the sword, she . . . never sheathed it without victory." [44] Stimson's memoirs make clear that he held a very low opinion of the American habit of diplomacy through international conference and "Pan-American junket." He felt that the Buenos Aires meeting had accomplished no permanent results and that North American "manners" had only angered the proper Argentines.[45]

The Ambassador also had his inner thoughts about Argentina's intentions in sponsoring the Conference. While officials of the Conservative government appeared pleased to entertain the delegates, he suspected that they hoped for no decisive actions.[46] Argentina's subsequent delay in constituting its section of the High Commission confirmed Stimson's suspicions. In spite of pressure from McAdoo, Lansing, and Stimson, President De la Plaza made no appointments and his successor took his time. Not until September 5, 1919, could Sumner Welles, then acting chargé, reply to an enquiry of April 5, 1917, that the commissioners had been selected.[47] Through three and one-half difficult years of war and postwar readjustment the delay effectively paralyzed the Commission's activities so far as Argentina was concerned.

Secretary McAdoo's subsequent evaluation of the High Commission's practical projects was not so favorable as his contemporary estimate. "In the end nothing, or next to nothing, came of them," he wrote in his reminiscences of "crowded years." He attached the blame, however, not to the Argentines or to any of the Latin Americans but to the war and the Harding administration's disinterest.[48]

The United States and Irigoyen's Latin American Conference

As America's rupture with Germany quietly closed the door on Wilson's Pan American Pact, so it opened the way for Irigoyen's conference of Latin American neutrals. Twice during the next year, he sought to promote meetings from which the United States would be excluded.[49] Both were fiascoes. The purposes of the conferences and the reasons for their failure, like Irigoyen's own intentions, remain obscure, for Argentina has still not published the correspondence. Stim-

---

[44] The phraseology and italics are Stimson's (*ibid.*, pp. 337-339).

[45] *Ibid.*, pp. 330, 342.

[46] *Ibid.*, p. 330.

[47] McAdoo to Secretary of State, April 3, 1917; Lansing to Embassy, April 5, 1917; Welles to Secretary of State, Sept. 5, 1919, NA, DS, 810.51/767, 946.

[48] McAdoo, *op. cit.*, p. 360.

[49] There are brief discussions of the conference attempts in Thomas A. Bailey, *The Policy of the United States toward Neutrals, 1917-1918*, pp. 315-317, and Percy Alvin Martin, *Latin America and the War*, pp. 255-257.

son's sketchy reporting at the time and his slighting of the matter in his memoirs betray the secrecy which prevailed.

Though feelers had been put out weeks before, the formal invitations were not sent until April and May.[50] They gave slight clue to Irigoyen's purposes. The Argentine government believes, they read, "that the American nations should concert a uniform opinion in this respect, realizing the desire to establish ties, whose cordial nature would strengthen the situation and aspect of the American states, in the general concert of nations." Stimson's first report was that the conference would seek to mediate in the war; later it was to be a peace congress, then a commercial congress, and finally a "Congress of the Nations of America." [51]

Before the invitations were issued, Foreign Minister Pueyrredón asked Stimson if the United States "would look with sympathy" on a conference of American neutrals. He expected, he said, that the congress would agree upon moral support for the United States and the Allies. The intentions of Secretary Lansing's reply were unmistakable: the Ambassador should tell the Minister that "he will readily see the impossibility of any expression of views on the part of the Government of the United States, particularly at the present time." In recalling that Argentina had just endorsed America's war aims, Pueyrredón betrayed his disappointment at Lansing's reactions. He then hinted to Stimson that Argentina's purpose was to align the other republics with Wilson's attitude.[52]

But leaders in Washington remained suspicious. After a conference with Ambassador Naón, President Wilson confided to Lansing that there was "a very poor chance for Argentina to pull anything off!" [53] In spite of Naón's reassurances on Argentina's friendly intentions, Lansing counselled his envoys in certain Latin American capitals that they should discreetly make use of the Department's judgment that the conference would serve no useful purpose.[54] In other capitals, especially

[50] Stimson reported the Foreign Minister as saying that some of the nations had been informally invited before the United States broke relations; Naón told Lansing that the idea originated after the United States was in the war (April 20, May 17, 1917, *For. Rel., 1917*, Sup. 1, pp. 260, 282).

[51] Stimson to Secretary of State, Feb. 27, April 20, 22, 1917, *ibid.*, pp. 235, 260, 263-264. An Argentine historian asserts that Irigoyen was really seeking to tighten the bonds among the Spanish American republics (Lucio M. Moreno Quintana, *La diplomacia de Yrigoyen*, pp. 396-399).

[52] Stimson to Secretary of State, April 20, 25, and Secretary to Stimson, April 22, 1917, *For. Rel., 1917*, Sup. 1, pp. 260-261, 263-265.

[53] NA, DS, 763.72119/587 1/2.

[54] Naón to Secretary of State, May 17, 1917, *For. Rel., 1917*, Sup. 1, pp. 282-283; Lansing to all American missions in Central and South America, except Argentina, Mexico, Panama, Cuba, Brazil, and Santo Domingo, May 25, 1917, NA, DS, 763.72110/608.

Panama and Tegucigalpa, the pressure exerted was less mild.[55]

As the attitude of the United States became known and as Germany's submarine campaign broadened, the early enthusiasm of most of the invited states tapered off. Brazil, Cuba, Panama, and the Dominican Republic declared war or broke relations. Bolivia, Peru, Guatemala, Nicaragua, and others resolved to concert their policies with the United States. Haiti and Venezuela categorically refused. Paraguay would participate only if all the American states were represented. Chile wished more specific information on the purpose of the conference. In the end, only Colombia and Mexico, each with understandable reason, still ardently supported a congress which would exclude the United States.[56] So lukewarm, in fact, was the reaction of most of the nations that the State Department might well have reserved the diplomatic pressure it authorized its agents to apply. By early July, itself involved with Germany over sinking of the *Toro*, the Argentine government seemed interested merely in justifying the initiative it had taken.[57]

The facts of Irigoyen's second proposal are equally obscure and the results even more barren. In late October and early November, the Peruvian chargé and the Chilean ambassador revealed to the State Department that Argentina had again invited their governments to a Latin American congress. Subsequently, the chargé reported that Irigoyen had insisted that Peru attend and had recommended that, as the first order of business, its delegates sponsor a resolution that all American states sever relations with Germany. In such a case, Irigoyen is alleged to have said, Argentina would be disposed to go along. If the United States would endorse attendance at the congress on this basis, Peru suggested, it would undertake to line up other South American states. Lansing, together with the governments of Bolivia, Brazil, Ecuador, and Uruguay, approved the ingenious Peruvian plan.[58]

In Buenos Aires, belatedly as before, Stimson was advised of Argentina's move, this time by the President himself. Indicating that he would gladly invite the United States if it would accept, Irigoyen earnestly assured Stimson that the purpose of the congress was not hostile to the United States and that he might at any time examine all the correspondence. Still skeptical of Irigoyen's intentions, Lansing directed the Ambassador not to visit the President except upon express invitation, lest his initiative be interpreted as an indication of American desire to

[55] Lansing to Legations in Panama and Honduras, May 12, 1917, *ibid.*, nos. 590, 592.

[56] The comments on responses are based on despatches from American envoys in the Latin American capitals (*ibid.*, nos. 595-596, 599, 606-608, 613, 625, 627, 667, 671, 681). Cf. Moreno Quintana, *op. cit.*, pp. 218-220.

[57] Stimson to Secretary of State, July 5, 1917, *For. Rel.*, *1917*, Sup. 1, p. 306.

[58] *Ibid.*, pp. 354-355, 367-368, 376-377, NA, DS, 763.72119/973, 1088.

participate. Unless Argentina agreed to adhere to the Peruvian plan, the United States felt the congress should not convene.[59]

By the end of December the fate of the conference was fixed. Only Mexico, whose delegates later arrived, had accepted definitely or without significant reservations.[60] It was evident that Irigoyen had fumbled, and fumbled badly. He had visualized an opportunity for Argentina but could not effectively exploit it. His failure, like his opportunity, grew out of the magnitude of national and international responsibilities which beset his immature administration.

In the midst of world war, Irigoyen had been elected by his followers to bring them long-needed social and political reforms. Suddenly, after four months in the Casa Rosada, like Wilson in August, 1914, he saw his domestic problem complicated by a grave international crisis. Without losing his grip on his party, therefore, or offending Argentina's national pride, he must implement the comprehensive internal program expected of him and fulfill the nation's traditional international destiny. Lacking in administrative experience, Irigoyen faced this appalling task as the head of an untried Cabinet and leader of a party that had never held the reins of national government.

In 1914 Irigoyen's predecessors had understood the threat brought by war to the political and economic security of the American nations. Mindful, like their contemporaries in other states, that the most effective countermeasure was common action, they had logically turned to the institutionalized means at hand, the Pan American organization and the leadership of the United States.[61] In response, the Wilson administration took the initiative in those areas in which it believed common policy desirable. It chose, therefore, to project the Pan American Peace Pact and to convene the Financial Conference but not to seek general accord on rules for neutrality. When this position became clear and as long as the United States remained at peace, neither Argentina nor any Latin American nation attempted to promote Pan American agreement on procedures for neutrals.

Once the United States broke with Germany, however, the other American states were left with a hard choice. Each might follow the lead of the United States, might act in agreement with the remaining neutrals, or might go it alone. To Argentina, long reluctant to play tail to the American kite and long ambitious to exercise leadership over the Latin American states, the second alternative seemed the logical course and

---

[59] Stimson to Secretary, Dec. 6, and Secretary to Stimson, Dec. 15, 1917, *For. Rel., 1917*, Sup. 1, 381-383, 388-389. One of Irigoyen's biographers indicts the United States for destroying the project before its birth (Manuel Gálvez, *Vida de Hipólito Yrigoyen, el hombre del misterio*, p. 287).

[60] Stimson to Secretary, Dec. 28, 1917, Jan. 12, 1918, *For. Rel., 1917*, Sup. 1, pp. 394-395, and NA, DS, 763.72119/1109.

[61] See above, p. 306.

an obvious opportunity. That President Irigoyen in making this choice gave support to the doctrine of Latin Americanism is clear; that, like Ugarte or other critics of the United States, he was anti-American does not necessarily follow.

His decision to call a conference of Hemisphere neutrals immediately after the American break with Germany was mistrusted by the Wilson administration. It was criticized by the American press [62] and has since been called in question by historians. In seeking agreement of the remaining neutrals on juridical problems of the war, Argentine apologists for his policy have pointed out, Irigoyen was only doing what Wilson could have done in 1914. Had he really wished to inspire Hemisphere unanimity on neutrality, Wilson could have utilized one of the instruments of the Pan American organization, such as the Fifth General Conference. Having failed to do so, his opposition to Irigoyen's leadership in a comparable situation was unjustified.[63]

But regardless of Irigoyen's intentions, still not divined or satisfactorily analyzed, his actions have had an enduring effect on Argentine-American relations. They played into the hands of anti-American propagandists. They provided a whipping boy for critics of Argentina's normal independence of views and actions. At a time when the United States was deeply involved elsewhere, they challenged its leadership of the American states. They widened the breach, perhaps irreparably, between the two rivals for Hemisphere hegemony, both within and without the Pan American organization.

Ambassador Naón: the End of a Mission

On the day World War I ended Ambassador Naón resigned his post.[64] With his passing from official position, the United States lost its most ardent Argentine friend and the Western Hemisphere one of its staunchest proponents of Pan Americanism. His resignation marked more than the end of a diplomatic mission; it symbolized the growing disharmony between Hemisphere rivals.

Through periods of peace, neutrality, and war, Naón's mission spanned eight difficult years in Washington. Appointed by a Conservative president, he served under his successor and survived the Radical Party's

[62] At the time of the first invitation, Naón was extremely concerned over the American reaction (Lansing to the President, May 21, 1917, NA, DS, 763. 72119/587 1/2).

[63] Moreno Quintana, *op. cit.*, p. 223; Ricardo Ryan, *La política internacional y la presidéncia Yrigoyen*, pp. 54-55. Irigoyen's invitation to belligerents as well as neutrals to the second conference deprives the argument of some of its cogency.

[64] República Argentina, Ministerio de Relaciones Exteriores y Culto, *Circular informativa mensual*, No. 18 (Nov., 1918), p. 1.

revolutionary changes in national administration. He adjusted to the divergent political philosophies of two American presidents and established close working relations with three secretaries of state. Upon the elevation of missions in 1914, he became Argentina's first Ambassador to the United States.

In diverse practical ways Naón had sought improvement of Argentine-American relations and growth of the inter-American spirit. Loyal to Argentina, through speeches and magazine articles he attempted to inform Americans about his nation. In an address to the American Bar Association, he stressed the unique humanitarian features of the Argentine constitution, especially its guarantees of complete equality to aliens and of unhampered navigation of inland waterways to ships of all nations.[65] At various times he offered realistic suggestions for the expansion of bilateral trade.[66]

On repeated occasions Naón made his services available to Secretaries Bryan and Lansing. At the time of the Mexican crisis in 1914, he suggested and participated in the ABC mediation. Through both the Department of State and the Governing Board of the Pan American Union he worked to secure a common policy for American neutrals. Believing in the merit of Wilson's Peace Pact, he assisted Lansing's search for a formula that would satisfy the Chileans and never wavered in his willingness to approve it. When suddenly advised of the State Department's decision to publish the three Luxburg telegrams, he worked closedly with Lansing in arranging joint release of the remainder.

After February, 1917, Naón's greatest diplomatic aim was to place Argentina at America's side, if not as a belligerent, then as a close economic ally. Each new affront to Argentine neutrality in 1917 renewed his hopes that Irigoyen would fulfill what the Ambassador believed to be his nation's international responsibility. In December, completely out of harmony with his government's policies, he resigned and returned to Argentina. When he returned to his post in July, 1918, after six months of restless activity in Buenos Aires, he was motivated by duty to Irigoyen's wishes and by hope that Washington would agree to some sort of economic alliance. To the end of the war, however, he remained frustrated by the adamant position of Irigoyen and by Allied disinterest

[65] His address appeared as an article, "International Democracy: a Guiding Principle in the Foreign Relations of Argentina," *World's Work*, XXIX (Dec., 1914), 147-148. The preamble to the Argentine constitution contains the singular expression, "securing the benefits of liberty to ourselves, our posterity, and to all people in the world who may wish to inhabit the Argentine soil." This guarantee to aliens is fortified in succeeding constitutional articles (A. F. Macdonald, *Government of the Argentine Republic*, pp. 132, 139-142).

[66] Naón, "Trade Expansion with Argentina," *The Pan-American Magazine*, XX (March, 1915), 10-16.

in his own vague proposals. On November 11, impelled, he said, by his aspirations and ideas, he resigned irrevocably.[67]

Three months later, Naón put on paper a testament of his beliefs in Pan Americanism. Though published as a pamphlet by the American Association for International Conciliation, it deserves to be better known.[68] As an expression of faith in the inter-American concept, it is a buoyant yet realistic appraisal.

Naón's thesis was that the European war and the Peace Conference would enormously modify the international organization of the world. By invoking exclusively national policies, the American states had ignored the principle of solidarity and lamentably reversed the tendencies of Pan Americanism. The entrance of the United States into the war, however necessary, interrupted its promising modification of the Monroe Doctrine into an international continental policy. The failure of other nations to follow the United States damaged growing continental solidarity and prejudiced, without destroying, the Pan American spirit.[69]

Two principal dangers, Naón believed, threatened the revival and extension of the idea. The first was the classification of nations by the Peace Conference into great powers and small powers. Complicity of the United States in this conception might weaken a basic condition of inter-American solidarity, the sovereign equality of all states. However significant at critical times the political interests of the United States in Europe, consolidation of the Pan American idea must be the *sine qua non* of its foreign policy.[70]

The second source of danger to resurgence of the continental spirit was internal: the promotion of Latin Americanism. To Naón this idea was unwholesome, Teutonic, and anarchical. "By pandering to paltry prejudices and flattering national vanities," it was capable of replacing continental solidarity by a continental equilibrium. This was the system which had brought Europe to war. "If there is no possibility now . . . for the international organization of the world," wrote Naón in his closing appeal, "let us at least see to it that it shall be the essential base of the international organization of America." [71]

But the troubled ambassador was casting bread upon dead seas. Long before his words saw print in New York, his own government had accepted his resignation and, in a verbose decree, refuted his strictures

[67] Copies of his resignation and Irigoyen's decree of acceptance were enclosed in Stimson to Secretary of State, Nov. 29, 1918, NA, DS, 701.3511/695.

[68] "The European War and Pan Americanism," *International Conciliation*, No. 20 (April, 1919). It was also published in *Columbia University Quarterly*, XXI (April, 1919), 85ff.

[69] *International Conciliation*, No. 20 (April, 1919), 3-9.

[70] *Ibid.*, pp. 12-17.

[71] *Ibid.*, pp. 18-19.

on Argentine conduct during the war.[72] In the United States, the Wilson administration was immersed in the problems of reconversion to peace and deeply committed to the European involvements Naón had warned against. The Ambassador's testament was probably little read, certainly soon forgotten.

The cleavage between the United States and Argentina over their international policies within the Western Hemisphere was not abrupt nor had it ever approached an open break. It was rather a fissure, opened in 1890, narrowed and widened at various times to 1917, then immeasurably broadened by the discordant policies of President Wilson and President Irigoyen.

[72] See above, p. 338, note 67.

X X I

THE RISE AND FALL OF COMMERCE: BUSINESS DURING WAR, BOOM, AND DEPRESSION, 1914-1939

The annual value of Argentine-American commerce between 1914 and 1939 fluctuated with the ebb and flow of world conditions. In reciprocal trade, as in their domestic economies, the two nations responded sensitively to the changing stages of global war, global prosperity, and global depression. The demands of World War I pushed total trade to heights that would remain unequalled until the late forties. Steadily rising prosperity in the middle twenties brought lush profits to exporters in both countries. World-wide depression lowered the value of two-way commerce to pre-1914 figures.

Persistent efforts by both nations gradually pared down many barriers that had obstructed their commercial exchange for a century. Yet the fundamental similarity of their agricultural and pastoral production, protected by new tariff walls, sanitary embargoes, or exchange restrictions, continued to forestall the growth of sound bases for mutual trade. Argentina in the twenties and both nations in the thirties frustrated hopeful attempts to replace the antiquated commercial treaty of 1853. After 1933 Democratic administrations in Washington were as unsuccessful in reaching agreement with Argentine Conservatives as Republicans had been with Radicals during the previous decade. As World War II approached, the accelerated trade drives of Britain and Germany cut deeply into American sales.

Expansion of Argentine Prosperity

With the products of its fields and pastures flowing out to the nations of the North Atlantic, Argentina between 1913 and 1929 enjoyed the greatest prosperity in its history. As the value of foreign trade tripled, it developed the highest standard of material comfort in Latin America.

340

It doubled the mileage of telegraph wire, quadrupled the number of telephones, and constructed highways and railways until, per thousand inhabitants, it led all the Latin republics. The citizens of Argentina enjoyed the advantages of a per capita purchasing power twice that of Cuba, next most prosperous Latin nation. In peacetime it enabled them to buy more foreign-made articles, per person, than even residents of the United States.

To replace the shortages of imported goods and petroleum caused by the war, domestic and foreign capital undertook the development of new industries and expansion of oil resources. The increased demand for labor brought higher wage scales and pushed Argentina's percentage of population in cities over 25,000 to the highest in Latin America. Its total population grew to nearly 10,700,000, an increase of 40 per cent. Through the construction of nearly four thousand schoolhouses, the nation almost doubled school attendance and raised its literacy rate until it approached that of Uruguay, the highest in Latin America. The growing cities and provinces raised foreign loans to support erection of new public buildings, widening of streets, and improvement of health and sanitary services.[1]

Growth of Two-Way Trade, 1914-1929

The United States shared Argentina's era of prosperity. During the years of war and recovery the volume of reciprocal commerce reached abnormal heights. In both directions, while Argentina fed the maw of America's wartime appetite and the United States replaced former European suppliers, the movement of trade increased year by year. The upward cycle reached its apogee in 1920, as the Argentines splurged for the luxuries and replacement goods of which war had deprived them and the Americans honored contracts already made for agricultural and livestock products. Not until 1947, a comparable postwar year, would total trade surpass the 1920 peak of $421,000,000. From 1914 through 1919 Argentina enjoyed the favorable balance.

Receding rapidly from the high-water mark of 1920, the flow of two-way trade levelled off to a decade of steady growth. Even the depression-year total of $171,000,000 in 1921 was more than twice that of the last prewar year. Rising annually, except in 1924, the figure nearly doubled again by 1929. In the total of Argentina's foreign trade, the United States had now outstripped all its rivals except the United Kingdom.[2]

---

[1] This interpretation of Argentina's economic development is based on statistical analyses made by Max Winkler, *Investments of United States Capital in Latin America*, pp. 286-287, and J. F. Rippy in A. C. Wilgus (ed.), *Argentina, Brazil and Chile Since Independence*, p. 141.

[2] Fourth Pan American Commercial Conference, *Foreign Trade of Latin America, 1910-1929*, p. 27.

TABLE 3

VALUE OF ARGENTINE TRADE WITH THE UNITED STATES
(IN THOUSANDS OF DOLLARS): 1913-1930

Year	Argentine Exports	Argentine Imports	Argentine Excess of Exports (+); of Imports (−)
1913	$ 25,576	$ 54,980	−
1914	56,274	27,128	+
1915	94,678	52,841	+
1916	116,293	76,874	+
1917	178,261	107,099	+
1918	228,388	105,105	+
1919	199,158	155,899	+
1920	207,777	213,726	−
1921	59,926	110,836	−
1922	85,678	95,542	−
1923	115,276	112,782	+
1924	75,298	117,093	−
1925	80,170	148,759	−
1926	88,058	143,575	−
1927	97,240	163,485	−
1928	99,438	178,899	−
1929	117,581	210,288	−
1930	71,891	129,862	−

SOURCE: *Statistical Abstract of the United States, 1920,* p. 411; *1925,* pp. 450-451; *1930,* pp. 492-493; *1935,* pp. 438-439.

The one-way movement of commerce followed much the same pattern. The value of Argentine exports to the United States in 1929 doubled that of 1921 and quadrupled that of 1913. But while the shares of the other major buyers remained relatively constant, the American portion increased from 4.7 to 9.8 per cent. Only Great Britain, Belgium, and Germany were now better customers, although the British still outbought the other three.[3]

On the other hand, a truly spectacular change took place in the growth of Argentina as a buyer of American goods. While in 1913 the United States supplied less than one-seventh of Argentina's imports to Britain's nearly one-third, in 1929 the American share had grown to more than one-fourth and the British dropped to barely one-sixth. By 1929 the dollar value of American sales was three times that of 1913; the value of British exports actually decreased. After 1916, except 1922-1924, the United States was the principal source of Argentine imports. Even ten years after the war Britain had not regained its prewar position as first supplier of Argentine needs.[4] Moreover, at least temporarily, Argentina had passed Cuba as America's best customer in Latin America.

[3] *Loc. cit.*

[4] *Loc. cit.;* Virgil Salera, *Exchange Control and the Argentine Market,* p. 42.

The balance of trade, therefore, adverse during most of the century, continued to run against the Argentines. From 1921 to 1929, in a total trade volume exceeding two billion dollars, they suffered an annual average deficit of more than fifty millions.

Causes of Growth: Sequel to War

This heightened flow of trade through channels that had been relatively stagnant for a century stemmed from a complex of influences: from the economic dislocations imposed by widespread war; from the whetting of new interest in foreign trade among American entrepreneurs; from the dissemination of knowledge in the United States about Argentina and its markets; from the reduction, if not the elimination, of frustrating obstacles; and from the increased movement of American capital to Argentina. These influences can be explained, if not evaluated.

The extent and duration of World War I placed insatiable demands upon the natural granaries and storehouses of the world. The eventual involvement of the United States served to increase its own dependence, as well as that of all the Allied nations, upon the agricultural and pastoral riches of neutral Argentina. To feed, clothe, equip, and house its troops, the United States reached into the Argentine reservoir for vast quantities of meat and corn, wool and skins, hides and tanning extract, and linseed.[5]

The eclipse of Germany both as a market and as a source of manufactured goods forced the Argentines to turn more and more to the United States. The inability of Britain to "deliver the goods" in wartime as in peace accelerated the trend. Moreover, the decline in normal imports of consumer goods stimulated the birth of local industries, especially those producing cigarettes, beer, soap and other toilet articles, textiles, and building materials.[6] Tools and equipment for these industries, as well as replacement parts for the transportation system and machines for expanding agriculture, were available, if at all, only in the United States.

These diverse wartime dislocations, therefore, deepened the shallow channels of Argentine-American trade. By forcing leaders of government and business in each nation, however belatedly and reluctantly, to recognize the indispensability of the other's production, the war served to minimize the natural repulsion of their noncomplementary economies. Quickened by the requirements of war, the current of bilateral trade maintained much of its momentum with the return of peace.

[5] The Chamber of Commerce of the United States of America in the Argentine Republic, *Trade Relations between Argentina and the United States of America*, pp. 24-25.

[6] *Ibid.*, p. 24.

Causes of Growth: Improved Intelligence

The expansion of trade naturally brought to the citizens of each country new knowledge about the other—and new demand for steadier flow of information. In the months after the war, spokesmen of both republics stressed the need for fuller mutual acquaintanceship if the United States wished to hold the trade supremacy it had won.

No American visualized the weakness of the State Department in these matters—or its appropriate mission—more effectively than Frederic J. Stimson, first Ambassador to Argentina, who served until the end of the Wilson administration. On February 18, 1919, in a long despatch to his secretary of state, he set forth his recommendations for the improvement of reporting procedures. Acutely aware, from his wartime service in Argentina, of the growing intimacy between commerce and diplomacy in Latin America, he scored the overlapping functions of the ambassador, the consul general, and the commercial attaché. In his view, consuls and attachés should be responsible to the diplomatic service and the chief of mission should see every report. Only by painstaking and coordinated reporting, he argued, could diplomacy assure the flow of reliable information upon which to base the nation's commercial policies.[7] These improvements, of course, would eventually come. In the meantime, sound studies of the Argentine economy by the Bureau of Foreign and Domestic Commerce partially filled the hiatus which concerned Stimson.[8]

When opportunity presented, Argentine leaders, too, pointed up the need for mutual understanding. Among others, Carlos Tornquist, speaking in 1920 before the newly organized Argentine-American Chamber of Commerce in New York, and Honorio Pueyrredón, Irigoyen's Foreign Minister and after 1923 Ambassador in Washington, urged greater exchange of information.[9]

Expansion of American press services in Latin America assured fuller coverage of news developments for both Argentines and Americans. The United Press, during the late months of the war, and the Associated Press in 1919 enlisted as subscribers the leading dailies of Buenos Aires. By gradually increasing the daily transmission of cabled news they helped to offset in Argentina the heavy coverage of European happenings which had long prevailed. Still, as Pueyrredón later reported

---

[7] NA, DS, Decimal File, 121.56/384.

[8] Such as L. B. Smith and H. T. Collings, *The Economic Position of Argentina during the War* (Washington, 1920), and M. A. Phoebus, *Economic Development in Argentina Since 1921* (Washington, 1923).

[9] "Argentine-American Relations Offer Field for Improvement: Opinions of a Distinguished Argentine," *The Pan-American Magazine*, XXX (March, 1920), 266-269; Pueyrredón to Angel Gallardo, Minister of Foreign Affairs, Jan. 1, 1926, *Memoria, 1925*, 691-692.

to his government, it took a revolution or an earthquake to interest most Americans in South America.[10]

The Chamber of Commerce of the United States in the Argentine Republic, founded at the close of the war and merged in 1920 with the Argentine-American Chamber of Commerce in New York, actively promoted the commercial interests of both countries. It answered requests from the United States, put American companies in touch with Argentine firms, maintained an employment service, informed members of legislative developments, and wired fortnightly cables to New York. It sent its monthly journal, *Comments on Argentine Trade*, and regular bulletins to the Departments of State and Commerce, the United States Chamber of Commerce, and the Pan American Union.[11]

Supplementing the *Comments* in its drive to foment trade, *The American Weekly of Buenos Aires* began publication in 1923. To serve a similar purpose in New York, a new periodical, *Argentina*, appeared in 1928, encouraged by the Argentine-American Chamber of Commerce and edited by Dr. Pedro Lainez. *The Pan-American Magazine*, founded some years before, continued its efforts to give Americans the facts of Argentine life.

Causes of Growth: Reduction of Barriers

The gradual removal during and just after the war of impediments that had plagued commercial interchange for decades contributed to the retention of the new Yankee share of the Argentine market. Improvement of shipping facilities was the greatest boon to reciprocal trade. First under the United States Shipping Board, then under private companies, scores of ships of American registry eliminated the hard choice between irregular sailings and the two-way crossing via Europe. In 1919 alone, 335 American merchant vessels docked in Argentine ports, where five years before the Yankee ensign rarely flew. In the twenties, the Munson and Norton Lines from east coast ports and Swayne and Hoyt from San Francisco offered direct, regular passenger service; the American Republics Line, with twelve vessels, and the Gulf-Brazil-River Plate Line, with fifteen, maintained fairly regular cargo service.[12]

[10] Pan American Union, *Pan American Commerce, Past—Present—Future, from the Pan American Viewpoint. Report of the Second Pan American Commercial Conference* . . . , p. 95; Pueyrredón to Gallardo, Jan. 1, 1926, *Memoria, 1925*, pp. 694-696.

[11] W. H. Robertson, Consul General to Buenos Aires, to Secretary of State, Dec. 16, 1920, NA, DS, 635.11171/25; *Comments on Argentine Trade*, V (May, 1926), 3, 6. An early editor of this periodical was John W. White, who was later to serve for many years as correspondent in Buenos Aires for *The New York Times* and who in 1942 was to publish *Argentina, The Life Story of a Nation*.

[12] P. A. Martin, *Latin America and the War*, pp. 546-547; *Comments on Argentine Trade*, II (Feb., 1923), 3-4, and VI (April, 1927), 52-56, 58; *Current History*, XVII (Dec., 1922), 529.

The opening in December, 1919, of the first direct cable communication between the United States and Buenos Aires represented another significant gain for American interests.[13] For fifty-one years secretaries of state had strongly supported the efforts of cable companies to break the British monopoly of east coast communications. James A. Scrymser, of the Central and South American Telegraph Company, devoted a lifetime to the struggle. Later, after this firm had merged with All America Cables, Inc., John L. Merrill took up the fight. Repeatedly urging the Department of State to bring diplomatic pressure upon Brazil, Uruguay, and Argentina, they finally curbed the British stranglehold on direct cable connections.[14] No longer would rival merchants hold the advantage of cheaper wire costs and free access to American commercial information.

Accompanying these advances in transportation and communications services, other developments strengthened the American position. The wider employment of trade acceptances, authorized by the Federal Reserve Act, together with expanded use of the new branches of two strong American banks in Buenos Aires, facilitated the financing of shipments in both directions and enabled the American manufacturer to compete with European companies in the granting of credits. By 1919 dozens of important American concerns established branch houses in Buenos Aires or contracted with agencies to conduct their sales. Argentine firms, although controlled in some cases by European capital, began to maintain permanent buyers in the United States.[15]

Besides its many other activities, the newly created Chamber of Commerce of the United States in Argentina worked to build up faith in the American manufacturer. Through its Arbitration Committee, which handled nearly six hundred complaints from 1919 to 1923, it sought to protect importers against ingenuous or "fly-by-night" American exporters. To reduce the number of complaints it advised merchants of the value of meeting consumer demands and the futility of deficient packing, tardy delivery, or noncompliance with specifications.[16]

Causes of Growth: Americans Invest in Argentina

Since the nineteenth century prominent Argentine leaders had advanced their own panaceas for increasing bilateral trade. They had

[13] Robert Lansing, Secretary of State, to Ministers of Foreign Affairs of Uruguay and Argentina, Dec. 19, 1919, NA, DS, 835.73/34a, 109.

[14] See above, pp. 231, 236. Hundreds of documents on the extended controversy are filed in NA, DS, 835.73.

[15] R. S. Barrett, "Will the United States Hold Its Present Trade in Argentina?" *The Pan-American Magazine*, XXIX (June, 1919), 98-100.

[16] White, "An American Reply to Dr. Zeballos," *The American Weekly of Buenos Aires*, I (Aug. 18, 1923), 5, 13.

repeatedly advocated that the United States, like Britain, should increase its capital in Argentina, especially in industrial establishments. American investors, however, were slow to follow this suggestion.

Even at the end of 1920 total American investment in Argentina was little larger than the $40,000,000 of 1913. During the war years American packing companies had consolidated and expanded their prewar position in the meat trade. The International Portland Cement and National Lead Companies had set up small enterprises. In 1917 American banking houses had taken up $15,000,000 in the bonds of the Central Argentine Railway. But few other important firms followed the paths of these pioneers. Although many well-known American concerns were doing business in Argentina, most operated through branch houses or local agents.[17]

The first substantial flow of Yankee venture capital began in the twenties. The Ford Motor Company erected several assembly plants. The Radio Corporation of America became part-owner of a porteño radio station. Through subsidiaries the Standard Oil Companies of New Jersey and California were seeking to uphold American interests in the world scramble for oil. Other firms were active in the areas of textiles, corn products, leather, and construction of public works. By 1924 the total industrial investment approached $100,000,000. The Chamber of Commerce of the United States in Argentina had grown to nearly two hundred members.[18]

During the middle-twenties American capital migration to Argentina went more largely into government securities than into direct investments. By 1928, however, as flush times induced investors to seek more speculative outlets, American money turned to Argentine business possibilities, especially the utilities of Buenos Aires and provincial communities.[19] Leading the new penetration, the International Telephone and Telegraph Corporation and the American and Foreign Power Company in 1928-1929 invested nearly $160,000,000. As a result of this dollar offensive, the total of American direct investments in Argentina reached $355,000,000, more than that in any of the Latin American republics except Cuba and Mexico.[20]

Only in the strategic matter of petroleum did the State Department pay more than routine heed to the activities of these investors. As early as April, 1919, it instructed its representatives in Buenos Aires to probe

[17] Winkler, *op. cit.*, pp. 68-72; W. R. Ingalls, *Wealth and Income of the American People: A Survey of the Economic Consequences of the War*, p. 51.

[18] R. W. Dunn, *American Foreign Investments*, pp. 64-65. For a partial list of American firms, see *The Argentine Annual, Including Lists of English Speaking Residents and Estancieros*, p. 223.

[19] H. E. Peters, *The Foreign Debt of the Argentine Republic*, p. 135.

[20] Winkler, *op. cit.*, pp. 69-74, and *Foreign Bonds: An Autopsy*, p. xv note.

rumors of British interest in Patagonia. Throughout the twenties, as the world powers stepped up the race for control of the world's oil resources, Washington officials maintained alertness to developments in Argentina.[21]

American companies were first to investigate the Argentine oil fields. By June, 1920, the Argentine-Bolivia Exploration Company had secured concessions and by August the Standard Oil Company of New Jersey was preparing to negotiate. Both were primarily interested in the potentialities of northwestern Argentina.[22] From the outset Washington directed the Embassy to render "all proper assistance and support" to the agents. Repeatedly in subsequent instructions, the Department revealed its desire that American companies push their projects with vigor. Meanwhile, reports of activities by English, French, and German nationals persisted.[23]

The sudden attraction of their oil fields for alien interests aroused the Argentines anew to the necessity of safeguarding their resources. Ten years before, under President Saenz Peña, the government had broadened the state's legal powers over its natural assets. Wartime shortages had driven home the evils of dependence upon foreign oil. Now, to forestall possible domination of oil resources by large foreign corporations, the Irigoyen administration placed restrictions on the size of holdings. Beyond this, moreover, rumors of possible nationalization or monopolistic grant to a foreign concern reached Washington.[24]

Confronted by these reports, the State Department promptly formulated its attitude toward a state or state-controlled monopoly of Argentine oil. It held that such a monopoly would violate the principle of reciprocity, would exclude American capital, and might reduce the flow of trade. As early as September, 1920, while cautioning against representations to the Argentine authorities on a domestic matter, the Secretary of State instructed his representative to suggest these views to the Irigoyen government. Whatever the reaction, he was to insist that

[21] Act. Sec. of State to Consul to Buenos Aires, April 7, 1919, NA, DS, 835.6363/12a.

[22] Stimson to Secretary of State, June 24, 1920, NA, DS, 163./845; Secretary of Commerce to Secretary of State, July 14, 1920; E. J. Sadler, Standard Oil Co. of N. J., to Secretary of State, Aug. 16, 1920; Memorandum of a conversation with Spruille Braden, Feb. 1, 1921; Francis White, Chargé d'Affaires ad interim to Argentina, to Secretary of State, June 22, 1921, 835.6363/21, 25, 45, 65. Mr. Braden stated that he and his father, William, were interested in the Argentine-Bolivia Exploration Company as advisory engineers, not as investors.

[23] A. A. Adee, Asst. Sec. of State, to Sadler, Sept. 3, and to C. W. Wadsworth, Chargé d'Affaires ad interim to Argentina, Sept. 9, 1920, NA, DS, 835.6363/25, 32a. On the Department's attitude toward European competitors, see many documents in this file.

[24] White to Secretary of State, June 27, 1921, *ibid.*, no. 67. A departmental memo. prepared in 1928, presents a comprehensive survey of the trend toward nationalization of oil resources from 1910 to 1928 (NA, DS, 810.6363/36).

American citizens should receive equal opportunity to participate in the monopoly.[25]

The American position, however, did not deter President Irigoyen. A few months later, acting in consonance with his characteristic nationalistic beliefs, he pushed through a law creating the Yacimientos Petrolíferos Fiscales (YPF), a state agency authorized to exploit and protect the nation's oil resources. Under his successor, President Marcelo T. de Alvear, the new agency did not immediately move toward nationalization or expropriation of existing private interests.[26]

Nevertheless, the trend toward nationalization continued, led after 1926 by the Director General of YPF, General Enrique Mosconi. "The Standard Oil Company" became the principal target of his virulent attacks on foreign oil interests. "Wherever this company obtains a foothold," he said in a Mexico City speech, "it becomes not only a Government within a Government but a Government over a Government." [27] Soon he moved to secure annulment of the company's concessions in Salta Province. Successful defender of the Standard's interests during a long court fight was Dr. Rómulo Naón, first Argentine Ambassador to Washington and long-time friend of the United States.[28]

Causes of Growth: Argentina Borrows in the United States

While American capital during and after World War I moved reluctantly into the Argentine industrial field, investors reacted more favorably toward issues of government securities. From 1915 to 1917 and again from 1921 to 1928 offers of portfolio investments found ready buyers in New York. By 1930 total holdings approached a half-billion dollars.[29]

The decline in foreign commerce in the early months of the war and the tardy financing of public improvements already under way had confronted Argentine governments with the necessity of floating foreign loans. Refused in London, the traditional source of funds, fiscal authorities turned for the first time to the United States. Reluctant to pay

[25] Memorandum from the Office of the Foreign Trade Advisor, Aug. 14; Colby to Embassy to Argentina, Sept. 15; Norman H. Davis, for the Secretary, to Embassy, Nov. 13, 1920, NA, DS, 835.6363/28, 36, 49.

[26] Departmental memo, 1928, NA, DS, 810.6363/36.

[27] T. R. Armstrong, Standard Oil Company of N. J., to Stokely Morgan, Chief, Division of Latin American Affairs, May 15, 1928, and enclosure, NA, DS, 835.6363/311.

[28] P. A. Jay, Ambassador to Argentina, to Secretary of State, Oct. 18, 1926, NA, DS, 835.631/5; R. W. Bliss, Ambassador to Argentina, to Secretary of State, June 10, 1931, RSC, DS, 835.6363/358. With the subsequent expansion of YPF activities, the State Department continued its insistence upon equality of opportunity for American oil companies operating in Argentina (*For. Rel., 1936*, V, 184-200).

[29] Winkler, *Foreign Bonds: An Autopsy*, p. xv note.

interest rates which usually approached 7 per cent, they resorted to a series of short-term funding operations. At the time of American entry into the war, American bankers headed by J. P. Morgan and Company and the National City Bank of New York held about $80,000,000 in bonds.[30]

After 1917 Argentina became a creditor nation itself and within three years liquidated all its outstanding American loans. Feelers for a new loan in early 1920 received a cold shoulder from the Wilson administration. This brief use of the New York money market, restricted largely to bankers and attended by little fanfare, left American investors with no deeper interest in Argentina than they had had before 1914.[31]

After changes of administration, however, in both Buenos Aires and Washington, and especially after the upturn in world business in 1923-1924, Argentine authorities again sought loans in New York. The principal borrowers were the national government and the provinces and cities of Buenos Aires, Córdoba, Santa Fe, and Tucumán. They issued bonds not only to cover refunding operations but also to finance construction of schoolhouses and other public buildings and improvement of streets, highways, and sanitary installations. With interest running often to 7 per cent, the banking houses of New York and Boston were eager bidders. The flow of dollars to support Argentina's era of public spending under President Alvear reached its zenith in 1928.[32] Then his onetime mentor, Irigoyen, returned to office. Government borrowing in New York suddenly stopped. Still seeking outlet for their gold in profitable Argentina, American investors turned from portfolio bonds to industrial stocks.

The combination of American investments in Argentina and Argentine borrowings in the United States had established the northern republic as the other's second-best creditor. From 1913 to 1929 its investment total had grown 1429 per cent to Britain's 15 per cent. Though the figure of $2,140,000,000 was still three and one-half times the American, no longer could the porteño spokesman chide the Yankee for his failure to stake his dollars on Argentina's future.[33]

Throughout the twenties the Department of State followed the practice of encouraging the bankers to inform it concerning each loan flotation before completion of the transaction. Refusing to participate

[30] Peters, *op. cit.*, pp. 95-97. I have relied upon this volume for my interpretation of American lending to Argentina.

[31] Peters, *op. cit.*, pp. 92, 95, 97, 100.

[32] For a summary of the issues floated, see Winkler, *Investments of United States Capital in Latin America*, pp. 72-74. The voluminous State Department correspondence on the subject—with the Embassy, with other government departments, and with the banks—is filed in NA, DS, 835.51 and subordinate numbers.

[33] Winkler, *op. cit.*, pp. 284-285.

in negotiations, however, it held firmly to the position that failure to interpose objections did not imply official endorsement.[34]

The movement of American capital in the twenties was roughly proportionate to the increase of sales to the Argentine market. Whether or not the exports followed the dollar is debatable. But at least the Americans had modified another barrier, real or alleged, to freer exchange of goods.[35]

Obstacles to Growth: Tariff Walls and Sanitary Embargoes

The reduction of these multiple obstacles, significant as they were, failed to place the structure of Argentine-American commerce on sound foundations. The trade trend of the twenties gave the appearance of solidity, but it was no more than a statistical façade masking basic faults. As they had done many times since 1867, Republican administrations again raised the wall of protection around domestic agricultural and pastoral products. Sometimes they acted through imposition of sanitary embargoes, but always they used the tariff. Repeated explanations that the measures were designed to protect domestic interests, not damage the Argentine, did not soften the blows.[36] The growing imbalance of their trade with the United States hurt Argentine pocketbooks but even more it stung porteño pride.

Following so closely the war-born boom in two-way trade, the tariff measures of 1921 and 1922 struck the Argentines with full force. Almost as soon as the last congressional session under President Wilson took up emergency tariff legislation, protests began to reach Washington. Prompted by influential agrarian interests in Argentina, the United States Chamber of Commerce in Buenos Aires urged its counterpart in Washington to use every means to defeat the bill. The Argentine Commercial Federation for Industry and Production suggested to President Irigoyen the possible use of reprisals.[37] On the day President Wilson

[34] Typical statements of this policy were contained in F. M. Dearing, Asst. Sec. of State, to Lewis Straus, of Kuhn, Loeb, & Company, Oct. 10, 1921, NA, DS, 835.51/274, and Frank B. Kellogg, Secretary of State, to Embassy to Argentina, Nov. 28, 1927, 835.51B861/36.

[35] Peters points out this relationship but doubts that the influence can be measured (*op. cit.*, pp. 147-149). At any rate, in their annual reports from Washington, Honorio Pueyrredón and Felipe Espil acknowledged the growing importance of the United States as a market for Argentine bonds (*Memoria, 1925*, p. 669; *1926*, p. 581; *1927*, pp. 754-755).

[36] For example, on the problem of hoof-and-mouth disease, see Memorandum of Division of Latin American Affairs, Dec. 24, and Memorandum of conversation with Espil, Dec. 30, 1926, NA, DS, 611.355/22, 29.

[37] C. D. Snow, Manager, Foreign Commerce Dept., Chamber of Commerce of the U.S.A., Washington, to Norman H. Davis, Asst. Sec. of State, Jan. 7, 1921, NA, DS, 611.3531/71; Stimson to Secretary of State, Dec. 31, 1920, and enclosures, 611.356/108.

vetoed the bill, an Argentine deputy introduced retaliatory tariff legislation.[38]

Neither Wilson's veto nor Argentine threats could prevent the new Republican Congress from promptly adopting (May 27, 1921) prohibitive rates on wheat, corn, meat, wool, hides, flax, and sugar.[39] The Argentine ambassador, Tomás A. Le Breton, protested the high emergency duties as well as those later prepared for the permanent tariff measure. Of the twenty products comprising 80 per cent of Argentina's exports to the United States, fifteen had been on the free list; only two now remained. The new levies would affect goods that had constituted 16 per cent of Argentina's total exports in 1920. Hides and meat were products of an Argentine business in which Americans had invested heavily. Wool and flaxseed were essential to important American industries.[40] Yet, committed to protection of the farmer, in September, 1922, Congress passed the Fordney-McCumber Act.

Argentine leaders, public and private, had lost their fight to forestall the new rates but not their will to protest. Throughout the decade, at conferences, in public addresses, in official correspondence, through the press, they raised their voices against American tariff policy.

Both in Buenos Aires and in Washington these protests reached a crescendo in 1926-1928 and presaged the reaction that would come with the world depression of 1929-1930. It was a series of restrictive orders on sanitary and kindred matters that provoked the sharpest irritations. In April, 1926, with the hope of determining adaptability to general use in the United States, the Department of Agriculture began to require the coloring, on a percentage basis, of all imported alfalfa and red clover seed.[41] In May, discovering shipments of white grapes to be infected with the Mediterranean fruit fly, it prohibited further importations.[42] Capping the succession of exclusive measures, four months later the Department prohibited the importation of fresh or frozen meats from regions of the world infected with foot-and-mouth disease.[43] In Argentina there were such regions.

[38] Stimson to Secretary of State, April 2, 1921, NA, DS, 635.003/114.

[39] In his veto message, the President expressed the belief that imports of grain, like those of wheat from Argentina, would not compete with the domestic crop (*Cong. Rec.*, 66 Cong., 3 sess., Vol. LX, pt. 4, pp. 4498-4499).

[40] To C. E. Hughes, Secretary of State, April 10, 1922, NA, DS, 611.3531/75; Memorandum of Division of Latin American Affairs, April 12, 1922, 611.003/1322.

[41] Espil called the law arbitrary and unnecessary (to Secretary of State, Dec. 6, 1926, NA, DS, 811.612/1329).

[42] In November, the Argentine government gave assurances that it would tighten up its inspection system and prohibit exportation of grapes from suspected areas (Jay to Secretary of State, Nov. 24, 1926, *ibid.*, no. 1339). The Department of Agriculture subsequently sent its own entomologist to investigate.

[43] Bureau of Animal Industry Order 298, Sept. 17, 1926, file copy in NA, DS, 611.355/40.

The progress of sanitary science, especially in plant and animal diseases and destructive pests, had given rise in the United States to advanced regulatory legislation. Charged with the administration of these laws, the Department of Agriculture secured strong farm support for rigorous enforcement. The agrarian groups at home could appreciate the ulterior advantage of sanitary restrictions on foreign competition. In countries like Argentina, where the new science was less publicized, the regulations appeared discriminatory.[44] The legitimate mission of the Department of Agriculture, therefore, seeking to protect the American farmer, rendered more difficult the task of the Department of State, confronted by the vexations produced in Argentina.

At the root of Argentine resentment was beef, heart of the popular diet, base of national prosperity, pride of the export trade, and joy of English tables. No true Argentine, from urban laborer to beef baron, could be brought to believe that the American embargo was more than a legal screen to protect home-grown beef of poorer quality and dearer price.[45] If they could not sell their meat, at least they would protect their reputation as world's first producer of top-quality beef.

The Department's action, effective on January 1, 1927, produced an angered outcry from the Argentine press, a dignified protest from the Argentine Rural Society, and a formal request for reconsideration from the Embassy. *La Nación* wrote sarcastically about Yankee talk of "Pan Americanism." [46] The president of the Rural Society, speaking in Washington, suggested that purchases of 350,000,000 pounds of Argentine beef, 28 per cent of its annual exports, would amount to only 5 per cent of American consumption.[47]

Assured that the order would apply only to meat from infected areas, not from the entire country, the Argentine chargé d'affaires nevertheless secured a suspension of the restrictions until March 1. By that time the Department of Agriculture agreed to accept Argentine certificates that beef exported to the American market came from noninfected cattle.[48] Over the objection of the State Department, however, already apprehensive over anti-American expressions in Argentina, the Bureau of Animal Industry decided to send an expert to determine the validity of the certificates. His report was extremely critical of the conditions he

[44] Memo of the Office of the Economic Adviser, Jan. 26, 1927, NA, DS, 811. 612/1384.

[45] For a description of press and official reaction, see P. L. Cable, Chargé d'Affaires ad interim to Argentina, to Secretary of State, March 9, 1927, NA, DS, 835.00/392.

[46] Dec. 21, 1926.

[47] Pan American Union, *Third Pan American Commercial Conference*, p. 182.

[48] Espil to Kellogg, Dec. 30, 1926; Memo of conversation between the Secretary and Pueyrredón, March 17, 1927, NA, DS, 611.355/20, 23.

found, especially the inadequacy of precautionary and inspection measures. The system of certification was unpalatable to both nations.[49]

Agricultural officials in Washington could find satisfaction when British authorities, too, revealed concern about the ineffectiveness of Argentine controls. But diplomatic representatives on the spot felt constrained to report that London approached the problem with greater caution and tact. In contrast to American bluntness and failure to smooth the way, Britain avoided hostile criticism by giving the *estancieros* and their government opportunity to develop effective controls.[50]

Hard on the heels of the annoying incidents over alfalfa seed, fruit, and meat, the Tariff Commission decided to implement the "flexible" rate clause of the 1922 tariff act. This novel provision authorized the president to raise or lower rates as much as 50 per cent, whenever the Commission found change necessary to equalize the cost of production at home and abroad. The flaxseed growers of Minnesota and the corn growers in the American Farm Bureau Federation pressed for action.[51]

Without consulting the State Department, the Commission in May, 1927, created a team of investigators to study the cost of flax production in Argentina, principal American supplier. Even before they received official notification, Argentine authorities indicated that the proposed mission would not be welcome.[52] When Secretary Kellogg took the matter directly to the President, Mr. Coolidge replied that he did

> not want to have foreign governments suppose that by intimating that they do not wish our representatives to make investigations there they can thereby suspend the operation of our flexible tariff. I do not feel that we can sacrifice the interests of agriculture for a possible benefit of making a market for manufactured products in the Argentine. I am making these suggestions as possible aids to you in arriving at some conclusion.[53]

[49] Memo of conversation with Bureau of Animal Industry, Department of Agriculture, March 26, 1927; file copy of report of Dr. S. O. Fladness, June 14-Nov. 7, 1927, NA, DS, 611.355/38, 51.

[50] U. Grant-Smith, Minister to Uruguay, to Secretary of State, Aug. 20, 1927, NA, DS, 611.355/47, and Bliss to Secretary, Jan. 6, 1928, 641.355/2.

[51] Francis White, Asst. Sec. of State, to Secretary, June 22, 1927, NA, DS, 103.802/140; C. H. Gray, Washington representative, American Farm Bureau Federation, to Kellogg, Sept. 29, 1928, 611.353 Corn/5.

[52] White to Secretary of State, June 8, and Bliss to Secretary, Sept. 7, 1927, NA, DS, 103.802/140, 158.

[53] Kellogg to the President, Aug. 22, and Coolidge to the Secretary, Aug. 29, 1927, NA, DS, 103.802/151, 159. The President was at the summer White House in Rapid City, North Dakota.

Nevertheless, in part perhaps because of Pueyrredón's firm position, the experts did not sail. Instead, the study of production costs went on in Washington.[54]

Some months later, when it seemed probable that the Tariff Commission would raise the duty on corn, Kellogg appealed again to the President. In a long, carefully composed memorandum, he pleaded the importance of Argentine friendship, especially when contrasted with an annual importation of less than 5,000,000 bushels to a nation producing 3,000,000,000.[55]

This iteration of galling actions—"pinpricks," the economic adviser of the State Department called them—gradually aroused among the Argentines a demand for retaliatory action.[56] The growth each year from 1926 to 1929 of the adverse trade balance provided tangible justification.[57] Though Pueyrredón and Espil were always tactful in their approaches to the secretary of state, they revealed in their annual reports to the minister of foreign affairs the extent of their official representations.[58] In Buenos Aires itself censure of American policies was not always so circumspect.

In his annual message to the Congress in May, 1927, President Alvear suggested the possibility of tariff legislation based upon the policy "Buy from those who buy from us!" [59] His proposal received strong support from all quarters, especially from the Argentine Rural Society, which advocated reciprocal tariffs, and from the less conservative Argentine Industrial Union, which urged open retaliation.[60] Frequently used by British spokesmen in Buenos Aires, the new slogan gained wide currency.[61] By the time new Presidents, Hoover and Irigoyen, assumed office, signs indicated its adoption as the basis of official policy.

Obstacles to Growth: Anglo-American Rivalry

Washington's exclusion of Argentine products, whether to enforce sanitary regulations or lessen competition, arrested the growth of a more solid base for commercial interchange. But throughout the twenties

[54] Bliss to Secretary of State, Sept. 17, 19, 1927, and enclosures, NA, DS, 103.802/170. During the period of study, Argentine representatives were in frequent communication with officials of the State Department and the Tariff Commission.
[55] Oct. 29, 1928, NA, DS, 611.353 Corn/11a.
[56] Memorandum to Secretary of State, Oct. 4, 1928, NA, DA, 611.353 Corn/7.
[57] See above, pp. 341-342.
[58] *Memoria, 1925*, pp. 543-544; *1926*, 568-569, 573, 579-580; *1927*, 724-747.
[59] Cable to Secretary of State, May 30, 1927, NA, DS, 635.1111/2.
[60] "Immediate Tariff Revisions Urged for Retaliation and Protection," *Comments on Argentine Trade*, VIII (Feb., 1929), 13-19.
[61] Cable to Secretary of State, Jan. 10, 1927, NA, DS, 635.1112/38; Ray Atherton, Chargé d'Affaires ad interim to England, to Secretary of State, April 19, 1929, 635.4117/33.

other restraining influences helped to determine the future shape of Argentine-American relations. Among these was the hard competition of Great Britain, which near the end of the decade stepped up its drive to thwart growing American penetration.

Britain's inability during World War I to supply Argentina with the fruits of its banks and factories opened the door to the American initiative it had surpassed for a century. Though the British outgunned the United States in enforcement of the black lists against Germany, Yankee packing houses moved heavily into the Argentine meat industry and Yankee banking houses temporarily monopolized the loan business. At war's end, Americans broke the British cable monopoly, cut into British shipping, and set out to compete in the quest for oil concessions. After 1923, in both direct and portfolio investments, American capital far outdistanced new English money. As Argentina recurrently strove to equalize Brazil's military strength, Anglo-American rivalry simmered in the bidding for airplanes, army equipment, new naval vessels, and even repair of the two battleships originally constructed in American yards.[62] Above all, after 1924 American exporters steadily outsold their rivals in Argentine markets.

In spite of all these advances, however, it was the British who, year in and year out, bought the greater share of Argentina's exports. In this way they supplied the liquid assets with which the Argentines could finance their purchasing and borrowing in the United States. When, therefore, in the late twenties Washington's "pinpricks" goaded porteño leaders toward retaliation, they found in Albion a willing accomplice.

The spearhead of Britain's efforts to win advantage from Argentina's rising anti-Americanism was its ambassador, Sir Malcolm Robertson. Friend of the landed and aristocratic elements as well as promoter of his own nation's interests, he allegedly coined the expression "Buy from those who buy from us!" Disturbed by American purchase of British-owned utilities in South America, he apparently feared that their railways, too, would fall into Yankee hands.[63]

During 1928-1929 State Department representatives reported frequently on pro-British developments, some of which they attributed to Sir Malcolm's influence. In May, 1928, they learned that a group of cattle raisers had organized to promote free entry of British goods. To preserve for British industry the market for transportation equipment,

---

[62] State Department materials on the arms business are filed in NA, DS, 635.11174; 835.24; 835.34; 835.51. A few key documents are published in *For. Rel., 1926,* I, 561-563; *1927,* I, 424-434. France, Germany, Italy, and Spain were also involved in phases of the competition.

[63] Ray Atherton, Chargé d'Affaires ad interim to Britain, to Secretary of State, April 19, and G. S. Messersmith, Consul General to Argentina, Sept. 19, 1929, NA, DS, 611.4117/33, 58.

several Argentine railroads in 1929 voted to limit ownership of voting stock to nationals of the two countries.[64]

London's campaign against American trade reached a climax with the sending of a strong mission to consider economic relations of broad interest. The timing of its visit clearly betrayed the hope that it would offset President-elect Hoover's earlier visit.[65] Under the chairmanship of Viscount D'Abernon, the mission remained in Argentina from August 20 to September 8, 1929. Its only tangible achievement, leaving no distinct advantage to either party, was an agreement providing reciprocal credits for the purchase of railway materials and cereals. A more significant result, however intangible, was its revelation of the attitude of Argentine leaders, especially the pro-British inclination of President Irigoyen.[66]

When *La Nación* published an Associated Press story of the "grave concern" the mission had given the Department of Commerce in Washington, Ambassador Bliss and Secretary Stimson agreed that it was no more than "a natural step for the British Government to take." [67] In evaluating the D'Abernon Mission two months later, American diplomats in Buenos Aires and London concluded that the British had overplayed their hand.[68] This was on October 23, 1929. Nevertheless, significant events already under way would prolong and intensify Anglo-American rivalry in Argentina.

Depression and the Fall of Trade

The depression which struck, then gripped, the world in 1929 and after staggered Buenos Aires and Washington, as it did the capitals of all exporting nations. Even before the collapse of the stock market in the United States, the prosperity of the Alvear administration had begun to fade. Boom, speculation, and overexpansion had already

[64] Bliss to Secretary of State, May 9, 1928, NA, DS, 635.4115/16; Messersmith to Secretary of State, Aug. 10, 1929, 835.77/180.

[65] Atherton to Secretary of State, May 28, and Albert Halstead, Consul General to Britain, to Department, Aug. 2, 1929, NA, DS, 635.4117/36, 38. The United States had long recognized the political importance in its Latin-American relations of sending official missions headed by distinguished leaders. In the previous ten years Theodore Roosevelt, Bainbridge Colby, and General Pershing had visited Buenos Aires. The Prince of Wales, in 1925, was the first member of the British royal family officially to set foot in South America (Woodbine Parish, "Britain's Royal Envoy in South America," *Current History*, XXII [Sept., 1925], 937-938).

[66] Messersmith to Department, Sept. 19, NA, DS, 635.4117/58; Atherton to Secretary of State, Oct. 1, 1929, 635.4115/21. The Argentine Congress refused to ratify the convention.

[67] Bliss to Secretary of State, Sept. 3, and White to Bliss, Sept. 13, 1929, NA, DS, 4117/45.

[68] Atherton to Secretary of State, Oct. 23, 1929, and enclosure, *ibid.*, no. 64.

brought deflation, retrenchment, and adverse balance of payments. The decline of its exports in 1929, combined with decreased inflow of new capital and heavy exports of gold, swelled the national debt and disorganized the public treasury. As the peso fell in foreign money markets, unemployment rose and wages went unpaid at home. Its financial stability threatened, the administration of the aged Irigoyen faced the world economic crisis in confusion and helplessness.[69] In 1930, as world prices for agricultural and pastoral products fell disastrously, the Argentine people saw the value of their exports plummet to the lowest annual total since the war.[70]

Argentine-American trade shared in the general collapse. By 1932 its dollar value skidded to a mere $47,000,000, lowest since 1908. Argentina sold to the United States goods worth less than $16,000,000, while American sales dipped to one-seventh those of 1929.

Even the subsequent recovery of domestic economies failed to restore their reciprocal commerce. Not once in the thirties did the annual trade approach the lush totals of 1927-1929; only in 1937, because of American droughts in the corn belt, did it exceed even the more normal figures of 1921-1926. Taking into account the depreciation of currencies, the annual volume of goods exchanged was probably no more than during the five years before World War I. Except in 1935-1937, when its cereals came to the aid of parched American fields, Argentina sold to the United States much less than it bought.

More damaging than this loss of business, however, especially to its

TABLE 4

VALUE OF ARGENTINE TRADE WITH THE UNITED STATES
(IN THOUSANDS OF DOLLARS): 1930-1940

Year	Argentine Exports	Argentine Imports	Argentine Excess of Exports (+); of Imports (−)
1930	$ 71,891	$129,862	−
1931	35,980	52,652	−
1932	15,779	31,133	−
1933	33,841	36,927	−
1934	29,487	42,688	−
1935	65,408	49,374	+
1936	65,882	56,910	+
1937	138,940	94,183	+
1938	40,709	86,793	−
1939	61,914	70,945	−
1940	83,301	106,874	−

SOURCE: *Statistical Abstract of the United States, 1930*, pp. 492-493; *1935*, pp. 438-439; *1940*, pp. 508-509; *1943*, pp. 534-535.

[69] Lawrence Smith, "Suspension of the Gold Standard in Raw Material Exporting Countries," *American Economic Review*, XXIV (Sept., 1934), 432-433; Peters, *op. cit.*, 152-153, 156-157.

[70] Pan American Union, *Argentina*, Foreign Trade Series No. 87, 1931, p. 1.

prestige in Buenos Aires, was America's forfeiture to the United Kingdom of its recently won position as Argentina's best supplier. After providing nearly one-fourth of Argentina's annual imports from 1925 to 1929, its share was halved in the period 1934-1938. During the same years Britain's portion rose from 20.5 per cent to 23.1 per cent. Retaking first place in 1931, it strengthened its lead through the trying thirties.[71]

Radicals and Republicans in Conflict

Hipólito Irigoyen, darling of the Argentine masses in his first term, was completely unfit to govern during his second. Approaching eighty, his mind failing, unable to understand what he read or to speak intelligently what he thought, he left administration to less honest aides. Needing a government that could act decisively to meet a grave international crisis, Argentina had one that could not even cope with routine domestic financing. Uncoordinated efforts to stabilize the peso by refunding loans and suspending the gold standard were wholly inadequate.

Passage in June, 1930, of the Smoot-Hawley Tariff Act, removing hides from the free list and raising duties on meat, flaxseed, corn, and wool, aggravated Irigoyen's deteriorating position. The Argentine press reacted with vigor and hostility. The Rural Society warned the American consul general that reprisals might follow.[72] To clear the way for presidential manipulation of current tariff rates, the Bolsa de Comercio recommended abrogation of the most-favored-nation clause in existing treaties. Beyond urging representatives to encourage American purchases of corn and flaxseed, Irigoyen did nothing. Apparently resigned to their government's ineptitude, the Argentines soon suspended their attacks on the higher rates.[73]

Spreading opposition to the President's incapacity, however, paved the way for military intervention. Even the popular masses abandoned the inscrutable leader they had long adored. In early September, 1930, an arch-conservative general, José Félix Uriburu, swept the Irigoyenistas from office and ended fourteen years of Radical administration. "Politically," wrote Federico Pinedo, one-time Socialist turned Conservative, "Irigoyen was annihilated, neither by oligarchs, nor capitalists, nor the military, but by the public opinion of the entire nation."[74]

[71] Salera, *op. cit.*, pp. 240-241.

[72] J. C. White, Chargé d'Affaires ad interim to Argentina, to Secretary of State, June 26, and Messersmith to Secretary of State, July 3, 1930, NA, DS, 611.003/2224, 2286.

[73] Bliss to Secretary of State, July 31, and White to Secretary, Aug. 27, 1930, NA, DS, 611.003/2344 and 611.353 Linseed/9.

[74] *En tiempos de la república*, I, 71. Felix J. Weil, on the other hand, asserts that the revolt was nurtured by banks and big business and possibly encouraged by the opposition of foreign oil interests to an alleged deal for Russian oil imports between the government petroleum monopoly (YPF) and the Soviet Trade Delegation (*Argentine Riddle*, pp. 41-42).

Once installed in the Casa Rosada, General Uriburu revived in modern Argentina the ruthless type of dictatorship Rosas had conceived a century earlier. By censoring the press, cancelling elections, dismissing or exiling opposition leaders, and "intervening" universities and provincial governments, he sought to undermine the democratic institutions in which he had little confidence.[75] Imbued, like many of his fellow patricians and Army colleagues, with tinges of fascist ideology, he obviously hoped to use military power to restore and perpetuate government by an aristocratic coterie.[76]

Turning promptly to the economic blight which had settled over the nation, Uriburu moved with vigor to forestall complete economic collapse. By suspending public works and paring the public payroll, he sharply cut government costs. Through domestic refinancing he amortized foreign loans and sought to stabilize the value of the peso. But declining foreign trade and growing unemployment forced the press to look for scapegoats. By December *La Prensa* renewed its attacks on the American tariff.[77] In February the government decreed extensive tariff increases on a variety of American exports.[78] Though it reacted coolly to the suggestion of a Pan American customs union to consider postponement of loan payments, it welcomed President Hoover's moratorium proposal of June, 1931.[79]

But if along with economic recovery Uriburu hoped to establish in Argentina a *criollo* model of the corporative state, his plans failed to capture adequate support. His proposals to eliminate the imperfections of democracy by modifying the constitution aroused the opposition of important party leaders and key Army officers.[80] Forced, therefore, by these pressures to abandon his pretensions, the Provisional President announced elections for November, 1931. Nevertheless, even by temporarily restoring the Army to its nineteenth-century role in government, General Uriburu had sown the seeds for subsequent creation of a military dictatorship on semi-totalitarian lines. Among the young officers who supported his 1930 coup was a still unknown captain, Juan Perón, who in the mid-1940's would assume the mantle his commander had laid aside.[81]

More immediately, however, General Uriburu's interregnum served

---

[75] Ricardo Levene, A *History of Argentina*, p. 512. On Uriburu's foreign policies, see below, p. 379.

[76] Pinedo, *op. cit.*, p. 81.

[77] Dec. 14, 1930.

[78] A. M. Warren, Consul to Buenos Aires, to Secretary of State, March 5, 1931, RSC, DS, 635.113/17.

[79] Reports that Chile was promoting a conference to discuss these subjects are filed in NA, DS, 551C1. See Pueyrredón to Hoover, July 4, 1931, 462.00R296/4709.

[80] Cf. Pinedo, *op. cit.*, pp. 81-82.

[81] See below, pp. 430ff.

another purpose. It permitted the return to power, after fourteen years of Radical presidents, of the Conservative oligarchy of the estancias. The November election brought to the presidency Agustín P. Justo, former general, cabinet member, and administrator of public works. Acceptable to business and agrarian leaders alike, he governed with efficiency and firmness. Both corruption and political opposition he kept at a minimum.

Conservatives and Democrats in Conflict

The return of the Conservatives to power in Buenos Aires preceded by only a few months the resurgence of the Democrats in Washington. The task of President Justo was as definable as that of Franklin D. Roosevelt: how to rescue a nation from the evils imposed by low prices, mortgage foreclosures, and reduced demand for exports. In measures which required only domestic enforcement—price-fixing, currency devaluation, exchange control, and tariff restrictions—they followed similar courses. In policies which demanded adjustment with other nations their paths sharply diverged. Justo, with Carlos Saavedra Lamas as foreign minister, went the way of nationalism and bilateralism, while Roosevelt, abetted by Cordell Hull, turned to the broader philosophy of multi-lateral trading.

Argentina's natural gravitation toward economic nationalism received strong encouragement from British policies—its accelerated drive for Argentine markets, its encouragement of suspension of foreign debt service, and its steady trend toward imperial preference.[82] The limited success of the D'Abernon Mission in 1929 did not end British efforts to win back their Argentine markets. In March-April, 1931, with much fanfare, they sponsored an extensive British Empire Trade Exhibition. The Prince of Wales and Prince George led the list of distinguished visitors. During forty-five days it attracted 700,000 paid customers, eager to inspect the machinery, airplanes, and other exhibits from England and the Dominions.[83]

By December, as reports reached Buenos Aires that Britain was contemplating expansion of imperial preference, the Argentines grew apprehensive about their markets in the United Kingdom.[84] Yet their proposal to send a trade mission to London received only discouragement from British leaders, who refused to discuss tariff questions until after

[82] T. W. Lamont, of J. P. Morgan & Co., to Secretary of State, Sept. 7, 1932, NA, DS, 835.51/841. Ambassador Bliss urged upon Foreign Minister Saavedra Lamas the advantages of continuing debt service (to White, Asst. Sec. of State, Oct. 14, 1932, *ibid.*, no. 857). The Argentine national government did not default.

[83] See Benjamin Thaw, Jr., First Secretary of the Embassy to London, to Secretary of State, April 10, 1931, NA, DS, 610.4115/14, and several despatches in 835.607 British Empire Trade Exhibition/25, 42, 51, 59.

[84] White to Secretary of State, Dec. 18, 1931, NA, DS, 635.4131/30.

the Ottawa Conference. This was the opportune moment, decided Ambassador Bliss, for the United States to curry favor by reducing duties on some Argentine staples. "Our tariff policy, especially of late," he wrote to the Secretary of State,

> has castigated Argentine products when import duties have been increased, . . . America cannot point to one instance in which our Government has shown consideration in this form for a country which offers a large market for our own manufactured articles.[85]

The agreements of the Ottawa Conference transformed apprehension into alarm in Buenos Aires. England's preference for the products of its own dominions would leave Argentine growers no place to turn. In this situation, the Anglophile press was perplexed. It could scarcely denounce the trade program of a nation to which Argentina still had to sell its beef and wheat. Instead, while lamenting Britain's turn to a selfish national trade policy, it blamed its own government's short-sightedness in erecting tariff walls to protect infant industries.[86]

The Justo administration moved with despatch now to send its mission to London. Because the announced purpose was to return the visit of the Prince of Wales, the Vice-President, Julio A. Roca, became its chairman. But Roca's wardrobe included a business as well as a dress suit.[87]

The Roca-Runciman Pact of May 1, 1933, to run for three years, placed trade between the two nations on a basis of virtual barter. By agreeing to buy as much chilled beef as it had in mid-1932 Britain secured a guaranteed market for its manufactured goods—and at 1930 tariff levels. Beyond this, Britain won assurance that the public service enterprises of its citizens would receive "benevolent treatment."[88] In exchange for a strengthened position in its traditional market, Argentina had pledged Britain protection of its investments and its export trade. Six years of preaching the text "Buy from those who buy from us!" had finally converted both nations. Within a short time, Argentina broadened its new commercial policy by concluding other such bilateral agreements.

In taking these decisive steps toward economic nationalism, nevertheless, the Argentines did not close the door to the possibility of better trading terms with the United States. The sweeping electoral victory of Roosevelt and the Democrats in 1932 gave them hope; they could remember the favorable rates of the Underwood-Simmons tariff. Twelve days after Roosevelt's inauguration, even with the Roca Mission active

[85] May 13, 1932, NA, DS, 641.3515/8.
[86] Bliss to Secretary of State, Aug. 26, 1932, NA, DS, 836.111/27.
[87] Bliss to Secretary of State, Nov. 18, 1932, NA, DS, 635.4131/64.
[88] Atherton to Secretary of State, May 2, 1933, *ibid.,* no. 81.

in London, the Justo government launched an offensive to secure improved American terms.[89] It appreciated, as Washington long had argued, that the Treaty of 1853 was obsolete and hopelessly unsuited to the economic complications of the nineteen-thirties.[90]

During the next ten months, with almost exasperating regularity, Foreign Minister Saavedra Lamas and Ambassador Espil approached State Department representatives to suggest negotiation of a reciprocal commercial agreement.[91] On October 5 Espil filed with the Department an exhaustive memorandum setting forth Argentina's position. It would undertake negotiations, he said, if the United States would restore the 1913 tariff rates, modify or remove sanitary and other restrictions, and give other assurances against future discrimination. The American chargé in Buenos Aires suspected Saavedra Lamas of trying to "club" the United States into reciprocity.[92]

But Roosevelt and Hull, weighted with problems of domestic and world recovery, wished to move more slowly and on a much broader basis. The Secretary thought it wiser to postpone reciprocity arrangements until first the World Economic Conference, then the Inter-American Conference, had cleared the air and approved general principles of freer commercial exchange. Though the President assured Espil in July that the United States would undertake exploratory conversations, the Department postponed indefinitely a reply to the Argentine proposals of October 5th.[93]

By the close of 1933 the Democratic leaders had hit upon a new approach to free world trade. Unable to reduce the high American tariff structure by unilateral action or lower trade barriers by common consent, they determined to attack the problem bit by bit through negotiation of reciprocal agreements with individual countries. By extension of unconditional most-favored-nation treatment, they sought both to reduce abnormal trade barriers and to remove discrimination against American goods. By thawing the frozen terms of bilateral trading, they hoped to minimize causes of international discord as well as to increase world trade. Passed in June, 1934, the Reciprocal Trade Agreements Act embodied their trade philosophy.

The issue between the two principal trading nations of the Americas was now clear-cut. Not only had they permitted mutual discrimination

---

[89] Memorandum by the Secretary of State, March 16, 1933, *For. Rel., 1933,* IV, 642.

[90] The Department of State had tried earnestly between 1923 and 1927 to negotiate a new treaty with Argentina. Unwilling to negotiate a new treaty, Argentina was then interested only in adding to the Treaty of 1853 a protocol providing the right of denunciation (Bliss to Secretary of State, Sept. 20, 1927, *For. Rel., 1927,* I, 421-422).

[91] *Ibid., 1933,* IV, 642-683 *passim; 1934,* IV, 510-511.

[92] *Ibid., 1933,* IV, 650, 661-681.

[93] Memorandum by the Act. Sec. of State, July 12, 1933, *ibid.,* p. 646.

to hamstring their own reciprocal commerce, but they had diverged on the appropriate solution to the world's trade problems. Reconciliation of their views would be long and tedious.

During the next seven years presidents and diplomats of both nations hammered away to forge a solution based upon good will. Each side put forth proposals and counterproposals. Each made specific offers, unacceptable to the other, to undertake formal negotiations. Both sent experts to assist the ambassadors in conversations. More than a thousand documents accumulated in appropriate files of the State Department.[94]

Whatever the ephemeral causes of disagreement, progress toward an accord invariably foundered on one immovable two-headed obstacle. The Argentines would not recede from their dependence on exchange control and bilateral balancing. The Americans would not lower the tariff bars or sanitary restrictions against Argentina's principal exports.[95]

Hope stirred from time to time as one nation or the other appeared ready to retreat from its affirmed position. In 1935 Secretary Hull submitted to the Senate the draft of a sanitary convention which proposed to restore the pre-1930 basis of regional, not country, quarantine.[96] Western cattle interests, however, effectively scotched this overture, which would have removed at least some of the stigma attached to Argentine meat.[97]

In 1936, when the Argentines indicated willingness to enter conversations with all reference to fresh and chilled beef excluded, the Department pleaded need for more time to study and reluctance to announce negotiations until the Trade Agreements Act was re-enacted.[98] A year later, when Washington asked assurance of "full equality of treatment to United States products with respect to exchange allotments," the ambassador suggested the impossibility of getting a decision in the last weeks of an administration.[99] So it went, from year to year.

America's failure to resolve its philosophical differences with Argen-

[94] Most of these are filed in NA, DS, 611.3531. Many have been published in *Foreign Relations* for the years 1933-1940.

[95] Secretary Hull incorporated a clear statement of the issue in his instruction to A. W. Weddell, Ambassador to Argentina, Feb. 12, 1938, *ibid., 1938*, V, 283-286.

[96] *Ibid., 1935*, IV, 296-299; *Memoria, 1935-1936*, I, 711-714; Department of State, *Press Releases*, May 24, 1935, XII, 367-369.

[97] The *Congressional Record* for the 74th and 75th Congresses abounds in memorials from such organizations as the National Grange, the National Livestock Marketing Association, and the American Farm Bureau Federation. The Argentine press was never sanguine that the U.S. Senate would ratify the treaty (Weddell to Secretary of State, July 5, 1935, and many subsequent despatches, NA, DS, 711.359 Sanitary/44). Debated from time to time, without successful issue, the agreement was returned to the White House on April 17, 1947 (*Cong. Rec.*, 80 Cong., 1 sess., XCIII, pt. 3, pp. 3583-3584).

[98] Memorandum by the Argentine Government, undated, and Act. Sec. of State to Secretary, Dec. 21, 1936, *For. Rel., 1936*, V, 179-183.

[99] Memorandum of conversation with Espil by Sumner Welles, Under Secretary of State, Dec. 6, 1937, *ibid., 1937*, V, 227-228.

tina played into the hands of its commercial rivals. While American sales languished at pre-World War I figures, the nations which had signed bilateral trading agreements with Argentina were rapidly recovering their predepression trade. Until the outbreak of war Britain retained the superiority it had regained in 1931. Nazi trade drives made substantial inroads into important Argentine markets, especially for machinery and vehicles, iron and iron manufactures, paper and cardboard, and chemical and pharmaceutical products. Brazil cut sharply into Yankee exports of lumber.[100]

Not until August, 1939, eight days before the invasion of Poland, did the State Department formally announce intention to negotiate its own bilateral agreement. The statement listed a variety of products, not including fresh or chilled meat, upon which it would consider granting concessions. Accepting the multilateral principles of the American reciprocal program, Argentina agreed that the proposed convention would assure full equality to American products and guarantee non-discrimination in government regulation of imports.[101]

The discussions lasted until January, 1940, without success. In the joint communique announcing their breakdown, the disputants emphasized Argentine unwillingness to accept the American proposal of customs quotas on such products as linseed and canned meat. The American negotiators felt impelled to protect domestic producers; the Argentines objected to limitation upon possible expansion of their exports.[102] Behind the announced reasons for failure, however, were the still reigning divergence in basic commercial philosophies and the financial uncertainties caused by the war's dislocations.

The heights and depths between which Argentine-American trade ranged in the interwar decades exposed the inadequacies of the Treaty of 1853. In seeking to modernize the basis of their reciprocal commerce, successive administrations in both republics, headed by the chiefs of whichever political party, had foundered on the continuing competitiveness of national economies. Even the modification of many ancient handicaps had not brought the stabilized commercial exchange both nations seemed to desire. Against the growing threat from the totalitarian powers this economic incompatibility hampered the quest of Pan American statesmen for the political foundations of Hemisphere security.

---

[100] The Chamber of Commerce of the U.S.A. in the Argentine Republic, *op. cit.*, pp. 40-41, 44-45, 80-81.

[101] Department of State, *Bulletin*, I (Aug. 26, 1939), 166-170.

[102] *Ibid.*, II (Jan. 13, 1940), 42. For Ambassador Armour's observations, see his despatch to Secretary of State, Jan. 29, 1940, *For. Rel., 1939*, V, 294-302. For the official Argentine statement on the termination of negotiations, see *The New York Times*, Jan. 14, 1940.

XXII

RIVALRY IN INTER-AMERICAN AFFAIRS: RELUCTANT PARTNERS IN PAN AMERICANISM, 1919-1939

In the two decades between world wars Argentina and the United States perpetuated and expanded their rivalry for leadership of the American republics. In the twenties, as they adjusted their economies to the new postwar world, they found little common ground for action within the Pan American organization. At the end of the decade, under President Irigoyen, Argentina virtually ceased to participate in the movement and left its mission to Washington without an ambassador. As each Republican administration turned its shoulder toward Europe, Buenos Aires seemed to accord the United States the same treatment.

In the thirties, as the people of both nations slowly came to understand the threat of the totalitarians in Europe, their leaders managed to agree on minimum measures for the security of the Western Hemisphere. But, when in 1939 the menace became real, their area of agreement was too small to assure effective cooperation to resist it. As President Roosevelt faced full-front toward Europe, the Argentine leaders seemed not to sense the danger.

Rarely during the interwar years did their rivalry permit the kind of working partnership which previously had produced for themselves and others settlement of boundary disputes or abatement of tensions. Even when they could agree on a desirable end, such as the negotiation of an antiwar pact or mediation in the Chaco War, they split over the means to achieve it. Issues like the Monroe Doctrine, commercial reciprocity, the right of intervention, and the rightful jurisdiction of the League of Nations obstructed the growth of harmony.

Argentina, the League, and the Monroe Doctrine

Early postwar actions in both Washington and Buenos Aires verified the philosophical analysis of Pan Americanism which Ambassador Rómulo Naón had composed at the close of his long tenure in Washington.[1] As he predicted, world war and the Peace Conference greatly altered the international organization of the world. In securing adoption of the Covenant of the League of Nations, President Wilson seemed to have justified the decision to drop his Pan American Pact in favor of a universal association of nations. Argentine leaders generally, including the semi-isolationist Irigoyen himself, approved this transition.[2] Even before the League's formal constitution and without congressional authorization, the President filed Argentina's declaration of adherence.[3]

But the League Covenant was not the ideal charter for which the Argentines had hoped. The success of Wilson's opponents in forcing incorporation of the article on "regional understandings like the Monroe Doctrine" stimulated the renewal of exclusively national policies Naón had forecast.[4] When congressional spokesmen reasserted the two-sphere basis of the Doctrine and reaffirmed America's exclusive right to apply it, Argentine leaders denied that it was a regional understanding and levelled attacks against its recognition in the Covenant. Some critics denounced the Doctrine as an attempt to divide the world into zones. Others termed it incompatible with true Pan Americanism.[5] The Under Secretary of the Ministry of Foreign Relations, Diego Luis Molinari, told the American Chargé that Argentina had long ignored the Doctrine, and implied that it would continue to do so if League decisions conflicted with it.[6]

In his zeal for the Pan American idea, Naón had revealed his apprehensions of the world's return to peace. Two great obstacles would spring up, he had warned, to hamper renewal of the promising continental solidarity interrupted by America's entrance into the war. One

[1] See above, pp. 338-339.

[2] Committee on Public Information, *The Official United States Bulletin*, Feb. 24, 1919, p. 4; W. H. Kelchner, *Latin American Relations with the League of Nations*, pp. 91-93.

[3] Argentina was the first nation in South America to accede to the League Covenant (*ibid.*, pp. 46-49). The Ministry of Foreign Relations advised Washington of its decision almost at once (Honorio Pueyrredón to Embassy to Washington, July 15, 1919, NA, DS, 763.72119/5770).

[4] Dexter Perkins, *Hands Off: A History of the Monroe Doctrine*, pp. 279-299.

[5] F. J. Stimson, Ambassador to Argentina, to Secretary of State, May 2, June 23, 1919, NA, DS, 710.11/399 and 763.72119/5415; L. M. Moreno Quintana, *La diplomacia de Yrigoyen*, pp. 416-418; Estanislao Zeballos, "United States' Diplomacy in South America," *The Living Age*, Vol. 307 (Nov. 20, 1920), pp. 446-448.

[6] Craig Wadsworth, Chargé d'Affaires ad interim to Argentina, to Secretary of State, Nov. 13, 1920, and enclosures, NA, DS, 500.C001/147.

was American acquiescence in the division of nations into great and small powers by the Versailles Conference. The other was the resurgence of Latin Americanism as a counterpoise to Pan Americanism. The prompt appearance of both realities quickly stirred waves of anti-American feeling in Argentina.

American insistence upon the unilateral character of the Monroe Doctrine, reinforced by perpetuation of interventions in the Caribbean republics, appeared to Argentine nationalists as denial of the sovereign equality of states. Though Secretary Charles Evans Hughes and his young associate, Sumner Welles, sought to pare down the interventions and to disentangle them from the Doctrine, their acts alone could not sway the convictions of Argentine and other Latin American critics.[7] Moreover, with its adverse balances of trade and payments, Argentina itself began to feel the bite of Yankee economic penetration.[8]

These diverse American attitudes stimulated the revival of Latin Americanism. Sometimes misunderstood, sometimes exaggerated, actions of the United States provided abundant thunder for its critics, whether friendly or deeply anti-American. Political leaders like Molinari and Zeballos, scholars like José Ingenieros,[9] and publicists like Manuel Ugarte renewed in 1921-1923 the verbal or literary shafts they had kept well-sheathed since prewar days. Of these it was Ugarte who cried out most persistently for the preservation of Spanish American culture against Yankee encroachments.[10]

These troublesome eddies of disagreement effectively concealed essentially similar points of view on basic foreign policies. While the United States clearly hoped to resuscitate the Pan American movement, like Argentina it shunned any form of continental union which involved political or military commitments. Though Argentina, unlike the United States, joined the League of Nations, its inactivity as a member rendered it equally uninfluential in world councils.[11] When in 1921 the League Assembly denied Irigoyen's bid for universality of membership, Argentina withdrew from active participation.[12] Reverting to semi-isolation, Republican administrations in Washington and Radical governments in Buenos Aires repeatedly sought to forestall multilateral decisions that

[7] Perkins, *Charles Evans Hughes and American Democratic Statesmanship*, pp. 129-132.

[8] See above, pp. 346-351.

[9] In a particularly bitter speech in Buenos Aires on Oct. 11, 1922, given in honor of José Vasconcelos, Mexican Minister of Public Instruction, Ingenieros said: "We are not, we do not want to be any longer, and we could not continue to be Pan-Americanists" (NA, DS, 710.E/171).

[10] As examples, see his article "L'Amérique latine après la guerre," *La Revue Mondiale*, Vol. 142 (May 15, 1921), 139-147, and his book, *The Destiny of a Continent*, esp. pp. xx, 285-286, 288-289.

[11] Cf. A. P. Whitaker, *The United States and Argentina*, pp. 101-102.

[12] Kelchner, *op. cit.*, pp. 93-103.

would limit their freedom of action within the Hemisphere. If the deflated Pan American spirit were to be renewed, therefore, it would require extensive artificial respiration by the United States and the Latin American nation.

The Santiago Conference

Representatives of the American republics had not met in full general conference since the Buenos Aires gathering of 1910. The interposition of war and the conflicting projects of Presidents Wilson and Irigoyen had interrupted whatever natural growth the movement might have attained. The possibility of reviving the regular meetings, therefore, rested largely upon the status of Argentine-American relations. In spite of attacks upon America's postwar policies, mostly by the press and private citizens, several events in the closing months of the Irigoyen administration gave hope that in Hemisphere affairs a cooperative spirit might be renewed.

Overthrow of the existing government of Bolivia in July, 1920, offered such an opportunity. Doubtful of the constitutionality of the revolutionary regime, Secretary Bainbridge Colby sought the advice of the Argentine Chancellery and suggested the possibility of joint recognition at the appropriate time. Flattered by this unexpected overture, Foreign Minister Pueyrredón responded eagerly, kept the American Embassy currently informed, and in early February, 1921, agreed to simultaneous recognition of the elected government of Bautista Saavedra.[13] During 1920-1921, too, the State Department complied with Argentine requests that American consuls represent its commercial interests in Kobe, Japan, Singapore, and Colombo.[14]

The official visit of Secretary Colby to Buenos Aires in January, 1921, interpreted by Ambassador Tomás A. Le Breton solely as a gesture of good will, served for a time to reduce growing friction.[15] Though the Secretary planned at the outset only to return recent state visits by Brazilian and Uruguayan presidents, Sumner Welles counselled the wisdom of adding Buenos Aires to his itinerary.[16] In the Argentine

[13] The essential correspondence is printed in *For. Rel., 1920*, I, 380-386, and República Argentina, Ministerio de Relaciones Exteriores y Culto, *Circular informativa mensual*, No. 60 (May, 1922), 221-224. Also see *Mensaje del presidente de la nación, Doctor Hipólito Yrigoyen, 1922*, p. 23.

[14] NA, DS, 704.3594/orig.; 704.3546c/1; 704.3546d/a. In 1923 the Argentine government requested similar services for Albania, Latvia, and Lithuania (704.3560m/orig.).

[15] Le Breton to Yrigoyen, Nov. 12, 1920, Luis Rodríguez Yrigoyen, *Hipólito Yrigoyen, 1878-1933*, pp. 361-362.

[16] Memo to Under Secretary, Oct. 1, 1920, NA, DS, 033.1132/12. See *For. Rel., 1920*, I, 228-235, and *Memoria, 1920-1921*, pp. 196-209. The Presidents were Epitacio da Silva Pessôa and Baltasar Brum.

capital Ambassador Stimson encountered some official coolness to the prospect of entertaining the Secretary. Skeptical himself at first about the sending of a lame-duck official on so important a mission, Stimson subsequently admitted Mr. Colby's success. His frankness and tact apparently pleased President Irigoyen, whose personal call upon the Secretary represented a compliment he had not paid to either McAdoo or Admiral Caperton.[17]

Twice during 1921 America's strained relations with Panama involved the Argentine Republic. First, the Argentine ambassador in Washington accepted a joint investigation to arbitrate the pecuniary claims of American citizens against the Panamanian government.[18] The second was more pregnant. As the climax of its long-standing boundary dispute with Costa Rica, Panama indicated in April-May, 1921, its refusal to abide by the earlier arbitral award of Chief Justice Edward D. White or to heed Secretary Hughes's warning against hostilities. Instead, it appealed directly to the good offices of the Irigoyen government. On July 16 Pueyrredón advised the Panamanian emissary that his country would interpose its services only upon the petition of both parties. Two days later the State Department politely reminded the Argentine Foreign Office of its special interest in Panama. With equal politeness Pueyrredón acknowledged this "friendly consideration." [19]

These isolated instances of cooperation received much less attention in Buenos Aires than the vulnerable American positions on the protective tariff, the League, the Monroe Doctrine, and the right of intervention. Moreover, as the eve of the Santiago Conference approached, the Harding administration committed a tactical blunder. Without preliminary notification to the Argentines, it sent a naval mission to Rio de Janeiro to aid the organization and instruction of the Brazilian Navy.

To Washington the agreement with Brazil was no more than routine application of a congressional act which authorized such aid to any South American government. It bore no political overtones. To the Argentines, always sensitive about Brazil's growing economic and military power, it was an affront. To the bewildered naval authorities who had ordered dreadnaughts and naval armaments in the United States it appeared an expression of ill will. Though Secretary Hughes directed a full and complete explanation of the Brazilian contract, Argentine reaction remained bitter.[20]

This disagreement of December, 1922, probably motivated Argentina's

---

[17] Stimson, *My United States*, p. 453.

[18] Le Breton to Pueyrredón, April 23, and Pueyrredón to Le Breton, April 26, 1921, *Memoria, 1921-1922*, p. 30.

[19] *Ibid.*, pp. 14-29; Moreno Quintana, *op. cit.*, pp. 438-439.

[20] J. W. Riddle, Ambassador to Argentina, to Hughes, Dec. 20, and Hughes to Riddle, Dec. 21, 1922, *For. Rel.*, 1922, I, 655-656; Riddle to Hughes, personal, Dec. 20, 1922, NA, DS, 832.30/97.

curt reply to Brazil's suggestion of a tripartite conference with Chile on the question of armaments. Brazilian leaders saw the conversations as an essential preliminary to discussion of disarmament at the full-scale Santiago Conference. In his refusal the Argentine Foreign Minister explained that the time was too short for adequate preparations. Then, ironically, he pleaded Argentina's aversion to disrupting continental solidarity by participation in a regional meeting.[21]

Under these circumstances, Argentina could look forward to the Fifth Pan American Conference no more sanguinely than it had to the first four. Among others, the acting foreign minister just returned from Washington, Tomás Le Breton, was flatly pessimistic.[22] The new president, however, Francophile Marcelo T. de Alvear, former minister to Paris and first Argentine delegate to the League Assembly, ensured a strong, well-briefed delegation.[23]

Fully aware of the opportunity presented by the Santiago meeting, Secretary Hughes hoped it might allay the distrust of the United States which had accumulated since the war. Yet he appointed a delegation which lacked both the appropriate experience and the peculiar temper to fulfill his desires. As chairman he named Henry P. Fletcher, career ambassador to Belgium, and among his associates Senator Frank B. Kellogg, secretary of state-to-be.[24]

Moreover, in the very areas in which it needed greatest freedom of action Mr. Hughes's comprehensive instructions circumscribed the delegation. "The function of these Pan American Conferences," he pointed out, "is to deal so far as possible with non-controversial subjects of general nature." More specifically, he warned the delegates against any discussion of the Monroe Doctrine and forbade their endorsing any arrangement, or resolution even, which would curtail in any way its application by the United States. He scrupulously characterized the Doctrine as a national policy of the United States and denied its status as a "regional understanding." [25]

Argentine and American views on such matters as reciprocal commerce, pecuniary claims, and pacific settlement of disputes remained as divergent as before. Yet, at Santiago, neither delegation seemed disposed to push disagreement to the showdown stage. In two committees, including that considering the Gondra Treaty on Pacific Settlement,

[21] Riddle to Secretary of State, Dec. 1, 1922, and enclosures, NA, DS, 710.L62/12. A copy of the Brazilian invitation is filed in *ibid.*, no. 5.

[22] Hughes to Embassy, Dec. 16, and Riddle to Secretary, Dec. 20, 1922, March 12, 1923, NA, DS, 710.E/131a, 133, and 835.00/321.

[23] Riddle to Secretary, Jan. 29, Feb. 3, 1923, NA, DS, 710.E002/12, 79; *Quinta Conferencia Internacional de las Repúblicas Americanas*, IV, 162ff.

[24] Perkins, *op. cit.*, p. 133; Hughes to Embassy, Jan. 30, 1923, NA, DS, 710.E002/16i.

[25] *Ibid.*, no. 68a.

Argentina's delegates revived the prewar drive for mandatory arbitration on a broad basis. Only when the Juridical Committee reported out a watered-down proposal substituting a commission of inquiry for obligatory arbitration did Hughes authorize American approval.[26]

Throughout the Conference Argentine representatives concentrated their fire on the arms reduction proposals of Chile. Setting limits under which their government would incur no additional expenditures, they strove for limitation of land as well as naval armaments.[27] Beyond its desire for a regional agreement on arms limitation among South American nations, Washington had little direct interest in this debate. Foreseeing a Conference deadlock on the subject, Mr. Fletcher sounded out the representatives of the ABC powers on the possibility of a subsequent meeting in Washington. Angel Gallardo, Alvear's foreign minister, reaffirmed Argentina's position that the issue should be settled in full conference.[28] As chairman of the Committee on Limitation of Arms, Fletcher presented its final report to the plenary session. It represented much less than the Argentines desired. Having anticipated effective Conference action, they derided the platitudes and abstractions of the report.[29]

On one item of Conference business at least, the Argentine and American delegates found common ground. Both reacted coolly to Uruguay's proposal for an American Association of Nations following the pattern outlined three years before by President Brum. In its far-reaching details the project went much beyond the contemporary Hemisphere aims of both Buenos Aires and Washington.[30]

Besides sixty-seven resolutions, the Santiago Conference approved one treaty and three conventions. The United States signed and ratified all four, as it had the majority of the seventeen agreements concluded at previous Conferences. Though it too signed the four, Argentina failed to ratify one. This was now its standard course of action, for of the seventeen agreements it had already signed it had approved only two.[31]

The fifth reunion of the American states, therefore, drew Argentina no nearer midstream of the Pan American movement. It had participated,

[26] Fletcher to Secretary, April 17, 27, 29, and Hughes to Delegation, April 21, May 1, 1923, NA, DS, 710.E1Jur./1, 4, 5.

[27] *Report of the Delegates of the United States of America to the Fifth International Conference of American States*, pp. 21-25, 195-197.

[28] Fletcher to Secretary, April 26, 29, May 1, and Hughes to Delegation, April 27, 1923, NA, DS, 710.E1Arm/3, 4, 8.

[29] *Actas de las sesiones plenarias de la Quinta Conferencia Internacional Americana*, I, 661-685.

[30] For the text of the proposal, see Juan Carlos Welker, *Baltasar Brum: verbo y acción*, pp. 204-217.

[31] Pan American Union, *Status of the Pan American Treaties and Conventions*, pp. 1-2.

as before, primarily to safeguard its own freedom of action and to inhibit unwanted multilateral measures. Moreover, no American had inspired the warm feeling Elihu Root had generated at Rio de Janeiro and no Argentine revealed the confidence in the State Department Martín García Merou had shown at Mexico City.

Boundaries and Other Hemisphere Problems

The state of Argentine-American relations in the half-decade between the Fifth and Sixth Conferences continued to impede recrudescence of the Pan American spirit. After the Santiago Conference the State Department kept a weather eye on Argentine attitudes, especially toward arms limitation and the American naval mission to Brazil. In directing the Embassy in Buenos Aires to step up its intelligence coverage, it requested comprehensive reports on all aspects of Argentine-Brazilian relations.[32] Meanwhile, the Argentine government continued to side-step any ABC agreement on disarmament and went ahead with its plans for an extensive rearmament program.[33]

The kind of Hemisphere problems which had previously produced cooperative action between Argentina and the United States failed now to engender even the transient harmony of 1910 or 1914. Resurgence of old boundary questions—Peru-Ecuador, Argentina-Bolivia, Argentina-Paraguay—brought forth no suggestion of joint action.

For a time in 1925-1926 diplomats of the two nations discussed possible steps to resolve the long-standing dispute between Chile and Peru over Tacna-Arica. When friction developed between the disputants over the plebiscite ordered by President Coolidge on March 4, 1925, Argentine diplomats in Washington and Santiago suggested several solutions to the American dilemma. First Hughes, then Kellogg, revealed amenability to an official proposal.[34] Much as it desired settlement of the persistent canker, however, the Argentine Foreign Office seemed eager to avoid involvement.[35] At any rate, it stood aside to let the United States struggle alone until the final division of Tacna-Arica in 1929. On the other hand, in using their good offices to resolve differences be-

[32] Nov. 6, 1923, NA, DS, 835.00/332a.

[16] Memo to Under Secretary, Oct. , 1920, NA, DS, 033.1132/12. See *For. Rel.*, L62/29. In November, 1923, the Argentine Congress appropriated $100,000,000 for armaments (Willing Spencer, Chargé d'Affaires ad interim to Argentina, to Secretary of State, Nov. 10, 1923, 835.51/444). Earlier in the year, it had contracted with American companies for repairs to its battleships *Rivadavia* and *Moreno*.

[34] Memo of conversation between Hughes and Argentine Ambassador, Dec. 3; William M. Collier, Ambassador to Chile, to Secretary of State, Dec. 17; Kellogg to Embassy to Chile, Dec. 22, 1925, NA, DS, 723.2515/1756-3/6, 1760.

[35] Jay to Secretary of State, Jan. 11, March 24, April 22, 1926, *ibid.*, nos. 1834, 2051, 2279.

tween Bolivia and Paraguay after 1924, neither Alvear nor Irigoyen suggested the assistance of the United States.[36]

Moreover, as the eve of the Havana Conference approached, a profusion of vexatious issues accumulated to becloud its prospects. In 1926 the United States nettled the Argentines with its limitation on alfalfa seed and its sanitary embargoes on fruit and meat. In 1927 it proposed the sending of experts to study the costs of corn and flaxseed production in Argentina. The steady rise of trade deficits after 1924 stimulated the retaliatory philosophy "Buy from those who buy from us!" American oil companies came under increasing attack. Argentina resisted Washington's overtures for a new commercial treaty.[37] Spasmodically through these years anti-Yankee newspapers and publicists berated American policies toward Mexico and Nicaragua.[38]

Havana: Pueyrredón vs. Hughes

Resentment over unresolved differences, therefore, sullied the Argentine-American air as the twenty-one republics prepared for the Sixth Pan American Conference. Rumors reached Washington from other Latin capitals that leaders were girding for frontal challenge to American policies, especially the right of intervention.

Fully sensitive to the delicacy of the situation, Secretary Kellogg recommended to President Coolidge that he appoint a delegation of "skill and prestige" and that he himself go to Havana for a day.[39] Appropriately, the President appointed Charles Evans Hughes as chairman and Oscar Underwood, Dwight Morrow, and Henry P. Fletcher as delegates.

Holding the United States clearly in mind, the Argentine government selected as representatives its ambassador to Washington, his counsellor of embassy, and the minister-designate to Cuba. As Foreign Minister under Irigoyen and as Ambassador since 1924, Honorio Pueyrredón had formed close associations with American leaders and developed broad awareness of American problems. Driving his own car, he had toured widely in the United States. Battle-tested adviser to Argentine executives, he was a probable presidential candidate in the elections of April, 1928. Veteran of many international conferences,

---

[36] Argentine efforts to mediate in 1907 had not succeeded. On the various aspects of its intercession between 1924 and 1928, see República Argentina, Ministerio de Relaciones Exteriores y Culto, *La política argentina en la guerra del Chaco*, I, 13-137.

[37] See above, pp. 347-349, 351-355. Upon his appointment as Ambassador in August, 1927, Robert W. Bliss asked for a list of topics he should avoid in his presentation speech to President Alvear. The Division of Latin American Affairs suggested all of these items (NA, DS, 123.B61/225).

[38] For a good example, see *La Prensa*, April 20, 1927.

[39] Aug. 19, 1927, NA, DS, 710.F/42a.

Felipe A. Espil had served nine years in Washington—and would serve many more. Laurentino Olascoaga, an eccentric who cultivated a resemblance to General San Martín, completed the delegation.[40]

It must have been with wishful thoughts, or perhaps with tongues in cheeks, that the two chancelleries instructed their delegations to adhere strictly to agenda items and to avoid controversial subjects.[41] In a supplementary instruction of January 13 on the focal problem of Nicaragua, the Argentine Foreign Minister added a prophetic, more realistic note. If any other delegation raised the issue, or created a situation which called for an Argentine statement, Pueyrredón at the opportune moment should assert his nation's traditional faith in "the sound doctrine of respect for the sovereignty of nations." [42] In spite of agenda and instructions, intervention and economic reorganization of the Pan American Union became central themes in conference debate. Pueyrredón moved upstage in both scenes. Charles Evans Hughes became his able adversary.

Efforts to incorporate the principle of nonintervention into public international law precipitated the most discordant clash between the rival leaders. It flared first in the meeting of the Committee on Codification of International Law. Avoiding a strong declaration against intervention, its chairman, Dr. Victor Maúrtua of Peru, asserted merely that "every nation has the right to independence in the same sense that it has a right to the pursuit of happiness." Chiding this mild statement, the Salvadoran representative countered with the bold proposal that "no state has the right to intervene in the internal affairs of another." [43]

Mr. Hughes supported the committee position. He maintained the right of a nation to "interpose" in another to protect the lives and property of its citizens. Political stability is essential to political independence, he argued, though interposition to secure stability must never become permanent. Moreover, the task of the Conference was to codify international law, not to make it.[44]

This was the moment for which the Argentines had prepared. For the first time in the history of the Pan American movement the Latin republics had succeeded in bringing the festering issue to the floor of a general conference. Unaffected itself by direct American intervention,

[40] Bliss to Secretary of State, Nov. 3, 1937, NA, DS, 710.F002/59.
[41] Instructions to the American delegation are printed in *For. Rel., 1928*, I, 534-585; a portion of the Argentine in *Circular informativa mensual*, No. 129 (Feb., 1928), pp. 67ff. See also Bliss to Secretary of State, Oct. 28, Nov. 3, 1927, NA, DS, 710.F1a/97; 710.F002/59.
[42] *Circular informativa mensual*, p. 75. Five days later, it instructed him to bring it up, if necessary.
[43] *Diario de la Sexta Conferencia Internacional Americana*, pp. 486-489.
[44] Hughes to Secretary of State, Feb. 4, 1928, NA, DS, 710.F Intervention/2, 3. On Hughes's relationship to the Rio Commission of Jurists and the Maúrtua report, see S. F. Bemis, *The Latin American Policy of the United States*, pp. 248-253.

Argentina came strongly to the support of El Salvador and the anti-interventionist delegations. "The sovereignty of states," Pueyrredón proclaimed,

> lies in the absolute right to full domestic autonomy and entire external independence. That right is guaranteed the powerful nations by their own strength; the weak by the respect of the strong. If this right is not respected and practiced in definite form, internal juridical harmony does not exist. Diplomatic or armed intervention, whether permanent or temporary, is an attack against the independence of these states, . . .[45]

In subsequent sessions the ex-Secretary of State renewed his defense of the American position. Upon the precarious sands of intervention the United States had based much of its hope for upholding the duties as well as the rights of states, for maintaining the integrity of the Roosevelt Corollary, and for safeguarding defense strategy in the Panama Canal area. To protect this policy structure Mr. Hughes resisted any declaration that would censure or outlaw the right of intervention.[46] Though the schism was now clear cut, other developments contributed to postponement of its resolution.

Even before their dispute over nonintervention, Pueyrredón and Hughes had duelled over economic problems of the Hemisphere. In debate on a preamble to the proposed convention on the nature of the Pan American Union, Pueyrredón proposed to insert a declaration favoring reduction of economic barriers. His two-hour speech was a thinly veiled attack upon American tariff barriers and sanitary embargoes. Unless the Conference incorporated his proposals in the preamble, he threatened, Argentina would not sign the convention.[47]

Attacked unexpectedly on this vulnerable salient, Mr. Hughes argued in support of American policy and current concepts of the Pan American Union. "Let us continue our cultural work," he said,

> our cooperation in those lines where we feel we have a community of interest; where we realize that good can be accomplished; and let us not destroy the Union by attempting to make it a tariff commission, or a tax commission, for the purpose of impinging upon our respective authority as independent States.[48]

[45] *Diario*, p. 492; Pueyrredón to Minister of Foreign Relations, Feb. 4, 1928, *Circular informativa mensual*, p. 76. Both the President and the Foreign Minister cabled Pueyrredón messages of congratulations for his "admirable defense." For an Argentine analysis of the conflicting Argentine-American views on intervention, see Carlos Saavedra Lamas, *La conception argentine de l'arbitrage et de l'intervention à l'ouverture de la Conférence de Washington*, pp. 37-41.

[46] Bemis, *op. cit.*, pp. 250-253.

[47] *Diario*, pp. 395-396; *Circular informativa mensual*, p. 67.

[48] *Diario*, p. 434.

The two nations had reversed their positions of an earlier day. Pueyrredón had revived something of Blaine's economic philosophy of 1889-1890. More confident now of its own industrial strength, the United States wished to avoid any multilateral action that might modify its national tariff policies. At this early stage of the proceedings, Mr. Hughes chose the tactful course. He complimented the Argentine's speech and proceeded to discuss the convention itself.[49] Pueyrredón won little support from the other delegations, even opposition from his own.

On the question of nonintervention the obdurate Argentine adhered strictly to his instructions. On the problem of economic barriers he sallied forth on his own and stubbornly defied orders to retreat. Disturbed by Pueyrredón's temerity, Felipe Espil appealed directly to President Alvear. On February 10 he cabled that refusal to sign the convention would damage relations with the United States and might wreck the Pan American Union.[50] Cautioning against unyielding action that would isolate Argentina from the Union or cause its collapse, both the President and the Foreign Minister ordered Pueyrredón to sign—with reservations, if necessary.[51]

Nevertheless, Pueyrredón persisted in his obstinate course. On the 15th he resigned both as delegation chief and as Ambassador to the United States.[52] His successor promptly signed the convention on organization and purposes of the Pan American Union. Returning to Washington at once, where he professed to both President Coolidge and Secretary Kellogg his continuing friendship for the United States, Pueyrredón received formal but cool farewells.[53]

In Buenos Aires the government sought to mend its broken diplomatic and political fences. Unable to conceal the administrative rift opened by Pueyrredón's action, it determined to publish the revealing correspondence.[54] By disclaiming complicity in his unexpected initiative, it hoped to minimize foreign criticism and protect its status before the Hemisphere. By underscoring his willfulness and insubordination, it apparently sought to prevent his use of the incident to enhance his own political fortunes.[55]

The electrifying Argentine-American clashes at Havana made more

[49] Hughes to Secretary of State, Jan. 23, 1928, NA, DS, 710.F1bPan American Union/2.
[50] *Circular informativa mensual*, p. 68.
[51] Feb. 10, 14, 1928, *ibid.*, pp. 68, 70.
[52] *Ibid.*, p. 70.
[53] Secretary's memorandum of conversation with the Ambassador, March 1, 1928, NA, DS, 710.F002/264; White to Bliss, March 21, 1928, 701.3511/309.
[54] It appeared in the Foreign Ministry's *Circular informativa mensual.* See Ambassador Bliss's analysis in his despatch of Feb. 22, 1928, NA, DS, 710.F002/281.
[55] *Circular informativa mensual*, pp. 74-75; Bliss to Secretary of State, April 16, 1928, NA DS, 710.F002/308.

transparent than ever the rivalry of the two republics for leadership of the Pan American organization. By plan in the case of nonintervention, by chance in that of economic barriers, Argentina had dramatized in open convention its two principal grievances against the United States. Regardless of the Pueyrredón incident, the Foreign Minister's published instruction of February 15 laid bare the nation's concept of its diplomatic tactics and aims. If the Conference were to fail, he suggested, his government wished responsibility to be charged against American intransigence on nonintervention, where Argentina counted on wide support, not to Argentine obstinacy on the tariff question, where it stood alone.[56]

Mr. Hughes had defended American policies, insofar as they were defensible, with tact and historical logic. His forthright admissions and expositions on American policies may have won more enduring support for the United States than Pueyrredón's histrionics for Argentina. Yet, viewed in perspective, the actions of both men were essential to Pan American progress. Face-to-face debate and stalemate on critical Hemisphere problems at Havana helped to pave the way for partial reconciliation at Montevideo.

Shifts in Three Governments

The sharp controversies between Hughes and Pueyrredón at the Sixth Conference cast a long shadow over United States-Argentine relations. Coupled with growing discord over economic problems, the disagreements at Havana produced a coolness unequalled since the Falklands affair. There was no incident or threatened rupture of intercourse. Rather, Argentine suspicion, even distrust, of the United States frustrated warm response to Washington's overtures.[57] Moreover, the inherent isolationism of the aged Irigoyen, returned to the Casa Rosada in October, 1928, tended to minimize all of Argentina's diplomatic contacts with the world. And the depression soon reduced its commercial interchange.

Though President Alvear immediately appointed a replacement for Pueyrredón he chose to leave to his successor action on the conventions and resolutions approved at Havana.[58] His administration showed no more enthusiasm when Secretary Kellogg urged Argentina to sign his treaty renouncing war.[59] The porteño press and officials in the Ministry

---

[56] To Pueyrredón, *Circular informativa mensual*, p. 77. On the American Ambassador's interpretation of Argentine policy, see his despatch of April 16, 1908, NA, DS, 710.F002/308.

[57] Bliss to Secretary of State, Aug. 18, 1928, NA, DS, 711.35/63.

[58] Bliss to Secretary of State, Aug. 21, 1929, NA, DS, 710.F/461.

[59] Bliss to Kellogg, personal, Sept. 30, 1928, *For. Rel., 1928*, I, 200-201.

of Foreign Relations continued to debate at long range with Mr. Hughes on the scope and content of the Monroe Doctrine.[60]

Through indifference, inertia, or opposition, President Irigoyen brushed aside repeated opportunities to renew cordiality. When Ambassador Manuel Malbrán made a hasty trip to Buenos Aires in December, 1928, the President did not permit his return to Washington. Although in response to American invitation to the Washington Conference on Conciliation and Arbitration, Alvear had appointed delegates, Irigoyen preferred not to send them.[61] He prevented Argentina's adherence to the Briand-Kellogg Pact, took no steps to encourage approval of the Havana agreements, and withheld support from Pan American attempts to settle the Chaco dispute.[62]

Even in entertaining President-elect Hoover on his preinaugural "good neighbor" tour, the Argentines displayed less than their usual unrestrained hospitality. Irigoyen sent his invitation belatedly and only at the last minute decided to deliver the address of welcome. Heavy security precautions and critical press comments revealed the continuing anti-Americanism of the Argentines. Nevertheless, by denouncing the "big brother" concept in inter-American affairs, Hoover created a favorable impression and raised popular hopes for improvement in relations.[63]

General Uriburu's overthrow of the Irigoyen government in September, 1930, reversed the extreme isolationism to which Argentina had reverted.[64] The provisional President quickly returned Argentine diplomats to world councils and offered the nation's services for settlement of disturbing disputes among its neighbors. By promising a more cordial attitude toward the United States, Uriburu also sought to restore diplomatic normalcy in Argentine-American relations.[65] After a hiatus of

[60] In the midst of the Havana Conference, the Ministry of Foreign Relations instructed its minister in Switzerland to issue a declaration decrying the Covenant's definition of the Monroe Doctrine as a regional understanding (*Circular informativa mensual*, No. 131 [April, 1928], p. 170). *La Prensa*, May 11, and *La Nación*, May 12, 1928, criticized passages of Hughes's lectures at Princeton University (Hughes, *Our Relations to the Nations of the Western Hemisphere*, pp. 11-20).

[61] Kellogg to Bliss, April 14, 1928, *For. Rel., 1928*, I, 623; Bliss to Secretary, Nov. 29, 1928, NA, DS, 710.1012WashP43/229. Unfortunately, this left Argentina without representation as the Conference sought methods to halt the Chaco War.

[62] *For. Rel., 1928*, I, 230-231; Bliss to Secretary of State, Aug. 21, 1929, NA, DS, 710.F/461. On the Chaco dispute, see below, pp. 385-389.

[63] Alexander DeConde, *Herbert Hoover's Latin-American Policy*, pp. 20-22; *The Memoirs of Herbert Hoover: The Cabinet and the Presidency, 1920-1933*, pp. 212-213; *Memoria, 1928*, pp. 656-664; Bliss to Secretary of State, Dec. 22, 1928, Jan. 5, 1929, NA, DS, 033.1110 Hoover, Herbert/280, 360.

[64] See above, pp. 359-360.

[65] Bliss to Secretary of State, Sept. 8, 1930, *For. Rel., 1930*, I, 381. Though expressions of anti-Americanism persisted, there were some evidences of better feeling, especially in such cultural activities as those of the Argentine–North American Cultural Institute (DeConde, *op. cit.*, p. 114).

nearly two years, Ambassador Malbrán returned to his post in Washington. Yet, in spite of Uriburu's promise and Hoover's modifications of Latin American policy, operation of the Smoot-Hawley tariff in the midst of depression prevented any real flowering of Argentine-American harmony.

Responsibility for resolving their differences, therefore, passed to new administrations with new political and economic orientations. In February, 1932, following fourteen years of Radical government and eighteen months of Army rule, the Argentine people restored the Conservative Party, with Agustín P. Justo as President. A year later, at the close of three terms of Republican restoration, Americans entrusted their depression-gripped economy to Franklin D. Roosevelt and the Democrats. And between these developments, on January 30, 1933, portentous for the future of both American nations, Adolph Hitler became Chancellor of the Third German Reich.

Montevideo: Hull and Saavedra Lamas

In appointing their respective Cabinets, Presidents Justo and Roosevelt placed in charge of foreign affairs two of the ablest, most tenacious Secretaries their governments had produced. That Carlos Saavedra Lamas and Cordell Hull should confront each other in the most trying moment of Argentine-American relationships was symbolic of the critical situation they inherited. From 1933 to 1938 inter-American affairs revolved to a great degree around the duel between these two determined antagonists.

With black mustache, high stiff collar, and imperious manner, Dr. Saavedra Lamas was a throwback to the diplomatic school of Disraeli and Bismarck. Like his father-in-law, former President Roque Saenz Peña, he clung to the traditional Argentine doctrine that while ties to Europe must come first, leadership of Spanish America should remain firm. Yet he was not, as so frequently pictured, an inveterate critic of Washington's actions. In June, 1931, for example, after a visit to the United States, he had openly lauded the Hoover-Stimson "rectification" of old policies.[66]

Legislator by experience rather than diplomat, Cordell Hull met the Argentine's reserve with American directness and his formal courtesy with Tennessee earthiness. In their face-to-face negotiations, circumstances forced the two men to overcome personal as well as international differences. Fortunately, each could count on the experience of an able lieutenant. Felipe Espil, veteran of nearly ten years in the Argentine Embassy, became ambassador in June, 1931, and served throughout the

[66] See his article, "Hoover's New International Policy: Its Transcendency," *La Nación*, June 1, 1931.

tenure of Saavedra Lamas. Sumner Welles, Assistant Secretary of State, had devoted most of his career, including two years in Argentina, to inter-American affairs.

During the trying months of mid-1933, as the two nations prepared for the Seventh Inter-American Conference, old differences remained to plague the new administrations: the Monroe Doctrine, intervention, trade policies, and peace machinery. When in September Argentina reactivated its membership in the League of Nations, it reiterated its objection to the Monroe Doctrine as a regional understanding.[67]

The outbreak of the Cuban revolution in August raised new alarms of intervention. Although the Argentine leaders responded enthusiastically to Roosevelt's policy of consulting the Latin diplomats and his decision to respect Cuba's sovereignty, they believed as firmly as ever in Hemisphere interdiction of the right to intervene.[68]

By signing the Roca-Runciman Pact in May and similar bilateral trading agreements in subsequent months the Justo administration revealed its plan for reviving foreign trade. In its note of October 5 to the State Department it renewed its attacks upon high tariff rates and sanitary embargoes. Hull's failure to reply pointed up Washington's slowness in mounting its own attack upon world depression.[69]

Through promotion of his Anti-War Pact Saavedra Lamas also captured the initiative in Hemisphere efforts to strengthen its peace machinery. Soon after taking office the Minister unveiled his project to neighboring states and subsequently to the United States and the remaining republics. Eventually he opened it to all nations.[70]

Described by a journalist as "a sort of grab-bag of odds and ends of earlier peace treaties," [71] the project pretended to coordinate essential peace machinery from five existing conventions, the Gondra Conciliation Treaty of 1923, the Kellogg-Briand Pact, the Washington treaties of 1929, and the League Covenant. Unlike the Pact of Paris, which denounced war as an instrument of national policy, it condemned only "wars of aggression." It also denied the validity of forceful acquisition of territory and prohibited the right of intervention.[72]

---

[67] Alexander Weddell, Ambassador to Argentina, to Secretary of State, Sept. 28, 1933, NA, DS, 500.C001/817.

[68] Argentine Ministry for Foreign Affaires to the Department of State, Sept. 8, 1933, *For. Rel., 1933*, V, 409.

[69] See above, pp. 361-362.

[70] Although it did not receive an official draft copy until late September, through Ambassador Espil the Department of State learned of Saavedra Lamas' proposal a month earlier (Memoranda by Asst. Sec. of State White, Aug. 22, 30, 1932, *For. Rel., 1932*, V, 260-261).

[71] *The New Republic*, LXXXVI (April 1, 1936), 219-220.

[72] A complete copy of the treaty is printed in *For. Rel., 1932*, V, 261-268. See also *Memoria, 1932-1933*, I, 148-244.

Dr. Saavedra Lamas apparently derived his inspiration from two sources: first, Pan American failure to halt the war between Bolivia and Paraguay and, secondly, his own desire to return Argentina to the midstream of international affairs, especially as the leader of the Latin American states. For the second purpose he used the Anti-War Pact with great effectiveness. In January, 1933, he succeeded in getting his draft proposal included on the agenda of the Seventh Conference, thus ensuring the Latin states another opportunity to attack the American position on intervention.[73] In February he met with Chilean leaders at Mendoza to discuss diverse problems including the peace proposal.[74]

Later in the year the Foreign Minister accompanied President Justo to Rio de Janeiro, where, amid appropriate fanfare, he secured the signatures of Brazil and five other nations to the treaty.[75] Without consulting the United States, therefore, Saavedra Lamas had effectively checkmated President Roosevelt's May 16th appeal for a general non-aggression pact. He was now prepared to confront Hull at Montevideo with an actual treaty rather than a mere proposal.[76]

Yet, until the eve of the Conference, the Argentine Foreign Minister harbored reservations about the wisdom of holding it. Recurrently during 1933 Washington received reports that Saavedra Lamas wished to see it postponed.[77] In his view, tensions generated by political disturbances in Cuba and Uruguay and by boundary disputes over the Leticia and Chaco territories dictated the advisability of delay.[78] At the same time, of course, he could reason that postponement of the Montevideo Conference would strengthen his own hand in dealing with the Chaco War, underscore Argentina's foresight in joining the League of Nations, and further weaken the inter-American organization.

With the Conference but five weeks away, while continuing to assure the American ambassador that he wished it to go on, Saavedra Lamas sought to interest Brazil, Chile, and Peru in its postponement. Though apparently unwilling that Argentina alone should bear responsibility

---

[73] See the useful analyses of Bemis, *op. cit.*, pp. 264-267, and P. C. Jessup, "The Saavedra Lamas Anti-War Draft Treaty," *The American Journal of International Law,* XXVII (Jan., 1933), 109-114.

[74] Bliss to Secretary of State, Feb. 3, 1933, NA, DS, 710.1012Anti-War/21.

[75] The treaty was signed on October 12 (Hugh Gibson, Ambassador to Brazil, to Secretary of State, Oct. 12, 1933, NA, DS, 835.001Justo, A. P./27).

[76] Bemis, *op. cit.*, p. 270. On one occasion Ambassador Espil suggested to Asst. Sec. of State Jefferson Caffery that if the United States wished to win Saavedra Lamas at Montevideo, it should adhere to his pact (Memorandum by the Asst. Sec., Oct. 31, 1933, *For. Rel., 1933*, IV, 233).

[77] H. L. Stimson, Secretary of State, to Bliss, Feb. 8, 1933, and Hull to Weddell, Oct. 10, *For. Rel., 1933*, IV, 2, 28. On May 4, 1932, the Governing Board of the Pan American Union had already postponed the Conference to December, 1933 (Francis White, Asst. Sec. of State, to American Diplomatic Officers in Latin America, June 4, NA, DS, 710.G/114).

[78] Weddell to Hull, Oct. 28, 1933, *For. Rel., 1933*, IV, 34.

for torpedoing the meeting, he used the long-distance telephone to sound out Ambassador Espil about the possibility of delay.[79]

In Washington, reservations on the timing of the Conference ran equally deep. Hard on the heels of its setback at the London Economic Conference, the young Roosevelt administration faced the probability of another diplomatic reverse at Montevideo. Its high hopes for spreading the doctrine of the "good neighbor" seemed about to collapse on the sharp peaks of Latin American unrest, economic nationalism, and widespread resentment against the United States.[80]

Almost alone among high Washington officials, Secretary Hull held out against scuttling of the Conference. Unless the Good Neighbor policy could demonstrate its effectiveness in the Western Hemisphere, he argued, it had no chance of moderating tensions in other parts of the world. If the Latin Americans remained bitter over past American policies, the Roosevelt administration must prove that its new attitude represented more than pretense. Since no other country had presented a genuine program, the United States must assume leadership. Assembly of Hemisphere diplomats at Montevideo offered the opportunity to meet this challenge frontally. He himself would become the first incumbent secretary of state to head an American delegation to an inter-American gathering. Fortified by such rationalization, the Secretary successfully weathered the efforts of Saavedra Lamas to bring about postponement.[81]

In full realization, therefore, of Argentina's aims and tactics and the probable hostility of other Latin states, Mr. Hull utilized the long sea voyage to Montevideo to draft a program and a plan of action. He organized his staff into study groups, conferred with other delegations aboard ship, communicated frequently with the White House, and drafted resolutions on key agenda items. In all these activities he concentrated on the problems of economic stagnation, inadequacy of Hemisphere peace machinery, and bitterness over past American interventions. He determined to build his program around two comprehensive resolutions: one would attack the problem of high tariffs and trade restrictions; the other would urge universal ratification of Saavedra Lamas' Anti-War Pact and all other peace instruments. As to the American policy of intervention, he was already prepared to accept the Latin American point of view.[82]

Profiting by his shipboard conversations with other delegations, Secretary Hull came to several other conclusions. He would work at Monte-

[79] Weddell to Hull, Oct. 27, 28, 1933, and Memorandum by Asst. Sec. of State Caffery, Oct. 31, *For. Rel., 1933*, IV, 33-34, 232-233.

[80] *The Memoirs of Cordell Hull*, I, 308-309.

[81] *Ibid.*, pp. 317-318.

[82] *Ibid.*, pp. 318-324.

video to broaden the principles and policies of Hemisphere relations. He would avoid the dramatic showdowns of past Conferences. He would encourage others to lead where he wished to go. Immediately upon his arrival in Montevideo, through his unprecedented "open-collar" interviews with Saavedra Lamas and other Latin leaders, he set out to achieve these purposes.[83]

On the paramount issues of economic recovery and peace machinery, Secretary Hull persuaded the Argentine Foreign Minister to undertake joint sponsorship of their proposed resolutions. "We shall be the two wings of the dove of peace," responded Saavedra Lamas, "you the economic and I the political." [84] Each fulfilled to the letter his commitment in the significant bargain of December 9-10.

On December 12 the Minister warmly seconded Hull's proposal for a broad attack upon harmful trade barriers and high tariffs through bilateral reciprocity agreements. Three days later the Secretary espoused the Argentine's suggestion that each delegation pledge its government to sign the five existing instruments for the organization of peace. The Conference gave unanimous approval to both resolutions.[85]

At critical points on divisive issues Saavedra Lamas kept the faith with Mr. Hull. When the topic of intervention came to the floor, he left to others leadership of the anti-American attacks.[86] When the Mexican delegation submitted a comprehensive program on debts and monetary problems, he reinforced Hull's position that the plan should be discussed at a later conference.[87] After failing to secure support for his proposal that bordering countries take up the Chaco War, the Minister supported Hull's resolution reminding Bolivia and Paraguay of their obligations under the League Covenant and requesting them to settle their differences by juridical methods.[88]

Through the efforts of its canny representative, Argentina contributed notably to the most successful of all inter-American conferences. By substituting the role of the catalyzer for that of the obstructionist, it effectively reasserted the leadership it coveted. Yet in departing from its traditional approach Argentina yielded no principles and sacrificed no goals. Saavedra Lamas secured American signature for his Anti-War

---

[83] *Ibid.*, pp. 310, 319-323, 325-331; Hull to Acting Sec. of State, Dec. 1, 1933, *For. Rel., 1933*, IV, 156; *The New York Times*, Dec. 18, 1933.

[84] Hull, *op. cit.*, pp. 327-329; memorandum of conversations between the Secretary and members of various delegations, undated, *For. Rel., 1933*, IV, 178-182.

[85] Seventh International Conference of American States, *Minutes and Antecedents with General Index*, ch. I, 20-23; ch. IX, 90-92; Hull, *Memoirs*, I, 331-333; Department of State, *Report of the Delegates of the United States of America to the Seventh International Conference of American States*, pp. 7-10, 54-57, 195-198.

[86] *Minutes and Antecedents*, ch. II, 107-115, 121-122; Hull, *op. cit.*, pp. 333-336.

[87] *Ibid.*, pp. 335-336; *Report of the Delegates*, pp. 26-31.

[88] *Ibid.*, pp. 11-16, 284; Hull, *op. cit.*, pp. 336-338.

Treaty.[89] He endorsed a program of bilateral reciprocity that at the time seemed essentially compatible with his own. Without aggressiveness on his part, he saw his Latin colleagues win Mr. Hull's assurance that no government need fear American intervention. In resisting Mexico's program on debts, he frustrated a strong challenge to Argentina's leadership. The success of the new Argentina approach, of course, fed also upon the attitudes of Franklin Roosevelt and the self-effacing diplomacy of Cordell Hull.[90]

War and Peace in the Gran Chaco

The cloud of war in the Gran Chaco hung low over the inter-American conference at Montevideo, as it had five years before at Washington. Between 1924 and 1938 the bitter conflict between Bolivia and Paraguay flared up repeatedly, each time a challenge to the new peace instruments of the League of Nations and the American states. Oratorical flights in congressional halls on improved Hemisphere peace machinery seemed hollow and pointless while two sister nations waged war in their tropical jungles.

For more than half a century the two inland republics had quarreled almost incessantly over El Chaco Boreal, the low alluvial plain between the rivers Paraguay and Pilcomayo. A half-dozen boundary treaties had gone unratified while bushfighters of the two proud nations battled snakes, jungle diseases, and impotable water to salvage national honor over a region largely useless. Uncomfortably close to its northern borders, the fighting involved an area Argentina itself had once claimed. However far removed from its shores, the United States had its own special interest in the struggle. The territory at stake was essentially that which President Hayes had awarded to Paraguay in 1878. Without reference at that time to Bolivia's claim, he had supported Asunción's contentions against those of Buenos Aires.[91]

Innumerable attempts by diverse agencies to reconcile the grim foes brought only frustration. Efforts by Argentina, acting alone, and by a Commission of Neutrals, authorized by the Washington Conference, ended in confusion and failure. A self-constituted group of bordering nations, the ABCP powers, and a League of Nations Commission fared

[89] He received the American adherence on April 27, 1934 (*Memoria, 1933-1934,* I, 226-227). Argentina ratified the Kellogg Pact in November (*Circular informativa mensual,* nos. 207-211 [Aug.-Dec., 1934], 160-161).

[90] While working in the archives of the Department of State, I enjoyed the opportunity of reading a manuscript by Robert C. Hayes, of the Historical Division, "Notes on the Conferences of Montevideo, Buenos Aires, and Lima, with Especial Reference to Argentine Policy." I am indebted to Mr. Hayes for phases of my interpretation of the Montevideo and later Conferences.

[91] See above, pp. 204-205.

no better. From time to time, factors of personal ambition, national rivalries, and organizational jurisdiction and prestige intervened to obstruct the progress of negotiations. At many points the aspirations and policies of Argentina conflicted with the views of the United States. In the end, however, it was the group of South American nations suggested by Saavedra Lamas and supported, sometimes under exasperating circumstances, by the United States, that produced a solution.

After a quiet period of several years in the early twenties, Bolivia and Paraguay had reopened their boundary conflict in 1924. Reports of Bolivian concessions to American oil companies raised apprehension in Asunción; Paraguayan plans for settlement of Mennonite colonies in the disputed area disturbed La Paz.[92] When both nations gave indications of inviting the United States to arbitrate, the Alvear administration moved quickly to submit its good offices. Though the rival nations reluctantly agreed to accept Argentina's services, extended negotiations in Buenos Aires finally broke down in July, 1928, five months before the opening of the Washington Conference on Conciliation and Arbitration.[93]

Fresh incidents placed the dispute squarely on the doorstep of the Conference. It acted with promptness. On December 10, appealing directly to Bolivia and Paraguay to settle their differences peacefully, it appointed a committee to study conciliatory action. On January 3 it created a Commission of Inquiry and Conciliation composed of representatives of Colombia, Cuba, Mexico, Uruguay, and the United States, as well as of the disputants.[94]

Argentina's untimely absence from the Conference presented complications. As Chairman, Secretary Kellogg was acutely conscious of Irigoyen's sensitivity to whatever decisions the delegates might make. After learning that the President had already offered Argentina's services as "friendly adjuster," he bombarded Ambassador Bliss with "rush—double priority" inquiries about subsequent actions.[95] Though he interposed no objections to the creation of the Commission of Inquiry, Irigoyen refused to authorize full Argentine participation.[96]

During the next four years, the Commission of Neutrals, meeting in Washington, undertook diverse methods of inquiry and conciliation.[97] Though at times it secured the cooperation of the two nations, as in

[92] *La política argentina*, I, 13.

[93] *For. Rel.*, *1924*, I, 282-287; *1928*, I, 673-675; *La política argentina*, I, 13-137.

[94] *For. Rel.*, *1928*, I, 685; *1929*, I, 835-837.

[95] On the frequent exchanges between the Department and the Embassy, see *ibid.*, *1928*, I, 682-690; *1929*, I, 827-830. Irigoyen's offers are described in *La política argentina*, I, 160-162.

[96] Bliss to Secretary of State, Jan. 2, 1929, *For. Rel.*, *1929*, I, 829-830. The Argentine "Blue Book" does not explain Irigoyen's refusal.

[97] The essential documents on the Commission's activities are published in appropriate volumes of *For. Rel.*; voluminous unprinted materials are filed in NA, DS, 724.3415.

the repatriation of prisoners, it made no headway toward settlement of the basic issues. The administrations of Irigoyen and Uriburu rendered routine assistance they could hardly avoid but in the main seemed to hope for the Commission's failure.[98] Frequent reports reached Washington, especially from Asunción, that Argentina was intriguing with Bolivia to frustrate negotiations.[99]

The renewal of open hostilities in June, 1932, brought into the arena of conciliation the whole galaxy of agencies. As the war intensified, well-meaning leaders obstructed each other's efforts. On August 3, led by the Commission of Neutrals, the nineteen American states addressed a supreme appeal to Bolivia and Paraguay, warning that they would recognize no territorial changes obtained by force.[100] At this point, a new group of nations—Argentina, Brazil, Chile, and Peru—entered the picture, pledged to aid the Commission. Actively led by Saavedra Lamas, they waited only three days to invite Bolivia and Paraguay to settle their differences by conciliation.[101] A showdown between the two groups, the one guided by Washington, the other sparked from Buenos Aires, was now approaching.

In mid-September the Commission of Neutrals proposed a broad plan of settlement which included an immediate armistice and arbitration of all points at issue. A Commission delegation would supervise the armistice in the field. In case of violation, it would declare an aggressor and suggest diplomatic isolation by all the American governments.[102] The Argentine Foreign Minister quickly picked up this cue. Lashing out at the proposal, he labelled it a form of intervention, even if diplomatic and multilateral, which Argentina could not countenance. Moreover, he said, since both Bolivia and Paraguay were members, the League of Nations should handle the Chaco controversy.[103]

The Council of the League chose this moment to inject itself more actively into the line-up of conciliators. Through its Committee of Three it repeatedly offered to cooperate with the Commission of Neutrals. From the American chairman, Mr. Francis White, however, it received no encouragement.[104]

Thus, by promoting the activities of the ABCP group, by denying

[98] *La política argentina*, I, 171, 174, 201, 234.

[99] NA, DS, 724.3415/780, 796, 829, 838, 878. See also *La política argentina*, I, 210, 219, 225.

[100] *For. Rel., 1932*, V, 159-160. Hailing the role of Saavedra Lamas in this declaration, the Argentine press gave him considerable credit for formulation of the doctrine of nonrecognition of territory acquired by force (Bliss to Secretary of State, Aug. 5, 1932, NA, DS, 724.3415/2072).

[101] *La política argentina*, I, 376-378, 392-393.

[102] *For. Rel., 1932*, V, 93-94. See also Bemis, *op. cit.*, pp. 265-267.

[103] *For. Rel., 1932*, V, pp. 203-206; *La política argentina*, I, 424-427, 438-442. Ambassador Espil toned down the Minister's indictment.

[104] *Ibid.*, pp. 420-422. On the League's activities in the Chaco dispute, see Helen P. Kirkpatrick, "The League and the Chaco Dispute," *Foreign Policy Reports*, XII (July 15, 1936).

support to the armistice proposal, by encouraging the intercession of the League of Nations, and by undertaking direct conversations with the representatives of Bolivia and Paraguay, Saavedra Lamas effectively blocked the efforts of the Commission of Neutrals. During these same months he used the war and the stalemated attempts to halt it to win South American support for his Anti-War Pact.[105]

Until June, 1933, the Commission of Neutrals and the ABCP group continued their halfhearted attempts to cooperate. Neither their separate nor their joint efforts produced progress in halting hostilities. When the combatants finally agreed to accept a League inquiry, the Commission resolved to withdraw.[106] For the moment at least the American republics surrendered to Geneva leadership of peace moves. For the first time the United States conceded jurisdiction in a Western Hemisphere dispute to the League of Nations.[107]

Yet the spirit of inter-American cooperation, revived at Montevideo, did not quickly die. Hull and Saavedra Lamas went immediately to work to extend the armistice engineered at the Seventh Conference. When this effort failed, the Secretary pressed the Argentines to undertake new moves. By the end of February, despairing of League success, Saavedra Lamas concluded that the American states must renew their activities.[108]

With the full knowledge of the League Commission, the Foreign Minister drafted a new conciliation formula based upon his own Anti-War Pact and the "no-transfer" principle of the August 3rd Declaration. Granting Hull's contention that all American republics should eventually be invited, he secured agreement of the United States and of Brazil to co-sponsor the formula. Saavedra Lamas could not bring it off, however, and in September, despite the Secretary's opposition, returned initiative to the League.[109]

After yet another season of abortive activities by the League, including the imposition of an arms embargo, final resolution of the Chaco dispute fell to the American states. As before, working closely this time with Chile, Saavedra Lamas took the lead. In February, 1935, the two nations sent exploratory missions to La Paz and Asunción. They enlisted the cooperation of Brazil, Peru, Uruguay, and the United States in a mediation group, which produced the truce agreement of June 12.

[105] See above, pp. 381-382.

[106] *La política argentina*, II, 7-66; *For. Rel., 1933*, IV, 343-344.

[107] On the activities of the League, see *ibid., 1932*, V, 220-259; *1933*, IV, 241-283 *passim; 1934*, IV, 32-135; and *La política argentina*, II, 167-193.

[108] Weddell to Secretary of State, Jan. 4, and enclosure, Jan. 17, Feb. 27; Secretary to Weddell, Feb. 25, *For. Rel., 1934*, IV, 32-35, 45, 56, 59; March 14, 1934, NA, DS, 724.3415/3600 1/2.

[109] *La política argentina*, II, 228-238; Secretary to Weddell, July 14, and Weddell to Secretary, Sept. 18, 1934, *For. Rel., 1934*, II, 144-145, 214-216. A translation of the formula is printed in *ibid.*, 140-142.

Its terms approved at once, representatives of the combatant nations on July 1 joined the mediating states in the peace conference it authorized. After six months of false starts, backtracking, and recesses, the delegates drafted the Protocol of January 21, 1936. Subject to legislative ratification, the parties agreed to exchange all prisoners and renew diplomatic relations.[110] Though the substantive question remained, the Conference had effectively concluded the Chaco War. It required nearly three more years, however, to write the definitive treaty and fix the frontier lines.[111]

Through more than a decade Argentina and the United States had tugged and pulled to settle a boundary dispute that often divided the Hemisphere. The difficulties which frustrated their collaboration stemmed in part, but only in part, from the eccentricities and ambitions of President Irigoyen and Foreign Minister Saavedra Lamas. The long, tangled series of diplomatic miscarriages between the two nations sprang primarily from their deep-seated rivalry for Hemisphere leadership and their divergent views on Pan Americanism and the League of Nations. Nevertheless, Saavedra Lamas, by his persistence and forcefulness, and Hull, by his never-failing firmness and patience, contributed notably to a major inter-American achievement.[112]

Buenos Aires: Roosevelt, Hull, and Saavedra Lamas

No one could have foreseen in February, 1933, that Adolph Hitler's accession to power in Germany would so directly affect relations between Argentina and the United States—between the Justo government, installed a few months before, and the Roosevelt administration, to be inaugurated a few weeks later. Yet, within two years the German drive for the minds, markets, and materials of Latin America raised the old specter of European intervention. To Franklin Roosevelt and other leaders these activities insinuated a threat to Hemisphere security that called for continental action.

Even apart from the menace of the dictators, the inter-American organization lacked the vigor and unity which Montevideo had promised. The Hull-Saavedra Lamas "dove of peace" had failed either to

[110] *Ibid.*, *1935*, IV, 7-198; *1936*, V, 35-39; *La política argentina*, II, 301-302, 310-321, 343-355, 384ff, 419-422; Hull, *op. cit.*, pp. 346-347.

[111] For copies of the treaty and the frontier award, see *For. Rel.*, *1938*, V, 168-170, and Department of State, *The Chaco Peace Conference, Report of the Delegation of the United States of America* . . . , annex 47, pp. 173-176. American representatives to the Conference, in order, were Hugh Gibson, Ambassador to Brazil, Weddell, and Spruille Braden, who served for three tedious years. Braden's reports reveal the human foibles and national rivalries which often obstructed the work (*For. Rel.*, *1937*, V, 4-45; *1938*, V, 89-174).

[112] The American delegates, Weddell and Braden, received credit for saving the peace talks at critical points (*The New York Times*, June 9, 1935, Oct. 30, 1938).

assure peace or rejuvenate trade. The protracted fumbling required to halt the Chaco War revealed basic flaws in Hemisphere peace machinery.[113] The heavy hand of discriminatory controls continued to obstruct the free flow of goods.

The key to a strong front on all these problems lay firmly in the hands of Argentina and its foreign minister. Resolving, therefore, once more to court Argentine support for continental unity, while alerting Hemisphere leaders to the growing danger of Nazi-Fascist penetration, Roosevelt and Hull projected the Conference for Maintenance of Peace at Buenos Aires.

In November, 1936, Franklin Roosevelt and Carlos Saavedra Lamas were world figures, each at the height of his prestige. Winner at home in an overwhelming re-election victory, the President could count upon a growing area of support in Europe and the Americas. By a series of practical measures his Good Neighbor policy had demonstrated its integrity.

As Argentine Foreign Minister since 1932, Saavedra Lamas had restored his nation to a position of influence in both Hemisphere and world councils. He had secured thirty adherents to his Anti-War Treaty and received credit for halting the Chaco War. He had returned Argentina to an active role in the League of Nations and become president of its Assembly. As a fitting climax, thanks in part to the support of Cordell Hull, he had received the Nobel Peace Prize.[114] Clearly, his primary international orientation had moved toward the universal while Roosevelt's remained continental.

As early as July, 1935, Saavedra Lamas learned of the President's consideration of a special conference to discuss inter-American peace machinery. Alternately he warmed and cooled to the idea, warming when he saw the possibility of throwing the Chaco dispute into its lap, cooling when he feared it might not convene in Buenos Aires.[115] Judiciously the President withheld his invitations until after the January 21st Protocol which formally ended the war. Responding to his suggestion, President Justo invited the Conference to Buenos Aires.[116] The date was later set for December.

President Roosevelt's decision to make the long voyage to Buenos

[113] Barely half the nations had ratified all five inter-American peace instruments. Though Saavedra Lamas' Anti-War Pact was the only treaty approved by all, Argentina had ratified no other (Pan American Union, *Status of the Pan American Treaties and Conventions*, p. 5).

[114] Dr. Saavedra Lamas had actively solicited the Secretary's support (NA, DS, 093.57N66/277, 280).

[115] Weddell to Secretary of State, Oct. 12, 1935, Feb. 6, 1936, and Braden to Secretary, Feb. 14, 1936, NA, DS, 710. Peace/10, 11: tel., 147. See *For. Rel., 1936*, II, 5-6.

[116] To Justo, Jan. 30, *ibid.*, pp. 3-5; Justo to Roosevelt, Feb. 22, 1936, NA, DS, 710.Peace/143; *Memoria, 1936-1937*, I, 205-206.

Aires for the opening of the Conference revealed the weight he attached to the project he had initiated. The popular reception he received in the Argentine capital demonstrated the high place he had attained as the champion of peace and democracy. If the porteños "threw their house out of the window" to welcome the American fleet in World War I, the Argentines threw their country out of the capital to greet the magnetic president. Special trains brought them from all directions. A hundred thousand packed the Plaza de Mayo to cheer the two executives.[117] All sectors of the press except the nationalist and pro-German hailed the man and his mission.[118]

But the warmth of the people toward President Roosevelt did not thaw the iciness with which their government received the American program. In preliminary meetings Secretary Hull found that Saavedra Lamas was no longer the friendly collaborator of Montevideo. He concluded that the Argentine had committed himself to inflexible opposition and that only by American concessions could the Hemisphere nations maintain unanimity.[119]

Early in the proceedings Mr. Hull introduced a comprehensive plan that would ensure inter-American solidarity in the face of war in Europe or menace to continental security. It embraced three specific propositions: (1) compulsory consultation among the American states in case of threat to Hemisphere peace; (2) a permanent consultative committee of all foreign ministers to determine the nature of common action; and (3) extension to Latin America of current United States neutrality principles.[120]

As early as the previous March Saavedra Lamas had drafted his own project for the maintenance of peace. It called for (1) close inter-American cooperation with the League of Nations, (2) consultation only by direct negotiation through regular diplomatic channels, and (3) absolute nonintervention, even "excessive diplomatic intervention." [121] Because the State Department had invited all delegations to exchange recommendations in advance, the American and Argentine delegations had steeled themselves for the clashes which came.[122]

---

[117] Weddell to Secretary of State, Jan. 7, 1937, NA, DS, 811.001Roosevelt Visit/302; *The New York Times*, Dec. 1, 1936.

[118] In their editions of November 30, *La Crítica* and *La Razón* devoted eleven and fourteen pages to Roosevelt and the Conference.

[119] Hull, *op. cit.*, p. 497.

[120] The text of the plan was printed in Department of State, *Press Releases*, XV (Dec. 12, 1936), No. 375. See also Hull, *op. cit.*, pp. 498-500.

[121] *Draft of a Convention for the Maintenance of Peace*, pp. 1-16. The Minister discussed his proposals at length in his *La Conferencia Interamericana de Consolidación de la Paz*, pp. 39-71.

[122] Saavedra Lamas received a copy of the American plan while still in Geneva (Hull to Legation to Switzerland, Oct. 5, 1936, NA, DS, Records of U.S. Delegation to Buenos Aires, 1936, General Records, Box 10; Saavedra Lamas, *La Conferencia Interamericana*, pp. 105-113).

Once Hull's project reached the floor, Saavedra Lamas assailed it with an intensity that official Conference records do not reveal.[123] He attacked the permanent consultative organ as an attempt to create a regional League of Nations. Besides opposing Geneva, he said, it would ascribe political functions to the Pan American Union. He struck out at the suggestions for obligatory consultation and mandatory collaboration. These steps would deprive the American states of their freedom of action. He opposed continentalization of American neutrality principles because they embodied arms and credits embargoes. The proposal contradicted the League policy which permitted export of arms to victims of aggression.[124]

As a result of the Minister's verbal forays, the Conference approved only a shadow of Hull's project. The Convention to Coordinate, Extend and Assure Fulfillment of the Existing Treaties Between the American States mandated no action, created no permanent organ, and referred to a common neutrality policy only as a desirable objective.

In two other important instances the Conference bowed to the intransigence of Saavedra Lamas. In the Convention for the Mainte- nance, Preservation and Re-establishment of Peace and the Declaration of Principles of Inter-American Solidarity and Cooperation, he persuaded his colleagues to remove all reference to aggression by a non-American power. Though the first of these prescribed consultation among the signatories, by inserting the phrase "if they so desire" Saavedra Lamas rendered it purely voluntary. As a corollary to this pact, moreover, the Conference approved a special protocol proscribing intervention by any of the contracting parties.[125] Thus, by linking the new plan of consultation to their coveted principle of nonintervention as well as to the Monroe Doctrine, the Latin leaders moved the United States even beyond the concessions it had made in the Montevideo Declaration of 1933.

In frustrating American objectives and elevating Argentina's leader- ship, Saavedra Lamas had conducted a masterly performance. He had set forth the Argentine line consistently and tenaciously. Unlike Roose- velt and the leaders of other American states, he saw little to fear in the actions of the European dictators. He refused to endorse a stronger inter-American organization unless to coordinate its system of collective

---

[123] See rather Hull, *op. cit.*, 498-502, and Saavedra Lamas' 741-page tract on the Conference, *La Conferencia Interamericana de Consolidación de la Paz*. This volume is a hodgepodge of resolutions, speeches, and critical analyses, extremely difficult to use.

[124] *Ibid.*, pp. 115, 135-136, 159-166, 199, 283-288, 327, 426, 734-736.

[125] The various conventions and resolutions are printed in Department of State, *Report of the Delegation of the United States of America to the Inter-American Conference for the Maintenance of Peace*. For effective analyses of the debates, see Bemis, *op. cit.*, pp. 284-293, and O. E. Smith, Jr., *Yankee Diplomacy: U.S. Inter- vention in Argentina*, pp. 26-36.

security with that of the League of Nations. He opposed any step that would isolate the Hemisphere from Europe.[126]

Strangely in this case, though consistent with its record, the Argentine Congress ratified none of the arrangements Saavedra Lamas had striven so stubbornly to achieve. The American Senate approved them all. Yet in spite of the Minister's gains and the Secretary's losses, the American states at Buenos Aires constructed the framework of their later solidarity. At Lima in 1938 they would implement the principle of consultation and after September, 1939, place it in effective operation during wartime. Unfortunately, however, the Foreign Minister's performance convinced Secretary Hull that Argentina was hopelessly recalcitrant, a conclusion that would hamper inter-American harmony for the indefinite future.[127]

Lima: Cantilo and Hull

Aggressive actions by the totalitarian states during 1937-1938 exemplified the menace President Roosevelt had sought to dramatize through the Buenos Aires Conference. Japan's undeclared war against China and Germany's occupation of Austria and the Sudetenland underscored the weakness of the League of Nations machinery Saavedra Lamas had struggled to shore up. Emboldened by these successes in Europe, German and Italian propagandists, cultural emissaries, and commercial agents stepped up their offensive in Argentina and other parts of Latin America.

Under the new administration of President Roberto M. Ortiz, the authorities became increasingly concerned about the activities of German nationals. Their meetings, parades, cultural programs, open use of uniforms, and teaching of Nazi ideals in German-language schools gradually aroused anti-German sentiment. Press criticism, even by the restrained *La Prensa*, grew more articulate.[128] The zealous Deputy Enrique Dickmann proposed to undertake a congressional investigation.[129] Germany's tactics reached a climax on April 10, 1938, day of Reichstag elections, when it conducted in its embassy and consulates an official registration of German nationals and *Volksdeutsche*. This offensive action the Argentine Ambassador in Berlin strongly protested, as he had numerous actions by the Germans since 1934. But in response to a request for friendly advice, the Nazi State Secretary reported the Ambassador as saying: "[The Germans] should simply re-organize our

[126] Cf. Hayes, *op. cit.*, pp. 50-51, 59-60.

[127] Cf. Whitaker, *op. cit.*, pp. 107-108.

[128] Edmund, Freiherr Von Thermann, German Ambassador to Argentina, to the Foreign Ministry, May 18, 1938, *Documents on German Foreign Policy, 1918-1945*, Series D, Vol. V, 848-852; *La Prensa*, April 6, 1938.

[129] See his *La infiltración Nazi-Fascista en la Argentina* (Buenos Aires, 1939).

[their] Party organizations in Argentina and replace them with less obtrusive organizations with an inoffensive appearance." [130]

During the same period a succession of expressions by Argentine authorities betrayed a friendlier attitude toward the United States. At the dinner of the American community in Buenos Aires on July 4, 1937, Saavedra Lamas endorsed the Monroe Doctrine to the extent that it bars from the Americas any political idea hostile to the republican form of government.[131] On two occasions he strongly supported Cordell Hull's candidacy for the Nobel Peace Prize.[132] In August, after first publicly deploring Hull's proposal to lease six decommissioned destroyers to Brazil, the Foreign Minister quickly reversed himself and sought to allay press and congressional resentment.[133]

After his inauguration in February, 1938, President Ortiz continued these friendly gestures. Like the Argentine people generally, he enthusiastically welcomed the flight of six "flying fortresses" sent to honor him.[134] Almost immediately he initiated negotiations for an Army Air Corps mission of eight flying instructors.[135] On March 21, in the presence of Ambassador Weddell and high government officials, he broadcast a good-will message directly to the American people. [136] At the time of the Czech crisis in September he sent to President Roosevelt a pledge of Argentine support for his peace appeal to Hitler and Beneš.[137]

But neither German encroachments on Argentina's sovereignty nor favorable Argentine expressions toward the United States altered the basic directions of the nation's foreign policy. Even before he left his post in Rome to become Foreign Minister, José M. Cantilo began to urge postponement of the Eighth Conference of the American States, scheduled for Lima in December, 1938. He gave the disturbed world situation as one of the reasons. Like his predecessors, he stressed the intimacy of Argentina's relations with Europe. He did admit, however,

---

[130] Two memoranda by the German State Secretary, May 18, 1938, *Documents on German Policy*, V, 845-848. A short time later the German ambassadors and *Auslandsorganisation* officials in southern South America determined "to proceed cautiously" (*ibid.*, pp. 863-867, 869-872).

[131] *The New York Times*, July 5, 1937. The *Times* described it as "undoubtedly the most laudatory speech made about the United States in any Latin-American country in the last generation." Dedicating a statue to George Canning in December, the Foreign Minister declared that protection of the Latin American states against outside aggression would always be based upon the United States and Great Britain (*ibid.*, Dec. 5, 1937).

[132] Weddell to Secretary of State, July 24, 1937, Feb. 9, 1938, NA, DS, 093.57N66/318, 343.

[133] Weddell to Secretary of State, Aug. 13, 1937, NA, DS, 810.34Leasing/60 Tel.; Aug. 18, 20, 1937, *For. Rel., 1937*, V, 162, 165-169.

[134] *Press Releases*, XVIII (March 5, 1938), 279-280.

[135] *For. Rel., 1938*, V, 313-320.

[136] Weddell to Secretary of State, March 22, 1938, NA, DS, 835.76/22.

[137] *Memoria, 1938-1939*, I, 285-287, 289.

that conditions in Europe might make desirable his nation's closer association with the American republics.[138]

The relationship of José Cantilo to the Lima Conference has been misinterpreted and greatly misunderstood. Unlike Pueyrredón at Havana or Saavedra Lamas at Buenos Aires, he did not lead the Argentine delegation into the Conference lists, there to collide with American foes. Rather, after giving one of the principal opening addresses, he steamed away in an Argentine warship, leaving a weak delegation to confront Secretary Hull, while he himself enjoyed a vacation at an unrevealed Chilean resort. In this phase he played the prima donna as effectively as his predecessors. But the coin of Cantilo's contribution to Lima has another side—and it is not the side of sheer obstructionism to the American position.

Consistent with Ortiz' gestures of good will, his foreign minister kept the State Department continuously informed of the position he proposed to take. Seven weeks before the Conference opened, he told Weddell he was considering a proposal to extend the principle of consultation. A week later he made available the text of a memorandum setting forth Argentine views on a variety of agenda items including consultation. Even before Hull's plans had crystallized, Felipe Espil reviewed this despatch point by point with Sumner Welles. Two weeks before the Conference, while Mr. Hull was en route, Cantilo forwarded the specific terms of his proposal to broaden the basis of consultation. He recommended meetings of the ministers of foreign affairs, on both universal and regional bases, "when they deem it advisable." [139] This was the consultative organ Hull had asked and Saavedra Lamas refused at Buenos Aires.[140]

Admittedly, from Hull's point of view, the Argentine's conduct at Lima was less exemplary. In his opening address, while admitting the need for continental solidarity, Cantilo re-emphasized Argentine ties with Europe and denied the need for any special pacts.[141] By rendering himself incommunicado during the critical debates, he hamstrung

[138] *For. Rel., 1938,* V, 3-4; Phillips to Secretary of State, Feb. 15, 1938, NA, DS, 835.00/802. For a detailed statement of Cantilo's views, see *Informaciones argentinas,* No. 8 (Sept. 15, 1938).

[139] Weddell to Secretary of State, Oct. 21, 27; Memorandum of conversation with Argentine Ambassador, Oct. 27; S. P. Tuck, Chargé, to Act. Sec. [undated; received Nov. 26, 1938], *For. Rel., 1938,* V, 31-36, 44-45.

[140] In his *Memoirs,* the Secretary described Cantilo's suggestions as "very weak and general" (I, 603).

[141] His extensive and enthusiastic endorsement of continental solidarity, including the statement, "We are prepared to repel . . . anything that implies a threat to the American order," is often overlooked (República Argentina, Ministerio de Relaciones Exteriores y Culto, *La República Argentina en la Octava Conferencia Internacional Americana,* pp. 71-73).

his own delegation and deepened the Secretary's convictions on Argentina's intractability.[142]

Working closely with Brazilian representatives, Hull strove for a much stronger declaration than Cantilo had proposed. He insisted upon an agreement that would assure the unity of the Americas. He wanted unity against "whatever kind of activities" the Old World might contrive. To prescribe the continental action, he sought regular as well as emergency meetings of the foreign ministers.[143]

After ten days of exasperating stalemate, the Secretary appealed to President Ortiz over Cantilo's head. This quickly brought from the Foreign Minister the draft of a new declaration which incorporated most of Hull's requirements. After further negotiations, inside and outside the plenary sessions, this draft became the basis of the "Declaration of Lima." [144]

Years later Hull denied that the Argentines had won at Lima the distinct victory hailed at the time by anti-American and antiadministration critics. He claimed that the final declaration resembled his own original draft much more closely than Cantilo's, as indeed it did. He did not concede, however, that even the Minister's original proposal was a long step beyond Argentina's position of two years before.[145]

Nevertheless, in justice to Secretary Hull's valiant efforts to maintain unanimity of the American states in the face of growing danger, it must be admitted that Argentina remained the most averse to strong measures of security. Its ultimate agreement to the Declaration of Lima and the companion "Declaration of American Principles" made possible the united front with which the Hemisphere met the first impact of World War II. But, consistent with its traditional policies, Argentina's reservations at Lima foreshadowed its later reluctance to enter the struggle in active defense of the principles it endorsed.[146]

During the interval between world wars the United States revived and effectively nurtured the Pan American idea. Under American initiative and guidance a frail international movement blossomed into a mature regional organization, a powerful influence in the Western Hemisphere and a swelling factor in world politics. At almost every stage of its growth through a succession of notable conferences, American leaders encountered in Argentine statesmen either shrugging indif-

---

[142] Hull, *op. cit.*, pp. 604-608.
[143] *Ibid.*, pp. 606-607; *Argentina en la Octava Conferencia*, pp. 97-98.
[144] *For. Rel., 1938*, V, 80-88; Hull, *op. cit.*, pp. 605-608. On Cantilo's various drafts, see *Argentina en la Octava Conferencia*, pp. 97-98, 101, 150, 348. For an Argentine analysis of its position on the Declaration, see *Memoria, 1938-1939*, I, 146-148.
[145] Hull, *op. cit.*, pp. 608-609.
[146] Hayes, *op. cit.*, pp. 77-78, 83.

ference, begrudging cooperation, or outright opposition. On rare occasions, as at Montevideo in 1933 and at Lima in 1938, when it chose to cooperate at all Argentina became, at best, a reluctant partner to Washington's aims. More often, driven by isolationism, by devotion to a universal organization, or by a deep urge to lead the Latin American states, it maintained a spirited rivalry to America's leadership of the Hemisphere. The origin and spread of World War II would put to severer test both the vitality of the inter-American system and the direction of Argentina's loyalties.

XXIII

WORLD WAR II:
NEUTRALITY AND BELLIGERENCY, 1939-1943

The German invasion of Poland in September, 1939, brought the governments and peoples of Argentina and the United States no such paralyzing shock as had the outbreak of war in 1914. The aggressions of the Axis nations in Asia, Africa, and Europe had long since toughened the American states against the debacle they were helpless to prevent. Through the broadened news coverage of press and radio, the people of the Americas were no longer uninformed of the diplomatic maneuverings of Old World chancelleries.

Yet the resources and the minds of both Argentines and Americans were as vulnerable as before. Their agricultural, industrial, and raw material reserves remained as essential to the demands of the belligerents. The calculated Nazi-Fascist use of mass media and underground organizations, while hardening the resistance of the far-seeing, had softened up large sectors of the population in both countries for the intensified psychological warfare to come.

Both nations were as determined to resist involvement as they had been a quarter-century earlier. Mindful of the profits brought in by World War I and of the nation's deep-set antagonism to foreign commitments, the entrenched oligarchs in Buenos Aires coveted neutrality as tenaciously as had their forebears. However much distrusted by President Roosevelt, the new neutrality legislation of the American Congress had won bipartisan and popular support in the United States.

To fortify their individual resolution to safeguard neutrality, unanimous action of the American republics at Buenos Aires and Lima had created the rudimentary machinery for multilateral action against war's impact. In Washington, the perpetuation in office of Roosevelt and Hull assured continuing support for the Hemisphere policies they had inspired. In Buenos Aires, on the other hand, a succession of administrative changes between 1940 and 1943 handicapped Argentina's participation in inter-American decisions.

Even during the season of "phony war" in 1939-1940, the conflict brushed Argentine and American shores far more quickly and threateningly than had World War I. Through subversion and fifth columnism, especially in Argentina, it invaded the core of each nation. As before, deepening awareness of the issues involved, together with the growing prospect of German triumph, wedded the Argentines to noninvolvement, while rousing Americans to take up the sword.

Argentine and American Commitments to Their Neighbors

At the outset of the war Argentina was a functioning, though hardly an exhorting, member of the Inter-American System. It had participated actively in all eight regular conferences, as well as the Conference on the Maintenance of Peace, and had signed all but two of the fifty-one treaties and conventions negotiated by them. Yet its Congress had ratified only two of these, one on the Status of Naturalized Citizens, the other on Codification of International Law. Even in the case of its own Anti-War Pact, promoted so assiduously by Carlos Saavedra Lamas, it deposited its ratification a year after the United States. No other state had bound itself so loosely to the treaty obligations of the Hemisphere. The American Congress, on the other hand, had ratified all but ten of the forty-one conventions which delegates of the United States had signed.[1]

More significant, however, than Argentina's record of nonperformance was the moral obligation it had assumed at the Eighth Conference of the American States. In signing the Declaration of Lima, which required no ratification, it had joined its sister states in reaffirming "their continental solidarity and their purpose to collaborate in the maintenance of the principles upon which the said solidarity is based." Beyond this, it had supported the unanimous resolution to defend these principles "against all foreign intervention or activity that may threaten them." Argentina had gone even further. It had introduced the suggestion of consultation by foreign ministers as the instrument to determine the measures necessary to resist a threat to Hemisphere security.[2]

The extent of Argentina's commitments on intracontinental affairs, therefore, was minimal. But its moral obligation to maintain the principles of continental solidarity against foreign intervention was as great as that of any American state. Its performance in the face of subversion and war betrayed even less loyalty to American principles than its record on ratification.

Argentina's failure to honor its inter-American pledges stemmed in

[1] Pan American Union, *Status of the Pan American Treaties and Conventions,* pp. 1-5.
[2] See above, pp. 395-396.

part from the untimely incapacity of President Roberto Ortiz. His succession of friendly gestures toward the United States before and after the start of the war created a more cordial atmosphere than had prevailed for a decade. His responsiveness to Secretary Hull's direct appeals from Lima in 1938 and Havana in 1940 intimated a new Argentine cooperativeness.[3] But the President's long illness removed him effectively from the executive office after July, 1940. Ortiz may or may not have been as democratic or as cooperative as Washington believed. Even if he were, it is doubtful that he could have carried the Argentine nation willingly into the war. In any case, his illness and resignation placed his administration in the hands of Vice-President Ramón S. Castillo, whose actions often betrayed anti-American and pro-Axis sentiments.

Inter-American Neutrality and Security

Declarations of war against Germany by England and France on September 3 brought immediate proclamations of neutrality from Buenos Aires and Washington. Almost without dissent in both countries the press and the people warmed to the support of their governments. From Buenos Aires Ambassador Norman Armour, capable career diplomat recently assigned to the post, reported general condemnation of the German aggression and great sympathy for the democratic powers. Sentiment for Hemisphere solidarity was increasing, he noted, and the people looked to President Roosevelt and the United States to lead the way to inter-American cooperation.[4]

Foreign Minister Cantilo, indeed, had already taken steps to put in motion the consultative machinery he had helped to create at Lima nine months before. Within hours after Hitler's armoured divisions rolled into Poland on September 1, Cantilo announced to the press his desire for inter-American consultation and instructed Argentine representatives in all American capitals to take up the matter with the various governments. On the same day, at a hastily assembled meeting of Hemisphere diplomats, he stated the Argentine position.[5] When, two days later, President Roosevelt suggested specific plans for a conference at Panama, the Foreign Minister readily assented. On the fifth, Argentina joined

---

[3] See above, p. 396, and below, p. 405. For other instances of Ortiz' friendliness, see Norman Armour, Ambassador to Argentina, to Secretary of State, July 11, 1939, NA, DS, 710.11/2401, and *The New York Times*, April 17, 1939.

[4] Armour to Secretary of State, Sept. 4, 5, 6, 12, 1939, NA, DS, 740.00111A. R./24, 40, 57, 284.

[5] República Argentina, Ministerio de Relaciones Exteriores y Culto, *Memoria, 1939-1940*, pp. 30-31, *Reuniones de consulta entre ministros de relaciones exteriores de las Repúblicas Americanas*, pp. 25-26, and *Informaciones argentinas*, No. 32 (Sept. 15, 1939), p. 2; No. 36 (Nov. 15, 1939), p. 2.

the United States and six other nations (Brazil, Chile, Colombia, Cuba, Mexico, and Peru) in sponsoring Panama's invitation to the First Consultative Meeting of the Foreign Ministers.[6] With Argentina's wholehearted cooperation, therefore, Panama became the hopeful sequel to Buenos Aires and Lima.

In his instructions to the delegation, led by Dr. Leopoldo Melo, Cantilo reiterated Argentina's traditional positions favoring freedom of the seas and opposing political and military commitments, especially any that might expose the continent to a state of belligerency.[7] But, most significant, he urged the delegates

to be guided by the same spirit which animated the Argentine Delegates to the Eighth Pan American Conference at Lima, that is to say, a determined purpose of working together for whatever may tend to tighten our bonds with the other American Republics, on the base of the principles of the Declaration of Lima.[8]

At the Panama meeting the new consultative machinery of the Western Hemisphere successfully passed its first test. Argentine obstructionism to Yankee proposals and continental desires was as unobtrusive as it had been at any inter-American conference. Unwilling to play the traditional Argentine prima donna, Dr. Melo worked hand in glove with Under Secretary of State Sumner Welles to achieve unanimity on a broad plan of Hemisphere security.

Argentina balked at only two phases of the American program. One was the novel concept of a three-hundred-mile "security zone" around the Hemisphere embodied in the "Declaration of Panama." Cantilo had no objection to the use of common action to secure pledges from the combatants that they would eschew acts of war in waters adjacent to the continent. He chose to withhold, however, lest it bring conflict with the vessels of belligerents, any Argentine obligation to patrol those waters.[9] But Melo refused to isolate his nation. He insisted upon placing Argentina "in complete harmony and in friendly understanding with the United States."[10]

The Foreign Minister also objected to the proposal to exclude all belligerent submarines from Hemisphere waters. He was willing to require them to sail on the surface and to exclude those that committed acts of hostility, but otherwise he wished to treat them like

---

[6] Armour to Secretary of State, Sept. 4, 1939, NA, DS, 740.00111A.R./19; *Memoria, 1939-1940*, pp. 32-35.

[7] *Ibid.*, pp. 40-43; *Reuniones de consulta*, pp. 36-39, 91-94.

[8] *Ibid.*, p. 36.

[9] *Ibid.*, pp. 57-58; Hull to Welles, Sept. 29, 1939, *For. Rel., 1939*, V, 32-33.

[10] Welles to Secretary of State, Oct. 3, 1939, NA, DS, 740.00111A.R./425.

any belligerent vessels.[11] When the Declarations of Panama and of Neutrality left the questions of patrolling and submarine exclusion to the will of each nation, Cantilo authorized Melo to sign.[12]

On all other key resolutions, such as those on Economic Cooperation, Coordination of Police and Judicial Measures, and Transfer of Sovereignty of Geographic Regions by Non-American States, Argentina joined the common front for security. It also gained a coveted point when the Conference agreed to oppose contraband lists which included foodstuffs and clothing intended for civilians.[13]

Deeply impressed by Melo's cooperativeness, Sumner Welles recommended to Secretary Hull that he send a note of appreciation to Buenos Aires.[14] Through the helpfulness of Melo, therefore, the United States and the other American republics reinforced their neutrality during the troublous times of world war with the continental unanimity which another Argentine, Rómulo Naón, had vainly sought in 1914.[15] At the same time, Cantilo's reluctance at Panama was a portent of Argentina's dissent after Pearl Harbor.

During the strange war interlude between the fall of Poland and the fall of France, Foreign Minister Cantilo revealed unexpected support for the new policies of continental neutrality.[16] The sinking of merchant ships within the security zone and the British engagement with the *Graf Spee* apparently converted him to the efficacy of the Declaration of Panama. The presence on Argentine soil of a thousand interned Germans drove home the immediacy of war's dangers to neutrals. When Washington proposed to all the American republics the despatch of a joint note on the *Spee* incident, Cantilo favored a strong and unequivocal statement.[17] When the belligerent nations refused to accept the security zone concept, he argued that neutral nations have the right to establish their own rules of neutrality.[18]

Germany's acceleration of the war on land and sea in the spring of

---

[11] *Reuniones de consulta*, p. 58. The United States excluded belligerent submarines after Nov. 4, 1939, Argentina, after May 13, 1941.

[12] Before signing the Declaration of Panama, Argentina made its traditional reservation on "legitimate titles and rights" to the Falkland Islands.

[13] The entire Act of Havana is printed in J. B. Scott (ed.), *The International Conferences of American States, First Supplement, 1933-1940*, pp. 343-377.

[14] Welles to Secretary of State, Oct. 3, 1939, NA, DS, 740.00111A.R./425; *Memoria, 1939-1940*, p. 53.

[15] See above, pp. 306-307.

[16] On Pan American Day, 1940, fiftieth anniversary of the movement's founding, he spoke in the most expansive terms of the contributions of Pan Americanism (*Informaciones argentinas*, No. 43 [May, 1940], pp. 2-3).

[17] Hull to Armour, circular, Dec. 15, and Armour to Hull, Dec. 16, *For. Rel., 1939*, V, 94-96, 100-101; Armour to Secretary, Dec. 20, 1939, NA, DS, 740.0011-European War/1361.

[18] *The New York Times*, Jan. 19, 1940.

1940 stirred Cantilo to further steps. Immediately after the swift conquest of the Low Countries, he suggested a new consultative conference to consider the replacement of neutrality by "nonbelligerency." Rebuffed by his own Congress and confronted by rising nationalist opposition to the Ortiz administration, the Foreign Minister became for a time more timid and defeatist.[19]

Two German actions against Argentina, however, temporarily strengthened Cantilo's hand. On May 27, in apparent reprisal against his nonbelligerency proposal, a German submarine sank the Argentine ship *Uruguay*. Even before public announcement, the Foreign Minister divulged to Ambassador Armour the terms of the Argentine demand for indemnification. Less than a week later, the Nazi ambassador presented a long memorandum of protest against Argentina's increasingly hostile attitude. Citing press criticism, internment of the *Graf Spee* crew, and toleration of pro-British acts, the note ridiculed published reports of German fifth-column activities. After Cantilo disclosed the memorandum to him, Mr. Armour termed it "a clumsy attempt to cover German intrigue and espionage by taking the offensive in placing the blame on Argentina." [20]

Meanwhile, revelations of extensive Nazi preparations in Uruguay stimulated both Buenos Aires and Washington to precautionary measures. Argentina reinforced its army units along the frontier and despatched gunboats to border rivers. The United States ordered the fast cruisers *Quincy* and *Wichita* to the South Atlantic.[21]

But this stiffening of Cantilo's will was extremely transitory. The combination of Hitler's continued successes in Europe, the growing strength of nationalist and pro-German elements in Argentina, and the illness of President Ortiz at the moment of crisis weakened the hand of the Foreign Minister on the eve of the Second Conference of Foreign Ministers at Havana.[22] His vacillation during the critical months of May and June aided Argentina's gradual retreat from the continental solidarity so promisingly begun at Panama.

The rapid spread of German divisions over Western Europe caused extreme disquiet to President Roosevelt and Secretary Hull. The occupation of Holland and France raised the question of sovereignty over their possessions in the Western Hemisphere, a contingency foreseen in Resolution XVI of the Act of Panama. Upon Hull's initiative the Congress

---

[19] *Ibid.*, May 13, 15, 1940. For Armour's comments on Cantilo's reactions, see his despatches of June 4, 7, 1940, NA, DS, 835.00/853; 835.857/11.

[20] See Armour's reports mentioned above, note 19, together with that of June 2 (*ibid.*, no. 10).

[21] *The New York Times*, May 31, June 12, 1940. For the correspondence on the visit of the cruisers to Buenos Aires, see NA, DS, 811.3335/94a, 95, 97, 99.

[22] Armour to Secretary of State, June 4, 1940, NA, DS, 835.00/853.

on June 18 resolved to refuse recognition to the transfer of any Hemisphere region from one non-American power to another. The State Department immediately warned both Berlin and Rome.[23]

Secretary Hull's call for an early consultative conference brought out the change which had occurred in Cantilo's policy since his nonbelligerency statement of early May. Though he reported to Norman Armour that Argentina would send delegates, once he learned of Washington's unilateral action on European colonies he professed to see no need for the meeting.[24] On July 3 he announced through the press that the Argentine delegates would adhere to the position he had defined at Lima: "Continental solidarity, individual policy." [25]

In the usual preconference fencing the Foreign Minister reacted strongly against Hull's draft of a comprehensive resolution to cover any forceful transfer of Hemisphere territory.[26] He denied that such a change in sovereignty was necessarily hostile to the peace and safety of the American republics. He questioned their right to sit in judgment on political shifts in Europe, certainly not in advance of their occurrence. He doubted the wisdom of any policy which guaranteed the *status quo* without considering the desirability of change. In any case, the people themselves should determine their future status. Thinking perhaps of the Falkland Islands, Cantilo suggested the alternative principle that no European colonies should exist in the Western Hemisphere.[27]

After conferring with the Foreign Minister on these views, Ambassador Armour analyzed the recent shift in his attitude. He felt that strong nationalistic groups were encouraging drift toward a more pronounced isolationism. Making full use of Germany's economic and military offensives, Italy's entrance into the war, and France's submission, these elements had accelerated their anti-American propaganda and were seeking to check further Argentine commitments to the American states.[28]

Foreign Minister Cantilo did not go to Havana personally to confront Mr. Hull with his arguments against the Secretary's program. As at Panama, he sent the veteran Leopoldo Melo to present the Argentine case. By this time President Ortiz had retired from active direction of affairs and Ramón S. Castillo had become Acting President. Circumscribed by the changed attitudes of his superiors, the cooperative Melo

---

[23] *The Memoirs of Cordell Hull*, I, 813-817.

[24] *Memoria, 1940-1941*, I, 15-16; M. B. Davis, First Secretary of Embassy to Argentina, to Secretary of State, June 21, 1940, NA, DS, 710.Consultation(2)/98.

[25] Armour to Secretary of State, July 5, 1940, *ibid.*, no. 276.

[26] The complete text of the draft is printed in *For. Rel., 1940*, V, 217-218.

[27] Armour to Secretary of State, July 20, *ibid.*, pp. 235-237; despatches 991 and 992, July 23, 1940, NA, DS, 710.Consultation(2)/491, 492.

[28] Armour to Secretary of State, July 26, 1940, NA, DS, 835.00/880.

of Panama became at Havana the spokesman for traditional Argentine opposition.[29]

When the Secretary introduced the resolution he had fostered, the Argentine delegate faithfully represented Cantilo's position. Moreover, like the delegates of several other states, he questioned American ability to defend the entire Hemisphere in event of retaliation against enforcement of the proposed policy. To relieve the stalemate Hull secured Melo's approval for direct appeal to President Ortiz. In this instance, however, unlike that at Lima, the appeal meant going over the head of an Acting President as well as that of the Foreign Minister. As at Lima, the appeal brought immediate results. Argentina joined the other states in approving the "Act of Havana" and its accompanying "Convention on the Provisional Administration of European Colonies and Possessions in the Americas." [30]

No other problem considered at Havana provoked a clash between the Americans and the Argentines. Dr. Melo himself headed the committee which prepared solutions prescribing common action to curb subversive activities. He raised no objection to a resolution calling for economic cooperation to meet the impact of war nor to that affirming the "all for one and one for all" principle.[31]

Though delayed for a year by administrative changes and internal politics, the Argentine Congress eventually ratified the Convention of Havana.[32] Express exclusion of the Falkland Islands and comparative disinterest in Caribbean colonies doubtless expedited the action.

The Second Meeting of the Foreign Ministers at Havana marked the culmination of the Roosevelt-Hull program to build Hemisphere solidarity against the threat from Europe. If the American republics had not continentalized the Monroe Doctrine, at least they had endorsed its essence. The Havana agreements also represented the zenith of Argentina's cooperation with the United States. After that it would join the common front only to the extent of its own minimum concessions.

[29] For a summary of Melo's instructions, see *Reuniones de consulta*, pp. 115-117. Mr. Hull did not hold Dr. Melo responsible for the role he played (*Memoirs*, I, 825).
[30] Hull to Act. Sec. of State, July 23, 27, 1940, *For. Rel., 1940*, V, 239-241, 250; Hull, *op. cit.*, pp. 823-827.
[31] *Ibid.*, pp. 827-828.
[32] Armour to Secretary of State, Jan. 3, July 30, 1941, NA, DS, 710. Consultation-(2)/738, 774. Up to this time Argentina had approved no other major inter-American treaty. Though endorsed by an inter-American conference, Saavedra Lamas had initiated his Anti-War Treaty as an Argentine project.

Hemisphere Security and Argentine Indecision

The eighteen months between the Second and Third Conferences of Foreign Ministers embraced the period of Hitler's greatest military conquests. In direct relationship to their successes on the battlefield, the Nazis intensified their subversive campaigns against Argentina and neighboring states.

The widening threat to Hemisphere security gradually pushed President Roosevelt and the Congress along the road to pro-Allies neutrality. While taking the first steps to improve the nation's own preparedness and transform its economy into the "arsenal of democracy," they also undertook to buttress the military and economic defenses of the Hemisphere.[33] Through the various new organs of the Inter-American System, as well as by direct approach, Washington sought to carry the Argentines into wholehearted cooperation.

During 1940-1941, therefore, though wedded to the policy of neutrality, the leaders and people of Argentina found themselves pulled and torn between the machinations of the Axis and their own commitments to the American states. Traditional economic and cultural ties with the Western democracies complicated their inner conflict. Behind this torment to the individual Argentine, moreover, lay the realistic national aim of avoiding involvement without alienating the eventual victors. It was a thorny, somewhat calloused, path to follow, leading at times to vacillation and indecision. Changing leadership in the Foreign Ministry between September and June, together with the anomalous position of an acting president, added to the inconstancy.

Even before the Havana Conference Washington had initiated a program of strengthening continental military defenses. Its decision to accomplish its ends by secret bilateral staff conversations led at first to confusion and misunderstanding among Argentine officials. Press reports in October, 1940, that Yankee representatives were negotiating with Uruguay for exclusive use of bases aroused in Buenos Aires both nationalist agitation and official concern.[34] Though Under Secretary Welles denied that the United States was seeking to lease bases and Uruguayan Foreign Minister Alberto Guani affirmed that any bases constructed would be available to all American nations, their statements did not quiet the pro-totalitarian press. They did, however, help to clear the official air.[35]

---

[33] On American efforts to prepare continental defenses, see W. L. Langer and S. E. Gleason, *The Undeclared War, 1940-1941*, pp. 147-174.

[34] *For. Rel., 1940*, V, 16-17, 20-39; Armour to Secretary of State, Nov. 13, 1940, NA, DS, 810.20Defense/334.

[35] Council on Foreign Relations, *Documents on American Foreign Relations*, III, 136-137; Armour to Secretary of State, Nov. 20, 1940, NA, DS, 811.34533/19 1/2.

Argentine reaction to the furor caused by the incident gave Washington a glimmer of hope for closer cooperation. Authorities in Buenos Aires seemed reassured that the United States sought no jurisdiction nor even exclusive use of bases in Uruguay or other American countries. They appeared to accept the distinction between inter-American security agreements and the commitments made by individual nations in bilateral understandings. By encouraging Uruguayan accommodation with Argentina in a regional defense pact Washington reduced another point of friction with Buenos Aires. At the end of the episode ailing President Ortiz gave public endorsement to the desirability of a plan of action for continental defense. Foreign Minister Julio Roca went further. He assured Ambassador Armour that Argentina would promptly renew staff conversations on continental defense matters.[36]

But neither the understanding attitude of Dr. Roca nor the warm approval accorded by prodemocratic Argentines to President Roosevelt's re-election changed the uncooperative attitude of Acting President Castillo. Beset by domestic pressures and internal frictions, his Cabinet underwent a series of shifts during the early part of 1941. Dr. Roca, who had replaced José Cantilo as Foreign Minister in September, and Federico Pinedo, Finance Minister, resigned their posts in late January. Roca's successor, appointed only in March, did not assume his duties until June. In the meantime, Guillermo Rothe served on interim appointment. President Ortiz' continued incapacity, caused now by near-total blindness, increased the government's instability.

This political uncertainty in Buenos Aires, therefore, hampered American efforts to assist Argentine rearmament and financial stability. With Britain getting first call on current inventories of munitions and the nation's industrial machine not yet geared to maximum production, the United States lacked the means to satisfy the needs of all the American republics. In any case, Argentina's procrastination in appraising its requirements and determining to present them handicapped its case in Washington.[37]

On the side of economic aid, where reserves were less scanty, American policy gained some headway, but in the end the results were the same. An Argentine financial mission to Washington in December concluded two financial agreements. One provided a loan of $60,000,000 to finance increased trade; the other created a fund of $50,000,000 for currency stabilization. By postponing legislative action upon these ar-

---

[36] Armour to Secretary of State, Nov. 20, 28, and Hull to Embassy to Argentina, Nov. 29, 1940, NA, DS, 811.34533/19 1/2 and 810.20Defense/379. Ortiz' statement of November 19 and Welles's commentary are printed in *Documents on American Foreign Relations*, III, 138-140.

[37] At the close of 1940 Argentina was the only South American country with which the United States had not concluded a defense agreement (Langer and Gleason, *op. cit.*, p. 158). See also *For. Rel., 1940*, V, 460-463.

rangements, however, Argentina failed to profit by the financial assistance it clearly needed.[38]

The epoch of administrative weakness in Buenos Aires during early
1941, combined with Axis superiority in Europe, provided a springboard
for intensified German activity in Argentina. Immediately upon his
return from Berlin late in February Ambassador Von Thermann stepped
up all phases of the Nazi program in South America. The American
Embassy reported in detail upon the plans to discredit the United
States, forestall fulfillment of the Lend-Lease Act, and deny Argentine
resources to Britain. Identifying officers and structure of the Nazi
organization, the reports described the "State within a State" ready
to take over the functions of Argentine government.[39]

Under these pressures of domestic unrest and Nazi subversion, the
Castillo government refused to take any step that might antagonize
the Germans. In diverse ways it tapered off its cooperation with the
other American republics. It took no action to approve the loan agreements recently concluded in Washington. It failed to renew military
staff conversations, as Roca had promised. It continued to oppose American use of bases in Uruguay. While denying British claims to Axis ships
interned in Argentine ports, it refused to confiscate them even to
prevent sabotage. The Senate postponed until late April, 1941, action
on a military appropriations bill passed by the Chamber of Deputies
the previous June.[40]

The sweeping Axis victories in the Balkans and North Africa in April
and May contributed new substance to the influence of the extreme
nationalists and apparently confirmed Castillo's adherence to strict
neutrality. In a public statement on April 23, presumably to counteract
pro-American declarations by respected opposition leaders, and again
in his annual message on May 28, the Acting President restated Argentine resolution.[41]

Yet defeatism did not absorb all sectors of Argentine public opinion.
Castillo's cautious neutralism, clearly more pro-Axis than pro-Allies,
aroused open criticism from distinguished Argentine leaders—ex-Presi-
dents Alvear and Justo, Supreme Court President Roberto Repetto, even

[38] Department of State, *Bulletin*, III (Dec. 28, 1940), p. 590. The mission was
headed by Raul Prebisch, Director General of the Banco Central de la Nación. Its
activities in Washington were extensively discussed in the porteño press (for
example, see *La Prensa*, Nov. 10, 14, 19, 25; *La Nación*, Nov. 15, 1940).

[39] Armour to Secretary of State, Feb. 28, March 18, 26, April 18, 1941, NA, DS,
862.20210/426, 467; 862.20235/402, 406.

[40] Cf. Langer and Gleason, *op. cit.*, p. 620. Their extended discussion of the
Argentine attitude is based on many despatches from Ambassador Armour. On the
problem of Axis ships, see Armour to Secretary of State, April 1, 1941, NA, DS,
865.85/269.

[41] Armour to Secretary of State, April 23, June 13, 1941, NA, DS, 862.20235/434;
810.20Defense/882.

Saavedra Lamas. Representing a strong body of opinion, these spokesmen denounced the government's policy and advocated stronger cooperation with the American states. By the middle of June Ambassador Armour reported a deepening impatience with Castillo's caution and timidity and by August a more insistent popular demand for collaboration with Great Britain, the United States, and the other American republics.[42]

A Trade Agreement at Last

During the months from June to the Japanese attack on Pearl Harbor, the Castillo administration appeared to shift slightly in the direction desired by the growing political opposition. In a public statement on July 7 to two thousand Army officers, without retreating from "prudent neutrality," the Acting President revealed that the door to inter-American cooperation remained open. "Although the clash of extra continental powers has upset our economy and modified our balance of trade," he said,

> we believe the correct course is to keep alive collaboration with the American nations in order that the atmosphere of harmony will prevail here where peace and order make nations great and men respected.[43]

As a matter of fact, even before his annual message of May 28 he had taken several collaborative steps. He had permitted the Chief of the Naval General Staff to participate in an inspection tour of American naval establishments. On May 13, belatedly to be sure, his government closed Argentine ports and waters to belligerent submarines. On the same day, Enrique Ruiz Guiñazú, Foreign Minister-designate en route from Vatican City to Buenos Aires, was a guest of Secretary Hull in Washington.[44] Even earlier Castillo had proposed to the United States and Brazil a tripartite mediation in the recurring boundary dispute between Ecuador and Peru.[45]

Meanwhile, supported strongly by the pro-Allies press, the Chamber of Deputies committee investigating Nazi penetration was preparing to force Castillo's hand. Through periodic disclosure of its startling find-

---

[42] To Secretary of State, June 13, Aug. 20, 1941, *ibid.*, nos. 882, 1402.

[43] S. P. Tuck, Chargé d'Affaires ad interim to Argentina, to Secretary of State, July 11, 1941, NA, DS, 810.20Defense/1066, sects. 1-2.

[44] Department of State, *Bulletin*, IV (April 5, May 10, 1941), 423, 553-556; Langer and Gleason, *op. cit.*, p. 621.

[45] Despatches on the progress of the mediation are filed in NA, DS, 722.2315. See also Department of State, *Bulletin*, IV (May 17, 1941), 596-598; V, 73, 93, 112-113. Through the joint efforts of Argentina, Brazil, Chile, and the United States, the dispute was settled at the time of the Third Meeting of Ministers of Foreign Affairs in Rio (Department of State, *Bulletin*, VI [Jan. 31, 1942], 94, 194-196).

ings on the anti-Argentine activities of the German Embassy, it laid
bare the extent to which Ambassador Von Thermann had abused his
diplomatic privileges. On September 15 the Chamber voted his censure
and recommended dissolution of all German cultural and trade union
organizations.[46]

In this charged atmosphere the Castillo administration accelerated
diplomatic negotiations already under way for closer cooperation with
the United States. These related principally to the problems of world
wheat control, shortage of military equipment, and changing trade
patterns.

To resolve expanding difficulties over world wheat supply and demand,
Argentine officials met for many months with representatives of Aus-
tralia, Canada, the United Kingdom, and the United States. By April,
1942, they had agreed to a draft convention covering such matters as
stocks, relief pool, and controls over production, exports, and prices.[47]

American efforts to meet Argentina's needs for military assistance confronted one hurdle after another. Not until late June did the Argentines
present their initial list of military shortages, principally chemicals and
metals. When, a month later, the State Department sought to relate
requirements to staff conversations on continental defense, Ambassador
Espil raised bitter objections. Department officials quickly agreed to
the complete separation of military needs and political commitments.
Assured upon this point, the Argentines decided in August to send a
mission to Washington, though it arrived only after the attack on
Pearl Harbor.[48]

By far the most significant action to draw Argentina closer to Hemisphere cooperation was the conclusion on October 14 of a reciprocal
trade agreement. Under the pressure of trade dislocations and shipping
shortages, the two neutral nations succeeded in concluding the modern
commercial treaty long thwarted by their contradictory policies.[49] The
agreement replaced the obsolete treaty of 1853.

The outbreak of war in Europe had not at once seriously altered
either the pattern or the volume of Argentine foreign commerce. Increased sales to Italy and the United States, while the markets of
Western Europe held firm, more than offset the loss of trade with

---

[46] In a series of despatches between late August and late November, Mr. Armour
summarized the contents of the committee's revelations (NA, DS, 962.20235/570,
583, 601; 701.6235/110, 119, 122, 124, 126, 146).

[47] *Documents on American Foreign Relations*, IV, 713-718. The Memorandum
of Agreement was printed in Department of State, Executive Agreement Series 384.

[48] Armour to Welles, May 21, NA, DS, 810.20Defense/1094; memos of conversations with Espil, June 24, July 31, 835.24/157, 170; Hull to Embassy to Argentina,
Sept. 26, and Armour to Secretary of State, Oct. 19, Nov. 26, 1941, nos. 177, 195,
214.

[49] See above, pp. 363-365.

Germany and Poland. In fact, the export tonnage during the first nine months of the war increased 12 per cent; the value rose, almost 20 per cent, over the corresponding period in 1938-1939.[50]

German occupation of Western Europe, however, shattered the customary channels of Argentina's export trade. Of the European markets which had normally absorbed 75 per cent of its exports, only those in Britain, Spain, and Portugal remained open. Shipping space available in the second half of 1940 was only 39 per cent that of January to June. The total export volume was cut in two. Because imports remained fairly steady, the export surplus changed to a dangerous deficit. The British policy of blocked sterling balances aggravated the financial situation.

To meet this emergency the Argentine government tried a variety of measures. It promoted increased exportation of goods not previously emphasized, such as dairy products, vegetable oils, sugar, cotton, minerals, and liquors. It fostered greater sales to Spain and the American republics, especially its immediate neighbors and the United States. To protect the Argentine farmer, the government purchased surpluses at fixed prices, urged the use of grains as fuel, and even destroyed large stocks. These policies prevented a collapse of prices but saddled the national treasury with rising obligations.[51]

In this situation, Argentine trade with the United States became of transcendent importance. American markets were the only hope for reduction of accumulating surpluses. With British goods increasingly scarce, Yankee industry became even more relied upon for such essential imports as iron and steel products, automobiles and parts, industrial machinery, and chemicals.[52]

By the end of 1940 the mounting import surplus brought Argentine finances to the point of crisis. As Yankee exporters again became Argentina's principal suppliers, purchases from the United States reached the highest figure since 1930.[53] Though sales also rose, the combination of trade deficits and debt service forced the Argentines during the year to ship $59,000,000 in gold to New York. In December, therefore, the Castillo government felt compelled to negotiate the Export-Import Bank credit of $60,000,000 and the United States Treasury stabilization loan of $50,000,000.[54]

[50] J. C. deWilde and Bryce Wood, "U.S. Trade with Argentina," *Foreign Policy Reports*, XVII (Dec. 1, 1941), pp. 223-224. I have relied on this study for the immediate background of the trade agreement negotiations.

[51] *Ibid.*, pp. 224-228.

[52] Chamber of Commerce of the United States in Argentina, *Trade Relations between Argentina and the United States of America*, pp. 57-59, 90-91; DeWilde and Wood, *op. cit.*, p. 228.

[53] See above, p. 358, Table 4.

[54] DeWilde and Wood, *op. cit.*, p. 227. Also see above, p. 407.

In 1941, however, the trade balance between the two countries shifted sharply. By revising its exchange-control regulations in February, Argentina maintained its level of imports at the 1940 figure. Increased demand for wool, hides, skins, and quebracho extract, stimulated by the defense program, pushed the value of American purchases to twice that of 1940, the highest figure in twenty years. As its share of Argentine exports rose to more than 36 per cent, the United States became Argentina's best customer.[55]

TABLE 5

VALUE OF ARGENTINE TRADE WITH THE UNITED STATES
(IN THOUSANDS OF DOLLARS): 1941-1945

Year	Argentine Exports	Argentine Imports	Argentine Excess of Exports (+); of Imports (−)
1941	$166,618	$109,314	+
1942	149,853	71,866	+
1943	144,864	31,818	+
1944	176,965	29,092	+
1945	170,035	38,765	+

SOURCE: *Statistical Abstract of the United States, 1947*, p. 915.

Circumstances were ripe, therefore, in 1941 for the negotiation of the long-postponed trade agreement. Though surpluses of grain and flaxseed remained, other Argentine products were finding ready markets in the United States. Its export surplus was running at the highest rate since the flush times of World War I. Needing the products of the other, neither nation now feared the danger of flooded markets. Moreover, leaders in Washington were seeking effective measures to draw Argentina into closer continental cooperation.

On May 12 the governments announced formal intention to negotiate the treaty. They required only five months to come to the agreement of October 14.[56] By the letter of its terms Argentina appeared to have won the greater concessions. While it secured reduced tariff rates on goods which comprised nearly 75 per cent of its 1940 exports to the United States, it lowered rates on products composing only 18 per cent of its imports from the United States in that year.[57]

Even at best, under wartime dislocations, the treaty was a gamble for both nations. It could have little immediate effect on the pattern of bilateral trade. Shipping shortages and American priorities would soon curtail available exports to Buenos Aires. Argentina had not won a new

[55] See above, pp. 341, Table 3, and 358, Table 4.

[56] For complete text of the agreement, see Department of State, Executive Agreement Series 277.

[57] DeWilde and Wood, *op. cit.*, pp. 229-231.

market for its grains or fresh beef. Nevertheless the agreement brought advantages to both parties. It laid the basis for future diversification of commercial exchange. It reduced the area of resentment which had long prevailed over discrimination against each other's products. It modified the basic philosophical conflict between the bilateral and multi-lateral concepts of trade.[58]

Hard on the heels of the trade agreement, other developments gave basis for hope that Argentina might be moving toward genuine participation in Hemisphere defense. At the end of October Acting President Castillo announced that the military mission would soon leave for the United States to make essential purchases. It would be accompanied by a financial expert prepared to discuss Lend-Lease aid on American terms.[59] A month later, in consonance with American plans for economic warfare, Foreign Minister Ruiz Guiñazú announced Argentine agreement to sell the United States all its tungsten production for three years.[60] During a tour of the United States by a delegation of Argentine deputies, ex-Foreign Minister Cantilo alluded to "the inescapable necessity of strengthening Pan American relations and particularly the friendship between the United States and the Argentine Republic." [61] On December 2 Castillo assured Ambassador Armour that the Argentine government was determined to comply fully with its continental commitments. The United States, he said, could count on Argentina's full support.[62] On the eve of Pearl Harbor, therefore, Argentina seemed ready to join its sister republics.

American Belligerency and Argentine Nonbelligerency

The Japanese attack upon Pearl Harbor forced Argentina, like each of the American republics, to define its attitude toward Hemisphere solidarity. In view of its slender relations with Japan, the course of its policy presented no difficult decisions. Subsequent declarations of war by Japan's European partners confronted Argentina with a graver problem —the stark necessity of choosing between Germany and the United States. Because of its continental commitments, its tolerance of Nazi activities, and its traditional devotion to noninvolvement, the choice would be hard. American ability to carry Argentina along the direction of its recent cooperative gestures would be put to the fullest test.

[58] Cf. *ibid.*, pp. 231-232.

[59] Armour to Secretary of State, Oct. 19, 1941, and other despatches, NA, DS, 835.24/195; *The New York Times,* Oct. 24, 1941.

[60] República Argentina, Ministerio de Relaciones Exteriores y Culto, *Instrumentos internacionales de carácter bilateral suscriptos por la República Argentina,* II, 981-982.

[61] Department of State, *Bulletin,* V (Oct. 18, 1941), p. 295; Armour to Secretary of State, Dec. 6, 1941, NA, DS, 033.3511/154.

[62] Armour to Secretary of State, Dec. 2, 1941, NA, DS, 810.20Defense/1732.

A variety of considerations, geographic, economic, and strategic, de-termined both the speed with which the American republics reacted to the war and the degree to which they complied with their inter-American obligations. Closely tied to the United States by bonds of commerce and defense, the nine small states of the Caribbean area declared war against all Axis nations by December 10. Equally important to the United States in matters of supply and strategy, but animated by more complicated crosscurrents, the larger Caribbean nations, Mex-ico, Colombia, and Venezuela, moved more slowly, though all severed diplomatic relations by the end of the year. A third group of states—Argentina, Bolivia, Chile, and Uruguay—remote from the North Atlantic and apprehensive about their defenses in case of involvement, neverthe-less granted the United States the status of nonbelligerency. The remain-ing nations, Brazil, Ecuador, Paraguay, and Peru, formally acknowledged their solidarity with the United States, but reserved further action until late January.[63]

Argentina's first reactions to the Japanese aggression were prompt and correct. On December 9 Acting President Castillo advised Secretary Hull that Argentina would adapt its policy to the reciprocal assistance provision of Resolution XV of the Final Act of Havana.[64] In forwarding notice to President Roosevelt of the decree on nonbelligerency, he con-veyed "the friendly wishes of the Argentine Government and people." [65] Four days later Castillo broadened the status to cover America's war with Germany and Italy.[66] In both decrees he reiterated Argentina's neu-trality stand of September 4, 1939.

Distinguished leaders outside the administration, however, and a strong sector of the press did not restrict their reactions to such formal-ities. Ex-President Justo sent a cordial telegram to President Roosevelt.[67] From representatives of all classes, including ex-Foreign Minister Cantilo, the Embassy in Buenos Aires received personal assurances of solidarity. Party leaders in the Chamber of Deputies sent similar expressions to Speaker Sam Rayburn. Strongly condemning the Japanese attack, the principal porteño dailies declared that the Argentine decision did not go far enough nor did it conform to the reciprocal spirit of Havana. Terming Castillo's telegram to President Roosevelt an inadequate re-flection of the depth of feeling of the Argentine people, *La Prensa* called

[63] *Documents on American Foreign Relations*, V, 359. See also D. H. Popper, "The Rio de Janeiro Conference of 1942," *Foreign Policy Reports*, XVIII (April 15, 1942), 27-28.

[64] Department of State, *Bulletin*, V (Dec. 13, 1941), 485. The Minister of Foreign Affairs had given this information to Armour on the previous day.

[65] Castillo's message of December 9 and a telegram from President Ortiz on the following day are printed in *ibid.*, pp. 485-486.

[66] *Ibid.*, pp. 545-546.

[67] *Ibid.*, p. 486.

for an early agreement upon a uniform policy to be adhered to by all American countries.[68]

The Castillo government responded sharply to these pro-American expressions. Its actions during the next ten days left Mr. Armour with grave doubts about the genuineness of Argentine intentions. On December 16 the Acting President invoked the "state of siege," ostensibly to safeguard neutrality and to permit effective maintenance of the position adopted toward the war. Under the suspension of constitutional guarantees, the government could now muzzle public expression and weaken popular demand for closer collaboration with the American republics. It could also strengthen its hand in the face of mounting criticism over provincial election frauds. The first outcome would please the nationalists. Either or both eventualities would satisfy Castillo's Conservative followers who wished no deviation from strict neutrality.[69]

The administration waited less than twenty-four hours to invoke the state of siege against American interests. Without explanation it cancelled an open-air mass meeting planned by the pro-British *Acción Argentina* to pay tribute to President Roosevelt. Besides preventing the American ambassador from reading his chief's message of appreciation, the cancellation effectively silenced anti-Castillo spokesmen who might have used the platform for partisan political attacks.[70]

Other developments in December contributed to Armour's growing conviction that the Argentines would procrastinate and evade. When the German Ambassador requested his passport, Castillo asked that Berlin arrange his departure in a less abrupt manner.[71] Later in the month, resolved to retain full diplomatic representation in Japan, Argentina announced its intention to use an immobilized Italian steamer to convey a new ambassador to Tokyo. With or without cargo, the ship would pick up the diplomat in San Francisco, where the war had stranded him, and carry him across the Pacific. Armour reminded the Foreign Minister of the recent regulation of the Inter-American Economic and Financial Advisory Committee that the nations could use immobilized ships only in inter-American trade.[72]

Under the restrictions of the state of siege, Acting President Castillo and his cabinet were able to consolidate the power they had held so falteringly for many months. As Radical President Ortiz steadily became a closer captive of his illness, the leader of the Conservative oligarchy,

[68] Armour to Secretary of State, Dec. 12, 1941, NA, DS, 740.0011Pacific War/1021.

[69] Armour to Secretary of State, Dec. 24, 1941, *ibid.*, no. 1512.

[70] Armour to Secretary of State, Dec. 19, 1941, NA, DS, 740.0011European War 1939/17974.

[71] Armour to Secretary of State, Dec. 11, 1941, NA, DS, 701.6235/144. See below, p. 420.

[72] Memorandum of interview with Foreign Minister, enclosure in Armour to Secretary of State, Dec. 24, 1941, NA, DS, 835.20/67.

Vice-President Castillo, had slowly strengthened his hold on the executive reins. Aptly known as *El Zorro* ("The Fox"), by practical and political shrewdness Castillo had reached the Casa Rosada after forty-five years as judge, interventor, senator, and cabinet officer.

In December, 1941, the key Ministries of War and Foreign Affairs remained in the hands of General Pedro P. Ramírez and Enrique Ruiz Guiñazú. Veteran of the revolution of 1930 and of military assignments to Germany and Italy, Ramírez was probably more hostile toward the Allies than Castillo himself. Ruiz Guiñazú, in the view of Sumner Welles, was strongly anti-American, a deep believer in authoritarian principles and the Hispanic tradition. To his foreign minister, strongly influenced by pro-Nazi elements in the Army and ultranationalist groups among civilians, Castillo assigned increasing responsibility for the determination of foreign policy.[73]

These were the leaders who through the month of December prepared the position Argentina would defend at the Third Meeting of Foreign Ministers. At the suggestion of Chile and the United States, the Governing Board of the Pan American Union had called the meeting soon after Pearl Harbor. It would meet in Rio de Janeiro on January 15.

The Department of State received abundant warning of the stand the Argentines would take at Rio. At a Cabinet meeting on December 23, Ruiz Guiñazú proposed that Argentina avoid closer cooperation with the United States and adhere to the strictest possible neutrality.[74] A few days later he advised the Brazilian ambassador that his nation was not ready to declare war or even break relations.[75] At the end of the month the Foreign Minister invited the Conference delegates from Bolivia, Chile, Paraguay, and Uruguay to meet in Buenos Aires, presumably to form a bloc which would oppose American objectives.[76] In a statement to the press on January 7, he announced that Argentina would agree to no acts of "pre-belligerency" at the Rio meeting.[77]

If the Argentine delegates hewed strictly to this line at Rio, they were certain to run full front against the objectives sought by President Roosevelt. To eliminate Axis espionage and subversion in the Hemisphere, he believed that all the American republics should sever diplomatic, commercial, and financial relations. To secure the Americas

---

[73] Sumner Welles, *The Time for Decision*, pp. 225, 229-230.

[74] Armour to Secretary of State, Dec. 24, 1941, NA, DS, 740.0011Pacific War/1512.

[75] Armour to Secretary of State, Dec. 27, 1941, NA, DS, 710.Consultation(3)/121.

[76] Welles, *op. cit.*, p. 230. In his *Memoirs* Hull mentioned Peru instead of Bolivia (II, p. 1144). Ruiz Guiñazú later denied that he had sought to create a bloc (*La política argentina y el futuro de América*, pp. 188-190). Published in 1944, this volume includes an appendix, which is described as a "necessary rectification" of Welles's chapter on "The Good Neighbor Policy" in *Time for Decision*.

[77] Quoted from *La Nación* in O. E. Smith, Jr., *Yankee Diplomacy: U.S. Intervention in Argentina*, p. 53.

against both military attack and economic strain, he believed that all should agree upon cooperative measures. Without seeking to influence any nation to declare war, Sumner Welles and the American delegates were instructed to try to persuade all to join in these actions.[78]

The showdown between the two confirmed positions developed quickly. Appropriately, the three republics which had broken diplomatic relations, but not declared war, Mexico, Colombia, and Venezuela, introduced a resolution which would extend their action to all. The controversial clause of the draft was Article 3, which categorically required severance of relations with the three Axis powers. "The American Republics," it read,

> declare that, by virtue of their solidarity and in order to protect and preserve their freedom and integrity, none of them may continue to maintain political, commercial, or financial relations with the governments of Germany, Italy, and Japan; and, in like manner, they declare that, in full exercise of their sovereignty, they will take the measures suitable to the defense of the New World which they may consider in each case practical and advantageous.[79]

The Argentine and Chilean delegates alone refused to approve this mandate.

Both by his actions at Rio and by his reports of the meeting Ruiz Guiñazú revealed the abyss which now separated Argentine and American views. A portion of his arguments related to international principles and national policies, a portion to methods of implementing them. In his interpretation, rupture of diplomatic relations was a step toward "pre-belligerency" and pre-belligerency a step toward war. The Argentine people, he said, favored neutrality and their delegation had come to Rio to talk of peace, not of war. In any case, the meeting was called for the purpose of consulting, not for adopting binding actions. Moreover, under the Argentine constitution, only Congress could declare war. Hence, the delegates could not approve a resolution which almost certainly would lead to involvement.[80]

The Foreign Minister asserted that Argentina wished to cooperate with the American republics and to comply with all of its inter-American obligations. Committed by these only to neutrality, it had already moved beyond this point to declare the United States a nonbelligerent. The status of nonbelligerency, he thought, would permit Argentina to lend

[78] Welles, *op. cit.*, pp. 225-226.
[79] *La Prensa*, Jan. 18, 1942. This *porteño* daily reported Conference activities in great detail. See especially the issues of Jan. 18, 20-25.
[80] República Argentina, Ministerio de Relaciones Exteriores y Culto, *Tercera reunión de consulta de ministros de relaciones exteriores de las Repúblicas Americanas,* pp. 10-11, 24: Ruiz Guiñazú, *op. cit.*, pp. 21, 35, 79-80.

collaboration which few other American nations could give. Defense of its own territory and sovereignty by each nation was the form of reciprocal assistance envisioned in the agreements of Havana.[81]

Ruiz Guiñazú reserved his harshest comments for an attack upon Washington's elaboration of the doctrine of solidarity. Its policies were tending to create an entity superior to the state, a kind of "super-sovereignty." If not checked, the tendency would destroy the individuality of nations and the corollary right of self-determination.[82]

Through committee sessions and extramural conferences Welles and the other leaders sought to find a compromise solution. To meet the Argentine reservation that a diplomatic break must have congressional approval, the committee inserted in Article 3 the phrase "in the exercise of their sovereignty and in conformity with their constitutional institutions and powers, provided the latter are in agreement." Five days after the introduction of the resolution, January 21, with the skillful intermediation of Brazilian Foreign Minister Oswaldo Aranha, Ruiz Guiñazú was brought to approve this draft.[83] In spite of Secretary Hull's suspicion that Argentina had made sure of another loophole in an inter-American agreement, Mr. Welles had been unable to find a more acceptable formula.

Meanwhile, in Buenos Aires, Acting President Castillo was closely following developments. On the 21st he told Ambassador Armour that Argentina would not approve a resolution which required a break with the Axis powers.[84] A day later, by withdrawing his approval of the modified article, Ruiz Guiñazú reflected the President's position. His substitute for Article 3, a thinned-out shadow of the original three-nation proposal, fell like a bombshell in Conference halls. While retaining the phrases protecting Argentina's constitutional processes, Castillo had replaced the obligatory clause with a recommendatory one.[85]

Confronted by the adamant stand of the Argentines, delegates of the other states found little space for maneuver. The key to the impasse lay in the hands of the Brazilian President, Getulio Vargas. Though himself eager to cooperate with the United States, his Army leaders refused to endorse any action that was not equally acceptable to Argentina. If the Conference could find a compromise formula, Vargas assured Welles, Brazil would soon break relations. Both men were aware that Bolivia,

---

[81] *Tercera reunión de consulta*, pp. 10, 15-16, 25-26; Ruiz Guiñazú, *op. cit.*, pp. 80-82.

[82] *Ibid.*, 15-16; *Tercera reunión de consulta*, p. 10.

[83] Welles, *op. cit.*, p. 232; Hull, *op. cit.*, pp. 1146-1147; *La Prensa*, Jan. 21-22, 1941.

[84] Hull, *op. cit.*, pp. 1147-1148; Popper, *op. cit.*, pp. 29-30. Welles's task at this critical point was not helped by Senator Tom Connally's ill-timed remark that "Mr. Castillo will change his mind or the Argentines will change their President" (*The New York Times*, Jan. 22, 1941).

[85] Welles, *op. cit.*, pp. 232-233.

Ecuador, Paraguay, and Peru would probably follow Brazil's lead. Under these circumstances, the delegates favoring the original resolution faced a hard choice: to hold the line and split the Conference or to accept the watered-down version and retain unanimity. In the interests of inter-American solidarity, Welles and nineteen other delegates acceded to Argentine obduracy.[86]

Secretary Hull, who had fathered the principle of unanimity since 933, was incensed by the Under Secretary's unapproved action. His vexation over Argentine obstructionism had been growing since the Buenos Aires Conference. By the opening of the Rio meeting he had come to believe that the time for compromise had passed. Argentina must agree to eliminate itself as a base for Axis operations, he had concluded, or must go its own way. In his *Memoirs* he insists that Mr. Welles understood his views.[87]

To the Under Secretary the choice had been difficult but clear-cut. Though he preferred the original draft resolution stipulating obligatory rupture of relations, in hour-by-hour negotiations with Ruiz Guiñazú, Aranha, and the other delegates he came to believe that unanimity, even on a less decisive resolution, would best serve the interests of continental security.[88] Mr. Hull's now famous telephonic dressing-down of his deputy, with President Roosevelt on the wire, came too late to affect the decision.[89] It did, however, open a rift between the two men which would steadily widen. After the Argentine revolution of June, 1943, it would lead to Welles's resignation and open the door to Hull's substitution of coercion for the Under Secretary's policy of persuasion and compromise.[90]

Upon other important items introduced at Rio Ruiz Guiñazú raised no vigorous dissent. He approved resolutions recommending severance of commercial and financial relations with Axis nations, closing of Axis-controlled telecommunication stations, and development of economic resources. He did not oppose the creation of either the Inter-American Defense Board or the Emergency Advisory Committee for Political Defense.[91]

Argentina, therefore, could register complete satisfaction with the results of the Rio Conference. It had approved only declarations and recommendations. Without violating its plighted word, it could comply

[86] Welles, *Seven Decisions That Shaped History*, pp. 109-114; Laurence Duggan, *The Americas: The Search for Hemisphere Unity*, pp. 88-89.

[87] II, 1144-1146. The Secretary does not refer to the dilemma presented the Conference by Brazil's domestic situation.

[88] Welles, *op. cit.*, pp. 233-234.

[89] Hull, *op. cit.*, pp. 1148-1149.

[90] Cf. A. P. Whitaker, *The United States and Argentina*, pp. 112-113, and Smith, *op. cit.*, pp. 63-64.

[91] *Tercera reunión de consulta*, pp. 38-39; Department of State, *Bulletin*, VI, 117-141.

with these as it chose. Together with Chile, it had avoided diplomatic isolation from both the American republics and the Axis powers. It had clung fast to its foreign policies of a century's making. Argentina was free to go its own way.

The Beginnings of Coercion

The policy of "prudent neutrality," to which Argentina held firm at the Rio Conference, remained the lodestar of President Castillo's course until his overthrow by military revolt on June 4, 1943. Unremitting pressure from Washington, exerted both through its own agencies and through the organs of the Inter-American System, failed to dislodge the Argentines from their charted path.

On the morrow of the Rio meeting only Argentina and Chile failed to carry out the recommended rupture of relations they had approved. The authorities at Buenos Aires refused even to fulfill the numerous lesser recommendations to which they had readily assented.[92] Steadfastly they maintained financial, economic, and telecommunication relations with the Tripartite nations. In February they denied refuge to Axis diplomats expelled from other American republics and dropped representation of Italian interests in Mexico and Central America.[93] They had finally agreed to the recall of the German ambassador.[94] But further steps they would not take.

In both Buenos Aires and Washington public officials had received abundant intelligence on the extent to which Axis agents had penetrated Argentine economic and cultural life.[95] To President Castillo and Foreign Minister Ruiz Guiñazú these activities represented no threat to Argentine sovereignty, at least none that justified fuller compliance with Washington's promptings. Lacking arms or a place to secure them, they contended, Argentina could risk no action that might lead to involvement.[96] In any case, the nation was fulfilling its inter-American commitments as fully as its national interests and constitutional processes would permit.[97] If any substantial portion of the Argentine people disagreed with these official views, enforcement of the "state of siege" effectively blunted their active opposition.

To Secretary Hull, on the other hand, preoccupied with making diplomacy the handmaiden of the armed forces, Castillo's policies left

[92] See above, p. 419.
[93] *The New York Times*, Feb. 25, 26, 1942.
[94] See above, pp. 410, 415.
[95] See above, pp. 409-410, and note 46.
[96] Armour to Secretary of State, April 10, 1942 NA, DS, 835.34/583.
[97] Even the Argentine-American Chamber of Commerce in Buenos Aires supported this position. On February 14 it issued an extensive declaration detailing Argentine actions favorable to the democracies (*La Prensa*, Feb. 15, 1942).

the Americas unguarded on a vulnerable flank. Unless Argentina could be closed to Nazi subversion, espionage, and financial machinations, the Secretary feared, the security of the Hemisphere would remain in jeopardy. Confident of the pro-Allies sympathies of the Argentine people, he apparently believed that they might be induced to prod their government from its inflexible position. By the spring of 1942, therefore, the resolute Tennessean prepared to exert pressure, economic and political, American and inter-American, against the unyielding Castillo.[98]

Argentina first felt the cutting edge of Washington's coercive policy when Ruiz Guiñazú approached Sumner Welles in Rio for Lend-Lease assistance. The Under Secretary promptly rebuffed his request for airplanes, warships, and arms and ammunition. Only by severing relations with the Axis, he said, and by contributing its share to the defense of the Hemisphere could Argentina qualify for American arms. To the foreign minister, this was unjustified discrimination; to Welles, it was discrimination called forth by Argentina's refusal to join its sister republics.[99]

In Washington Secretary Hull enlisted the cooperation of the War and Navy Departments to forestall the requests of the Argentine military mission which had arrived in December. This decision dealt a hard blow to the Navy Department, earnestly desirous of close cooperation with the Argentine Navy. It hoped to assure transit, if it became necessary, through the Strait of Magellan as well as to offset the pro-German leanings of the Argentine Army. When in April Washington suggested that Argentine vessels might assist in convoy of shipping to the United States, Ruiz Guiñazú refused to risk the possible creation of a state of belligerency.[100] Their failure to secure arms in Washington, together with the reported arrival of war materials in Brazil and Uruguay, aroused the concern of Argentine military and naval leaders but did not sway the Castillo government.[101]

In withholding military aid, Washington played its highest trump, but it did not lack other strong cards. In April, in May, and again in June, the State Department directed Ambassador Armour to make representations to the Argentine government—against Axis espionage, on behalf of Argentine convoys, in support of the American black list of Axis firms.[102] When the Inter-American Conference on Coordination of Police and Judicial Measures met in Buenos Aires in May-June, it placed the force of collective action behind the American desire for continental solidarity. In a series of resolutions, the Conference successfully over-

[98] Hull, *op. cit.*, p. 1377.
[99] Welles, *op. cit.*, pp. 228-229.
[100] Hull, *op. cit.*, p. 1378; *The Christian Science Monitor*, May 4, 1942.
[101] Armour to Secretary of State, NA, DS, 835.34/583.
[102] Hull, *op. cit.*, pp. 1377-1380.

came Argentine opposition to proposed surveillance measures against Axis nationals.[103]

Meanwhile, by the middle of 1942, the spread of war cut more sharply into the mainstream of Argentine life. Lack of shipping space reduced imports of manufactured goods. Submarine sinkings destroyed essential cargoes of tin plate, crude rubber, newsprint, iron, and steel. Scarcity of newsprint halved the size of the great porteño dailies. Shortage of fuel kept homes and offices even cooler than usual. Rising costs, both of imported and home-produced goods, lowered the standard of living.[104]

The sinking of the Argentine freighter *Tercero* on June 22, two months after the German attack on the *Victoria*, dramatized anew the plight of neutrals in modern war. The Chamber of Deputies unanimously approved a resolution calling upon the foreign minister to explain the action taken against the Nazi government. Within the harsh limits imposed by the "state of siege," press and congressional spokesmen called for implementation of the Rio recommendations.[105]

These appeals for action only deepened Castillo's resolution. While extending the blackout against popular expression, his government accepted German promises to pay damages for the *Tercero* and to avoid future attacks on Argentine vessels. When in late June Germany announced its submarine blockade of the United States Atlantic seaboard, the Navy Ministry knuckled under by ordering Argentine merchant ships to avoid east coast ports.[106] In July a special representative of President Castillo formally approached the German chargé d'affaires for military assistance.[107]

The death of President Roberto Ortiz in early July left Castillo firmly ensconced in the presidential saddle. The passing in this critical year of former Presidents Alvear and Justo and former Vice-President Roca removed the last vestiges of effective opposition leadership.

During the late months of 1942, however, in a series of unrelated steps, the Castillo government seemed to veer toward cooperation with the American states. When Brazil declared war against Germany and Italy in late August, Argentina promptly gave it nonbelligerent status. In September the Ministry of Interior dissolved the German Federation of Cultural and Welfare Societies, alleged front for the Nazi Party. By executive decree of October 8th Castillo intervened telecommunica-

---

[103] *Documents on American Foreign Relations*, IV, 366-376.

[104] See a series of reports from Buenos Aires, Montevideo, and Asunción in *The Christian Science Monitor*, April 16, 18, 20, May 13, 23, June 2, 1942.

[105] *Memoria, 1942-1943*, pp. 23-29; *The New York Times*, June 26, 1942.

[106] *Memoria, 1942-1943*, p. 50; *The New York Times*, June 15, July 8, 1942.

[107] Department of State, *Consultation among the American Republics with Respect to the Argentine Situation*, (Dept. of State Publication 2473, Inter-American Series 29), p. 6.

tion enterprises, created military zones around national ports, and directed registration of personnel connected with maritime activities.[108]

But all these measures were but straws in the face of strong pro-Axis winds blowing from the Casa Rosada. Repeatedly during the same period President Castillo and Foreign Minister Ruiz Guiñazú reavowed their faith in the kind of neutrality they had fashioned. When in July the Chamber of Deputies asked him to explain why Argentina had not carried out the Rio recommendations, the Foreign Minister charged the United States with trying to dominate the whole continent and reiterated Argentine friendship with the Axis countries. When in late September the deputies finally approved a resolution calling for rupture of relations with the Axis, Castillo rested content to "take note" of the recommendation.[109] Returning to Washington in October from a visit to Buenos Aires, Ambassador Espil reported to Under Secretary Welles "that President Castillo was completely satisfied that the policy he had been pursuing to now was the policy which was desired by the great majority of the Argentine people and was in fact the policy which would prove to be the most beneficial to Argentine national interests." [110]

Confronted by this wall of resistance, State Department officials acted to tighten the pressure against the Argentines. Blunt speaking now replaced diplomatic niceties. Two days after his conference with Espil, in a speech delivered in Boston, Welles publicly rebuked both Argentina and Chile. "I cannot believe," he said,

> that these two republics will long continue to permit their brothers and neighbors of the Americas, engaged as they are in a life-and-death struggle to preserve the liberties and integrity of the New World, to be stabbed in the back by Axis emissaries operating in the territory and under the free institutions of these two republics of the Western Hemispere.[111]

Secretary Hull chose this moment to transmit to the Argentine government additional revelations of Nazi propaganda and espionage directed from Buenos Aires. On November 3, 4, and 10, Ambassador Armour delivered three extensive memoranda to the Foreign Office. When on the 9th Espil officially requested that the documents not be released, Hull indicted the Argentine government for its dereliction in suppressing subversive activities.[112]

To these proddings, for a time, the Castillo regime again seemed to

[108] *Memoria, 1942-1943*, pp. 37-44; *The New York Times*, Sept. 15, 1942.
[109] *Ibid.*, July 22, Sept. 30, Oct. 2, 1942.
[110] Memorandum of conversation, Oct. 6, 1942, NA, DS, 835.00/291. See also Hull, *op. cit.*, p. 1381.
[111] *The New York Times*, Oct. 9, 1942.
[112] Hull, *op. cit.*, p. 1382; *Memoria, 1942-1943*, p. 29.

edge in the direction desired by Washington. It promptly ordered curbs against all activities by representatives of the Tripartite states and their satellites which might be detrimental to the security of the American republics. In December the federal courts preferred charges against thirty-eight alleged Axis espionage agents, including several German diplomats. On Pearl Harbor Day the government permitted a great public rally to pay "homage to Roosevelt." In January it declared *persona non grata* the German naval attaché.[113]

In spite of these actions, Secretary Hull believed that the Argentine government had not taken adequate steps to halt the subversion which threatened the Hemisphere.[114] Axis agents, the Department's intelligence sources had revealed, were operating from Argentine bases under orders from the German High Command. They were collecting vital data on Allied ship and troop movements, American armaments and war production, and Latin American defense measures. They operated clandestine radio stations to relay their findings to Germany. Their espionage had resulted in grave loss of life and property to the United States and its allies.[115]

Concluding that the full weight of Hemisphere influence must be brought to bear upon the Castillo government, the State Department now prepared a timetable of actions. First, it compiled an extensive memorandum embodying charges against Argentina's neglect. On January 21, it transmitted the document to the Inter-American Emergency Advisory Committee for Political Defense, which had been created in Montevideo as a result of Resolution XVII of the Rio Conference of Foreign Ministers. Argentina received a copy on the same day.[116]

To wring the fullest impact from its incriminating disclosures, the State Department had timed delivery of the memorandum with meticulous care. It reached Montevideo and Buenos Aires on the day following Chile's rupture of relations with Germany and Japan. The Inter-American Committee voted to release it immediately.[117] To these developments Argentina reacted with indignation. In a special communiqué, while underscoring the government's recent actions against German nationals, the Foreign Office protested the Committee's procedures. President Castillo bluntly announced that Chile's decision would bring no change in Argentina's attitude toward the war.[118] At the end of January, 1943,

---

[113] *The New York Times*, Nov. 19, Dec. 5, 9, 1942; Jan. 12, 1943.

[114] Hull, *op. cit.*, p. 1382.

[115] Emergency Advisory Committee for Political Defense, *Annual Report Submitted to the Governments of the American Republics, July, 1943*, pp. 107-110.

[116] Hull, *op. cit.*, pp. 1382-1383.

[117] *Ibid.*, p. 1383, the entire document, together with the covering resolution of the Committee, is printed in its *Annual Report, 1943*, pp. 105-129.

[118] Hull, *op. cit.*, p. 1383; Armour to Secretary of State, Feb. 5, 1943, NA, DS, 835.00/1358.

therefore, now the lone American state from which Axis agents could operate with impunity, Argentina stood isolated in the Hemisphere.

After this failure to bring Argentina to book through collective political pressure, Washington turned again to its own economic devices. Eying the war boom upon which the ruling classes continued to grow fat, the State Department's Latin America experts recommended the toughening of economic restrictions. American exporters and importers, including companies firmly established in the Argentine trade, pressed for decisive action against the last Hemisphere neutral.[119] Ambassador Armour urged closer Anglo-American cooperation to threaten Argentina with loss of its rich markets for meat surpluses. Expanding food demands, however, of British consumers and Allied armies frustrated American exploitation of this vulnerable Argentine salient.[120]

Unwilling yet to adopt economic sanctions, Washington acted in February to restrict succor to the strained Argentine economy. The Board of Economic Warfare invoked a tight system of export controls to limit shipments of much-needed consumer goods, machine equipment, and transportation replacements. Only essential materials for the maintenance and operation of meat packing plants and mines producing tungsten and beryllium escaped the stringent regulations.[121] In April the United States and its allies barred Argentine participation in the United Nations Food Conference in Hot Springs, Arkansas. On his circle tour of South America Vice-President Henry A. Wallace bypassed the Argentine capital.[122]

To these economic pressures the Castillo government responded by increasing its dependence upon Axis-influenced nationalist elements. Ruiz Guiñazú clung to his position that Argentina had fulfilled all its inter-American obligations. By subscribing to Hemisphere principles and resolutions, he maintained, Argentina had not sacrificed its right of self-determination.[123]

As the months of 1943 wore on, Castillo's swelling intransigence and open flirtation with pro-totalitarian influences deepened the cleavages which had long rent Argentine society. To whatever extent they agreed with his political philosophy, many Conservative supporters could not accept the President's support of the more flagrant nationalist groups. The nationalists themselves were riven by sharp divisions. The Radical opposition was leaderless and disorganized. Like the government itself, each political faction lacked a program and a purpose. Without friends

[119] *The New York Times,* Jan. 26, 1943.

[120] To Secretary of State, Feb. 5, 1943, NA, DS, 835.00/1358.

[121] *Documents on American Foreign Relations,* V, 143-144. The licensing system became effective on April 1, 1943.

[122] *The New York Times,* April 18, 1943; *Documents on American Foreign Relations,* V, 297ff.

[123] Ruiz Guiñazú, *op. cit.,* pp. 14-15, 30.

and without a mission, Argentina was drifting—drifting in a world that demanded firmness and decision.[124]

Winds blowing off the North Atlantic throughout the early years of World War II gave the Argentine nation a harsh buffeting. Relentless pressure from the United States repeatedly forced the Castillo regime to reconsider its determined neutrality. Whistling Axis propaganda through the streets of Buenos Aires itself, the *pampero* effectively stiffened official resistance to these urgings.[125] A proud, energetic people, possessed of a rich land and a noble tradition, seemed incapable of uniting to express the national will. Throughout the trying period they indulged in the untimely luxury of empty factionalism. The great majority appeared content to accept the dictates of leaders without a program. Finally, in June, 1943, a party with little to show for its thirteen-year tenure succumbed to another luxury the nation could ill afford—military revolt in the midst of world-wide war.

[124] Cf. Rennie, *The Argentine Republic*, p. 342.
[125] This violent southwest wind gave its name to one of the most pernicious pro-German newspapers, *El Pampero.*

XXIV

WORLD WAR II AND AFTER:
COERCION OF A RELUCTANT ALLY, 1943-1947

Diplomatic relations between Argentina and the United States during and after the late months of World War II dipped to the lowest level in their century and a half of intercourse.[1] Two proud nations, which during the thirties had subordinated their mutual aversions to the larger cause of Hemisphere security, now imperilled the very protective machinery they had helped to assemble. For nearly four years after the Argentine Army throttled constitutional government in Buenos Aires in June, 1943, leaders of the two nations indulged in a ceaseless round of bitter charge and countercharge. Neither in war nor in peace were they able to agree on common objectives or lay aside national goals for the general welfare.

The Argentine military leaders who succeeded President Castillo in office willfully refused to place their nation at the side of the other American republics in the prosecution of the war. They refused even to move convincingly against the propaganda and espionage activities of Axis agents within their own borders. As they entrenched themselves in all branches of government, they imposed upon Argentine life more and more of the authoritarian philosophy against which the Allied nations were fighting.

To Secretary Hull, who had endured a decade of irritation at the hands of Argentina, its conduct now appeared to menace the solidarity of the Americas and the war efforts of the Allies. He and his successors in office utilized every method short of force to bring the Argentines into line—denial of military aid, economic sanctions, moral suasion, verbal castigation, unilateral and collective nonrecognition, even diplomatic intervention.[2]

[1] Two American historians have written detailed accounts of Argentine-American relations in these years: O. E. Smith, Jr., *Yankee Diplomacy: U.S. Intervention in Argentina*, pp. 77-168, and A. P. Whitaker, *The United States and Argentina*, pp. 115-150, 209-219.

[2] Cf. Edward O. Guerrant, *Roosevelt's Good Neighbor Policy*, p. 36.

In the end, every form of coercion failed. Though pressed into a diplomatic break with the Axis and ultimately into a declaration of war, the Argentines avoided to the last active participation in hostilities. Even after the return of peace, the military adventurers in Buenos Aires pertinaciously resisted Washington's efforts to moderate their totalitarian tendencies.

The Army Revolt of June 4, 1943

The strong Army units which left their big base at Campo de Mayo in the early hours of June 4, 1943, swiftly occupied the Casa Rosada and other important government office buildings.[3] The ease with which they ousted the fading administration of President Castillo belied the breadth and depth of the changes their leaders were soon to bring to every phase of Argentine life, public and private. A powerful military clique would soon scuttle the traditions, overturn the way of life, and destroy the hard-won values of an energetic people. The revolt they spawned would come to be viewed as one of the epochal events of Argentine history.

To American leaders who for many months had struggled against Argentine recalcitrance, as well as to pro-Allies sympathizers in the southern republic, it was natural to see in the revolt what they wished to see. To them an attempt to unseat President Castillo was an attack upon the policies he had supported—neutralism, anti-Americanism, and pro-totalitarianism. That the leaders who replaced him would move to implement Argentine commitments to the Inter-American System they hoped and expected.

Even in the welter of confusion which attended the creation of a provisional government, Ambassador Norman Armour observed hopeful signs that these expectations might be realized.[4] General Arturo Rawson, first provisional President, who appointed as Minister of Foreign Affairs a former chief of police of Buenos Aires, soon gave way to General Pedro P. Ramírez. In a general reshuffling of the Cabinet, Ramírez named to two key positions men who promptly asserted that Argentina would break relations with the Axis. The new Minister of Foreign Affairs was Admiral Segundo R. Storni, who had spent several years in Philadelphia during the building of the battleship *Rivadavia*. The new Minister of Finance, the only civilian, was Jorge Santamarina, president of the Banco de la Nación and guardian of the interests of the landholding oligarchy. Both were said to be pro-American.[5]

[3] Two interesting accounts of the revolution by American observers on the spot are Ruth and Leonard Greenup, *Revolution Before Breakfast* (Chapel Hill, 1947) and Ray Josephs, *Argentine Diary* (New York, 1944).

[4] To Secretary of State, June 7, 8, 14, 1943, NA, DS, 835.00/1483, 1496, 1560.

[5] Armour to Secretary of State, June 14, 1943, *ibid.*, no. 1563; Ysabel F. Rennie, *The Argentine Republic*, pp. 347-348; Bernardo Rabinovitz, *Sucedió en la Argentina (1943-1956): lo que no se dijo*, pp. 18-19.

When the Ramírez government promptly ended martial law, returned the Army to its barracks, and banned the use of code messages to Axis embassies and nationals, the American republics moved toward immediate recognition.[6] Just one week after the revolt, following Foreign Minister Storni's public statement that Argentina wished "to pursue a policy of most complete collaboration with all the Republics of the Continent, particularly with the United States," Washington joined the other states in recognition.[7] Ramírez and Storni soon indicated to Ambassador Armour that Argentina would break relations with the Axis, probably by August 15.[8]

But, in spite of this quick recognition of the revolutionary government, the Roosevelt administration did not hasten to change its basic attitude toward Argentina. Hesitant to shift tactics with the speed Armour seemed to be recommending, the Latin America experts in the State Department urged restraint. They believed that modification of policy should await tangible implementation of the words of Ramírez and Storni.

State Department officials could have known—and probably did—that the Argentine revolt stemmed primarily from domestic, not international, conditions. It did not spring from an insistent popular demand that the nation change its foreign policy; the new government would cling to neutrality as tenaciously as the old. It did not spring from righteous indignation over the widespread corruption in the Castillo administration; the new leaders did not bring the guilty to book for "crimes" that were traditional in Argentine public life.[9]

Of many causes suggested for the June revolt, the most convincing is that of the deep-seated economic conflicts in the Argentine nation. Aided by the impingement of wartime import shortages, industrialization was spreading rapidly in Argentina. As immigration ceased, factories recruited their laborers from the hinterland. Because Conservative presidents since 1930 had ignored social reform, the growing working class was ripe for unionization. Organization might lead to increased ballot-box pressure. This was the specter that haunted the great estancieros as the election of September, 1943, approached.[10]

Target of the agrarian oligarchy was Robustiano Patrón Costas, the heir apparent selected by President Castillo. As a grower of sugar in the Province of Tucumán, the candidate was of the great landholding class; but as a refiner of sugar, he was more industrialist than estanciero.

[6] Sumner Welles, *Where Are We Heading?*, p. 195.
[7] Department of State, *Bulletin*, VIII (June 12, 1943), 520; Rabinovitz, *op. cit.*, p. 26.
[8] *The Memoirs of Cordell Hull*, II, 1384.
[9] Felix J. Weil, *Argentine Riddle*, p. 54.
[10] *Ibid.*, pp. 42-44; Robert J. Alexander, *The Perón Era*, pp. 3-11. Each of these volumes contains an excellent analysis of the background of the revolt. Weil emphasizes the economic factors, Alexander the position of labor.

The choice presented the nation seemed that between a strong proponent of industrialization and an opposition candidate, still unnamed,
who might seek to grant the demands of the growing laboring class.[11]

To the oligarchy either of these alternatives was class-suicide. Their
best interests, it appeared, could be more effectively served by avoiding both choices. This they could do by resorting to the tested Latin
technique of revolution and dictatorship to forestall the election. If
the growth of industrialization was inexorable, then the estancieros must
move into position to control it. Known since the Uriburu revolt of
1930 for his opposition to democracy, General Ramírez might fit the
specifications of the diehard landowners. When rumors spread that
Castillo might be preparing to sack his minister of war, the seeds of
revolt sprouted.

Whether the military men who fostered the June revolt were merely
agents of the scheming oligarchs or ruthless exploiters of a situation
made to order for the attainment of their own ends is not clear. Without question, in any case, what the Army first posed as a routine provisional government soon transformed itself into a Frankenstein monster
the Argentine people were helpless to control.

Argentina Breaks Relations

The confusion and improvisation which marked the early days of the
new government suggested that the military leaders themselves were
jousting over the objectives of their movement. Independent actions
by newly designated officials seemed to contradict each other. In the
Casa Rosada itself, without clear explanation General Arturo Rawson
gave way to General Ramírez after two days. The Cabinet of Rawson,
allegedly pro-Ally, contained the names of two men on the American
black list. The Cabinet of his successor, believed to be pro-Axis, included
figures of pro-American tendencies.

Once established in the driver's seat, Ramírez held the reins of an
unmatched and unmanageable team. Hoping for military aid that
would assist Argentine equalization of Brazil's advancing military
preparations, General Rawson's supporters seemed to favor closer
cooperation with the United States. Pulling in the opposite direction, a
group of nationalistic young colonels and majors (the GOU) were conniving to take Argentina down the road to criollo totalitarianism.[12] One
of the behind-the-scenes leaders of this conspiratorial band was Colonel
Juan D. Perón, veteran of the Uriburu revolt in 1930, student of fascist

[11] Weil, op. cit., pp. 42-43.
[12] The initials were commonly understood to signify both the name of the group,
Grupo de Oficiales Unidos, and its slogan, *Gobierno, Orden, Unión*. An occasional
Argentine writer refers to the *Grupo Obra de Unificación*.

methods in Italy, Germany, and Spain, born leader of men.[13] Throughout the rest of the war period, as factions waxed and waned, these divergent elements struggled for the seats of power.

The leaders of the GOU made no secret of their plans for Argentina.[14] "As in Germany, our government will be an inflexible dictatorship," they boldly announced in a proclamation widely distributed weeks before the revolt. Stridently they proclaimed their intentions toward Argentina's neighbors. "Alliances will be our next step," they promised.

> Paraguay is already with us. We will get Bolivia and Chile. Together and united with these countries, it will be easy to exert pressure on Uruguay. These five nations can easily attract Brazil, due to its type of government and its important groups of Germans. Once Brazil has fallen, the South American continent will be ours. . . .[15]

Against this backdrop of confusion and intrigue Secretary Hull sought to shape effective action. His first step, on June 18, was to transmit to Ambassador Armour eleven specific measures the new government must take to demonstrate its sincerity. Besides severance of relations, diplomatic, financial, and commercial, these included effective control of subversive activities, foreign funds, clandestine radio stations, commercial aviation, and press and radio propaganda. These and other actions, thought the Secretary, Argentina had already committed itself to carry out.[16]

The Ramírez government, however, appeared to move in the opposite direction. During the next month it lifted the ban on use of coded messages, closed several pro-Allies newspapers, and disbanded important organizations working for the Allied cause that even Castillo had tolerated. At the same time, by postponing elections, censoring outgoing news reports, and barring discussion of foreign policy, it began to clamp down on civil liberties.[17]

When, toward the end of July, the government had taken no steps toward rupture with the Axis, Secretary Hull recalled Armour to Washington. He and President Roosevelt had determined "to re-examine the whole question of our relations with Argentina." Before his departure, while informing Foreign Minister Storni that he was being recalled for consultation, the Ambassador requested a clear, written statement of Argentina's position.[18]

---

[13] Rennie, *op. cit.*, pp. 347-349.

[14] For a comprehensive analysis of their program, as subsequently developed by Perón, see George I. Blanksten, *Perón's Argentina*, pp. 161-439.

[15] As quoted in Alexander, *op. cit.*, p. 13. See also Comisión Nacional de Investigaciones, *Libro Negro de la segunda tiranía, Decreto ley No. 14.988/56*, pp. 31-32.

[16] Hull, *op. cit.*, pp. 1384-1385.

[17] *The New York Times*, June 19, 26, July 16, 17, 1943; Smith, *op. cit.*, p. 80.

[18] Hull, *op. cit.*, pp. 1385-1386.

Through a long, importunate letter to Secretary Hull on August 5, Storni complied with Armour's request. The letter revealed on the part of its authors an extraordinary combination of naïveté, self-righteousness, and reluctance to face the facts of international life. Storni assured the Secretary of the democratic convictions of the Argentine leaders and their indissoluble links with the other American republics. He detailed the extensive collaboration with which the nation had served the Allied cause. He pleaded the need of time to clean up the corruption of the Castillo regime and to reorient the people to international realities. To break relations with the Axis at the present stage of the war, he argued, would be as unchivalrous an act as Italy's attack upon France.

Nevertheless, Storni concluded, President Roosevelt could hasten the evolution of anti-Axis opinion by making "a gesture of genuine friendship toward our people." The gesture would take the form of "airplanes, spare parts, armaments, and machinery to restore Argentina to the position of equilibrium to which it is entitled with respect to other South American countries." [19]

In his reply of August 30, Secretary Hull resorted to the ungloved fists of denunciation and indictment. Item by item he recited Argentina's failure to abide by its own inter-American commitments. Acknowledging its contributions of food and raw materials to the United Nations, he underscored the profits which accrued to the producers. As to the request for Lend-Lease arms and munitions, Hull insisted that these were available only for the defense of the Hemisphere, not for the maintenance of the balance of power among American states.[20] Hull's rebuff of the Argentine overture led immediately to the resignation of Foreign Minister Storni and the dismissal of two Ministry officials, the under secretary and the head of the American Affairs Section. The removal of these moderating influences and the appointment of General Alberto Gilbert as Storni's successor hastened extremist control of the military government.[21]

The exchange with Storni exposed to Secretary Hull the true nature of the "Argentine question." Until his retirement in November, 1944, he sought to meet the problem head-on. Simultaneously he pursued three policies: to press the Argentine government into effective collaboration with the Allies; to forestall its efforts to extend its influence in South America; and to secure British support for his coercive steps.[22]

Ambassador Armour returned to Buenos Aires in October in time to witness new extensions of GOU influence and effective consolidation of

[19] Department of State, *Bulletin,* IX (Sept. 11, 1943), 160-162.
[20] *Ibid.,* pp. 162-166.
[21] *The New York Times,* Sept. 10, 11, 1943.
[22] Cf. Whitaker, *op. cit.,* pp. 125-126, 130.

its power. On the 13th the Ramírez administration closed all newspapers published in the Yiddish language; four days later it removed all public employees and professors among the one hundred and fifty prominent citizens who signed a manifesto calling for restoration of constitutional government and compliance with Hemisphere obligations. At the same time three anti-Axis cabinet ministers resigned and the government recalled Felipe Espil, Ambassador to Washington since 1931. In November it withdrew its representative to the Inter-American Commission of Women, set up a new agency to regulate the activities of foreign correspondents and the local press, and threatened exile to Patagonia for anyone caught spreading propaganda against the government. In December it dissolved all political parties and made compulsory the teaching of the Catholic religion in all elementary and secondary schools.[23]

Of all these and other acts, by far the most portentous was the creation of the Secretariat of Labor and Social Security and the appointment of Colonel Juan Perón to head it. Retaining his post as Secretary General of the War Ministry, Perón was clearly moving into position to make his bid for power.

This succession of events, together with innumerable other decrees restricting the activities of Argentine citizens, convinced Mr. Armour that the GOU completely dominated President Ramírez and could now proceed to bend Argentina to its will.[24] The recall of Ambassador Espil and the retirement of Under Secretary Welles removed from the Washington scene two of the staunchest advocates of moderation in Argentine-American relations. Though Welles had continued to hope for Argentine vindication of his policy at the Rio Conference and had stood squarely behind Hull's crushing blow to Storni, his resignation left the supporters of patience without the effective leadership of a principal architect of the Good Neighbor policy.[25] The path was open for Secretary Hull's acts of coercion.

As he returned from Moscow late in the year, two revelations of Argentine duplicity provided him opportunity to renew pressure. First, in October the British disclosed the apprehension in Trinidad of Oscar Hellmuth, an Argentine national of German descent, who was en route to Berlin to negotiate for arms and mutual assistance. The GOU had determined to renew the efforts to secure Germany military assistance

[23] *The New York Times,* Oct. 8, 13, 14, 16, 17, 20, Nov. 11, 24, 30, Dec. 1, 1943, Jan. 1, 1944; Department of State, *Bulletin,* IX (Oct. 16, 1943), 264; Rabinovitz, *op. cit.,* pp. 32-41. Shortly after sharp criticism by President Roosevelt of the suspension of Jewish newspapers, the Ramírez government lifted the ban (*The New York Times,* Oct. 16, 1943).

[24] To Secretary of State, Oct. 23, 1943, NA, DS, 835.00/2091.

[25] Laurence Duggan, *The Americas: The Search for Hemisphere Security,* pp. 102-104. Duggan, Assistant Secretary for Inter-American Affairs, resigned in frustration some months later.

which Castillo had initiated a year before. Hellmuth undertook his mission with the full confidence of both Argentine officials and German secret agents.[26]

The second revelation related to suspected Argentine-Nazi complicity in subverting the pro-Allies government of Bolivia. When sudden revolt unseated President Enrique Peñaranda on December 20, Secretary Hull immediately suspected that outside influence had been at work. At this point, the Emergency Advisory Committee for Political Defense, sitting in Montevideo, came to Hull's assistance. It promptly framed and secured the approval of nineteen American states to resolutions embodying a new continental policy on recognition. These provided that they would recognize no new government instituted by force without prior consultation on its compliance with inter-American obligations. On January 7 Hull announced publicly that forces outside Bolivia appeared to have abetted the revolution.[27]

These developments pushed the Ramírez government into a vulnerable corner. American publication of the evidence it held on GOU plotting against Argentina's neighbors would damage its prestige throughout Latin America. Hull's threat, delivered through Ambassador Armour, achieved its purpose. When, on January 24, General Alberto Gilbert, new Foreign Minister, promised rupture with Germany and stern action against collaborationists, Washington agreed to withhold announcement of Argentine plotting against Bolivia. Two days later, the last American republic to fall into line, Argentina broke relations with Germany and Japan.[28]

Secretary Hull and the GOU

Argentina's formal severance of diplomatic and telecommunications relations with the Axis, of itself, settled nothing so far as Secretary Hull was concerned. Until the government rid itself completely of its Axis affiliations, ended its toleration of pro-Axis activities, and halted subversive actions of its citizens against neighboring governments, he proposed to continue his campaign against anti-Allies activities in Argentina. Even before public announcement of the break, Hull instructed Armour to ensure that President Ramírez understood the Amer-

---

[26] Hull, *op. cit.*, p. 1391; Department of State, *Consultation among the American Republics with Respect to the Argentine Situation* (Dept. of State Publication 2473, Inter-American Series 29), pp. 6-17 (hereafter cited as "Blue Book on Argentina"); *Memoria, 1943-1944*, pp. 32-33.

[27] Hull, *op. cit.*, pp. 1388-1392; Emergency Advisory Committee for Political Defense, *Second Annual Report Submitted to the Governments of the American Republics*, pp. 13-20, 79-92.

[28] Armour to Secretary of State, Jan. 24, 1944, NA, DS, 835.00/2275; *Memoria, 1943-1944*, pp. 57-58; Hull, *op. cit.*, p. 1392.

ican position and invited the British, Brazilian, and Chilean Foreign Offices to take parallel action.[29] On three occasions during the next week he repeated his expectations of a "complete housecleaning" in Argentina.[30]

In Buenos Aires the young officers of the GOU promptly justified Hull's skepticism, if not his policies. By March 10, apparently fearful that Ramírez would declare war against Germany and Japan, the Perón faction forced the resignation of the President and Foreign Minister Gilbert. The powerful clique took no more chances with the office of chief executive. They elevated to the post a front man they could manage, General Edelmiro Farrell. Perón's star was rising. Already successor to Farrell as Minister of War, he would soon follow him in the vice-presidency.

The State Department elected to regard the Farrell regime as a revolutionary government and hoped to invoke the new inter-American doctrine of no recognition without consultation. It ordered Ambassador Armour to avoid formal relations with the Argentine government. Bolivia, Chile, and Paraguay, however, viewing the shift as one of officials and not of governments, continued normal intercourse. The new consultative policy which was working so effectively in the Bolivian case broke down when applied to economically important Argentina.[31]

Though Armour remained in Buenos Aires until June, the Roosevelt administration refused until March, 1945, to recognize the Farrell government. Ambassador Escobar was recalled from Washington in July. In the midst of war the two nations waged a year-long duel over interpretation of the related doctrines of recognition and nonintervention. Hull maintained that fulfillment of Ramírez' promises on the Axis break must precede recognition; Farrell's Foreign Minister, General Orlando Peluffo, insisted that recognition must come first. The Argentines alleged that nonrecognition constituted intervention in their domestic affairs; Secretary Hull argued that the right to invoke the doctrine of nonintervention did not adhere to any government which shielded pro-Axis activities menacing to continental security.[32]

During the next three months, as the Farrell regime dug itself in, Secretary Hull and other State Department officials settled down to a policy of watchful waiting. In Buenos Aires, where he observed in-

[29] Hull to Embassy to Argentina, Jan. 25, 1944, NA, DS, 835.00/2275; Hull, *Memoirs*, II, 1393.

[30] These included his cable to express gratification to Foreign Minister Gilbert, his reply to official notification of the break by Chargé d'Affaires Don Rodolfo García Arias, and his remarks upon receiving the new Ambassador, Adrian Escobar (*ibid.*, pp. 1393-1394).

[31] Edward Stettinius, Acting Secretary of State, to Embassies to American Republics, Feb. 26, March 4, 1944, NA, DS, 835.00/2423A, 2528A; Welles, *op. cit.*, pp. 196-199; Hull, *op. cit.*, pp. 1394-1395.

[32] *Ibid.*, p. 1396.

creased Argentine pressure against its neighbors, Ambassador Armour questioned the advisability of continued nonrecognition. He revealed several well-grounded fears: unfavorable reaction among friendly Argentines; loss of American prestige if the nonrecognition front should be broken; and even Argentine embargo on meat, hides, and strategic materials. He recommended positive acts, such as recognition of Bolivia and economic assistance to Uruguay.[33]

In Washington Latin America experts debated alternative courses of action. One point of view held that Argentine economic aid was essential to the winning of the war and that, to whatever extent justified on moral grounds, mere nonrecognition and tongue lashings contributed little to this end. The contrary view was that the Farrell regime was deeply totalitarian, basically hostile to American policy, and a menace to American security. The choice for the United States lay between a modus vivendi which would permit the Argentine government to contribute its resources to Axis defeat or tighter economic sanctions which would precipitate its fall and hasten its replacement.[34]

Secretary Hull leaned toward the second view. On June 22 he recalled Ambassador Armour and persuaded Britain and the majority of the Latin American republics to take similar action. On the following day, led by the United States, nineteen American republics recognized the government of Bolivia, which after six months had presumably eliminated its alleged Argentine-Nazi ties.[35]

The Argentines responded to these measures with a determined bid for United States recognition. Through the Chilean chargé in Washington, on June 22 and July 10 they submitted memoranda reciting the actions they and their predecessors had taken to fulfill their promises and commitments.[36] In Buenos Aires, while underscoring the importance of national sovereignty, President Farrell, Colonel Perón, now Vice-President as well as Minister of War, and Foreign Minister Peluffo used the public platform to dramatize Argentine sincerity and rectitude.[37]

But Foreign Office memoranda and official statements did not dissuade Secretary Hull. Between late July and early October he and his colleagues unloosed a heavy broadside of verbal preachments and economic restrictions. He enlisted the assistance of President Roosevelt and Under Secretary Edward Stettinius in the issuance of condemnatory

---

[33] To Secretary of State, April 1, May 4, 1944, NA, DS, 835.01/313; 835.00/2824.
[34] Sumner Welles commented upon this debate in his syndicated newspaper columns and later in *Where Are We Heading?*, pp. 197ff.
[35] Hull, *op. cit.*, pp. 1397-1399; Emergency Advisory Committee, *op. cit.*, p. 97.
[36] Hull, *op. cit.*, p. 1400; Smith, *op. cit.*, p. 108.
[37] Edward L. Reed, Chargé d'Affaires ad interim to Argentina, to Secretary of State, July 7, 1944, NA, DS, 835.00/7-744; Argentine Republic, *Speech Pronounced, on July 26, by the Minister for Foreign Affairs*, . . . Orlando L. Peluffo, p. 3; *The New York Times*, July 28, 1944.

statements.[38] Prime Minister Churchill joined the cacophony of castigation and the Emergency Advisory Committee for Political Defense issued
a sharp rebuke of Argentine conduct.[39] On August 16 the United States
announced the freezing of over $400,000,000 in Argentine gold stocks.
A month later it ordered a deep cut in licenses for chemicals, steel, and
lumber exports to Argentina and forbade American ships to touch
Argentine ports after October 1.[40]

Britain Foils Hull's Hopes

Secretary Hull's actions against Argentina from the June revolt to the
time of his retirement were clearly the least successful of all his Latin
American policies. His resort to nonrecognition, mild economic sanctions,
and sharp-tongued rebukes failed to force Argentina's full-fledged
cooperation with the United Nations. Though his threats to reveal the
extent of GOU complicity in the Bolivian revolution induced severance
of relations with the Axis, the break brought little change. It did not
end Argentina's plotting against its neighbors nor lessen appreciably
its toleration of pro-Axis activities. Mr. Hull failed to achieve the two
prime objectives of his three-pronged attack because of his inability
to gain the third—support of Britain for economic restrictions against
Argentina.[41]

Beginning in December, 1942, the Secretary strove for two years to
swing Britain into line behind his anti-Argentine policy.[42] Repeatedly
he pressed the British Ambassador, Lord Halifax, to urge decisive action
upon his government. When response was slow, he stimulated President
Roosevelt to appeal directly to Prime Minister Churchill. On three
occasions Hull stepped up the pressure on Downing Street.

The first of these began in December, 1942, following repeated reports
from Ambassador Armour that the Castillo government was assuring
its people of British acquiescence in continued Argentine neutrality.
State Department officials responded to Armour's suggestion that the
British should act to neutralize this propaganda. In late December they
persuaded the Foreign Office to issue a public statement supporting

[38] On the preparation and issuance of these statements, including one by President
Roosevelt on September 29, see Hull, *op. cit.,* pp. 1400-1403. For the statements,
see Department of State, *Bulletin,* XI (July 30, Aug. 13, Oct. 1, 1944), 107-111,
158, 337.

[39] *The New York Times,* Aug. 4, 1944; Department of State, *Bulletin,* XI (Aug. 6,
1944), 133; Emergency Advisory Committee, *op. cit.,* pp. 7, 97-102.

[40] *The New York Times,* Aug. 17, Sept. 27, 1944; Guerrant, *op. cit.,* p. 44.

[41] Cf. above, p. 432.

[42] He describes these activities in great detail in his *Memoirs,* II, 1409-1419.
E. Louise Peffer has summarized "Cordell Hull's Argentine Policy and Britain's Meat
Supply," in *Inter-American Economic Affairs,* X (Autumn, 1956), 3-21.

American regret that Argentina had not joined its sister republics.[43] Ultimately agreeing to attach political considerations to their negotiations for a new meat contract, the Foreign Office secured Argentina's agreement to ban the use of coded radio messages.[44] Even the Castillo administration could see that continued loss of Allied ships to Axis submarines might materially reduce Argentina's food exports to Britain.

Throughout 1943, both before and after the June revolt, Argentine officials maintained cordial relations with the United Kingdom.[45] Britain retained its position as Argentina's best customer.[46] The new Army government had been in office less than three months when on August 23 it secured Britain's signature to the fattest meat contract in history, 1,500,000 tons by October, 1944.[47] Coupled with an agreement to purchase eggs, this contract took the sting from a subsequent Foreign Office statement deprecating Argentina's dalliance with the Axis.

Again, at the time of the crises over the Hellmuth arrest and the Bolivian revolution, Hull repeatedly urged that Britain join the United States in a general embargo against Argentina. He now believed that the time had come for the British government to "go against the Argentine Government with a battering ram." Prime Minister Churchill assured President Roosevelt of his eagerness to cooperate with American plans, but reiterated English and Allied dependence upon Argentine meat supplies.[48] Strategic studies of the Combined Food Board supported this conclusion. The Ministry of Food refused to approve any reduction in food reserves. The United States War Food Administration would not support a proposal to make up loss of Argentine supplies through a 10 per cent reduction of American consumption.[49]

By the time of Argentina's break with the Axis, it had become clear, even to Secretary Hull, that British and American views on the Argentine problem were virtually irreconcilable. Mr. Hull considered deepening subversion in Argentina as malignant, already threatening to infect the continent. In his view, failure to check the Argentine government would injure the war effort, undermine the security of other South American nations, and discredit the prestige of the United States. On the contrary, Churchill and Eden regarded Argentine totalitarianism as a passing phenomenon, to be dealt with at the end of the war. They

[43] *Memoria, 1942-1943*, pp. 67-69.

[44] Hull, *op. cit.*, pp. 1409-1410.

[45] *Loc. cit.*

[46] Chamber of Commerce of the United States in Argentina, *Trade Relations between Argentina and the United States of America*, p. 57; *The New York Times*, July 25, 1943.

[47] *Time*, XLII (Sept. 6, 1943), 32.

[48] Hull, *op. cit.*, pp. 1410-1413.

[49] Peffer, *op. cit.*, pp. 11-12. In his extensive defense of his efforts to win British support for his Argentine policy, Secretary Hull makes no allusion to the recommendations of these powerful wartime agencies.

were willing to adopt any position the State Department believed necessary as long as it did not jeopardize the flow of Argentine supplies to English tables and Army kitchens.[50] But like their nation's press, they had little sympathy with Hull's measures of coercion. As *The Manchester Guardian* later expressed it, the United States

> has barred its ships from calling at Argentine ports and no doubt would like us to follow suit. We like the Argentine brand of Fascism as little as does Mr. Cordell Hull, but we also prefer Argentine beef to American pork. When our food situation is as generous as that of the Americans, we can think about the luxuries of a blockade which may not hit the right people.[51]

Nevertheless, Hull made a third sustained effort to enlist British support. On June 23, after the decision to withdraw Ambassador Armour, he urged the British government, through Halifax, to recall Sir David Kelly. Failing to get results, the Secretary secured Roosevelt's intervention with Churchill. Confronted by what he called a *"fait accompli,"* the Prime Minister gave grudging and angered assent, though he still regarded collective nonrecognition of the Farrell regime as futile.[52]

When Ambassador Kelly passed through Washington on July 17, en route to London, Hull made another lengthy exposition of the American position.[53] Once again the Combined Food Board refused to let political considerations interfere with British renewal of negotiations for a meat contract. Again the War Food Administration failed to support Hull's position that the United States could make up any British deficiency.[54]

Though he harbored no illusions about the Farrell government, Prime Minister Churchill clearly kept his eyes on long-range, as well as immediate, British relationships with Argentina. In reviewing the war situation before the House of Commons on August 2, he requested that,

> as an Englishman, I may be pardoned at this moment for thinking of another South American country with which we have had close ties of friendship and mutual interest since her birth to liberty and independence. I refer to Argentina. We all feel deep regret and also anxiety, as friends of Argentina, that in this testing time for nations she has not seen fit to declare herself wholeheartedly, unmistakeably and with no reserve or qualification upon the side of freedom, and has chosen to dally with the evil, and not

[50] Hull, *op. cit.*, pp. 1411-1414, 1417.
[51] Sept. 30, 1944.
[52] *Ibid.*, pp. 1414-1416; David Kelly, *The Ruling Few*, pp. 300-301.
[53] Hull, *op. cit.*, pp. 1416-1417. Though he got little chance to express his own views, the Ambassador disagreed with Hull's main premises about the Argentine government (Kelly, *op. cit.*, pp. 302-304).
[54] Peffer, *op. cit.*, pp. 15-16.

only with the evil, but with the losing side. I trust that my remarks will be noted, because this is a very serious war. It is not like some small wars in the past where all could be forgotten and forgiven. Nations must be judged by the part they play. Not only belligerents but neutrals will find that their position in the world cannot remain entirely unaffected by the part they have chosen to play in the crisis of war.[55]

Britain's latest contract for Argentine meat was scheduled to expire on October 30. With the fortunes of war now swinging heavily in favor of the Allies, porteño leaders, too, began to look to their postwar situation. Fearing the possibility that Britain might return to the import quota system of the Ottawa Agreements, they hoped to secure a four-year arrangement. When on the eve of Hull's resignation as Secretary the British opened negotiations for a new contract, it was clear that Hull had suffered complete defeat in his two-year campaign to tighten the Anglo-American economic belt around Argentina.[56] The loss of this struggle signalized his failure to solve the Argentine problem.

Apart from the critical matter of meat supplies, other influences helped to shape Britain's attitude and ensure miscarriage of Hull's program.[57] English economic interests in Argentina, both commercial and financial, had never been keen about American policies that might place the "sixth dominion" wholly within the inter-American bloc and under the influence of their rivals in the United States.[58] In postwar commercial competition, Argentina would rank high in English plans.[59] Moreover, it remained one of the few areas in the world where English capital appeared to retain a secure foothold.[60] Whatever public statements British statesmen might issue from time to time on Anglo-American solidarity toward Argentine obduracy, to the English trader and overseas investor Hull's economic warfare against Argentina appeared suspiciously like economic warfare against Britain itself.[61]

Chapultepec and San Francisco

Long the target of verbal rebukes and economic sanctions from the North Atlantic, the military regime in Buenos Aires ultimately determined

[55] *Parliamentary Debates (Hansard)*, 5th Series, Vol. 402, House of Commons, p. 1484.

[56] Hull, *op. cit.*, p. 1419.

[57] Peffer, *op. cit.*, pp. 19-21.

[58] Reed to Secretary of State, July 22, 1944, NA, DS, 835.01/7-2244; "Britain and Argentina," *The Economist*, Vol. 147 (Aug. 5, 1944), 174-175.

[59] For a useful contemporary article on this aspect, see Ricardo Setaro, "The Argentine Fly in the International Ointment," *Harper's*, Vol. 189 (Aug., 1944), 204-209.

[60] Reed to Secretary of State, July 22, 1944, NA, DS, 835.01/7-2244; Welles, *op. cit.*, p. 200.

[61] *The Economist*, Vol. 147, p. 175; Peffer, *op. cit.*, p. 20.

to seize the diplomatic initiative from Washington. On October 27, 1944, it aimed a well-conceived counterblow at an unexpected sector. Without advance notification it requested the Governing Board of the Pan American Union to convene a meeting of the foreign ministers to consider the "misunderstanding" that existed between the Argentine Republic and other American nations.[62]

From the point of view of national self-interest, the Argentine leaders dropped their bombshell with an acute sense of timing. The request reached Washington during a moment of administrative shifts in the Department of State. Seriously ill since early October, Secretary Hull would shortly resign the office he had held for nearly twelve years. Inexperienced leaders, therefore, would direct American reaction to the overture—Mr. Edward R. Stettinius, Acting Secretary of State, soon to be Hull's successor, and Mr. Nelson Rockefeller, Assistant Secretary for American Republics Affairs. Motivated partly perhaps by choice, but also by pressures, both from inside and outside the Department, these new officials would move toward a softening of American policy toward Argentina. Though the departure of Secretary Hull marked the temporary passing of Washington's coercive policy, it did not settle the Argentine question.

As Allied armies drove more deeply into German-occupied territory, leaders in both Washington and Buenos Aires felt compelled to strengthen their nations against the impact of war's end. While straining to fulfill its military and political commitments in all parts of the world, the United States had already involved itself deeply in plans for a postwar international organization. Still quarantined by a majority of its traditional friends, its liquid assets tied up largely in British and American vaults, Argentina must gird itself against inevitable postwar economic dislocations.

Many of the Latin American nations had long since begun to grow restless over the continuing stalemate produced by Hull's policy of coercion. Some leaders feared the eventualities to which collective non-recognition might lead. Others resented the extent to which Washington's wartime actions, usually undertaken without consulting the other republics, dominated inter-American diplomacy and economics. Already broken through recognition of the Farrell government by three bordering states, the united Hemisphere front, on the eve of the war's end, seemed in jeopardy. The Latin Americans were eager for Hemisphere consultation on postwar problems.[63]

The Argentine request of October 27, therefore, served to bring to a focus obvious desires for a consultative meeting of Hemisphere foreign ministers. Yet, even under the goad of wartime pressures, the slow

[62] Pan American Union, *Bulletin*, LXXIX (Jan., 1945), 48-49.
[63] Welles, *op. cit.*, pp. 204-205.

wheels of diplomatic action forced the Argentines to wait more than two months for their reply. At its November meeting the Governing Board of the Pan American Union referred the request to the various chancelleries. The State Department sought opinions from its representatives in the field. Within the Department the Acting Secretary was buffeted between Secretary Hull, still in touch with policy-making, who favored denial of the request, and lesser officials who believed that coercion had failed. From outside the Department diverse interests— businessmen, politicians, and others whom Hull characterized as "malcontents" and "marplots"—pressed Stettinius for favorable action on the Argentine overture.[64] The Acting Secretary repeatedly announced to the press that the United States had no objection to a consultative conference, but he appeared to hedge on the question of Argentine participation.[65]

Latin American leaders offered Stettinius a way out. A proposal for dealing with the problem of Argentina without permitting its delegates to carry the issue to the floor of a full-dress conference stemmed from the persistence of Dr. Ezequiel Padilla, Foreign Minister of Mexico. Throughout 1944 the idea of a consultative conference had been germinating in his mind. In a memorandum of November 6 he formally presented to the State Department his plan for a limited foreign ministers conference. It would include only those American republics which had joined the war effort. Secretary Stettinius promptly approved the Mexican proposal.[66] By agreeing that an Argentine representative might be present to state his nation's case, he would avoid the necessity of a face-to-face debate with the spokesman of the Farrell government. At this point Hull's anti-Argentine policies seemed still to be controlling his successor's course.[67]

The Governing Board of the Pan American Union finally announced its plans on January 8. It would abstain "for the time being from acting on the Argentine request." On the other hand, it would soon invite

[64] Hull, *op. cit.*, pp. 1404-1405.

[65] *The New York Times*, Oct. 31, Nov. 2, 3, 19, 25, 1945.

[66] Hull, *op. cit.*, p. 1404.

[67] In a memorandum on the genesis of the Chapultepec Conference, dated April 11, 1945, State Department officials summarized the American position on the Argentine request as follows: ". . . contrary to the public impression, the United States favored hearing the Argentine case and the other republics felt that this would be inadvisable." In three circular telegrams to the other American republics, dated Nov. 12, 28, and Dec. 22, the memorandum notes that "we stated that if the other American Republics were disposed to grant such a hearing we would be prepared to participate, on the understanding that it would be a full and free discussion of the fundamental issues involved. At the same time we expressed our opinion that the Argentine request for a hearing could not be justified on its merits, and that the utility of such a hearing seemed doubtful." (Division of River Plate Affairs to John M. Cabot, Chargé d'Affaires to Argentina, April 11, 1945, NA, DS, 835.00/4-1145.)

those American republics collaborating in the war effort to consider a conference on urgent and postwar problems. By this action the Board chose deliberately to exclude Argentina from the meeting that would consider its proposal.[68] Rebuffed by this warping of the machinery of "consultation" which Argentina had helped to create, its leaders promptly withdrew from participation in the meetings of the Pan American Union.[69]

In sequel to these decisions, the Governing Board scheduled the Inter-American Conference on Problems of War and Peace for Mexico City on February 21. Deeply enmeshed in the diplomacy of the Yalta Conference and other transcendent problems, Secretary Stettinius gave no public indication that the United States proposed to moderate its "tough" policy toward the Farrell government.

Soon, however, according to Sumner Welles, the Secretary effected a secret understanding with Argentine leaders. Prior to the Conference, he relates, the State Department sent a special mission to Buenos Aires to confer with Vice-President Perón and Foreign Minister Juan Cooke. Under the agreement made in these conversations, Argentine compliance with the conditions to be drafted at Mexico City would assure relaxation of Washington's anti-Argentine policies. The United States would discard its coercive attitude, revoke its restrictive economic measures, and lift its embargo on military matériel.

Meanwhile, the Farrell government seemed to manifest an eagerness to mollify anti-Argentine opinion in the Hemisphere. It banned indefinitely the two most notorious anti-American newspapers, *Cabildo* and *El Pampero*. It reinstated the university professors who had signed the prodemocratic manifesto of October, 1943. It intimated the possibility of a return to constitutional government. It pressed vigorously for German payment of sums owed for submarine damages and cost of maintaining *Graf Spee* internees. When it protested the German threat to deny safe conduct to Argentine diplomats seeking exit from Sweden, the press suggested that the nation might be edging toward a declaration of war.[71]

The exclusion of Argentina from the deliberations at Chapultepec did not preclude the resolution of high-level Hemisphere problems. The "Act of Chapultepec" greatly strengthened existing machinery for re-

[68] *Report of the Delegation of the United States of America to the Inter-American Conference on Problems of War and Peace,* p. 5. For the American view, see Stettinius to Secretary, Governing Board, Jan. 6, 1945, Department of State, *Bulletin,* XII (Jan. 21, 1945), 91.

[69] *The New York Times,* Jan. 11, 1945.

[70] Welles, *op. cit.,* p. 206.

[71] *The New York Times,* Feb. 11, 17, 19, 21, 1945; "Blue Book on Argentina," p. 78.

ciprocal assistance and continental solidarity and laid the groundwork
for the Rio Pact of 1947. The "Economic Charter of the Americas"
enunciated guiding principles for winning the war and aiding orderly
return to peacetime economy. In a variety of ways the American republics sought to get their regional house in order before convening
of the San Francisco Conference of the United Nations.

Yet, throughout the deliberations, no delegation could ignore the
influence of the nation which since 1889 had persistently given leadership to Latin American views. Even though treated as an afterthought,
the Conference could not side-step the Argentine problem. Its final
action, therefore, provided for Argentina's readmission to the continental
family of nations.

The terms for Argentina's restoration to good standing were clear
and succinct, though general enough to allow all parties to save face.
In underscoring the necessity of solidarity among all the American
states, the Conference recognized Argentina's rightful place as an integral
part of the Inter-American System. It called upon the errant member
to cooperate with its sister republics and to identify itself "with the
common policy these nations are pursuing." By adhering to the Final
Act, which the Conference now invited Argentina to do, presumably it
would bind itself to declare war on Germany and Japan and to enforce
the diverse Hemisphere agreements against Axis activities.[72]

On the other hand, without the least change in the government
Roosevelt and Hull had been censuring for many months, Argentina
could rejoin the American republics and count on their support for
its incorporation into the United Nations. Both by his vote and by
specific comments in his closing address, Secretary Stettinius assured
United States endorsement of these terms.[73]

With the conclusion of the formal arrangements at Chapultepec,
events moved swiftly in Buenos Aires and Washington to bring about
at least a semblance of Hemisphere unity. In the southern capital,
where preparatory beating of the war drums barely dented public
apathy, the Farrell government on March 27 declared war on Germany
and Japan. Within twenty-four hours it notified the Director General of
the Pan American Union that it was ready to comply with the terms
of the Conference resolution. A week later, by signing the Act of
Chapultepec, it rejoined the inter-American organization.[74]

In Washington the State Department moved toward prompt recognition. On March 31 Assistant Secretary Rockefeller proclaimed satisfac-

---

[72] The Final Act of the Conference is printed in *Report of the Delegation,* pp. 68-
136. Resolution LIX provided for Argentina's readmission (pp. 133-134).

[73] Department of State, *Bulletin,* XII (March 11, 1945), 400.

[74] Council on Foreign Relations, *Documents on American Foreign Relations,* VII,
753-757.

tion with Argentina's actions. It has taken over all Axis firms, he announced, and blocked Axis funds. Four days later the United States cancelled its economic restrictions against Argentina and on April 19, without waiting for fuller demonstration of Argentine good faith, recognized the Farrell government, with which it had had no formal contact since March 14, 1944.[75]

The American republics had now cleared the decks for the approaching action of the United Nations at San Francisco. The Latin American states approached the meeting with three well-formulated purposes: to secure the admission of Argentina; to safeguard the integrity of their regional organization; and to limit as much as possible the extension of Great Power control. With two-fifths of Conference voting strength, they were in a good position to exert their influence.[76]

The United States, on the other hand, entered the Conference heavily weighted with the responsibilities of global military and political leadership. Moreover, to complicate its prestige in the Western Hemisphere, it had committed itself to three entangling agreements. At Mexico City it had promised to work for Argentina's incorporation into the United Nations. At Yalta it had consented to the admission of the Ukrainian and Byelorussian Soviet Socialist Republics. With the British government it had agreed to oppose the Soviet Union's bid for the admission of the Lublin government of Poland. Of these secret arrangements the Secretary of State had not advised his colleagues in the American republics. Indeed, since the Dumbarton Oaks conferences they had frequently complained of lack of information about maturing plans for a world organization. These developments served only to deepen the Latin American discontent which had long been accumulating over dissatisfaction with Hull's unilateral Argentine policy.[77]

This tangled web of Latin goals and American commitments involved both Argentina and the United States, as well as the Latin American bloc. Argentina won admission to the United Nations but only after a fresh blackening of its name in the American and world press. Though remaining faithful to its diverse commitments, the United States suffered damage to its position of world and Hemisphere leadership. While gaining recognition of their regional system, the Latin Americans lost many of their battles to limit the influence of the Great Powers. At San Francisco the Hemisphere nations contributed notably to the founding of the United Nations, but in the process they remuddied the newly becalmed waters of the continental system.[78]

---

[75] *Ibid.*, pp. 776, 786.
[76] J. A. Houston, *Latin America in the United Nations*, pp. 14, 27.
[77] *Ibid.*, pp. 14, 27-29; Welles, *op. cit.*, pp. 198-199, 210-211.
[78] *Ibid.*, pp. 212-214.

Braden vs. Perón

The State Department's choice of an ambassador to restore formal diplomatic contacts with the Farrell government was Spruille Braden, veteran American entrepreneur and diplomat in Latin America. Since 1933 he had faithfully fulfilled one diplomatic mission after another— from delegate to the Conference of the American States at Montevideo to wartime Ambassador to Colombia and Cuba. Prior to 1945 he was best known to Argentines for his effective leadership of the long-stalemated Chaco Peace Conference in the thirties. This diplomatic success had won him an honorary degree from the University of Buenos Aires and honorary membership in several distinguished Argentine societies.

Big and buoyant, Spruille Braden undertook all of his activities with intensity and gusto, whether water polo at Yale, courtship and copper mining in Chile, or defense of American principles wherever he might be. His love of democracy was as strong as his huge frame. He had fought involvement of American businessmen in the corruption of Cuban politics as vigorously as he had resisted penetration of Nazi interests into Colombia. In the State Department he was something of an incongruity—a militant, bare-fisted diplomat.[79] His interpretation of the inter-American principles of "nonintervention" and "respect for national sovereignty" diverged sharply from that of his critics.[80] To Braden nonintervention did not mean acquiescence, and respect for national sovereignty did not demand support for dictatorship. His appointment to the long-vacant, supersensitive post in Buenos Aires could hardly portend continuance of the new "soft" policy of Stettinius and Rockefeller.

Braden's arrival in Buenos Aires in mid-May coincided with a resurgence of domestic turmoil under the military dictatorship. Now serving simultaneously as Vice-President, Minister of War, and Secretary of Labor and Social Security, Juan Perón was preparing to move up from key man behind the throne to the throne itself. The declaration of war against the Axis provided excuse for him to act more harshly against those elements whose dissidence had recently grown more clamorous.

Just prior to Braden's arrival, the Argentine government had rounded up General Rawson and seventy other persons accused of conspiring against the regime. To keep news of the arrests from the people it had reimposed political censorship. On the eve of the fall of Berlin, allegedly to forestall a possible antigovernment coup, the police announced that they would use violent methods to disperse any public demonstrations.

[79] Colorful contemporary portraits of Braden appeared in *Time*, XLVI (Nov. 5, 1945), 42-47, and Joseph Newman, "Diplomatic Dynamite," *Collier's*, Vol. 116 (Nov. 10, 1945), 11, 43-45.

[80] Notably Sumner Welles, who severely censured Mr. Braden's activities in Argentina (*op. cit.*, pp. 215-218).

Only recently whipped up to accept declaration of war against Germany, the people of Buenos Aires now received in beaten silence the news of Berlin's capitulation. Soon after Braden's official reception, the dictatorship stepped up its intimidation of foreign correspondents and repression of pro-Allied activities.[81]

The situation which confronted Braden openly challenged his principles and his love of action. Pulling no punches, he quickly warmed to the task. In his first meeting with foreign correspondents he announced that the United States would like to see democratic governments established everywhere. In public speeches he reminded government officials that they had still not expelled Axis-controlled firms and declared that diplomatic recognition did not imply blanket approval of their policies.[82]

State Department officers appeared to support Braden's reversion to Mr. Hull's belief that outside assistance might encourage overthrow of the nationalist government. Speaking in San Francisco on May 28, after bitter press attacks on his vote for Argentina's admission to the United Nations, Mr. Stettinius sought to reassure the American people that the United States had not changed its attitude toward the Farrell government.[83] On the following day Washington reversed an earlier decision to supply much-wanted arms to Argentina.[84] Testifying before a Senate subcommittee on June 25, Assistant Secretary of State Will L. Clayton submitted evidence that Argentina had not eliminated a single one of the 104 Axis companies suspected of spearheading German economic penetration.[85]

Braden's openly declared sympathies for democratic elements in Argentina and his vigorous defense of freedom of the press served as rallying points for antigovernment groups. In a sharply phrased manifesto on June 16, 321 commercial and industrial organizations levelled an attack at Perón's social and economic policies. The signers ranged from the Argentine Chamber of Commerce to the Society of Barbers and Hairdressers of Mendoza. During succeeding weeks opposition forces used every opportunity to lash out at the Farrell-Perón regime— a banquet of the Radical Party, a rally in honor of ex-President Roque Saenz Peña, the surrender of Japan, and the return of distinguished political exiles.[86]

To whatever extent they were interrelated, the activities of Braden and the anti-Peronistas were bound to stimulate sharp reaction from

[81] *The New York Times,* April 24, 26, 28, May 4, June 1, 6, 1945.

[82] *Ibid.,* June 6, 1945; Greenup, *op. cit.,* p. 142.

[83] *Documents on American Foreign Relations,* VII, 437; Welles, *op. cit.,* p. 213.

[84] The recommendation to send military aid to Argentina had been made by Avra Warren, Chief of the State Department's Office of American Republics, after a visit to Buenos Aires in April (*The Inter-American,* IV [July, 1945], 6; *The Evening Star* [Washington], April 24, 1945).

[85] *Ibid.,* May 25, 1945.

[86] *The New York Times,* June 17, July 2, Aug. 10, 15, Sept. 3, 1945.

government leaders.[87] On the one hand, under this recurrent and widespread pressure, the dictatorship seemed to relax its restrictions upon the populace. President Farrell announced in July that the government would hold elections before January 1st. For the first time in more than three years and a half it lifted the state of siege. It felt called upon to issue a ten-thousand-word defense of measures taken to comply with its Chapultepec commitments.[88]

On the other hand, already an announced candidate for the presidency, Perón could not ignore Braden's overt challenge to his personal ambitions nor the deep-seated ferment he had stirred. In the middle of July, while the Ambassador was on a hard-hitting speaking tour in the provinces, a flood of scurrilous anti-Braden posters and leaflets inundated the streets of central Buenos Aires. Diverse porteño groups, including students, businessmen, a portion of organized labor, and ex-Foreign Ministers Saavedra Lamas and Cantilo, now came to Braden's defense.[89] Clearly, the jovial but forceful democrat had drawn blood. The issue was now Braden vs. Perón.

Administrative shifts in the State Department during these developments in Buenos Aires indicated the end of Washington's brief period of trying to do business with Argentina. James Byrnes replaced Edward Stettinius as Secretary in early July. Acknowledging his unfamiliarity with Hemisphere affairs and his deep involvement with events in Europe and Asia, he expressed his intention to leave guidance of inter-American policies to a qualified subordinate. He found his man in Spruille Braden. Late in August, after publicly indicting the Argentine regime and admitting the failure of his own policy of tolerance, Nelson Rockefeller resigned as Assistant Secretary to open the way for Braden's appointment.[90] At a farewell luncheon in Buenos Aires some time later the Ambassador trumpeted his future intentions: "Let no one imagine that my being transferred to Washington means the abandonment of the task I have undertaken." [91]

In his analysis of these changes, Sumner Welles was extremely critical of the State Department's return to its policy of coercion.[92] He believed that pressure from two principal sources was largely responsible: first, from those officials within the Department who still hoped to justify

[87] Cf. the views of Alexander, *op. cit.,* pp. 203-204; Blanksten, *op. cit.,* pp. 410-412; and Greenup, *op. cit.,* pp. 143-145.

[88] *The New York Times,* July 7, Aug. 7, Sept. 12, 1945. The complete text of Argentina's apologia appeared in República Argentina, Ministerio de Relaciones Exteriores y Culto, *Informaciones argentinas,* Aug. 1945, pp. 2-4, 8-10, 17.

[89] *The New York Times,* July 20, 21, 24, Aug. 3, 1945.

[90] Department of State, *Bulletin,* XIII (Sept. 2, 1945), 326. Mr. Rockefeller appeared to have revised the clean bill of health he had given the Argentine government five months before (see above, p. 445).

[91] See complete text of his speech in Department of State, *Bulletin,* XIII (Aug. 26, 1945), 285-289, 291.

[92] *Washington Post,* Sept. 6, 1945.

the hard policy they had developed under Secretary Hull; and second, the Committee on Latin American Affairs of the CIO, which professed to represent the views of 6,000,000 organized workers.[93] "Our committee asks," its chairman wrote, "for vigorous and unequivocal official action to prevent Argentina from continuing as a source of fascist infection in the Western Hemisphere." [94]

Colonel Perón's bid for total power over the Argentine government reached both its nadir and its zenith in the weeks after Braden's departure. The greatest display of opposition to his ambitions came on September 19. In what they hailed as a "March of the Constitution and Liberty," several hundred thousand aroused porteños thronged downtown Buenos Aires. Following up this popular demonstration, key officers of the Campo de Mayo garrison promptly besieged Perón's weakened position. On October 9 they forced him to resign his three civil offices and "banished" him to Martín García Island.[95]

In this moment of apparent defeat, Perón revealed the magic of his personality and the solidity of the structure he had created. Divided and inept, the Army officers could not form a new government. Their indecision gave the henchmen of Perón time to rally the laboring masses he had assiduously cultivated. By their stimulated, yet almost uncontrolled, surge into the Plaza de Mayo on October 17, the *descamisados* ("shirtless ones") forced President Farrell to recall their leader from exile.[96]

Within a week Perón had moved from threatened oblivion to near-unassailable control of Argentina. He had demonstrated the Army's incapacity to rule without him. He had revealed his ability to pit the new power of organized labor against the waning political strength of the Army and the oligarchy. He could now openly avow his marriage to Eva Duarte, confirmed foe of the old order and his accomplice-to-be in demagogic appeal to the masses. Unfettered by government office, though represented in high positions by his associates, he could conduct his campaign for the presidency with confidence and unconcern. Above all, he could renew his resistance to Yankee interventionism, still personified by Spruille Braden, and perhaps add the satisfaction of personal revenge to his numerous other conquests.[97]

---

[93] *Op. cit.*, pp. 219-220. He reprints the text of a letter, dated Aug. 5, 1945, sent to Mr. Byrnes by George Michanowsky, Executive Secretary of the Committee.

[94] Letter from Jacob S. Potofsky, Chairman of the Committee, to the editor, *The New York Times*, June 28, 1945. In the following January the Committee further indicated its deep interest in the Argentine situation by publishing a 166-page tract entitled *The Argentine Regime: Facts and Recommendations to the United Nations Organization*.

[95] *The New York Times*, Sept. 20, Oct. 10, 1945; Rabinovitz, *op. cit.*, pp. 60-61.

[96] Whitaker recounts Perón's "descent to the underworld—and return" (*op. cit.*, pp. 134-138). See also *The New York Times*, Oct. 12, 13, 18, 19, 1945.

[97] Cf. Whitaker, *op. cit.*, pp. 137-138.

"Perón o Braden!"

The duel between Perón and Braden, which in its opening phase had featured almost face-to-face exchange, now switched to long-range diplomatic fencing between Buenos Aires and Washington. The advantages of surprise and initiative, which the Ambassador had used so effectively in the first round, gave way to Perón's new self-assurance and firmer control of his own government. As a declared candidate for chief executive in Argentina's first presidential election since 1938, he bore a constitutional status he had previously lacked. At the same time, as Assistant Secretary of State, Braden, too, led from a position of greater authority. In the second round, as in the first, citizens of both nations, like the leaders of all the American republics, were eager spectators. The stakes remained high—the unity and solidarity of the Hemisphere.

Argentines have called the election of 1946 the freest and most honest in their history. Far more strikingly even than that of 1916, it brought into the open the deep-rooted social and economic cleavages rending Argentine life. Serving as the spearhead of social change and economic nationalism, Colonel Perón represented the hopes of the newly articulate descamisados and members of government-controlled labor unions. As the events of October, 1945, revealed, he had aroused in them an almost mystical faith. To assure his hold on this popular base, he could count at this time upon strong support from leaders in the armed forces and the Roman Catholic Church and from the whole apparatus of labor, information, and police agencies in the national government.[98]

Against this formidable combination, supporting a candidate of admired virility and demonstrated fascination, the opposition held out the attractions of a return to prerevolutionary normality. This approach had its appeal for strong sectors of Argentine life—the former ruling oligarchy, most industrialists and businessmen, the majority of civic leaders and civic organizations, the university communities, and the displaced political parties. However weakened by more than two years of Army dictatorship, these influences remained powerful. In an effort to coalesce their forces, four opposition parties in November, 1945, formed the Democratic Union. As their candidate they nominated a sixty-year-old veteran of Congress and Cabinet, a respected figure of little popular appeal, José Tamborini.[99]

[98] John J. Kennedy, *Catholicism, Nationalism, and Democracy in Argentina*, pp. 205-207.

[99] Whitaker has written extensively of the domestic crosscurrents involved in the election (*ibid.*, pp. 140-148). See also Alexander, *op. cit.*, pp. 50-51.

With the war over and the Army dictatorship now two and a half years old, Argentina seemed prepared to decide an election on purely domestic issues. But in Washington, where the Truman administration suspected the continuing power of Nazi agents in the Hemisphere, the Byrnes-Braden team would not let it be so. They felt that the Allies had fought the war, at least in part, to rid the world of the totalitarian virus. Argentina continued to be Braden's particular whipping boy.

The new Assistant Secretary had barely hung his hat in the State Department when Acting Secretary Dean Acheson announced that the United States would not sign a treaty of military assistance with the Argentine regime. Negotiation of such a pact was the sole purpose of a Conference of Foreign Ministers already scheduled for October 20, 1945 in Rio de Janeiro. Without consulting the other republics, the State Department had suggested its cancellation to the host government.[100]

Confirmation of Mr. Braden's new appointment already before the Senate Foreign Relations Committee, its senior members forced him to bear the brunt of their dissatisfaction with the administration's unilateral action. Senators Tom Connally and Arthur Vandenberg, delegates to the Mexico City and San Francisco Conferences, castigated this "bull in a china shop" approach and insisted on future Department compliance with "the spirit and letter" of inter-American agreements. Meanwhile, the Latin American governments had no choice but to accept postponement of the meeting.[101]

Soon, however, through one public statement after another, Braden renewed his open attacks upon the Farrell government. He declared that the United States would use "every means at its disposal" to answer "the cry of the Argentine people for a democratic government." Repeatedly he appealed for elimination of Nazi-Fascist ideology in Argentina.[102]

Late in November Mr. Braden received broadened support for his anti-Perón policy. Under the guise of a new extension of the Act of Chapultepec, inspired perhaps by the United States, the Foreign Minister of Uruguay, Alberto Rodríguez Larreta, introduced a project for collective intervention, to be used whenever an American nation denied its citizens their essential rights or defaulted its international obligations. His timing of the suggestion indicated Argentina as the immediate target. To this revolutionary doctrine Secretary Byrnes and other high

---

[100] Department of State, *Bulletin*, XIII (Oct. 7, 1945), 552.

[101] *Cong. Rec.*, 79 Cong., 1 sess., XCI, pt. 8, pp. 9899-9908; Welles, *op. cit.*, p. 225.

[102] Department of State, *Bulletin*, XIII (Oct. 28, 1945), 658; XIV (Jan. 6, 13, 1946), 26-32; *The New York Times*, Oct. 28, Nov. 15, 1945, Jan. 6, 1946. See also his article "The Germans in Argentina," published in *The Atlantic Monthly*, Vol. 177 (April, 1946), 37-43.

Department officials gave immediate and unqualified adherence.[103] Stamping the proposal as a negation of the Hemisphere principle of nonintervention, other Latin American states refused to endorse it. Argentina in particular, through its Foreign Minister, Juan I. Cooke, denounced the proposal as precipitate, confusing, and destructive of the spirit of cooperation.[104]

Yet, however intense the heat generated against Argentina during these months, Washington's actions were chiefly verbal and diplomatic. Except the ban on arms shipments, it made no attempt to restore economic sanctions or wartime controls. Europe's kitchens and factories, even Spruille Braden admitted publicly, required the surplus food products and raw materials of Argentina's farms, fields, and forests. If its exports were to relieve the shortages in devastated Europe, vast quantities of coal, oil, tires, replacement equipment, and trucks and automobiles must reach Buenos Aires. Eager to compete with European exporters re-entering the Argentine market in the days of flush postwar trade, American manufacturing, shipping, and financial interests would not tolerate official resumption of economic curbs.[105]

Neither the repeated fulminations of Washington officials nor Perón's confirmed views against Yankee interventionism played a significant part in the early stages of the presidential campaign. A fortnight before election day, however, when Perón's victory seemed increasingly a possibility, the State Department deliberately injected the issue of Nazi-Fascist influences in the Argentine regime. Through the eighty-six pages of its "Blue Book on Argentina," it released to the world its "proof positive" of Argentina's complicity with the enemy. Based in considerable part upon captured German documents, the pamphlet exposed the pattern of Argentina's "aid to the enemy, deliberate misrepresentation and deception in promises of Hemisphere cooperation, subversive activity against neighboring republics, and a vicious partnership of Nazi and native totalitarian forces." [106] The State Department presented the document as its contribution to the consultation among the American republics it had requested on October 3.

Though President Truman and Secretary Byrnes promptly accepted

---

[103] Department of State, *Bulletin*, XIII (Nov. 25, 1945), 864-866; XIV (Jan. 6, 13, 1946), 28; *The New York Times*, Nov. 28, 29, 1945. Welles suggests that Rodríguez Larreta may have been stimulated by the United States (*op. cit.*, p. 226).

[104] Welles, *op. cit.*, p. 227. For Cooke's criticism, which appeared on November 29, see the pamphlet issued by the Foreign Office, *Three Statements on the International Policy of Argentina* . . . , pp. 17-25.

[105] *The New York Times*, Nov. 15, 1945; Olive Holmes, "Argentina—Focus of Conflict in the Americas," *Foreign Policy Reports*, XXI (Feb. 1, 1946), 305.

[106] "Blue Book on Argentina," p. 4. Photographic reproductions of documents allegedly implicating the Peróns and other Argentines in Nazi intrigues are printed in Silvano Santander, *Técnica de una traición: Juan Perón y Eva Duarte, agentes del nazismo en la Argentina*, pp. 34-35, 42-43, 46, 50-51, 59, 66-67.

responsibility for the publication, Colonel Perón added it to the list of his grievances against Assistant Secretary Braden. With fiery words and heated charges he now heaped invective upon his adversary. He denounced the former ambassador as "the inspirer, creator, organizer, and true head of the Democratic Union" which opposed him.[107] As the culmination of his drive to the presidency, he made Braden his chief rival in the campaign. *"Perón o Braden!"* became the cry of his followers.

In this national election, bristling with domestic issues, the influence of the State Department's eleventh-hour intervention cannot be accurately measured. It may or may not have assured Perón's election; obviously it did not prevent his resounding triumph. No nationalistically minded people, least of all the sensitive Argentines, could avoid resentment over such patent violation of their national pride.

Among the remaining Latin American states the Truman administration won little support. Advised of the "Blue Book" only after release of its text to the press, they looked upon it, not as the result of the consultation the document seemed to indicate, but as an exclusive State Department project. Some regarded it as a renewal of Yankee intervention. Now that the people of Argentina had expressed their will in free election, most of the Latin states saw no choice but to admit the nation to its rightful place in all Hemisphere councils. They were eager to proceed with the Conference of Foreign Ministers long since planned to consider a Hemisphere treaty of mutual assistance and already once postponed.[108]

Clearly, Perón's unexpected success in winning the presidency shook policy-makers in Washington. By refusing to unseat the nationalist regime the Argentine people had effectively repudiated the State Department's principal justification for its policies of coercion and intervention. The United States had suffered a diplomatic defeat of the highest order. Unless to strengthen the power of Colonel Perón, the Hull-Braden policies had failed to alter the course of events in Argentina.[109]

Once the furor of the election had receded, the leaders of each nation began to make guarded conciliatory gestures toward the other. Even before official verification of his election, reports leaked out of Buenos Aires that Perón was contemplating an approach to the United States to relieve shortages of tires, farm machinery, industrial equipment, even arms. He appeared to assume that Argentina's only enemy in the United States was Spruille Braden and that his removal was imminent.[110] When, on March 29, the Argentine Foreign Office issued

---

[107] *The New York Times*, Feb. 13, 16, 1946.

[108] Welles, *op. cit.*, pp. 230-231; Whitaker, "Blue Book Blues," *Current History*, X (April, 1946), 295-296.

[109] Welles, *op. cit.*, p. 230.

[110] *The New York Times*, March 11, 1946.

its rebuttal to the "Blue Book," it concluded its argument with an appeal for restoration of good neighborliness. It would be absurd, declared Foreign Minister Cooke, to prolong the controversy. "It is the duty of the strong to be tolerant with the weak. The United States cannot disregard this concept." [111]

In Washington, Assistant Secretary Braden publicly declared in March that "we would look silly" if we now broke relations with Argentina. Restoration of economic sanctions, he said, would only stop the flow of food to starving Europe. In accepting the Director Generalship of UNNRA, Fiorello H. LaGuardia announced that he would go straight to Juan Perón for wheat.[112]

Senior members of the Senate Foreign Relations Committee, who had voiced their opposition to Braden's policies in the previous October, again expressed their dissatisfaction with the handling of the Argentine problem. Pressure on the White House brought about the appointment of an ambassador to Buenos Aires, where only a chargé d'affaires had been accredited since Braden's departure.[113] The appointee was George S. Messersmith, Ambassador to Mexico and veteran career officer with wide experience in Latin America. His selection assured skillful and temperate direction of the sensitive post.

Messersmith and Truman Make Peace with Perón

In spite of Colonel Perón's decisive electoral victory and Washington's convincing diplomatic defeat, the Hull-Braden policy of coercion required yet another year to run its full course. Only in June, 1947, when Mr. Braden resigned his post as Assistant Secretary of State, did President Truman announce unqualified American willingness to enter a Hemisphere defense pact with Argentina.[114] In the meantime, as Washington licked its wounds and Perón consolidated his power, the two nations continued their intermittent sparring over unsettled postwar problems.

The State Department did not wait until Perón's inauguration to reaffirm its postelection attitude. In a memorandum of April 1, noting the forthcoming renewal of constitutional government in Argentina, it reminded the other American republics that Axis influences still threat-

[111] The Argentine reply to the "Blue Book," entitled *La República Argentina ante el "libro azul,"* was a hastily assembled collection of documents, speeches, and other materials, most of which the Foreign Office had published previously, especially in Cooke, *Three Statements,* and in *Board for the Vigilance and Final Disposal of Enemy Property, Precis of Its Activities from Its Creation to January 15, 1946.* Portions of the report were reprinted in *The New York Times,* March 30, April 18, 1946.
[112] *Ibid.,* March 28, 30, 1946.
[113] Welles, *op. cit.,* p. 233.
[114] See below, pp. 457-458.

ened the security of the Hemisphere. Only when the new Argentine administration had complied fully with its Chapultepec commitments, it made clear, by "deeds and not merely promises," would the United States consent to negotiation of a mutual assistance pact.[115]

Strengthened by his restoration to the active Army list and his promotion to the rank of brigadier general, President-elect Perón could approach his inauguration with assurance of wide support for whatever program he proposed. Though in his inaugural address he dealt chiefly with domestic affairs, he tersely reasserted Argentina's traditional foreign policy foundations. It would continue to respect all other countries, he said, but only in return for consideration of its own sovereignty. Since "victory does not give rights," as Argentina had maintained for a century, it would continue to rely on negotiation as the means for prevention or settlement of international disputes. To the extent that they were consistent with the national laws and constitution, it would fulfill all its international obligations. From this point of view, Perón declared, the Congress would scrutinize the Act of Chapultepec and the United Nations Charter. Beyond this, in what he presented as the "very simple philosophy which guides our international relations," he mentioned no individual nation nor specific international problem.[116]

However vague or generalized, Perón's statements on Argentina's foreign policy seemed slanted toward Washington. Spurning the opportunity to gloat over his recent diplomatic victory or reopen the sores of previous controversy, he held out the possibility of reconciliation.

Promptly, however, the new president set a fresh arrow in his bow. Two days after his inauguration he formally opened diplomatic relations with the Soviet Union, ruptured since February, 1918.[117] Timing this action with a period of increased world tension over Russian threats to Iran, Perón was beginning to prepare the groundwork for his "Third Position" in world diplomacy, which he would seek to maintain throughout his term in office.

In his official relations with Washington, President Perón proceeded to play one angle after another. First, he demanded that the Truman administration free Argentina's more than a half-billion dollars in frozen gold assets. Then, professing genuine friendship for the United States but only a mercantile interest in the Soviet Union, he promised to bring to early trial Nazi refugees in Argentina. On June 26, though without

---

[115] Department of State, *Bulletin*, XIV (April 21, 1946), 666-667; *The New York Times*, April 9, 1946. A few weeks later, even in the wake of President Truman's revolutionary proposal for a program of inter-American military collaboration, Under Secretary Dean Acheson spurned an Argentine overture for arms aid (Council on Foreign Relations, *The United States in World Affairs, 1945-1947*, p. 230).

[116] The entire address appears in *Informaciones argentinas*, 1946, No. 105, p. 18. See Whitaker, *op. cit.*, pp. 216-217.

[117] *The New York Times*, June 7, 1946.

specific recommendation, he transmitted to the Argentine Congress both the Act of Chapultepec and the Charter of the United Nations. On August 1 he publicly announced that in any future war Argentina would fight with the United States and the other American nations.[118]

Early ratification of the two multilateral pacts by the Peronista legislature, however, served to clarify the President's intentions. Whatever the state of its relations with the Soviet Union or other individual nations, he manifestly wished to secure Argentina's place in both the inter-American organization and the United Nations. In this he acted consistently with the nation's long-standing record toward international bodies—always join up, whatever actions collective deliberations or decisions might later dictate.

To these diverse overtures from the resourceful Perón, Byrnes and Braden showed no signs of relaxing their stubborn position. Though they agreed to free Argentina's blocked funds and to lift the black list against Axis firms, they remained as staunchly opposed as before to entering a security pact with Perón's government.[119] In spite of pressures from Capitol Hill and the Latin capitals, they secured further postponement of the Rio meeting as well as of the Ninth Inter-American Conference, tentatively scheduled for Bogotá in 1946. To counteract growing criticism of Mr. Braden and his tenacious position, in late October both President Truman and Secretary Byrnes issued strong public statements in his defense. In Buenos Aires, endeavoring faithfully to fulfill the special mission which had fallen to his lot, Ambassador Messersmith sought to convince porteño leaders that the United States would not sacrifice principles for harmony or accept promises for deeds.[120]

In the meantime, heady with new power, Perón plunged aggressively forward with his bold personal and nationalistic designs. Before the end of September his government had purchased the American-owned United River Plate Telephone Company, signed a rich, new meat contract with Britain, secured release of large stocks of blocked funds in London, and taken the first steps toward nationalization of British-owned railroads. By demanding larger portions of Bolivia's rubber and tin exports in return for adequate food supplies, by exerting diverse pressures against Uruguay, by tightening economic collaboration with Chile, and by reviving its claim to the Falkland Islands, the Perón government seemed to be aiming at redemption of the lands once included in Spain's Viceroyalty of the Río de la Plata. Before the end of the year Perón's Congress had written into law a gigantic five-year

---

[118] *Ibid.*, June 22, 25, 27, Aug. 2, 1946.
[119] *Ibid.*, June 26, July 9, 1946.
[120] *The United States in World Affairs, 1945-1947*, pp. 230-231; *The New York Times*, July 5, Oct. 23, Nov. 1, 1946.

plan, comprising an omnibus of twenty-seven separate laws. By giving the state power over everything from education to property, the blueprint spelled out the plans for the new scheme of state socialism.[121]

While the success of President Perón's domestic program did nothing to relieve the stalemate with Washington, other forces were pressing the State Department to modify its unyielding position. Increasingly disturbed by postwar economic and social dislocations, the Latin American states pleaded the urgency of assistance and leadership from the United States. The widening deterioration of Soviet-American relations increased the concern of American military leaders for improved Hemisphere defenses. Critical of Mr. Braden's continuing "tough policy," Senators Connally and Vandenberg and other congressional leaders decried the weakening of inter-American solidarity in the face of spreading communism.[122]

The recall of Ambassador Messersmith to Washington at the close of the year, after barely seven months on his trouble-shooting mission, encouraged these groups to hope that a change in State Department policy might be imminent. Secretary Byrnes's replacement by General George Marshall on January 8 buoyed their hopes. At the outset of his tenure, the transparent disagreement between Braden and Messersmith confronted the new Secretary. While the Ambassador admitted that Argentina had not completely eradicated Axis influences, he apparently had confidence in Perón's intentions to fulfill his nation's Hemisphere commitments. Braden had not receded in the slightest from his rock-ribbed conviction that to gain full readmission to Hemisphere councils Argentina must purge itself of all Axis ties.[123]

Faced with the choice of changing policy, sacking a valued official, or postponing a decision, President Truman and Secretary Marshall chose to procrastinate. While retaining Spruille Braden as Assistant Secretary, they ordered Ambassador Messersmith to return to Buenos Aires. But, the state of the world's affairs in early 1947 would not let this deadlock endure. With diverse forces pressing for an end to coercion of Argentina, the State Department could not long postpone the inevitable.[124]

By gradual steps the Truman administration moved toward full reconciliation with the Argentine regime. In late January the State Department hailed Perón's decree providing elimination of enemy control over sixty spearhead Axis firms.[125] Three months later, as Ambas-

---

[121] *Ibid.,* Sept. 18, 22, Oct. 6, 24, Nov. 17, 20, Dec. 14, 1946. The United River Plate Telephone Company was owned by the International Telephone and Telegraph Company.

[122] Smith, *op. cit.,* p. 166; *The New York Times,* Dec. 24, 1946, Jan. 12, 1947.

[123] Department of State, *Bulletin,* XVI, pt. 1, (Jan. 19, 1947), 83, 86-87; *The New York Times,* Dec. 24, 1946, Jan. 8, 1947.

[124] *The United States in World Affairs, 1945-1947,* pp. 231-232.

[125] Department of State, *Bulletin,* XVI, pt. 1 (Feb. 2, 1947), 214.

sador Oscar Ivanissevich prepared to return to Buenos Aires, President Truman went out of his way to invite him to the White House. He expressed his desire to end Argentine-American misunderstandings and to proceed with the inter-American defense agreement.[126] Speaking before representatives of all the American republics on Pan American Day, Senator Vandenberg renewed his long-standing plea that Hemisphere unity demanded the collaboration of "all" the republics. A month later General Marshall overruled Assistant Secretary Braden's opposition to Army-Navy plans for transfer of military equipment to other American states.[127]

The climax to four years of strained relations came on June 3, when President Truman declared that "no obstacle remained to discussions looking toward the treaty of mutual assistance contemplated by the Act of Chapultepec." Hard on the heels of this White House statement, the State Department announced the completion of Messersmith's mission and the resignation of Mr. Braden. To the assistant secretary's post it appointed the officer who had preceded him in Buenos Aires, Norman Armour, veteran diplomat recently retired.[128]

During the first four years of the Army-Perón regime the Argentine government pursued with undeviating consistency the nation's traditional foreign policies. Like its predecessors, civilian or military, Radical or Conservative, it resisted all foreign pressures, especially those from the United States, that threatened impairment of national sovereignty. No matter what the issues at stake, it spurned all measures which might have committed it to active participation in a war of the Great Powers. Through war and peace alike it sought to renew Argentine leadership of the Latin American republics, sometimes at the expense of weak neighboring states, always with a weather eye on Brazil's power. Except on occasion to preserve the national interests, it clung to its routine of bilateral diplomacy. At the same time, United States policy toward Argentina and Latin America revealed essential inconsistencies. Fresh from its reluctant acceptance of the doctrine of nonintervention, Washington resorted to diverse forms of coercion, including both individual and collective sanctions, to bring Argentina into the war and to cleanse it of prototalitarian influences. In its deep concern over Argentina's plight, the State Department ignored even the new machinery of Hemisphere consultation, conceived and developed by statesmen of the two nations. Temporary retreat from coercion in 1944 and tacit confession of its failure in 1947 only underscored this lack of consistency.

[126] *The New York Times*, April 15, 1947. The President invited Under Secretary Acheson, but not Assistant Secretary Braden, to attend this conference.

[127] *Ibid.*, April. 15, May 23, 1947.

[128] Department of State, *Bulletin*, XVI, pt. 2 (June 15, 1947), p. 1177; *The New York Times*, June 4, 6, 10, 1947.

X X V

COLD WAR IN THE AMERICAS:
RIVALRY FOR HEMISPHERE LEADERSHIP,
1947-1955

By the time President Truman had mended Washington's diplomatic fences with General Perón in June, 1947, circumstances had cast the shape of the postwar world. From pole to pole, in the Eastern Hemisphere and the Western, the world was in ferment.

To the east and west of the great Soviet heartland utter defeat of once-powerful enemies left gigantic power vacuums to be filled by the victors, singly or in collaboration. Across the onetime colonial areas of South and Southeast Asia, the Middle East, and Africa native nationalist leaders surged to free their peoples from exploitive bondage, political or economic. Through social revolutions, which often utilized some form of collectivist politics, the underprivileged peoples scrambled to modernize and industrialize their backward economies.

To cope with the manifold problems of both vanquished nations and rising peoples, most Americans, North and South, for two years had hopefully relied on the agencies of international cooperation, especially the new organs of the United Nations. But, by the spring of 1947, the failure to attain Soviet-American agreement in Korea, the breakdown of four-power collaboration in Germany, Soviet domination of the satellite areas, and American decision to contain communism through the Truman Doctrine had exposed the futility of these hopes. Already the polarization of lesser states around the great power centers of Moscow and Washington had begun. In what came to be called "the Cold War," the two gigantic nuclei lost the powers of mutual attraction with which the exigencies of World War II had cloaked them.[1]

More than other peoples of the world, the Latin American republics lay outside the mainstream of these postwar developments in power

[1] I have adapted this general interpretation from William G. Carleton, *The Revolution in American Foreign Policy* (New York, 1954, 1957).

politics. Unlike the rising peoples of Asia and Africa, they had long since escaped from political servitude to colonial powers. Unlike Poland or Hungary, Greece or Turkey, Iran or Korea, they were far removed from the path of Soviet expansion. They had not yet felt the sharpest edges of Moscow's propaganda or infiltration.

Yet, even in their diplomatic backwater, the Latin Americans faced frustrations and dangers. Allied purchases of the sinews of war slowed down. Essential imports of production equipment and consumers' goods, still in short supply, demanded high prices. Vast backlogs of foreign exchange accelerated inflation. Combined with rising populations and leashed opposition to entrenched administrations, these economic dislocations produced social unrest and political dissatisfaction.

In this situation most of the Latin American states were ripe for Hemisphere leadership that would bring them the security, stability, and satisfaction of "rising expectations" they desired. Since V-J Day they had looked to Washington, but vainly, for a revival of the Pan American spirit they had so hopefully endorsed. With suspicious but attentive eyes they looked to Buenos Aires, where the constitutional president, Juan Perón, was already promoting the Hemisphere hegemony to which Argentina had long aspired.

President Truman's decision to come to terms with Perón, therefore, stemmed directly from Washington's expanding responsibilities in world affairs and from Argentina's growing influence in the Western Hemisphere. The President's willingness to proceed, at last, with the oft-postponed inter-American conference to regularize the Act of Chapultepec demonstrated his determination to reinvigorate United States leadership. At the same time, by consolidating his power at home and by injecting his nation into Hemisphere and world affairs, President Perón revealed his own eagerness to reassert Argentina's claim to importance. After 1947, even more than before, the two nations became rivals for leadership in the Americas.[2]

[2] For the study of Argentina and its relations with the United States since 1947 no official manuscript materials and few official published sources are available. In the preparation of this and the following chapters, therefore, I have leaned heavily upon several secondary volumes, each based in part upon the author's contemporary observation and investigation in Argentina. More often than I have cited them, I owe a special debt to: R. J. Alexander, *The Perón Era* (New York, 1951); G. I. Blanksten, *Perón's Argentina* (Chicago, 1953); George Pendle, *Argentina* (London, 1955); and A. P. Whitaker, *The United States and Argentina* (Cambridge, 1954) and *Argentine Upheaval: Perón's Fall and the New Regime* (New York, 1956). For the setting of United States foreign policy toward Latin America, I have used extensively the annual volumes of the Council on World Relations, *The United States in World Affairs*. For the day-to-day sequence of events, I have drawn upon *The New York Times*. The most useful study of Perón and Peronismo is the one-volume summary of the five volumes of findings of the Argentine Comisión Nacional de Investigaciones (latter not publicly available), both published by the Provisional Government in 1958, *Libro Negro de la segunda tiranía, Decreto ley No. 14988/56* (hereafter cited as *Libro Negro*). The Lonardi government created the Commission on October 7, 1955.

Perón's Program at Home

Months before his return to the good graces of the White House, Juan Perón had revealed to Argentina and the world the distinctive character of his leadership and the comprehensive nature of his revolutionary program. On repeated occasions, through his charm, masculinity, and demagogic appeal, he had shown his capacity to rekindle the ardor of the laboring masses he had organized and to renew the loyalty of the armed forces from which he had sprung.

Perón's lifetime in the Argentine army, as his critics maintained, may have saddled him with the normal limitations of the professional soldier and indoctrinated him with the tactics of the barracks and the drill field. But, interrupted frequently by periods of teaching, writing, advanced study, and foreign service, his military career had also given him a deep interest in history, its leaders, and the lives of people.[3] "The words 'national defense,'" he said in 1944,

> may make some of you think this is a problem whose presentation and solution are of interest only to the nation's armed forces. The truth is very different: into its solution go all the inhabitants, all their energies, all their industries and production, all their means of transport and communication, the armed forces being merely . . . the fighting instrument of that great whole which is 'the nation in arms.'[4]

From the experiences of Mussolini, Hitler, Franco, Vargas, Rosas, and Uriburu, the General knew how to adapt what was most suitable for Argentina. Yet he made his dictatorship distinctively his own and uniquely criollo.[5]

To assure the fulfillment of his program for the "new Argentina," Perón had first to secure, then consolidate, a position of power. Throughout his years of tenure, he gave almost unremitting attention to this task. Prior to his election to the presidency in 1946, he used his positions as Secretary of Labor and Social Security, Minister of War, and Vice-President to build up a personal following in the ranks of labor, the Army, and the inarticulate masses and to raise his friends to key government posts.[6]

Once elevated, by a convincing popular majority, to the Casa Rosada, the President had at his command the broad constitutional powers granted to the Argentine chief executive. Promptly and efficiently he pro-

---

[3] Whitaker, *The United States and Argentina*, pp. 118-121; *Libro Negro*, pp. 37-42.
[4] Ysabel F. Rennie, *The Argentine Republic*, p. 375.
[5] Whitaker, *op. cit.*, pp. 116-121. Cf. Bernardo Rabinovitz, *Sucedió en la Argentina (1943-1956): lo que no se dijo*, pp. 49-50.
[6] Alexander, *The Perón Era*, pp. 84-102, 115-132; Blanksten, *Perón's Argentina*, pp. 306-328; Pendle, *Argentina*, pp. 85-86; Whitaker, *op. cit.*, pp. 140-145.

ceeded to bend to his will all branches and agencies of government. His sweeping electoral victory brought Peronista majorities to both houses of Congress. His control of the legislative branch assured the successful purge in 1947 of the Supreme Court and by 1949 of all inferior national courts.

After decisive triumph by his followers in the congressional elections of March, 1948, Perón took steps to ensure his perpetuation in office and the continuance of his program. Broad revision of the constitution by March, 1949, repealed the prohibition against immediate re-election of the president, granted the state expanded economic powers, especially over foreign trade, natural resources, and public services, and elevated to supreme law of the land important phases of the social revolution. Four months later, by organizing the *Partido Peronista,* under his own leadership, Perón introduced to Argentina the one-party system familiar in European dictatorships.[7]

Once in effective control of all the instrumentalities of government, the dictator could move easily to muzzle potential sources of dissidence. Very soon he exercised his constitutional right to "intervene" the six national universities, gradually purged their faculties of liberal-minded professors, and ultimately took over appointment of their rectors. At the lower educational levels, by dictating the choice of textbooks and dismissing noncompliant teachers, the government effectively controlled instruction of youth. Sensitive, like all dictators, to public criticism, Perón moved against the articulate Argentine press. Through intimidation, excessive regulation, or outright suspension, he gagged journalistic opposition. Ultimately, by 1951, he closed even the famous Socialist *La Vanguardia* and turned the distinguished *La Prensa* over to the government-directed General Confederation of Labor.[8]

By broadening existent laws against treason and *desacato* ("disrespect" for the regime or its officials), the dictatorship made it possible to arrest or imprison almost any opponent or even alleged critic. By greatly enlarging the Federal Police, it undergirded the quasi-totalitarian control that gradually sapped the vitality of proud Argentina and violently shocked its friends in the other American republics.[9]

Firmly entrenched in all the seats of power, Perón and his henchmen could accelerate the manifold phases of their social and economic program. Through hundreds of laws and decrees they undertook the systematic renovation of Argentine life. By 1949 they had begun to refer to *justicialismo,* their new revolutionary philosophy. As Perón's critics

---

[7] *Libro Negro,* pp. 56-61, 68-70, 110-122, 124, 131-134; Whitaker, *op. cit.,* pp. 153-158.

[8] *Ibid.,* pp. 152-153, 158-161; *Libro Negro,* pp. 93-101, 163, 168-169, 175-176; Blanksten, *op. cit.,* pp. 186-219.

[9] Pendle, *op. cit.,* pp. 96-97.

alleged, justicialismo may have been nothing more than "gobbledygook" or intellectual mishmash.[10] Or it may have been, as his followers claimed, a worthy innovation in the field of social and political philosophy. In any case, to foes and friends alike, it became a useful label. It might denominate either the dictator's sins against the Argentine people or his efforts to improve their lives.

Interpreters of Argentine history have most often defined justicialismo as the "Third Position" taken by Perón's administration. This, writes one American analyst, may have several allusions. It may refer to Perón's domestic economic policies—to his "third position" between the oligarchy and the underprivileged. It may refer to his domestic political actions—to his avoidance of extremism, neither the full protection nor the complete destruction of personal liberties, political parties, or federal principles. Or it may refer to his foreign policies—to his "third position" between the United States and the Soviet Union, between capitalism and communism.[11] But the Third Position was not centrism or neutralism. It did not advocate fence-straddling or middle-of-the-road policies. As Perón himself characterized it, justicialismo was fluid, not fixed, and, as circumstances demanded, might veer to the right or to the left.[12]

In whatever way it is defined, the two main ends of justicialismo, often proclaimed by Peronista spokesmen, were "social justice" and "economic independence." To each of these, before and after his election to the presidency, Perón gave continuing obeisance. To bring about social justice, the Peronista Congress enacted a broad program of welfare legislation. It committed the nation to support minimum wages, the forty-hour week, pay for holidays, dismissal and compensation payments, retirement and pension benefits, restriction of child labor, and aid to expectant and nursing mothers. Though not always successful, Perón sought to stabilize the cost of living and to tie pensions to rising price indices.[13]

Through her warmhearted, but obviously demagogic, appeal, Señora Eva Perón championed the cause of her favored descamisados. Using her offices in the Ministry of Health and the Secretariat of Labor and Social Welfare, she encouraged the expansion of hospital facilities and abetted campaigns against prevalent diseases. Through her private Social Aid Foundation, supported principally by funds raised through her own efforts, Evita carried her philanthropies to all parts of the

---

[10] For several recent criticisms see Rabinovitz, *op. cit.*, p. 212, and Humberto Zamboni, *Peronismo, justicialismo: juicio crítico*, pp. 11-12, 63-64, 71, 75-76.

[11] Blanksten, *op. cit.*, pp. 292-293. Cf. *Libro Negro*, pp. 125-126.

[12] O. D. Confalonieri, *Perón contra Perón*, pp. 247-248; Whitaker, *op. cit.*, pp. 209-210.

[13] *Libro Negro*, pp. 152-154; Pendle, *op. cit.*, pp. 104-106.

nation.[14] By her personal fire and indefatigable energy she helped to create the myth of Perón—and the myth of Evita, "the spiritual chief of the nation." [15]

At the expense of the wealthy, these various schemes for social amelioration improved for the masses of unskilled workers and their families a palpably low standard of living. In return, they gave to Perón the support he sought. The middle classes, including professional people, tradesmen, and skilled workers, were left to fend for themselves.[16]

In seeking his second goal, economic independence, Perón aimed even more sharply at the creation of a new Argentina. Ever conscious of the dramatic, the President selected July 9, 1947, anniversary of political independence, and Tucumán, site of its proclamation, to issue Argentina's "Declaration of Economic Independence." In ringing language it boldly reasserted

> the firm purpose of the Argentine people to gain their economic independence from the capitalistic foreign powers which have exercised their tutelage, control and command, in the form of condemnable economic hegemony, and of those in the country who might be connected with them.[17]

In these terms Perón proclaimed his determination to eliminate foreign ownership of public utilities, decrease Argentine dependence on foreign imports, and weaken further the position of the agrarian oligarchs.

In seeking to fulfill these strongly nationalist purposes, the Argentine administration created two types of governmental economic instrumentalities. First, it founded the *Instituto Argentino de Promoción del Intercambio* (IAPI), a gigantic purchasing agency with almost unlimited powers to buy and sell Argentine crops and to use the profits in foreign trading. Secondly, it formed semigovernmental corporations to promote and stimulate domestic economic activities. In addition, by nationalizing the Central Bank (1946) and centralizing the insurance business (1947), the government virtually monopolized the nation's money stocks.[18]

With all these agencies at his command, Perón now occupied a formidable position from which to dominate the economic life of the nation. He consummated the purchase of the English-owned railways. He took steps to pay off Argentina's foreign debt. He vastly expanded the government-owned merchant marine and moved into the production of electric power and the operation of civil airlines.

Under the authority of the revised constitution (1949) and the battery

---

[14] *Ibid.*, pp. 103-104; James Bruce, *Those Perplexing Argentines*, pp. 280-287.

[15] *Libro Negro*, pp. 44-45.

[16] Whitaker, *op. cit.*, pp. 204-208.

[17] *Perón expone su doctrina*, pp. 151-152.

[18] Pendle, *op. cit.*, pp. 87-91; Whitaker, *op. cit.*, pp. 177-180; *Libro Negro*, pp. 155-156, 195-202.

of laws embodied in the first Five-Year Plan, these extensive actions would carry Argentina far along the road to the economic independence proclaimed at Tucumán. They would also strengthen Perón's hand as he sought to broaden Argentina's leadership in the Hemisphere and forge its Third Position in world affairs.

Truman's Program in the Hemisphere

For the American people, however, in the early months of 1947 there was a greater foreign danger than Perón's disquieting activities. The opening skirmishes of the Cold War, signalized by pronouncement of the Truman Doctrine and Secretary Marshall's trial balloon on economic aid, dictated to the White House the urgency of putting Western Hemisphere affairs in order. To the cause of continental solidarity, therefore, in the face of the new threat from Europe, Americans would have to subordinate their concern over Argentina. President Truman's tentative *rapprochement* with Perón in June, 1947, removed the last barrier to inter-American negotiations for the treaty of mutual assistance contemplated in the Act of Chapultepec.[19]

In seeking to recapture the Pan American spirit and shore up the crumbling structure of the Inter-American System, the Truman administration now revived or re-emphasized four goals it had cherished since the end of the war: military collaboration, Hemisphere security, economic stability, and political solidarity. To each of these, in spite of deepening involvement in Europe and the Far East, Washington directed its attention during the next year.

As to military collaboration among the American republics, the War and Navy Departments had not waited upon the grinding wheels of diplomacy. Even before V-J Day, the War Department had initiated studies aimed at standardization of equipment, training, and organization of Hemisphere armies. Though lacking explicit directives for its operations, the Inter-American Defense Board had recommended consolidation of continental defenses. Influenced by these pressures, President Truman had presented to Congress on May 8, 1946, the Inter-American Military Cooperation bill, which would authorize the president to negotiate bilateral agreements with the other American states. These might cover the sending of arms, ships, supplies, technical information, and training missions. Shelved at one session of Congress, the bill was reintroduced by the President a year later, with the same result.[20]

Mindful of Brazil's military expansion during the war and of their own failure to share in Lend-Lease aid, Argentine leaders could not rejoice

[19] See above, pp. 443-444.
[20] Ernesto Galarza, "The Standardization of Armaments in the Western Hemisphere," *Inter-American Reports,* No. 1 (Oct., 1947).

over this proposal. Such a plan, they were quick to see, might freeze the very military inferiority that had long vexed their armed services. And standardization, however free the flow of American equipment, might hamstring their own growing armaments industry and tie their entire defense establishment to their northern rival. Moreover, they had not forgotten the rebuff given their former chief of staff, General Carlos von der Becke, in May, 1946, when he had approached General Eisenhower and Under Secretary of State Acheson about the purchase of arms.[21]

Fixing of August 15 as the date for the Rio Conference on Hemisphere security pushed aside for the time being the question of military collaboration. It represented, too, a personal diplomatic triumph for Juan Perón over Washington. Without demanding the slightest shift in policies it had opposed for two years, the United States now consented to treat the Argentine nation as an equal worthy of inclusion in a mutual security pact. With blithe confidence, therefore, on the eve of the Conference, Perón's foreign minister, Juan Bramuglia, could assure Argentina's commitment to "absolute and complete American solidarity."[22] His delegation bore the Argentine sun to its first important inter-American conference since January, 1942. Besides Bramuglia, soon to win prestige in the United Nations Security Council, the delegation included the Argentine ambassadors to Brazil and the United States. Among its advisors were General Von der Becke, only a few months returned from Washington, and Colonel Eduardo Lonardi, leader-to-be of the anti-Perón movement of 1955.

President Truman named as distinguished a delegation as had represented the United States at any inter-American gathering. Secretary of State George C. Marshall headed a group composed of William D. Pawley, Ambassador to Brazil, Senators Arthur H. Vandenberg and Tom Connally, Representative Sol Bloom, and Warren R. Austin, Representative to the United Nations.[23] The lone agenda item facing these and other delegations was the Treaty of Reciprocal Assistance. In the debates on the American proposal, Argentina readily resumed its well-worn place as principal opponent of Washington's intentions, though with less intransigence and less success than usual.

Foreign Minister Bramuglia raised his voice on four basic points. First, he proposed that collective sanctions should be applied against aggression only by a non-American nation. Senator Vandenberg dubbed this

---

[21] *The United States in World Affairs, 1945-1947*, pp. 227-230; *1947-1948*, pp. 109-112. See above, p. 455, note 115.

[22] *The New York Times*, Aug. 9, 1947.

[23] *Inter-American Conference for the Maintenance of Continental Peace and Security, . . . Report of the Delegation of the United States of America*, pp. 163-164, 168-170. Norman Armour was a political adviser to the American delegation.

proposal "an armed alliance against the rest of the world." [24] Secondly, the Foreign Minister insisted upon the right of each nation to veto any collective action against an aggressor.[25] Uruguay favored decision by simple majority, but all others agreed to the compromise two-thirds vote.[26] Thirdly, the Argentine sought to preclude collective action in case an American nation were attacked outside the Hemisphere zone defined in the treaty. The Conference agreed only that action in such cases should not be automatic. On his fourth sally, Bramuglia fared better. Renewing Argentina's oft-stated claims to the Falkland Islands and asserting its sovereignty over a sector of Antarctica, he gained the inclusion of these areas in the Hemisphere defense zone.[27] On the key issues of the debate, Argentina led a losing cause, but, in the end, as Bramuglia had forecast, it accepted in good grace the will of the majority.

In two instances unrelated to the official agenda, Argentina managed to capture the spotlight. During the early stages of the deliberations Bramuglia pressed vigorously for a Conference decision to call a special inter-American meeting on urgent economic matters. Introducing Perón's Third Position, he called for a kind of "Marshall plan" for the Americas to eliminate "capitalist and totalitarian extremes, whatever their origin and their particular constituents." Just five minutes before Secretary Marshall's scheduled reply to these overtures, Argentina staged its most dramatic act of the Conference. Fresh from her publicized visits to Rome, Madrid, and Paris, Eva Perón entered the conference hall at Quitandinha to capture a significant, if fleeting, moment of glory for Argentina and her husband.[28]

The third of President Truman's goals for revivifying Pan Americanism—economic stability—involved the most tortuous and the least successful proceedings of the four. By 1947, in contrast with their early postwar prosperity, most of the Latin American nations were suffering from inflation, depletion of dollar reserves, overexpansion of wartime industries, and need to replace production equipment. Moreover, they sought capital for power development, improved transportation, and broadened industrialization. Their search for needed funds was discouraging. The International Bank had given them no loans. The Export-Import Bank had loaned them comparatively little. The European Recovery Program offered hope, but its help would be indirect and slow

[24] *Report of the Delegation,* pp. 16-17, 84-87; *The New York Times,* Aug. 23, 1947.

[25] On this point Argentina betrayed its inconsistency. On several occasions, both before and after the Rio meeting, it proposed to the United Nations General Assembly abolition of the veto in the Security Council (*The New York Times,* July 19, 1947, March 17, Sept. 7, Dec. 2, 1948).

[26] *Report of the Delegation,* pp. 33, 195.

[27] *Ibid.,* pp. 56, 61.

[28] *The New York Times,* Aug. 17, 21, 1947.

in arriving. Believing its public funds should go first to Western Europe, then to China, Washington persistently sought to quiet the Latin clamor by urging them to seek private funds, domestic and foreign.[29]

Washington's dilemma again became Argentina's opportunity. Blessed with high prices for its bumper food crops, its wartime balances of foreign exchange still not exhausted, Argentina was riding the crest of a boom. Perón did not miss the opening. Through the use of bilateral agreements, he granted long-term loans or credits to neighbors Bolivia and Chile and to half a dozen European nations.[30] Peronista spokesmen began to refer to the "Perón plan."

The climax to Perón's bid for economic leadership of the Latin American states came in late 1947 at the United Nations Conference on Trade and Employment in Havana. Though Argentina had joined the United Nations, it had still not affiliated with the International Bank for Development, the International Monetary Fund, the Food and Agriculture Organization, or UNESCO, nor had it ratified the General Agreement on Tariffs and Trade. But the Havana meeting to consider methods of reducing barriers to easy flow of international trade offered Argentina the chance to win prestige among the underdeveloped nations.[31]

The draft charter for the proposed International Trade Organization, supported by the United States and other nations, promptly came under barbed attack by the Argentine delegates. Leader of the assault, aimed without quarter at the United States, was Diego Luís Molinari, long a figure in Argentine public life and now an ardent Peronista. Arrogating to himself spokesmanship for the less privileged nations, he hurled a challenge at United States leadership of social and economic reconstruction, not only in Latin America, but in the world. He portrayed the American type of capitalism as "an international spider web of Shylocks squeezing the heart of hungry multitudes." [32] Instead of the principles of the International Trade Organization, he proposed freedom to use import quotas, exchange controls, preferential tariffs, and state trading. Though the statement was subsequently reinterpreted in different vein in Buenos Aires, Molinari announced that Argentina was ready to provide economic aid to the extent of $5,000,000,000.[33]

At the close of the Conference on March 23, 1948, Argentina and Poland alone refused to sign the Havana Charter. Though they had

[29] *The United States in World Affairs, 1947-1948*, pp. 127-136; *1948-1949*, pp. 367-368.

[30] *The New York Times*, Oct. 14, 1947, March 14, 1948; Whitaker, *op. cit.*, pp. 175-176, 227.

[31] *Ibid.*, pp. 225-227; *The United States in World Affairs, 1947-1948*, pp. 266-273.

[32] *The New York Times*, Dec. 3, 1947.

[33] What Molinari apparently meant to say was that, if furnished with adequate supplies of vital materials and equipment, Argentina could provide $5,000,000,000 worth of meat and grains within the next five years. His statement assumed, therefore, that outright sale of food supplies constituted "economic aid" (*ibid.*, Dec. 19, 1947).

failed to win the adherents they had hoped for, Perón's representatives had staked out afresh their anti-United States position. Argentina, they proclaimed, would continue to do business only on its traditional bilateral basis.

Hemisphere economic questions still unresolved, therefore, the Truman administration turned to the fourth of its goals for the rejuvenation of the Inter-American System—political solidarity. Since its founding in 1889-1890, the organization had lacked permanent constitutional status. To replace the omnibus of treaties and resolutions upon which authority had rested, the Chapultepec Conference (February, 1945) officially acknowledged the need for a charter. It directed the Governing Board of the Pan American Union to prepare such a document for consideration by the Ninth Inter-American Conference, scheduled to meet in Bogotá. Recognition of regional organizations in the United Nations Charter had dictated prompt action upon this task. But delay on the proposed mutual assistance pact postponed the Bogotá Conference until March, 1948.

Perón's representatives at Bogotá maintained the principles which long since had become the hallmark of Argentine foreign policy: resist all efforts to strengthen the regional system; emphasize the efficacy of bilateral rather than multilateral diplomacy; and check the slightest attempt to impair national sovereignty.

Concentrating fire on the long-contemplated draft charter, Foreign Minister Bramuglia termed it an attempt to create a "superstate" and opposed proposals to give the organization more than administrative powers. Failing on this point, he did succeed in preventing an Advisory Defense Committee from becoming a permanent organ of the newly established Council.[34] On the issue of Hemisphere defense against international communism, the Argentine stood staunchly by Perón's developing Third Position. Communism could be frustrated, he argued, only by sound economic policies. Each nation must deal with its communists in its own way. On the issue of recognition, he opposed a resolution which seemed to him to revive the "collective action" principle of the scotched Rodríguez Larreta doctrine.[35]

Joining Guatemala and Chile in twisting the tail of the weakened British lion, the Argentines lent their support to a resolution calling for the end of European colonies in the Americas. As so often in the past, they were thinking of the "illegally occupied" Falkland Islands as well as their new claims to Antarctica. They sought to characterize European colonies as incompatible with American ideals and menacing

[34] *Ninth International Conference of American States . . . , Report of the Delegation of the United States,* pp. 14, 26. In the debate over a name for the organization, the Argentines opposed such proposals as "union," "association," or "community."
[35] *Ibid.,* pp. 82-84; 266-267. Also see above, pp. 451-452.

to Hemisphere security. Though the resolution adopted was considerably milder than the Argentines proposed, the United States delegates were unwilling to affront their British ally by approving it. To avoid opposing what the Argentines and others called their "just aspiration," therefore, the Americans abstained from the final vote.[36]

By April, 1948, the Truman administration could regard with some satisfaction its efforts of the previous ten months to refurbish the tarnished shield of Pan Americanism. Conclusion of the Rio Defense Pact, soon to come into force, seemed to render more secure a vulnerable Hemisphere flank.[37] Approval of the Charter of the Organization of American States appeared to put the capstone on more than half a century's search for political solidarity through a regional organization. Yet, in spite of these successes, military collaboration and economic stability remained as elusive goals. Deep-seated differences over economic issues, especially, left a possible avenue of threat for extremist movements in the Hemisphere. And though Perón's Argentina had returned as a functioning member of the Inter-American System, its participation was as arrogant and as vexing as before. Perón's drive for prestige and recognition left Washington no room for complacency.

Perón's Program in the Hemisphere

To the extent that it violated human liberties and introduced to the Western Hemisphere features of European totalitarianism, Perón's domestic program dismayed the American government and people. But, by itself, it did little harm to Washington's leadership of the inter-American movement. Rather, it was the dictator's moves against neighboring states and his growing influence throughout the continent that demanded the closest attention of the Truman administration.

Argentina's foreign policy after the election of 1946 was dictated largely by the international ostracism into which the nation had fallen. To regain the prestige it had lost through support of the vanquished powers, Perón saw the need of restoring Argentina's voice to the highest councils of Hemisphere and world. To accomplish this, without weakening the flaming nationalism he had aroused at home, he developed his flexible policy of the Third Position. Without tying his nation or its economy to either communism or capitalism, he could "roll with the punch" while spreading Argentine influence among the nations around him.[38]

Perón's most dramatic pronouncement of his Third Position took the

[36] *Ibid.*, pp. 84-86, 268-269.
[37] With the ratification of the fourteenth nation on December 3, 1948, the Pact became effective.
[38] Cf. Whitaker, *op. cit.*, pp. 209-210.

form of a radio message to the nations of the world on July 6, 1947, when he called for an end to all "capitalistic and totalitarian extremism." He offered Argentina's aid to peoples ravaged by the war and its support for the cause of world peace. In a sequel to this broadcast, Foreign Minister Bramuglia transmitted to all the American republics and the Vatican a special message outlining Argentina's specific proposals for action.[39] Though the appeal fell mainly on arid ground, it served to clarify for the world Argentina's unique position.

Consistent with his justicialist philosophy, therefore, Perón eagerly sent his emissaries to the Rio and Bogotá Inter-American Conferences. While satisfying Washington's hopes for restoration of the united Hemisphere front, the Argentines resourcefully found issues with which to confront the United States and to seek support from the Latin American republics. At the same time, his earlier resumption of diplomatic relations with the Soviet Union, ruptured since 1918, his subsequent trade negotiations with Moscow and satellite nations, and his opposition to inter-American action against communism revealed Perón's willingness to do business on both sides of the street.[40]

In the United Nations, Argentina's representatives were never able to regain the stature Saavedra Lamas had held during his heyday in the League of Nations. Yet, during his brief tenure as President of the Security Council in 1948, Juan Bramuglia emerged as the effective leader of the six-nation group seeking a compromise solution of the West's dispute with Moscow over the Berlin blockade.[41] Otherwise, however, Argentina's voice was heard principally in the General Assembly, where José Arce repeatedly urged abolition of the Great Power veto and enlargement of the Economic and Social Council.[42] Most activities of the United Nations' subsidiary bodies were incompatible with Perón's concepts of Argentine sovereignty and nationalism.

Whatever tactics he may have used to extend Argentine influence in the Western Hemisphere, it is doubtful that President Perón ever seriously contemplated steps to reconstitute the old Viceroyalty of the Río de la Plata. Yet leaders of the neighboring republics could remember the GOU proclamation of 1943 and could hear the chauvinistic preachments of Peronista spokesmen.[43] Faced with disturbed social and political conditions, their nations exposed vulnerable flanks to Argentine pressures. Its own strong economic position after World War II, coupled

[39] Secretary Marshall's reply was a kind of oblique exhortation that Argentina itself contribute more actively to world restoration (Department of State, *Bulletin*, XVII, [Aug. 17, 1947], 337-340).

[40] *The New York Times*, June 7, 16, 1946; March 26, June 12, 1948.

[41] *Documents on American Foreign Relations*, X, 83, 99-100; *The United States in World Affairs, 1948-1949*, pp. 456-464.

[42] See above, p. 431 and note 25.

[43] Bruce, *op. cit.*, pp. 315-316. Also see above, p. 431.

with its traditional propensity for Latin American leadership, offered Perón the chance to spread his doctrines while exporting consumers' goods and capital.

In fishing for effective ways to penetrate the Latin American countries with his ideas of Peronismo and the Third Position, Perón used four principal techniques: negotiation of bilateral economic pacts, assignment of labor attachés to Argentine embassies, spreading of propaganda, and stimulation of, or at least providing a model for, the creation of military governments in other Latin American nations.

After 1946 Perón sought to perpetuate the intensified intracontinental trade the war had forced upon the South American states. To Chile, Paraguay, Bolivia, and other countries he proposed pacts that would abolish tariff barriers, increase trade, and provide funds for loans and investments. If consummated, these would promote the formation of an economic bloc under Argentine hegemony.[44] But distrust of Perón led the Chilean Congress to reject the treaty negotiated in 1946.[45] Its transportation and food sources already linked with Argentina, Bolivia accepted some new provisions for limited free trade and porteño financing. Even if it chose, Paraguay could not escape Argentina's grip on its economic life. Uruguay's position was as exposed as ever, but its doughty people could normally count on the assistance of Brazil and the United States. Except to pay higher prices for bread when Perón withheld wheat shipments, Brazil's economy was relatively immune to Argentine tinkering.[46] Resistance to Perón's tactics of penetration, therefore, combined with poor harvests and fuel shortages after 1949, left plans for an austral bloc illusory.

The strength of his own regime based heavily on the support of organized labor, Perón determined to spread Peronismo by appeals to the workingmen of other nations. To carry out this purpose he conceived the scheme of assigning labor attachés to all Argentine embassies in the New World. Indoctrinated for their special missions, they moved into the Latin capitals prepared to work with union leaders, speak before labor rallies, assist friendly newspapers, and arrange pilgrimages to Buenos Aires. In Peru, Mexico, Cuba, and Costa Rica especially, the attachés achieved disturbing influence. Condemned, however, by both

[44] *Ibid.*, p. 317; Alexander, *op. cit.*, p. 184.

[45] In his reminiscences of his mission to Chile, Claude Bowers describes the origins of this mistrust. While serving as Military Attaché to Santiago, Perón was expelled because of his attempts to secure Chilean defense plans. His successor in the post and, according to Bowers, reluctant accomplice in the plot was Lieutenant Colonel Eduardo Lonardi (Bowers, *Chile Through Embassy Windows*, pp. 139-140).

[46] *The United States in World Affairs, 1945-1947*, pp. 241-246; Olive Holmes, "Perón's 'Greater Argentina' and the United States," *Foreign Policy Reports*, XXIV (Dec. 1, 1948), 164-165.

the CIO and the AFL, Perón's government made less headway in seeking to penetrate powerful international labor bodies.[47]

At no time during his career as a public figure did Perón lack broad public relations coverage. Almost from the start, his regime controlled the national press and radio. His colorful personality, his quick rise to power, his facility for straddling many fences, his ability to dodge oblivion, even his personal affairs—all these assured him open-sesame to the foreign press. His propaganda pieces, in several languages, flowed to all parts of the Hemisphere. Though the evidence is vague, he appears to have subsidized newspapers and radio stations in other countries. Perón's name, like his actions, was always headline news. And with his name went his propaganda for justicialism and the Third Position.[48]

Allegations of Perón's connivance with the military authorities of other nations grew out of the epidemic of right-wing coups which struck Latin America during 1948.[49] In three countries—Peru, Venezuela, and El Salvador—military regimes displaced civilian authorities, and in eight others the governments quelled revolts or incipient uprisings.[50] The charges against Perón may have rested on nothing more than suspicion, but certainly his success at home must have inspired emulation by other dictator-aspirants. On the other hand, no one of them sought to build the kind of proletarian base upon which the Argentine had assured his power.[51] Nonetheless, the widespread use of force to threaten or unseat constitutional governments drew the condemnation of the State Department in Washington. On December 21 it instructed its ambassadors in all capitals of Latin America, except Buenos Aires and those directly involved, to confer with foreign ministers on steps to restore continental stability.[52] The exclusion of Argentina, along with those states where military coups had succeeded, revealed something of the unique attitude with which President Truman still regarded the Perón dictatorship.

Truman's Policy Toward Argentina

The Truman administration's reversal of policy toward Argentina in early 1947 had served to restore, however shakily, the united Hemisphere front against Cold War threats. But return of the recalcitrant member

[47] Ernesto Galarza, "Argentine Labor Under Perón," *Inter-American Reports*, No. 2 (March, 1948), 13-14; Alexander, *op. cit.*, pp. 187-193.

[48] *Ibid.*, pp. 193-195; *Libro Negro*, pp. 246-252.

[49] Bruce, *op. cit.*, p. 316; Alexander, *op. cit.*, pp. 193-197.

[50] *The New York Times*, Dec. 22, 1948.

[51] Whitaker, *op. cit.*, pp. 230-231.

[52] *The New York Times*, Dec. 22, 1948.

to the bosom of the American family did not assure complete harmony between its two most aggressive leaders, rivals as they were for the leadership of kindred states. Quite apart from Perón's relationship to the Inter-American System, Washington still faced an Argentine problem. While promoting the Conferences at Rio and Bogotá, therefore, President Truman also sought to find a more amicable basis for adjusting bilateral relations with Buenos Aires.

Pressures from many sources impinged upon the White House to make a clear-cut break with the coercive policies of the Hull-Braden era. The War and Navy Departments continued their concern over Hemisphere military collaboration, sources of food supplies for the armed forces, and emergency access to strategic areas like the Strait of Magellan.[53] Latin America experts in the Department of State argued that continued moral lashing of Argentina only bolstered the position of the extremists; they tended to favor adjustment of trade and financial relations rather than perpetuation of ideological differences with the Perón government.[54] For many months key members of Congress had urged an end to the "tough" policy.[55]

In addition to these official pressures, the American business community, both at home and in Argentina, pumped for restoration of more normal business relations.[56] As the Perón government expanded its program of economic nationalism, strict regulations of the Central Bank and the IAPI threatened the independence of American companies or at least snarled their management in red tape. Difficulties of securing import licenses to get goods in and remittances to get profits out handicapped American importers and manufacturers. The multiplicity of bank, price, and exchange restrictions discouraged plant expansion and new investments. Special problems beset American petroleum companies, packing houses, airlines, and motion-picture producers.[57]

In the hope of easing some of these strains, President Truman determined in June, 1947, to try to do business with Perón through businessmen rather than career diplomats. Since 1941 three veteran ambassadors—Armour, Braden, Messersmith—while faithfully fulfilling their

[53] In 1948 the United States Army invited a group of Argentine Army officers, including the Minister of War, Major General José Humberto Sosa Molina, to visit the United States. Later in the year the Air Force brought a hundred Argentine air cadets to travel and study. (Alexander, *op. cit.*, p. 215; *The New York Times*, May 16, 1948).

[54] Laurence Duggan, *The Americas: The Search for Hemisphere Security*, pp. 212-215; *The United States in World Affairs, 1949*, p. 481.

[55] See above, pp. 457, 458.

[56] After the war a parade of American businessmen invaded Buenos Aires in search of opportunities (Alexander, *op. cit.*, pp. 208, 215).

[57] *Sen. Rep.*, No. 1082, 83 Cong., 2 sess., p. 36 ("Study of Latin American Countries," prepared by the Senate Committee on Banking and Currency after a tour of the area in October-December, 1953); *The New York Times*, Nov. 1, 5, 1947, May 20, 1948.

respective missions in the political sphere, had failed to harmonize Argentine-American economic affairs. Perhaps, therefore, Perón would respond to the approach of the American businessman in striped pants. During the next five years three Yankee tycoons sought to sell good will and free-enterprise ideas to Argentine consumers.

The first of these was James Bruce, big and friendly executive of the National Dairy Products Corporation and the Baltimore Trust Company, who soon established backslapping and *abrazo* relationships with Juan Perón and many of his officials. Interrupted by two trips to Washington, Bruce managed to last out two years of a difficult mission. To bail him out so that he could regain touch with Washington politics, he persuaded an old friend, Stanton Griffis, to assume his mantle in Buenos Aires.[58] Owner of Brentano's, closely associated with Madison Square Garden, Paramount Pictures, and other entertainment activities, Griffis was a partner in the investment firm of Hemphill, Noyes & Company. Before arriving in Buenos Aires, he had held briefly the ambassadorships to Poland and Egypt. Last of the trio, serving, like Griffis, just over a year, was Ellsworth Bunker, president of the National Sugar Refining Company.[59]

When James Bruce departed for his post in August, 1947, he bore instructions from President Truman and Secretary Marshall "to be as friendly as possible with the Argentines." [60] In this portion of his mission, he was eminently successful. He was soon publicly referring to President Perón as "a great leader of a great nation." Two years later, when he left Argentina, Peronista papers hailed Mr. Bruce as "a great diplomat" and "a great friend of Argentina." [61] During the interim he worked assiduously, in his way, to restrain the Argentines from their nationalistic course.

As Bruce arrived in Buenos Aires, Argentina was just beginning to feel the pinch of postwar problems that had already plagued most of the other Latin American republics—declining production, shrinking markets, shortage of dollars. By working with American businessmen and with Perón's advisers, the Ambassador sought to persuade the Argentines to liberalize their price policies and state trading practices.[62] While trying earnestly to speed the immediate flow of goods and dollars, he apparently saw Argentina's only salvation in long-range improvement of trade relations.[63]

[58] Stanton Griffis, *Lying in State*, p. 244. Griffis' book is a forthright and entertaining account of his experiences in the business and diplomatic worlds.
[59] Each of the three moved on to larger fields, Bruce to Paris, Griffis to Madrid, and Bunker to Rome.
[60] Bruce, *op. cit.*, p. 343.
[61] *The New York Times*, Nov. 5, 1947, Aug. 20, 1949.
[62] Bruce, *op. cit.*, pp. 346-348.
[63] *The New York Times*, Nov. 5, 1947, April 3, June 20, Aug. 28, 1948, May 18, 1949.

A succession of developments, however, in both Buenos Aires and Washington, molested the progress Bruce was able to achieve. Late in 1948 Perón renewed his attacks on the United States, first by accusing a former American diplomat of conspiracy to kill him and his wife, then by withdrawing transmission privileges from five Yankee journalists. Recurrently, because of its shortage of dollars, Argentina froze imports or embargoed remittances.[64]

Policy conflicts between agencies of his own government, however, hampered Bruce's efforts as much as Perón's economic nationalism. Because of Mr. Marshall s position at the Bogotá Conference, Argentina had come to believe that it would share generously in the Secretary's plan for aid to Europe. Ambassador Bruce, too, had proceeded on this assumption. These hopes received a thorough dousing in June, 1948, when the European Cooperation Administration sent ex-Assistant Secretary of the Navy H. Struve Hansel to give the Argentines the cold truth. Wheat crops in Europe, Canada, and the United States, he reported, could meet Europe's needs; Argentina might sell its wheat, if it wished to meet market prices, end monopolistic trading policies, and contribute its share to European recovery.[65]

Of the first $155,665,750 ECA aid spent in Latin America, Argentina received only $1,274,456. At the end of 1948, it had contracted for sales of barely $3,000,000. Behind this situation lay a deep-seated conflict between the State Department and ECA, which apparently even President Truman was unable to resolve. Department officials alleged at least thirty instances of outright discrimination against Argentina by ECA officials.[66]

Renewal of Anglo-American rivalry played into Perón's hands and further handicapped Bruce's efforts. In the years after the war Britain took prompt steps to protect its financial interests and to rebuild its trade with the former "sixth dominion." It no longer had stomach for cooperating with Washington's "crack down" policies. Each of the commercial agreements it signed with Argentina in 1946, 1947, and 1949 moved the two nations closer to the pure bilateralism the United States had long opposed.

The climax to this trend came with the signing in June, 1949, of a five-year trade agreement, in which Argentina committed itself to take a considerable volume of English-made luxury goods on strictly bilateral terms. Combined with the Andes Agreement (1948), by which Argentina had purchased the British-owned railways, this pact brought

---

[64] *Ibid.*, Sept. 25, Oct. 3, 1948, Feb. 2, May 26, 1949.

[65] *Ibid.*, Feb. 10, May 30, June 20, 1948.

[66] In an attempt to iron out these difficulties with President Truman, the Ambassador returned to Washington in August, 1948 (*ibid.*, July 23, Oct. 11, 1948, June 11, 1949).

an end to the historic Anglo-Argentine-American triangle. No longer would Britain permit the Argentines to convert their sterling into dollars for purchase of American exports. Protests at this development by officials of both the State Department and ECA only aggravated the problems of Bruce and his successors.[67]

In spite of these adverse circumstances, Bruce's mission was not without success. On May 16, 1949, as a result of his initiative some months earlier, the two governments announced the creation of a joint committee to study problems related to the increase of trade. During the following months experts from the two Foreign Offices projected measures for overcoming obstacles to economic cooperation, including the possibility of a modernized trade treaty to replace the obsolete agreement of 1853.[68] Consummation of these negotiations, however, remained for Bruce's successors and the active leadership of Edward G. Miller, Jr., Assistant Secretary of State for American Republics Affairs.[69] The Ambassador's departure in September, 1949, coincided approximately with Argentina's plunge to its lowest economic level since the war.

Perón Blows Hot and Cold

Argentina escaped the harsh effects of postwar economic dislocations longer than any of the other Latin American republics. Its policies of pro-Axis neutralism had enabled it to emerge from the war period with rich reserves of dollars and pounds. Heedless, perhaps, of the limits of any largess, or, more likely, imperceptive of the shape of the future world, the Perón government proceeded to squander its huge stocks of foreign exchange. It liquidated the bulk of its funded debts, internal and external.[70] It granted large credits to American and European nations. It purchased the British-owned railroads and the American-owned telephone system. It nationalized shipping lines, airlines, and other public services.[71] It inaugurated a broad plan of industrialization and launched new schemes of social welfare.

Yet, in their zeal to lead and haste to reform, Perón's planners made a number of miscalculations. They failed to discern the effects of rapid industrialization and a growing population on the farm labor supply and the capacity to export foodstuffs.[72] They did not foresee that emphasis upon armaments and public works would divert capital and machinery from basic activities. They overlooked the possible deleterious effects

[67] Department of State, *Bulletin*, XXII (May 29, 1950), 860-861.
[68] *Ibid.*, XX, (June 5, 1949), 734.
[69] See below, p. 480.
[70] Griffis, *op. cit.*, p. 259.
[71] *Sen. Rep.*, No. 1082, p. 33.
[72] *Ibid.*, pp. 11, 14.

of nationalization on economic initiative. They neglected to buttress their softened-up economy against the impact of overseas developments they might at least have anticipated. English financial policies rendered inconvertible Argentine stocks of sterling exchange. The Anglo-Iranian dispute over oil brought a severe fuel shortage.[73] Shifts in the pattern of foreign trade and failure to receive the expected volume of Marshall Plan aid caught them unprepared.

By 1948 the national economy began to slip from its bounteous state of prewar and postwar plenty.[74] Severe droughts in 1949 and after cut deeply into exportable surpluses of meat and cereals. During 1951-1952 acute depression brought food shortages, fuel rationing, inflation, and unemployment. Adverse trade balances prevented remission of profits earned by foreign-owned companies and slowed importation of capital goods for basic industries.[75]

The Argentines were equally unprepared for the striking changes which took place in the pattern of their foreign trade. The nation whose lush farms and grazing lands in 1937 had provided exports of 18,200,000 metric tons of agricultural, animal, and other products could ship a bare 3,000,000 tons in 1952. Even its exports of meat were one-third less than in 1920.[76] Beginning in 1950 the United States took over Britain's habitual position as Argentina's best customer, a relationship which seemed likely to persist.[77] In 1952 American importers purchased 26 per cent of Argentina's total exports, double their prewar proportion. At the same time, the United States retained the pre-eminence it had won before the war as Argentina's greatest supplier. After 1951 it began to maintain about a three-to-one margin over Great Britain.[78]

In the bilateral trade between the two American countries, equally surprising changes appeared. While wool normally represented Argentina's first export to the United States, meat—canned meat—began to challenge it as the leading commodity for Yankee purchase. By 1952 Americans were eating twice as much Argentine meat as the English, whose roast beef and lamb chops had long savored of the pampa.[79] Along with its South American neighbors, therefore, Argentina's northern rival was helping it to replace lost European markets. In 1949

[73] Whitaker, *op. cit.*, pp. 176, 181.

[74] For a broad analysis of Argentina's deteriorating economy, see E. J. Chambers, "Some Factors in the Deterioration of Argentina's External Position, 1946-1951," *Inter-American Economic Affairs*, VIII (Winter, 1954), 27-62.

[75] *Libro Negro*, p. 158; *Sen. Rep.*, No. 1082, pp. 40-41.

[76] On the shortage of beef for export see E. Louise Peffer, "Less Beef in the Plate?" *Inter-American Economic Affairs*, XI (Summer, 1957), 3-35.

[77] *Sen. Rep.*, No. 1082, pp. 12, 14, 18, 22.

[78] Cf. Whitaker, *op. cit.*, pp. 195-196. In 1952 the United States furnished about 18 per cent of Argentina's total imports.

[79] *Ibid.*, pp. 196-197; *Sen. Rep.*, No. 1082, pp. 31-32.

American sales to the southern republic, which only two years before had reached the highest figure in history, fell off to a postwar low. In the same year Argentine exports to the United States reached their lowest point since 1940. During most of the postwar period the balance of trade ran against Argentina, though in some years its system of controls forestalled American superiority.

TABLE 6

VALUE OF ARGENTINE TRADE WITH THE UNITED STATES
(IN THOUSANDS OF DOLLARS): 1946-1954

Year	Argentine Exports	Argentine Imports	Argentine Excess of Exports (+); of Imports (−)
1946	$194,380	$191,144	+
1947	154,637	679,851	−
1948	179,765	380,866	−
1949	97,523	130,843	−
1950	206,060	141,996	+
1951	219,754	233,083	−
1952	158,669	148,028	+
1953	181,896	104,550	+
1954	103,043	123,190	−

SOURCE: *Statistical Abstract of the United States, 1954*, p. 925; *1958*, p. 895.

Perón's program of economic independence contributed to another sharp shift in Anglo-American competition in Argentina. Predominant among foreign investors since the 1820's, Great Britain by 1950 conceded first place to the United States. Sale of its railroads and other properties had reduced Britain's proportion of total foreign investments from 60 per cent to 18. The rise of the American portion from 15 per cent to 25, however, concealed an actual decrease in dollar value. While sending nearly a billion dollars into the other Latin American nations after the war, Americans by 1950 had actually reduced by nearly 10 per cent their 1940 Argentine investments of $388,000,000.[80] So long as Perón persisted in his policies of economic nationalism, this figure seemed unlikely to increase.

Through these years of fading prosperity and deepening depression, Juan Perón repeatedly shifted his nation's attitude toward the United States. Almost as if by pressing buttons, "blow hot" or "blow cold," he directed cooperation or noncompliance with Washington's intentions, while his press and spokesmen turned on praise or wrath. These shifts

[80] Whitaker, *op. cit.*, pp. 200-201. It should be noted, however, that the figure had fallen through the period of the war (1946) to $202,000,000, then risen again by 1950 to $356,000,000 (Office of Business Economics, Department of Commerce, *U. S. Investments in the Latin American Economy*, p. 112).

sometimes reflected Perón's reactions to domestic conditions, sometimes to his own Hemisphere ambitions, sometimes to world developments. Or perhaps they represented his adroit use of the shifting nature of his Third Position.

Argentina's deep financial plight, especially its inability to meet overdue commercial obligations to American suppliers, forced Perón in 1949-1950 to bow to more intimate ties with his northern rival. In January, 1950, he accepted many of the recommendations of the Joint Committee on Commercial Studies, created eight months before to design proposals for reducing barriers to normal commercial intercourse.[81] Prompt implementation of these recommendations followed an exchange of visits between high-ranking officials of the two nations, Assistant Secretary Edward G. Miller, Jr., to Buenos Aires in February, and Dr. Ramón A. Cereijo, President of the National Economic Council of Argentina, to Washington a month later.[82]

First, the Argentine government moved to improve the climate for foreign investments. In March and April it agreed to liquidate the grievances of Swift International and the Braniff, Panagra, and Pan American airlines. A short time later it worked out more satisfactory operating arrangements for American petroleum and motion-picture companies. Meanwhile, searching for more permanent solutions, representatives of the two nations discussed the possibilities of a new commercial treaty and agreements on investment and double taxation.[83]

By far the most striking result of the Miller-Cereijo visits, however, was Washington's decision in May to accord the Perón government a loan of $125,000,000. Granted to a consortium of Argentine commercial banks, this Export-Import Bank credit would permit delinquent business houses to refund their financial obligations to American exporters. It would also place the nation on a current paying basis.[84] "The extension of these credits," the State Department announced, "should be looked upon as an indivisible part of the foundation of a new era of economic collaboration between the two countries." [85] Clearly, the Truman administration had taken a calculated financial risk to attain what it considered a desirable political goal. Though widely approved in American business circles, labor organizations condemned the loan "as a compromise with democratic principles and an appeasement of dictatorships." [86] In Buenos Aires, where he had toned down the anti-United States press during

---

[81] Department of State, *Bulletin*, XXII, (Jan. 2, 1950), 31. (Also see above, on p. 477.)

[82] *Ibid.*, XXII (May 29, 1950), 860-862.

[83] *Ibid.*, XXII (May 22, 29, 1950), 801-803, 860-861; XXIII (Aug. 7, 1950), 216-217.

[84] *Sen. Rep.*, No. 1082, pp. 25-26.

[85] Department of State, *Bulletin*, XXII (May 29, 1950), 861.

[86] *Ibid.*, XXII (May 22, 1950), 801.

the negotiations, Juan Perón insisted that his governme
a credit, not a loan.[87]

Washington's willingness to gamble a multimillion-dolla
the hope of redirecting Perón's errant ways brought only one i
gain. On June 28, three days after the outbreak of the Korean
the Peronista Congress ratified the Rio Defense Treaty, which it h
shelved for nearly two years. Beyond this formality, apparently a *quid
pro quo* of the loan agreement, the Perón government disdained to
move.

President Truman's decision to check the aggression in Korea placed
Perón in an awkward position. Compliance in the form of active participation would contradict a time-tested Argentine policy and arouse
opposition from his Radical critics and nationalist supporters. Less than
hearty cooperation with UN and OAS calls for assistance might jeopardize his nation's already weakened economy. Yet, perpetuation of
the "police action" offered the prospect of increased demand for Argentine products and escape from mounting economic troubles. In the end,
Perón remained true to his Argentine heritage and to his own Third
Position. He sent minor contributions of foodstuffs, not fighting men,
to Korea.[88]

When in late 1950 the Chinese Communists intervened in the Korean
action, a new challenge confronted both Washington and Buenos Aires
—the possible spreading of conflict. Eager to strengthen Hemisphere
unity in the face of aggressive international communism, the Truman
administration promptly requested a consultation of OAS Foreign Min·
isters. For Argentina and its Third Position, on the other hand, a policy
decision would be less clear-cut. Fortunately for Perón, the meeting
did not convene until March 26, 1951. In this long interim the threat
of general war subsided and the risk of Argentine involvement cor-
respondingly declined.

The Argentine delegates, nonetheless, approached this inter-American
gathering with far less truculence than did their predecessors in 1942.
Perón's recent seizure of the venerable newspaper *La Prensa* placed
them clearly on the defensive before their Hemisphere colleagues.[89]
Even the announcement on the eve of the meeting that Argentine
scientists had found a new and cheaper way to produce atomic energy
failed to check the angered outcry against Perón from Washington and
many parts of the free world.[90]

Throughout the sessions of the Washington Conference the Argentine

---

[87] *The New York Times*, May 18, 1950.

[88] Whitaker, *op. cit.*, pp. 232-236. In this instance, to be sure, except Colombia
at a much later date, no other Latin American republic did more.

[89] The Editors of *La Prensa, Defense of Freedom*, p. 10.

[90] *The New York Times*, March 25, 1951. The announcement was fatuous.

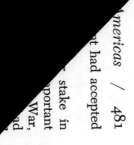

ly inconspicuous part. In the renewal of
eavage between American emphasis on
n concern over economic welfare, they
o of the thirty resolutions considered by
e protests. And on each of these they
er their approval with reservations. On
the Defense of the American Republics
of the United Nations," the Argentines
heir armed forces anywhere in the world
of their congress and their people. On
European colonies and possessions, they
reasserted their sovereignty over the Falkland Islands and other territories in the South Atlantic.[91]

After the interlude of somewhat friendlier contacts during the loan negotiations and the early stages of the Korean crisis, Perón in 1951 again turned the cold shoulder toward the United States and its objectives. He manifested this changed attitude, in part, by strengthening his grip on the Argentine nation, in part by renewing his drive for leadership of the Latin American republics. Besides twisting the screws ever tighter on the press, educational institutions, labor organizations, and the armed forces, he permitted the Yankee-hating Evita to foment a boom for her candidacy as his running mate in the November presidential elections. Though Army pressure forced her withdrawal and some dissident officers attempted a halfhearted coup, resurgence of descamisado support strengthened the dictator's position.[92]

After his electoral triumph in November, President Perón wasted no time in launching new steps to widen Argentine influence in Latin America. By exploiting nationalist aspirations and widespread anti-United States sentiment he radiated throughout the continent the authoritarian tendencies of his own regime. The presidential victories of Carlos Ibáñez in Chile and Víctor Paz Estenssoro in Bolivia, both of whom had consulted with the Argentine president, seemed to manifest the extension of Peronismo. Elsewhere, he continued his pressure against Paraguay and Uruguay and viewed with satisfaction political trends in Brazil, Ecuador, and Venezuela.[93]

At the same time, the dictator took steps to accelerate his demagogic appeals to the Latin American laboring man. Repelled by two international labor federations, the one led by the communist-tainted Lombardo Toledano, the other endorsed by the AFL-CIO, he determined

[91] *Fourth Meeting of Consultation of Ministers of Foreign Affairs of American States, . . . Report of the Secretary of State,* pp. 68-69, 71-72, 87-88.
[92] *The New York Times,* April 10, June 22, Aug. 12, 19, 23, Sept. 1, 29, 30, Oct. 3, Nov. 15, 1951.
[93] *Libro Negro,* pp. 246-252; Whitaker, *op. cit.,* pp. 239-240.

to create his own inter-American body. Consistent with the justicialist philosophy of the Third Position, the *Agrupación de Trabajadores Latino-Americanos Sindicalistas* (ATLAS) sought to pick up middle-ground support in diverse parts of the Hemisphere.[94]

The death of Eva Perón on July 26, 1952, brought a perceptible slackening of the new wave of aggressive Peronismo. The passing of this once-powerful woman, loved and mourned by millions of Argentine workers, forced her dictator-husband to attend to the sources of strength which had given and assured him the reins of power. The pseudo deification of Evita was part and parcel of Perón's plans for retaining the loyal following she had recruited. Yet, in shoring up this foundation stone of his regime, he ran the danger of alienating his indispensable support among Army leaders. To accomplish this delicate balancing he quickly removed from their positions of authority powerful exponents of Evita's influence and studiedly wooed leaders of opposition parties. Reassured by these moves, Perón could turn again to the economic woes which still gripped his nation.[95]

Meanwhile, beset by its responsibilities in Europe and Asia, the Truman administration tended to neglect or ignore Argentina and its sister republics. Assistant Secretary Miller had earnestly tried to come to terms with the Argentine leaders. President Truman had repeatedly revealed his deep interest in continuing the Good Neighbor policy. Yet, like his Secretary of State, Dean Acheson, he was absorbed with urgent world tasks that demanded priority. As the presidential elections of 1952 approached, the Democrats permitted the Argentine problem to drift.

On the other hand, after eight years of trying, the Department of State seemed convinced that nothing it could do would alter Argentina's course or produce friendly relations with its leader. It had failed to find either the coordination or the continuity its Argentine policy wanted. Like the erratic dictator himself, it had blown hot and cold. The Hull-Braden attempts at coercion had backfired. The four-year tenure of businessmen-diplomats had gained only passing success. Overtures for new commercial and economic agreements had proved barren. Even Argentina's economic distress had not modified Perón's intentions. Thus, Washington offered no new loans. It suggested no program of military assistance.[96] Instead, President Truman sent to Buenos Aires a career diplomat, Albert F. Nufer, who had recently served as chairman of the Joint Argentine-United States Committee on Commercial Studies. In fluent Spanish he announced upon his arrival in July that he hoped

---

[94] *Libro Negro,* pp. 252-257; Pendle, *op. cit.,* pp. 124-125.

[95] Rabinovitz, *op. cit.,* pp. 144-146; Whitaker, *op. cit.,* pp. 166-172. The principal officials removed were José Espejo, head of the General Confederation of Labor, and Evita's brother, Juan Duarte, private secretary to Perón.

[96] *The United States in World Affairs, 1952,* pp. 268-269.

he represented an end to the quick turnover of ambassadors that had prevailed since 1945.[97] Presumably Nufer would symbolize a policy of "correct friendliness."

The Eisenhower-Dulles Policy

The return of a Republican administration to Washington in January, 1953, promised fresh efforts to restore vitality and momentum to the inter-American movement. During the election campaign General Eisenhower had indicted Truman's Latin American policy as "feeble" and had pledged strengthening of inter-American ties. In a radio address soon after assuming the secretaryship of state, John Foster Dulles accused his predecessors of neglecting South America. The new Assistant Secretary of State for Inter-American Affairs, John Moors Cabot, urged stronger American leadership for progressive social reform in the Latin American countries.[98]

In the observance of Pan American Day in April, President Eisenhower became the first United States chief executive since 1946 to address the Council of the OAS. "I am profoundly dedicated," he said, "personally to doing all that I can to perfect the understanding and trust upon which this community must rest." In closing his address, he announced that his brother, Dr. Milton Eisenhower, would soon visit a number of the republics in search of ways of "strengthening the bonds between us and all our neighbors in this Pan-American Union." [99]

In Buenos Aires, however, Juan Perón did not wait to see which way the Republican winds would blow. Plagued by growing food shortages, rising unemployment, and spreading discontent, he faced the continuing decay of Argentina's economic structure. While the new administration in Washington was planning a fresh approach to Hemisphere problems, therefore, Perón was actively seeking to combat dangerous inflation and bolster the national economy.

To regain foreign markets for Argentina's exportable foodstuffs, the dictator inaugurated a new campaign for bilateral trade agreements. In February, the first Argentine president to visit Chile in forty years, he persuaded his friend Carlos Ibáñez to sign the "Act of Santiago." By easing customs barriers, coordinating production, and improving all forms of transport and communication, the two presidents hoped to increase exchange of mineral and agricultural products. On a return visit of the Chilean executive to Buenos Aires in July, they formalized an agreement embodying their objectives. Looking toward the possibility of a broader

---

[97] *The New York Times,* July 17, 1952.
[98] Department of State, *Bulletin,* XXVIII (Feb. 9, March 30, 1953), 214-215, 460-462; *The New York Times,* March 23, 1953.
[99] Department of State, *Bulletin,* XXVIII (April 20, 1953), 563-564.

"economic union," they soon persuaded Paraguay and Ecuador to adhere to the Act. At the same time, Perón was signing other trade agreements, notably with the Soviet Union, France, and Japan.[100]

At home, Argentine leaders began to implement key provisions of the second Five-Year Plan, passed by Congress in December, 1952. Far more comprehensive than its predecessor, the new Plan revealed the striking reorientation of Perón's broad economic policy. He would now favor the pastoral and agricultural activities he had long discouraged, slow down the industrialization he had spurred, freeze the wages of the urban workers he had supported, and force back to the ranches and farms the laborers he had drawn to the cities. Most revolutionary in the new program, however, was the bid it made for the return of private investment to the Argentine economy. With unproclaimed candor, the dictator was baiting his hook to lure United States capital.[101]

But paper programs for reviving agriculture and expanding exports brought no immediate relief to the Argentine consumer and taxpayer. To meet the food demands of porteño laborers Perón now resorted to drastic measures. On April 2 he ordered stock growers to provide adequate meat supplies within a week or face seizure of their cattle. To enforce price regulations against the spiraling cost of living he threatened the use of rifle butts or even his own services as street-corner butcher.[102]

After the fashion of dictators in such emergencies, Perón sought scapegoats, both domestic and foreign. Climaxing an April fortnight of threats against the rural oligarchs and the urban profiteers, he used a bomb-punctuated rally in the Plaza de Mayo to incite gangs of young nationalists to an orgy of arson and pillage against buildings symbolizing his opposition.[103] In his May Day message to Congress, he charged three American news services with treachery, slander, and rumormongering about the economic crisis. Almost at once despatches from the Associated Press, United Press, and International News Service began to disappear from the pages of Argentine newspapers. On May 12 the Ministry of Communications suspended the licenses of the three agencies.[104]

His position temporarily strengthened by this blast of terror, Perón

---

[100] *The New York Times,* Feb. 2, July 9, 1953; *The United States in World Affairs, 1953,* pp. 338-339. Brazil, Peru, and Uruguay refused to sign the Act; Bolivia signed up in 1954.

[101] Pendle, *op. cit.,* pp. 108-110.

[102] *The New York Times,* April 2, 3, 9, 1953.

[103] These included the headquarters of the Conservative, Radical, Intransigent Radical, and Socialist parties and the palatial center of the aristocratic opposition, the Jockey Club (*ibid.,* April 16, 17, 19, 1953).

[104] *Ibid.,* May 2, 10, 13, 1953. The early restoration of the licenses did not at once halt the boycott.

could return to the objectives of his Five-Year Plan, especially the quest for private capital. Just a week before the scheduled visit of Dr. Eisenhower, he submitted to Congress a bill he hoped would restore Argentina's attractiveness to foreign investors. For government-approved projects the proposal promised fair treatment on introduction of capital, whether hard money or equipment, remission of profits, and repatriation of capital. Mindful of the Plan's objective of self-sufficiency in fuel, the bill's authors were looking primarily for aid to the petroleum industry.[105]

On Dr. Eisenhower's two-day visit to Buenos Aires in late July, President Perón was on his best behavior. At a luncheon, a dinner, a boxing show, and a soccer game, he turned on the warmth and charm of which he was so capable. Besides the top-level conversations, economic experts of the two nations discussed trade, finance, and implications of the proposed legislation on private investments.

The enthusiastic reception accorded the mission of Dr. Eisenhower seemed to herald fairer weather in the long-clouded Argentine-American atmosphere. Both executives ventured further gestures of good will. Almost at once, despite his announced intention to replace him, President Eisenhower determined to retain Albert Nufer as ambassador, an apparent concession to Perón as well as to American businessmen. In August the Argentine Congress enacted the much-discussed law to attract foreign capital. A month later President Perón directed the preparation of a general amnesty law which would free all political prisoners and encourage the return of hundreds of exiles. On a state visit to Paraguay in October, after proclaiming that "America is a great homeland which does not have any boundaries," the dictator went out of his way to praise the powerful leadership of President Eisenhower. Later in the month he lifted a long-standing ban on *The New York Times* and fifteen American magazines.[106]

When at last, in November, the White House released Dr. Eisenhower's report, Argentine leaders at first felt disappointment that it ignored their reformed attitude.[107] But they could bask in other evidences of its recognition. Assistant Secretary Cabot, who had accompanied Dr. Eisenhower, publicly acclaimed the "constructive attitude of President Perón" and promised earnest efforts "to consolidate the improvement which has taken place in our relations with Argentina." [108] More important for Argentina's fortunes, the trickle of Yankee business repre-

[105] *Ibid.*, July 15, 1953; Pendle, *op. cit.*, pp. 109-110.
[106] *The New York Times*, July 29, Sept. 26, Oct. 6, 29, Nov. 12, 1953. The Amnesty Law was passed in November.
[107] Department of State, *Bulletin*, XXIX (Nov. 23, 1953), 695-717.
[108] Cabot, *Toward Our Common American Destiny*, p. 92.

sentatives which had begun to flow toward Buenos Aires now swelled to a stream. Agents of leading corporations like Standard Railway Equipment, Westinghouse, John Deere, Caterpillar, and International Harvester reportedly signed agreements, made offers, or looked over the prospects. Negotiators for American oil companies were among the early harbingers of this new migration of American capital. Perón's "new look" seemed to be attracting customers—customers with purchasing power and an eagerness to spend.[109]

Like the executive branch and the American businessman, the United States Senate suddenly found an interest in Argentina's new financial prospects. Heading a seven-week swing around Latin America for the Committee on Banking and Currency, Senator Homer E. Capehart, with a staff of experts, spent four days in Buenos Aires. Argentine emphasis upon its desire for private industrial development, particularly of its oil and steel industries, impressed the millionaire senator from Indiana. In his report of the following March, he added his influential Republican voice to those advocating increased economic aid to Latin America.[110]

As the Eisenhower administration moved into its second year, therefore, a more favorable climate governed Argentine-American relations. In view of Washington's concern over expanding communism, this circumstance gave hope that the approaching Tenth Inter-American Conference might fortify Hemisphere solidarity. Nevertheless, such agenda items as European colonies, economic development, commercial cooperation, and especially the intervention of international communism in the American republics opened the possibility of continued cleavage.[111]

Secretary Dulles journeyed to Caracas and his first inter-American conference convinced that in Guatemala international communism was establishing, or perhaps had already established, a beachhead in the Western Hemisphere.[112] With the resoluteness that was to become the hallmark of his long diplomatic career, he determined to seek an anti-communist resolution that would provide a basis for whatever collective action might be necessary to expunge subversive threats. Argentina and most of the other Latin American governments, on the other hand, as strongly opposed to communism as the United States, preferred to attack the problem at its roots. The most effective way to combat the

[109] *Time*, LXII (Nov. 30, 1953), 47.

[110] *Sen. Rep.*, No. 1082, pp. 26-38, 647. In visiting fourteen countries to study the relationship of the Export-Import Bank and the International Bank for Reconstruction and Development to the expansion of foreign trade, the Committee gathered an abundance of useful data.

[111] *Tenth Inter-American Conference. . . . Report of the Delegation of the United States of America*, pp. 7, 15.

[112] Some of the evidence was later published in Department of State, *Intervention of International Communism in Guatemala*, pp. 35-96.

evil, they had long maintained, was to encourage economic development and promote higher standards of living, not pass new anti-communist resolutions.[113]

Debate on the American proposal absorbed most of the first two weeks of the Conference sessions (March 1-28). Argentina and other republics came to the support of Guatemala's contention that condemnation of any specific kind of political arrangement in the Hemisphere would jeopardize the principle of nonintervention. They opposed any new extension of collective action into the internal affairs of national states. On the problem of a specific threat to an American nation, they refused to endorse the proposal that "appropriate action in accordance with existing treaties" be automatic; they would go no further than to provide consultation for consideration of such action. To this position of the Argentines and their colleagues Secretary Dulles eventually bowed. But, even after his reassurances on Washington's devotion to nonintervention and good economic relations, the Secretary failed to win unanimity. Guatemala, of course, voted against the resolution; Perón's delegates joined the Mexicans in abstaining.[114]

When, however, the Latin Americans began to introduce their favorite resolutions on foreign trade, tariff concessions, and economic aid, the shoe was on the other foot. Handicapped by White House delay in acting on Dr. Eisenhower's recommendations or even in defining the directions of its economic policy, the American delegation was forced to discourage, postpone, or oppose action on insistent Latin American projects. Even to their urgent request for international cooperation in the disposal of agricultural surpluses the Argentines failed to win American support.[115] And when they introduced their customary demand for an end to colonialism in the Hemisphere, they found Republican diplomats as refractory as their Democratic predecessors.[116]

Although the Caracas Conference had pared down his anti-communist proposal, Secretary Dulles could find satisfaction in its deliberations. In warning his colleagues of the imminent danger in Guatemala, he had effectively dramatized what he believed to be a dire threat to Hemisphere security. He had taken advantage of his opportunity to reassure them of his concern over their economic welfare and political independence. At no point had he aroused the Argentines to sheer obstructionism or leadership of an opposition bloc. On the other hand, Perón's delegates had forthrightly maintained their traditional policy positions and won as many contests as they lost. Without its usual intransigence,

---

[113] *The United States in World Affairs, 1954*, p. 369.

[114] *Ibid.*, pp. 371-377; *Report of the Delegation*, pp. 7-9, 156-157.

[115] *Ibid.*, pp. 15-21, 140-142; *The United States in World Affairs, 1954*, pp. 67, 374, 377-378.

[116] *Report of the Delegation*, pp. 10-11, 159-160.

Argentina had remained a counterpoise to United States intentions in the Hemisphere.

Nothing that happened at Caracas served to disturb the newborn calm that had settled over Argentine-American relationships. During the next year the Eisenhower administration seemed content to continue the policy of correct friendliness President Truman had inaugurated in mid-1952. While it took few steps to implement the excellent recommendations of Milton Eisenhower, it steadily refrained from verbal criticism of Juan Perón's continuing authoritarianism.

Meanwhile, seeking deals under Argentina's new investment law, Yankee businessmen like Henry Kaiser and Atlas Corporation's Floyd Odlum continued to move freely in and out of Buenos Aires. Yet, until March, 1955, except Kaiser's agreement to introduce assembly-line manufacture of cars, jeeps, and trucks at Córdoba, contracts materialized slowly. Perón chose this moment to step up the pace by opening the door to foreign exploitation of oil reserves. Finally convinced that without assistance Argentina's oil monopoly, the YPF, could not produce self-sufficiency in fuel, Perón signed a contract with a subsidiary of the Standard Oil Company of California. This arrangement for the exploration and exploitation of oil lands in Patagonia, combined with similar deals under consideration with Royal-Dutch Shell and the Standard Oil Company of New Jersey, might eliminate Argentina's petroleum deficit. Shortly before announcement of this development, the Argentine public had learned of negotiations with the Export-Import Bank for a $60,000,-000 loan to purchase steel-mill equipment.[117]

By the Washington springtime of 1955 Argentine foreign policy had distantly receded from the high tide of blatant nationalism, Hemisphere hegemony, and economic independence Juan Perón had flaunted in the late forties. The toning down of public statements, the restrained position at inter-American gatherings, and the decision to lift the ban against foreign oil companies marked his retreat from the jingoism of earlier years. The failure to reap ripened fruit from the bilateral pacts with neighbor nations bared the bankruptcy of his plans for an economic bloc. The cordiality shown to the parade of American businessmen and public officials suggested that his declaration of economic independence had been premature. In seeking financial aid and technical skills from the United States, Perón was trading the boasted fluidity of his Third Position for cooperation with the nation he had often baited. His once-vigorous challenge to American leadership of the Hemisphere had petered out; he would soon be pressed even to retain power at home.

[117] Marcos Kaplan, *Economía y política del petróleo argentino (1939-1956)*, pp. 113-114; *The New York Times*, April 3, May 10, 1955.

XXVI

A PROUD NATION IN DISTRESS: THE END OF PERON AND THE BEGINNING OF RECONSTRUCTION, 1955-1960

By the middle months of 1955, it can be seen in retrospect, Juan Perón's once-impressive authoritarian state had become little more than a hollow shell. Though to the outside world, and perhaps to most Argentines, the dictator may have appeared as buoyant and self-confident as ever, he was only the stout façade masking a decadent structure. Deep clefts, inadequately repaired, had weakened its underpinnings. In this condition the edifice could withstand the ill-planned attack against its walls in the revolt of June 16. But, its fissures probed and widened by this initial assault, it could not resist the more determined onslaught of the following September. Within a matter of days, its architect driven into exile, the once-impregnable fortress crumbled.

Slowly, perhaps shamefully, the proud Argentine people had come to a reluctant realization—that Perón had repudiated the very philosophical aims he had preached.[1] In his vaunted quest for social justice, he had permitted scarcity of food, rising cost of living, and loss of personal freedoms to counterbalance whatever benefits he had given. At the same time, the decline of agriculture, loss of foreign markets, and growing reliance upon foreign capital had transformed his economic independence into a mirage. Whether applied to foreign policies or domestic economic and political actions, Perón's justicialist philosophy of the Third Position had grown more and more illusory. Somehow, somewhere, by ways and means not yet disclosed, multiple eddies of discontent suddenly merged and, in their merging, found the power to unseat the dictator who had used these shibboleths to bring misfortune to Argentina. To these developments the United States was an interested—and an involved—spectator.

[1] Cf. prefatory statement in Comisión Nacional de Investigaciones, *Libro Negro de la segunda tiranía*, pp. 21-22.

Accumulating Discontent

The nucleus of forces which in 1955 brought an end to Perón spawned in the opposition he aroused to his changed directions after the election of 1951 and the death of Evita. As long as his policies reflected his promises to emancipate the masses from poverty and the nation from foreign controls, he retained the loyalty of adequate millions. But when droughts and loss of foreign markets drove him to emergency measures, disaffection took root. Opposition gradually formed around dissatisfaction with his actions in three principal areas: his efforts to bolster the domestic economy, his handling of relations with other nations, and his attacks upon the Roman Catholic Church.

After their profligate use of the monetary reserves Argentina had accumulated during World War II, neither Perón nor his advisers were able to cope with the economic problems that beset the nation. By 1955 his economic programs had eaten up all but $450,000,000 of the $1,682,-000,000 reserves of 1946 and had multiplied the national debt nearly eight times.

Perón's emphasis upon industrialization, without adequate stimulus to the oil and steel industries, had aggravated the shortages of fuel and electric power. Foreign purchases of petroleum and coal in 1954 jumped to 20 per cent of total imports, double the prewar proportion. Available electric power supplied less than three-fourths of demand. Neglect of agricultural and pastoral activities forced a near-catastrophic decline in cereal and livestock production. Partly because of serious droughts, the total of grain produced in the years 1950-1955 fell off 33,000,000 tons from the 90,000,000 tons of 1939-1944. In the seven years after 1948 acreage under cultivation decreased by nearly one-fourth.[2]

Together with the 15 per cent population growth during Perón's ten years, these circumstances held to a mere 3.5 per cent Argentina's per capita increase in production.[3] Dismal statistics like these, of course, were unknown in 1955 to the porteño in the street. Even had they been available, he might not have appreciated their true significance. But he could understand meatless days, scarce goods, rising prices, and

[2] The First National Bank of Boston, Buenos Aires Branch, *The Situation in Argentina*, Oct. 31, 1955, p. 1. These statements are based on the preliminary report submitted to the Provisional President, General Eduardo Lonardi in late October, 1955, by his special adviser, Dr. Raul Prebisch. Serving as Director of the United Nations Commission for Latin America, he had been General Manager of the Argentine Central Bank. The recommendations for Argentine economic recovery which Prebisch based upon these data later came under stiff attack. For example, see Luis V. Sommi, *El Plan Prebisch y el destino argentino* (Córdoba, 1956).

[3] This was barely equal to a single year's growth in comparable countries like Brazil, Colombia, and Mexico (José Santos Gollan, "Argentine Interregnum," *Foreign Affairs*, XXXV [Oct., 1956], p. 93).

transport difficulties. So, too, could the man of the middle class, who had received none of the favors once lavished on the descamisado. And even without the statistics, the owner of the great estancia had known what was happening.

When, to ease his economic troubles, Perón relaxed his attacks on the United States and sought its financial assistance, he stimulated a second source of opposition. The $125,000,000 loan of 1950 had aroused criticism, but, still firmly in the saddle, the dictator had been able to pass it off as a credit. Moreover, he had earmarked those funds for the liquidation of overdue commercial accounts; they did not represent foreign investments.

Rather, it was the second Five-Year Plan and its corollary investment law of 1953 that provoked, first, murmurs of discontent, then a chorus of opposition. In April-May, 1955, when the government disclosed its proposed agreement with the Standard Oil Company of California, this criticism swelled to a climax.[4] Submission of the contract to the Peronista Congress and announcement that similar deals were under negotiation with other American companies forced into the open critics who would no longer remain muzzled. Along with Perón, the United States became the target of their animus.

More than any other natural resource, petroleum stood as a symbol of Argentina's economic sovereignty. For half a century its exploitation had been reserved for Argentine enterprise; since the close of World War I it had been a state monopoly.[5] Perón's nationalization of railroads, airlines, steamship lines, telephone services, and other public utilities had effectively promoted his aim of economic independence and pleased both moderate and rabid nationalists. But now, by opening the doors of the petroleum industry to foreign capital, he raised fears of new expatriation of Argentina's resources.

The most vocal critic of the oil deals was Arturo Frondizi, chairman of the National Committee of the Radical Party and future president. On the day Perón submitted the proposed contract to Congress, the Radical leader attacked his new surrender to American imperialists. Other critics, like the distinguished Socialist leader Alfredo Palacios and the mining lawyer Adolfo Silenzi de Stagn, condemned this deviation from traditional national policy.[6]

---

[4] See above, p. 487. For examples of pamphlets and broadsides, published anonymously, see Féliz Lafiandra, *Los panfletos: Su aporte a la revolución libertadora*, pp. 443-462.

[5] See above, pp. 348-349.

[6] For Frondizi's views on the Argentine oil question at this time, see his *Petróleo y política* (Buenos Aires, 1954). Palacios and Silenzi de Stagni have expressed their opinions in books that have gone through several editions: Palacios, *Petróleo, monopolios y latifundios* (Buenos Aires, 1957), and Silenzi de Stagni, *El petróleo argentino* (Buenos Aires, 1955). Numerous other postrevolutionary publications

Frondizi used the oil contract as the basis for levelling a broadside against Yankee intentions and Perón's complicity with them. In the heat of his anti-Peronism, perhaps, he professed to see American interest in oil and industry as part of a master plan to establish a sphere of influence in Argentina, the South Atlantic, and Antarctica. He recalled Washington's wartime efforts to establish bases on the Strait of Magellan. Although he did not mention them, the recent industrial contract with Henry Kaiser, the pending loan for a steel mill, and the rumored negotiation of a mutual assistance pact were perhaps cases in point.[7]

Argentina, of course, had long concerned itself with "repatriation" of the Falkland Islands and more recently had staked out claims in Antarctica. Since 1833 porteño statesmen had nursed a grievance against the United States for its loss of the Falklands to England.[8] Now, Frondizi and others added the new complaint of Antarctica, where Argentine ships had recently established a string of bases.[9] They questioned American intentions in sending a new exploring expedition and in refusing either to assert or recognize territorial claims to the area.[10] At successive inter-American conferences Argentine delegates had restated, in one form or another, their reservations to all these territories.

The United States, therefore, by June, 1955, was paying the penalty for its decade of vacillation toward Perón. Washington's earlier tendency to moralize, to praise or to condemn him, now rendered it vulnerable to the attacks of his opponents. Its current emphasis upon correct friendliness, as well as its disposition to do business with him, seemed a calculated guess that Peronismo was better than an unknown alternative. At any rate, in linking the United States with Perón they professed to find Yankee financial penetration no more palatable a form of intervention than the political and economic coercion of ten years before.

The third source of opposition to Perón stemmed from his persecution of the Catholic Church. Though the last to develop, this force was perhaps the decisive one. At any rate, the shame and bitterness engendered by his anti-Church policies had a catalytic effect on the diverse types of opposition accumulating against him.

---

revealed the hostility to Perón's oil policy (see Fritz L. Hoffman, "Perón and After: A Review Article," *The Hispanic American Historical Review,* XXXVI [Nov., 1956], 520-521, and XXXIX [May, 1959], 229-232).

[7] For fuller discussion of Frondizi's attack, see A. P. Whitaker, *Argentine Upheaval: Perón's Fall and the New Regime,* pp. 101-105.

[8] See above, pp. 114-120, 467, 482, 488.

[9] *The New York Times,* Jan. 13, 18, 1955.

[10] Whitaker, *op. cit.,* p. 103. Great Britain, too, came in for renewed criticism, after it had submitted the problem of Antarctic claims to the International Court at The Hague. Refusing to accept the Court's jurisdiction, the Argentine government in June passed a law declaring the Falklands and Dependencies to be part of a new province embodying all the mainland and islands south of latitude 46° (George Pendle, *Argentina,* p. 131).

The feud between President Perón and the Church was concentrated largely in the months from September, 1954, to June, 1955. Prior to that time relations between the two had been first friendly, then formal. In February, 1944, through a pastoral letter, the bishops had strongly commended the military government's recent revival of religious instruction in the schools. Two years later they supported Perón's candidacy for the presidency.[11] From that time on the Argentine hierarchy appears to have clung to its traditional position—avoid general opposition to the government in power or official intrusion as a political force.[12] This is not to say, of course, that individual priests, lay groups, or Catholic opinion in general did not take firm positions. Some Argentine Catholics undoubtedly recognized the evil in Perón earlier than others.[13]

In his sudden offensive against the Church in 1954-1955, the General ordered both flank and frontal attacks. He opened the controversy in September by flaunting the Catholic concept of family life through a law granting equal rights to all children, illegitimate as well as legitimate. In successive steps, then, he legalized divorce, authorized government-controlled prostitution, removed many religious festivals from the list of public holidays, abolished compulsory religious instruction in the schools, and moved toward the permanent separation of Church and State.

During the same months, in similar step-by-step tactics, President Perón directed his frontal assault on the Church and its functions. He accused parochial schools of fraud, cut their subsidies to a trickle, and threatened to withdraw tax exemption from all Church property. He ordered the dismissal of teaching priests and nuns, the arrest and imprisonment of scores of clerics, and the banning of religious processions and outdoor masses.[14] The climax came on June 15, when he deported two monsignors for alleged incitement of demonstrations against his regime. This was the step that precipitated his excommunication and helped to touch off the abortive June revolt.[15]

Why, it must be asked, did Perón undertake this campaign against the Argentine Catholic Church? Why, since it had not opposed him, since it had held to its traditional stand of avoiding politics, did he risk angering its supporters? In a series of public statements, the dictator made allegations that provide possible explanations. First, he

[11] John J. Kennedy, *Catholicism, Nationalism, and Democracy in Argentina*, pp. 206-207. A law of 1884 had removed religious instruction from the school curriculum (*ibid.*, p. 187). For a newspaper correspondent's view, see Herbert L. Matthews, "Juan Perón's War With the Catholic Church," *The Reporter*, XII (June 16, 1955), 19-22.

[12] Kennedy, *op. cit.*, pp. 205, 207, 211-212.

[13] *Ibid.*, pp. 205-206; Whitaker, *The United States and Argentina*, p. 143.

[14] Kennedy, *op. cit.*, pp. 207-208; Pendle, *op. cit.*, pp. 101-102.

[15] *Libro Negro*, pp. 238-242; *The New York Times*, June 16, 1955. See below, p. 495.

claimed that Catholic forces were infiltrating diverse lay organizations, especially labor groups, with the intent of alienating them from support of the government. Later he accused the professedly nonpolitical *Acción Católica Argentina* of conniving with the communists to undermine his regime. He referred to a Christian Democratic movement, burgeoning in Córdoba, that might grow into a political party. And finally, on the eve of the revolt, he charged the Church with reviving its old ties with the oligarchy. This appears, now, to have been a desperate gambit to regain strength among those who might assume that in attacking the Church he was preparing to renew his assault upon the other still-unbroken citadel of Argentine life, the oligarchy. Right or wrong, these explanations lend some support to Perón's insistence that his quarrel was with Catholic laymen and a few clergy, not with the hierarchy itself.[16]

In arousing opposition to his policies in three broad areas—foreign affairs, domestic economy, the Church—Perón had cut across all sectors of Argentine society. But previous actions of the dictator, such as the use of terror and brutality, the suppression of *La Prensa*, and the destruction of civil liberties, had offended citizens of all classes without goading them to revolt. In this instance, too, unless the forces of accumulating opposition could coalesce, either by plan or chance, and win the support of the armed forces or the descamisados, or both, they could not hope successfully to challenge the dictatorship. Sooner than expected, this coincidence happened.

The Fall of the Despot

The revolt which brought an end to Perón and his ten years of repression lasted from June 16 to September 20. Its military phases, though bloody, were brief, almost fleeting—a few hours in the preliminary skirmish of June, four days in the September denouement. The three-months interim was a kind of winter truce, punctuated by retaliatory verbal fireworks and desperate preparations for spring combat. The issue was the perpetuation or destruction of Argentina's harshest regime in a century. At stake was the proud dignity of the Argentine people.

The date of June 16 marks the first junction, however fortuitous, of the forces of opposition which had been accumulating against the dictator's policies. The almost simultaneous announcement of the Holy See's excommunication of Perón and the thudding of naval air force

---

[16] Kennedy discusses the first two explanations (*op. cit.*, pp. 208-210); Whitaker, although in a slightly different context than that in which I have placed them, refers to the second and third, along with others (*Argentine Upheaval*, pp. 74-75). For excerpts from Perón's important speech of June 13, 1955, see *ibid.*, pp. 151-152.

bombs on the Casa Rosada symbolized this merging.[17] The Vatican's decree could not have caused the Navy's bombing, but both actions stemmed from the disaffection Perón had stimulated.

At noontime on the 16th bombardiers of the naval planes, swooping low over the Plaza de Mayo, set their sights on the President's executive offices and nearby government buildings. Joined by a few Air Force planes and a detachment of marines, they attacked air bases and other objectives. During the afternoon their sorties rallied some civilian support. To this ill-planned attack the government reacted swiftly. Loyal under their Perón-picked commanders, the Army quickly despatched armored units to defend the Casa Rosada and besiege the Navy Ministry. The descamisados turned out in Perón's support. Later that night mobs ransacked Catholic churches. The government had survived the Navy's uncoordinated attack. Without support from the Army's ground troops or the Navy's ships, the rebel planes could not finish what they had started.[18]

At midnight Perón announced the complete crushing of rebellion. His radio report to the nation revealed the course he would now take to mend obvious cracks in his regime. First, he appealed to his "fellow workers" for calmness and restraint. Then he delivered a paean to the loyalty of the Army. "Not one man has deserted," he declared, and

> all the Generals of the Republic, chiefs, officers, noncommissioned officers and troops have brilliantly done their duty. With this I achieve one more passionate aim of my life: that our Army should be loved by the people, and our people loved by the Army.[19]

If the opposition was determined to storm his citadel, he could meet force only with force. To Perón this reality dictated greater reliance upon his one pillar, the Army, and dissuasion of the other, the descamisados.

To the Army, therefore, under its minister, General Franklin Lucero, went the task of mopping up and restoring order. Under the state of siege which Perón decreed on the 17th, it received total control over Argentine security forces, the Federal Police, the National *Gendarmería*, and the Maritime Port Police. The cleaning up quickly accomplished, on June 22 Army units returned to their quarters. A week later General Perón reassumed command and ended the state of siege.[20]

---

[17] *The New York Times*, June 17, 1955.
[18] For brief summaries of the June revolt, see Whitaker, *op. cit.*, pp. 8-11, and eyewitness accounts in a book by ten Argentine journalists, *Así cayó Perón: crónica del movimiento revolucionario triunfante*. Useful details are found in the Army's communique, printed in *The New York Times*, June 18, 1955.
[19] *Ibid.*, June 17, 1955.
[20] *Ibid.*, June 19, 23, 30, 1955.

In Washington official reaction to the short-lived rebellion was routine. The White House reserved comment. Reasserting American policy of nonintervention, the State Department contemplated no involvement. In the Congress several members of the House subcommittee on Inter-American Affairs suggested a resolution to condemn Perón's persecution of religion; others called into question the administration's economic policy toward his regime. Under interrogation, Assistant Secretary of State Henry F. Holland defended the government's twin policies of economic assistance and nonintervention as applied to Latin America.[21]

During the next six weeks Perón reiterated his earlier tender of conciliation. First, by displacing two prominent anti-Church and pro-descamisado officials—Angel G. Borlenghi, Minister of the Interior, and Eduardo Vuletich, Secretary General of the General Confederation of Labor—he appeared ready to moderate his attacks on the Church. The concomitant boon derived by the Army from these changes may not have been incidental.[22]

Meanwhile, as other high officials resigned and rumors spread of Perón's replacement by a military junta, tension in Buenos Aires steadily mounted. On July 5 the uneasy president again resorted to the radio, not, however, to resign, but to exhort the opposition to accept a political truce and coexistence with the Peronistas. This new offer of conciliation only spurred his enemies, especially the leaders of the Radical Party.[23] In radio reply on July 28 to Perón's olive branch, Arturo Frondizi lashed out courageously against any new submission. He then proceeded to lay down a prohibitive series of prerequisites to true pacification. In the area of foreign relations, he called for "an independent international policy . . . based on an understanding of the political sovereignty of the country, as well as on the economic and political sovereignty of the people." Specifically, without naming the United States, he demanded rejection of the proposed petroleum agreement.[24] Frondizi's rebuttal was a spirited performance, clearly not acceptable to Perón, probably not intended to be.

Stung by this rebuff to his boldest offer of pacification, Perón did not long respect the truce he had initiated. Promptly he arrested Frondizi for disrespect to the government. In the following weeks, as ferment continued and the opposition grew bolder, Perón returned more and more to his former techniques of repression. On August 15, after announcing failure of an armed plot, the Federal Police arrested two hundred suspects, from communists to members of the *Acción Católica*

[21] *Ibid.*, June 17, 22, 1955.
[22] *Ibid.*, June 29, 1955.
[23] *Ibid.*, July 6, 1955.
[24] Whitaker lists many points from the speech and quotes it at length (*op. cit.*, pp. 12-13, 153-155).

Argentina. Hours later, the Peronista Party, from whose leadership both President Perón and Vice-President Admiral Alberto Teissaire had recently resigned, proclaimed its intention to revive its fighting role of 1946.[25] Late in the month Perón reorganized the Argentine security forces. He placed all branches, except the Army, Navy, and Air Force, under a new National Security Board, headed by Major General Félix María Robles, once military attaché to Washington. On September 1, by re-subjecting Buenos Aires to a state of siege, the Peronista Congress wrote a formal end to the period of truce.[26]

In spite of these defensive moves, Perón still faced a major decision—how to rebalance his two principal sources of strength. Although the Army had preserved his administration in June, there were now indications that he had swung too heavily in its favor. For example, in the extended sequence of resignations of high Peronista officials during July and August he seemed to be bowing to Army pressures.[27] On the other hand, rumblings in the ranks of organized labor disclosed unrest among the descamisados.[28] As in October, 1945, and September, 1951, the time had come to demonstrate his command of the "shirtless ones." Perón projected two actions. On August 31, after offering to resign, he mobilized them in another gigantic labor rally. When they demanded his continuance as President, he delivered the most inflammatory speech of his career, laden with threats of violence, even "annihilation" of the opposition.[29] Seven days later the General Confederation of Labor offered its 6,000,000 members to the Army as a civil militia for "the defense of law, the Constitution and constituted authorities." In the first instance, Perón acceded to the "demands" of his followers; in the second, the Army scornfully rejected their proffer of assistance.[30] The tactics so successful in 1945 and 1951 had failed him in 1955. Perón was at the mercy of the Army.

The major streams of opposition were now approaching confluence. Whether or not the merging took place would be the decision of the Army, in this case its post and unit commanders, not its minister or commander in chief. If the Army remained loyal, it might or might not choose to perpetuate the President in office. On the other hand, if even its major units renounced him and joined the insurgents to whom they

[25] Both men announced that they were resigning their party posts so that they might become leaders of the whole nation (*The New York Times*, July 16, 1955).
[26] The events in this paragraph are described in *ibid.*, Aug. 16, 17, 27, Sept. 2, 4, 1955.
[27] Among the six Cabinet members replaced was Jerónimo Remorino, Foreign Minister since 1951 (*ibid.*, Aug. 26, 1955).
[28] A group of fifty-three displaced labor leaders, all with followings in their twenty unions, on August 25 indicted the General Confederation of Labor as a political appendix of the Peronista Party (*ibid.*, Aug. 25, 1955).
[29] Whitaker, *op. cit.*, pp. 19-23, 156-158.
[30] *The New York Times*, Sept. 1, 8, 10, 1955.

had denied aid in June, the swollen opposition might sweep Perón from office. The first signs of dissidence appeared on September 8 among troops stationed in the Province of Córdoba, soon to be a prime center of revolt and hard fighting.

The actual junction of the opposition elements waited another week. The final revolt, when it came on September 16, was the work of the armed forces, however widespread the civilian discontent which impelled them. In contrast to the uncoordinated effort of June, Navy and Air Force planes now received indispensable ground support from important Army contingents. Though the powerful forces in and near Buenos Aires remained loyal, their strength was partly neutralized by the offshore firepower of the Navy's guns. The decisive element in the military situation was probably the insurgency of units stationed in the interior, particularly in Córdoba, Bahía Blanca, and the mountain provinces. The hardest, most heroic fighting took place in Córdoba, where the chief of the revolution, Major General Eduardo Lonardi, established his headquarters.

After three days of bloody battle, the rebels forced the resignation of President Perón and his government. On the 19th a military junta of four loyalist generals replaced him and immediately sought to end hostilities. Three days of negotiation with the insurgents followed. On the 22nd they passed the scepter of government to provisional President Lonardi. Perón had already fled to a Paraguayan gunboat; two weeks later he flew to Asunción. Sooner than most observers expected, the rivulets of opposition had coalesced to wash away his repressive dictatorship.[31]

Military Guardians of the State

The toppling of the giant monolith which for a decade had cast its shadow over the Argentine people did not at once free them from military rule. The Army leaders who took over custodianship of the state would require yet another two and a half years to prepare for return to constitutional government. Fortunately for Argentina, the two generals who served as provisional presidents were able, high-minded men, eager not to wield power but to revive their stricken country.

Major General Lonardi, who had successfully led the revolutionary forces, became the first guardian of the liberated state. Veteran of varied Army assignments at home and abroad, he had spent a year in Washington as Argentina's representative on the Inter-American Defense Board. Retired from the Army in 1951 for alleged plotting against

---

[31] A full account of the September revolution is contained in Arturo J. Zabala, *La revolución del 16 de setiembre: antecedentes, gestación y victoria del movimiento de liberación nacional*, pp. 45-116. See also Whitaker, *op. cit.*, pp. 28-33.

Perón, he had apparently continued his machinations as a civilian. The dictator had once imprisoned him for eight months and later kept him under surveillance.[32] Lonardi evidently long remembered the humiliation he had suffered as an unwilling accomplice to Perón's efforts to gain Chilean defense plans.[33]

Even before removing his headquarters from Córdoba, President Lonardi announced that the military government would rule by law and at the earliest possible moment surrender its power. Promising elections within 180 to 220 days, he promptly dissolved the Peronista Congress and restored freedoms of speech, press, and assembly. With almost equal promptness, he presented to Ambassador Nufer a formal request for American recognition.[34] Pleased with the broad magnanimity of Lonardi's early actions, eager to demonstrate its good will, and possibly hopeful of regaining prestige lost through its intermittent cooperation with Perón, the Eisenhower administration immediately recognized the new regime.[35]

Lauded at home and recognized abroad, Lonardi's government could set to work on the mountain of problems it faced, some immediate, others long-range.[36] First, of course, must come the "de-Peronization" of the agencies of government and the auxiliary organs upon which Perón had built and maintained his power. This process meant not only apprehension and punishment of guilty officials but elimination of the corruption and thievery the Peronistas had condoned.

Of the other problems demanding instant attention most fell in the areas around which the opposition to Perón had recently polarized. Weakened by unbalanced budgets, mounting debts, and declining gold reserves, the nation was approaching insolvency. Inflation endangered its standard of living. Its state-owned transportation system operated under accumulating deficits. Its industrial system lacked fuel and power. In relations with foreign states or their nationals, the problems ranged from pending contracts with overseas oil companies to maturing payments on financial commitments and unremitted profits of private corporations. Perón's controversy with the Church left beclouded the current status of its rights under the law, the state's relations with the Vatican, and even the principle of religious freedom.

Its own revolutionary origins and provisional character required the Lonardi government to face a variety of constitutional and legal questions. Had it replaced a *de facto* or a constitutional regime? Was the constitution of 1949 or that of 1853 the supreme law of the land? If a

---

[32] Zabala, *op. cit.*, pp. 151-152; *Time*, LXVI (Oct. 3, 1955), 31.

[33] See above, p. 472, note 45.

[34] *The New York Times*, Sept. 23, 24, 1955.

[35] Department of State, *Bulletin*, XXXIII (Oct. 10, 1955), 560.

[36] For American readers, Lonardi explained his aims in an article in *Life*, XXXIX (Oct. 17, 1955), 147-149.

constitutional convention was in order, should it convene before or after national elections? Should the decisions of the Perón-packed federal courts be honored? If the new government acted by decree to return property seized by its predecessor, as in the case of *La Prensa,* would it not be as guilty of illegal procedures as Perón had been? Or could the courts possibly cope with the crowded dockets the alternative procedure would entail? [37] In the absence of a Congress, who should decide all these knotty legal questions?

Most of the long-range problems were extensions of those demanding immediate action: reconstruction of a balanced economy; restoration of Argentina's prestige in the eyes of other nations; clarification of the Church's role in all sectors of national life; revision of the constitution, with special consideration to the powers of the central government and the principle of federalism itself. But more basic than all these problems, Lonardi and his successors would have to attend the wounds inflicted one could divine how deeply Perón had warped the national character to the moral fiber, perhaps even the ethos, of the Argentine nation. No on the national mind. No one could adequately appraise the harm done by his debasement of the public official, emphasis upon the class struggle, and extension of state control over the proletariat.[38]

Sincerely and courageously Lonardi bent to the task before him. In his first speech to the nation, delivered soon after his arrival in Buenos Aires, he demonstrated his awareness of Argentina's predicament.[39] During the following weeks he took many of the steps that had to be taken: he sought to bolster the sagging peso; he reopened the universities under more acceptable interventors; he decreed general amnesty; authorized intensive investigation of Peronista graft and corruption; appointed Raul Prebisch to survey the nation's economy; dissolved the Supreme Court and appointed new judges; removed the outward symbols of Peronismo and declared Perón and his congressional supporters guilty of treason; gradually took a firmer stand against Peronista labor organizations; and released to the public the bald facts uncovered by commissions investigating corruption and economic ills.[40]

Interested as were the State Department and the American people in Lonardi's acts to rejuvenate his nation, they felt greater concern about his reorientation of foreign policy. For some time, as was to be expected,

---

[37] On the legal aspects of the *La Prensa* case, see Whitaker, *op. cit.,* pp. 44-46.

[38] In the post-Perón era the Argentines themselves have written of many of these problems. For a comprehensive discussion of their publications, see Fritz L. Hoffman's bibliographical articles mentioned above, p. 492, note 6.

[39] Whitaker, *op. cit.,* pp. 35-36.

[40] *The New York Times,* Sept. 27, 29, 30, Oct. 3, 6, 16, Nov. 13, 1955; Whitaker, *op. cit.,* pp. 161-164. The extensive findings of the Comisión Nacional de Investigaciones, however, were not released until 1958 (see Hoffman, *op. cit.,* XXXIX, 212-215).

they had only words, not deeds, to guide their reactions, but what they heard was mainly encouraging. At a press conference with American journalists on September 28 President Lonardi avowed his desire for firmer cordiality with the United States and pledged that the State Department's cooperation with Perón would not affect future friendship. As to private investments, he promised a favorable climate for American capital, though he proposed to re-examine the pending contract with the Standard Oil Company of California.[41] As to its broader foreign relationships, Lonardi's foreign minister announced that Argentina would stand squarely with the West, drop its opposition to the colonial powers in the UN, and ratify the 1948 Bogotá Charter of the OAS.[42]

But, though the State Department might regard with satisfaction the public statements of Lonardi and his advisers, they could only view with misgivings the presence in his government of nationalists of the extreme Right. Foremost among these were the Foreign Minister himself, Mario Amadeo, long a stormy figure in Argentine politics, and Lonardi's press secretary, Juan Carlos Goyaneche, former Peronista cultural officer in Madrid. The Department's "Blue Book on Argentina" in 1946 had specifically cited both men, Amadeo as "a trusted collaborator of the [Nazi] SD" and Goyaneche as an "ardent pro-Nazi" and "quasi-official representative of the Argentine government" to interview Mussolini, Ciano, Von Ribbentrop, Himmler, Franco, and Laval.[43]

Among the liberal elements in the Argentine government this situation soon provoked genuine alarm. Led by the Vice-President, Admiral Isaac Rojas, a hero of the September revolt, they became increasingly suspicious of President Lonardi's policy of conciliation and his lagging efforts to cleanse his administration of Peronista influences. In a bloodless coup on November 13, therefore, they displaced the first military guardian of the provisional government and substituted another, Major General Pedro Eugenio Aramburu.[44]

The new President, who was to serve until May, 1958, had spent all but sixteen of his fifty-two years in the Argentine Army. Besides the usual sequence of school, post, and staff assignments, he had studied armored tactics in Paris and served as military attaché to the United States and Brazil. Though not regarded as more honest or better intentioned than his predecessor, he seemed to represent the more energetic and democratic force his faction now believed necessary.[45]

[41] *Ibid.*, pp. 36, 110-113; *The New York Times*, Sept. 28, 1955. Lonardi made no immediate comment on the Kaiser enterprises or the proposed Export-Import Bank loan for a steel mill.
[42] *Ibid.*, Oct. 12, 1955. The Minister did not commit himself on the subject of a mutual defense pact to implement the Rio Defense Treaty.
[43] "Blue Book on Argentina," pp. 28-29.
[44] Whitaker, *op. cit.*, pp. 47-51, 164-166.
[45] *The New York Times*, Nov. 14, 1955.

To guide the changed course desired by the liberal group, Aramburu created a five-man revolutionary junta, consisting of himself, the Vice-President, and the Ministers of Army, Navy, and Air Force. By insisting that the differences with Lonardi centered about personnel and not revolutionary aims, the President sought to avoid the necessity of re-recognition by foreign powers.[46] In contrast with its action in the Ramírez-Farrell shift of 1944, the United States willingly accepted the Argentine interpretation.[47]

With less regard for the legalisms that had restrained Lonardi, the new regime moved decisively to eliminate the Peronista influences and Rightist personalities to which it had objected. By arresting leaders, censoring the press, and using the military, Aramburu quickly broke a general strike declared by the Perón-dominated General Confederation of Labor. Soon he dissolved the deposed dictator's propaganda machine and abolished the security law which he had used to harass his opposition. Before the end of November he decreed the return of *La Prensa* to its former owners and ordered the dissolution of the Peronista Party. In remodeling the Cabinet, he removed the tainted Amadeo as foreign minister and appointed Dr. Luis A. Podestá Costa, veteran diplomat and international lawyer.[48]

If the State Department expected Aramburu to issue a comprehensive foreign policy statement, it waited in vain. Nevertheless, in pursuing his program of reconstruction at home, the President scrupulously avoided actions that would seriously impair Argentina's standing abroad. His prompt handling of the *La Prensa* issue, of course, pleased broad sectors of American opinion. Announcement at a press conference in late November that Argentina would live up to its commitments at future inter-American conferences seemed a hopeful sign. Although his decree freezing assets of scores of private companies listed Industria Kaiser Argentina and several affiliates of American corporations, Washington raised no protests.[49]

In the absence of more concrete evidence, the Eisenhower administration could only assume that Aramburu contemplated no sharp departure from Lonardi's stated aims. Its willingness to acknowledge his assumption of power without specific recognition and its acceptance of his first acts without comment or stricture seemed to reveal determination to keep hands off—even "words off"—the Argentine problem. In any case, the State Department wasted no time in sending Henry F. Holland, Assistant Secretary of State for Inter-American Affairs, to Buenos Aires, presumably to discuss financial assistance.[50]

[46] Whitaker, *op. cit.*, pp. 124-125.
[47] See above, p. 435.
[48] *The New York Times*, Nov. 15, 16, 19, 25, 29, Dec. 1, 1955.
[49] *Ibid.*, Nov. 29, Dec. 10, 27, 1955.
[50] *Ibid.*, Nov. 29, 1955.

Meanwhile, the provisional government gave unremitting attention to acute economic problems demanding solution. Early in January its special economic adviser, Dr. Prebisch, submitted proposals for recovery based on the grim findings he had revealed the previous October. Nothing less than a 10 per cent increase in per capita production within a year, he argued, and another 20 per cent within three or four years would restore the general situation. He suggested specific goals to be reached in agriculture, industry, and mining, as well as in the production of petroleum and electric power. He emphasized the repair and construction necessary to relieve the transport bottleneck. Included in his formidable series of proposals for these increases in production and services were recommendations for higher wages for the lower-income group, establishment of a free-exchange market, extension of bilateral trade agreements on a multilateral basis, liquidation of public investment in commercial and industrial enterprises, membership in international monetary organizations, and agreements for at least $1,200,000,000 in foreign loans, especially for machinery and other capital goods. On January 28 government experts approved the Prebisch reports.[51]

By the end of its third month in office the Aramburu government had clearly outlined the pattern it would follow during its interregnum: (1) maintain order and a reasonable standard of living, while reconstructing Argentina's straitened economy; (2) avoid any impairment of the favorable opinion generated abroad, while smoothing the way for large-scale foreign borrowings; and (3) erase from public life the vestiges of Peronista influence, while consolidating the disorganized nation and preparing the people for general elections.[52] The accomplishment of these steps, however, especially the last, required much longer than either Lonardi or Aramburu foresaw.

After a year of implementing the Prebisch recommendations for economic recovery, the Argentine people found themselves facing a more dire economic plight than before. Though beef and wheat production were increasing, a new drought had damaged the corn crop. The Suez Canal crisis had cost them $100,000,000 in higher oil prices and freight rates. Foreign trade ran a deficit of $210,000,000, almost the equivalent of current gold reserves of $237,000,000. President Aramburu had no choice but to warn his people that they were on the brink of economic disaster. His finance minister recommended additional austerity measures to take the form of reduced government expenditures, new and higher taxes, elimination of subsidies, and postponement of salary increases.[53]

[51] *The Situation in Argentina,* Jan. 20, 1956, pp. 1-2.

[52] Cf. Santos Gollan, *op. cit.,* pp. 84-94.

[53] *The Situation in Argentina,* March 25, 1957; *The New York Times,* March 20, 1957.

At the end of another year, as it prepared to hold presidential elections, the Aramburu regime could still not boast of tangible results from its economic program. Though the people ate well, agricultural production had reached only 90 per cent of prewar levels. Petroleum imports cost a quarter of a billion dollars and the deficit in electric power continued to grow. Gold reserves had fallen to $150,000,000. With the United States alone the adverse trade balance rose to more than $150,000,000. The government's middle-of-the-road policies seemed to

TABLE 7

VALUE OF ARGENTINE TRADE WITH THE UNITED STATES
(IN THOUSANDS OF DOLLARS): 1955-1960

Year	Argentine Exports	Argentine Imports	Argentine Excess of Exports (+); of Imports (−)
1955	$125,995	$149,028	—
1956	133,980	211,586	—
1957	129,331	284,735	—
1958	130,741	249,584	—
1959	125,784	231,107	—
1960	98,216	349,143	—

SOURCE: *Statistical Abstract of the United States, 1960,* 897; *1961,* 893.

satisfy neither the free-enterprise group nor the advocates of wider government operation.[54]

This disheartening progress in surmounting economic problems occurred in spite of Aramburu's persistent efforts to increase exports and secure foreign loans and investments. Though he met with some success in both areas, his main contribution was to ease the path for his successors. During his tenure trade and financial missions moved regularly in and out of Buenos Aires, the Argentine to seek loans or trade agreements, the American and others to assess possibilities or assist planning.

By sedulous attention to the climate of foreign opinion, especially in the United States, Aramburu prepared the way for favorable consideration of his requests. In April, 1956, after eight years of delay, Argentina deposited its ratification of the Bogotá Charter of the OAS. Five months later, by joining the World Bank and the International Monetary Fund, it reversed Perón's obstinate stand against international organizations. At the end of the year Argentina displayed an unprecedented willingness to cooperate with the United States Armed Forces. In quick succession it signed an agreement for an Air Force mission to assist its aeronautical development, sent a ninety-man Army mission to study American techniques, and authorized its Navy to conduct joint anti-submarine exercises with an American task force. In other areas during

[54] *Ibid.,* Jan. 8, 1958.

subsequent months it signed a Point Four agreement with the United States and cooperated closely in fulfilling the scientific purposes of the International Geophysical Year in Antarctica.[55]

To this transformed attitude of a regime in Buenos Aires, American officials and businessmen responded in kind. The first fruit born of the improved climate (September, 1956) was an Export-Import Bank loan of $100,000,000. Though, considering Argentina's total needs, it was only a token of Yankee good will, it would provide American equipment and services for immediate relief to transportation, industry, and agriculture. Besides $75,000,000 from the International Monetary Fund, the Argentine government received loans of over $50,000,000 from American banks and credits of $30,000,000 from the Standard Oil Company.[56]

During this era of Argentina's painful recovery, unfortunate events in both countries disturbed, without permanently damaging, the growing friendliness. To the dismay of thinking Argentines, spokesmen for both political parties in the American presidential campaign of 1956 indulged in mutual recriminations over which had appeased Perón the more.[57] On the other hand, Aramburu's summary execution of pro-Perón rebels in June, 1956, and the government's seizure of foreign-owned electric power plants in 1957 temporarily incensed American opinion.[58] And, as newly won freedoms allowed their paperbacks to roll off the presses, Argentine nationalists of varied hues vilified the new penetration by *"los trusts yanquis."* [59]

Meanwhile, in his efforts to reunify the nation and re-establish civilian government, President Aramburu confronted one hurdle after another. These ranged from recurring dissidence in the armed forces and unrest in labor organizations to revision of the national constitution and preparations for presidential and congressional elections. To ride out the storms raised over these matters, while seeking to rebuild internal stability and external respect, required an administrator with patience, courage, and respect for the popular will. As he sat atop the crater of Argentine volatility and economic distress, Aramburu revealed his strength.

After twelve years of favored attention under a military dictatorship,

[55] Department of State, *Bulletin,* XXXIV (May 7, 1956), 782; XXXV (Oct. 15, 1956), 604-605; XXXIX (Aug. 4, 1958), 210-211; *The New York Times,* Nov. 11, Dec. 30, 1956; *The Situation in Argentina,* Sept. 24, 1956, p. 1.

[56] Department of State, *Bulletin,* XXXV (Oct. 1, 1956), 515; *The New York Times,* Jan. 8, 1958. In December, 1955, Washington had authorized the sale, under long-term contracts, of $25,300,000 worth of surplus rice and edible oils, proceeds from which were to be used to stimulate Argentine economic potential (Department of State, *Bulletin,* XXXIV [Jan. 2, 1956], 28).

[57] *The United States in World Affairs, 1956,* pp. 240-241.

[58] *The New York Times,* June 11, 1956, March 26, July 25, 1957.

[59] A prime example was Jaime Fuchs, *La penetración de los trusts yanquis en la Argentina* (Buenos Aires, 1957).

the Army was saturated with moral bankruptcy and honeycombed with leaders hungry for power. Even among the officers who had promoted the revolution against Perón there were those who opposed the liberal tendencies of the Aramburu faction. For the group in power these circumstances required constant vigilance against plotting, frequent shifts in the Army command, and an occasional purge.[60]

Long pampered by Perón and touched perhaps by a sense of nostalgia for the power of descamisado days, Argentine labor maintained a steady pace of strikes, threats to strike, and agitation for new benefits. Under his program of national economic austerity, Aramburu found it difficult to meet even justifiable demands for wage increases or to encourage a trade-union movement free of government sponsorship. Forceful action against the General Confederation of Labor and its pro-Perón leaders did not remove all Peronista influences nor eliminate the possibility of Perón's meddling from afar in Argentine politics.[61]

The provisional President's determined efforts to streamline the top-heavy bureaucratic structure he inherited met the normal outcry from displaced officeholders. In the interests of both economy and efficiency, he cut down the federal rolls, scrapped mushroomed agencies, and reduced the size of the unwieldy Cabinet. Twice during a six-month period, he reshuffled his ministers; steadily he resisted pressure from the armed forces to appoint more officers to Cabinet posts.[62]

But it was in the arena of practical politics, so long closed to unfettered activity, that the General confronted his most articulate opposition. Freed from restrictions by the return of civil liberties, repressed politicians and political parties burst out in full play. As leaders jockeyed for position, new parties blossomed and old parties splintered. Aramburu's determination to hold a constituent assembly prior to the general elections of 1958 opened the door to tactical experimentation before the showdown of the presidential campaign.[63]

Resistance to the President's plans began with the first announcement of his intentions in late October, 1956, and continued to the eve of the election on July 28. The most strenuous opposition emanated from the fiery Arturo Frondizi, who with Ricardo Balbín had opposed Perón in the election of 1951 and who was already the nominee of the Intransigent wing of the Radical Party. To him, the convening of the assembly meant postponement of presidential elections and possible damage to his chances. To him, as to others who hoped to capture Peronista support, the provisional administration had already acted

---

[60] For examples, see *The New York Times*, May 30, June 10, Oct. 28, 1957.

[61] *Ibid.*, June 10, 1956, Oct. 13, 1957.

[62] *Ibid.*, July 26, 1956, Jan. 26, 1957; *The Situation in Argentina*, June 25, 1956, p. 1; Jan. 28, 1957, p. 1.

[63] *The New York Times*, June 12, Aug. 22, Nov. 30, 1956; *Buffalo Courier Express*, Sept. 4, 1956.

illegally in abrogating the Perón constitution and reverting to the constitution of 1853. Lesser parties took up the cry as they tried out their wings for the general elections. However specious his arguments, Frondizi exploited them to his own advantage and to Aramburu's concern.[64]

In the election of July 28 the parties favoring the President's plans for constitutional reform polled a clear-cut majority over its opponents. In the test for the presidential campaign, Frondizi's Intransigent Radicals ran second to Balbín's People's (Moderate) Radicals. A disturbing factor to both parties, however, was the 24 per cent blank-vote total presumably cast by diehard Peronistas. Their attitude might well hold the key to the 1958 contest.[65]

The actions of the Constituent Assembly fell far short of Aramburu's hopes. After endorsing his abrogation of the Perón constitution, the reformers were unable to muster the necessary votes to modernize the constitution of 1853. Such projected reforms as curbing the executive power through a ban on re-election, strengthening the legislative and judicial branches, elevating the status of the provinces in the federal system, creating an effective civil service, and fortifying guarantees of civil rights must await future action. Promptly upon the assembly's adjournment, President Aramburu announced a detailed timetable for national and provincial elections and reaffirmed his decision to dissolve the provisional government on May 1, 1958.[66]

The Return of Civilian Government

By appealing to a conglomeration of voters, from Peronistas and right wing groups to communists and his own left wing Radicals, Arturo Frondizi swept to an easy victory in the elections of February 23, 1958. While he was piling up impressive popular and Electoral College majorities, his party won control of Congress and captured all twenty provincial governorships at issue. As if in celebration of the return to civilian control after fifteen years of military executives, nearly 90 per cent of approximately ten million registered voters went to the polls.[67] Within thirty months the liberating revolution of Lonardi, Aramburu, and their colleagues had established foundations for stable government and materially reinvigorated the democratic spirit among the Argentine people. In building stability on these foundations Frondizi faced a formidable task.

When the new President entered the Casa Rosada on May 1, at the age of fifty-nine, he carried with him the experience of years of rugged

[64] *The New York Times*, Oct. 27, Nov. 4, 1956, April 13, 14, June 23, July 17, 1957.
[65] *Ibid.*, July 31, Aug. 4, 1957.
[66] *Ibid.*, Oct. 27, 1956, Nov. 5, 16, 1957.
[67] *Ibid.*, Feb. 2, 25, 1958.

infighting under military governments. Earlier, he had witnessed from his law school classroom the excesses of the Uriburu dictatorship and, like many of his university contemporaries, turned to the writings of leftist thinkers. By the time Perón began to erect his authoritarian regime, the lawyer was ready to forsake his practice for active opposition to the dictatorship. Elected to the showcase Radical minority in the Peronista Congress, he joined Ricardo Balbín in leading what opposition they could muster. As candidates for president and vice-president in the election of 1951, Balbín and Frondizi bowed to the power of the administration machine. Holding the spotlight by writing and speaking on nationalist and anti-imperialist themes, especially the need to safeguard Argentina's oil resources, Frondizi reached the zenith of his anti-Perónism in his courageous radio attack of July 28, 1955.[68] Later, after taking over leadership of the Radical Party, he continued to expose his leftist tendencies and began to court the favor of many groups, even the followers of Perón. In Aramburu's 1956 proposal for a constituent assembly, Frondizi found the cause he needed for rallying support to his ultranationalism.

Through his long career of opposition, therefore, Arturo Frondizi had become known in the United States not only as a valiant fighter against authoritarian government, but as a leftist, a nationalist, and a caterer to Peronistas and communists. To American officials and businessmen these were not encouraging recommendations for the leader of a near-bankrupt nation whose solvency might depend upon their willingness to supply financial succor. To whatever extent Washington and New York might wish to aid a democratic neighbor in distress, they would insist upon knowing the intentions of its executive. Under these circumstances Vice-President Nixon's trip to President Frondizi's inauguration was much more than a courtesy call.

Mr. Nixon may not have been surprised, though certainly reassured, by the temper of the new executive's inaugural address. With bold vigor Frondizi disclosed to the Argentines and their distinguished guests that the national treasury was empty, the state oil monopoly floundering, and imports of vital supplies threatened. More startling even than these revelations was the action program he proposed. He would encourage production through private enterprise. Without surrendering state control, he would accept private investment in the oil industry. He would avoid new expropriations of foreign capital. He would promote austerity in the operation of his government.[69]

Vice-President Nixon and the experts who accompanied him apparently made no commitments. While suggesting to a group of bankers

---

[68] *Time*, LXXI (March 10, 1958), 30. On his radio speech of 1955, see above, p. 497.
[69] *Time*, LXXI (May 12, 1958), 34; *The New York Times*, May 1, 3, 1958.

and businessmen that Argentina's chances for financial aid were "better today than they have been for ten years," they insisted that it must first demonstrate its ability to repay. Mr. Nixon emphasized Washington's policy of denying government loans to state oil monopolies which banned private capital. Samuel C. Waugh, president of the Export-Import Bank, suggested the availability of loans should Frondizi's policies enable Argentina to earn more dollars. The Export-Import Bank stood ready, the Americans said, to send a study mission within sixty days.[70] The Vice-President's public welcome in Buenos Aires was warm, though not tumultuous; at least he received none of the indignities later heaped upon him in Lima and Caracas.

President Frondizi lost no time in making a direct approach to the White House. In a personal letter on June 4 he assured President Eisenhower of his government's "earnest desire for cooperation toward achieving the fullest possible development of our relations." In alluding to Argentina's wealth, resources, and legal guarantees, he appeared to be offering the reassurance Mr. Nixon and Mr. Waugh had solicited. The onetime Argentine ultranationalist offered Argentine support for any cooperative effort to attack economic dislocation in the Hemisphere. In his acknowledgment, Mr. Eisenhower singled out for emphasis the Argentine's overture on inter-American cooperation.[71]

The critical shortage of petroleum demanded Frondizi's first attention. In fact, press despatches indicated that even before his inauguration he had given tacit approval to foreign participation in the oil industry.[72] The Argentine public soon learned of his about-face. In a speech to the nation on July 24 he lamented Argentina's annual bill of $300,000,000 for petroleum imports. Dramatically, then, he announced that the YPF had already concluded agreements (either contracts or letters of intent) for more than a billion dollars of private investments in the oil industry. Largest of the proposed contractors were: the "United States Group," a consortium of American and European firms headed by the Atlas Corporation; the Pan American Oil Co., a subsidiary of the Standard Oil Co. of Indiana; and Carl M. Loeb, Rhoades and Co., an investment concern of New York. These and numerous smaller agreements covered equipment and machinery, exploration, drilling, laying of pipelines, and construction of plants. Under the program of attaining self-sufficiency, the YPF planned to drill nearly 10,000 wells by 1964, twice the number "shot" in fifty years.[73] In addition, the President announced

---

[70] *Ibid.*, May 3, 1958.

[71] Department of State, *Bulletin*, XXXIX (Aug. 4, 1958), 209-211. In reply to his message of appreciation for Argentine hospitality, Vice-President Nixon received a letter in similar vein from the Foreign Minister (*ibid.* [Sept. 1, 1958], p. 348).

[72] *The New York Times*, March 2, 5, 1958. Apparently provisional President Aramburu had taken the initiative.

[73] *The Situation in Argentina*, May 26, 1959, p. 1.

conclusion of a barter purchase of petroleum from Colombia and pending deals for oil or machinery with the Soviet Union and other oil-producing countries. Though it could hardly have appeased the nationalists he had long exhorted, Frondizi pledged that YPF had granted no special concessions and retained complete sovereignty over petroleum reserves.[74]

In spite of his landslide presidential victory, the President enjoyed the briefest of honeymoons with the Argentine electorate. Buffeted between Peronistas grumbling over unpaid obligations and revolutionaries resisting any concessions, he rode billows of strife and confusion. Combined with the *volte-face* on petroleum, labor discontent and galloping inflation generated a succession of crises that hampered economic recovery and threatened internal stability. To hold his seat and accomplish his reforms, Frondizi would need the continuing support of the military leaders who three years before had ousted Juan Perón.

The first of the crises reached a climax in November. Touched off by Peronista agitation against living costs, unrest quickly spread to petroleum workers protesting the new oil-development program. Imposition of a state of siege to meet the emergency signalized return of the armed forces to Argentine politics after a hiatus of six months. The price they exacted for support was the curbing of strong Peronista influence in Frondizi's government. At the height of the crisis, alleged plotting by Vice-President Alejandro Gómez and his forced resignation split the administration. As discontent spread to railroad workers demanding retroactive wage increases, only their mobilization under the Army forced the strikers back to work.[75]

These difficulties coincided with the culminating negotiations in Washington for a cluster of multimillion-dollar loans. Argentina's acquisition of financial assistance hinged upon its ability to contrive an anti-inflation program that would prove convincing to American and international lending agencies. During the late months of 1958 Frondizi's minister of economy, Emilio Donato del Carril, commuted between Buenos Aires and Washington in quest of a satisfactory formula.[76] On December 29 public and private officials in Washington announced consummation with Argentina of a massive complex of stabilization and development loans totalling $329,000,000.

As "one of the most comprehensive operations ever undertaken by the United States in Latin America," the program of credits would assist Argentina to increase production, develop new export goods, reduce import requirements, and stimulate private investments. The largest of

---

[74] The details of these arrangements are discussed in *ibid.,* July 28, 1958, p. 1, and *The New York Times,* Jan. 18, 1959.

[75] *Ibid.,* Oct. 18, Nov. 10, 12, 14, 19, 29, Dec. 4, 1958.

[76] *Ibid.,* Nov. 3, Dec. 1, 1958.

the five arrangements was the $125,000,000 Export-Import Bank credit, most of which would be reserved for case-by-case loans to expansion projects in the areas of cement, paper, rubber, meat, petrochemicals, and electric power. The Development Loan Fund credit of $25,000,000 would be used for capital goods to assist improvement of waterworks, transportation, and electric power. The remaining credits from eleven private banks ($54,000,000), the Treasury Department ($50,000,000), and the International Monetary Fund ($75,000,000) were earmarked for short-term requirements such as stabilization of the peso and liquidation of the foreign exchange shortage.[77]

For this huge "package loan" President Frondizi's administration could thank the joint efforts of three United States government agencies, eleven private financial institutions, and the International Monetary Fund. As a cooperative venture in the field of international financing, it represented a significant development in American postwar programs of economic aid. By hitching its own loans to that of the IMF, Washington revealed its confidence in the international agency's policy of demanding sound national monetary practices as a prerequisite for financial aid. At the same time, its support added to the growing stature of the IMF as an effective force in the fiscal affairs of the free nations.[78]

Upon announcing the cooperative program, the State Department emphasized that "it has been the Argentine Government's initiative in analyzing and dealing with its current economic situation in sound and realistic terms which has made this joint undertaking possible." [79] On its part, therefore, the Argentine government committed itself to freeing the peso, ending import restrictions, and knuckling down to a program of national austerity.[80] For the Argentine people these steps would mean higher prices, fewer luxuries, scarcity of meat, reduced government payrolls, and general reduction in the standard of living. This was another of the prices they would pay for the improvident policies of Juan Perón.

Inauguration of the stabilization program on January 1 provoked the second major crisis of Frondizi's young administration. With the peso freed and controls ended, prices began to soar. The workingman sud-

[77] Department of State, *Bulletin*, XL (Jan. 19, 1959), 105-106. The eleven participating banks were the Bank of America, Chase Manhattan Bank, First National Bank of Boston, First National City Bank of New York, Grace National Bank, Guaranty Trust Company of New York, The Hanover Bank, Manufacturers Trust Company, J. P. Morgan and Company, Philadelphia National Bank, and the Royal Bank of Canada (New York Agency). The statement quoted at the beginning of the paragraph was made by Under Secretary of State Robert Murphy.

[78] *Loc. cit.* See also Secretary of the Treasury Robert B. Anderson's remarks to the Board of Governors of the IMF, Sept. 28, 1959 (*ibid.*, XLI [Oct. 19, 1959], 533).

[79] *Ibid.*, XL (Jan. 19, 1959), 105.

[80] Gold reserves at this time had fallen to less than $100,000,000.

denly felt the full impact of the austerity plan. Approved only by business organizations and the conservative parties, the emergency measures stirred wide resistance throughout the nation. The Socialist newspaper, *La Vanguardia*, questioned the government's sincerity in calling for national sacrifice. The People's Radical Party attacked the stabilization plan itself. A Peronista manifesto described it as a "yoke of foreign capitalism." Communists and nationalists condemned the "sellout" to the United States. Exploited by Peronista leaders, a sit-down strike in the national meat packing plant threatened to touch off a general walkout. Yet, supported as before by the armed forces, President Frondizi weathered his second crisis without retreating from his stand on reform.[81] By using force, however, he had perhaps only postponed the inescapable showdown with Perón's followers over control of organized labor.

In refusing to let domestic strife interfere with his scheduled visit to the United States, the redoubtable Argentine demonstrated the confidence he placed in the loyalty of the armed forces and in the security of his own regime.[82] As the first President of Argentina ever to set foot on the land of its long-time rival, Frondizi would establish himself as the symbol of the new turn in Argentine-American relations. From White House to Wall Street and Broadway, public officials, bankers, and throwers of confetti prepared to welcome him in this vein. Pennsylvania Avenue might at last reciprocate the greeting the Avenida de Mayo had bestowed upon Franklin Roosevelt in 1936.

President Frondizi reached Charleston on January 19 for a twelve-day tour of the United States. Moving on to Washington, he delivered a memorable address to the members of Congress. Reflecting the fighting democrat he had always been, he shunned the ultranationalism and Yankee-baiting he had flaunted before entering the Casa Rosada. Skirting former differences, he stressed the similarities of the two countries: the same political organization, federal system, and government of limited powers; similar histories of independence, individual freedom, and democratic enterprise; identical capacity to assimilate universal culture and defend national sovereignty and self-determination; the same population growth from currents of European immigration. He praised the United States for its early recognition of Argentine nationhood and for the stimulus Domingo Sarmiento had found in its system of public education.

The Argentine's speech was a ringing endorsement for the Western

[81] *Hispanic American Report*, XII (March, 1959), 49; *The New York Times*, Jan. 5, 8, 18, 1959.
[82] The Department of State had announced plans for the visit on Nov. 28, 1958 (*Bulletin*, XXXIX [Dec. 15, 1958], 954).

Hemisphere idea and inter-American solidarity. "The American continent," he said,

> is a community of nations linked by geographical facts, by history, and by a spiritual identity. . . . [This] hour finds us all, the Americans of the Americas, united by the same solidarity, the same confidence, and the same hope that made of this hemisphere a community of sovereign republics.

In less idealistic vein, he alluded to the misery and backwardness of millions of Latin Americans. Their welfare will require "the same process of expansion and integration of domestic economy which has led the United States to the present and magnificent level of development." This, he said, is the road Argentina has chosen. After reminding the members of Congress that the United States could not stand aloof from Latin America and extending thanks for recent credits, President Frondizi assured them of the hospitable climate foreign investors would find in Argentina.[83]

But the Argentine president had not departed Buenos Aires in crisis to display porteño gallantry in Washington, nor did he seek additional government credits. On his tour of American cities, especially New York and Chicago, he conferred with leading bankers in diligent search for private investment capital. Besides his personal entourage of the Foreign Minister, the Economy Minister, and financial experts, delegations of businessmen and military officials accompanied him. In addition to investment funds, the Argentines sought bilateral agreements on civil aviation and exchange of uranium ore for fissionable fuel. Needing modern equipment, representatives of the armed forces were searching for ways to acquire it without the signature of a military pact that would arouse a leftist storm at home.[84] The closer military cooperation which President Aramburu had initiated in 1956 seemed certain of perpetuation under Frondizi.

Back in Buenos Aires from his notably successful mission, President Frondizi dug himself in for the day-to-day struggle to hold power while fulfilling the harsh requirements of economic reconstruction. At the end of three months under the austerity program, salutary results began to appear. Compared with the adverse figure of $46,000,000 in 1958, the favorable trade balance of $86,000,000 helped to reverse the outflow of foreign exchange. A 50 per cent decline in beef consumption swelled available supplies for export. The rate of infusion of new pesos into the monetary stream fell off 90 per cent from late 1958. Petroleum production rose 33 per cent over the first quarter of the previous year.[85]

---

[83] The entire speech is reprinted in *ibid.*, XL (Feb. 23, 1959), 280-283.
[84] *The New York Times*, Jan. 16, Feb. 10, 1959.
[85] *Ibid.*, March 7, 1959; *The Situation in Argentina*, May 26, 1959, pp. 1-2.

These statistical gains, however, only aggravated the strain on the Argentine people. The official cost-of-living index had risen 38 per cent in three months and 107 per cent in a year. The government enforced two beefless days each week and luncheon menus began to feature sandwiches and milk instead of steak. The meat-loving Argentines heard exhortations to eat more fish and fruit. Trebled gasoline prices forced people to walk or get bicycles out of storage. At the beginning of March two million government employees found their 35-hour work week lengthened to 40 hours for office workers and 44 for manual laborers; they heard of administration plans to reduce the civil service rolls. These hard realities soon provoked a new round of labor agitation. Bank employees in Buenos Aires and municipal workers in Rosario staged long strikes. Violence at the Kaiser automotive plants in Córdoba aroused the concern of other American companies. Unions dominated by Peronista or communist leaders reconsidered the strategy that had failed to produce the general strikes they had planned for January and earlier.[86]

Undeterred by the storm he had roused, President Frondizi pushed ahead with the two-year program he hoped would restore stability and prosperity. In April he sent his chief economic adviser, Rogelio Frigerio, to the United States to round up additional aid and investment capital. Upon his return, Frigerio announced that he had secured about $350,-000,000 in loans, contracts, and letters of intent. Three American oil companies, he reported, would advance $100,000,000 to YPF. Other American and Canadian firms had agreed to invest in plants for the production of pulp, paper, petro-chemicals, and other products.[87] The United States government would provide, on long-term credit, another $33,000,000 of rice and edible oils.[88]

When President Frondizi went before the Congress on May 1 to deliver his state-of-the-union message, however, he had little but gloom to report to the Argentine people. The opposition of minority groups, he said, had hampered the progress of his economic reforms and postponed the stability he hoped to achieve. Decrying the threats and violence which persisted, he urged the necessity of preserving constitutional government even in the face of two more years of austerity.[89]

During the following months Frondizi confronted the third and most dangerous crisis of his presidency. Growing criticism by leaders of the armed forces, especially the former Vice-President, Admiral Rojas,

[86] *Ibid.*, April 27, 1959, p. 1; *Hispanic American Report*, XII (April, May, 1959), 110, 112, 169; *The New York Times*, April 11, 15, 1959.

[87] *Ibid.*, May 6, 1959; *Hispanic American Report*, XII (June, July, 1959), 228, 288. The three petroleum companies were the Pan American Oil Co., Standard Oil Co. of New Jersey, and the Continental Oil Co.

[88] Department of State, *Bulletin*, XL (June 29, 1959), 977.

[89] *Hispanic American Report*, XII (July, 1959), 284.

threatened the unified support they had given in earlier crises. Rojas and others had consistently objected to Frondizi's retention of pro-Peronists in influential positions. They focused their opposition now on Rogelio Frigerio, whom they had already driven from his position as Minister of Economy. Though he had masterminded the stabilization program and fulfilled a successful mission to the United States, he retained the stigma incurred for his alleged deals with the Peronistas during Frondizi's presidential campaign. By the middle of May military pressure forced Frigerio's retirement as the President's principal economic adviser.[90]

Nevertheless, neither the removal of the controversial aide nor shifts in the Cabinet stilled the clamor of the dissidents. Opposition parties denounced the President and individual critics demanded his resignation. Even under the state of siege, military leaders continued their attacks and their plotting. Although former provisional President Aramburu and War Minister General Héctor Solanas Pacheco urged the necessity of preserving constitutional government, Army units grew increasingly restive. They resented their role of enforcing unpopular administrative measures against an unwilling public. First in May and again in late June only the loyalty of the Air Force, most Army units, and some naval officers saved Frondizi's government from attempted coups by naval forces and the Córdoba Army garrison.

The Road to Economic Recovery

The military men who enabled President Frondizi to survive his third crisis again demanded a price for their loyalty—a comprehensive house cleaning of Peronista and communist elements, not the piecemeal removals that had followed previous crises. Among the new figures soon appointed to the Cabinet, the foremost were General Elbio C. Anaya as Minister of War and Alvaro Alsogaray as Minister of Economy and acting Minister of Labor and Welfare. As engineer and minor-party candidate for the presidency in 1958, Alsogaray was a strong advocate of free enterprise and large-scale foreign investments. To him President Frondizi assigned complete power to administer the stabilization program.

The new Minister promptly breathed fresh life into Frondizi's program. By means of radio broadcasts and news releases he sought to win public approval of the stabilization measures. He gave the people the hard facts of economic life, even the shocking news that only foreign loans enabled the government to meet its payrolls. To regain the support of labor, he announced the end of Army control of railroads and

[90] *Ibid.*, p. 285; *The New York Times*, May 14, 1959.

railroad workers, in effect since December, and suggested further steps to eliminate the complaints of other unions.[91]

Yet neither Frondizi's concessions to the military leaders nor Alsogaray's forthright actions relieved the pressures against the faltering administration. Factions within the Army immediately resumed the dangerous game that threatened both the political stability and the economic development they seemed to favor. One of these cliques, known as the *gorilas,* renewed its claims of continuing Peronista influence in the government and the armed forces. Committed to the perpetuation of their own dominant position in the government, the gorilas levelled their fire at the Green Dragon Lodge, a new group of nationalist officers which appeared to be supporting the President. The rivalry between these groups precipitated in early September a crisis more serious than that of the previous June. Faced with imminent civil strife, Frondizi bowed to the power of the gorilas, sacked his newly appointed minister of war, and subordinated his administration even more pliantly to the dictates of the powerful Army group.[92]

Though the civilian government weathered these critical events, the Argentine nation suffered new jolts in its quest for return to normal living. Constitutional government would remain, though increasingly subject to the caprice of military factions. The President's lowered prestige would weaken his efforts to allay social unrest and to broaden the base of his political support. Continuing cleavages within Argentine society would impede progress toward the essential goals of the austerity program. Generated by popular turmoil and dissatisfaction over government policies, the succession of crises would continue.

Nevertheless, the Frondizi administration pushed its relentless search for foreign loans and capital investments to speed Argentine recovery. Before the end of 1959 Alsogaray returned from trips to the United States and Europe with a portfolio of new commitments for loans from American and European banks and international lending agencies. Besides the re-extension of old loans, these promises totalled more than $250,000,000. In supplying large stocks of electrical-generating, road-building, and railroad equipment, the Soviet Union fulfilled the last of the credits granted under an earlier loan of $100,000,000.[93] In addition, Argentina joined the International Finance Corporation, tightened its relations with the International Monetary Fund, and signed a common-market agreement with six Latin American republics.[94]

Meanwhile, impressed by the growing stability of the Argentine peso and the steady increase of monetary reserves, foreign investors accel-

[91] This discussion of the May-June crisis is based upon *ibid.,* June 25, 29, 1959, and *Hispanic American Report,* XII (Aug., 1959), 341-343.
[92] *Ibid.,* XII (Nov., 1959), 509-511.
[93] *Ibid.,* XIII (March, 1960), 55; *The Situation in Argentina,* Dec. 28, 1959, p. 1.
[94] *Ibid.,* Oct. 26, 1959, p. 1; Dec. 28, 1959, p. 1; Feb. 22, 1960, p. 1.

erated the flow of new capital into Argentine industry. In early 1960 Economic Minister Alsogaray announced that during 1959 the Argentine government had approved 120 foreign investments totalling $202,000,000 and promising employment to 60,000 persons.[95] As the Eisenhower administration scrupulously refrained from criticism or overt action, American capitalists further loosened their purse strings. Automobiles and trucks stood high on the list of Argentine production priorities, with General Motors, Ford, Chrysler, and Kaiser Industries leading the way. In such vital industries as chemicals, paper manufacturing, and meat packing, other American companies were founding new enterprises or expanding old ones. Companies representing German, French, Dutch, Swiss, Italian, and Japanese capital were equally active.[96]

During his first two years in office, therefore, Argentina's straitened circumstances forced President Frondizi to move gingerly from crisis to crisis, constantly beset by pressures from the armed forces and by public clamor for an end to austerity. Yet, however thorny and tortuous his political path at home, the dogged Argentine persisted in an economic program that won the confidence of bankers, businessmen, and government leaders abroad. Especially to the White House and the State Department, Frondizi's steadfastness against recurrent frustrations provided justification for the assistance they had given him. When, therefore, in early 1960 President Eisenhower decided to visit South America, Buenos Aires seemed an appropriate stop on his itinerary. Moreover, as a token of growing harmony between the two recently estranged nations, the visit would reciprocate the Argentine president's friendly tour of the United States a year before.

In the light of half a century of Argentine-American rivalry, President Eisenhower's reception in Buenos Aires was far more fervent than might have been expected. Belying the alleged natural reserve of the Argentine populace, nearly a million porteños thronged the streets of the capital to extend their welcome. Whether this outpouring represented belated tribute to a military hero of World War II or honor to the chief of state of a newly respected neighbor nation, none could say. Though a few minor demonstrations punctuated the orderly proceedings, these appeared to be more pro-Perón and anti-Frondizi than anti-United States. For a time at least, the Frondizi-Eisenhower exchange of official state visits seemed to presage a smoother course in relations between their countries.

In his address to the Argentine Congress, President Eisenhower emphasized the policies that had guided the United States in the Cold

---

[95] *Ibid.*, Mar. 28, 1960, p. 1. By June the figures had grown to 144 investments for projects involving $277,000,000 (*Ibid.*, June 27, 1960, p. 1).
[96] *Ibid.*, Sept. 28, 1959, p. 1; Oct. 26, 1959, p. 1; *Hispanic American Report*, XII (Aug., Nov., 1959; Jan., 1960), 346, 512, 626.

War. He was careful to congratulate the legislators on Argentina's extraordinary efforts to restore its national economy and improve its living standards. He expressly reminded them of the United States share in "the most intensive program of financial cooperation to have been carried out in the history of the Hemisphere." His closing remarks conveyed additional assurance

> of the continued readiness of my Government to cooperate with you to the extent that such cooperation is feasible, is welcomed and may contribute to the well-being of your great country.[97]

The joint statement issued by the two presidents from San Carlos de Bariloche contained little more than a superficial expression of their mutual hopes for the political, economic, and social progress of the Americas. Yet its very issuance, together with President Eisenhower's public statements, revealed the extent of the revolutionary turn President Frondizi had given to Argentine-American relations. Even at the risk of alienating powerful sectors of Argentine opinion, he had dared to solicit vast American support for his unpopular austerity measures. On his part, President Eisenhower had used an Argentine platform to proclaim his official endorsement of Frondizi's program of economic stabilization. Now, through a solemn declaration issued on Argentine soil, the head of the nation which had scorned collaboration with the United States in two world wars and frequently frustrated effective American action in the Western Hemisphere agreed to share in the Cold War against the Soviet Union.[98]

During the remaining months of 1960, there was little change in either the directions of national life in Argentina or the pattern of its relations with the United States. In diverse ways the Eisenhower administration broadened its policy of aid and support for the activities and needs of the Frondizi government. It approved a $100,000,000 loan for much-needed highway and housing construction. Recurrently, it entered negotiations for other long-term borrowings and for stretch-out of short-term indebtedness. Through signed agreements or exchanges of notes it consented to loan two submarines to the Argentine Navy, to assist the instruction of the Argentine Army, and to provide equipment and materials for nuclear research and training.[99]

Meanwhile, the accelerated flow of durable goods from American suppliers revealed the buying power of Argentina's vast new credits. The 50 per cent increase in 1960 exports over 1959 consisted principally of manufactured goods essential to economic and industrial development —machinery, vehicles, metals, and replacement parts. As its share of the

[97] Department of State, *Bulletin*, XLI (Mar. 28, 1960), 477-480.
[98] *Ibid.*, p. 480; *The New York Times*, Feb. 29, 1960.
[99] *Ibid.*, Oct. 24, 1960; Department of State, *Bulletin*, XLII (May 9, 1960), 766; XLIII (July 11, Sept. 5, 1960), 73, 387.

Argentine market grew from 19 to 26 per cent, the United States out-stripped its closest competitor, West Germany, more than two to one. Unfortunately for Argentina, a decline in its exports to American buyers aggravated its trade deficit and compelled greater attention to European and Latin American markets.[100] In this situation, the United States found it expedient to endorse President Frondizi's personal negotiations with the European Common Market for protection of Argentina's farm exports.[101]

Its slow recovery from the economic stagnation produced by Juan Perón compelled Argentina to reconsider its attitudes toward international organizations it had once shunned or grudgingly supported. During the late months of 1960 it became a provisional member of the General Agreement on Tariffs and Trade, signed the 1959 International Wheat Agreement, and submitted a bid for membership in the International Sugar Agreement.[102] Within the OAS the Argentine representatives consistently refrained from the Yankee-baiting tactics of former days. At the San José Meeting of the Foreign Ministers in August they joined in the collective actions against the Trujillo regime in the Dominican Republic and against extracontinental intervention in the Americas.[103] Though officially cool to Fidel Castro, the Argentines adhered to their affirmed position that Cuban-American problems must not be permitted to hamper relations between the United States and the other republics. Subsequently, at the Bogotá Economic Conference, they initiated and assisted efforts to meet the social and economic problems of the Hemisphere.[104]

At the same time, the President and his economic minister gave no signs of slowing down their domestic program. Month by month, they maintained their efforts to streamline government departments, reduce the personnel of overstaffed agencies, and transfer state-operated monopolies to private enterprise. To erase national budget deficits and halt inflation, they sought new ways to expand exports, contract imports, and hasten the attainment of self-sufficiency in petroleum. They hinted at new foreign investments to develop the steel industry. They and their emissaries travelled to the United States and Europe in search of new loans and risk capital.[105]

By the end of 1960 the Argentine economy revealed clear-cut signs that thirty months of austerity had begun to accomplish the intended results. The gross domestic product for the year had increased 4.2 per

---

[100] *Foreign Commerce Weekly*, LXV (May 1, 1961), p. S-19.
[101] *The New York Times*, Sept. 10, 1960.
[102] *Hispanic American Report*, XIII (Oct., 1960; Jan., Feb., 1961), 558, 832, 920.
[103] *The New York Times*, Aug. 30, 1960.
[104] *Hispanic American Report*, XIII (Oct., 1960), 653-655.
[105] *The Situation in Argentina*, May 30, 1960, p. 1; July 25, p. 1; Sept. 26, p. 1; Nov. 28, p. 1.

cent over 1959. Exports, especially to Europe, were increasing and the balance of payments improving. The budgetary deficit had been reduced. The exchange rate remained relatively stable. The cost of living had risen less than expected. Petroleum production surpassed the previous year's output by 44 per cent, and self-sufficiency before the end of 1961 seemed probable.[106] This progress toward economic stabilization had raised Argentine prestige in the money markets of the North Atlantic nations.

Yet however encouraging these signs to foreign eyes, they did little to stem popular discontent or halt disturbing crises at home. In the congressional elections of the previous March—the first general electoral test since the President's sweeping victory of 1958—Argentine voters in large numbers had registered their dissatisfaction. Though the administration retained an adequate working majority in the Congress, the size of the opposition vote and the proportion of blank ballots (25 per cent) betrayed the force of deepening unrest and the continuing influence of Peronistas.[107]

Neither the rise in national prestige abroad nor the demonstrable gains of the austerity program, nor even the patriotic events attending observance of Argentina's sesquicentennial during the year, served to quiet the opposition. At least five times between March and December, the government faced new threats of varying intensity. Expressed through strikes, plotting, Army demands, Cabinet resignations, Peronista uprisings, and waves of terrorism, dissidents continued to confront the administration with one crisis after another.[108]

As Argentina's 1960 spring passed into summer, two great uncertainties shadowed President Frondizi's position. First, would the Argentine laboring and middle classes, oppressed by hard times and continuously agitated by rabble-rousing leaders, concede to the President and his advisers the time and patience they asked for fulfillment of their recovery program? A military uprising at year's end, abetted by Peronista elements, seemed to indicate that crises were not yet over. Secondly, as new crises occurred, would the proadministration military leaders persist in their ability and willingness to suppress attempted coups by their disgruntled colleagues? Repeated efforts by the President to allay rampant mistrust in the armed forces revealed his awareness of their indispensability as a stabilizing force.

In full view of the inter-American world as well as of his Argentine constituents, Arturo Frondizi was balancing perilously on the tightrope of Argentina's floundering economy and scrambled politics. In Washing-

[106] *Foreign Commerce Weekly*, LXV (Mar. 20, 1961), p. 7; (May 15), p. 3; LXVI (July 3), p. 1.

[107] *Hispanic American Report*, XIII (May, 1960), 201-202.

[108] *Ibid.*, XIII (May, 1960), 203; (Aug.), 410-412; (Dec.), 732-734; (Jan., 1961), 827-830; (Feb.), 916-917.

ton and the other American capitals sympathetic governments could only wish him well while avoiding any semblance of interference. In Buenos Aires the choice seemed to lie between an era of austerity administered by an unpopular civilian government and an era of austerity enforced by an unwanted military dictatorship. Strange though it seemed, the civilian-democrat Arturo Frondizi found himself riding the same precarious balance between the armed forces and organized labor as had his onetime opponent Juan Perón, the general-dictator. Yet, through one crisis after another, he had shown consummate courage and skill in maintaining his equilibrium. For want of a more acceptable solution, these cleavages might keep Frondizi in power. Perhaps —but only perhaps—Argentina could muddle through without resort to military dictatorship.[109]

During the years of revolution, provisional regimes, and return to constitutional government, Washington's policy seemed to be one of alert sideline watchfulness. It fulfilled its normal commercial and diplomatic obligations. It responded helpfully and understandingly to Argentina's overtures, especially for financial aid. It offered advice only when requested and refrained from passing official judgments. It obviously hoped for President Frondizi's success in his unenviable task and for Argentina's full-fledged return to prosperous neighborliness. In the continuing tensions of the Cold War, it was good to find the Argentine problem in abeyance; it would be even better if a civilian president could achieve its solution.

---

[109] In late March, 1962, after this book had been completed, President Frondizi came to the end of his resolute but frustrating presidential tenure. Allegedly to forestall a resurgence of Peronista influence, in just less than four years after they had returned the reins of government to civilian control, the Argentine armed forces summarily deposed the constitutional President and installed as his successor the President of the Argentine Senate, José María Guido.

Part Seven: Conclusion

XXVII

TWO AMERICAN NATIONS IN 1960:
CONTRASTS

By the close of 1960 the Argentine Republic and the United States of America had rounded out a century and a half of diplomatic and commercial intercourse. Suspended on occasion, though never overtly ruptured, their reciprocal relationships had expanded from the first tenuous contacts of the early nineteenth century to the current web of commercial, financial, military, and cultural ties. Lacking both ancient traditions and physical power, the two relatively amorphous nationalities of 1776 and 1810 had overcome both internal dissensions and external threats to establish themselves as recognized members of the family of nations. Long before it added its fiftieth state, the northern republic had achieved pre-eminence as a world power. At the same time, though far less influential in world affairs, the southern nation stood forth as a leader of the Latin American states.

As an Argentine president had said to the American Congress, the two countries had followed roughly parallel courses of evolution. Revolutionary offspring of European parentage, they had developed similar political institutions, immersed themselves in the same heritage of human freedoms, and received comparable currents of Old World immigrants. They had shown the capacity to assimilate universal culture patterns they admired, to resist ideological influences they abhorred, and to defend the national sovereignty they cherished. On the soil of both countries, Arturo Frondizi submitted, there had occurred the "miracle of America"—the intermingling of people from diverse latitudes, languages, and creeds.[1]

Had he chosen, the Argentine executive might have given the American legislators an even more impressive list of historical similarities: the redemption and defense of national territories; the elimination of

[1] *The New York Times,* Jan. 22, 1959. See above, pp. 513-514.

the Indian menace; partial dependence upon foreign capital and technology; the struggle to achieve balance between industrial and agricultural-pastoral sectors of the economy; the emphasis upon material comforts and good living; the long-time devotion to isolationism in international relations; and the infusion of popular drive and initiative into all phases of national life. Yet, as President Frondizi tactfully refrained from pointing out, relations between nations hinge upon differences as well as similarities. In the case of Argentina and the United States, the contrasts occasionally overshadowed the likenesses to produce misunderstanding, irritation, and even menacing rivalry. In recent decades divergences in the economic, political, and cultural realms have replaced the geographic separation which for a century minimized their contacts.

Symbolic of these contrasts between the two proud, energetic nations are their capital cities themselves. As the nerve center of the anti-Axis coalition during World War II and the heart of Free World defense in the Cold War, Washington had built upward and outward until in 1960 its population of 746,958 ranked ninth in the nation. Spilling beyond the federal district into Maryland and Virginia, the metropolitan area included an additional 1,221,604 people. Its proliferation of public services to the nation and world had brought gigantic expansion of federal payrolls and government buildings.

Yet neither in population, extent, nor national functions could Washington match the fantastic expansion of Buenos Aires. Surpassed by only half-a-dozen world cities, its population in 1960 approximated five million, roughly one-fourth of the nation's total. Pushing outward into the flat pampa rather than upward from its river shores, the porteño population sprawled over an area probably greater than any metropolitan district in the world. As to its place in national life, Buenos Aires combined the functions of Washington, New York, and Chicago. Far more than Washington, it had assumed responsibility for a nation's political system; the central government dominated the provinces and municipalities. Like New York, it served as the country's greatest port, its principal avenue to the outside world, and a fountainhead of cultural inspiration; unlike New York, however, it virtually monopolized these functions. Like Chicago, the focal point of a vast agrarian heartland, the Argentine capital functioned as the center of the meat packing industry and principal transfer point in the shipment of foodstuffs and manufactured goods. As so often pointed out, Buenos Aires was not Argentina, but without it, as the head, heart, and soul, there would be no Argentine body. And yet, strangely, the capital city often found itself isolated, cut off from the mainstreams of world affairs, insulated even from its own hinterland.

Like the nations they served, both capitals had come a long way since President Madison invited Joel Roberts Poinsett to bear good wishes to the revolutionary leaders of the southern land. From colorless, uninfluential towns on ugly river banks they had grown into two of the world's most beautiful seats of government. Lacking the natural advantages of Santiago or Rio de Janeiro, Argentine and American planners had transformed drab streets into tree-lined boulevards and flat plots into elegant parks and plazas. By recurrently tearing down and reconstructing, energetic builders in both cities maintained a steady pace of civic face lifting. While Buenos Aires had become the more cosmopolitan, with features borrowed from Paris and Madrid, Washington had become the more influential in world politics, with power that had once belonged to London.

Though the Argentine metropolis had far outstripped Washington in area and population, the reverse was true of the nations whose fortunes they guided. At least in the eyes of porteño critics, the United States had frequently revealed its imperialist tendencies, usually at the expense of Argentina's kindred nations. The territorial accretions of the Floridas, Texas and the Mexican lands, Puerto Rico, and the Philippines, not to mention the unique relationships with Cuba and Panama, both contemporaneously and afterwards provided useful thunder for the chants of anti-Yankee nationalists.

On the other hand, expansionist ambitions of porteño statesmen had foundered from the beginning, usually on the rock-ribbed resistance of neighboring nationalities. When later leaders agreed to the arbitration of allegedly unredeemed lands, it was American presidents who frustrated their hopes. Since 1833 the Argentines had attributed their loss of the Falkland Islands to Yankee interference and more recently they had encountered Washington's refusal to recognize their claims to a sector of Antarctica. Even Juan Perón's schemes for an economic sphere of influence proved abortive. Thus, after a century and a half, Argentina's size remained essentially unchanged—half again as great as Mexico but less than a third as large as the United States or Brazil.

While Argentina, therefore, occupied only its original limits, the United States expanded to the Pacific and far beyond, gradually increasing to fifty its seventeen states of 1810. The unchecked expansion of the northern republic in no way belittled the other's achievement in securing its territorial integrity, but success of the one in fulfilling its self-confessed "manifest destiny" accentuated the failure of the other. To whatever degree jealousy has stimulated Argentine-American rivalry, this circumstance has been a contributing cause.

The contrasts in national population are even sharper than those of area. Argentina's estimated twenty millions probably represent no more than one-ninth of the United States population of 1960. While Americans have pushed inexorably westward to engulf all their lands except the mountain regions, Argentines have tended to concentrate within a 300-mile semicircle about Buenos Aires. Four-fifths of the population live within this narrow belt of the pampa, leaving relatively unpeopled vast stretches of Patagonia, the Chaco, and the foothills of the Andes. On the other hand, Argentina's long-range rate of population increase—4,000 per cent in a century and a half—far exceeds that of the United States.

While, like its northern counterpart, Argentina received great waves of immigrants, especially between 1880 and 1930, the newcomers were overwhelmingly Latin and Roman Catholic, 80 per cent Spanish and Italian. These factors of common race and religion and kindred nationalities and languages should have contributed to the growth of a homogeneous people, and in the long run probably would. Immediately, however, another factor—the economic—stimulated the restratification of Argentine society, or perhaps hardened the class lines that were already forming. Many of the new immigrants, seeking to improve their economic fortunes, found their paths barred by the prevailing system of land tenure. Already firmly entrenched on its landed estates and in the seats of political power, the oligarchic class tightened its strangle hold against the penetration of the immigrant tide. Content at first to furnish the human resources for Argentina's great economic upsurge, the alien group and its offspring would not always remain a shapeless, voiceless mass. Forced into the cities, frustrated and disillusioned, the new arivals tended to make common cause with the mass of Creoles, still unenfranchised and impotent, against the power of the ruling aristocracy. As their economic fortunes slowly improved and class lines grudgingly thawed, these groups contributed from their number and their influence to the enlargement of the rudimentary middle class. Vertical mobility, fortunately, became more fluid than in most Latin American countries. Unable to rise from their socioeconomic status, however, the less fortunate of the Creole-immigrant group remained to provide the broad base of the social pyramid.[2]

By 1900, therefore, circumstances had cast Argentine society into the mold that would shape its twentieth-century lines: the oligarchy, the middle class, and the descamisados—or the rich, the comfortable, and the poor.[3] Embroiled by the penetration of political ideologies from Europe, these social cleavages helped to determine the character of the party system and to pave the way for the dictatorships of Uriburu

[2] José Luis Romero, *Las ideas políticas en Argentina*, pp. 170-183. See above. pp. 219-220.
[3] See A. P. Whitaker, *The United States and Argentina*, pp. 9-14, and Hubert Herring, *Good Neighbors*, pp. 38-44.

and Perón. The United States, in contrast, thanks to its freer land policies, its greater experience with democratic institutions, and its larger proportion of native population, escaped Argentina's harsh experience with social stratification.

The formidable task of absorbing the millions of European émigrés did not prevent the Argentines from developing a superior level of culture. Though it would be unfair to compare the cultural achievements of the younger nation with those of the United States, even the obvious indices of intellectual activity reveal its pre-eminence among the Latin American outposts of Western civilization. Before the era of Peronista decadence, at least, it had the highest literacy rate, the greatest newspaper circulation, and the best schools and universities south of the United States. As a publishing center, Buenos Aires exceeded even Madrid or Barcelona; its presses produced the works of more and more native writers, as well as reprints of imported classics. In the fields of education, the fine arts, and even medicine, Argentina was rearing more than its share of leaders. Far beyond most Latin American countries, these developments reached wide sectors of the population.[4]

Considering culture in broader sociological terms, the contrast with the United States appears more vivid. The concentration of settlement in and around Buenos Aires and other cities contributed to the evolution of an urban culture in the heart of an agricultural paradise. The preponderance of Spaniards and Italians gave it essentially a Latin and Roman Catholic tone. The declining proportion of Indians and Negroes left the population basically white. Yet Argentine culture was eclectic too, with heavy borrowings from English commercial practices, German military doctrines, and especially French architecture, literature, and society.[5] Though the influence of the United States did not reach Argentina with force until the middle third of the twentieth century, it threatened in 1960 to become the most pervasive of all. In spite of their devotion to Creole adaptations of European forms, the Argentines were finding it difficult to resist the impact of North American movies, news services, technology, science and medicine, and investment dollars.[6]

In striking a desirable balance between agriculture and industry, the Argentines consistently lagged behind their Yankee contemporaries. The oligarchs who dominated the nation's policies in the late nineteenth and early twentieth centuries made Argentina the world's greatest surplus food-producing country. By so doing, they tied their economy to English and European markets, perpetuated Argentina's colonial-type status, and postponed essential industrialization. Long before Perón in-

---

[4] Whitaker, *op. cit.*, pp. 72-76, 79-81.
[5] *Ibid.*, p. 7.
[6] Cf. James Bruce, *Those Perplexing Argentines*, pp. 333-339.

augurated his program of nationalization, however, even during and before World War I, his predecessors had begun to diversify the economy.
But, for good or evil, it was Perón who lighted the fires of industrialization and sought to liberate the nation from dependence upon foreign
markets, supplies, and capital.[7]

The dictator's headlong and misguided policies pushed Argentina too
fast along the nationalist course apparently approved by most of its
citizens. The economic blight he produced has compelled his successors,
military and civilian, to retreat, consolidate, and start anew. Even the
onetime-fiery nationalist spokesman, Arturo Frondizi, has been forced,
as President, to negate the very campaign oratory by which he rose
to power. Convinced that his country can regain economic stability
only with outside financial aid, he has openly courted foreign lenders
and investors, especially in the United States. By inviting large-scale
overseas investments to develop the nation's oil industry he has reversed traditional policy. By contracting loans with American and international lending agencies he has mortgaged the economy for the indefinite future. Able to borrow only by promising a program of national
austerity, he has committed his people to a drastic frugality they are
ill-equipped to accept.

Since World War II Argentina's financial and commercial relations
with the North Atlantic powers have undergone revolutionary shifts.
After trailing Great Britain for more than a century, the United States
has become Argentina's best customer, its greatest supplier of goods,
and its most fruitful source of loans and investments. Though American
sanitary restrictions still bar fresh beef from the pampa, purchases
of canned meat outrank any other single item of import from the
southern republic.[8] As its prewar share of world exports of corn and
wheat has gradually tapered off, Yankee growers have moved in to take
up the slack.[9] National economies which have long competed appear to
be growing more and more complementary.

Perhaps the deepest divergence in the two national cultures grows
out of the contrasting operation of their political systems. The Argentines seem never to have been able to decide, once and for all, whether
to abide by the spirit of their constitution or to revive the nineteenth-
century pattern of the dictator Rosas. As in most Latin countries, strong
administrators have been the rule, even when constitutionally elected,
and both legislators and voters have been content to let it be so. Either
the electorate has failed to exert its capacity for democratic action or

[7] George Pendle, *Argentina*, p. 138.
[8] Whitaker, *op. cit.*, pp. 195-197.
[9] Economic Commission for Latin America, *Economic Survey of Latin America,
1957*, p. 262.

executives have been unable to relate their administrations to the factor of public opinion.[10] The pervasive power vested in the Casa Rosada, whether exercised by civilian presidents or military dictators, has extended to the provinces and even nonpolitical institutions like the universities and the press, as well as to individual citizens.

These contrasts in the practical functioning of two governments under similar constitutions have sprung in part from Argentine variations on the American model, in part from differences in popular traditions. Though the 1853 constitution created a government based on separation of powers, it cloaked the executive branch with far greater authority than its counterpart and, at the same time, deprived the legislative branch of adequate checks. Though ostensibly it authorized a federal system, with appropriate division of powers between nation and provinces, the president's right of intervention, by decree or law, virtually assured the development of a centralized state. Beyond the literal constitutional authorization of these broad powers, of course, the very history and traditions of the Argentine people encouraged the conception of a strong chief of state and overcentralization of authority in Buenos Aires. Thanks to their Anglo-Saxon origins and their fortunate colonial experiences in self-government, the Americans successfully bridged most of these problems in the nineteenth century.

Out of this welter of demographic, social, economic, and political crosscurrents, the Argentines in the twentieth century have struggled to mold a national character, a process the Americans had pretty well completed before 1900. Neither Argentine nor American analysts agree on what that character is, nor even if it has yet emerged. Most observers content themselves with listing its specific traits or appraising the influences that have shaped it.

James Bruce, the only recent American ambassador to write extensively of Argentina, has recorded impressions of two years of observation. In his view, the Argentines are a keen, alert, and energetic people; peaceable, honest in their own way, and eager for self-respect; law-abiding though resistant to discipline. They admire power, yet are suspicious of its exercise. They are realistic, mercenary, and comfort-seeking. They learn how to reason effectively but remain indecisive; love to know but not to dig for the facts; praise the creative but borrow their culture. They love sports, conversation, and argumentation. Their lives tend to be active, hurried, and businesslike, yet their outlook sad and puzzled. They worship their heroes and zealously guard their sovereignty. They display concern with international affairs, but as spectators, not participants. They have deep interest in themselves, excessive

[10] F. L. Hoffman, "Perón and After: A Review Article," *The Hispanic American Historical Review*, XXXIX (May, 1959), 218, 225.

pride in their nation, and indelible faith in the correctness of their own position.[11]

The leading historian of Argentine-American relations is less categoric in his analysis. Among the distinctive traits of Argentine character, he selects for emphasis energy, versatility, sensitivity to criticism, lack of a well-developed sense of humor, ebullient patriotism, and love of peace.[12] But in refusing to see in these qualities the emergence of a national character, Professor Arthur P. Whitaker is at one with a leading Argentine intellectual, José Luis Romero. Writing in the time of Perón of what he called "the alluvial era" (after 1880), he confesses that "nothing [would] be more ingenuous than to hazard a forecast about a process whose characteristics, at this moment, are originality and instability." [13]

For the foreseeable future, it appears, the popular American view of the Argentine character must necessarily remain piecemeal and inconclusive. Knowing little of Argentina—and that mostly bad—and given few opportunities to learn more, Americans will probably continue to form harsh, and often unfair, judgments. Certainly their recent conception of the Latin nation as a cantankerous, willfully uncooperative member of the Hemisphere community, conniving to sabotage the well-laid plans of the United States, does less than justice to the Argentine people.

Many of the factors which have contributed to the younger nation's difficulties in forming a national character have also handicapped its quest for national unity. Deep-seated conflicts over traditional issues in public life continue to molest honest efforts to attain economic balance and political stability: the new industrialization vs. the old specialization in agriculture and grazing; state control vs. private ownership; Buenos Aires vs. the provinces; strong centralization in government vs. true federalism; Army control vs. civilian dominance; cleavages within the armed forces; Peronistas vs- anti-Peronistas; the descamisados anud organized labor vs. the still potent oligarchy. On most of these issues the divisions cut across both class and party lines.

While impeding the growth of a satisfying national spirit, these conflicts have also complicated Argentina's search for a pattern of foreign relations that would rally all elements of the population. Changes in the structure of society during the past century, accompanied by class gropings for imported ideologies, have deeply confused the tone of modern Argentine nationalism. The strident calls for a revival of

---

[11] Bruce, *op. cit.*, pp. 4-39.
[12] Whitaker, *op. cit.*, pp. 14-16.
[13] Romero, *op. cit.*, p. 227.

Peronismo clash with the continuing echoes from the voice of a former generation.

The post-Rosas cluster of leaders who transformed Argentina from its colonial primitivism to modern productive greatness possessed an unquenchable attachment to the land that reared them. They gloried in the achievements of the May revolution and shared with its authors the aim of exploiting economic riches under a liberal government. By fostering the cult of San Martín and proclaiming his contributions to Spanish American independence, they perpetuated the nation's claims to Hemisphere leadership. In emphasizing economic and racial superiority over neighboring nations, they nurtured national pride and promoted cultural, as well as geographic, insularity. Though they adopted the culture pattern and production methods of the North Atlantic nations, they believed increasingly in Argentina's destiny and their own role in shaping it.

This generation of builders drank deeply of the tenets of liberal democracy but created a government that would enhance their own class and perpetuate it in the seats of power. Their precepts seemed to be "liberty for the governing class, order for the rest of the people, and progress for the individual who could make the most of the economic free-for-all." [14] In firm control of society and culture, of economy and government, the oligarchs evolved a distinctive nationalism and determined the character of foreign relations. Their constancy toward the nation and fidelity to its mission would permit them to borrow from Europe, vie with the United States, and seek leadership of fellow Spanish Americans but never to temper optimism, concede inferiority, nor sacrifice national sovereignty.

Even as the Generation of Eighty rose and clung to power, however, new social currents began to lap at the structure they had created. By opening the gates in the late nineteenth century to a flood tide of immigrants, the oligarchy had prepared the way for a social realignment that would eventually undermine its own entrenched position. Gradually through succeeding decades, without ever forming a truly coherent class, the immigrants and Creoles exerted increasing influence in the body politic. Rarely able to agree on attainable social goals or to unite in effective political opposition, the growing middle class nevertheless voiced stronger and stronger protests against the policies of the ruling group.[15]

Largely without cohesion or effective leadership, the poorer classes became pawns in the widening political strife. Ripe for appeals from

[14] T. F. McGann, *Argentina, the United States, and the Inter-American System, 1880-1914*, p. 45.
[15] See above, p. 528.

Europe's totalitarian ideologies and Argentina's latter-day demagogues, they responded avidly after 1943 to the specious promises of Juan Perón. Their hopes lifted and their latent power aroused, the descamisados provided the substance for a vigorous labor movement and a dictator's reliable following.

This ferment in Argentine society rendered the nation vulnerable to sudden transformation of the liberal nationalism of the oligarchy. Joined at times by diverse dissidents from aristocratic and intellectual groups and supported by sectors of the German-trained Army and pro-Spanish clergy, the new classes gave increasing support to a more aggressive nationalism. However disparate these factions, they generally opposed free speech, free trade, free private enterprise, republican government, and all aspects of traditional liberalism. They favored adoption of totalitarian principles, creation of a corporate state, speeding-up of industrialization, and closer union between Church and State. In reappraisal of nineteenth-century leaders, they glorified the dictator Rosas and depreciated the liberals Alberdi, Mitre, and Sarmiento. They coveted restoration of all territory in the old Viceroyalty of the Río de la Plata and advocated the necessary rearmament to accomplish it. They fostered the rejuvenated Hispanism of General Franco and assailed the Pan Americanism of the United States. They became anti-British and anti-American. Uniquely Argentine but with European overtones, this extremist nationalism led inexorably to extremist actions in foreign relations. At many points, during and after World War II, the aggressive goals of Argentine nationalists clashed with the broad aims of the United States.[16]

This brief résumé of the predominant contrasts between the two countries does not wholly explain why their reciprocal relations have produced periods of tension or crisis. It does, however, serve to underscore two salient facts: (1) in evolving from colonial status to modern nationhood, each state has proceeded in its own way and at its own pace; and (2) in developing its distinguishing tone, each has sought to exploit the peculiar advantages of its geographic position and its cultural heritage. That the United States, with the boon of an early start, matured more rapidly and arrived more promptly at satisfactory definition of its national character should imply no criticism of Argentina's historical evolution. Nevertheless, these disparities help to explain why the foreign policies of the two nations sometimes collided, and occasionally provoked irritations or incidents.

---

[16] For fuller discussion of the impact on Argentine nationalism and foreign relations of changes in class structure, see diverse passages in the works of Romero and Whitaker, previously cited in this chapter, and Ysabel Rennie, *The Argentine Republic*.

Until the eighteen-nineties, with the world generally at peace, each country grasped the opportunity to consolidate its national position. Each sympathized, if no more, with the other's efforts to confirm the independence it had declared; Argentines responded favorably to early American recognition. In seeking to round out its continental domain, neither appreciably affected the interests of the other. The contradiction between the unilateral Monroe Doctrine and the Argentine belief in the right of nonintervention caused little controversy. The competitive nature of their economies held reciprocal trade to a minimum; both operated largely on bilateral terms. Their desires to avoid international commitments were mutual. In expression of their peaceful inclinations, the United States repeatedly offered its services as mediator, while Argentina invited American arbitration of vexatious boundary disputes.[17]

Yet even during this early era of their relationships incidents occurred that would grow, fester, and become increasingly irritating. The first of these was Yankee interference in 1832 with Argentine settlements on the Falkland Islands—a grievance that porteño statesmen and nationalists frequently nurtured.[18] The second was the imposition in 1867 of high duties on wool—original basis for the continuing contention that the United States discriminated against their most productive exports.[19]

These incidents might have remained relatively uninfluential, however, had not Yankee initiative in later decades cut directly athwart Argentina's cherished foreign policies. At the close of the century America's drive to find foreign markets for the output of its expanding industry heightened criticism of Republican import policies. As American tariffs rose and Argentine trade deficts mounted before and during World War I, the nineteenth-century grievance grew into a twentieth-century obsession. In the twenties and thirties Washington's use of the sanitary embargo on beef and increasing emphasis on unconditional most-favored-nation trading only aggravated what was already a running sore.[20]

After 1890 the Pan American movement provoked even greater irritation. Whether to promote commercial intercourse within the Hemisphere or to erect a regional security system against European threats, the Inter-American System clashed with Argentina's prejudice against multilateral diplomacy. Even during World War I, but especially before and

[17] See above, pp. 10, 194ff., 213-214, 239ff., 266-267. Cf. Whitaker, *op. cit.*, pp. 85-88.
[18] See above, pp. 105ff., 467, 482, 488.
[19] See above, pp. 224-229.
[20] See above, pp. 235, 352-355, 359-365.

during World War II, its leaders frequently looked upon the State Department's inter-American policies as unwarranted pressure, coercion, or even intervention.[21]

These and other grievances and the facts behind them have been little known to the American public, sometimes not even to public officials. Herein lies another source of vexation toward the United States—the tendency of its people to ignore or disregard the Argentines and its failure to seek understanding of their culture or national aims. With the exception of a few newspapers and periodicals, the American press rarely reports on the southern republic, unless to record its revolutions or hostile attitudes. A former president of the Buenos Aires Rotary Club and editor of *La Prensa*, Rodolfo Luque, once chided a group of visiting American educators, in friendly fashion, by saying: "On a recent trip to New York I made a point of examining a number of history textbooks. I was impressed by American fascination with archaeological research in ancient Egypt and Greece, but I did not find my country even mentioned. When you return to your homes, I hope you will correct this."

On its part, of course, especially since the nineteen-thirties, the United States has had abundant basis for criticism of is rival: its failure or refusal to implement even the inter-American agreements it signed; the toleration of Axis influences and activities during World War II; and the inflammatory anti-Americanism engendered by President Perón. Against these actions administrations in Washington felt they had no alternative but that of protest. Sometimes the Argentines thought the protests went too far.

Yet discussions of contrasts and emphasis upon discordant episodes should not blind either the Argentines or the Americans to their century and a half of essentially peaceful intercourse. Crises have caused coolness and even recall of diplomats but never complete breakdown in intercourse. And along the way representatives of each country have distinguished themselves by notable records of service to the other: for Argentina, President Domingo F. Sarmiento, Foreign Minister Luis María Drago, and diplomats Martín García Merou at the turn of the century and Rómulo Naón during World War I; for the United States, President Franklin D. Roosevelt, Secretary Cordell Hull during his first two terms, and diplomats William I. Buchanan in the nineties, Frederic Stimson during World War I, and Norman Armour during the trying era of World War II.

Where the coming 1960's are concerned, new and difficult problems are already arising, and will continue to arise. As José Luis Romero wrote

[21] See above, pp. 275ff., 322ff., 366ff., 416-454.

in 1946, so in 1960 we see Argentina as "uncertain and enigmatic, although abounding with possibilities, with promises, and with hopes." [22] We may be prophetic, however, with some certainty: For a long time to come, Argentina cannot escape the influence of the United States and the United States will continue to face some form of Argentine problem.

[22] *Op. cit.*, p. 183.

Appendices

APPENDIX A

ARGENTINE MINISTERS OF FOREIGN RELATIONS *

1822, Feb. 5—[?]	Bernardino Rivadavia
1824, May 14—1826, Feb. 10	Manuel José García
1826, Feb. 10—1827, July 7	Francisco de la Cruz
1827, July 7—1827, Aug. 13	Manuel Dorrego
1827, Aug. 13—1828, July 10	Juan Ramón Balcarce
1828, July 10—1828, Oct. 8	José Rondeau (acting)
1828, Oct. 8—1828, Oct. 8	Juan Ramón Balcarce (reassumed office)
1828, Oct. 8—1828, Dec. 3	Tomás Guido
1828, Dec. 3—1829, May 4	José Miguel Díaz Vélez
1829, May 4—1829, Aug. 7	Salvador María del Carril
1829, Aug. 7—1830, March 9	Tomás Guido
1830, March 9—1832, Jan. 30	Tomás Anchorena (acting)
1832, March 6—1832, June 13	Vicente López
1832, June 13—1833, Aug. 6	Manuel Vicente de Maza (acting)
1833, Aug. 6—1833, Nov. 6	Manuel José García
1833, Nov. 6—1835, April 30	Tomás Guido
1835, April 30—1852, April 6	Felipe Arana
1852, April 6—1852, April 7	Luis José de la Peña
1852, April 7—1852, June 22	Vicente López (acting)
1852, June 22—1853, Feb. 3	Luis José de la Peña (reassumed office)
1853, Feb. 3—1853, Feb. 26	José Miguel Galán (acting)
1853, Feb. 26—1853, Aug. 29	Luis José de la Peña (reassumed office)

* I am indebted for this list to the following officials of the Ministry of Foreign Relations and Worship of the Argentine Republic: to Abelardo Arenas Fraga, former Chief, Division of Archives, Buenos Aires; to Alberto Benegas Lynch, Chargé d'Affaires ad interim, Argentine Embassy, Washington, and Santos Goñi Demarchi, Secretary of Embassy, both in 1956; and to Francisco R. Bello, Minister of Embassy in 1960.

1853, Aug. 29—1854, March 7	Facundo Zuviría
1854, March 7—1856, Aug. 1	Juan María Gutiérrez
1856, Aug. 1—1858, Sept. 30	Bernabé López (acting)
1858, Sept. 30—1858, Sept. 30	Luis José de la Peña
1858, Sept. 30—1859, March 1	Juan Francisco Seguí (acting)
1859, March 1—1859, April 12	Luis José de la Peña (reassumed office)
1859, April 12—1859, April 18	Pedro Lucás Funes (acting)
1859, April 18—1859, May 9	Santiago Derqui (acting)
1859, May 9—1859, June 22	Elías Bedoya (acting)
1859, Aug. 3—1859, Nov. 7	Baldomero García (acting)
1859, Nov. 7—1860, March 5	Luis José de la Peña (reassumed office)
1860, March 5—1860, Dec. 8	Emilio de Alvear
1860, Dec. 14—1861, Feb. 4	Francisco Pico
1861, Feb. 6—1861, June 3	Nicanor Molinas (acting)
1861, June 3—1861, Aug. 6	José S. de Olmos (acting)
1861, Aug. 6—1861, Dec. 12	Nicanor Molinas (reassumed office)
1862, April 12—1862, Oct. 13	Eduardo Costa
1862, Oct. 15—1867, Sept. 6	Rufino de Elizalde
1867, Sept. 6—1868, Jan. 25	Marcelino Ugarte
1868, Jan. 25—1868, Oct. 12	Rufino de Elizalde
1868, Oct. 12—1870, Aug. 17	Mariano Varela
1870, Aug. 17—1874, Oct. 12	Carlos Tejedor
1874, Oct. 12—1874, Oct. 12	Félix Frías
1874, Oct. 12—1875, Aug. 2	Pedro A. Pardo (acting)
1875, Aug. 2—1877, Oct. 2	Bernardo de Irigoyen
1877, Oct. 2—1878, May 8	Rufino de Elizalde
1878, May 8—1879, Sept. 6	Manuel A. Montes de Oca
1879, Sept. 6—1879, Oct. 8	Domingo F. Sarmiento (acting)
1879, Oct. 9—1880, June 7	Lucás González
1880, June 7—1880, Oct. 12	Benjamín Zorrilla (acting)
1880, Oct. 12—1882, Feb. 11	Bernardo de Irigoyen
1882, Feb. 11—1883, Oct. 25	Victorino de la Plaza
1883, Oct. 25—1886, Oct. 12	Francisco J. Ortiz
1886, Oct. 12—1889, Feb. 14	Norberto Quirno Costa
1889, Feb. 14—1889, Feb. 25	Mariano A. Pelliza
1889, Feb. 25—1889, Sept. 10	Norberto Quirno Costa
1889, Sept. 10—1890, April 18	Estanislao S. Zeballos
1890, April 18—1890, June 30	Amancio Alcorta (acting)
1890, June 30—1890, Aug. 4	Roque Saenz Peña
1890, Aug. 6—1891, Oct. 21	Eduardo Costa
1891, Oct. 22—1892, Oct. 12	Estanislao S. Zeballos
1892, Oct. 12—1893, June 7	Tomás Anchorena

1893, June 7—1893, June 27	Miguel Cané
1893, June 27—1893, July 5	Norberto Quirno Costa
1893, July 5—1893, Dec. 16	Valentín Virasoro
1893, Dec. 16—1895, Jan. 10	Eduardo Costa
1895, Jan. 10—1899, Dec. 7	Amancio Alcorta
1899, Dec. 7—1900, April 5	Felipe Yofre (acting)
1900, April 5—1902, May 9	Amancio Alcorta
1902, May 9—1902, Aug. 11	Joaquín González (acting)
1902, Aug. 11—1903, July 18	Luis María Drago
1903, July 20—1903, Sept. 9	Joaquín González (acting)
1903, Sept. 9—1904, Oct. 12	José A. Terry
1904, Oct. 12—1906, March 15	Carlos Rodríguez Larreta
1906, March 15—1906, Nov. 21	Manuel A. Montes de Oca
1906, Nov. 21—1908, June 22	Estanislao S. Zeballos
1908, June 22—1910, Aug. 9	Victorino de la Plaza
1910, Aug. 9—1910, Oct. 12	Carlos Rodríguez Larreta
1910, Oct. 12—1910, Dec. 17	Epifanio Portela (acting)
1910, Dec. 17—1914, Feb. 16	Ernesto Bosch
1914, Feb. 16—1916, Oct. 12	José Luis Murature
1916, Oct. 12—1917, Feb. 2	Carlos A. Becú
1917, Feb. 2—1918, Sept. 13	Honorio Pueyrredón (acting)
1918, Sept. 13—1920, Oct. 8	Honorio Pueyrredón
1920, Oct. 8—1921, Feb. 15	Pablo Torello (acting)
1921, Feb. 15—1922, Oct. 12	Honorio Pueyrredón (reassumed office)
1922, Oct. 12—1922, Dec. 26	Tomás A. Le Breton (acting)
1922, Dec. 26—1924, Jan. 5	Angel Gallardo
1924, Jan. 5—1924, Jan. 25	Tomás A. Le Breton (acting)
1924, Jan. 25—1927, Sept. 12	Angel Gallardo
1927, Sept. 12—1928, Feb. 1	Antonio Sagarna (acting)
1928, Feb. 1—1928, Oct. 12	Angel Gallardo
1928, Oct. 12—1930, Sept. 5	Horacio B. Oyhanarte
1930, Sept. 6—1931, Oct. 9	Ernesto Bosch
1931, Oct. 9—1932, Feb. 20	Adolfo Bioy
1932, Feb. 20—1933, Oct. 1	Carlos Saavedra Lamas
1933, Oct. 1—1933, Oct. 21	Leopoldo Melo (acting)
1933, Oct. 21—1933, Dec. 1	Carlos Saavedra Lamas
1933, Dec. 1—1933, Dec. 28	Leopoldo Melo (acting)
1933, Dec. 28—1936, Aug. 28	Carlos Saavedra Lamas
1936, Aug. 28—1936, Nov. 18	Ramón S. Castillo (acting)
1936, Nov. 18—1938, Feb. 20	Carlos Saavedra Lamas
1938, Feb. 20—1938, Feb. 20	José María Cantilo
1938, Feb. 20—1938, April 20	Manuel R. Alvarado (acting)

1938, April 20—1938, April 29	José María Cantilo (assumed office)
1938, April 29—1938, May 7	Manuel R. Alvarado (acting)
1938, May 7—1938, Nov. 29	José María Cantilo
1938, Nov. 29—1938, Dec. 24	Manuel R. Alvarado (acting)
1938, Dec. 24—1940, Sept. 2	José María Cantilo
1940, Sept. 2—1941, Jan. 28	Julio A. Roca
1941, Jan. 28—1941, June 13	Guillermo Rothe (acting)
1941, June 13—1943, June 4	Enrique Ruiz Guiñazú
1943, June 7—1943, Sept. 9	Segundo R. Storni
1943, Sept. 10—1943, Oct. 21	Alberto Gilbert (acting)
1943, Oct. 22—1944, Feb. 15	Alberto Gilbert
1944, Feb. 16—1944, Feb. 26	Benito Sueyro (acting)
1944, Feb. 26—1944, May 2	Diego I. Mason (acting)
1944, May 2—1945, Jan. 15	Orlando L. Peluffo
1945, Jan. 18—1945, May 6	César Ameghino (acting)
1945, May 7—1945, Aug. 9	César Ameghino
1945, Aug. 9—1945, Aug. 21	Amaro Avalos (acting)
1945, Aug. 21—1945, Aug. 27	César Ameghino
1945, Aug. 28—1945, Sept. 12	Juan I. Cooke
1945, Sept. 13—1945, Sept. 18	J. Hortensio Quijano (acting)
1945, Sept. 18—1945, Oct. 14	Juan I. Cooke
1945, Oct. 14—1945, Oct. 17	Vernengo Lima (acting)
1945, Oct. 18—1946, June 4	Juan I. Cooke
1946, March 6—1947, Aug. 7	Juan Atilio Bragmuglia
1947, Aug. 9—1947, Sept. 9	Fidel L. Anadon (acting)
1947, Oct. 20—1948, March 22	Juan Atilio Bramuglia
1948, March 22—1948, May 7	Fidel L. Anadon (acting)
1948, May 7—1948, Sept. 3	Juan Atilio Bramuglia
1948, Sept. 3—1948, Sept. 23	Fidel L. Anadon (acting)
1948, Sept. 23—1948, Dec. 27	Humberto Sosa Molina (acting)
1948, Dec. 27—1949, Aug. 13	Juan Atilio Bramuglia
1949, Aug. 13—1951, March 21	Hipólito J. Paz
1951, March 21—1951, April 16	Franklin Lucero (acting)
1951, April 16—1951, June 28	Hipólito J. Paz
1951, June 28—1955, Aug. 25	Jerónimo Remorino
1955, Aug. 25—1955, Sept. 16	Ildefonso Cavagna Martínez
1955, Sept. 16—1955, Nov. 14	Mario Octavio Amadeo
1955, Nov. 14—1957, Jan. 28	Luis A. Podestá Costa
1957, Jan. 28—1958, Jan. 14	Alfonso de Laferrere
1958, Jan. 14—1958, May 1	Alejandro Ceballos
1958, May 1—1959, May 23	Carlos Alberto Florit
1959, May 23— *	Diógenes Taboada

* Served until April, 1961.

APPENDIX B

ARGENTINE REPRESENTATIVES AT WASHINGTON *

Special Agents

Date of
Appointment

1814, Dec. 7	Juan Pedro Aguirre ⎱ (Commissioned to Diego de Saavedra ⎰ purchase arms)
1815 **	Thomas Taylor (Commissioned to fit out privateers)
1816, Sept. 4	Martín Thompson (Confidential Agent)
1817, May 18	Manuel Hermenegildo de Aguirre (Confidential Agent)
1818 **	David C. DeForest (Commissioned Consul General)
1818 **	William H. Winder (Special Deputy)

Ministers Plenipotentiary

1823, Dec. 28	Carlos M. de Alvear
1825–1826	No representative
1826, April 26	Manuel Moreno (Ill health prevented assumption of office)
1826–1832	No representative

Envoys Extraordinary and Ministers Plenipotentiary

1832, Nov. 10	Carlos M. de Alvear (Illness prevented assumption of office)
1832–1835	No representative
1835, Sept. 17	Manuel Moreno (Ill health prevented assumption of office)

* For source, see note, p. 541.
** These agents were not included in the official list prepared for me by the Division of Archives, Ministry of Foreign Relations, Buenos Aires, although there is correspondence to and from them in the Archivo General de la Nación.

1835–1837	No representative
1837, July 28	Carlos M. de Alvear (Died in U.S. in 1852)
1852–1860	No representative
1860, Nov. 4	Emilio de Alvear
1863, Dec. 4	Domingo F. Sarmiento
1868, Oct. 16	Manuel Rafael García
1882, Jan. 1	Luis L. Domínguez
1885, May 22	Vicente G. Quesada
1893, March 29	Estanislao Zeballos
1896, Jan. 10	Martín García Merou
1900, Jan. 11	Eduardo Wilde
1901, March 20	Martín García Merou
1905, May 17	Epifanio Portela
1910, Dec. 20	Rómulo S. Naón (see below, 1914)

Ambassadors

1914, Sept. 24	Rómulo S. Naón
1918, Dec. 5	Tomás A. Le Breton
1923, Aug. 31	Honorio Pueyrredón
1928, March 31	Manuel Malbrán (Declared *"en disponibilidad"* on Dec. 6, 1928)
1930, Sept. 25	Manuel Malbrán (Designated anew)
1932, June 16	Felipe A. Espil
1943, Oct. 6	Adrian C. Escobar
1945, Apr. [?]	Oscar Ibarra García
1946, June 26	Oscar Ivanissevich
1948, April 17	Jerónimo Remorino
1951, Aug. 10	Hipólito Jesús Paz
1956, Oct. 19	Adolfo A. Vicchi
1957, June 12	Mauricio L. Yadarola
1958, April 22	César Barros Hurtado
1959, Sept. 15 *	Emilio Donato del Carril

* Still in office, Jan., 1962.

APPENDIX C

UNITED STATES REPRESENTATIVES AT BUENOS AIRES *

Special Agents

1810–1815 Joel Roberts Poinsett (Agent for Seamen and Commerce)
1811–1813 William Gilchrist Miller (Consul)
1814–1818 Thomas Lloyd Halsey (Consul)
1816–1817 John Devereux (Commercial Agent)
1817–1820 W. G. D. Worthington (Special Agent)
1817–1818 Caesar A. Rodney
      Theodoric Bland }(Special Commissioners)
      John Graham
1819–   Commodore Oliver H. Perry (Special Agent; died en route)
1819–1820 Commodore Charles Morris (Special Agent)
1819–1820 John B. Prevost (Special Agent)
1820–1823 John M. Forbes (Special Agent)

Chargés d'Affaires

1823–1824 Caesar A. Rodney (Commissioned Minister; died in Buenos
      Aires, 1824)
1824–1831 John M. Forbes (Secretary of Legation, Jan. 27, 1823; acting
      Chargé, June 10, 1824; commissioned Chargé, March 9, 1925)
1832, Jan. 3–Sept. 3 Francis Baylies
1832–1843 No diplomatic representation (a succession of consuls ex-
      ercised semi-diplomatic functions)
1843–1844 Harvey M. Watterson (Special Agent; Senate refused ap-
      proval as Chargé)
1844–1846 William Brent, Jr.

* I have assembled these data from appropriate records in Department of State archives.

1846–1851 William A. Harris
1851–1854 John S. Pendleton

Ministers Resident *

1854–1858 James A. Peden
1857– Mirabeau B. Lamar (transferred to Nicaragua before assuming duties)
1858–1859 Benjamin C. Yancey
1859–1861 John F. Cushman
1861–1862 Robert M. Palmer
1862–1866 Robert C. Kirk
1866–1868 Alexander Asboth
1868–1869 Henry G. Worthington
1869–1871 Robert C. Kirk
1871–1873 Dexter E. Clapp
1873–1874 Julius White
1874–1885 Thomas O. Osborn
1885–1887 Bayless W. Hanna (see below, 1887–1889)

Envoys Extraordinary and Ministers Plenipotentiary

1887–1889 Bayless W. Hanna
1889–1893 John R. G. Pitkin
1894–1899 William I. Buchanan
1900–1903 William P. Lord
1903–1904 John Barrett
1904–1908 Arthur M. Beaupré
1908–1909 Spencer F. Eddy
1909–1911 Charles H. Sherrill
1911–1914 John W. Garrett

Ambassadors

1914–1921 Frederic J. Stimson
1921–1925 John W. Riddle
1925–1927 Peter A. Jay
1927–1933 Robert W. Bliss
1933–1939 Alexander W. Weddell
1939–1944 Norman Armour
1945–1945 Spruille Braden (recalled in September to become Assistant Secretary of State)
1946–1947 George S. Messersmith

* I have not included chargés d'affaires ad interim.

1947–1949   James Bruce
1949–1950   Stanton Griffis
1951–1952   Ellsworth Bunker
1952–1956   Albert F. Nufer
1956–1960   Willard L. Beaulac
1960 ——— * Roy R. Rubottom

* Resigned in Jan., 1961; resignation accepted, Oct., 1961.

Bibliography

BIBLIOGRAPHY

I. MANUSCRIPTS

A. Argentina: Archives of the Ministry of Foreign Relations

(Deposited in the Archivo General de la Nación, Buenos Aires, unless otherwise indicated)

Archivo del General Tomás Guido, 1958, 1859.

Archivo de Don Luis Vernet. Expediente para esclarecer su proceder en los asuntos de las Malvinas, 1832. (S1-A4-A5-núm. 10a).

Archivo de Don Luis Vernet. Malvinas. Papers relative to the origen [sic] and present state of the questions pending with the United States of America, on the subject of the Malvinas. 1832. (S1-A4-A5-núm. 10e).

Archivo de Luis Vernet. Malvinas y documentos Vernet. 1824-1866. (S1-A4-A5-núm. 10f).

Archivo de Sr. Luis Vernet. Malvinas Costa Patagónica—Colonización—Documentos administrativas navegación—Memoriales y varios. 1670-1831; 1832-1840. (S1-A4-A5-núm. 2-3).

Archivo del Sr. Luis Vernet. Recortes de periódicos. (S1-A4-A5-núm. 8).

Archivo Sr. Luis Vernet. Documentos particulares. 1770-1852. (S1-A4-A5-núm. 5).

Correos. 1816. División Nacional. Documentos orginales sobre las opiniones vertidas para la formación de un estado confederado e independiente. (S.V.-C.XXIII-A8-núm. 5).

Correspondencia del Comisionado Aguirre en Washington. (Copies deposited with the Instituto de Investigaciones Históricas, Facultad de Filosofía y Letras, Buenos Aires.)

Donación Alvear. Archivo de los documentos del General Carlos de Alvear. 1766-1852. (S1-A1-A1-núm. 6).

Donación Alvear. Documentos diplomáticos del General Alvear. 1823-1852. (S1-A1-A1-núm. 5).

Donación Alvear. Documentos particulares del Archivo del Gl. Alvear. 1815-1852. (S1-A1-A1-núm. 4).

Estados Unidos. 1810-1823. Correspondencia con los cónsules y agentes. S1-A2-A4-núm. 8).

Estados Unidos. Ministro Alvear. 1833-1852. (S1-A2-A4-núm. 13).

Estados Unidos. Ministro plenipotenciario en Buenos Aires D. Juan M. Forbes. 1824-1831. (S1-A2-A4-núm. 11).

Estados Unidos. Misión Alvear. 1823-1825. (S1-A2-A4-núm. 10).

Estados Unidos. Representantes diplomáticos y consulares en Buenos Aires. 1826-1851. (S1-A2-A4-núm. 12).

Estados Unidos. 1811-1854. Misiones diplomáticas . . . [y] correspondencia del gobierno argentino con el de E.E. U.U. (S1-A2-A4-núm. 9).

Intervención Anglo-Francesa mediación de los agentes de EE. UU. 1845-1846. (Copies deposited with the Instituto de Investigaciones Históricas, Facultad de Filosofía y Letras, Buenos Aires.)

B. Chile: Archives of the Ministry of Foreign Relations

(Deposited in the Archivo Nacional, Santiago)

Cónsules de Chile en el extranjero. 1881. Vol. XLVI.

Copiador oficios diplomáticos chilenos. 1898, Vol. I; 1899.

Correspondencias a los cónsules chilenos. 1879-1882.

Diplomáticos estranjeros. 1880-1883.

Gobierno y agentes diplomáticas de E. U. de Norte América en Chile. 1881-1882. Vol. XII.

Gobierno y legación de los Estados Unidos en Chile, 1898; 1899.

Gobierno y legación de la República Arjentina en Chile. 1898-1899.

Legación de Chile en la Arjentina. 1893-1907.

Legación de Chile en los Estados Unidos de Norte América. 1898, Vol. II; 1899.

C. Great Britain: Archives of the Foreign Office

(Photostatic reproductions deposited in the Library of Congress, Washington)

Public Record Office. Foreign Office 5. Vols. 197, 273, 593, 673.

D. Paraguay: Archives of the Ministry of Foreign Relations

(Deposited in the Archivo General de la Nación, Sección Histórica, Asunción)

Decretos circulares de gobierno sobre prohibición de comprar de esclavos por los estrangeros y consiguiente libertad de los que tenían: . . . 1854. Vol. IX, no. 23.

Espediente creado á consequencia de la compra ílegal que hizo el Norte Americano D. Eduardo A. Hopkins, de las tierras de San Antonio. . . . 1854. Vol. LXXIV, no. 4.

Espediente que trata sobre el asunto del Norte Americano Eduardo Hokis [Hopkins] contra el gobierno de López. 1859. Vol. LII, no. 2.

Legajo de correspondencias oficiales con E. U. al del Paraguay con los gobiernos de los López desde 1845 hasta 1864. Vol. LXXXVI, no. 2.

Legajo de papeles del interior relativos á las bárbaras tropelias de Hokis [Hopkins]: . . . 1854. Vol. CXVI, no. 21.

E. United States: Archives of the Department of State

(Deposited in the National Archives, Washington)

Appointment Papers. Recommendations for Office. Edward A. Hopkins.

Buenos Ayres Claims, Miscellaneous.

Consular Letters (Despatches from Consuls):
Buenos Aires, Vols. I-XXIV; Rosario, I.

Correspondence of Capt. Voorhees, Commodore Turner, etc., 1844.

Decimal File, 1910-1945. (Includes documents on more than 500 cases involving Argentina. Specific references in footnotes.)

Despatches from Ministers:
Argentina, Vols. I-XLVII.
Brazil, Vols. XI, XIX, XX; Chile, X, XXXI, XLVI; Great Britain, LXVII; Paraguay, I-V (some volumes include Uruguay).

Domestic Letters, Vol. XVI.

Instructions to Consuls, Vols. I, II, VI, IX, XVI, XXXIII.

Instructions to Special Missions, Vols. I, III.

Instructions to Ministers:
United States Ministers, Vols. VII-XIII.
United States Ministers, American States, Vol. XIV.
United States Ministers, Argentina, Vols. XV-XVI, Brazil XV-XVI; Paraguay, I; Uruguay, I.

Minor File, 1906-1910, Vols. III, X.

Miscellaneous Letters, 1807, Jan.-Dec.; 1832, July-Dec.; 1833, Jan.-Mar.; 1844, Nov.-Dec.; 1845, Jan.-Mar., Apr.-Aug., Oct.; 1851, June; 1855, Sept.

Notes from Foreign Legations:
Argentina, Vols. I-V; Brazil, VII; Chile, IV, VI; Uruguay, I.

Notes to Argentine Legation, Vol. VII.

Notes to Foreign Legations, Vols. II-VI.

Numerical File, 1906-1910. (Includes documents on more than 175 cases involving Argentina. Specific references in footnotes.)

Records of the United States Delegation to the Second International Conference of American States, 1901-1902.

The South American Mission.

Special Agents Series, Vols. III, VI, VII, XIII.

F. United States: Archives of the Navy Department

(Deposited in the National Archives, Washington)

Brazilian Squadron, Commodore Daniel Turner, 1843-1845.

Captain's Letters, 1838, Apr., May, Oct., Nov., Dec.; 1839, Mar., Apr.

Confidential Letters, No. 2 (1849-1853); No. 4 (1857-1861).

Letters, etc., from Lieutenant Thomas J. Page, Commanding U.S. Steamer "Water Witch." . . . Jan. 6, 1853 and Aug. 4, 1856.

Letters from Masters Commandant, 1832, Jan.-June.

Letters to Flag Officers and Commandants of Vessels, No. 5 (1865-1867); No. 6 (1867-1870).

Letters to Officers of Ships of War, Vols. XIII, XX, XXVII.

Paraguay Expedition and Brazil Squadron, Flag Officer Wm. B. Shubrick, Sept., 1858-May, 1859.

Private Letters, 1813-1840.

South Atlantic Squadron, Rear Admiral S. W. Godon, 1865-1867; Rear Admiral Ch. H. Davis, 1867-1868, 1868-1869.

G. United States: Library of Congress, Division of Manuscripts

Broadsides, 310. Argentina.

Forbes Papers.

Monroe Papers, Johnson Collection.

The Papers of James Madison, Vol. LXIV.

The Papers of James Monroe
  Writings of Monroe, Vol. V.
  Writings to Monroe, Vols. XVI-XVII.

Papers of Jeremy Robinson
  Diaries, 1818.
  Portfolios, 1810-1820.

Poinsett Papers. Notes and memoranda on conditions in Chile, the Plate, etc. Two portfolios.

Rodney Papers.

South American Pamphlets.

Toner Collection. Diaries of W. G. D. Worthington (after return from South America in 1819). 3 vols.
Webster Papers, Vol. XII.

G. United States: Grosvenor Library, Buffalo, New York

Buchanan Papers. Chilian-Argentine Boundary Arbitration: Private Papers, W. I. Buchanan, Deciding Member of the Commission, 1899.

H. United States: Historical Society of Pennsylvania, Philadelphia

Gratz Collection, Case 2, Box 20; Case 3, Box 25; Case 6, Box 9.
Poinsett Papers, Vols. I, II, IX, XIII, XVII.

II. GOVERNMENT AND SEMIOFFICIAL PUBLICATIONS

A. Argentina

Argentine Confederation, *Documentos oficiales. Mediación del encargado de negocios de los Estados Unidos de América D. Benjamin Yancey, en la cuestión de la integridad nacional y proclama del Presidente de la Confederación Argentina.* Montevideo, 1859.

——*Registro oficial de la República Argentina que comprende los documentos espedidos desde 1810 hasta 1873.* Buenos Aires, 1879-1884; 6 vols.

Boletín oficial de la República Argentina, 1893——. Buenos Aires, 1894——.

Comisión Nacional de Investigaciones, *Libro Negro de la segunda tiranía, Descreto ley No. 14988/56.* Buenos Aires, 1956.

Congreso Nacional, Cámara de Diputados, *Diario de sesiones de la Cámara de Diputados, 1854——.* Buenos Aires, 1886——.

——Cámara de Senadores, *Diario de sesiones de la Cámara de Senadores, 1854——.* Buenos Aires, 1883——.

Cooke, Juan Isaac, *Three Statements on the International Policy of Argentina.* Buenos Aires, 1946.

Delegación á la Segunda Conferencia de la Paz, *La República Argentina en la Segunda Conferencia Internacional de la Paz, Haya, 1907.* Buenos Aires, 1907.

Delegación á la Segunda Conferencia Pan-Americana, *Report Which the Delegation of the Argentine Republic Submits to the Second Pan-American Conference.* [Mexico, 1901.]

Delegación á la Tercera Conferencia Internacional Americana, *Memoria de la delegación de la República Argentina, presentada a la Tercera Conferencia Internacional Americana. . . .* Rio de Janeiro, 1906.

Mabragaña, H., *Los mensajes. Historia del desenvolvimiento de la Nación Argentina, redactada cronologicamente por sus gobernantes, 1810-1910.* [Buenos Aires, 1910]; 6 vols.

Memoria presentada al tribunal nombrada por el gobierno de Su Majestad Británica "para considerar é informar sobre las diferencias suscitadas respecto á la frontera entre las Repúblicas Argentina y Chilena". . . . London, 1902; 2 vols.

Ministerio de Relaciones Exteriores y Culto, *Board for the Vigilance and Final Disposal of Enemy Property; Precis of Its Activities from Its Creation to January 15, 1946.* . . . Buenos Aires, 1946.

——*Boletin mensual, 1884*——. Buenos Aires, 1884——.

——*Circular informativa mensual destinada al cuerpo diplomático y consular de la República Argentina, 1917-1935.* Buenos Aires, [1917-1936]; Nos. 1-223.

——*Colección de documentos oficiales con que el gobierno instruye al cuerpo legislativo de la provincia del origen y estado de las cuestiones pendientes con la república de los E. U. de Norte América, sobre las Islas Malvinas.* Buenos Aires, 1832.

——*Correspondence Sustained between the Government of Buenos-Aires, Charged with the Foreign Affairs of the Argentine Confederation, and Captain John B. Nicolson, Commander of the U. States' Naval Forces on the Coast of Brazil and River Plate, Respecting the Question Produced by the Agents of France.* Buenos Aires, 1839.

——*Digesto de relaciones exteriores, 1810-1913.* Buenos Aires, 1913.

——*Documentos y actos de gobierno relativos a la guerra en Europa.* Buenos Aires, 1919.

——*La frontera argentino-brasileña. Estudios y demarcación general, 1887-1904.* Buenos Aires, 1910; 2 vols.

——*Instrumentos internacionales de carácter bilateral suscriptos por la República Argentina (hasta el 30 de junio de 1948).* Buenos Aires, 1950; 2 vols.

——*Memoria de relaciones exteriores presentada al Congreso Nacional.* . . . Buenos Aires, 1860——.

——*Papers Relative to the Origin and Present State of the Questions Pending with the United States of America, on the Subject of the Malvinas,* . . . Buenos Aires, 1832.

——*La política argentina en la guerra del Chaco.* Buenos Aires, 1937; 2 vols.

——*La República Argentina ante el "Libro Azul."* Buenos Aires, 1946.

——*Speech Pronounced, on July 26, by the Minister for Foreign Affairs of the Argentine Republic, Brigadier General Orlando L. Peluffo.* Buenos Aires, 1944.

——Dirección de Investigaciones, Archivo y Propaganda, *Informaciones argentinas, 1938*——. Buenos Aires, 1938——.

———División de Asuntos Jurídicos, *La República Argentina en la Octava Conferencia Internacional Americana Reunida en Lima.* . . . Buenos Aires, 1939.

———División de Asuntos Jurídicos, *Reuniones de consulta entre ministros de relaciones exteriores de las Repúblicas Americanas, Panamá,* . . . *1939, la Habana,* . . . *1940. Participación argentina.* Buenos Aires, 1941.

———División de Asuntos Jurídicos, *Tercera reunion de consulta de ministros de relaciones exteriores de las Repúblicas Americanas, Rio de Janeiro,* . . . *1942. Participación argentina.* Buenos Aires, 1942.

Oficio del cónsul encargado interinamente del consulado general de Francia en Buenos-Aires, al Sr. Ministro de Relaciones Exteriores de la Confederación Argentina, . . . Buenos Aires, 1838.

Presidente, *Mensaje del presidente de la nación.* . . . Buenos Aires, 1837-1940.

Provincia de Buenos Aires, Archivo Histórico, *Documentos del Congreso de Tucumán.* (Documentos del Archivo, Vol. XII.) La Plata, 1947.

Tratados, convenciones, protocolos, actos y acuerdos internacionales. Buenos Aires, 1911-1912; 11 vols.

Zeballos, Estanislao S., *Arbitration on Misiones,* . . . Buenos Aires, 1893.

———*Argument for the Argentine Republic upon the Question with Brazil in Regard to the Territory of Misiones,* . . . Washington, 1894.

———*Cuestiones de límites entre las Repúblicas Argentina, el Brasil y Chile,* . . . Rosario, 1892.

———*Demarcación de límites entre la República Argentina y Chile,* . . . Buenos Aires, 1892.

B. Brazil

Statement Submitted by the United States of Brazil to the President of the United States of America as Arbitrator, under the Provisions of the Treaty Concluded September 7, 1889, between Brazil and the Argentine Republic. New York, 1894; 6 vols.

C. Chile

Chilo-Argentine Boundary. The Puna de Atacama. Memorandum Presented by the Government of Chile to the Government of the United States of America. Washington, [1898?].

Esposición que por parte de Chile i en respuesta a la esposición arjentina se somete al tribunal que constituyó el gobierno de su Majestad Británica en su carácter de árbitro nombrado por el acuerdo de 17 de abril de 1896. Paris, 1902; 6 vols.

Memoria de relaciones esteriores i de colonización presentada al Congreso Nacional en 1881, 1899. Santiago, 1882, 1900.

President, Discurso de su excelencia el presidente de la república en la apertura del Congreso Nacional de 1881. Santiago, 1881.

D. France

Bureau de la Statistique Générale, Annuaire statistique de France. Paris, 1878——.

E. Great Britain

Board of Trade, Statistical Abstract for the United Kingdom. London, 1854——.

Foreign Office, British and Foreign State Papers, 1812——. London, 1841——.

Hansard's Parliamentary Debates, 5th Series, Vol. 402, House of Commons.

F. Paraguay

Mensajes de Carlos Antonio López, primer presidente constitucional de la república. Asunción, 1931.

Ministerio de Relaciones Exteriores, Appendix and Documents Annexed to the Memoir Filed by the Minister of Paraguay, on the Question Submitted to Arbitration. New York, 1878.

——Chaco Paraguayo: memoria presentada al arbitro por Benjamín Aceval. . . . Asunción, 1896.

G. United States

American State Papers: Foreign Relations. Washington, 1832-1859; 6 vols.

American State Papers: Naval Papers. Washington, 1834-1861; 4 vols.

Annals of Congress. Washington, 1834-1856; 42 vols.

Commission under the Convention between the United States & Paraguay: Statements and Arguments for Claimants and for the Republic, and Opinion and Award of Commissioners. Washington, 1860.

Committee on Public Information, The Official United States Bulletin, May 10, 1917—March 31, 1919. [Washington, 1917-1919]; 3 vols.

Congressional Documents (figures in parentheses represent the Congress and session).

House Documents, Nos. 155 (15.1), 48 (15.2).

House Executive Documents, Nos. 281 (20.1), 211 (25.3), 212 (29.1), 69 (40.3), 79 (40.3), 226 (48.2), 50 (49.1).

House Journal, (25.3), (29.1).

House Reports, Nos. 65 (41.2), 2263 (54.1).

Senate Documents, Nos. 1 (21.2), 744 (61.3), 2, 3, (62.1).

Senate Executive Documents, Nos. 18 (35.2), 1859-60, III (36.1), 112 (41.2), 7 (45.3), 232 (51.1).

Senate Journal, (29.1).

Senate Reports, Nos. 60 (35.1), 1082 (83.2).

Congressional Globe. Washington, 1834-1873.

Congressional Record. Washington, 1873——.

Curtis, W. E., *Trade and Transportation between the United States and Spanish America.* Washington, 1889.

Department of State, *Bulletin.* Washington, 1939——.

——*The Chaco Peace Conference, Report of the Delegation of the United States of America to the Peace Conference Held at Buenos Aires, July 1, 1935—January 23, 1939.* Washington, 1940.

——*Consultation among the American Republics with Respect to the Argentine Situation.* Washington, 1946.

——*Fourth Meeting of Consultation of Ministers of Foreign Affairs of American States, Washington, D. C., March 26—April 7, 1951. Report of the Secretary of State.* [Washington, 1953.]

——*Inter-American Conference for the Maintenance of Continental Peace and Security, Quitandinha, Brazil, August 15—September 2, 1947. Report of the Delegation of the United States of America.* Washington, 1948.

——*Intervention of International Communism in Guatemala.* Washington, 1954.

——*List of Treaties Submitted to the Senate, 1789-1931, Which Have Not Gone into Force, October 1, 1932.* Washington, 1932.

——*Ninth International Conference of American States, Bogotá, Colombia, March 30–May 2, 1948. Report of the Delegation of the United States of America. . . .* [Washington, 1948.]

——*Papers Relating to the Foreign Relations of the United States, with the Annual Message of the President.* Washington, [1862——].

——*Papers Relating to the Foreign Relations of the United States. The Lansing Papers, 1914-1920.* Washington, 1939-1940; 2 vols.

——*Press Releases, October 5, 1929—June 24, 1939.* [Washington, 1929-1939.]

——*Reciprocal Trade Agreement and Supplemental Exchanges of Notes between the United States of America and Argentina Signed at Buenos Aires, October 14, 1941.* Washington, 1943.

——*Report of the Delegates of the United States of America to the Fifth International Conference of American States, Held at Santiago, Chile, March 25, to May 3, 1923.* Washington, 1923.

——*Report of the Delegates of the United States of America to the*

Seventh International Conference of American States, Montevideo, Uruguay, December 3-26, 1933. Washington, 1934.

―――*Report of the Delegation of the United States of America to the Inter-American Conference for the Maintenance of Peace, Buenos Aires, Argentina, December 1-23, 1936.* Washington, 1937.

―――*Report of the Delegation of the United States of America to the Inter-American Conference on Problems of War and Peace, Mexico City, Mexico, February 21—March 8, 1945.* Washington, 1946.

―――*The Statutes at Large of the United States of America, . . .* Boston and Washington, 1845――.

―――*Tenth Inter-American Conference, Caracas, Venezuela, March 1-28, 1954. Report of the Delegation of the United States of America, with Related Documents.* [Washington, 1955.]

Federal Trade Commission, *Food Investigation. Report of the Federal Trade Commission on the Meat-Packing Industry.* Washington, 1919-1920; 6 vols.

Halsey, Frederic M., *Investments in Latin America and the British West Indies.* Washington, 1918.

Malloy, William M., *Treaties, Conventions, International Acts, Protocols, and Agreements between the United States of America and Other Powers, 1776-1909.* Washington, 1910; 2 vols.

Melvin, A. D. and G. M. Rommel, "Meat Production in the Argentine and Its Effects upon the Industry in the United States," *Yearbook of the United States Department of Agriculture, 1914,* pp. 381-390.

Moore, John B., *A Digest of International Law. . . .* Washington, 1906; 8 vols.

―――*History and Digest of the International Arbitrations to Which the United States Has Been a Party.* Washington, 1898; 6 vols.

Navy Department, *Annual Report.* Washington, [1824――]. (Title varies.)

Phoebus, M. A., *Economic Development in Argentina Since 1921.* (Trade Information Bulletin, No. 156.) Washington, 1923.

Pizer, Samuel and Frederick Cutler, *U. S. Investments in the Latin American Economy.* Washington, [n.d.].

Richardson, J. D. (ed.), *A Compilation of the Messages and Papers of the Presidents, 1789-1897.* Washington, 1896-1899; 10 vols. Washington, 1913; 11 vols.

The "Santissima Trinidad," 7 *Wheaton* 283, 5 L. Ed. 454 (1822).

Smith, L. B., H. T. Collings, and Elizabeth Murphey, *The Economic Position of Argentina during the War.* (Bureau of Foreign and Domestic Commerce, Miscellaneous Series, No. 88.) Washington, 1920.

Treasury Department, *American Commerce: Commerce of South Amer-*

ica, Central America, Mexico, and West Indies . . . , 1821-1898.
[Washington, 1899.]
Statistical Abstract of the United States. Washington, 1878——.

H. Miscellaneous

Documents on German Policy, 1918-1945. Series D (1937-1945), Volume
V, Poland; The Balkans; Latin America; The Smaller Powers——
June, 1937—March, 1939. Washington, 1953.
Fourth Pan American Commercial Conference, *Foreign Trade of Latin
America, 1910-1929.* Washington, 1931.
Inter-American Emergency Advisory Committee for the Political Defense
of the Hemisphere, *Annual Reports, 1943, 1944.* Washington, 1943,
1945.
International American Conference, 1889-1890, *Minutes of the Interna-
tional American Conference.* Washington, 1890.
——*Reports of Committees and Discussions Thereon.* Washington,
1890; 4 vols.
International American Conference, 1901-1902, *Second International
American Conference, Mexico: 1901-1902. Organization of the Con-
ference, Projects, Reports, Motions, Debates and Resolutions.*
Mexico City, 1902.
International American Conference, 1910, *Cuarta Conferencia Interna-
cional Americana, 1910.* Buenos Aires, 1911; 2 vols.
International American Conference, 1923, *Actas de las sesiones plenarias
de la Quinta Conferencia Internacional Americana.* Tomo 1. Diario
de sesiones. Santiago, 1923.
——*Quinta Conferencia Internacional de las Repúblicas Americanas.
Informes de las delegaciones presentados en cumplimiento del tema
I del programa.* Vol. IV; Santiago, 1923.
International American Conference, 1928, *Diario de la Sexta Conferencia
Internacional Americana.* Havana, 1928.
International American Conference, 1933, *Minutes and Antecedents with
General Index.* Montevideo, 1933.
Pan American Financial Conference, *Proceedings of the First Pan-
American Financial Conference, May 24 to 29, 1915.* Washington,
1915.
Pan American Union, *Argentina: Latest Reports from Argentine Official
Sources.* (Foreign Trade Series, No. 87.) Washington, 1931.
——*Pan American Commerce, Past—Present—Future, from the Pan
American Viewpoint. Report of the Second Pan American Commer-
cial Conference Held in the Building of the Pan American Union,
Washington, D. C., June 2-6, 1919.* Washington, 1919.

————*Proceedings of the Pan American Commercial Conference, February 13-17, 1911.* Washington, 1911.

————*Status of the Pan American Treaties and Conventions* (Revised to January 1, 1947 by the Juridical Division of the Pan American Union.) Washington, [n.d.].

————*Third Pan American Commercial Conference, May 2nd-5th, 1927. Proceedings.* Washington, 1927.

United Nations, Economic Commission for Latin America, *Economic Survey of Latin America, 1951-1957.* United Nations, N. Y., 1954-1959; 6 vols.

III. UNOFFICIAL PUBLICATIONS

A. Documents, Correspondence, Memoirs, Diaries, and Travels

Adams, Charles F. (ed.), *Memoirs of John Quincy Adams, Comprising Portions of His Diary from 1795 to 1848.* Philadelphia, 1874-1877; 12 vols.

Adams, John Quincy, "Diary of John Quincy Adams," in *Proceedings* of the Massachusetts Historical Society, 2nd series, XVI (1902), 291-464.

Alberdi, Juan B., *Escritos póstumos.* Buenos Aires, 1895-1901; 16 vols.

————*Obras selectas.* New ed.; Buenos Aires, 1920; 18 vols.

Bacon, Robert, and J. B. Scott, *Latin America and the United States. Addresses by Elihu Root.* Cambridge, 1917.

Baker, Ray S., *Woodrow Wilson: Life and Letters.* Garden City, N. Y., 1927-1939; 8 vols.

Bliss, P. C., *Historia secreta de la misión del cuidadano norte-americano Charles A. Washburn, cerca del gobierno de la República del Paraguay.* [n. p., 1868.]

Bowers, Claude, *Chile Through Embassy Windows, 1938-1953.* New York, 1958.

[Brackenridge, Henry M.?], "North American Pamphlet on South American Affairs," *The Pamphleteer, Respectively Dedicated to Both Houses of Parliament,* XIII (Feb. 6, 1818), 36-83.

Brackenridge, Henry M., *Voyage to South America, Performed by Order of the American Government, in the Years 1817 and 1818, in the Frigate Congress.* Baltimore, 1819; 2 vols.

Bruce, James, *Those Perplexing Argentines.* New York, 1953.

Buchanan, William I., "Latin America and the Mexican Conference," *Annals of the American Academy of Political and Social Science,* XXII (July, 1903), 47-55.

Bunkley, Allison W. (ed.), *A Sarmiento Anthology*. Princeton, 1948.

Burr, Robert N. and Roland Hussey, *Documents on Inter-American Cooperation*. Philadelphia, 1955; 2 vols.

Cabot, John M., *Toward Our Common American Destiny*. Medford, Mass., 1955.

Caldcleugh, Alexander, *Travels in South America, during the Years 1819-20-21; Containing an Account of the Present State of Brazil, Buenos Ayres, and Chile*. London, 1825; 2 vols.

Carnegie Endowment for International Peace, *The Proceedings of the Hague Peace Conferences; . . .* New York, 1920-1921; 5 vols.

Charter and By-Laws of the United States and Paraguay Navigation Company. Providence, 1853.

Congress of Industrial Organizations, Committee on Latin American Affairs, *The Argentine Regime. Facts and Recommendations to the United Nations Organization*. New York, 1946.

Correspondencias generales de la Provincia de Buenos Aires relativas a relaciones exteriores (1820-1824). (Documentos para la historia argentina, Vol. XIV.) Buenos Aires, 1921.

Council on Foreign Relations, *Documents on American Foreign Relations, 1938———*. Boston, 1939———.

Drago, Luis M., *Discursos y escritos, compilados y prededidos de una introducción por su hijo Mariano J. Drago*. Buenos Aires, 1938; 3 vols.

———*La República Argentina y el caso de Venezuela: documentos, juicios y comentarios relacionados con la nota pasada al ministro argentino en Washington*. Buenos Aires, 1903.

A Five Years' Residence in Buenos Ayres during the Years 1820 to 1825: . . . By an Englishman. 2nd ed.; London, 1827.

Ford, Worthington C. (ed.), *Writings of John Quincy Adams*. New York, 1913-1917; 7 vols.

García, Manuel R., *Cartas confidenciales de Sarmiento a M. R. García (1866-1872)*. Buenos Aires, 1917.

[García, Manuel R.], *Paraguay and the Alliance against the Tyrant Francisco Solano López*. New York, 1869.

———*Remarks Concerning the Means to Re-establish the Declining State of Commerce between the United States and the Argentine Republic by the Proper Reduction of the Present Tariffs*. Washington, 1869.

García Merou, Martín, *Estudios americanos*. Buenos Aires, 1900.

General McMahon's Opinions in Regard to the Paraguayan War. [Washington ?, 1869?]

Gillespie, Alexander, *Gleanings and Remarks: Collected during Many Months of Residence at Buenos Ayres, and within the Upper Country; . . .* Leeds, 1818.

Griffis, Stanton, *Lying in State*. New York, 1952.

Gulick, Charles A., Jr., *The Papers of Mirabeau Buonaparte Lamar.* Austin, [1921-1925].

Hamilton, S. M. (ed.), *The Writings of James Monroe, . . .* New York, 1898-1903; 7 vols.

Hendrick, Burton. J., *The Life and Letters of Walter H. Page, Containing the Letters to Woodrow Wilson.* Garden City, 1925-1926; 3 vols.

Herrera, Luis Alberto de, *La diplomacia oriental en el Paraguay; correspondencia oficial y privada del Doctor Juan José de Herrera, ministro de relaciones exteriores de los gobiernos de Berro y Aguirre.* Montevideo, 1908-1927; 5 vols.

Hill, Henry, *Recollections of an Octogenarian.* Boston, 1884.

Historia documentada de la cuestiones entre el gobierno del Paraguay y el de los Estados Unidos. Asunción, 1858.

Hoover, Herbert, *The Memoirs of Herbert Hoover.* New York, 1951——; 3 vols.

Hopkins, Edward A., *Historico-Political Memorial upon the Regions of the Río de la Plata, and Coterminous Countries, to James Buchanan, President of the United States.* New York, 1858.

——"The La Plata and the Paraná-Paraguay," *DeBow's Review,* XIV (March, 1853), 238-251.

——"Memoir on the Geography, History, Productions, and Trade of Paraguay," *Bulletin of the American Geographical and Statistical Society,* I (1852), 14-42.

——"Navigation of the Confluents of the Río de la Plata," *The Merchants' Magazine and Commercial Review,* XXI (July, 1849), 80-87.

——"The Republic of Paraguay; since the Death of the Dictator Francia," *The American Review,* VI (July, 1847), 245-260.

——*La tiranía del Paraguay, a la faz de sus contemporáneos.* Buenos Aires, 1856.

Hull, Cordell, *The Memoirs of Cordell Hull.* New York, 1948; 2 vols.

Humphreys, R. A., *British Consular Reports on the Trade and Politics of Latin America, 1824-1826.* (Camden Third Series, Vol. LXIII.) London, 1940.

Hunt, Gaillard (ed.), *Writings of James Madison, . . .* New York, 1908; 8 vols.

[Irigoyen, Bernardo de], *La cuestión de límites entre la República Argentina y Chile.* Buenos Aires, 1881.

Kelly, Sir David, *The Ruling Few or The Human Background to Diplomacy.* London, 1852.

Kenway, Mary W., "Correspondence between General William Winder and President Monroe with reference to proposals made by the United Provinces of South America," *The Hispanic American Historical Review,* XII (Nov., 1932), 457-461.

Lansing, Robert, *War Memoirs of Robert Lansing, Secretary of State.* Indianapolis, 1935.

Luiggi, Alice H., "Some Letters of Sarmiento and Mary Mann, 1865-1876," *The Hispanic American Historical Review,* XXXII (May, Aug., 1952), 187-211, 347-375.

McAdoo, William G., *Crowded Years: The Reminiscences of William G. McAdoo.* Boston, 1931.

Manning, William R. (ed.), *Arbitration Treaties among the American Nations to the Close of the Year 1910.* New York, 1924.

————*Diplomatic Correspondence of the United States Concerning Independence of the Latin-American Countries.* New York, 1925-1926; 3 vols.

————*Diplomatic Correspondence of the United States: Inter-American Affairs, 1831-1860.* Washington, 1932-1939; 12 vols.

Mason, Amos L. (ed.), *Memoir and Correspondence of Charles Steedman, Rear Admiral, United States Navy, with his Autobiography and Private Journals, 1811-1890.* Cambridge, 1912.

Masterman, George F., *Seven Eventful Years in Paraguay.* London, 1869.

A Memorial on the National and Territorial Unity of the Argentine Republic, . . . Hartford, 1857.

Mitre, Bartolomé, *Archivo del General Mitre.* Buenos Aires, 1911-1914; 28 vols.

Moore, John B. (ed.), *The Works of James Buchanan, . . .* Philadelphia, 1908-1911. 12 vols.

Moreno, Manuel, *Vida y memorias del Doctor Don Mariano Moreno.* Buenos Aires, 1918.

Naón, Rómulo S., "The European War and Pan Americanism," *International Conciliation,* Interamerican Division Bulletin, No. 20. New York, April, 1919.

————"International Democracy: a Guiding Principle in the Foreign Relations of Argentina," *World's Work,* XXIX (Dec., 1914), 147-148.

————"Trade Expansion with Argentina," *The Pan-American Magazine,* XX (March, 1915), 10-16.

Page, Thomas J., *La Plata, the Argentine Confederation, and Paraguay. . . .* New York, 1859.

————*Report of the Exploration and Survey of the River "La Plata" and Tributaries, . . . to the Secretary of the Navy, 1856.* Washington, 1856.

Parish, Sir Woodbine, *Buenos Ayres and the Provinces of the Rio de la Plata: . . .* London, 1839. 2nd ed.; London, 1852.

Pazos, Vicente, *Letters on the United Provinces of South America, Addressed to the Hon. Henry Clay, Speaker of the House of Representatives in the U. States.* London, 1819.

Perón, Juan, *Perón expone su doctrina.* Buenos Aires, 1948.

Piñero, Norberto, *Escritos de Mariano Moreno*. Buenos Aires, 1896.

La política exterior de la República Argentina. (Estudios Editados por la Facultad de Derecho y Ciencias Sociales de la Universidad de Buenos Aires, Vol. XIX.) Buenos Aires, 1931.

Polk, James K., *The Diary of James K. Polk during his Presidency, 1845 to 1849,* . . . Chicago, 1910; 4 vols.

Quesada, Vicente G., *Recuerdos de mi vida diplomática; misión en Estados Unidos (1885-1892).* (Anales de la Facultad de Derecho y Ciencias Sociales de la Universidad de Buenos Aires, Vol. VI.) Buenos Aires, 1904.

The Reports on the Present State of the United Provinces of South America; Drawn up by Messrs. Rodney and Graham, ... London, 1819.

Robertson, William S., "Documents concerning the Consular Service of the United States in Latin America, with Introductory Note," *Mississippi Valley Historical Review,* II (March, 1916), 561-568.

Rojas, Ricardo, *Doctrina democrática de Mariano Moreno.* (Biblioteca argentina, Vol. I.) Buenos Aires, 1915.

Ruiz Guiñazú, Enrique, *La política argentina y el futuro de América.* Buenos Aires, 1944.

Saavedra Lamas, Carlos, *La Conferencia Interamericana de Consolidación de la Paz (celebrada en Buenos Aires, del 1.º al 23 de diciembre de 1926).* Buenos Aires, 1938.

———*Draft of a Convention for the Maintenance of Peace.* . . . Washington, 1936.

Saenz Peña, Roque, *Escritos y discursos.* Buenos Aires, 1914-1915; 2 vols.

Saladías, Adolfo (ed.), *Papeles de Rozas.* La Plata, 1904-1907; 2 vols.

Sarmiento, Domingo F., *Obras de D. F. Sarmiento.* Paris, 1899-1909; 54 vols.

Scott, James B. (ed.), *The International Conferences of American States, 1889-1928;* . . . New York, 1931.

———*The International Conferences of American States, First Supplement, 1933-1940.* Washington, 1940.

Seymour, Charles (ed.), *The Intimate Papers of Colonel House.* Boston, 1926-1928; 4 vols.

Stewart, Charles S., *Brazil and La Plata: the Personal Record of a Cruise.* New York, 1856.

Stimson, Frederic J., *My United States.* New York, 1931.

Strictures on a Voyage to South America, as Indited by the "Secretary to the Late Mission" to La Plata; . . . Baltimore, 1820.

Summary of the Public Exercises and Honors at the Interment of the Honorable Caesar A. Rodney, Minister Plenipotentiary of the United States of America. Buenos Aires, 1824.

Thompson, George C. E., *The War in Paraguay, with a Historical Sketch of the Country and Its People and Notes upon the Military Engineering of the War.* London, 1869.

Universidad de Buenos Aires, *Comisión de Bernardino Rivadavia ante España y otras potencias de Europa (1814–1820).* (Documentos para la historia argentina, Vols. XXI-XXII.) Buenos Aires, 1933-1936; 2 vols.

Washburn, Charles A., *The History of Paraguay, with Notes of Personal Observations, and Reminiscences of Diplomacy under Difficulties.* Boston, 1871; 2 vols.

Washington, H. A. (ed.), *Writings of Thomas Jefferson;* . . . New York, 1853-1854; 9 vols.

Welles, Sumner, *The Time for Decision.* New York, 1944.

Wilson, Hugh, *The Education of a Diplomat.* New York, 1938.

Zeballos, Estanislao S. (ed.), "Diario del Brigadier General Tomás Guido durante su misión al Paraguay (1858-1859)," *Revista de Derecho, Historia y Letras,* VI (June, 1900), 485-510; VII (July, 1900), 34-52; (Aug., 1900), 195-208.

B. Other Books and Pamphlets

Adams, Henry, *History of the United States of America.* New York, 1891-1898; 9 vols.

Akers, Charles E., *A History of South America, 1854-1904.* New York, 1905.

Alberdi, Juan B., *The Life and Industrial Labors of William Wheelwright in South America.* Boston, 1877.

Alexander, Robert J., *The Perón Era.* New York, 1951.

Antokoletz, Daniel, *La diplomatie pendant la révolution: politique extérieure de la junte provisoire de gouvernement du Triumvirat (1810-1814).* (Histoire de la diplomatie argentine, Vol. I.) Paris, 1914.

Arciniegas, Germán (ed.), *The Green Continent: A Comprehensive View of Latin America by Its Leading Writers.* New York, 1944.

Babson, Roger W., *The Future of South America.* Boston, 1915.

Bacon, Robert, *For Better Relations with Our Latin American Neighbors. A Journey to South America.* Washington, 1915.

Bailey, Thomas A., *The Policy of the United States toward Neutrals, 1917-1918.* Baltimore, 1942.

Barreda Laos, Felipe, *Roque Saenz Peña.* Buenos Aires, 1954.

Barros Arana, Diego, *Esposición de los derechos de Chile en el litijio de límites sometido al fallo arbitral de S. M. B.* Santiago, 1899.

——*Historia jeneral de Chile.* Santiago, 1884-1902; 16 vols.

Bealer, Lewis W., *Los corsarios del Buenos Aires: sus actividades en las guerras hispano-americanas de la independencias, 1815-1821.* (Publicaciones del Instituto Investigaciones Históricas, Facultad de Filosofía y Letras, Vol. LXXII.) Buenos Aires, 1937.

Beccar Varela, Adrián, *Juan Martín de Pueyrredón*. Buenos Aires, 1924.

Belgrano, Mario, *La Francia y la monarquía en el Plata (1818-1820)*. Buenos Aires, 1933.

Bemis, Samuel F., *Early Diplomatic Missions from Buenos Aires to the United States, 1811-1824*. Worcester, Mass., 1940.

———*The Latin American Policy of the United States; An Historical Interpretation*. New York, 1943.

———(ed.), *The American Secretaries of State and Their Diplomacy*. New York, 1927-1929; 10 vols.

Bernstein, Harry, *Origins of Inter-American Interest, 1700-1812*. Philadelphia, 1945.

Blakeslee, George H., *The Recent Foreign Policy of the United States; Problems in American Cooperation with Other Powers*. New York, 1925.

Blanksten, George I., *Perón's Argentina*. Chicago, 1953.

Box, Pelham Horton, *The Origins of the Paraguayan War*. (University of Illinois Studies in the Social Sciences, Vol. XV, Nos. 3-4.) Urbana, Ill., 1927.

Boyson, V. F., *The Falkland Islands*. Oxford, Great Britain, 1924.

Brown, John H. (ed.), *Lamb's Biographical Dictionary of the United States*. Boston, 1900-1903; 7 vols.

Buchanan, A. W. P., *The Buchanan Book. The Life of Alexander Buchanan, Q. C., of Montreal, Followed by an Account of the Family of Buchanan*. Montreal, 1911.

Bunkley, Allison W., *The Life of Sarmiento*. Princeton, 1952.

Burgin, Miron, *The Economic Aspects of Argentine Federalism, 1820-1852*. Cambridge, 1946.

Cady, John F., *Foreign Intervention in the Río de la Plata, 1838-50: A Study of French, British, and American Policy in Relation to the Dictator Juan Manuel Rosas*. Philadelphia, 1929.

Carleton, William G., *The Revolution in American Foreign Policy*. New York, 1957.

Chamber of Commerce of the United States of America in the Argentine Republic, *Trade Relations between Argentina and the United States of America*. Buenos Aires, 1946.

Chandler, Charles L., *Inter-American Acquaintances*. 2nd ed.; Sewanee, Tenn., 1917.

Cline, Howard F., *The United States and Mexico*. Cambridge, 1953.

Confalonieri, Orestes D., *Perón contra Perón*. Buenos Aires, 1956.

Correa Luna, Carlos, *Alvear y la diplomacia de 1824-1825 en Inglaterra, Estados Unidos y Alto Perú, con Canning, Monroe, Quincy Adams, Bolívar y Sucre*. Buenos Aires, 1926.

Council on Foreign Relations, *The United States in World Affairs: An Account of American Foreign Relations, 1931——.* New York, 1932——.

Crawford, William R., *A Century of Latin-American Thought.* Cambridge, 1944.

Currier, Theodore S., *Los corsarios del Río de la Plata.* (Instituto de Investigaciones Históricas, Universidad Nacional de Buenos Aires, Vol. XLV.) Buenos Aires, 1929.

Curti, Merle, *The Growth of American Thought.* New York, 1943.

Davis, Thomas B., *Carlos de Alvear, Man of Revolution.* Durham, N. C., 1955.

DeConde, Alexander, *Herbert Hoover's Latin-American Policy.* Stanford, Cal., 1951.

DeForest, J. W., *The De Forests of Avesnes (and of New Netherland). A Huguenot Thread in American Colonial History, 1494 to the Present Time.* New Haven, 1900.

Dickmann, Enrique, *La infiltración nazi-fascista en la Argentina.* Buenos Aires, 1939.

Dictionary of American Biography. New York, 1928-1936; 20 vols.

Duggan, Laurence, *The Americas: The Search for Hemisphere Security.* New York, 1949.

Dunn, Robert W., *American Foreign Investments.* New York, 1926.

Frondizi, Arturo, *Petróleo y política.* Buenos Aires, 1954.

Fuchs, Jaime, *La penetración de los trusts yanquis en la Argentina.* Buenos Aires, 1957.

Gálvez, Manuel, *Vida de Hipólito Yrigoyen, el hombre del misterio.* Buenos Aires, 1939.

De Gandía, Enrique, *Las ideas políticas de Mariano Moreno: autenticidad del plan que le es atribuido.* (Publicaciones del Instituto de Investigaciones Históricas, Facultad de Filosofía y Letras, Vol. XCVI.) Buenos Aires, 1946.

Gleed, Charles S., "Thomas A. Osborn," *Transactions of the Kansas Historical Society, 1897-1900.* Vol. VI. Topeka, 1900.

Goebel, Julius, *The Recognition Policy of the United States.* (Columbia University Studies in History, Economics and Public Law, Vol. LXVI, No. 1.) New York, 1915.

——*The Struggle for the Falkland Islands: A Study in Legal and Diplomatic History.* New Haven, 1927.

Graham, Malbone W., *American Diplomacy in the International Community.* Baltimore, 1948.

Greenup, Ruth and Leonard, *Revolution before Breakfast: Argentina, 1941-1946.* Chapel Hill, 1947.

Griffin, Charles C., *The United States and the Disruption of the Spanish Empire, 1810-22.* New York, 1937.

Groussac, Paul, *Les Iles Malouines: nouvel exposé d'un vieux litige*. Paris, 1910.

Guerrant, Edward O., *Roosevelt's Good Neighbor Policy*. Albuquerque, 1950.

Hayes, Carlton J. H., *Essays on Nationalism*. New York, 1928.

Herring, Hubert, *Good Neighbors, Argentina, Brazil, Chile, & Seventeen Other Countries*. New Haven, 1941.

——*A History of Latin America from the Beginning to the Present*. New York, 1955.

Hill, Lawrence F., *Diplomatic Relations between the United States and Brazil*. Durham, N. C., 1932.

Holdich, Col. Sir Thomas Hungerford, *The Countries of the King's Award*. London, 1904.

Houston, John A., *Latin America in the United Nations*. New York, 1956.

Hughes, Charles E., *Our Relations to the Nations of the Western Hemisphere*. Princeton, 1928.

Hyde, Charles C., *International Law: Chiefly As Interpreted and Applied by the United States*. Boston, 1951; 3 vols.

Ibarguren, Carlos, *En la penumbra de la historia argentina*. Buenos Aires, 1932.

Ingalls, Walter R., *Wealth and Income of the American People: A Survey of the Economic Consequences of the War*. York, Pa., 1923.

Ingenieros, José, *La evolución de las ideas argentinas*. Buenos Aires, 1918-1920; 2 vols.

Ireland, Gordon, *Boundaries, Possessions, and Conflicts in South America*. Cambridge, 1938.

Iriarte, General Tomás de, *Memorias: Rivadavia, Monroe y la guerra argentino-brasileña*. Buenos Aires, 1945.

James, Preston, *Latin America*. New York, 1942.

Jeffrey, William H., *Mitre and Argentina*. New York, 1952.

Johnson, Emory R., *et al.*, *History of Domestic and Foreign Commerce of the United States*. Washington, 1915; 2 vols.

Josephs, Ray, *Argentine Diary, the Inside Story of the Coming of Fascism*. New York, 1944.

Kaplan, Marcos, *Economía y política del petróleo argentino (1939-1956)*. Buenos Aires, 1957.

Kay-Shuttleworth, Nina Louisa, *A Life of Sir Woodbine Parish (1796-1882)*. London, 1910.

Keen, Benjamin, *David Curtis DeForest and the Revolution of Buenos Aires*. New Haven, 1947.

Kelchner, Warren H., *Latin American Relations with the League of Nations*. Philadelphia, 1930.

Kennedy, John J., *Catholicism, Nationalism, and Democracy in Argentina*. South Bend, Ind., 1958.

Kirkpatrick, F. A., *A History of the Argentine Republic.* Cambridge (England), 1931.

Klein, Julius, *Frontiers of Trade.* New York, 1929.

Koebel, William H., *Paraguay.* London, 1917.

———*The Romance of the River Plate.* London, 1914; 2 vols.

Krout, John A. and Dixon R. Fox, *The Completion of Independence, 1790-1830.* New York, 1944.

Lafiandra, Félix (ed.), *Los panfletos: su aporte a la revolución libertadora.* Buenos Aires, 1955.

Lamar, Clarinda P., *The Life of Joseph Rucker Lamar (1857-1916).* New York, 1926.

Langer, William L. and S. Everett Gleason, *The Undeclared War, 1940-1941.* New York, 1953.

Levene, Ricardo, *Ensayo histórico sobre la revolucion de mayo y Mariano Moreno.* Buenos Aires, 1920-1921; 2 vols.

———*Historia de la Nación Argentina (desde los orígenes hasta la organización definitiva en 1862).* Buenos Aires, 1939-1947; 10 vols.

———*A History of Argentina.* Chapel Hill, 1937.

Link, Arthur S., *Woodrow Wilson and the Progressive Era, 1910-1917.* New York, 1954.

Lockey, Joseph B., *Pan Americanism: Its Beginnings.* New York, 1920.

López, Vicente F., *Historia de la República Argentina, su origen, su revolución, y su desarrollo político hasta 1852.* Buenos Aires, 1911; 10 vols.

Macdonald, Austin F., *Government of the Argentine Republic.* New York, 1942.

McGann, Thomas F., *Argentina, the United States, and the Inter-American System, 1880-1914.* Cambridge, 1957.

MacKenzie, Alexander S., *The Life of Commodore Oliver Hazard Perry.* New York, 1840; 2 vols.

McMaster, John B., *The Life and Times of Stephen Girard, Mariner and Merchant.* Philadelphia, 1918; 2 vols.

Martin, Charles E., *The Policy of the United States as Regards Intervention.* (Columbia University Studies in History, Economics, and Public Law, Vol. XCIII, No. 2.) New York, 1921.

Martin, Percy A., *Latin America and the War.* Baltimore, 1925.

Matienzo, José N., *El gobierno representativo federal en la República Argentina.* (Biblioteca de Ciencias Políticas y Sociales, Vol. XIV.) Madrid, [1917?].

Mitre, Bartolomé, *Historia de Belgrano y de la independencia argentina.* Buenos Aires, 1927-1928; 4 vols.

Moreno Quintana, Lucio M., *La diplomacia de Yrigoyen; relación técnica, objetiva y documentada de la política internacional argentina durante el período de gobierno, 1916-1922.* La Plata, 1928.

Moses, Bernard, *The Intellectual Background of the Revolution in South America, 1810-1824.* New York, 1926.

Nevins, Allan, *Henry White: Thirty Years of American Diplomacy.* New York, 1930.

Normano, J. F. *The Struggle for South America: Economy and Ideology.* New York, 1931.

Padilla, Alberto, *La constitución de Estados Unidos como precedente argentino.* Buenos Aires, 1921.

Palacios, Alfredo L., *Las Islas Malvinas: archipiélago argentino.* Buenos Aires, [1934].

———*Petróleo, monopolios y latifundios.* Buenos Aires, 1957.

Palomeque, Alberto, *Oríjenes de la diplomacia arjentina, misión Aguirre á Norte América.* Buenos Aires, 1905; 2 vols.

Parker, William Belmont (ed.), *Argentines of To-Day.* Buenos Aires and New York, 1920; 2 vols.

Paxson, Frederic L., *The Independence of the South American Republics: A Study in Recognition and Foreign Policy.* 2nd ed.; Philadelphia, 1916.

Pecquet du Bellet, Louise, *Some Prominent Virginia Families.* [Lynchburg, Va., 1907]; 4 vols.

Pelliza, Mariano A., *Historia argentina desde su origen hasta la organización nacional.* Buenos Aires, 1910; 2 vols.

Pendle, George, *Argentina.* London, 1955.

Pereira Salas, Eugenio, *La misión Worthington en Chile (1818-1819).* Santiago, 1936.

Perkins, Dexter, *Charles Evans Hughes and American Democratic Statesmanship.* Boston, 1956.

———*Hands Off: A History of the Monroe Doctrine.* Boston, 1941.

———*The Monroe Doctrine, 1823-1826.* Cambridge, 1927.

———*The Monroe Doctrine, 1826-1867.* Baltimore, 1933.

———*The Monroe Doctrine, 1867-1907.* Baltimore, 1938.

Peters, Harold E., *The Foreign Debt of the Argentine Republic.* Baltimore, 1934.

Peterson, Harold F., "Urquiza y el enredo paraguayo-norteamericano," Academia Nacional de la Historia, Junta de Historia y Numismática Americana, *IIº congreso internacional de historia de América reunido en Buenos Aires en los días 5 a 14 de junio de 1937,* IV, 320-330. Buenos Aires, 1938; 6 vols.

Pinedo, Federico, *En tiempos de la república.* Buenos Aires, 1946; 4 vols.

Piñero, Norberto, *La política internacional argentina.* Buenos Aires, 1924.

Pratt, Julius W., *A History of United States Foreign Policy.* New York, 1955.

La Prensa, Editors of, *Defense of Freedom.* New York, 1952.

Putnam, Herbert E., *Joel Roberts Putnam: A Political Biography*. Washington, 1935.

Quesada, Ernesto, *La política argentino-paraguaya*. Buenos Aires, 1902.

Quesada, Vicente G., *Historia diplomática latino-americana*. Buenos Aires, 1918-1920; 3 vols.

Rabinovitz, Bernardo, *Sucedió en la Argentina (1943-1956): lo que no se dijo*. Buenos Aires, 1956.

Ramos-Mejía, Francisco, *El federalismo argentino*. Buenos Aires, 1887.

Ravignani, Emilio, *Historia constitucional de la República Argentina*. Buenos Aires, 1926-1927; 3 vols.

Read, William T., *Biographical Sketch of Caesar Augustus Rodney, . . .* Wilmington, Del., 1853.

Rebaudi, A., *Guerra del Paraguay; la conspiración contra S. E. el presidente de la república, Mariscal Don Francisco Solano López*. Buenos Aires, 1917.

Rennie, Ysabel F., *The Argentine Republic*. New York, 1945.

Rippy, J. Fred, *Joel R. Poinsett, Versatile American*. Durham, N. C., 1935.

———*Latin America and the Industrial Age*. New York, 1944.

———*Rivalry of the United States and Great Britain over Latin America (1808-1830)*. Baltimore, 1929.

Robertson, William S., *France and Latin-American Independence*. Baltimore, 1939.

———*Hispanic-American Relations with the United States*. New York, 1923.

Robison, Edgar and Victor J. West, *The Foreign Policy of Woodrow Wilson, 1913-1917*. New York, 1917.

Rodríguez Yrigoyen, Luis (ed.), *Hipólito Yrigoyen, 1878-1933: documentacion historica de 55 años de actuación por la democracia y las instituciones*. Buenos Aires, 1934.

Romero, José Luis, *Las ideas políticas en Argentina*. Mexico, 1946.

Rowe, Leo S., *The Federal System of the Argentine Republic*. Washington, 1921.

Ryan, Ricardo, *La política internacional y la presidencia Yrigoyen*. Buenos Aires, 1921.

Saavedra Lamas, Carlos, *La conception argentine de l'arbitrage et de l'intervention à l'ouverture de la Conférence de Washington*. Paris, 1928.

Saldías, Adolfo, *La evolución republicana durante la revolución argentina*. Madrid, 1919.

———*Historia de la Confederación Argentina: Rozas y su época*. 2nd ed.; Buenos Aires, [1892]; 5 vols.

Salera, Virgil, *Exchange Control and the Argentine Market*. New York, 1941.

Santander, Silvano, *Técnica de una traición: Juan Perón y Eva Duarte, agentes del nazismo en la Argentina.* 2nd ed.; [Montevideo], 1953.

Severance, Frank H., "The Peace Conference at Niagara Falls in 1914," *Peace Episodes on the Niagara.* (Buffalo Historical Society Publications, Vol. XVIII.) Buffalo, 1914.

Sherrill, Charles H., *Modernizing the Monroe Doctrine.* Boston, 1919.

——*The Sherrill Genealogy: the Descendants of Samuel Sherrill of East Hampton, Long Island, New York.* [New Haven], 1932.

Silenzi de Stagni, Adolfo, *El petróleo argentino.* 3rd ed.; Buenos Aires, 1955.

Silva, Carlos A., *La política internacional de la Nación Argentina.* . . . . Buenos Aires, 1946.

Smith, O. Edmund, Jr., *Yankee Diplomacy: U. S. Intervention in Argentina.* Dallas, Tex., 1953.

Sommi, Luis V., *El plan Prebisch y el destino argentino.* Córdoba, [1956].

Teele, A. K., *The History of Milton, Mass., 1840 to 1887.* [Milton, Mass., 1887.]

Ten Argentine Journalists, *Así cayó Peron: crónica del movimiento revolucionario triunfante.* Buenos Aires, 1955.

Torres Lanzas, Pedro, *Independencia de América: fuentes para su estudio.* 1st series; Madrid, 1912; 6 vols.

Udaondo, Enrique, *Diccionario biográfico argentino.* Buenos Aires, 1938.

Ugarte, Manuel, *The Destiny of a Continent.* New York, 1925.

——*La patria grande.* Madrid, 1924.

Une question du droit des gens. M. Washburn, ex-ministre des Etats-Unis a l'Assomption et la conspiration paraguayenne. Paris, 1868.

Varela, Luis V., *Histoire de la démarcation de leurs frontières despuis 1843 jusqu'á 1899;* . . . Buenos Aires, 1899; 2 vols.

Vera y González, Enrique, *Historia de la Repúblic Argentina desde el gobierno del General Viamont hasta nuestros días.* Buenos Aires, 1926; 3 vols.

Warren, Harris G., *Paraguay, An Informal History.* Norman, Okla., 1949.

Webster, C. K., *Britain and the Independence of Latin America, 1810-1830.* London, 1938; 2 vols.

Weil, Felix J., *Argentine Riddle.* New York, 1944.

Welker, Juan C., *Baltasar Brum: verbo y acción.* Montevideo, 1945.

Welles, Sumner, *Seven Decisions That Shaped History.* New York, 1950.

——*Where Are We Heading?* New York, 1946.

Whitaker, Arthur P., *Argentine Upheaval: Perón's Fall and the New Regime.* New York, 1956.

——*The United States and Argentina.* Cambridge, 1954.

——*The United States and the Independence of Latin America, 1800-1830.* Baltimore, 1941.

——*The Western Hemisphere Idea.* Ithaca, N. Y., 1954.

White, John W., *Argentina, the Life Story of a Nation.* New York, 1942.
Wilder, D. Webster, *The Annals of Kansas.* Topeka, 1886.
Wilgus, A. Curtis (ed.), *Argentina, Brazil and Chile Since Independence.* Washington, 1935.
Williams, John H., *Argentine International Trade under Inconvertible Paper Money, 1880-1900.* Cambridge, 1920.
Winkler, Max, *Foreign Bonds: An Autopsy. A Study of Defaults and Repudiations of Government Obligations.* Philadelphia, 1933.
————*Investments of United States Capital in Latin America.* Boston, 1929.
Wriston, Henry M., *Executive Agents in American Foreign Relations.* Baltimore, 1929.
Ynsfran, Pablo M., *La expedición norteamericana contra el Paraguay, 1858-1859.* Mexico, 1954, 1958; 2 vols.
Zabala, Arturo J., *La revolución del 16 de setiembre: antecedentes, gestación y victoria del movimiento de liberación nacional.* Buenos Aires, 1955.
Zamboni, Humberto, *Peronismo, justicialismo: juicio crítico.* Córdoba, 1956.

IV. PERIODICALS AND NEWSPAPERS

(* Indicates specific references in footnotes)

Aldoa, Carlos A., "American Politics: Argentina and the United States," *Inter-America,* VII, 126-127.
The American Weekly of Buenos Aires, 1923-19——.*
The Annual Register: A Review of Public Events at Home and Abroad, 1758——. London, 1761——.
Archivo Americano y Espíritu de la Prensa del Mundo. Series 1, Buenos Aires, 1843-1846; series 2, Buenos Aires, 1847-1851.
"Argentine-American Relations Offer Field for Improvement," *The Pan-American Magazine,* XXX (March, 1920), 266-269.
The Argentine Annual, including Lists of English Speaking Residents and Estancieros, 1921——. Buenos Aires, [1921——].
The Argentine Year Book, 1902. Buenos Aires, 1902——.
*El Argos de Buenos Ayres.**
Barrett, Robert S., "Will the United States Hold Its Present Trade in Argentina?" *The Pan-American Magazine,* XXIX (June, 1919), 98-100.
*Boston Patriot and Morning Advertiser.**
Braden, Spruille, "The Germans in Argentina," *The Atlantic Monthly,* Vol. 177 (April, 1946), 37-43.

Brady, George S., "American Shipping in Argentina," *The American Weekly of Buenos Aires*, I (April 12, 1924), 5-7.

"Britain and Argentina," *The Economist*, Vol. 147 (Aug. 5, 1944), 174-175.

"Britain's Royal Envoy in South America," *Current History*, XXII (Sept., 1925), 936-940.

*The Buenos Aires Herald.**

*Buenos Ayres Standard.**

*The Buffalo Courier-Express.**

Bulletin of the Pan American Union, Washington, 1893——.

Chambers, E. J., "Some Factors in the Deterioration of Argentina's External Position, 1946-1951," *Inter-American Affairs*, VIII (Winter, 1954), 27-62.

Chandler, Charles L., "Americans were active in Argentine Trade more than a century ago," *Comments on Argentine Trade*, VIII (July, 1929), 34-41.

———"The First Three Yankee Consuls in B.A.," *The American Weekly of Buenos Aires*, I (July 14, 1923), 5-7.

———"La influencia de los Estados Unidos de América en el Río de la Plata, 1799-1802," *Revista de Ciencias Económicas*, V (Sept., 1917), 133-145.

———"The River Plate Voyages, 1798-1800," *American Historical Review*, XXIII (July, 1918), 816-826.

———"San Martín and the Early Yankee Consuls," *Comments on Argentine Trade*, II (May, 1923), 3-4.

———"United States Commerce with Latin America at the Promulgation of the Monroe Doctrine," *Quarterly Journal of Economics*, XXXVIII (May, 1924), 466-486.

———"United States Merchant Ships in the Río de la Plata (1801-1808)," *The Hispanic American Historical Review*, II (Feb., 1919), 26-54.

———"United States Shipping in the La Plata Region, 1809-1810," *The Hispanic American Historical Review*, III (May, 1920), 159-176.

*The Chicago Daily Tribune.**

The Christian Science Monitor, Boston.*

Comments on Argentine Trade, Buenos Aires.*

Commercial Advertiser, New York.*

La Crítica, Buenos Aires.*

Current History, New York, 1915—.*

Cushing, Caleb, "English and French Intervention in the Río de la Plata," *United States Magazine and Democratic Review*, XVIII (March, 1846), 163-184.

Daily National Intelligencer, Washington.*

The Daily Union, Washington.*

DeBow's Review, New Orleans, 1846-1867.*

DeWilde, J. C. and Bryce Wood, "U.S. Trade Ties with Argentina," *Foreign Policy Reports*, XVII (Dec. 1, 1941), 221-232.

Dickens, Paul D., "Argentine Arbitrations and Mediations with Reference to United States Participation," *The Hispanic American Historical Review*, XI (Nov., 1931), 464-484.

Espil, Courtney Letts de, "John Pendleton and His Friendship with Urquiza," *The Hispanic American Historical Review*, XXXIII (Feb., 1953), 152-167.

The Evening Star, Washington, D.C. (Title varies.) *

Foreign Commerce Weekly, Washington, D.C.*

Gaceta de Buenos Aires, 1810-1821, Buenos Aires, 1910. 6 vols.*

Galarza, Ernesto, "Argentine Labor under Perón," *Inter-American Reports*, No. 2 (March, 1948).

——"The Standardization of Armaments in the Western Hemisphere," *Inter-American Reports*, No. 1 (Oct., 1947).

Gil, Enrique, "The Point of View of Latin-America on the Inter-American Policy of the United States," *The American Political Science Review*, VI (Feb., 1912, supplement), 164-172.

The Globe, Washington, D.C.*

Goebel, Dorothy B., "British Trade to the Spanish Colonies, 1796-1823," *American Historical Review*, XLIII (Jan., 1938), 276-318.

Greenhow, Robert, "The Falkland Islands: A Memoir: Descriptive, Historical, and Political," *The Merchants' Magazine and Commercial Review*, VI (Feb., 1842), 105-151.

Griffin, Charles C., "Privateering from Baltimore during the Spanish-American Wars of Independence," *Maryland Historical Magazine*, XXXV (March, 1940), 1-25.

Harper's Weekly, New York, 1857-1916.*

Harrison, John P., "Science and Politics: Origins and Objectives of Mid-Nineteenth Century Government Expeditions to Latin America," *The Hispanic American Historical Review*, XXXV (May, 1955), 175-202.

Hill, David J., "The Luxburg Secret Correspondence," *The American Journal of International Law*, XII (Jan., 1918), 135-140.

Hispanic American Report, Stanford, Cal., Nov. 1948——.*

Hoffman, Fritz, "Perón and After: A Review Article," *The Hispanic American Historical Review*, XXXVI (Nov., 1956), 510-528; XXXIX (May, 1959), 212-233.

Holmes, Olive, "Argentina—Focus of Conflict in the Americas," *Foreign Policy Reports*, XXI (Feb. 1, 1946), 297-307.

——"Perón's 'Greater Argentina' and the United States," *Foreign Policy Reports*, XXIV (Dec. 1, 1948), 157-172.

"Immediate Tariff Revisions urged for Retaliation and Protection," *Comments on Argentine Trade*, VIII (Feb., 1929), 13-19.

The Inter-American Monthly, Washington, D.C., 1942———.*

The Inter-Ocean, Chicago.*

Jessup, Philip C., "The Saavedra Lamas Anti-War Draft Treaty," *The American Journal of International Law*, XXVII (Jan., 1933), 109-114.

Johnson, Victor L., "Edward A. Hopkins and the Development of Argentine Transportation and Communication," *The Hispanic American Historical Review*, XXVI (Feb., 1946), 19-37.

Kirkpatrick, Helen P., "The League and the Chaco Dispute," *Foreign Policy Reports*, XII (July 15, 1936), 109-120.

Life, New York.*

Livermore, S. W., "Battleship Diplomacy in South America," *The Journal of Modern History*, XVI (March, 1944), 31-48.

El Lucero, Buenos Aires.*

*The Manchester Guardian.**

*Massachusetts Centinel.**

Matthews, Herbert L., "Juan Perón's War with the Catholic Church," *The Reporter*, XII (June 16, 1955), 19-22.

Mecham, J. Lloyd, "Conflicting Ideals of Pan-Americanism," *Current History*, XXXIII (Dec., 1930), 401-404.

The Merchants' Magazine and Commercial Review, New York, 1839-1870. (Title varies.) *

Mercury, Boston.*

Mock, James R., "The Creel Committee in Latin America," *The Hispanic American Historical Review*, XXII (May, 1942), 262-279.

La Nación, Buenos Aires.*

El Nacional Argentino, Paraná, Argentina.*

National Intelligencer, Washington. (Triweekly.) *

Newman, Joseph, "Diplomatic Dynamite," *Collier's, the National Weekly*, Vol. 116 (Nov. 10, 1945), 11, 43-45.

The New Republic, Vol. 86 (April 1, 1936), 219-220.

*The New York Times.**

Niles' Weekly Register, Baltimore and Philadelphia, 1811-1849. 75 vols.

The North American Review, Boston and New York, 1815———.*

Peffer, E. Louise, "Cordell Hull's Argentine Policy and Britain's Meat Supply," *Inter-American Economic Affairs*, X (Autumn, 1956), 3-21.

———"Less Beef on the Plate?" *Inter-American Economic Affairs*, XI (Summer, 1957), 3-35.

Peterson, Harold F., "Edward A. Hopkins: A Pioneer Promoter in Paraguay," *The Hispanic American Historical Review*, XXII (May, 1942), 245-261.

———"Efforts of the United States to Mediate in the Paraguayan War," *The Hispanic American Historical Review*, XII (Feb., 1932), 2-17.

————"Mariano Moreno: The Making of an Insurgent," *The Hispanic American Historical Review*, XIV (Nov., 1934), 450-476.

Popper, David H., "The Rio de Janeiro Conference of 1942," *Foreign Policy Reports*, XVIII (April 15, 1942), 25-36.

Pratt, Edwin J., "Anglo-American Commercial and Political Rivalry on the Plata, 1820-1830," *The Hispanic American Historical Review*, XI (Aug., 1931), 302-335.

La Prensa, Buenos Aires.*

Pueyrredón, Honorio, "Argentine-American Relations Offer Field for Improvement: Opinions of a Distinguished Argentine," *The Pan-American Magazine*, XXX (March, 1920), 266-269.

La Razón, Buenos Aires.*

La Reforma Pacífica, Asunción.*

*Richmond Enquirer.**

Robertson, William S., "South America and the Monroe Doctrine, 1824-1828," *Political Science Quarterly*, XXX (March, 1915), 82-105.

Santos Gollan, José, "Argentine Interregnum," *Foreign Affairs*, XXXV (Oct., 1956), 84-94.

Scott, James B., "Argentina and Germany: Dr. Drago's Views," *The American Journal of International Law*, XII (Jan., 1918), 140-142.

El Seminario de Avisos y Conocimientos Utiles, Asunción, 1853————.*

Setaro, Ricardo, "The Argentine Fly in the International Ointment," *Harper's*, Vol. 189 (Aug., 1944), 204-209.

Sherrill, Charles H., "Practical Mediation and International Peace," *The North American Review*, Vol. 200 (Dec., 1914), 887-892.

————"The South American Point of View," *International Conciliation*, [July, 1914?], pp. 1-12.

The Situation in Argentina. Monthly Bulletin of the Buenos Aires Branch of the First National Bank of Boston, Boston.*

Smith, Lawrence, "Suspension of the Gold Standard in Raw Material Exporting Countries," *American Economic Review*, XXIV (Sept., 1934), 430-449.

The Southern Cross, Buenos Aires.*

The Standard, Buenos Aires.*

Stewart, Watt, "Activities of Early Argentine Agents in the United States," *The Southwesten Social Science Quarterly*, XVIII (March, 1938), 1-10.

————"Argentina and the Monroe Doctrine, 1824-1828," *The Hispanic American Historical Review*, X (Feb., 1930), 26-32.

————"The Diplomatic Service of John M. Forbes at Buenos Aires," *The Hispanic American Historical Review*, XIV (May, 1934), 202-218.

————"The South American Commission, 1817-18," *The Hispanic American Historical Review*, IX (Feb., 1929), 31-59.

———"United States-Argentine Commercial Negotiations of 1825," *The Hispanic American Historical Review*, XIII (Aug., 1933), 367-371.

———and William M. French, "The Influence of Horace Mann on the Educational Ideas of Domingo Faustino Sarmiento," *The Hispanic American Historical Review*, XX (Feb., 1940), 12-31.

El Tiempo, Buenos Aires.*

El Tiempo, Caracas, Venezuela.*

Time, New York.*

Tribuna, Buenos Aires.*

Ugarte, Manuel, "L'Amérique latine après la guerre," *La Revue Mondiale*, Vol. 142 (May 15, 1921), 139-147.

The Union, Washington, D. C. (Triweekly.)*

Victórico, Julio, "Los Estados Unidos, el Paraguay y la mediación argentina de 1859," *Revista de Derecho, Historia y Letras*, VII (Sept., 1900), 365-379.

The Washington Post.*

The Washington Star.* (See *The Evening Star*.)

Wast, Hugo (Martínez Zuviría, Gustavo A.), "President Irigoyen of Argentina," *Current History*, XXX (Aug., 1929), 869-875.

Weekly National Intelligencer, Washington, D.C.*

Whitaker, Arthur P. "Blue Book Blues," *Current History*, new series, X (April, 1946), 289-297.

White, John W., "An American Reply to Dr. Zeballos," *The American Weekly of Buenos Aires*, I (Aug. 18, 1923), 5, 13.

Wilgus, A. Curtis, "James G. Blaine and the Pan American Movement," *The Hispanic American Historical Review*, V (Nov., 1922), 662-708.

Ynsfran, Pablo M., "Sam Ward's Bargain with President López of Paraguay," *The Hispanic American Historical Review*, XXIV (Aug., 1954), 313-331.

Zeballos, Estanislao S., "Gobierno radical: incidente del Conde Luxburg," *Revista de Derecho, Historia y Letras*, LVIII (Oct., 1917), 254-265.

———"Gobierno radical: política internacional," *Revista de Derecho, Historia y Letras*, LX (May, 1918), 118-120.

———"Gobierno radical: la visita de la escuadra americana," *Revista de Derecho, Historia y Letras*, LVII (Aug., 1917), 526-538.

———"Theodore Roosevelt y la política internacional americana," *Revista de Derecho, Historia y Letras*, XLVI (Dec., 1913), 545-604.

———"United States' Diplomacy in South America," *The Living Age*, Vol. 307 (Nov. 20, 1920), 440-448.

Zinny, Antonio (ed.), *La Gaceta Mercantil de Buenos Aires, 1823-1852*. Buenos Aires, 1912; 3 vols.

Index

INDEX

Commerce and Labor, Department of, studies Argentine needs and resources, 235; concerned by British trade drive, 357

Commercial Bureau of the American Republics, 225, 286; created at Washington Conference, 284

Commission of Inquiry and Conciliation, *see* Commission of Neutrals

Commission of Neutrals, attempts mediation in Chaco War, 385-88

Committee on Banking and Currency, United States Senate, sends experts to South America, 487

Committee on Codification of International Law, 375

Committee on Commercial Studies, Joint Argentine-United States, recommends proposals for reducing trade barriers, 480; chaired by Nufer, 483-84

Committee on Inter-American Affairs, House, members propose resolution condemning Perón's persecution of religion, 497

Committee on Latin American Affairs, CIO, opposes Perón, 449

Communications, Ministry of, suspends U.S. press services, 485

Communism, Argentine, and Perón's Third Position, 463; and Perón's attacks on Catholic Church, 495; attacked by Perón, 497; and Frondizi government, 508, 509, 513, 515, 516, 536

Communism, international, and Perón's "Third Position," 463, 469; at Bogotá Conference, 469; offers threat to Hemisphere, 481, 487; at Caracas Conference, 487-89

Compañía Alemana Transatlántica de Electricidad, 319

Conciliation and Arbitration, Washington Conference on (1928), Argentina fails to attend, 379; and the Chaco War, 386

Confederación General del Trabajo, see CGT

Conference for Maintenance of Peace, *see* Buenos Aires Conference (1936)

Conference of Hemisphere Neutrals, proposed by Irigoyen, 332ff.

Conference of Latin American Neutrals, invited to Buenos Aires by Irigoyen, 316, 322, 332-35

Congress, Argentine, offers subvention for direct shipping line to U.S., 157, 230; and tariff reciprocity, 227-28; approves arms-building program, 294; Peronista majorities in, 462; passes second Five-Year Plan, 485; passes new

investment law, 486; addressed by Frondizi, 515

Congress, Brazilian, and boundary dispute with Argentina, 247

Congress, Chilean, 244

Congress, U.S., 205; considers Spanish American revolutions, 5, n.9, 43, 46, 48, 51-53, 62, 63-64, 68-69; delays recognition of Argentina, 46, 52-53; approves recognition of Argentine independence, 72-73; protectionist views of, after 1867, 159; probes U.S.-Paraguayan relations, 192; affects Argentine relations by its tariff laws, 224-29, 351-55; passes high postwar tariffs, 352, 359; ratifies inter-American agreements, 399; urges end to "tough" policy, 474; addressed by Frondizi, 513-14, 525

Congress of the Nations of America, proposed by Irigoyen, 333ff.

Congress (U.S. ship), conveys South American mission to Buenos Aires, 41; protects U.S. commerce off Montevideo, 129

Connally, Tom, criticizes Braden's approach, 451, 457; at 1947 Rio Conference, 466

Conservative Party, 323, 331; leaders favor U.S. in World War I, 321; fails to reach sound trade basis with U.S. after World War I, 340, 361-65; disapproves Castillo's support of nationalist groups, 425; ignores social reform, 429

Constituent Assemblies, Argentine: (1813) attempts to reform Argentine government, 22; seeks U.S. aid, 22; (1817) adopts unpopular constitution, 62; (1852) drafts constitution of Argentine Confederation, 148; (1957) fails to modernize Constitution of 1853, 508

Constitutions, Argentine: (1853) drafting and adoption of, 148; resembles that of U.S., 148; modified by Perón, 462; Lonardi questions status of, 500-501; restored by Aramburu, 507-8; (1949) shaped by Perón, 464-65; Lonardi questions status of, 500-501; displaced by Aramburu, 507-8

Consular service, U.S., inadequacy of, in Argentina, 232

Consultation, as policy approved at Buenos Aires Conference, 391-92; extended at Lima Conference, 393, 395; broadened by Cantilo, 395; at Panama, 400-402; at Havana, 403-5; at Rio, 416-20; on Argentine question at Chapultepec, 441-443; at Washington, 481-82; at San José, 520

Consultative Meetings of Ministers of